D1474111

A New Architecture for the U.S. National Accounts

Studies in Income and Wealth
Volume 66

National Bureau of Economic Research
Conference on Research in Income and Wealth

A New Architecture for the U.S. National Accounts

Edited by **Dale W. Jorgenson,
J. Steven Landefeld, and
William D. Nordhaus**

The University of Chicago Press

Chicago and London

DALE W. JORGENSON is the Samuel W. Morris University Professor at Harvard University. J. STEVEN LANDEFELD is director of the Bureau of Economic Analysis of the U.S. Department of Commerce. WILLIAM D. NORDHAUS is the Sterling Professor of Economics at Yale University and a research associate of the National Bureau of Economic Research.

The University of Chicago Press, Chicago 60637
The University of Chicago Press, Ltd., London
© 2006 by the National Bureau of Economic Research
All rights reserved. Published 2006
Printed in the United States of America
14 13 12 11 10 09 08 07 06   1 2 3 4 5
ISBN: 0-226-41084-6 (cloth)

Library of Congress Cataloging-in-Publication Data

Conference on a New Architecture for the U.S. National Accounts
(2004 : Washington, D.C.)
A new architecture for the U.S. national accounts / edited by Dale W.
    Jorgenson, J. Steven Landefeld, and William D. Nordhaus.
        p.   cm. — (Studies in income and wealth ; v. 66)
    "National Bureau of Economic Research, Conference on Research
    in Income and Wealth"—Ser. t.p.
    Proceedings of the Conference on New Architecture for the U.S.
    National Accounts, held April 16–17, 2004 in Washington, D.C.
    Includes bibliographical references and index.
    ISBN 0-226-41084-6 (pbk : alk. paper)
    1. National income—United States—Accounting—Congresses.
    2. Finance, Public—Econometric models—Congresses. 3. National
    income—Accounting—Mathematical models—Congresses I. Jorgen-
    son, Dale Weldeau, 1933– II. Landefeld, J. Steven. III. Nordhaus,
    William D. IV. Conference on Research in Income and Wealth.
    V. Title. VI. Series.

    HC106.3 .C714 vol. 66
    [HC110.I5]
    330 s—dc22
    [339.373]
                                                        2005053859

♾ The paper used in this publication meets the minimum requirements of
the American National Standard for Information Sciences—Permanence
of Paper for Printed Library Materials, ANSI Z39.48-1992.

Relation of the Directors to the
Work and Publications of the
National Bureau of Economic Research

1. The object of the NBER is to ascertain and present to the economics profession, and to the public more generally, important economic facts and their interpretation in a scientific manner without policy recommendations. The Board of Directors is charged with the responsibility of ensuring that the work of the NBER is carried on in strict conformity with this object.

2. The President shall establish an internal review process to ensure that book manuscripts proposed for publication DO NOT contain policy recommendations. This shall apply both to the proceedings of conferences and to manuscripts by a single author or by one or more co-authors but shall not apply to authors of comments at NBER conferences who are not NBER affiliates.

3. No book manuscript reporting research shall be published by the NBER until the President has sent to each member of the Board a notice that a manuscript is recommended for publication and that in the President's opinion it is suitable for publication in accordance with the above principles of the NBER. Such notification will include a table of contents and an abstract or summary of the manuscript's content, a list of contributors if applicable, and a response form for use by Directors who desire a copy of the manuscript for review. Each manuscript shall contain a summary drawing attention to the nature and treatment of the problem studied and the main conclusions reached.

4. No volume shall be published until forty-five days have elapsed from the above notification of intention to publish it. During this period a copy shall be sent to any Director requesting it, and if any Director objects to publication on the grounds that the manuscript contains policy recommendations, the objection will be presented to the author(s) or editor(s). In case of dispute, all members of the Board shall be notified, and the President shall appoint an ad hoc committee of the Board to decide the matter; thirty days additional shall be granted for this purpose.

5. The President shall present annually to the Board a report describing the internal manuscript review process, any objections made by Directors before publication or by anyone after publication, any disputes about such matters, and how they were handled.

6. Publications of the NBER issued for informational purposes concerning the work of the Bureau, or issued to inform the public of the activities at the Bureau, including but not limited to the NBER Digest and Reporter, shall be consistent with the object stated in paragraph 1. They shall contain a specific disclaimer noting that they have not passed through the review procedures required in this resolution. The Executive Committee of the Board is charged with the review of all such publications from time to time.

7. NBER working papers and manuscripts distributed on the Bureau's web site are not deemed to be publications for the purpose of this resolution, but they shall be consistent with the object stated in paragraph 1. Working papers shall contain a specific disclaimer noting that they have not passed through the review procedures required in this resolution. The NBER's web site shall contain a similar disclaimer. The President shall establish an internal review process to ensure that the working papers and the web site do not contain policy recommendations, and shall report annually to the Board on this process and any concerns raised in connection with it.

8. Unless otherwise determined by the Board or exempted by the terms of paragraphs 6 and 7, a copy of this resolution shall be printed in each NBER publication as described in paragraph 2 above.

Contents

	Prefatory Note	ix
	Introduction Dale W. Jorgenson, J. Steven Landefeld, and William D. Nordhaus	1
1.	**Blueprint for Expanded and Integrated** **U.S. Accounts: Review, Assessment, and Next Steps** Dale W. Jorgenson and J. Steven Landefeld	13
2.	**The Architecture of the System of National** **Accounts: A Three-Way International Comparison** **of Canada, Australia, and the United Kingdom** Karen Wilson	113
3.	**Principles of National Accounting for** **Nonmarket Accounts** William D. Nordhaus	143
4.	**A Framework for Nonmarket Accounting** Katharine G. Abraham and Christopher Mackie	161
5.	**The "Architecture" of Capital Accounting:** **Basic Design Principles** Charles R. Hulten	193
6.	**Integrating Industry and National Economic** **Accounts: First Steps and Future Improvements** Ann M. Lawson, Brian C. Moyer, Sumiye Okubo, and Mark A. Planting	215

7.   **Aggregation Issues in Integrating and Accelerating
        the BEA's Accounts: Improved Methods for
        Calculating GDP by Industry**   263
        Brian C. Moyer, Marshall B. Reinsdorf, and
        Robert E. Yuskavage
        Comment: W. Erwin Diewert

8.   **Integrating Expenditure and Income Data:
        What to Do with the Statistical Discrepancy?**   309
        J. Joseph Beaulieu and Eric J. Bartelsman

9.   **An Integrated BEA/BLS Production Account:
        A First Step and Theoretical Considerations**   355
        Barbara M. Fraumeni, Michael J. Harper,
        Susan G. Powers, and Robert E. Yuskavage
        Comment: Carol Corrado

10.   **The Integration of the Canadian Productivity
        Accounts within the System of National Accounts:
        Current Status and Challenges Ahead**   439
        John R. Baldwin and Tarek M. Harchaoui

11.   **Integrated Macroeconomic Accounts for the
        United States: Draft SNA-USA**   471
        Albert M. Teplin, Rochelle Antoniewicz,
        Susan Hume McIntosh, Michael G. Palumbo,
        Genevieve Solomon, Charles Ian Mead,
        Karin Moses, and Brent Moulton

12.   **Micro and Macro Data Integration:
        The Case of Capital**   541
        Randy A. Becker, John Haltiwanger, Ron S. Jarmin,
        Shawn D. Klimek, and Daniel J. Wilson

        Panel Remarks   611
        Thomas L. Mesenbourg, U.S. Census Bureau
        Kathleen P. Utgoff, Bureau of Labor Statistics
        Larry Slifman, Board of Governors of the Federal
            Reserve System
        Katharine G. Abraham, University of Maryland
            and National Bureau of Economic Research
        J. Steven Landefeld, Bureau of Economic Analysis

        Contributors   625
        Author Index   629
        Subject Index   633

Prefatory Note

This volume contains the proceedings of the Conference on Research in Income and Wealth on "A New Architecture for the U.S. National Accounts." The conference was held at the Board of Governors of the Federal Reserve System in Washington, D.C., on April 16–17, 2004. Funds for the Conference on Research in Income and Wealth are provided by the Bureau of Labor Statistics, the Bureau of Economic Analysis, the Federal Reserve Board, and the Bureau of the Census; we are indebted to them for their support. We are also grateful to Dale W. Jorgenson, J. Steven Landefeld, and William D. Nordhaus, who served as conference organizers and editors of the volume. We thank the National Bureau of Economic Research staff and the University of Chicago Press editors for their assistance in organizing the conference and editing the volume.

The editors of this volume, who also served as the organizing committee for the conference on "A New Architecture for the U.S. National Accounts," are grateful to Carl Beck and Denis Healy of the National Bureau of Economic Research (NBER) conference staff for their excellent work in organizing the conference. In preparing the proceedings for publication we have benefited greatly from the expert assistance of Helena Fitz-Patrick, coordinator of book publishing at the NBER, and Catherine Beebe of the editorial staff of the University of Chicago Press. We are very grateful to two anonymous referees for their comments on the individual contributions. Finally, we would like to express our gratitude to the authors for helping us produce the volume in a timely fashion.

Executive Committee, July 2005

Charles R. Hulten (Chair), University of Maryland
John M. Abowd, Cornell University

Susanto Basu, University of Michigan
Ernst R. Berndt, Sloan School of Management, MIT
Carol A. Corrado, Board of Governors of the Federal Reserve
Robert C. Feenstra, University of California, Davis
John Greenlees, Bureau of Labor Statistics
John C. Haltiwanger, University of Maryland
Michael J. Harper, Bureau of Labor Statistics
Ron Jarmin, Bureau of the Census
John Bradford Jensen, Institute for International Economics
Lawrence Katz, Harvard University
J. Steven Landefeld, Bureau of Economic Analysis
Brent Moulton, Bureau of Economic Analysis
Mark J. Roberts, Pennsylvania State University
Matthew Shapiro, University of Michigan
David W. Wilcox, Board of Governors of the Federal Reserve

Introduction

Dale W. Jorgenson, J. Steven Landefeld, and
William D. Nordhaus

From its inception, the Conference on Research in Income and Wealth (CRIW) has focused much of its attention on the U.S. national accounts, now officially entitled the National Income and Product Accounts (NIPAs). Notwithstanding this historical focus, the most recent CRIW volume devoted entirely to the national accounts was *The U.S. National Income and Product Accounts: Selected Topics,* edited by Murray Foss and published in 1983. This reported the proceedings of a conference held in Washington, DC, on May 3–4, 1979, more than a quarter of a century ago!

The present volume contains the proceedings of the conference "A New Architecture for the U.S. National Accounts," held in Washington, DC, on April 16–17, 2004. The purpose of the conference was to initiate the development of a comprehensive and fully integrated system of U.S. national accounts. Attainment of this objective will require a great deal of effort, a substantial amount of time, and the collaboration of many individuals and institutions. It is important to emphasize that while this effort is in one sense a new architecture, in another it is the latest in a series of steps to update, supplement, and reconcile different components of our evolving system of national accounts.

The purpose of a new architecture is to integrate the existing systems of accounts, identify gaps and inconsistencies, and expand and integrate systems of nonmarket accounts with the core system. We are fortunate in building on a history of success. Samuelson and Nordhaus (2005, 429) and

Dale W. Jorgenson is the Samuel W. Morris University Professor at Harvard University. J. Steven Landefeld is the director of the Bureau of Economic Analysis. William D. Nordhaus is Sterling Professor of Economics at Yale University and a research associate of the National Bureau of Economic Research.

the Department of Commerce have characterized the gross domestic product (GDP) as one of the great inventions of the twentieth century.[1]

America's economy is not only large and diverse but is also becoming increasingly interrelated with the rest of the world in both its current and financial accounts. The diversity of the U.S. economy is reflected in the decentralization of its statistical system. The major agencies involved in providing data and generating the accounts include the Bureau of Economic Analysis (BEA) in the Department of Commerce, the Bureau of Labor Statistics (BLS) in the Department of Labor, the Census Bureau (also in the Commerce Department), the board of governors of the Federal Reserve System, and the Statistics of Income (SOI) division of the Internal Revenue Service.

Without being exhaustive we can enumerate some of the major assignments of the leading contributors. The BEA has responsibility for the NIPAs, the core system of accounts. The BLS generates employment; wage and salary data; productivity statistics, including labor productivity and multifactor productivity; as well as almost all of the underlying price data. The board of governors produces the flow-of-funds accounts, including the balance sheets. The Census Bureau collects and reports much of the primary information through its business and population censuses and surveys. The SOI generates tax-based data and incomes used in calculating gross domestic income. In addition, many other agencies and private-sector organizations provide source data for the national accounts.

The NIPAs, the productivity statistics, and the flow-of-funds have different origins, reflecting different objectives and data sources. However, they are intimately linked. For example, the BLS multifactor productivity statistics employ data on output, income, and investment from the NIPAs. The flow-of-funds incorporates BEA data on investment and stocks of tangible and reproducible assets and the U.S. international investment position. An important part of the motivation for developing a new architecture for the national accounts is to integrate the different components and make them consistent.

Emerging measurement issues have also motivated reconsideration of the architecture of the national accounts. Examples would include attempts to understand the recent decline in saving and the rebound in productivity growth and potential economic growth. Alternative and sometimes inconsistent perspectives on these issues are provided by different data sources. In addition, ownership-based accounting for international transactions and linked micro and macro accounts continue to pose chal-

---

1. At a press conference on December 7, 1999, the Department of Commerce selected "the development of the national income and product accounts as its achievement of the century." See Landefeld (2000).

lenges. These are symptomatic of issues that need attention by the national accounting community.

The key elements of the new architecture are outlined in chapter 1, "Blueprint for Expanded and Integrated U.S. Accounts," by Dale W. Jorgenson and J. Steven Landefeld. This chapter presents a prototype system of accounts that integrates the NIPAs with the productivity statistics generated by the BLS and balance sheets produced by the Federal Reserve Board. The system features GDP, as does the NIPAs; however, GDP and gross domestic income (GDI) are presented in both current and constant prices, together with multifactor productivity. Similarly, the BEA's accounts for reproducible assets and the U.S. international investment position are extended to encompass a balance sheet for the U.S. economy.

Jorgenson and Landefeld provide an overview of the current system of accounts and an explanation of the existing architecture. Chapter 1 also compares the NIPAs with the principal alternative, the international accounting guidelines in the *System of National Accounts* (United Nations et al., 1993; hereafter SNA). Finally, this chapter presents a brief history of the U.S. national accounts, beginning with the seminal work of Simon Kuznets at the National Bureau of Economic Research (NBER) and continuing through the most recent developments. These include the new seven-account system for the NIPAs, illustrated by table 1.1 of the chapter. The tables present the accounts for 2002, the year of the most recent benchmark revision.

Chapter 2, "The Architecture of the System of National Accounts: A Three-Way International Comparison of Canada, Australia, and the United Kingdom," by Karen Wilson, provides a comparison among three systems of national accounts that implement the United Nations SNA. These systems are organized around the supply and use framework employed in constructing input-output accounts. Financial accounts and balance sheets are an integral part of the system in all three countries. However, the architecture is quite different from the U.S. national accounts, which emphasize the expenditure definition of GDP, the familiar $C + I + G + X$, personal consumption expenditures, gross private domestic investment, government expenditures, plus net exports.

Australia, Canada, and the United Kingdom have highly centralized statistical systems with a single agency in each country responsible for the system of national accounts. Table 5 in the paper summarizes and compares the sequence of accounts in the three countries. This begins with GDP and continues with income and expenditures and capital accounts. The financial accounts, including balance sheets, and the external accounts are integrated with the income and product accounts in all three countries. The SNA and the NIPAs are compared in greater detail in chapter 11.

The U.S. national accounts are not limited to the core system of accounts for market activity, centering on the NIPAs and including the productivity statistics and the flow-of-funds accounts. In chapter 3, "Principles of National Accounting for Nonmarket Accounts," William D. Nordhaus considers the major conceptual issues in nonmarket accounting. This builds on the principles developed for environmental accounts in the National Research Council study, *Nature's Numbers,* edited by Nordhaus and Edward Kokkelenberg (1999). Nordhaus recommends the National Economic Accounts (NEA) as a guiding principle for the nonmarket accounts. Under this principle, nonmarket goods and services should be treated as if they were produced and consumed as market activities. The accounts would include a full set of current and capital accounts, modeled after those of systems of market-based accounts.

Nordhaus emphasizes that the single most important source of data for nonmarket accounts is the American Time Use Survey initiated by the BLS in 2003. An important challenge is evaluating the time used in activities not covered by labor markets. Nordhaus and James Tobin (1973) employed marginal after-tax labor compensation, and this approach has been adopted in most approaches to time valuation. Drawing appropriate boundaries is a central issue in augmented accounts for nonmarket activities. A narrow view could confine these boundaries to near-market goods and services, where there is a direct counterpart to market goods and services. A broad definition would also include personal goods and services for which there are no market transactions, but also public goods with benefits spreading over the entire community.

The Committee on National Statistics (CNStat) of the U.S. National Academies has recently published a comprehensive survey of nonmarket accounting, *Beyond the Market,* edited by Katharine G. Abraham, chair of the CNStat panel, and Christopher Mackie of CNStat (Abraham and Mackie 2005). This report is summarized by Abraham and Mackie in chapter 4, "A Framework for Nonmarket Accounting." Like Nordhaus, Abraham and Mackie favor modeling nonmarket accounts on the core system of national accounts, preserving double-entry bookkeeping and relying on market transactions insofar as possible in the valuation of nonmarket inputs and outputs. An important goal is to include prices, quantities, and values for nonmarket activities that can be compared with corresponding estimates for market activities.

Beyond the Market recommends the development of "satellite" systems of accounts for nonmarket activity in five areas—household production, education, health, the nonprofit and government sectors, and the environment. The report makes specific recommendations for systems of accounts in each of these areas and presents detailed references to the relevant literature. Abraham and Mackie identify the American Time Use Survey (BLS 2004) as an important new source of data on nonmarket activity. This could be exploited in many areas, including home production, investments in health and education, volunteer activity, and environmental accounting.

The conceptual issues in designing capital accounts are discussed in Charles R. Hulten's paper, "The 'Architecture' of Capital Accounting: Basic Design Principles." Hulten outlines the standard model of capital introduced by the BLS (1983) in its multifactor productivity program. The key concepts are the flow of capital services and the user cost of these services. These complement the older concepts of the stock of capital and the price of assets, employed in the BEA's accounts for reproducible tangible wealth. Incorporation of capital services and user costs into the NIPAs would be an important step in the integration of the productivity statistics with the core system of accounts. This would also open the way to accounting for capital income, much of it imputed, in the household, nonprofit, and government sectors.

Hulten employs a circular flow model (CFM) as the framework for capital accounting. Capital is a stock of productive assets for producers, as well as a store of wealth for consumers. Investment is defined as expenditure made with the intention of increasing future, rather than current, consumption. This leads to considering research and development and other intangible forms of investment as part of capital. It also focuses attention on the necessity of treating the cost of capital or user cost as an integral part of the production account for an integrated and consistent system of accounts. Gross output is the natural measure for the production sector, while net output is appropriate as a measure of welfare. Both are required in a complete system of accounts. Finally, the division between production and consumption suggests that capital should be identified both by the production sector where it is employed and the consumer sector where it is owned.

The most important barrier to an integrated and consistent production account at the industry level for the United States is the construction of consistent input-output and national income accounts. This important and challenging topic is the subject of three chapters. Chapter 6, "Integrating Industry and National Economic Accounts: First Steps and Future Improvements," by Ann M. Lawson, Brian C. Moyer, Sumiye Okubo, and Mark A. Planting, presents an initial integration of the BEA's annual input-output accounts with GDP by industry. Many countries produce integrated accounts by assuming that industry ratios of intermediate inputs to gross output do not change from the most recent benchmark input-output table. The BEA uses a very different approach, combining the available source data to estimate a balanced set of annual input-output accounts and GDP-by-industry accounts.

The integration of GDP-by-industry accounts with the annual input-output accounts is the latest is a series of improvements in the BEA's industry accounts. These include, first, resuming the publication of annual input-output tables and accelerating their release to within three years after the reference year. Second, the GDP-by-industry accounts have been expanded to include gross output and intermediate input for all industries. Third, accelerated GDP-by-industry accounts are available with a lag of only four months after the end of the reference year. The BEA's long-run goal is to integrate GDP-by-industry accounts with the benchmark input-output accounts compiled every five years and the NIPAs, as well as the annual input-output accounts. Achievement of this objective will require several years of effort by the BEA, as well as the continuing participation and cooperation of other statistical agencies, especially the Bureau of the Census and the BLS, to further enhance the quality and timeliness of the underlying source data. Much more information is provided on initiatives already underway by Thomas L. Mesenbourg of the Bureau of the Census and Kathleen P. Utgoff, Commissioner of Labor Statistics, in their contributions to the panel discussion reported at the end of this volume.

Chapter 7, "Aggregation Issues in Integrating and Accelerating the BEA's Accounts: Improved Methods for Calculating GDP by Industry," by Brian C. Moyer, Marshall B. Reinsdorf, and Robert E. Yuskavage considers aggregate measures of GDP obtained from the GDP-by-industry accounts. These differ from the expenditure-based measure of the GDP featured in the NIPAs. An important conclusion is that differences in source data and methodology account for most of the differences in the growth of aggregate output. Few of the differences are attributable to the treatment of the statistical discrepancy or aggregation methods. Another important finding of the chapter is that the formula employed by the BEA for calculating the contributions of final expenditures to real GDP growth can be used to calculate industry contributions based on value added. With a consistent set of source data this formula would yield the same estimate of real GDP from the income side and the expenditure side.

The BEA's objective is a full integration of industry and expenditures accounts that reduces or eliminates the existing discrepancies. Chapter 7 identifies options for fuller integration of the industry accounts and the NIPAs and improvements in source data that will be required. The authors recommend using a consistent set of source data within the framework provided by balanced annual input-output accounts, together with the aggregation methods currently used by the BEA. This would require major improvements in the source data for gross output, final uses, and intermediate inputs. The Census Bureau has several initiatives in the 2002 Economic Census that would contribute to this goal. The BLS continues to expand and improve service-sector producer price indexes. However, incorporation of the new data and full integration will require substantial time and effort.

Chapter 8, "Integrating Expenditure and Income Data: What to Do with the Statistical Discrepancy?" by J. Joseph Beaulieu and Eric J. Bartlesman, is the third chapter dealing with integration of the industry accounts and the NIPAs. This chapter compares the expenditure estimates of GDP with value added estimates derived by adding over industries. This comparison is carried out within the framework of annual input-output accounts derived from a variety of source data. The initial estimate is converted into a final estimate by eliminating the statistical discrepancies. This requires methods for "balancing" the accounts; the results enable the authors to identify possible improvements in the underlying source data that would be useful in setting priorities.

Beaulieu and Bartlesman show that conflicting measurements of deliveries to final demand and value added in a few problem industries explain most of the aggregate statistical discrepancy. Many of the industry-level statistical discrepancies arise from personal consumption expenditures. These are associated with specific industries such as trade, finance and insurance, chemicals, petroleum refining, rubber and plastics, and communications industries. In addition, the machinery and instruments industry contributes to the statistical discrepancy in private fixed investment. Finally, there are significant issues in the measurement of value added in the mining and health services industries. Beaulieu and Bartlesman propose methods for combining expenditure and income data to create an integrated data set.

A more specific agenda for designing a new architecture for the U.S. national accounts would include an integrated production account presenting the GDP and GDI, as in the NIPAs. Both would be given in current and constant prices, as in the BLS multifactor productivity statistics. These would be extended to the industry level by introducing gross output and intermediate input by industry, as in the BEA's annual input-output accounts. The production account is the subject of chapter 9, "An Integrated BEA/BLS Production Account: A First Step and Theoretical Considerations," by Barbara M. Fraumeni and Robert E. Yuskavage of the BEA and Michael J. Harper and Susan G. Powers of the BLS. The authors compare data sources employed in the BEA production accounts and the BLS productivity accounts and discuss the methodology required to integrate the two systems.

Chapter 9 is an important first step in collaboration between the BEA and BLS. This chapter describes a framework for the production account based on Jorgenson, Gollop, and Fraumeni (1987). This framework incorporates data on the production of commodities by individual industries, as well as the interindustry flows available in the input-output accounts. Data in current prices are deflated by commodity prices and aggregated to provide measures of real input and output and productivity by industry. The chapter presents an integrated and consistent aggregate production account for U.S. private business and private nonfarm business sectors. Finally, the chapter documents and presents alternative measures of industry output available from the BEA and BLS. These comparisons could be used by the two agencies in reconciling and eliminating the remaining differences. The chapter identifies the conversion of the NIPAs and the productivity statistics to the North American Industry Classification System (NAICS) as an important opportunity to achieve more thorough going integration.

John R. Baldwin and Tarek M. Harchaoui present Statistics Canada's system of integrated production and productivity accounts in chapter 10, "The Integration of the Canadian Productivity Accounts within the System of National Accounts: Current Status and Challenges Ahead." This provides a paradigm for measuring productivity within a system of national accounts based on the SNA. The industry-level estimates are based on gross output and intermediate input from the input-output accounts in current and constant prices. Capital and labor inputs are defined in a similar manner to the BLS multifactor productivity program, but cover the whole of the Canadian economy. The Canadian system of productivity accounts has important implications for an integrated and consistent production account in the U.S. system of national accounts, but differences between the NIPAs and the SNA would have to be eliminated in order to use the Canadian accounts as a model.

Baldwin and Harchaoui emphasize the advantages of integrating the productivity accounts with the national accounts. This requires a consistent set of data on outputs and inputs that conforms to the system of national accounts. These data help to eliminate the common difficulty of "different stories," like those arising from differences between the BEA and BLS industry data. The construction of productivity accounts also provides an important quality check on data from the national accounts and helps to identify and fill data gaps. A system of productivity accounts integrated with the system of national accounts enhances the national accounts through improvements in accuracy, coherence, relevance, and interpretability. Baldwin and Harchaoui conclude by calling for the integration of productivity accounts into the United Nations SNA framework.

The final topic in developing new architecture for the U.S. national accounts is an integrated and consistent system of financial and income accounts. This is presented in chapter 11, "Integrated Macroeconomic Accounts for the United States: Draft SNA-USA," by Albert M. Teplin in collaboration with Susan Hume McIntosh, and Michael G. Palumbo of the Federal Reserve Board; Genevieve Solomon of the Federal Reserve Bank of Dallas; Rochelle Antoniewicz of the Investment Company Institute; and Charles Ian Mead, Brent Moulton, and Karin Moses of the BEA. This paper integrates the NIPAs and the U.S. international investment position generated by BEA with the flow-of-funds accounts produced by the Federal Reserve Board. Fuller integration would involve harmonizing sector boundaries, exploiting the same data sources, and treating transactions uniformly. The chapter presents a prototype integrated and consistent system that resolves many of these issues and identifies others for future work. Larry Slifman of the Board of Governors comments on the different meanings of integration, especially in the work of Teplin and his colleagues and Beaulieu and Bartlesman.

Chapter 11 provides integrated financial and income accounts for 1985–2002, based on official data as of June 10, 2004, and a few unofficial estimates by the authors. These accounts are presented for seven sectors—households and nonprofit institutions serving households; nonfinancial, noncorporate businesses; nonfinancial corporate businesses; financial businesses; federal government; state and local governments; and the rest of the world. Each sector has production and income accounts in current prices, a capital account giving data on accumulation, a revaluation account, and a balance sheet account. Relative to current publications of the BEA and the Board of Governors, the integrated accounts go considerably further in implementing the United Nations SNA. The new accounts also advance the goal identified by Richard and Nancy Ruggles (1982) of integrating the NIPAs, the U.S. international investment position, and the flow of funds.

A final methodological issue, the integration of micro and macro accounts for capital, is discussed by Randy Becker, John Haltiwanger, Dan Wilson, Ron Jarmin, and Shawn D. Klimek in chapter 12, "Micro- and Macrodata Integration: The Case of Capital." This chapter focuses on the empirical basis for the allocation of investment flows by industry and by asset. New information collected in the Census Bureau's Annual Capital Expenditures Survey (Bureau of the Census 2004; hereafter ACES) will enhance the empirical foundations for capital accounts at both aggregate and industry levels. This information will also facilitate the integration of micro- and macrodata for investment, capital stocks, and capital services.

A key theme of chapter 12 is that inconsistencies between industry and asset measures of capital and firm and establishment measures reflect dramatically different methodologies. Estimates of investment by industry and asset are constructed form commodity flow data for capital goods. The perpetual inventory method is employed in constructing estimates of capital stocks. An important empirical issue is the basis for the allocation of investment and capital by industry. The ACES provides direct evidence on investment by firms and establishments and these have been incorporated into the most recent benchmark table of capital flows by industry and asset. The chapter identifies a number of obstacles to reconciliation of the industry and asset data with firm and establishment data, such as the limited asset detail available from business surveys and the enormous sample rotation, especially for younger businesses. Finally, the chapter recommends integration of micro and macro approaches to capital measurement and re-design of surveys to generate better microdata on investment flows and capital stocks.

We conclude that the Conference on a New Architecture has accomplished the objective of initiating the lengthy process that will be required to produce an integrated and consistent system of U.S. national accounts. This process will involve steps within the BEA to integrate the components of the core system of accounts—the NIPAs, the input-output accounts, and the international accounts. It will also involve collaboration between the BEA and BLS on an integrated and consistent production account and between the BEA and the Federal Reserve Board on integrated and consistent income and expenditures, capital, and wealth accounts. An open question that deserves immediate attention is how to create an institutional framework for successful interagency collaboration within the highly decentralized U.S. statistical system. The requisites for ongoing collaborations are obviously very different from those for one-time efforts through interagency task forces. These issues are addressed in greater detail by Abraham and Landefeld in their contributions to the panel discussion.

The institutional framework for collaboration on satellite systems of accounts is a less urgent matter, but also requires attention. The BEA has already established collaborative relationships in the areas surveyed by Jorgenson and Landefeld, but many unexploited opportunities remain, such as those identified by Abraham and Mackie. A third area that must be addressed by the national accounting community is international harmonization through implementation and revision of the SNA. This is the focus of the chapters by Teplin and his colleagues and by Wilson. The next objective for the national accounting community will be to set priorities and a schedule for accomplishing the goal identified in this volume: creating an integrated and consistent system of U.S. national accounts.

References

Abraham, Katharine, and Christopher Mackie, eds. 2005. *Beyond the market.* Washington, DC: National Academies Press.

Bureau of the Census. 2004. *Annual Capital Expenditures Survey, 2002.* Washington, DC: Bureau of the Census.

Bureau of Labor Statistics (BLS). 1983. *Trends in multifactor productivity, 1948–1981.* Washington, DC: U.S. Government Printing Office.

———. 2004. *American Time-Use Survey, 2003.* Washington, DC: Bureau of Labor Statistics.

Foss, Murray F. 1983. *The U.S. National Income and Product Accounts: Selected topics.* Chicago: University of Chicago Press.

Jorgenson, Dale W., Frank M. Gollop, and Barbara M. Fraumeni. 1987. *Productivity and U.S. economic growth.* Cambridge, MA: Harvard University Press.
Landefeld, J. Steven. 2000. GDP: One of the great inventions of the 20th century. *Survey of Current Business* 80 (1): 6–14.
Nordhaus, William D., and Edward Kokkelenberg, eds. 1999. *Nature's numbers.* Washington, DC: National Academy Press.
Nordhaus, William D., and James Tobin. 1973. Is growth obsolete? In *The measurement of economic and social performance,* ed. Milton Moss, 509–32. New York: Columbia University Press.
Ruggles, Richard, and Nancy D. Ruggles. 1982. Integrated economic accounts for the United States, 1947–80. *Survey of Current Business* 62 (5): 1–53.
Samuelson, Paul A., and William D. Nordhaus. 2005. *Economics.* 18th ed. New York: McGraw-Hill.
United Nations, Commission of the European Communities, International Monetary Fund, Organisation for Economic Co-operation and Development, and World Bank. 1993. *System of national accounts 1993.* Series F, no. 2, rev. 4. New York: United Nations.

1

Blueprint for Expanded and Integrated U.S. Accounts
Review, Assessment, and Next Steps

Dale W. Jorgenson and J. Steven Landefeld

1.1 Introduction

The United States possesses some of the best-developed sets of economic accounts in the world. These accounts have been regularly updated and have served researchers and policymakers well. Certain components of these sets of accounts, however, were developed independently to meet differing policy and analytical needs. As a result, while the flow of funds and balance sheet accounts produced by the Federal Reserve Board (FRB), the productivity statistics produced by the Bureau of Labor Statistics (BLS), and the rest of the national accounts produced by the Bureau of Economic Analysis (BEA) are among the best in the world, they are not completely comprehensive or fully integrated. The lack of integration and problems of consistency have hampered analysis of such issues as the downtrend in personal saving and the sources of the improvement in growth and productivity in the latter half of the 1990s.

Longer-standing issues also raise questions about the scope and structure of the nation's economic accounts. Since their inception, there have been suggestions to expand the scope of the accounts to include nonmarket activities. Simon Kuznets, one of the primary architects of the U.S. accounts, recognized the limitations of focusing on market activities and excluding household production and a broad range of other nonmarket activities and assets that have productive value or yield satisfaction. The need to better understand the sources of economic growth in the postwar era led to the development—much of it by academic researchers—of various supplemental series, such as investments in human capital.

Dale W. Jorgenson is the Samuel W. Morris University Professor at Harvard University. J. Steven Landefeld is the director of the Bureau of Economic Analysis.

13

More recently, some data users have suggested that the overall architecture of the accounts—which has been regularly updated throughout its history but whose basic structure has remained largely unchanged for over fifty years—needs to be reexamined. Alternative structures, such as ownership-based accounting for international transactions or macro accounts that are linked to micro accounts, are examples.

In this chapter, we examine these issues in the context of a review and assessment of the accounts and find that the existing accounts have served the nation well, but they have required continuing incremental updates, supplements, and reconciliation.[1] At this point in time, we believe that there is need not for a new paradigm but for an expansion and integration of the accounts produced by the BEA, BLS, and FRB in coordination with the U.S. Census Bureau ("Census"), a primary supplier of source data. This effort would consist of (a) an expansion and integration of the accounts to include a complete production account for the analysis of growth and productivity; (b) an expansion of the accounts to cover goods and services that are important to the analysis of growth and productivity but not fully captured in the existing accounts, such as mineral resources, human capital, and R&D; and (c) an expansion of the accounts to nonmarket goods and services that are important to the economy, but also have large welfare implications—such as environmental and health accounts.

In the last section of the chapter, we present an illustrative framework and set of estimates that build on the work of Jorgenson et al. and on the BEA's seven-account framework, estimates introduced as part of the BEA's 2003 benchmark revision of the National Income and Product Accounts (NIPAs). The framework's scope is restricted to the existing boundaries of market accounts and is focused on presenting an integrated, complete, and consistent set of accounts, but the framework can be expanded to cover intangible assets important to the analysis of growth and productivity, such as R&D, as well as nonmarket activities, such as household production.

1.2   Measuring Economic Activity in the Market Sector

1.2.1   Introduction: Overview of Existing Sets of U.S. Accounts

The existing sets of U.S. accounts are already interrelated through their use of and sharing of the same data. The BEA has responsibility for most of the U.S. economic accounts, including the national income, product, and reproducible wealth accounts; the balance of payments and international investment position accounts; the gross domestic product (GDP)–

---

1. "We" is used to describe the cumulative work discussed in Christensen and Jorgenson (1996), Jorgenson and Fraumeni (1996a, 1996b), and Jorgenson, Gollop, and Fraumeni (1987) to build integrated accounts as well as the continuation of that work discussed in this article.

by-industry and input-output accounts; the regional accounts; and a number of related accounts. These are estimated using Census, BLS, Internal Revenue Service (IRS), U.S. Treasury, FRB, and other data. The FRB uses the BEA's estimates of reproducible wealth and international balance-of-payment flows and positions, in combination with FRB estimates of domestic financial stocks and flows, to produce the nation's flow of funds and balance sheets accounts. The BLS uses BEA estimates of real output, investment, and capital and labor income as inputs into its aggregate, multifactor, and industry estimates of output and productivity.

The BEA's NIPAs record the value and composition of national production as measured by expenditures and the distribution of incomes generated in producing that output. The BEA's input-output and industry accounts measure national output by each industry's value added to production, estimate each industry's gross output and intermediate inputs, trace the flow of goods and services among industries in the production process, and provide a detailed commodity breakdown of national production. BLS productivity estimates measure labor productivity, multifactor productivity, and related measures, thereby providing a picture of each industry and labor, capital, and other inputs contributions to productivity growth.

The BEA's wealth accounts measure stocks and changes in stocks of reproducible assets, while the BEA's international investment position accounts measure international assets and liabilities and changes in these assets and liabilities. The FRB's flow-of-funds accounts detail the role of financial institutions and financial instruments in intermediating saving and investment and the changes in assets and liabilities across sectors that result. The FRB balance sheets record the distribution of these assets and liabilities at the end of each quarter.

The BEA's supporting international accounts measure U.S. residents' transactions with the rest of the world and trace those transactions by types of goods and services, incomes, and transfers as well as by type of payment for those transactions. The BEA's regional accounts disaggregate the national accounts by geographic area, providing many of the same types of information and serving the same purposes as the national accounts.

Taken together, these sets of national accounts paint a comprehensive picture of economic activity. The system provides an interconnected set of accounts that measures the flow of current economic transactions (expenditures, incomes, and production), prices, and stocks of productive assets and wealth. The accounts are double-entry accounts that are linked to one another so as to give users an integrated and comprehensive picture of economic activity for macroeconomic monitoring, analysis, and decision making. In an evaluation conducted by the United Nations (UN) and the International Monetary Fund (IMF) in the late 1990s, the United States and Canada were the only countries to receive a rating of 6 out of 6 in terms of the completeness of their sets of accounts as specified by the internationally recognized System of National Accounts (United Nations et al. 1993; hereafter SNA 1993). The U.S. accounts are also regarded as among the most accurate, up-to-date, and timely sets of accounts (as measured by GDP revisions, incorporation of new measurement concepts and methods, and release of GDP data).

The three most commonly cited difficulties with the U.S. accounts have been (a) incomplete integration, consistency, and gaps in the U.S. accounts that can for certain purposes reduce their analytic value; (b) inconsistency with the sectoring, structure, and presentation recommended by the SNA 1993 that reduces international comparability and analyses (a real problem when the U.S. economy is the benchmark and numeraire for cross-country comparisons); and (c) lack of expanded—and integrated—measures of economic activity (and welfare). A fourth and more recent complaint is that the U.S. accounts have moved ahead too fast in updating concepts and methods to measure the U.S. economy, resulting in reduced comparability of the U.S. accounts with other nations that have been slower in updating their accounts.

1.2.2   The BEA's NIPAs

While there are many summary statistics, accounts, and subaccounts in the NIPAs and SNA 1993, the best known is gross domestic product (GDP). GDP is an unduplicated measure of domestic production and can be measured in the following three ways: (a) by final expenditures, (b) by incomes earned in production, or (c) by the production approach, which is measured by industry value added, the value of gross output less the value of intermediate input. In concept, all three measures should be the same; in practice, they differ because they rely on different and incomplete source data.

The BEA prepares variants of all three of these measures of output. The BEA's final expenditures-based estimate is GDP; the income-based measures are gross domestic income (GDI), nominal GDP by industry, and gross state product (GSP); and the production value-added estimates come from BEA's input-output accounts and real GDP by industry.

The BEA's seven summary accounts in the NIPAs feature the GDP and GDI estimates and include quarterly and annual re-estimates in nominal and real terms. The NIPAs are double-entry sets of accounts in which the use of resources (expenditures) recorded in one account for one sector are also recorded as a source of resources (receipts) in the account of another sector or, if it is an intrasectoral transaction, in the same sector.

The first account is the domestic income and product account presented in table 1.1. This shows the consolidated (unduplicated) production of all sectors of the economy as the sum of goods and services sold to final users on the right-hand side of the account and the income generated by that production on the left side of the account. The other six accounts are consistent with and map into the domestic income and product account,

Table 1.1   NIPA summary accounts, 2002

Row
No.

Account 1. Domestic Income and Product Account

Row		Value
1	Compensation of employees, paid	6,024.3
2	Wage and salary accruals	4,979.8
3	Disbursements (3-12 and 5-11)	4,979.8
4	Wage accruals less disbursements (4-9 and 6-11)	0.0
5	Supplements to wages and salaries (3-14)	1,044.5
6	Taxes on production and imports (4-16)	760.1
7	*Less:* Subsidies (4-8)	38.2
8	Net operating surplus	2,523.2
9	Private enterprises (2-19)	2,520.3
10	Current surplus of government enterprises (4-26)	2.8
11	Consumption of fixed capital (6-13)	1,288.6
12	**Gross domestic income**	10,558.0
13	Statistical discrepancy (6-19)	−77.2
14	**GROSS DOMESTIC PRODUCT**	10,480.8
15	Personal consumption expenditures (3-3)	7,385.3
16	Durable goods	911.3
17	Nondurable goods	2,086.0
18	Services	4,388.0
19	Gross private domestic investment	1,589.2
20	Fixed investment (6-2)	1,583.9
21	Nonresidential	1,080.2
22	Structures	266.3
23	Equipment and software	813.9
24	Residential	503.7
25	Change in private inventories (6-4)	5.4
26	Net exports of goods and services	−426.3
27	Exports (5-1)	1,006.8
28	Imports (5-9)	1,433.1
29	Government consumption expenditures and gross investment (4-1 and 6	1,932.5
30	Federal	679.5
31	National defense	438.2
32	Nondefense	241.2
33	State and local	1,253.1
34	**GROSS DOMESTIC PRODUCT**	10,480.8

Account 2. Private Enterprise Income Account

Row		Value
1	Income payments on assets	2,316.7
2	Interest and miscellaneous payments (3-20 and 4-21)	2,267.7
3	Dividend payments to the rest of the world (5-14)	42.1
4	Reinvested earnings on foreign direct investment in the U.S. (5-15)	6.9
5	Business current transfer payments (net)	89.8
6	To persons (net) (3-24)	42.6
7	To government (net) (4-24)	46.8
8	To the rest of the world (net) (5-19)	0.4
9	Proprietors' income with inventory valuation and capital consumption adjustments (3-17)	797.7
10	Rental income of persons with capital consumption adjustment (3-18)	173.0

(continued)

Table 1.1   (continued)

Row No.		
11	Corporate profits with inventory valuation and capital consumption adjustments	904.2
12	Taxes on corporate income	195.0
13	To government (4-17)	185.9
14	To the rest of the world (5-19)	9.2
15	Profits after tax with inventory valuation and capital consumption adjustments	709.1
16	Net dividends (3-21 and 4-22)	398.3
17	Undistributed corporate profits with inventory valuation and capital consumption adjustments (6-10)	310.8
18	USES OF PRIVATE ENTERPRISE INCOME	
19	Net operating surplus (1-9)	2,520.3
20	Income receipts on assets	1,761.1
21	Interest (3-20)	1,558.7
22	Dividend receipts from the rest of the world (5-6)	81.5
23	Reinvested earnings on U.S. direct investment abroad (5-7)	121.0
24	SOURCES OF PRIVATE ENTERPRISE INCOME	4,281.5

Account 3. Personal Income and Outlay Account

Row No.		
1	Personal current taxes (4-15)	1,053.1
2	Personal outlays	7,674.0
3	Personal consumption expenditures (1-15)	7,385.3
4	Personal interest payments (3-20)	194.7
5	Personal current transfer payments	94.0
6	To government (4-25)	58.6
7	To the rest of the world (net) (5-17)	35.4
8	Personal saving (6-9)	183.2
9	PERSONAL TAXES, OUTLAYS, AND SAVING	8,910.3
10	Compensation of employees, received	6,019.1
11	Wage and salary disbursements	4,974.6
12	Domestic (1-3 less 5-11)	4,971.4
13	Rest of the world (5-3)	3.2
14	Supplements to wages and salaries (1-5)	1,044.5
15	Employer contributions for employee pension and insurance funds	680.4
16	Employer contributions for government social insurance	364.1
17	Proprietors' income with inventory valuation and capital consumption adjustments (2-9)	797.7
18	Rental income of persons with capital consumption adjustment (2-10)	173.0
19	Personal income receipts on assets	1,378.5
20	Personal interest income (2-2 and 3-4 and 4-7 and 5-5 less 2-21 less 4-21 less 5-13)	982.4
21	Personal dividend income (2-16 less 4-22)	396.2
22	Personal current transfer receipts	1,292.2
23	Government social benefits (4-4)	1,249.5
24	From business (net) (2-6)	42.6
25	*Less:* Contributions for government social insurance (4-19)	750.3
26	PERSONAL INCOME	8,910.3

Account 4. Government Receipts and Expenditures Account

Row No.		
1	Consumption expenditures (1-29)	1,595.4
2	Current transfer payments	1,271.1

Table 1.1   (continued)

Row
No.

3	Government social benefits	1,252.3
4	To persons (3-23)	1,249.5
5	To the rest of the world (5-18)	2.7
6	Other current transfer payments to the rest of the world (net) (5-18)	18.8
7	Interest payments (3-20)	319.3
8	Subsidies (1-7)	38.2
9	*Less:* Wage accruals less disbursements (1-4)	0.0
10	Net government saving (6-12)	−243.3
11	Federal	−240.0
12	State and local	−3.2
13	GOVERNMENT CURRENT EXPENDITURES AND NET SAVINGS	2,980.7
14	Current tax receipts	2,006.2
15	Personal current taxes (3-1)	1,053.1
16	Taxes on production and imports (1-6)	760.1
17	Taxes on corporate income (2-13)	185.9
18	Taxes from the rest of the world (5-18)	7.2
19	Contributions for government social insurance (3-25)	750.3
20	Income receipts on assets	116.1
21	Interest and miscellaneous receipts (2-2 and 3-20)	114.0
22	Dividends (3-21)	2.1
23	Current transfer receipts	105.3
24	From business (net) (2-7)	46.8
25	From persons (3-6)	58.6
26	Current surplus of government enterprises (1-10)	2.8
27	GOVERNMENT CURRENT RECEIPTS	2,980.7

Account 5. Foreign Transactions Current Account

1	Exports of goods and services (1-27)	1,006.8
2	Income receipts from the rest of the world	299.1
3	Wage and salary receipts (3-13)	3.2
4	Income receipts on assets	296.0
5	Interest (3-20)	93.5
6	Dividends (2-22)	81.5
7	Reinvested earnings on U.S. direct investment abroad (2-23)	121.0
8	CURRENT RECEIPTS FROM THE REST OF THE WORLD	1,306.0
9	Imports of goods and services (1-28)	1,433.1
10	Income payments to the rest of the world	277.6
11	Wage and salary payments (1-3)	8.4
12	Income payments on assets	269.2
13	Interest (3-20)	220.2
14	Dividends (2-3)	42.1
15	Reinvested earnings on foreign direct investment in the U.S. (2-4)	6.9
16	Current taxes and transfer payments to the rest of the world (net)	59.3
17	From persons (net) (3-7)	35.4
18	From government (net) (4-5 and 4-6 less 4-18)	14.3
19	From business (net) (2-8 and 2-14)	9.6
20	Balance on current account, national income and product accounts (7-1)	−464.1
21	CURRENT PAYMENTS TO THE REST OF THE WORLD AND BALANCE ON CURRENT ACCOUNT	1,306.0

(continued)

Table 1.1   (continued)

Row
No.

	Account 6. Domestic Capital Account	
1	Gross domestic investment	1,926.3
2	Private fixed investment (1-20)	1,583.9
3	Government fixed investment (1-29)	337.1
4	Change in private inventories (1-25)	5.4
5	Capital account transactions (net) (7-2)	1.3
6	Net lending or net borrowing (–), national income and product accounts (7-3)	–465.4
7	GROSS DOMESTIC INVESTMENT, CAPITAL ACCOUNTS TRANSACTIONS, AND NET LENDING	1,462.2
8	Net saving	250.8
9	Personal saving (3-8)	183.2
10	Undistributed corporate profits with inventory valuation and capital consumption adjustments (2-17)	310.8
11	Wage accruals less disbursements (private) (1-4)	0.0
12	Net government saving (4-10)	–243.3
13	*Plus:* Consumption of fixed capital (1-11)	1,288.6
14	Private	1,077.8
15	Government	210.8
16	General government	177.6
17	Government enterprises	33.2
18	*Equals:* Gross saving	1,539.4
19	Statistical discrepancy (1-13)	–77.2
20	GROSS SAVING AND STATISTICAL DISCREPANCY	1,462.2
	Account 7. Foreign Transactions Capital Account	
1	BALANCE ON CURRENT ACCOUNT, NATIONAL INCOME AND PRODUCT ACCOUNTS (5-20)	–464.1
2	Capital account transactions (net) (6-5)	1.3
3	Net lending or net borrowing (–), national income and product accounts (6-6)	–465.4
4	CAPITAL ACCOUNT TRANSACTIONS (NET) AND NET LENDING, NATIONAL INCOME AND PRODUCT ACCOUNTS	–464.1

Source: BEA (2004a).

Note: Table 1.1 is consistent with the 2002 benchmark revision of the U.S. National Accounts, while subsequent tables and figures are based on the 2003 annual revision, which appears in BEA (2004b).

providing additional detail on the aggregates presented in account 1. These supporting summary accounts include nearly 300 detailed supporting tables and subaccounts.

Accounts 2 through 5 present the receipts and expenditures of the major sectors of the economy. The second account, for example, is the private enterprise income account that provides additional information on the sources of funds (receipts) to private companies and other business enterprises on the right-hand side and information on the uses of those funds (payments) on the left-hand side. Account 3 is the personal-sector account (including households and nonprofit institutions serving households); account 4 is the government sector, and account 5 is the external, or foreign, sector.

Account 6, the domestic capital account, shows the sources of domestic saving and their use in domestic investment and capital transfers. Net borrowing from the foreign sector is the balancing item that fills the shortfall between domestic investment and domestic saving. Account 7 is the external, or foreign, sector capital account.

The United States has a rich set of monthly and quarterly indicators on both the income and the expenditure side of the U.S. accounts. As a result, while the U.S. national accounts are benchmarked to the U.S. benchmark input-output accounts every five years, the expenditure and income estimates in the quarterly and annual NIPAs are estimated independently from the annual production (value-added) estimates of GDP by industry and input-output estimates, which in turn are benchmarked to each other but also estimated separately. The result is a set of interrelated accounts that are highly consistent with the current indicators of the economy normally associated with each set of estimates (such as the expenditure estimates and the current data from Census on trade sales, inventories, capital goods shipments, international trade, and corporate profits). This relationship is very important to U.S. financial markets, business analysts, and planners who focus heavily on the most recent data.

A number of countries—many with less current period indicators and direct measures—depend heavily on their input-output accounts to develop current-period GDP and GDI estimates tied more directly to the production or value-added approach. The result is a highly consistent set of national accounts, but one in which current period estimates are based on fixed proportions of value added to gross output by industry. This method may be inconsistent with direct measures of wages and profits or of final expenditures from monthly or quarterly indicators, which are likely to vary from month to month and quarter to quarter. Although lacking direct measures for these variables, it is often impossible to tell. Sometime after the initial estimates—often once a year—such countries balance their production accounts with their expenditure and income-based estimates.

The NIPAs feature the expenditure-based GDP and income-based GDI estimates mainly because BEA believes that the quality of the U.S. source data for expenditures and income are, in general, superior to the value-added estimates (mainly due to inadequacies in the data on intermediate inputs). Clearly, a better approach would be the joint estimation of the expenditure, income, and production (value-added) estimates on a concurrent basis using a methodology that weights the relative quality of the source data and methods used in each technique. This would produce a common and, presumably, more accurate set of estimates that is balanced on an ongoing basis and consistent over time.

1.2.3   The BEA's Other Flow Accounts

BEA international and regional accounts map into the NIPAs, providing further detail on the associated components that appear in the NIPAs. The concepts, source data, and methods used are generally consistent across the accounts, although there are still some differences and reconciliation tables are available to compare the alternative estimates. The remaining differences largely reflect the differing needs in these areas. These differences have been reduced over time, particularly in the international area, as a result of efforts to harmonize the IMF's balance-of-payments manual and SNA 1993.

1.2.4   The BEA's Capital and Financial Accounts

The BEA produces what SNA 1993 describes as capital stocks. These estimates include real, current-cost, and historical-cost estimates of reproducible household, business, and government wealth, including opening and closing net stocks, investment flows, depreciation, average age, and valuation adjustments. The estimates are available by type of asset, by sector, and by industry. They are all consistent with the NIPAs.

The BEA also produces capital and financial accounts as part of its international accounts. Within the balance of payments, the current account records flows of goods and services, income, and transfers, while the capital account records transactions related to tangible assets—such as the transfer of the assets of the Panama Canal to Panama. The financial account records changes in U.S. international assets and liabilities, and the international investment position displays the year-end levels for those assets and liabilities.

1.2.5   BLS Productivity Estimates

The NIPAs and the associated industry accounts contain many components of a production account, but they, like SNA 1993, lack a measure of capital services. The BLS multifactor productivity estimates address this gap and present estimates for the value of capital services based on imputed rental prices, as well as measures of labor services that adjust for differences in labor quality and measures of intermediate inputs, all within the structure of a neoclassical production function. The BLS multifactor productivity estimates build on the large body of work by U.S. researchers, notably Denison and later Jorgenson and his colleagues, that extended and reformulated the NIPAs in an attempt to better explain the sources of economic growth.[2] The BLS accounts follow this tradition, and the estimates are largely consistent with the NIPAs.

---

2. See Denison (1967), Jorgenson (1996b), and Christensen and Jorgenson (1996).

1.2.6   FRB Flow-of-Funds and Balance Sheet Accounts

The NIPAs and the BEA's wealth estimates contain stock and flow data on reproducible wealth by sector. The BEA's balance-of-payments accounts contain stock and flow data on international financial assets and liabilities, but neither set of accounts contains data on domestic financial assets and liabilities. The FRB takes these data and adds estimates on domestic financial assets and liabilities and changes in those balances to create the flow-of-funds and balance sheet accounts. These accounts are generally consistent with the NIPAs, with the balance-of-payments accounts, and with the wealth accounts and cover most of the economy.

1.2.7   Overview of the International System of National Accounts

SNA 1993 is a highly articulated integrated accounts structure that is the international guideline for national accounts around the world. The accounts are jointly sponsored by the UN, IMF, the Organisation for Economic Co-operation and Development (OECD), and the European Union (EU). As shown in table 1.2, they present flow and stock information similar to that presented in the U.S. accounts. The structure of SNA 1993 differs from the U.S. accounts mainly with respect to its focus on the production account, the degree of consolidation, and its sectoring.

Whereas the U.S. accounts feature GDP as measured by the expenditure approach, the SNA 1993 structure features value-added measurement as estimated by the production approach. Like the NIPAs, it then details the distribution of the incomes earned in production by sector and details the sources and uses of those funds. The familiar GDP as measured by $C + I + G + (X - M)$ is not presented, except in a disaggregated fashion in the auxiliary goods and services transactions accounts. In practice, while most countries (as described above) use the production approach in estimating value-added output and GDP, when reporting national accounts estimates and GDP estimates, countries—and organizations including the UN, OECD, and IMF—feature GDP and its expenditure components, which are balanced to their production-based estimates, in their presentations of the national accounts. Also, most countries do not produce all of the highly detailed information specified by SNA 1993.

The U.S. accounts differ from SNA 1993 in that they are more consolidated. SNA 1993, for example, presents household incomes in several separate accounts (generation of income, allocation of primary income, secondary distribution of income, redistribution of income, and use of income accounts). In NIPA account 3, the personal income and outlay account, all sources of personal income are consolidated. For example, wages, salaries, dividends, taxes, and transfer payments are all included in the consolidated personal income and outlay account. There are also counterentries for

Table 1.2   System of national accounts 1993

	Nonfinancial corporations	Financial corporations	General government	Households	NPISHs	Total economy	Rest of the world	Total
Current accounts								
Production/external account of goods and services				Uses & resources				
Distribution and use of income accounts								
Generation of income account								
Allocation of primary income account								
Secondary distribution of income account								
Redistribution of income in kind account								
Use of income account								
Accumulation accounts			Changes in assets & changes in liabilities and net worth					
Capital account								
Financial account								
Other changes in volume of assets account								
Revaluation account								
Balance sheets			Assets & liabilities					
Opening balance sheet								
Changes in balance sheet								
Closing balance sheet								

Source: United Nations et al. (1993), pp. 28, 60–65.

Note: NPISH = nonprofit institutions serving households.

these transactions in the other sectoral accounts (private enterprise, government, and foreign).

Finally, the U.S. accounts differ from SNA 1993 in sectoring. SNA 1993, for example, breaks out nonprofit institutions serving households (NPISH) from households. The U.S. accounts are moving in this general direction, in this area, with the introduction of such a separation in the 2003 comprehensive revision. The BEA introduced separate estimates of the income and outlays of the households and of the NPISHs. However, in other areas, institutional arrangements in the United States suggest that current BEA definitions are better suited for the United States than SNA 1993.

1.2.8   Evolution of the U.S. National Income and Product Accounts: Responses to Changes in the Economy and Policy Needs

Prior to the development of the NIPAs, policymakers had to guide the economy using limited and fragmentary information—such as stock prices, freight car loadings, and incomplete indexes of industrial production—about the state of the economy. The Great Depression and the growing role of government in managing the economy during World War II underlined the problems of incomplete data and led to the development of the national accounts.

In response to the lack of economic data in the 1930s, the Department of Commerce commissioned Nobel laureate Simon Kuznets to develop national income estimates, which later evolved into a set of national economic accounts. This work was a coordinated effort with the National Bureau of Economic Research (NBER), and the Conference on Research in Income and Wealth (CRIW) was founded—with Simon Kuznets as its first chair—to assist in the formation of the accounts. Kuznets headed a small group within the Bureau of Foreign and Domestic Commerce's Division of Economic Research. Kuznets coordinated the work of researchers at the NBER in New York and his staff at Commerce. The original set of accounts was presented in a report to Congress in 1934 and in a research report, *National Income, 1929–32.*

Early in 1942, annual estimates of gross national product (GNP) were introduced to complement the estimates of national income and to facilitate wartime planning. Wartime planning needs also helped to stimulate the development of input-output accounts. Nobel laureate Wassily Leontief developed the U.S. input-output accounts that subsequently became an integral part of the NIPAs. In commenting on the usefulness of the national accounts, Wesley C. Mitchell, director, NBER, said: "Only those who had a personal share in the economic mobilization for World War I could realize in how many ways and how much estimates of national income covering twenty years and classified in several ways facilitated the World War II effort."

Over time, in response to policy needs and changes in the economy, the accounts have been expanded to provide quarterly estimates of GDP and monthly estimates of personal income and outlays, regional accounts, wealth accounts, industry accounts, and expanded international accounts.

In the 1940s, World War II planning needs were the impetus for the development of product or expenditure estimates (at that time gross national product). By 1947, the accounts had evolved into a consolidated set of income and product accounts, providing an integrated bird's-eye view of the economy. In the late 1950s and early 1960s, interest in stimulating economic growth and in the sources of growth led to the development of official input-output tables, capital stock estimates, and more detailed and timely state and local personal income estimates. In the late 1960s and 1970s, accelerating inflation prompted the development of improved measures of prices and inflation-adjusted output.

In the 1980s, the internationalization of trade in services led to an expansion of the estimates of international trade in services in the NIPAs. In response to rapid technological innovation and the increasing importance in computers—and problems in measuring their prices—the BEA did pioneering work with IBM in the development of quality-adjusted price and output measures for computers. In the 1990s, the BEA introduced more accurate chain-weighted measures of prices and inflation-adjusted output, developed estimates of investments in computer software, and incorporated updated measures of high-tech products and banking output.

The BEA has continued to update its accounts in recent years, developing more accurate measures of changing aspects of the economy ranging from finance and insurance to corporate profits and pensions. The BEA has worked to improve the accuracy, expand the scope, and improve the timeliness of the BEA's industry (production-based) accounts. Finally, the BEA has—as noted above—changed the basic national accounts structure to increase international comparability and to provide expanded information in an easier to use format.

In general, most observers reviewing the history of the accounts have concluded that the basic structure and concepts are sound and that the Department of Commerce and BEA have done a good job of updating the accounts to keep pace with changes in the economy and in policy needs. As Federal Reserve Board Chairman Alan Greenspan said in reviewing the history of the accounts:

> the Department of Commerce has treated the national income accounts, and specifically the GDP, as living documents; that is, an endeavor to recognize that the American economy is continuously changing. Its nature is being altered by technology and all sorts of other institutional effects. And as a result, how one measures the notion of what is the market value of goods and services produced, of necessity, has been chang-

ing over the years. And I must say that it is really quite impressive the extent to which the Department of Commerce has been able to keep up with the various changes that have evolved.[3]

1.2.9   Remaining Challenges

Although over time the accounts have mainly addressed users' needs, there have been gaps relating to scope, to integration, and to nonmarket goods and services. As economists attempted to chronicle and analyze the sources of economic growth in the post-WWII era, it became clear that important sources of economic growth were omitted from the accounts. The accounts were directed more to issues of Keynesian fiscal policy than to accounting for the sources of growth. As a result, the focus was on expenditure and income flows with limited focus on capital inputs and capital stocks.

Lacking complete data from the NIPAs, Denison, Jorgenson, Griliches, and other researchers used the national accounts data on income shares, investment, and other information to build a rich set of data and analytical findings on the sources of economic growth. As noted above, the BLS multifactor productivity estimates built upon this important work and developed a comprehensive and consistent official framework and data set for the analysis of productivity growth.

The BEA NIPA and industry account data and the BLS productivity data are widely used to study economic growth, productivity, and structural change. The general picture of economic activity is consistent regardless of which data sources are used, but there are some differences. These differences largely arise from the disparate purposes for which the data are constructed, which are reflected in agency choices on methodology, coverage, and index number procedures.

For example, within the BEA sets of accounts, the current-period NIPAs, as noted above, are—except for benchmarking—estimated independently from the annual production-based input-output accounts and GDP by industry. This independence reflects decisions about the focus of each of the accounts, the quality of the underlying source data, and the need for each set of accounts to be consistent with its own set of methods and current indicators—Census data in the case of the input-output accounts and income data in the case of the GDP-by-industry accounts. The resulting set of accounts are less accurate and consistent than they might otherwise be and present differing results to researchers depending on which account's data are used. Examples of complications include uncertainty in budgeting, in monetary policy, and in business planning or analyses of sources of

---

3. December 7, 1999, press conference in Washington, DC. Full remarks were reprinted in Landefeld (2000).

growth across industries during the latter half of the 1990s when trend growth using the income approach exceeded that derived using the expenditure approach.[4]

Further variations between BEA and BLS data also reflect differences in the focus of each series. The BEA strives to provide complete and consistent coverage of the entire economy in the NIPAs, whereas the BLS primarily seeks to achieve maximum reliability in its various measures of productivity. These differing goals are not necessarily inconsistent with one another, since both require reliable output and input measures, but they can lead to differences in definition and coverage as well as in methodology. The BEA covers all industries, even those for which output measures are sometimes at best tenuous. The BLS, on the other hand, can focus on those industries for which measures are quite robust.

Part of the differences, especially at detailed industry levels, also reflects different choices for underlying source data and aggregation techniques. For example, the BEA uses a Fisher index-number formula to aggregate components of the NIPA price and quantity indexes consistently, decomposing the nominal change in GDP. The BLS, on the other hand, uses a Tornquist index to aggregate components of its multifactor productivity accounts because it is an exact and superlative index that matches the econometric and statistical properties needed for multifactor productivity analysis. The BEA and BLS use depreciation formulas that can differ for specific industries and types of assets. Until the recent NIPA comprehensive revision, moreover, the BEA and BLS defined the business sector differently to suit their particular needs.

In general, the quantitative importance of the differences caused by dissimilarities in index number formula and depreciation method is small, and the change in the BEA definition of the business sector has removed the sometimes significant differences in growth rates caused by the old definitional difference for that sector. As Diewert and others have shown, all superlative numbers closely approximate each other. Even over long periods, indexes produced by Tornquist and Fisher indexes are identical to the fifth decimal place.[5] Differences in depreciation rates can have an effect on capital services and multifactor productivity, but even the large changes in depreciation for non-residential buildings introduced by the BEA and BLS in 2001 had extremely small effects on capital inputs and multifactor productivity. In addition, the BLS and BEA work together to ensure consistency in depreciation rates.[6]

Most of the significant differences between the BEA and BLS estimates are the result of decisions made over time by individual analysts regarding

---

4. See, for example, the Council of Economic Advisers (1997), Office of Management and Budget (1997), and Congressional Budget Office (1997).

5. See Diewert (1978).

6. See Bureau of Labor Statistics (2003).

source data, mainly for price deflators rather than any agency views regarding the use of hedonics, or other broad methodological issues. Indeed, most of the differences between BEA and BLS estimates for manufacturing industries were eliminated by a concerted effort in recent years to agree on common deflators for industries where real growth rates differed. However, there are remaining differences in selected manufacturing industries and in a number of nonmanufacturing industries.

These remaining differences between the BEA and BLS estimates have led many researchers to construct their own measures of productivity, particularly for studying the "new economy" of the late 1990s. Results of these studies have sometimes differed significantly, depending partly on data sources and the level of detail provided, leading to differing interpretations of the sources of productivity growth. For example, Nordhaus (2002) found faster labor productivity growth for the nonfarm business sector using the BEA's value-added by industry data rather than the official BLS measure. Baily and Lawrence (2001), also using the BEA's value added by industry data, and Stiroh (2002), using the BEA's gross output by industry data, concluded that the post-1995 productivity acceleration had spread from information technology (IT)–producing industries to IT-using industries. Gordon (2001), however, questioned whether such a spillover actually occurred after finding conflicting evidence from several BEA and BLS output measures. Triplett and Bosworth (2004) have documented how productivity estimates may differ significantly for broad sectors and for individual industries, depending upon whether BEA or BLS data are used. These differences can hinder integrated analysis of the sources of productivity growth. Divergences in the data force researchers to either choose one set of estimates over the other, or to develop their own estimates.[7]

Similar issues arise regarding differences between the BEA's and the FRB's measures of saving and each agency's measure of wealth stocks. The BEA's and the FRB's measures of saving and wealth stocks are developed in concert, and taken as a whole, they both provide consistent and integrated information on trends in saving and wealth. There are, however, important differences between the two series and issues in reconciliation. Similar to the differences between the BEA and BLS, many issues relate to the different purposes for which the data are used. For example, the FRB definition of saving includes saving in the form of purchases of consumer durables. The NIPAs do not, largely because this definition would logically require the treatment of consumer durables as investment and require the estimation of the capital services from these consumer durables, as well as the further step of a full household production account that measures household labor as well as capital services.

7. Jorgenson, Ho, and Stiroh (2005) use a hybrid of BEA and BLS data to construct estimates of productivity.

These and other statistical and methodological differences between the two agencies' data have led economists to generate their own series. In the early 1980s, Ruggles and Ruggles (1982) developed an integrated version of the NIPAs and flow-of-funds accounts. More recently, Gale and Sabelhaus (1999) made adjustments to the BEA and FRB data to create an alternate definition of savings in order to analyze the decline in U.S. saving over the last decade. These adjusted measures showed that saving had fallen less than the official measures and the sectoral composition of the decline was different. Their analysis also underlined the importance of an integrated presentation of saving, capital gains, and other changes in household wealth.

1.2.10   Expanding the Boundary of the Accounts

Over the years, researchers interested in issues other than the sources of growth have advocated and developed expanded and better-integrated sets of accounts. Kendrick (1961), Ruggles and Ruggles (1982), and Eisner (1989) extended the NIPAs to better analyze business, household, and governmental decision making. This section discusses the various extensions of the existing accounts required to meet some of the needs raised by these researchers and those raised by the needs of researchers interested in the sources of economic growth.

Expanded Price and Quantity Measures

The BEA's accounts are presented in nominal and real terms, but the presentation is incomplete. A complete production account requires price and quantity measures for all stocks and flows. The NIPAs present prices and quantities for output (expenditures, gross output), intermediate inputs, certain assets (residential and nonresidential fixed capital, inventories, consumer durables, and government fixed capital), and selected income aggregates (GDI, GNP, and disposable personal income). What is missing—for a complete production account and other purposes—is price and quantity measures for all factor inputs (all components of labor and capital income and of value added), saving, and financial assets and liabilities.

The problem with developing such price and quantity measures has been the absence of clear conceptual or empirical guidance on the appropriate deflators for these measures. For goods sold in markets, there are observable prices per unit, but what is the appropriate per-unit price for corporate profits, or saving? Alternatively, while one can measure the price of residential houses to deflate the nominal value of the fixed stock of residential structures, what price should be used to deflate the value of corporate equities? One answer has been to use some form of a purchasing power index. The BEA, for example, deflates the value of disposable personal income with the price index for consumer spending. Deflating other incomes, however, is more difficult. Deflating corporate profits, for example, might require a weighted average of the deflators for consumer spending (dividends), fixed and inventory investment (retained earnings), and government (taxes).

Consumer Durables, Government, and Nonprofit Capital Services. Other required components for a complete production account, as well as expanded accounts for the analysis of household and government, are (a) the capitalization of investments in consumer durables and the addition of a service value from these consumer durables and (b) the addition of a complete service value for government and nonprofit fixed assets.

In the existing accounts (SNA 1993 and the NIPAs), investments in consumer durables are treated as current consumption, despite the fact that—like investments by business—they yield a flow of benefits over time. The rise in motor vehicle leasing has further highlighted this inconsistency. If, for example, a vehicle is leased by a household, it is treated as investment in the year it is purchased—by the leasing company—and then yields a flow of capital services (rental payments) that add to GDP over the term of the lease. In contrast, if the car is purchased by the household it is treated as consumption in the year it is purchased, and there is no additional flow of capital services over the life of the car.

The inconsistency related to government capital is similar. While the existing accounts do treat government expenditures on capital goods as investment, they include only a partial value for the services of government capital by counting the value of depreciation on government capital (no value is included for the services of nonprofit capital). In theory, the value of any capital service should be at least equal to the rent that would have to be paid to the owner of an asset: the return that the owner could make if the current market value of the asset were invested elsewhere, or the compensation to the owner for the decline in the value of the asset due to its use in production.[8] The present treatment of government capital implicitly assumes that the net return to government capital is zero, despite a positive opportunity cost. (And the treatment of nonprofits assumes no service value, net return, or depreciation.)

If leasing markets and data were complete then including complete service values for consumer durables and government would not be difficult. The BEA already has estimates of capital stocks and depreciation and could use market rents to estimate the implicit return to apply to the net stocks of capital. However, the absence of such data means that the net return to the capital stock must estimated and added to depreciation to develop a service value. This estimation raises conceptual issues relating to

---

8. This is a simplified view of the service value for an asset. As noted below, the formula for the service value becomes more complicated when taxes and capital gains and losses are considered.

the appropriate opportunity cost and empirical issues in estimating this cost.

There is a long-standing debate in the economic literature on the opportunity cost of government capital, which includes suggestions to use the household rate of return, the government borrowing rate, the rate of return to business, or some weighted average rate. Also, there are significant empirical difficulties in determining the appropriate values for these alternative rates. What government borrowing rate, for example, should one use— short-term rates, long-term rates, or some weighted average—and over what time period?

As a result of this uncertainty, many researchers have simply picked a rate, applied it to the net stock of capital, and added depreciation to estimate the return. The resulting indirectly estimated service values tend to move in line with movements in the capital stocks and tend to smooth movements in GDP. Such imputations are considered an undesirable characteristic to business, tax, and other analysts interested in movements in the business cycle and the "cash" components of the economy.

An example of how the inclusion of nonmarket transactions influences the national accounts can already be seen in the current calculation of GDP. One of the largest nonmarket activities included in GDP is owner-occupied housing, the rent that owners "pay" themselves to use their property. Although market rents are available, the imputation methodology results in a series that moves roughly in line with the growth in the stock of housing. Owner-occupied housing is a large addition to market-sector GDP (as would be an imputed rent for consumer durables), has ranged in size from 5 to 8 percent of GDP since 1960, and has experienced less volatility in real growth than GDP. During quarters of recessions between 1960:I and 2003:IV (quarters of recession as defined by NBER), GDP declined 1.6 percent on average while implicit housing grew 3.6 percent. Excluding owner-occupied housing, GDP during recessionary quarters would have declined by 1.9 percent, 0.3 percent more decline than stand-alone GDP. During the expansions of the same time frame (1960:I– 2003:IV), owner-occupied housing moderated growth. Stand-alone GDP grew 4.2 percent on average. Excluding owner-occupied housing, GDP would have grown 4.3 percent. Volatility also decreases by including owner-occupied housing in GDP. Absolute quarter-to-quarter change in real growth is lower for stand-alone GDP at 3.3 percent versus 3.5 percent if owner-occupied housing is excluded.

Because of this smoothing effect and the uncertainty regarding the appropriate rate of return, the solution for nonbusiness capital services may be the initial introduction of supplemental, or satellite, accounts estimates accompanied by further research and data collection of market rental values. Ultimately, after experimenting with different source data and methods and after vetting by users, hybrid estimates—that utilize a mix of market and imputed returns—could be integrated into an expanded set of core accounts.

Valuing Output in Both Consumers and Producers Prices. Sales, excise, and other taxes charged against output (output taxes) drive a wedge between the prices paid by consumers and the prices for the same products received by producers. Analysis of production or expenditures suggests that the valuation of output and expenditures should be done using the prices each of these sets of economic actors confronts. SNA 1993 recommends this treatment, with industry and sectoral output value at the prices received by producers (what they call *basic prices,* or market prices less output taxes) and final expenditures at the market prices (including output taxes) confronted by consumers, investors, and government.

While the BEA's input-output accounts decompose sectoral and industry output into producer and purchases prices, the GDP-by-industry accounts value industry and sectoral output at market prices. This treatment is largely motivated by a desire to completely—in one step—decompose GDP, which is valued at market prices. Given the BEA's new procedures (described elsewhere in this volume) of estimating and producing consistent annual I-O and GDP estimates that are available simultaneously, sectoral and industry estimates are now available on both basis. An aggregate production account using the NIPAs, however, requires deducting output taxes from consumption and each of the other components of GDP to transform it from an expenditure to a production account valued at producer prices.

Decomposition of Proprietor's Income into Labor and Capital Components

The NIPAs present a single estimate for proprietor's income with no decomposition of the return to the proprietor for his or her labor and the return to the capital invested in the business. A complete production account, however, requires the decomposition of returns from production into labor and capital. The difficulties with developing such a breakdown are twofold. First, proprietors do not break down their income and report the total amount as business income to the tax and statistical authorities. Second, indirect estimates that apply average wages to estimates of hours worked by self-employed persons or capital returns to estimates of capital stocks employed by proprietors result in negative returns to either capital or labor depending upon which imputation is estimated first. The reasons for this are not clear, but may be related to the extent to which proprietors underreport income to tax and statistical authorities, problems in measuring hours worked and capital invested by the self-employed, and the nonpecuniary benefits of self-employment.

Better data on proprietor income will have to await improvements in the reporting of self-employment income and hours, but in the meantime various methods can be employed to produce estimates that correctly capture the rough order of magnitude of labor and capital income and changes in these returns. The BLS in their productivity estimates assume that proprietors' labor and capital returns are distributed in the same proportions as in the corporate sector. In the estimates presented below, wages specific to the characteristics of the self-employed are employed, and the resulting residual for capital is lower than average returns to capital, but still positive.

R&D and Other Intangibles, Human Capital, and Other Expansions

Other important expansions to the accounts are human capital (Jorgenson and Fraumeni 1996a; Eisner 1989; and Kendrick 1961), research and development (Christensen and Jorgenson 1996, Eisner 1989), and natural resources (Wright 1990). More recent work (Hall and Hall 1993; and Corrado, Haltiwanger, and Sichel 2005) has also pointed to the importance of counting the value of management innovations and other intangibles. While it is clear that all of these assets are important to growth, investments in these assets are normally made by the individuals or the firms that use the capital and the "finished" assets are rarely bought and sold. The result is that although these are all economic assets that are "produced" by markets they are often regarded as nonmarket assets because there are no significant third-party markets and associated market prices for these assets that can be used to value either the assets or the services provided by these assets.

As is the case with consumer durables and government capital, what is needed is the development of an expanded set of satellite accounts that include R&D and other intangibles, human capital, and natural resources accompanied by a research program to improve the valuation basis for these expanded accounts.

1.3   Measuring Economic Activity in the Nonmarket Sector

1.3.1   Economic versus Welfare Accounts

Since the founding of the U.S. national accounts, there has been an ongoing debate regarding the treatment of natural resources and the environment, as well as the treatment of a whole set of broader welfare-based measures of economic and social progress, including some of the items discussed above. One school, exemplified by Kuznets (1946), favored development of a much broader set of welfare-orientated accounts that would focus on sustainability and address the externalities and social costs associated with economic development. Another, exemplified by Jaszi (1971), insisted that the national accounts must be objective and descriptive and thus based on observable market transactions. Jaszi felt that, conceptually, the accounts should be extended to treat the economic discovery, depletion, and stocks of natural resources symmetrically with plant and equipment and other economic resources. The absence of observable market transactions and the subjectivity associated with such estimates led him to conclude, however, that they should not be included in the accounts. As a result—as described above—analysts such as Jorgenson et al. developed their own extensions to the accounts for production analysis—as opposed to welfare analysis.

In the 1960s and early 1970s another more environmentally focused move to broaden the accounts arose out of concern about environmental degradation and fears that the world was running out of resources and approaching the "limits to growth."[9] Externalities associated with economic growth also prompted renewed interest in broader social accounting. Work by Nordhaus and Tobin (1973), among others, on adjusting traditional economic accounts for changes in leisure time, disamenities of urbanization, exhaustion of natural resources, population growth, and other aspects of welfare produced indicators of economic well-being. However, the seemingly limitless scope, the range of uncertainty, and the degree of subjectivity involved in such measures of nonmarket activities limited the usefulness of and interest in these social indicators. It was felt that inclusion of such measures would sharply diminish the usefulness of traditional economic accounts for analyzing market activities. Attention subsequently focused on more readily identifiable and directly relevant market issues, such as the extent to which expenditures that relate to the protection and restoration of the environment (and other so-called defensive expenditures) are identifiable in the economic accounts.

1.3.2   Satellite Accounting

The development of the UN system of environmental and economic accounting (SEEA) and the use of supplemental, or satellite, accounts went a long way toward resolving the long-standing impasse between those who advocated broader sets of accounts and those concerned with maintaining the usefulness of the existing economic accounts (see United Nations 1993). The supplemental accounts allowed conceptual and empirical research to move forward with estimates that can be linked to the existing accounts without diminishing their usefulness. Satellite accounts are also useful in expanding the level of detail of certain sectors or broadening the definition of an industry. For example, transportation appears much smaller in the national accounts than that actual industry since many companies own their own trucking fleet or other delivery system and transportation is often times not a final product.

---

9. See Meadows et al. (1972), which summarizes the running out of resources. In addition, Nordhaus and Tobin (1973) discuss the broader issue of the measurement of economic growth.

The SEEA is a flexible, expandable satellite system. It draws on the materials balance approach to present the full range of interactions between the economy and the environment. This accounting approach attempts to take inventory of assets or stocks by measuring initial levels and tracking additions to or subtractions from those levels. The SEEA builds on, and is designed to be used with, SNA 1993.

1.3.3   Integrated Economic and Environmental Satellite Accounts (IEESA)

In the 1990s, the BEA presented a prototype integrated economic and environmental satellite account (Landefeld et al. 1994).[10] In constructing this account, the BEA built on several key lessons from the social accounting experience of the 1970s and on the framework of the SEEA. First, such accounts should be focused on a specific set of issues. Second, given the kind of uses to which the estimates would be put, the early stage of conceptual development and the statistical uncertainties (even if the estimates are limited to the environment's effects on market activities), such estimates should be developed in a supplemental, or satellite, framework. Third, such accounts should not focus on sustainability or some normative objective but should cover those interactions that can be tied to productive market activities and valued using market values or proxies thereof. Fourth, in keeping with the focus of the existing accounts, the supplemental accounts should be constructed in such a manner as to be consistent with the existing accounts and thus allow analysis of the effects of the interactions between the environment and the economy on production, income, consumption, and wealth. Tables 1.3 and 1.4 show the structure of the BEA's IEESAs.

The existing economic accounts do not provide normative data, and neither did the integrated economic and environmental accounts developed by the BEA. They would describe activities that bear upon the market in the monetary terms of the market, without implying any conclusions about whether the reflected situation is "right." The IEESAs were designed to report either market values or proxies for market values. If a problem with property rights leads to the undervaluation and overexploitation of a resource, a set of integrated economic accounts will not reveal the right price or the correct level of stocks. However, they will provide the data for objective analysis of the problem for items such as the changes in the value of stocks or the share of income to be attributed to a resource. Integrated economic and environmental accounting aims to provide a picture of the

---

10. In addition to the IEESAs, the BEA has developed satellite accounts in a number of other areas, including household production (Landefeld and Howell 1997), research and development (Fraumeni and Okubo 2005), tourism (Okubo and Planting 1998), transportation (Fang et al. 2000), and ownership-based accounts for international transactions (Landefeld, Whichard, and Lowe 1993).

Table 1.3   IEESA production account

| | | Industries | | | | Final uses (GDP) | | | | | | |
| | Row No. | Agriculture, forestry, and fisheries (1) | Mining, utilities, water, and sanitary services (2) | Other industries (3) | Total (4) | Final consumption | | Gross domestic capital formation (7) | Exports (8) | Imports (9) | GDP (5 + 6 + 7 + 8 + 9) (10) | Total commodity output (= + 10) (11) |
						House-hold (5)	Govern-ment (6)					
				Commodities								
Made	1											
Assets	2											
Fixed assets	3											
Environmental management	4											
Pollution abatement and control	5											
Other	6											
Inventories	7											
Government	8											
Nonfarm	9											
Farm	10											
Other	11											
Environmental cleanup and waste disposal services	12											
Other	13											
Natural and environmental assets	14											
Fixed	15											
Cultivated biological resources: Natural growth	16											
Proved subsoil assets	17											
Developed land	18											

(*continued*)

Table 1.3   (continued)

	Row No.	Industries				Final uses (GDP)						
		Agriculture, forestry, and fisheries (1)	Mining, utilities, water, and sanitary services (2)	Other industries (3)	Total (4)	Final consumption		Gross domestic capital formation (7)	Exports (8)	Imports (9)	GDP (5 + 6 + 7 + 8 + 9) (10)	Total commodity output (4 + 10) (11)
						House-hold (5)	Govern-ment (6)					
Uncultivated biological resources: Natural growth	19											
Unproved subsoil assets	20											
Undeveloped land	21											
Water	22											
Air	23											
Work-in-progress inventories (natural growth products)	24											
Total intermediate inputs	25											
Compensation of employees	26		*Value added*									
Indirect business taxes, etc.	27											
Corporate profits and other property income	28											
Depreciation of fixed made assets: Structures and equipment	29											
Environmental management	30											
Pollution abatement and control	31											
Other	32											

Depletion and degradation of fixed natural and environmental assets	33
Growth products: Fixed	34
Proved subsoil assets	35
Developed land	36
Uncultivated biological resources	37
Unproved subsoil assets	38
Undeveloped land	39
Water	40
Air	41
Gross value added (GDP) (rows 25 + 27 + 28 + 29 + 33)	42
Depreciation, depletion, and degradation (rows 29 + 33)	43
Net value added (NDP) (rows 42–43)	44
Total industry output	45

Source: Survey of Current Business, April 1994, p. 47.

Table 1.4 IEESA asset account

	Row No.	Opening stocks (1)	Total, net (3 + 4 + 5) (2)	Change			Closing stocks (1 + 2) (6)
				Depreciation, depletion, degradation (3)	Capital formation (4)	Revaluation and other changes (5)	
Produced assets							
Made assets	1						
Fixed assets	2						
Residential structures and equipment, private and government	3						
Fixed nonresidential structures and equipment, private and government	4						
Natural resource related	5						
Environmental management	6						
Conservation and development	7						
Water supply facilities	8						
Pollution abatement and control	9						
Sanitary services	10						
Air pollution abatement and control	11						
Water pollution abatement and control	12						
Other	13						
Inventories	14						
Government	15						
Nonfarm	16						
Farm (harvested crops, and livestock other than cattle and claves)	17						
Corn	18						
Soybeans	19						
All wheat	20						
Other	21						
Developed natural assets	22						
Cultivated biological resources	23						
Cultivated fixed natural growth assets	24						

Livestock for breeding, dairy, draught, etc.	25
Cattle	26
Fish stock	27
Vineyards, orchards	28
Trees on timberland	29
Work-in-progress on natural growth products	30
Livestock raised for slaughter	31
Cattle	32
Fish stock	33
Calves	34
Crops and other produced plants, not yet harvested	35
Proved subsoil assets	36
Oil (including natural gas liquids)	37
Gas (including natural gas liquids)	38
Coal	39
Metals	40
Other minerals	41
Developed land	42
Land underlying structures (private)	43
Agricultural land (excluding vineyards, orchards)	44
Soil	45
Recreational land and water (public)	46
Forest and other wooded land	47

Nonproduced/environmental assets

Uncultivated biological resources	48
Wild fish	49
Timber and other plants of uncultivated forests	50
Other uncultivated biological resources	51
Unproved subsoil assets	52
Undeveloped land	53
Water (economic effects of changes in the stock)	54
Air (economic effects of changes in the stock)	55

Source: Survey of Current Business, April 1994, p. 41.

interactions between the economy and the environment, including uses of resources and feedback effects.

In accordance with the first criterion, the BEA limited the IEESAs to those interactions that directly affect the economy and are thus relevant to the objective of economic accounts. From this standpoint, the environment can be thought of as consisting of a range of natural resource and environmental assets that provide an identifiable and significant flow of goods and services to the economy. The economy's uses of these productive natural assets and the goods and services they provide can be grouped into two general classes. When use of the natural asset permanently or temporarily reduces its quantity, this is viewed as involving a flow of a good or service, and the quantitative reduction in the asset is called *depletion*. When use of the natural asset reduces its quality, the qualitative reduction in the asset is called *degradation*. However, the use of natural assets describes only part of the interaction between the economy and the environment. There are also feedback effects, such as the reduction in the future yield of crops, timber, fisheries, and the like from current pollution or overharvesting. Materials balance and energy accounting highlight both the use of the natural assets and the feedback effects from the use; thus, they capture the full interaction between the economy and the environment. In the case of environmental assets, feedback is more complicated, with effects that often fall on other industries and consumers. While this picture has numerous elements and is complex, by definition it does not cover many of the transformations and interactions within the environment itself—for example, the disposal of waste products from wild fish and mammals or the conversion of natural carbon dioxide into oxygen by plant matter on land and in the oceans.

In accord with the second criterion, the IEESAs had two main structural features. First, natural and environmental resources are treated like productive assets and only the economically productive aspects of the resources are considered. These resources, along with structures and equipment, were treated as part of the nation's wealth, and the flow of goods and services from them is identified and their contribution to production measured. Second, the accounts are designed to provide substantial detail on expenditures and assets relevant to understanding and analyzing the production process. Fully implemented IEESAs would permit identification of the economic contribution of natural and environmental resources by industry, by type of income, by product, and ultimately by region.

The BEA's decision to treat natural and environmental resources like productive assets in the IEESAs was based on their similarity to man-made capital for labor and materials in that they are devoted to producing fixed assets and then yield a flow of services over time. Inventories, on the other hand, are stocks held pending further processing, sale, delivery, or intermediate use.

The distinction between fixed assets and inventories is not always clear. Proved mineral reserves may seem to be similar to inventories since they are a set number of units waiting to be used up in production. Yet they also fit the classic characteristics of fixed capital expenditures in that materials and labor are needed to produce ("prove") them, and they yield a stream of product over long periods of time. Further, like a fixed asset such as a machine, the number of units extracted from a new mine or field is uncertain and varies over time and over the service life used up in production. Finally, the treatment of mineral reserves as fixed assets serves equally well as a reminder of the reproducibility of proved reserves.

The valuation basis for the IEESAs is market prices or proxies thereof. While alternative methods such as maintenance cost and contingent valuation have attractive theoretical characteristics, they are not appropriate for the BEA's purpose, and the associated practical difficulties outweigh their pluses. In keeping with the goals and criteria stated above, market pricing was the optimal choice for the IEESAs. First, market pricing maintains objectivity by avoiding the biases that may be inherent in "willingness to pay" surveys. Second, market pricing is consistent with conventional accounts, as well as the SEEA, and facilitates international comparability. Finally, market pricing is consistent with the limits placed on included interactions because it values those interactions from the perspective of the market.

1.4   What Is Now Required

1.4.1   Building an Integrated and Consistent
System of National Accounts

The foregoing review identifies a clear need to update, integrate, and extend the U.S. system of national accounts. Our first and most important objective is to make the NIPAs consistent with the accounts for productivity compiled by the BLS and the flow-of-funds accounts constructed by the FRB. The boundaries of production, income and expenditures, accumulation, and wealth accounts must be identical throughout the system in order to achieve consistency. Development of a fully integrated and consistent system of accounts will require close collaboration among the BEA, BLS, and FRB, as well as coordination with Census, the most important agency for generating primary source data.

This section lays out a blueprint for revamping the U.S. national accounts that builds directly on the new seven-account NIPA framework and the work of Jorgenson et al., as well as the estimates presented in the 2003 benchmark revision of the NIPAs. While this blueprint does not include nonmarket extensions to the accounts, it could be extended to near-market and nonmarket sectors along the lines outlined by Abraham and Mackie (chap. 4 in this volume) and Nordhaus (chap. 3 in this volume). Building on the lessons of the past, any such extension should be in the form of satellite, or supplementary, accounts. These accounts could then focus on non-market goods and services that contribute to production, can be valued in market prices, and are consistent with the economic concepts in the existing accounts.

Our initial goal is to integrate the BLS multifactor productivity measures with the production account of the NIPAs, as proposed by Fraumeni et al. (chap. 9 in this volume). Following the BEA, our measure of output represents the GDP, while our measure of input corresponds to GDI. The GDP is given in current and constant prices, as in the NIPAs, while GDI is given in current and constant prices, as in the BLS productivity accounts. Multifactor productivity is defined as the ratio of GDP to GDI in constant prices. This reformulation of the production account has been advocated, historically, by Denison (1967) and Christensen and Jorgenson (1996). More recently, the proposal has been supported by Hill (1999), Jorgenson (2001), and Moulton (2004).

The major challenge in implementing a consistent and integrated production account is the construction of a measure of GDI in constant prices. SNA 1993 and BLS (1993) have provided appropriate measures of the price and quantity of labor services. These can be combined with the price and quantity of capital services introduced by BLS (1983) to generate price and quantity indexes of GDI, as well as multifactor productivity. The primary obstacle to constructing capital service measures is the lack of market rental data for different types of capital. Although rental markets exist for most types of assets, such as commercial and industrial real estate and equipment, relatively little effort has been made to collect rental prices, except for renter-occupied housing.

An alternative approach for measuring rental prices, employed by the BLS, is to impute these prices from market prices for the assets, utilizing the user cost formula introduced by Jorgenson (1963). This requires estimates of depreciation and the rate of return, as well as asset prices. Measures of asset prices and depreciation, as well as investment and capital stocks, are presented in the BEA's (1999) reproducible wealth accounts. The BLS has generated estimates of the rate of return by combining property income from the NIPAs with capital stocks derived from the BEA's estimates of investment. The BLS employs the imputed rental prices to weight accumulated stocks of assets in generating price and quantity measures of capital services.

Our second goal is to integrate estimates of tangible wealth and the U.S. international position into a wealth account for the U.S. economy. This balance sheet represents an extension and consolidation of the balance sheets for individual sectors given by Teplin et al. (chap. 11 in this volume). Tangible wealth includes equipment, structures, inventories, and land in private business, household, and government sectors. Consolidation of these sectors eliminates claims among the sectors and requires only U.S. claims on the rest of the world (ROW) and ROW claims on the United States in addition to tangible assets. Estimates of these claims are presented in the U.S. International Position, generated by BEA, so that the international accounts for the U.S. economy can be incorporated into our blueprint without alternation.

An important issue, discussed at length by Fraumeni and Okubo (2001) and Moulton (2004), is the appropriate treatment of consumer durables. Moulton (2004) endorses the BEA's current practice of including this investment in the tangible assets accounts but excluding the services of these durables from the GDP. Starting from the premise that the boundaries of production, income and expenditure, accumulation, and wealth accounts should be the same, we treat the services of consumers' durables as an output as well as an input in the production account. These services are also a source of income and a form of expenditures in the income and expenditures account.

Our proposed treatment of consumer durables has the advantage of accounting for owned and rented assets in the same way, following the BEA's treatment of owner-occupied and renter-occupied housing. The principal disadvantage is that the scope of the GDP and the corresponding measure of GDI must be increased. The argument for this change is that the BEA already compiles detailed accounts for investment and stocks of consumer durables as part of its accounts for reproducible assets. The only additional step required to make the accounts for housing and consumer durables fully consistent is to introduce imputed rental prices for consumer durables based on asset prices, like those employed in the BLS productivity accounts.

Similar, but distinct, issues arise for intangible forms of investment such as software and research and development. We follow SNA 1993 and the NIPAs in treating software as a form of investment, but extend this treatment by imputing a flow of services from stocks of software in household, government, and business sectors. This requires an extension of the scope of the GDP and the GDI for the output and input of capital services in the household and government sectors. While we could account for research and development in the same way, we follow Fraumeni and Okubo (2005) and Moulton (2004) in recommending that this be treated as part of a satellite accounting system until more satisfactory data are available on the prices of assets generated by research and development activities.

1.4.2   Blueprint for a Complete Accounting System

A schematic representation of our prototype accounting system is given in figure 1.1. The complete accounting system includes a production account, incorporating data on output and input; an income and expenditures account, giving data on income, expenditures, and saving; and an accumulation account, allocating saving to various types of capital forma-

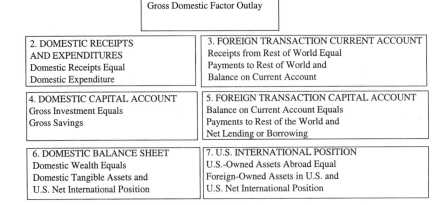

Fig. 1.1   Blueprint for an expanded and integrated set of accounts for the United States

tion. A national balance sheet contains data on national wealth. The production, income and expenditures, and accumulation accounts are linked through markets for commodities and factor services. Finally, the accumulation accounts are related to the wealth accounts through the accounting identity between period-to-period changes in wealth and the sum of net saving and the revaluation of assets.

The structure of our prototype system is similar to the NIPAs. The NIPAs currently present current price measures for outputs and inputs, but constant price measures only for outputs. The key innovation in the BLS accounts for multifactor productivity is to present both outputs and inputs in current and constant prices. Constant price measures of inputs and multifactor productivity are essential in accounting for the sources of economic growth. We also provide current and constant price measures of income and expenditures in order to account for the generation of income and its disposition as uses of economic growth. Finally, we present current and constant price measures of saving and capital formation to provide the necessary link between current economic activity and the accumulation of wealth.

Following the NIPAs, we generate a Domestic Income and Product Account for the U.S. economy, featuring GDP and GDI. Both GDP and GDI are presented in current and constant prices. The fundamental accounting identity is that GDP is equal to GDI in current prices. Multifactor productivity, a summary measure of economic performance, is defined as the ratio of GDP to GDI in constant prices. The interpretation of output, input, and productivity requires the concept of a production possibility frontier.[11] In each period the inputs of capital and labor services are transformed into outputs of consumption and investment goods. This transformation depends on the level of productivity.

The most important difference between our prototype system and the NIPAs is the creation of a consolidated Income and Expenditures Account. By consolidating the income and expenditures accounts for household, business, and government sectors presented in the NIPAs, we obtain a single account presenting income and its disposition. This has the advantage of radically simplifying the accounts by excluding all transactions among the sectors. For example, the taxes paid by private business are expenditures by the business sector and sources of income to the government sector. In the consolidated Income and Expenditures Account, these tax payments cancel out.

For the Income and Expenditures Account the fundamental accounting identity is that income is equal to expenditures in current prices. Income includes labor and property income from the Domestic Income and Product Account, evaluated at market prices, income received from the rest of the world, net of income payments to the rest of the world, and net current taxes and transfers to the rest of the world. Expenditures include personal consumption expenditures, government consumption expenditures, and saving, net of depreciation. Income and expenditures are presented in current and constant prices in order to account for the generation of income and its disposition through expenditures and saving and uses of economic growth. The interpretation of these magnitudes in constant prices requires the notion of a social welfare function.[12] Consumption expenditures in constant prices represent the current flow of goods and services for consumption, while net saving in constant prices corresponds to increments in the current period of future flows of consumption.

The Domestic Capital Account allocates saving to various forms of investment. The fundamental accounting identity is that saving is equal to investment in current prices. We take saving and investment in constant prices to be identical as well. Investment in constant prices is an essential link between current economic activity and the accumulation of stocks of capital. As in the Income and Expenditures Account, we radically simplify the Domestic Capital Account by consolidating the capital accounts for household, business, and government sectors. Claims among the sectors cancel out, so that we present only investment in tangible assets and changes in the U.S. International Position.

The Wealth Account completes the domestic side of our prototype system of U.S. national accounts. Our Wealth Account is consistent with the

---

11. This interpretation is developed by Jorgenson (1996a, 2001) and Jorgenson and Stiroh (2000).

12. This interpretation is developed by Samuelson (1961), Nordhaus and Tobin (1973), and Weitzman (1976, 2003).

balance sheets for financial sectors presented by Teplin et al. (chap. 11 in this volume). We have augmented these balance sheets by including all tangible wealth of business, government, and household sectors, as well as the U.S. International Position. The principal difference between our system of accounts for capital and wealth and SNA 1993 is that we have combined the SNA's capital and revaluation accounts into a single accumulation account. This account also includes period-to-period changes in wealth. Our treatment of consumer durables also differs from the international system (SNA 1993, chap. 9, para. 40, p. 208).

Although it will eventually be desirable to provide a breakdown of our prototype system of U.S. national accounts by industrial sectors, our initial blueprint is limited to aggregates for the U.S. economy as a whole. Disaggregating our production account by industrial sector will require a fully integrated system of input-output accounts and accounts for gross product originating by industry, as described by Lawson et al. (chap. 6 in this volume). This can be combined with measures of capital, labor, and intermediate inputs by industry, like those presented by Jorgenson, Ho, and Stiroh (2005), to generate production accounts by sector.[13] The principles for constructing these production accounts are discussed by Fraumeni et al. (chap. 9 in this volume).

Our Foreign Transactions Current and Capital Accounts are identical to the NIPAs. Similarly, we incorporate the U.S. International Position from the NIPAs without modification. The income and expenditures, capital, and wealth accounts in our prototype system are limited to national aggregates. This has the advantage that transactions among domestic sectors are not required in accounting for income and expenditures and claims among domestic sectors are not required in accounting for capital formation and wealth. The basic similarities between our approach and current accounting practice can be recognized through our reliance on data from the most recent benchmark revision of the NIPAs, published in December 2003.

The first step in implementing an accounting system is to develop accounts in current prices. In section 1.4.3 we present production, income and expenditures, accumulation, and wealth accounts for the U.S. economy for 1948–2002. In section 1.4.4, we introduce accounts in constant prices with a description of index numbers for prices and quantities. Our accounts in constant prices begin with the Domestic Income and Product Account in section 1.4.5. The product side includes consumption and investment goods output in constant prices. The income side includes labor and capital inputs in constant prices. The ratio of real product to real input is multifactor productivity. In section 1.4.6 we give income and expen-

---

13. A system of production accounts for industrial sectors of the U.S. economy is given by Jorgenson, Gollop, and Fraumeni (1987) and has been updated and revised by Jorgenson, Ho, and Stiroh (2005).

ditures, accumulation, and wealth accounts in constant prices for the U.S. domestic economy and the rest of the world.

1.4.3 Income and Wealth

Introduction

The measurement of income and wealth requires a system of seven accounts. These must be carefully distinguished for the new system of seven accounts employed in presenting the U.S. NIPAs. Our Domestic Income and Product Account provides data on the outputs of the U.S. economy, as well as inputs of capital and labor services. Incomes and expenditures are divided between two accounts—the Income and Expenditures Account and the Foreign Transactions Current Account. Capital accumulation is recorded in two accounts—the Domestic Capital Account and the Foreign Transactions Capital Account. Finally, assets and liabilities are given in the Wealth Account and the U.S. International Position.

Production Account

We implement the Domestic Income and Product Account for the U.S. domestic economy, including business, household, and government sectors.[14] In order to achieve consistency between investment goods production and property compensation we introduce imputations for the services of consumer durables and durables used by nonprofit institutions, as well as the net rent on government durables and government and institutional real estate. The services of these assets are included in the output of services, together with the services of owner-occupied dwellings; both also appear in property compensation. This assures that the accounting identity between the value of output and the value of input is preserved.

Gross Domestic Product is divided among nondurable goods, durable goods, and structures, as well as services, in the NIPAs. The output of durables includes consumer durables and producer durables used by governments and nonprofit institutions, as well as producer durables employed by private businesses. The output of structures includes government structures, private business structures, institutional structures, and new residential housing. The purpose of our imputations for the property compensation of governments, households, and nonprofit institutions is to provide a consistent treatment of investment goods output and property compensation throughout the system.

In the NIPAs the rental value of owner-occupied residential real estate, including structures and land, is imputed from market rental prices of renter-occupied residential real estate. The value of these services is allo-

---

14. Our estimates are based on those of Jorgenson (2001), updated through 2002 to incorporate data from the 2003 benchmark revision of the U.S. national accounts.

cated among net rent, interest, taxes, and consumption of fixed capital. A similar imputation is made for the services of real estate used by nonprofit institutions, but the imputed value excludes net rent. Finally, depreciation on government capital is included, while net rent on this capital is excluded. No property compensation for the services of consumer durables or producer durables used by nonprofit institutions is included. By imputing the value of these services and the net rent of government capital and real estate used by nonprofit institutions, we align the treatment of property compensation for these assets with that for assets used by private businesses.

We distinguish between taxes charged against revenue, such as excise or sales taxes, and taxes that are part of the outlay on capital services, such as property taxes. We exclude output taxes from the value of output, reflecting prices from the producers' point of view. However, we include taxes on input, since these taxes are included in the outlay of producers. Taxes on output reduce the proceeds of the sector, while subsidies increase these proceeds; accordingly, the value of output includes production subsidies. To be more specific, we exclude excise and sales taxes, business nontax payments, and customs duties from the value of output and include other indirect business taxes plus subsidies. Our valuation of output corresponds to the value of output at basic prices in SNA 1993. The Domestic Income and Product Account for 2002 is presented in table 1.5.

Gross Domestic Income includes income originating in private enterprises and private households and institutions, as well as income originating in government. We add the imputed rental value of consumer durables, producer durables utilized by institutions, and the net rent on government durables and real estate and institutional real estate, together with indirect taxes included in the value of these inputs. The value of capital inputs also includes consumption of fixed capital and the statistical discrepancy; consumption of fixed capital is a component of the rental value of capital services. The value of GDI for 2002 is presented in table 1.5.

Product and income accounts are linked through capital formation and property compensation. To make this link explicit we divide GDP between consumption and investment goods and GDI between labor and property compensation. Investment goods production is equal to the total output of durable goods and structures. Consumption goods production is equal to the output of nondurable goods and services from the NIPAs, together with our imputations for the services of consumer and institutional durables and the net rent on government durables and real estate, as well as institutional real estate.

Property income includes the statistical discrepancy and taxes included in property compensation, such as motor vehicle licenses, property taxes, and other taxes. The imputed value of the services of government, consumer and institutional durables, and the net rent on government and institu-

Table 1.5   **Domestic income and product account, 2002**

Row No.	Product	Source	Total
1	GDP (NIPA)	NIPA 1.1.5 line 1	10,487.0
2	+ Services of consumers' durables	Our imputation	1,082.2
3	+ Services of durables held by institutions	Our imputation	31.8
4	+ Services of durables, structures, land, and inventories held by government	Our imputation	340.6
5	– General government consumption of fixed capital	NIPA 3.10.5 line 5	178.0
6	– Government enterprise consumption of fixed capital	NIPA 3.1 line 38–3.10.5 line 5	33.2
7	– Federal taxes on production and imports	NIPA 3.2 line 4	87.3
8	– Federal current transfer receipts from business	NIPA 3.2 line 16	14.0
9	– S&L taxes on production and imports	NIPA 3.3 line 6	675.3
10	– S&L current transfer receipts fom business	NIPA 3.3 line 18	32.8
11	+ Capital stock tax	—	0.0
12	+ MV tax	NIPA 3.5 line 28	6.9
13	+ Property taxes	NIPA 3.3 line 8	291.5
14	+ Severance, special assessments, and other taxes	NIPA 3.5 line 29, 30, 31	47.8
15	+ Subsidies	NIPA 3.1 line 25	38.2
16	– Current surplus of government enterprises	NIPA 3.1 line 14	2.8
17	= Gross domestic product		11,303.1

Row No.	Income	Source	Total
1	+ Consumption of fixed capital	NIPA 5.1 line 13	1,303.9
2	+ Statistical discrepancy	NIPA 5.1 line 26	–15.3
3	+ Services of consumers' durables	Our imputation	1,082.2
4	+ Services of durables held by institutions	Our imputation	31.8
5	+ Services of durables, structures, land, and inventories held by government	Our imputation	340.6
6	– General government consumption of fixed capital	NIPA 3.10.5 line 5	178.0
7	– Government enterprise consumption of fixed capital	NIPA 3.1 line 38–3.10.5 line 5	33.2
8	+ National income	NIPA 1.7.5 line 16	9,225.4
9	– ROW income	NIPA 1.7.5 line 2–3	27.1
10	– Sales tax	Product Account	463.2
11	+ Subsidies	NIPA 3.1 line 25	38.2
12	– Current surplus of government enterprises	NIPA 3.1 line 14	2.8
13	= Gross domestic income		11,303.1

tional real estate are also included. Labor income includes the compensation of employees of private enterprises, households, and nonprofit institutions, as well as government. The value of labor input also includes the labor compensation of the self-employed. We estimate this compensation from the incomes received by comparable categories of employees.[15] Gross

15. Details are provided by Jorgenson, Ho, and Stiroh (2005).

Domestic Product, divided between investment and consumption goods output, and GDI, divided between labor and property income, are given for 1948–2002 in table 1.6.

Income and Expenditures Accounts

We define Net Income as proceeds from the sale of factor services from the Domestic Income and Product Account, plus income receipts from the result of the world, less income payments, and net current taxes and transfers to the rest of the world, less depreciation. We define Net Expenditures as personal and government consumption expenditures from the Domestic Income and Product Account, evaluated at market prices, plus net saving. These expenditures exclude purchases of durable goods but include the services of accumulated stocks of these durables. The value of Net Income for the year 2002 is presented in table 1.7.

Consumption expenditures include personal and government expenditures on services and nondurable goods, together with our imputation for the services of consumer, institutional, and government durables and the net rent of institutional and government real estate. Purchases of consumer durables, included in personal consumption expenditures in the NIPAs, are excluded from expenditures and included in investment in the Domestic Capital Account described below. The value of personal and government consumption includes taxes and excludes subsidies on output, reflecting prices from the purchasers' point of view. The value of Net Expenditures for the year 2002 is presented in table 1.7.

Income and expenditure accounts are linked through saving and the resulting property income. To make this link explicit we divide Net Income between labor and property income, net of depreciation, and Net Expenditures between net saving and consumption. Net income and expenditures in current prices for 1948–2002 are given in table 1.8. Income is divided between labor and property income, net of depreciation, while expenditures are divided between personal and government consumption and net saving.

The Foreign Transactions Current Account in the NIPAs gives receipts from exports and income receipts from the rest of the world. This is balanced against outlays for imports, income payments, current taxes and transfers to the rest of the world, and the balance on current account. Receipts, outlays, and the balance on current account are presented for the year 2002 in table 1.9. These data are given in current prices for 1948–2002 in table 1.10.

Accumulation Accounts

The NIPAs include a Domestic Capital Account that presents investment and saving. We implement this account by consolidating the accounts of business and government sectors with those of households and institutions. Financial claims on the business sector by households and

Table 1.6   Domestic income and product account, 1948–2002 (billions of current $)

Year	Gross domestic product	Investment goods product	Consumption goods product	Labor income	Capital income
1948	290.8	78.7	212.1	173.2	116.9
1949	285.6	72.2	213.5	173.6	111.2
1950	319.9	92.4	227.5	187.0	132.0
1951	366.3	106.3	260.0	213.6	152.1
1952	387.1	103.8	283.3	228.7	158.0
1953	409.6	110.7	298.8	244.4	165.0
1954	415.5	107.2	308.3	244.5	171.2
1955	448.0	127.0	321.0	262.7	185.4
1956	475.7	132.0	343.8	283.6	192.6
1957	493.5	134.8	358.6	297.5	195.3
1958	512.7	126.8	385.9	299.3	213.7
1959	542.1	145.0	397.1	323.5	218.7
1960	576.9	148.5	428.5	339.5	237.2
1961	588.8	150.3	438.5	348.7	239.8
1962	626.4	165.7	460.7	371.3	255.2
1963	658.4	176.1	482.4	388.9	269.3
1964	713.4	190.8	522.6	416.2	297.0
1965	779.9	212.9	567.0	446.6	333.2
1966	864.4	234.7	629.6	490.3	374.1
1967	900.4	236.8	663.5	522.6	377.9
1968	980.9	257.1	723.8	575.2	405.7
1969	1,063.0	276.5	786.5	632.1	431.1
1970	1,096.3	272.9	823.5	673.1	422.9
1971	1,197.6	303.5	894.0	719.0	478.5
1972	1,350.5	343.8	1,006.7	789.3	561.1
1973	1,525.7	398.2	1,127.5	880.9	644.9
1974	1,652.2	415.5	1,236.7	966.1	686.0
1975	1,789.6	427.3	1,362.4	1,029.5	760.0
1976	2,012.7	508.6	1,504.1	1,147.5	865.3
1977	2,265.3	590.8	1,674.5	1,279.4	986.0
1978	2,558.3	687.3	1,871.0	1,448.6	1,109.5
1979	2,803.2	774.9	2,028.2	1,628.4	1,174.9
1980	3,000.7	784.8	2,215.9	1,792.6	1,207.8
1981	3,338.3	884.9	2,453.4	1,980.5	1,358.1
1982	3,489.8	837.4	2,652.4	2,090.2	1,399.4
1983	3,845.2	904.1	2,941.1	2,219.2	1,626.1
1984	4,308.4	1,093.3	3,215.0	2,447.9	1,860.6
1985	4,575.2	1,140.4	3,434.9	2,626.0	1,949.2
1986	4,814.6	1,177.1	3,637.5	2,785.0	2,030.0
1987	5,105.7	1,241.1	3,864.6	2,978.8	2,126.7
1988	5,546.9	1,320.5	4,226.4	3,214.1	2,332.7
1989	5,939.4	1,413.9	4,525.5	3,402.5	2,537.1
1990	6,245.4	1,436.7	4,808.7	3,610.4	2,635.2
1991	6,427.8	1,377.5	5,050.2	3,733.9	2,693.6
1992	6,790.5	1,454.4	5,336.1	3,931.5	2,858.8
1993	7,087.0	1,552.1	5,534.8	4,118.3	2,968.7

(continued)

Table 1.6   (continued)

Year	Gross domestic product	Investment goods product	Consumption goods product	Labor income	Capital income
1994	7,501.0	1,705.2	5,795.8	4,332.5	3,168.3
1995	7,859.4	1,782.8	6,076.5	4,535.5	3,323.9
1996	8,340.0	1,934.2	6,405.8	4,749.1	3,591.2
1997	8,908.0	2,132.6	6,775.4	5,035.2	3,872.7
1998	9,366.3	2,266.8	7,099.5	5,409.0	3,956.9
1999	9,943.0	2,409.0	7,534.0	5,763.1	4,180.0
2000	10,525.6	2,528.8	7,996.8	6,204.4	4,321.6
2001	10,958.6	2,476.4	8,482.3	6,367.8	4,590.7
2002	11,303.1	2,439.4	8,863.7	6,493.5	4,809.4

institutions are liabilities of the business sector; in the consolidated accounts these assets and liabilities cancel out. Similarly, financial claims on the government sector by households and institutions cancel out.

Investment includes gross private domestic investment, government investment, and expenditures on durable goods by households and institutions, all evaluated at market prices, and the balance on current accounts. Net saving includes gross saving, as defined in the NIPAs, less consumption of fixed capital for households, institutions, and governments. Domestic saving and investment are given for 2002 in table 1.11, together with the revaluation of fixed assets and the change in wealth. Domestic investment is presented in current prices for 1948–2002 in table 1.12. Gross saving, depreciation, net saving, revaluation of assets, and the change in wealth are given in table 1.13.

Our estimates of revaluations for net claims on foreigners are based on accounts at market prices included in the U.S. International Position. We estimate revaluations as the difference between the period-to-period changes in these stocks and the deficit of the ROW sector. The NIPAs include a Foreign Transactions Capital Account that links net claims on foreigners to the balance on current account from the NIPAs. Data from the Foreign Transactions Account are given for 2002 in table 1.14 and for the period 1948–2002 in table 1.15.

Wealth Accounts

All of the accounts we have considered up to this point contain data on flows. The wealth accounts contain data on stocks. These accounts are presented in balance sheet form with the value of assets equal to the value of liabilities as an accounting identity. The Wealth Account includes the tangible assets of household, business, and government sectors and net claims on the rest of the world. The U.S. International Investment Position includes

Table 1.7   Income and expenditures account, 2002

Row No.	Income	Source	Total
1	+ Gross income	Product Account	11,303.1
2	+ Sales tax	Product Account	463.2
3	− Subsidies	NIPA 3.1 line 25	38.2
4	+ Current surplus of government enterprises	NIPA 3.1 line 14	2.8
5	= Gross domestic income at market prices		11,730.9
6	+ Income receipts from the rest of the world	NIPA 1.7.5 line 2	301.8
7	− Income payments to the rest of the world	NIPA 1.7.5 line 3	274.7
8	− Current taxes and transfers to the rest of the world (net)	NIPA 4.1 line 25	59.8
9	= Gross income		11,698.2
10	− Depreciation	Our imputation	1,934.3
11	= Net income		9,763.9

	Expenditures	Source	Total
1	+ Personal consumption expenditures		7,574.0
2	PCE nondurable goods (NIPA)	NIPA 2.3.5 line 6	2,080.1
3	PCE services	NIPA 2.3.5 line 13	4,379.8
4	Less space rental value of inst building and nonfarm dwellings	Our imputation	3,605.9
5	Services of consumers' durables	Our imputation	1,082.2
6	Services of structures and land	Our imputation	773.9
7	Services of durables held by institutions	Our imputation	31.8
8	+ Government consumption expenditures		1,738.7
9	Government consumption nondurable goods	NIPA 3.10.5 line 8	162.4
10	Government intermediate purchases, durable goods	NIPA 3.10.5 line 7	47.7
11	Government consumption services total		226.4
12	Government consumption services	NIPA 3.10.5 line 9	498.7
13	Less sales to other sectors	NIPA 3.10.5 line 11	272.3
14	Services of durables, structures, land, and inventories held by government	Our imputation	340.6
15	Less government enterprise consumption of fixed capital	NIPA 3.1 line 38–3.10.5 line 5	33.2
16	Government compensation of employees excluding force account labor	NIPA 3.10.5 line 4–10	994.8
17	+ Gross national saving and statistical discrepancy	Capital Account	2,385.2
	− Depreciation	Our imputation	1,934.3
18	= Net domestic expenditures		9,763.6

Table 1.8   Income and expenditures account, 1948–2002 (billions of current $)

Year	Net income	Labor income	Net capital income	Personal consumption expenditures	Government consumption expenditures	Net saving and statistical discrepancy
1948	262.5	173.2	89.2	179.0	39.5	43.9
1949	252.2	173.7	78.5	176.8	43.3	32.0
1950	285.6	187.1	98.5	189.6	47.3	48.6
1951	327.2	213.6	113.6	213.3	56.4	57.4
1952	347.0	228.7	118.3	227.0	68.4	51.4
1953	367.1	244.4	122.7	234.4	79.5	53.1
1954	369.7	244.5	125.2	247.1	76.4	46.1
1955	400.3	262.6	137.6	262.0	74.9	63.4
1956	423.1	283.5	139.6	282.7	77.2	63.1
1957	435.0	297.4	137.6	290.2	83.8	60.9
1958	452.5	299.2	153.3	308.4	96.5	47.4
1959	478.0	323.4	154.6	318.1	96.8	63.2
1960	512.1	339.4	172.7	343.8	104.0	64.4
1961	521.3	348.6	172.7	355.5	102.6	63.4
1962	558.4	371.2	187.2	371.4	110.3	76.9
1963	588.0	388.9	199.1	388.2	115.7	84.3
1964	640.5	416.2	224.3	417.5	127.1	96.0
1965	702.9	446.7	256.2	454.6	136.0	112.5
1966	778.6	490.3	288.3	500.1	153.9	124.4
1967	805.8	522.6	283.2	519.9	170.1	115.7
1968	879.4	575.2	304.1	567.5	187.2	124.8
1969	951.2	632.2	319.1	626.6	194.1	130.5
1970	970.2	673.2	297.1	664.8	193.0	112.5
1971	1,061.5	719.0	342.5	723.1	208.2	130.1
1972	1,198.8	789.3	409.6	799.0	248.1	151.7
1973	1,368.7	880.9	487.8	886.2	281.1	201.3
1974	1,470.3	966.1	504.2	969.8	321.7	178.9
1975	1,569.5	1,029.5	540.0	1,054.9	360.6	153.9
1976	1,778.7	1,147.4	631.3	1,167.2	405.5	206.0
1977	2,006.2	1,279.4	726.8	1,319.7	439.4	247.1
1978	2,264.5	1,448.5	816.0	1,479.0	477.8	307.8
1979	2,469.1	1,628.4	840.7	1,641.7	485.3	342.1
1980	2,611.0	1,792.5	818.5	1,815.2	513.0	283.0
1981	2,903.1	1,980.4	922.8	1,998.5	572.9	331.8
1982	2,999.8	2,090.0	909.7	2,134.0	632.2	233.7
1983	3,341.3	2,219.1	1,122.2	2,310.4	755.3	275.4
1984	3,786.1	2,447.7	1,338.4	2,527.0	838.8	420.2
1985	4,005.2	2,625.8	1,379.4	2,732.5	868.9	403.6
1986	4,178.9	2,783.2	1,395.7	2,920.0	879.1	379.9
1987	4,413.2	2,977.4	1,435.8	3,122.3	918.7	372.5
1988	4,814.2	3,213.2	1,601.0	3,396.2	998.8	419.2
1989	5,159.3	3,401.2	1,758.1	3,654.8	1,044.4	460.3
1990	5,423.5	3,608.1	1,815.4	3,914.2	1,086.2	423.2
1991	5,609.3	3,731.2	1,878.2	4,072.7	1,158.4	378.1
1992	5,915.5	3,928.5	1,987.0	4,310.9	1,211.3	393.2
1993	6,171.5	4,115.0	2,056.5	4,587.3	1,146.1	438.1
1994	6,548.1	4,328.5	2,219.5	4,816.9	1,193.0	538.2
1995	6,848.3	4,531.4	2,316.9	5,097.0	1,188.1	563.3
1996	7,279.1	4,745.0	2,534.2	5,362.9	1,274.6	641.4
1997	7,796.5	5,030.8	2,765.7	5,695.1	1,336.4	765.1
1998	8,184.8	5,404.4	2,780.3	6,023.6	1,355.5	805.9
1999	8,695.5	5,757.9	2,937.6	6,438.3	1,422.5	834.8
2000	9,174.5	6,199.8	2,974.8	6,907.1	1,504.3	762.9
2001	9,492.4	6,362.6	3,129.7	7,269.0	1,632.2	591.3
2002	9,763.5	6,488.0	–3,275.4	7,574.0	1,738.7	450.8

Table 1.9   **Foreign transactions current account, 2002**

Row No.	Receipts from the rest of the world	Source	Total
1	+ Exports of goods and services	NIPA 4.1 line 2	1,005.0
2	+ Income receipts from the rest of the world	NIPA 4.1 line 7	301.8
3	Wage and salary receipts	NIPA 4.1 line 8	2.9
4	Income receipts on assets	NIPA 4.1 line 9	298.8
5	= Current receipts from the rest of the world	NIPA 4.1 line 1	1,306.8

	Payments to the rest of the world and balance on current account	Source	Total
1	+ Imports of goods and services	NIPA 4.1 line 14	1,429.9
2	+ Income payments to the rest of the world	NIPA 4.1 line 19	274.7
3	Wage and salary payments	NIPA 4.1 line 20	8.4
4	Income payments on assets	NIPA 4.1 line 21	266.3
5	+ Current taxes and transfer payments to the rest of the world (net)	NIPA 4.1 line 25	59.8
6	+ Balance on current account	NIPA 4.1 line 29	−457.7
7	= Current payments to the rest of the world and balance on current account		1,306.7

foreign holdings of U.S. domestic assets and U.S. holdings of foreign assets. The Wealth Account for 2002 is presented in table 1.16, and annual data on domestic wealth for the period 1948–2002 are presented in table 1.17. The U.S. International Position for 2002 is given in table 1.18, while the U.S. International Investment Position for this period is given in table 1.19.

1.4.4   Price and Quantity Indexes

Introduction

We have presented data in current prices for our prototype system of U.S. national accounts in the preceding section. To express any accounting magnitude in constant prices we must separate the value in current prices between components associated with price and quantity indexes. Data in constant prices are associated with the quantity index, while the implicit deflator is associated with the price index. As an illustration, GDP in current prices in the Domestic Income and Product Account is the product of GDP in constant prices and the implicit deflator for GDP. Similarly, GDI in current prices is the product of GDI in constant prices and the implicit deflator for GDI.

As a second illustration, income in current prices from the Income and Expenditures Account can be separated between income in constant prices and the implicit deflator for income. Similarly, the value of expenditures can be separated into price and quantity components. Market prices that

Table 1.10   **Foreign transactions current account, 1948–2002 (billions of current $)**

Year	Balance on current account	Current receipts from the ROW	Exports of goods and services	Income receipts from the ROW	Current payments to ROW and balance on current account	Imports of goods and services	Income payments to ROW	Current taxes and transfers to ROW (net)
1948	2.4	17.6	15.5	2.0	17.6	10.1	0.6	4.5
1949	0.9	16.4	14.5	1.9	16.5	9.2	0.7	5.6
1950	−1.8	14.5	12.4	2.2	14.6	11.6	0.7	4.0
1951	0.9	19.9	17.1	2.8	19.9	14.6	0.9	3.5
1952	0.6	19.3	16.5	2.9	19.3	15.3	0.9	2.5
1953	−1.3	18.2	15.3	2.8	18.1	16.0	0.9	2.5
1954	0.2	18.9	15.8	3.0	18.8	15.4	0.9	2.3
1955	0.4	21.2	17.7	3.5	21.1	17.2	1.1	2.5
1956	2.8	25.2	21.3	3.9	25.3	18.9	1.1	2.4
1957	4.8	28.3	24.0	4.3	28.3	19.9	1.2	2.3
1958	0.9	24.4	20.6	3.9	24.4	20.0	1.2	2.3
1959	−1.2	27.0	22.7	4.3	27.0	22.3	1.5	4.3
1960	3.2	31.9	27.0	4.9	31.9	22.8	1.8	4.1
1961	4.3	32.9	27.6	5.3	32.9	22.7	1.8	4.2
1962	3.9	35.0	29.1	5.9	35.0	25.0	1.8	4.3
1963	5.0	37.6	31.1	6.5	37.6	26.1	2.1	4.4
1964	7.5	42.3	35.0	7.2	42.2	28.1	2.3	4.3
1965	6.2	45.0	37.1	7.9	45.0	31.5	2.6	4.7
1966	3.9	49.0	40.9	8.1	49.0	37.1	3.0	5.0
1967	3.6	52.1	43.5	8.7	52.2	39.9	3.3	5.4
1968	1.7	58.0	47.9	10.1	58.0	46.6	4.0	5.7
1969	1.8	63.7	51.9	11.8	63.7	50.5	5.7	5.8
1970	4.0	72.5	59.7	12.8	72.5	55.8	6.4	6.3
1971	0.6	77.0	63.0	14.0	77.0	62.3	6.4	7.6
1972	−3.6	87.1	70.8	16.3	87.1	74.2	7.7	8.8
1973	9.3	118.8	95.3	23.5	118.8	91.2	10.9	7.4
1974	6.6	156.5	126.7	29.8	156.4	127.5	14.3	8.1
1975	21.4	166.7	138.7	28.0	166.8	122.7	15.0	7.6
1976	8.9	181.9	149.5	32.4	181.9	151.1	15.5	6.3
1977	−9.0	196.6	159.4	37.2	196.6	182.4	16.9	6.2
1978	−10.4	233.1	186.9	46.3	233.2	212.3	24.7	6.7
1979	1.4	298.5	230.1	68.3	298.4	252.7	36.4	8.0
1980	11.4	359.9	280.8	79.1	359.9	293.8	44.9	9.8
1981	6.3	397.3	305.2	92.0	397.2	317.8	59.1	14.1
1982	−0.2	384.2	283.2	101.0	384.2	303.2	64.5	16.7
1983	−32.1	378.9	277.0	101.9	378.8	328.6	64.8	17.5
1984	−86.9	424.2	302.4	121.9	424.3	405.1	85.6	20.5
1985	−110.8	414.5	302.0	112.4	414.5	417.2	85.9	22.2
1986	−139.2	431.9	320.5	111.4	432.0	453.3	93.6	24.3
1987	−150.8	487.1	363.9	123.2	487.1	509.1	105.3	23.5
1988	−112.2	596.2	444.1	152.1	596.2	554.5	128.5	25.5
1989	−88.3	681.0	503.3	177.7	681.0	591.5	151.5	26.4
1990	−70.1	741.5	552.4	189.1	741.4	630.3	154.3	26.9
1991	13.5	765.7	596.8	168.9	765.8	624.3	138.5	−10.6
1992	−36.9	788.0	635.3	152.7	788.0	668.6	123.0	33.4
1993	−70.4	812.1	655.8	156.2	812.1	720.9	124.3	37.3
1994	−105.2	907.3	720.9	186.4	907.3	814.5	160.2	37.8
1995	−91.0	1,046.1	812.2	233.9	1,046.1	903.6	198.1	35.4

Table 1.10   (continued)

Year	Balance on current account	Current receipts from the ROW	Exports of goods and services	Income receipts from the ROW	Current payments to ROW and balance on current account	Imports of goods and services	Income payments to ROW	Current taxes and transfers to ROW (net)
1996	−100.3	1,117.3	868.6	248.7	1,117.3	964.8	213.7	39.1
1997	−110.2	1,242.0	955.3	286.7	1,242.0	1,056.9	253.7	41.6
1998	−187.4	1,243.1	955.9	287.1	1,242.1	1,115.9	265.8	48.8
1999	−273.9	1,312.1	991.2	320.8	1,312.0	1,251.7	287.0	47.2
2000	−396.6	1,478.9	1,096.3	382.7	1,479.0	1,475.8	343.7	56.1
2001	−370.4	1,355.2	1,032.8	322.4	1,355.2	1,399.8	278.8	47.0
2002	−457.7	1,306.8	1,005.0	301.8	1,306.7	1,429.9	274.7	59.8

Note: ROW = rest of world.

Table 1.11   **Domestic capital account, 2002**

Row No.	Investment	Source	Total
1	+ Private fixed investment, nonresidential structures	NIPA 5.4.5 line 2	271.6
2	+ Private fixed investment, equipment and software	NIPA 5.5.5 line 1	799.9
3	+ Change in private inventories, nonfarm	NIPA 5.6.5 line 19	12.7
4	+ Change in private inventories, farm	NIPA 5.6.5 line 2	−1.5
5	+ Private fixed investment, residential structures	NIPA 5.4.5 line 35	496.6
6	+ Personal consumption expenditures, durable goods	NIPA 1.1.5 line 3	916.2
7	= Gross private domestic investment		2,495.5
8	+ Government investment, structures	NIPA 5.8.5 line 6	222.6
9	+ Government investment, equipment and software	NIPA 5.8.5 line 46	124.9
10	= Gross domestic investment		2,843.0
11	+ Net lending or borrowing on rest of world account	NIPA 4.1 line 30	−458.9
12	+ Capital accounts transaction (net)	NIPA 4.1 line 32	1.3
13	= Gross investment		2,385.4

Row No.	Saving	Source	Total
1	+ Net saving (NIPA)	NIPA 5.1 line 26	180.4
2	Personal saving	NIPA 2.1 line 33	159.2
3	Undistributed corporate profits with IVA and capital consumption adjustments	NIPA 5.1 line 5	300.7
4	Wage accruals less disbursements (private)	NIPA 5.1 line 9	0.0
5	Net government saving	NIPA 5.1 line 27	−279.5
6	+ Consumption of fixed capital	NIPA 1.7.5 line 5	1,303.9
7	= Gross saving (NIPA)	NIPA 5.1 line 1	1,484.3
8	+ Personal consumption expenditures, durable goods	NIPA 1.1.5 line 3	916.2
9	= Gross saving		2,400.5
10	+ Statistical discrepancy	NIPA 5.1 line 26	−15.3
11	= Gross saving and statistical discrepancy		2,385.2
12	− Depreciation	Our imputation	1,934.3
13	= Net saving		450.9
14	+ Revaluation	Our imputation	2,123.2
15	= Change in wealth		2,574.0

Table 1.12   **Domestic capital account, investment, 1948–2002 (billions of current $)**

Year	Gross investment	Private investment	Government investment	Balance on current account
1948	81.2	71.7	7.1	2.4
1949	73.4	62.7	9.8	0.9
1950	93.8	85.7	9.9	−1.8
1951	109.2	90.8	17.5	0.9
1952	106.8	83.9	22.3	0.6
1953	112.4	89.7	24.0	−1.3
1954	108.5	85.8	22.5	0.2
1955	129.1	107.7	21.0	0.4
1956	135.5	109.7	23.0	2.8
1957	140.2	111.0	24.4	4.8
1958	128.9	101.5	26.5	0.9
1959	149.2	121.1	29.3	−1.2
1960	153.7	122.3	28.2	3.2
1961	155.8	120.0	31.5	4.3
1962	172.1	135.0	33.2	3.9
1963	183.9	145.3	33.6	5.0
1964	200.8	158.7	34.6	7.5
1965	223.1	181.4	35.5	6.2
1966	243.2	199.5	39.8	3.9
1967	245.5	199.0	42.9	3.6
1968	267.3	222.1	43.5	1.7
1969	287.5	242.4	43.3	1.8
1970	285.0	237.3	43.7	4.0
1971	317.5	275.1	41.8	0.6
1972	357.0	318.0	42.6	−3.6
1973	424.1	368.0	46.8	9.3
1974	434.6	371.7	56.3	6.6
1975	448.3	363.8	63.1	21.4
1976	526.3	451.0	66.4	8.9
1977	601.1	542.5	67.6	−9.0
1978	706.3	639.7	77.0	−10.4
1979	797.2	707.3	88.5	1.4
1980	805.4	693.7	100.3	11.4
1981	916.7	803.6	106.8	6.3
1982	869.7	757.5	112.4	−0.2
1983	935.8	845.0	122.8	−32.0
1984	1,114.6	1,062.2	139.3	−86.9
1985	1,147.7	1,099.7	158.8	−110.8
1986	1,183.4	1,149.4	173.2	−139.2
1987	1,240.2	1,206.7	184.3	−150.8
1988	1,349.1	1,275.2	186.1	−112.2
1989	1,456.2	1,346.8	197.7	−88.3
1990	1,480.9	1,335.2	215.7	−70.0
1991	1,490.7	1,256.8	220.4	13.5
1992	1,534.5	1,348.4	223.0	−36.9
1993	1,628.7	1,480.1	219.0	−70.4
1994	1,795.5	1,679.4	221.3	−105.2
1995	1,897.3	1,755.6	232.7	−91.0
1996	2,037.4	1,892.8	244.9	−100.3
1997	2,224.2	2,082.4	252.1	−110.3
1998	2,334.4	2,259.4	262.4	−187.4
1999	2,456.2	2,443.2	286.9	−273.9
2000	2,506.5	2,598.7	304.4	−396.6
2001	2,451.7	2,498.1	324.0	−370.4
2002	2,385.3	2,495.5	347.4	−457.6

Table 1.13   **Domestic capital account, change in wealth, 1948–2002 (billions of current $)**

Year	Gross saving	Depreciation	Net saving	Revaluation	Change in wealth
1948	81.2	36.5	44.7		
1949	73.4	40.5	32.9	4.5	37.4
1950	93.8	44.1	49.7	25.4	75.1
1951	109.2	51.1	58.1	71.7	129.8
1952	106.8	54.9	52.0	13.6	65.6
1953	112.4	58.8	53.6	42.8	96.4
1954	108.5	62.4	46.1	8.8	54.8
1955	129.1	65.9	63.2	31.5	94.7
1956	135.5	72.7	62.8	101.1	164.0
1957	140.2	78.7	61.5	79.0	140.6
1958	128.9	81.8	47.1	32.1	79.2
1959	149.2	86.2	63.0	45.0	108.0
1960	153.7	89.4	64.3	54.9	119.3
1961	155.8	92.1	63.7	59.8	123.5
1962	172.1	95.4	76.7	68.3	145.0
1963	183.9	99.7	84.2	34.6	118.8
1964	200.8	104.9	95.9	−9.4	86.5
1965	223.1	110.9	112.2	38.7	150.9
1966	243.2	118.9	124.3	78.4	202.8
1967	245.5	129.8	115.7	60.4	176.1
1968	267.3	142.6	124.7	191.2	315.9
1969	287.5	156.9	130.6	239.4	370.0
1970	285.0	172.5	112.5	158.1	270.5
1971	317.5	187.3	130.2	196.1	326.3
1972	357.0	205.3	151.7	259.8	411.4
1973	424.1	222.8	201.3	361.6	562.8
1974	434.6	255.8	178.8	606.4	785.3
1975	448.3	294.2	154.1	546.6	700.7
1976	526.3	320.2	206.1	326.5	532.5
1977	601.1	353.9	247.2	624.1	871.3
1978	706.3	398.5	307.8	860.5	1,168.3
1979	797.2	455.0	342.2	1,073.8	1,416.0
1980	805.4	522.1	283.3	1,069.9	1,353.2
1981	916.7	585.1	331.6	842.5	1,174.0
1982	869.7	635.9	233.8	527.6	761.4
1983	935.8	660.5	275.3	361.8	637.1
1984	1,114.6	694.4	420.2	333.9	754.2
1985	1,147.7	744.0	403.8	568.6	972.3
1986	1,183.4	803.6	379.8	917.9	1,297.7
1987	1,240.2	867.7	372.5	1,102.7	1,475.2
1988	1,349.1	929.9	419.2	1,193.6	1,612.9
1989	1,456.2	995.9	460.3	1,056.1	1,516.4
1990	1,480.9	1,057.7	423.2	744.5	1,167.7
1991	1,490.7	1,112.4	378.3	352.2	730.5
1992	1,534.5	1,141.3	393.2	311.6	704.8
1993	1,628.7	1,190.5	438.2	990.0	1,428.2
1994	1,795.5	1,257.3	538.2	793.8	1,332.1
1995	1,897.3	1,334.1	563.2	781.1	1,344.3
1996	2,037.4	1,396.0	641.4	801.9	1,443.3
1997	2,224.2	1,459.3	764.9	468.6	1,233.5
1998	2,334.4	1,528.5	805.9	626.0	1,431.9
1999	2,456.2	1,621.4	834.8	1,320.6	2,155.4
2000	2,506.5	1,743.7	762.8	1,654.1	2,416.9
2001	2,451.7	1,860.4	591.3	1,560.4	2,151.7
2002	2,385.3	1,934.3	451.0	2,123.2	2,574.1

Table 1.14   Foreign transactions capital account, 2002

Row No.	Balance on current account	Source	Total
1	Balance on current account	NIPA 4.1 line 29	−457.7
	Capital account transactions and net lending	Source	Total
1	Capital account transactions (net)	NIPA 4.1 line 32	1.3
2	Net lending or borrowing	NIPA 4.1 line 30	−458.9
3	= Current account transactions and net lending		−457.6

include production and sales taxes are used in evaluating private and government consumption expenditures, reflecting the purchasers' perspective. We extend the price and quantity decomposition to saving and investment in order to link investment in constant prices to the change in wealth.

Index Number Systems

To illustrate the construction of price and quantity index numbers we consider the value of output in the Domestic Income and Product Account. Suppose that m components of output are distinguished in the accounts; the value of output, say qY, can be written:

$$qY = q_1 Y_1 + q_2 Y_2 + \ldots + q_m Y_m.$$

Our system of index numbers consists of a price index for output q and a quantity index for output Y, defined in terms of the prices (q_i) and quantities (Y_i) of the m components. We choose the base for all price indexes as 1.000 in 2000, following the December 2003 benchmark revision of the NIPAs. The base for the quantity indexes is the corresponding value in 2000.

Gross Domestic Product is presented in current and constant prices in the NIPAs. The index number system is based on the Fisher ideal index, a geometric average of Laspeyres and Paasche index numbers. The Laspeyres index of quantity of output, say Y^L, is defined by

$$Y_1^L = \frac{\sum q_{i0} Y_{i1}}{\sum q_{i0} Y_{i0}}.$$

The Paasche index uses current prices, rather than base-period prices, as weights:

$$Y_1^P = \frac{\sum q_{i1} Y_{i1}}{\sum q_{i1} Y_{i0}}.$$

The corresponding price index is obtained by dividing GDP in current prices by the Fisher ideal quantity index.

Table 1.15   Foreign transactions capital account, 1948–2002 (billions of current $)

Year	Balance on current account	Capital account transactions (net)	Net lending or borrowing
1948	2.4		2.4
1949	0.9		0.0
1950	−1.8		−1.8
1951	0.9		0.9
1952	0.6		0.6
1953	−1.3		−1.3
1954	0.2		0.2
1955	0.4		0.4
1956	2.8		2.8
1957	4.8		4.8
1958	0.9		0.9
1959	−1.2		−1.2
1960	3.2		3.2
1961	4.3		4.3
1962	3.9		3.9
1963	5.0		5.0
1964	7.5		7.5
1965	6.2		6.2
1966	3.9		3.9
1967	3.6		3.6
1968	1.7		1.7
1969	1.8		1.8
1970	4.0		4.0
1971	0.6		0.6
1972	−3.6		−3.6
1973	9.3		9.3
1974	6.6		6.6
1975	21.4		21.4
1976	8.9		8.9
1977	−9.0		−9.0
1978	−10.4		−10.4
1979	1.4		1.4
1980	11.4		11.4
1981	6.3		6.3
1982	−0.2	−0.2	0.0
1983	−32.1	−0.2	−31.8
1984	−86.9	−0.2	−86.7
1985	−110.8	−0.3	−110.5
1986	−139.2	−0.3	−138.9
1987	−150.8	−0.4	−150.4
1988	−112.2	−0.5	−111.7
1989	−88.3	−0.3	−88.0
1990	−70.1	6.6	−76.6
1991	13.5	4.5	9.0
1992	−36.9	0.6	−37.5
1993	−70.4	1.3	−71.7
1994	−105.2	1.7	−106.9
1995	−91.0	0.9	−91.9
1996	−100.3	0.7	−101.0
1997	−110.2	1.0	−111.3
1998	−187.4	0.7	−188.1
1999	−273.9	4.8	−278.7
2000	−396.6	0.8	−397.4
2001	−370.4	1.1	−371.5
2002	−457.7	−1.3	−458.9

Table 1.16   **Wealth account, 2002**

Row No.	Wealth	Source	Total
1	+ Private domestic tangible assets	Our imputation	38,111.6
2	+ Government tangible assets	Our imputation	9,331.4
3	= Domestic tangible assets		47,443.0
4	+ Net international investment position of the United States		–2,553.4
5	= Wealth		44,889.6

Landefeld and Parker (1997) provide a detailed exposition of the chained Fisher ideal price and quantity indexes employed in the NIPAs, and Moulton (2001) discusses the implications of this index number system. Erwin Diewert (1976) has defined a superlative index number as an index that exactly replicates a flexible representation of the underlying technology (or preferences). A flexible representation provides a second-order approximation to an arbitrary technology (or preference system). Konus and Byushgens (1926) first showed that the Fisher ideal index employed in the NIPAs is superlative in this sense. Laspeyres and Paasche indexes are not superlative and fail to capture substitutions among products in response to price changes.

The BLS multifactor productivity program employs a superlative quantity index for measuring real input that replicates a translog representation of technology:

$$\log Y_t - \log Y_{t-1} = \overline{w}_{it} (\log Y_{it} - \log Y_{i,t-1}).$$

The relative share of the ith output in the value of total output, say w_i, is

$$w_i = \frac{q_i Y_i}{\sum q_i Y_i}.$$

The weights ($\overline{w}_{it}$) are arithmetic averages of the relative shares in the two periods,

$$\overline{w}_{it} = \frac{1}{2} w_{it} + \frac{1}{2} w_{i,t-1}.$$

The corresponding price index is obtained by dividing the value of output by the translog quantity index.[16]

In SNA 1993, superlative systems of index numbers like those employed in the U.S. national accounts are recommended for the output side of the production account. As the base period is changed from time to time, chain-linking of the resulting price and quantity indexes is recommended.

16. Translog index numbers were originally discussed by Fisher (1922).

Table 1.17   Wealth account, 1948–2002 (billions of current $)

Year	Wealth	Private domestic tangible assets	Government tangible assets	Net international investment position of the United States
1948	770.6	492.0	265.7	12.9
1949	799.8	526.9	259.1	13.8
1950	875.6	605.5	257.0	13.1
1951	1,008.0	698.5	295.5	14.0
1952	1,079.6	747.3	318.0	14.2
1953	1,175.6	816.3	343.9	15.4
1954	1,234.5	859.9	359.8	14.8
1955	1,328.3	934.5	379.1	14.7
1956	1,483.1	1,043.2	422.6	17.3
1957	1,619.5	1,141.1	456.4	22.0
1958	1,697.6	1,199.0	475.2	23.3
1959	1,799.3	1,280.2	496.4	22.7
1960	1,902.0	1,365.4	509.9	26.7
1961	2,008.6	1,446.6	533.8	28.1
1962	2,144.7	1,547.5	563.2	34.1
1963	2,266.2	1,632.2	597.2	36.8
1964	2,363.7	1,694.8	626.6	42.2
1965	2,512.4	1,807.2	657.8	47.4
1966	2,714.1	1,961.2	701.5	51.4
1967	2,900.6	2,098.9	751.5	50.2
1968	3,194.2	2,340.4	806.0	47.8
1969	3,547.4	2,614.4	885.4	47.7
1970	3,836.9	2,826.6	980.9	39.3
1971	4,152.6	3,062.1	1,064.5	26.0
1972	4,687.3	3,477.1	1,188.8	21.4
1973	5,299.0	3,944.9	1,304.7	49.3
1974	5,784.9	4,168.6	1,542.5	73.7
1975	6,626.8	4,816.6	1,721.0	89.2
1976	7,202.4	5,295.1	1,829.0	78.2
1977	8,138.9	5,999.0	1,986.0	153.8
1978	9,356.8	6,965.8	2,179.0	212.0
1979	10,898.7	8,110.1	2,455.3	333.3
1980	12,428.1	9,220.9	2,828.6	378.6
1981	14,106.3	10,582.0	3,224.2	300.1
1982	15,009.3	11,349.4	3,424.0	235.9
1983	15,628.4	11,841.8	3,529.2	257.4
1984	17,081.0	13,278.8	3,668.2	134.1
1985	18,650.4	14,799.9	3,753.6	96.9
1986	19,987.4	15,884.1	4,002.5	100.8
1987	21,339.8	17,007.2	4,282.1	50.5
1988	23,005.1	18,427.1	4,567.6	10.5
1989	24,721.6	19,883.7	4,884.9	−47.0
1990	25,194.5	20,351.1	5,007.9	−164.5
1991	25,919.0	20,993.3	5,186.5	−260.8
1992	26,170.7	21,336.5	5,286.5	−452.3
1993	27,067.8	21,811.2	5,400.8	−144.3
1994	27,581.6	22,210.7	5,506.2	−135.3
1995	29,373.4	23,803.1	5,876.1	−305.8
1996	30,426.3	24,677.9	6,108.5	−360.0
1997	31,726.5	26,110.0	6,439.3	−822.7
1998	33,951.7	28,159.2	6,867.8	−1,075.4
1999	36,550.3	30,224.8	7,372.2	−1,046.7
2000	39,504.6	33,046.6	8,046.6	−1,588.6
2001	41,629.9	35,371.8	8,566.2	−2,308.2
2002	44,889.6	38,111.6	9,331.4	−2,553.4

Table 1.18   U.S. international position, 2002

Row No.	Wealth	Source	Total
1	+U.S. owned assets abroad		6,613.3
2	−Foreign-owned assets in the United States		9,166.7
3	=Net international investment position of the United States		−2,553.4

Our index numbers are chain-linked Fisher ideal indexes of components from the NIPAs.

Taxes

At a number of points we present data net and gross of taxes, reflecting differences between sellers and buyers that result from tax wedges. As one illustration, consumer expenditures on goods and services in the Income and Expenditures Account include sales and excise taxes, reflecting the purchasers' point of view. Sales of the same goods and services in the Domestic Income and Product Account exclude these taxes, reflecting the perspective of producers. The prices net of taxes are denoted basic prices in SNA 1993. We treat sales and excise taxes as part of the price paid by consumers, so that we can separate the value of transactions into three components—price, quantity, and tax rate.

To illustrate the construction of price, quantity, and tax indexes we consider the value of consumer expenditure as it enters the Income and Expenditures Account. Suppose that m components of consumer expenditure are distinguished in the account; the value of output, gross of tax, say $q^+ Y$, may be written:

$$q^+ Y = q_1^+ Y_1 + q_2^+ Y_2 + \ldots + q_m^+ Y_m.$$

The prices (q_i^+) include sales and excise taxes; the quantities (Y_i) are measured in the same way as in the Domestic Income and Product Account. Price and quantity indexes based on these prices and quantities are defined as before.

To introduce taxes into the system of index numbers we let the market price of output q^+ be equal to the price received by the producer, say q, multiplied by unity plus the effective tax rate, t; the value of output at market prices is

$$(1 + t)qY = \sum (1 + t_i)q_i Y_i,$$

where the prices paid by the consumers (q_i^+) are expressed in terms of prices received by producers (q_i) and tax rates (t_i). Accordingly, we construct an index of taxes $1 + t$ by dividing the value of transactions at purchasers' prices by the value of transactions at producers' prices. The price and quantity indexes at market prices differ from the corresponding indexes at

Table 1.19   **U.S. international position, 1948–2002 (billions of current $)**

Year	U.S. owned assets abroad	Foreign owned assets in the United States	Net international investment position of the United States
1948	29.4	16.5	12.9
1949	30.7	16.9	13.8
1950	32.8	19.7	13.1
1951	34.8	20.9	14.0
1952	37.2	23.0	14.2
1953	39.5	24.1	15.4
1954	42.2	27.4	14.8
1955	45.0	30.4	14.7
1956	49.8	32.5	17.3
1957	54.3	32.4	22.0
1958	59.4	36.1	23.3
1959	64.8	42.1	22.7
1960	71.4	44.7	26.7
1961	75.0	46.9	28.1
1962	80.3	46.3	34.1
1963	88.3	51.5	36.8
1964	99.1	56.9	42.2
1965	106.2	58.7	47.4
1966	111.8	60.4	51.4
1967	119.9	69.7	50.2
1968	131.1	83.2	47.8
1969	138.5	90.8	47.7
1970	136.7	97.4	39.3
1971	151.9	125.9	26.0
1972	181.0	159.6	21.4
1973	232.0	182.7	49.3
1974	276.9	203.2	73.7
1975	321.3	232.1	89.2
1976	343.4	265.2	78.2
1977	488.4	334.6	153.8
1978	645.9	434.0	212.0
1979	844.8	511.5	333.3
1980	1,003.8	625.2	378.6
1981	944.7	644.6	300.1
1982	961.0	725.1	235.9
1983	1,129.7	872.3	257.4
1984	1,127.1	993.0	134.1
1985	1,302.7	1,205.8	96.9
1986	1,594.7	1,493.9	100.8
1987	1,758.7	1,708.2	50.5
1988	2,008.4	1,997.9	10.5
1989	2,350.2	2,397.2	−47.0
1990	2,294.1	2,458.6	−164.5
1991	2,470.6	2,731.4	−260.8
1992	2,466.5	2,918.8	−452.3
1993	3,091.4	3,235.7	−144.3
1994	3,315.1	3,450.4	−135.3
1995	3,964.6	4,270.4	−305.8
1996	4,650.8	5,010.9	−360.0
1997	5,379.1	6,201.9	−822.7
1998	6,174.5	7,249.9	−1,075.4
1999	7,390.4	8,437.1	−1,046.7
2000	7,393.6	8,982.2	−1,588.6
2001	6,898.7	9,206.9	−2,308.2
2002	6,613.3	9,166.7	−2,553.4

producer prices since taxes enter the weights (w_i) employed in constructing the indexes.

1.4.5   Domestic Income and Product Account in Constant Prices

Introduction

Our principal innovation in presenting the Domestic Income and Product Account in constant prices is to introduce a user cost formula for imputing the rental price of capital services. Systems of national accounts have traditionally relied on market rental prices for making these imputations, but data on market rentals are too limited in scope to cover the capital services required for an integrated and consistent system of U.S. national accounts. In this section we present the Domestic Income and Product Account in constant prices.

Output and Labor Income

To construct a quantity index for GDP we first allocate the value of output between consumption and investment goods. Investment goods include durable goods and structures. Consumption goods include nondurable goods and services. Data for prices and quantities of consumption and investment goods are presented in the NIPAs. We construct price and quantity index numbers for the services of consumer, institutional, and government durables, as well as institutional and government real estate, as part of our imputation for the value of the capital services.

The value of output from the point of view of the producing sector excludes sales and excise taxes and includes subsidies. We have allocated these taxes and subsidies in proportion to the consumption and investment goods output in current prices. The price index for each type of output is implicit in the value and quantity of output included in the GDP. We construct price and quantity indexes of GDP by applying chained Fisher ideal index numbers to price and quantity data for consumption and investment goods product. The results are given in table 1.20.

Construction of a quantity index of labor income begins with data on hours worked and labor compensation per hour. We obtain hours worked and labor compensation by sex, age, educational attainment, and employment class from the Census of Population and the Current Population Survey. These data are based on household surveys. Control totals for hours worked and labor compensation are taken from the NIPAs. These totals are based on establishment surveys and reflect payroll records.[17]

Denoting the labor income quantity index by L and the corresponding price index by p_L, we represent the value of labor input as the sum over all categories of labor input:

---

17. Details are given by Jorgenson, Ho, and Stiroh (2005).

Table 1.20   **Domestic income and product account, product, 1948–2002 (constant prices of 2000)**

Year	Gross domestic product		Investment goods product		Consumption goods product	
	Price	Quantity	Price	Quantity	Price	Quantity
1948	0.178	1,634.2	0.256	307.4	0.159	1,332.9
1949	0.171	1,674.2	0.254	284.6	0.151	1,415.3
1950	0.175	1,825.2	0.255	362.1	0.156	1,456.8
1951	0.185	1,980.1	0.282	376.5	0.162	1,608.1
1952	0.186	2,080.0	0.284	365.1	0.163	1,742.5
1953	0.188	2,181.3	0.283	390.8	0.165	1,813.6
1954	0.191	2,176.0	0.284	377.8	0.168	1,829.7
1955	0.193	2,319.8	0.287	441.7	0.170	1,884.8
1956	0.201	2,372.3	0.304	433.6	0.176	1,958.5
1957	0.203	2,427.1	0.314	428.8	0.177	2,029.9
1958	0.212	2,421.9	0.319	397.5	0.186	2,078.6
1959	0.211	2,572.0	0.318	456.5	0.185	2,148.3
1960	0.219	2,633.0	0.321	462.4	0.194	2,207.6
1961	0.218	2,700.9	0.322	466.4	0.193	2,277.6
1962	0.220	2,847.7	0.323	513.4	0.195	2,365.4
1963	0.223	2,956.9	0.324	543.3	0.198	2,439.4
1964	0.229	3,121.1	0.326	584.7	0.204	2,556.5
1965	0.236	3,303.1	0.331	643.7	0.213	2,666.5
1966	0.245	3,530.3	0.336	699.2	0.222	2,832.7
1967	0.248	3,626.7	0.342	691.6	0.225	2,950.5
1968	0.259	3,791.1	0.356	721.5	0.235	3,086.4
1969	0.272	3,909.9	0.372	744.1	0.247	3,183.2
1970	0.279	3,927.2	0.389	701.8	0.252	3,266.7
1971	0.295	4,057.0	0.405	749.1	0.268	3,337.8
1972	0.316	4,268.4	0.419	820.3	0.291	3,464.2
1973	0.338	4,511.6	0.436	912.8	0.313	3,596.9
1974	0.367	4,496.2	0.477	871.7	0.340	3,637.7
1975	0.398	4,495.4	0.537	795.8	0.364	3,745.9
1976	0.425	4,740.1	0.563	903.6	0.390	3,855.7
1977	0.455	4,974.6	0.594	994.2	0.421	3,981.0
1978	0.488	5,242.4	0.633	1,086.2	0.452	4,141.1
1979	0.519	5,401.8	0.691	1,120.9	0.476	4,264.6
1980	0.557	5,382.5	0.756	1,038.6	0.508	4,364.5
1981	0.607	5,500.1	0.825	1,073.0	0.552	4,442.4
1982	0.644	5,416.4	0.870	962.2	0.587	4,515.6
1983	0.681	5,649.0	0.869	1,040.9	0.632	4,656.2
1984	0.711	6,057.5	0.878	1,245.1	0.667	4,819.3
1985	0.722	6,337.2	0.888	1,284.3	0.678	5,065.8
1986	0.729	6,600.0	0.888	1,324.8	0.687	5,292.5
1987	0.746	6,845.6	0.901	1,378.2	0.705	5,484.2
1988	0.780	7,115.3	0.916	1,442.4	0.743	5,687.8
1989	0.806	7,365.1	0.940	1,504.3	0.770	5,873.7
1990	0.831	7,518.0	0.958	1,500.0	0.796	6,038.7
1991	0.857	7,502.9	0.972	1,417.4	0.825	6,121.4
1992	0.878	7,736.1	0.971	1,498.5	0.851	6,268.8
1993	0.892	7,943.7	0.982	1,581.3	0.866	6,543.5
1994	0.910	8,245.4	0.992	1,719.2	0.886	6,543.5
1995	0.928	8,471.2	1.001	1,780.3	0.906	6,707.0
1996	0.947	8,806.8	1.005	1,923.7	0.929	6,893.1
1997	0.966	9,220.6	1.004	2,124.6	0.954	7,099.0
1998	0.971	9,645.6	0.995	2,277.8	0.963	7,368.7
1999	0.983	10,111.7	0.993	2,425.4	0.980	7,686.4
2000	1.000	10,525.6	1.000	2,528.8	1.000	7,996.8
2001	1.027	10,670.5	1.010	2,452.7	1.032	8,216.7
2002	1.034	10,927.1	1.006	2,423.8	1.043	8,499.6

$$p_L L = \sum p_{L,j} L_j,$$

where $p_{L,j}$ is the price of the jth type of labor input and L_j is the number of hours worked by workers of this type. Price and quantity indexes of labor income are constructed from chained Fisher ideal quantity indexes, as recommended by SNA 1993.

Price and quantity indexes of labor income for 1948–2002 are given in table 1.21, along with employment, weekly hours, hourly compensation, and hours worked. Labor quality in table 1.21 is defined as the ratio of the quantity index of labor income to hours worked. Labor quality captures changes in the composition of the work force by the characteristics of individual workers, as suggested by BLS (1993). A more detailed description of our estimates is provided by Jorgenson, Ho, and Stiroh (2005).

Capital Income

Estimates of capital income, property compensation, depreciation, and capital assets in constant prices require data on both prices and quantities of capital goods. We next describe the construction of these data.[18] The starting point for a quantity index of capital income is a perpetual inventory of capital stocks. Under the assumption that efficiency of capital assets declines geometrically with age, the rate of depreciation, say δ, is a constant. Capital stock at the end of every period can be estimated from investment and capital stock at the beginning of the period:

$$K_t = A_t + (1 - \delta)K_{t-1},$$

where K_t is end of period capital stock, A_t the quantity of investment, and K_{t-1} the capital stock at the beginning of the period. To transform capital stocks into flows of capital services, we introduce an assumption about the time required for new investment to begin to contribute to production, namely that the capital service from each asset is proportional to the arithmetic average of current and lagged capital stocks.[19]

Our perpetual inventory estimates of capital stocks are based on the BEA's reproducible wealth accounts, described by Herman (2000). These data include investment by asset class for sixty-one types of nonresidential assets from 1901 to 2000, forty-eight types of residential assets for the same period, and thirteen types of consumers' durables from 1925 to 2000. As described by Fraumeni (1997), the reproducible wealth accounts use efficiency functions for most assets that decline geometrically with age. To simplify the accounts for tangible wealth, we approximate age-efficiency profiles that are not geometric by best geometric average (BGA) profiles

---

18. Further details are given by Jorgenson, Ho, and Stiroh (2005).
19. This assumption is employed by Jorgenson and Stiroh (2000), Jorgenson (2001), Jorgenson, Ho, and Stiroh (2005), and Oliner and Sichel (2000). Jorgenson, Gollop, and Fraumeni (1987) had assumed that capital services were proportional to lagged capital stocks.

Table 1.21   Domestic income and product account, labor income, 1948–2002 (constant prices of 2000)

Year	Labor income				Employment	Weekly hours	Hourly compensation	Hours worked
	Price	Quantity	Value	Quality				
1948	0.077	2,246.1	173.2	0.734	61,536	38.9	1.4	124,616
1949	0.079	2,184.5	173.6	0.734	60,437	38.6	1.4	121,201
1950	0.082	2,277.2	187.0	0.746	62,424	38.3	1.5	124,336
1951	0.087	2,462.7	213.6	0.761	66,169	38.3	1.6	131,846
1952	0.090	2,534.9	228.7	0.775	67,407	38.0	1.7	133,284
1953	0.094	2,597.5	244.4	0.788	68,471	37.7	1.8	134,352
1954	0.096	2,536.8	244.5	0.794	66,843	37.4	1.9	130,070
1955	0.100	2,613.8	262.7	0.797	68,367	37.6	2.0	133,520
1956	0.106	2,677.8	283.6	0.803	69,968	37.3	2.1	135,779
1957	0.111	2,684.3	297.5	0.811	70,262	36.9	2.2	134,783
1958	0.114	2,618.6	299.3	0.817	68,578	36.6	2.3	130,526
1959	0.119	2,709.3	323.5	0.822	70,149	36.8	2.4	134,240
1960	0.124	2,748.1	339.5	0.827	71,128	36.6	2.5	135,346
1961	0.125	2,788.2	348.7	0.842	71,183	36.4	2.6	134,905
1962	0.128	2,893.7	371.3	0.855	72,673	36.5	2.7	137,903
1963	0.133	2,930.9	388.9	0.859	73,413	36.4	2.8	139,032
1964	0.138	3,008.3	416.2	0.865	74,990	36.3	2.9	141,729
1965	0.144	3,105.4	446.6	0.865	77,239	36.4	3.1	146,304
1966	0.151	3,239.6	490.3	0.869	80,802	36.2	3.2	151,932
1967	0.159	3,290.3	522.6	0.875	82,645	35.7	3.4	153,260
1968	0.170	3,375.8	575.2	0.880	84,733	35.4	3.7	156,187
1969	0.183	3,463.6	632.1	0.881	87,071	35.4	3.9	160,067
1970	0.198	3,407.3	673.1	0.883	86,867	34.8	4.3	157,112
1971	0.211	3,408.2	719.0	0.887	86,715	34.7	4.6	156,454
1972	0.226	3,499.8	789.3	0.888	88,838	34.7	4.9	160,480
1973	0.242	3,640.8	880.9	0.889	92,542	34.7	5.3	166,760
1974	0.265	3,643.4	966.1	0.889	94,121	34.1	5.8	166,881

(continued)

Table 1.21 (continued)

Year	Labor income				Employment	Weekly hours	Hourly compensation	Hours worked
	Price	Quantity	Value	Quality				
1975	0.287	3,586.8	1,029.5	0.899	92,575	33.8	6.3	162,482
1976	0.311	3,689.2	1,147.5	0.901	94,922	33.8	6.9	166,754
1977	0.335	3,814.1	1,279.4	0.901	98,202	33.8	7.4	172,399
1978	0.363	3,985.8	1,448.6	0.900	102,931	33.7	8.0	180,360
1979	0.395	4,120.2	1,628.4	0.901	106,463	33.6	8.7	186,235
1980	0.437	4,104.6	1,792.6	0.904	107,061	33.2	9.7	184,922
1981	0.478	4,145.3	1,980.5	0.910	108,050	33.0	10.7	185,539
1982	0.509	4,105.2	2,090.2	0.918	106,749	32.8	11.5	182,161
1983	0.532	4,168.7	2,219.2	0.919	107,810	33.0	12.0	184,781
1984	0.555	4,413.4	2,447.9	0.928	112,604	33.1	12.6	193,754
1985	0.580	4,531.0	2,626.0	0.32	115,201	33.1	13.3	198,072
1986	0.608	4,578.9	2,785.0	0.932	117,158	32.9	13.9	200,164
1987	0.628	4,743.4	2,978.8	0.938	120,456	32.9	14.5	206,046
1988	0.657	4,889.3	3,214.1	0.942	123,916	32.8	15.2	211,493
1989	0.674	5,047.1	3,402.5	0.947	126,743	33.0	15.7	217,179
1990	0.705	5,121.8	3,610.4	0.956	128,290	32.7	16.5	218,341
1991	0.737	5,069.2	3,733.9	0.964	127,022	32.4	17.4	214,106
1992	0.774	5,076.2	3,931.5	0.965	127,100	32.4	18.4	214,183
1993	0.737	5,236.2	4,118.3	0.974	129,556	32.5	18.8	218,916
1994	0.803	5,393.0	4,332.5	0.977	132,459	32.6	19.3	224,790
1995	0.819	5,539.7	4,535.5	0.982	135,297	32.7	19.7	229,741
1996	0.841	5,644.8	4,749.1	0.988	137,571	32.5	20.4	232,695
1997	0.857	5,804.6	5,035.2	0.989	140,432	32.7	21.1	239,043
1998	0.907	5,964.9	5,409.0	0.993	143,557	32.8	22.1	244,667
1999	0.944	6,105.2	5,763.1	0.996	146,468	32.8	23.1	249,676
2000	1.030	6,204.4	6,204.4	1.000	149,364	32.5	24.5	252,730
2001	1.032	6,168.4	6,367.8	1.005	149,166	32.2	25.5	250,029
2002	1.065	6,098.7	6,493.5	1.005	147,885	32.1	26.3	247,080

Table 1.22   Benchmarks, depreciation rates, and deflators

Row No.	Asset class	2002 benchmark (billions of 2000 dollars)	Depreciation rate	Deflator
1	Consumer Durables	3,846.0	0.201	NIPA
2	Nonresidential Structures	11,482.5	0.024	NIPA
3	Residential Structures	10,639.4	0.016	NIPA
4	Equipment and Software	5,561.2	0.144	NIPA
5	Nonfarm inventories	1,573.3		NIPA
6	Farm inventories	124.7		NIPA
7	Land	10,193.5		Implicit price of household land, flow of funds

that are geometric, following Hulten and Wykoff (1982). Benchmark estimates of capital stocks in 2002, expressed in constant prices of 2000, rates of depreciation, and the sources of price indexes for each type of capital are presented in table 1.22.

The official price indexes for computers provide the paradigm for economic measurement. These indexes capture the steady decline in information technology prices and the recent acceleration in this decline. The official price indexes for central office switching equipment and prepackaged software also hold performance constant. Our price indexes for reproducible assets are taken from the NIPAs. An important assumption is that these prices are measured in "efficiency" units, holding the quality of assets constant over time. For example, we hold the performance of computers and peripheral equipment constant, using the constant quality price indexes constructed by a BEA-IBM team and introduced into the NIPAs in 1985. Triplett's (1986) discussion of the economic interpretation of these indexes brought the rapid decline of computer prices to the attention of a very broad audience.

Dulberger (1989) presented a more detailed report on her research on the prices of computer processors for the BEA-IBM project. Speed of processing and main memory played central roles in her model. Triplett (1989, 2005) has provided exhaustive surveys of research on hedonic price indexes for computers. Gordon (1989, 1990) gave an alternative model of computer prices and identified computers and communications equipment, along with commercial aircraft, as assets with the highest rates of price decline.

Communications technology is crucial for the rapid development and diffusion of the Internet, perhaps the most striking manifestation of information technology in the American economy. Flamm (1989) was the first to compare the behavior of computer prices and the prices of communications equipment. He concluded that the communications equipment prices fell only a little more slowly than computer prices. Gordon (1990) compared Flamm's results with the official price indexes, revealing substantial bias in the official indexes. Unfortunately, constant quality price indexes cover only a portion of communications equipment. Switching and terminal equipment rely heavily on semiconductor technology, so that product development reflects improvements in semiconductors. Grimm's (1997) constant quality price index for digital telephone switching equipment was incorporated into the national accounts in 1996. The output of communications equipment in the NIPAs also incorporates a constant quality price index for cellular phones.

Much communications investment takes the form of the transmission gear, connecting data, voice, and video terminals to switching equipment. Technologies such as fiber optics, microwave broadcasting, and communications satellites have progressed at rates that outrun even the dramatic pace of semiconductor development. Mark Doms (2005) has provided comprehensive price indexes for terminals, switching gear, and transmission equipment. These have been incorporated into the Federal Reserve's Index of Industrial Production, as described by Corrado (2003), but are not yet included in the NIPAs.

Both software and hardware are essential for information technology, and this is reflected in the large volume of software expenditures. The eleventh comprehensive revision of the national accounts, released by the BEA on October 27, 1999, reclassified computer software as investment.[20] Before this important advance, business expenditures on software were treated as current outlays, while personal and government expenditures were treated as purchases of nondurable goods. Software investment is growing rapidly and is now much more important than investment in computer hardware.

Parker and Grimm (2000) describe the new estimates of investment in software. The BEA distinguishes among three types of software—prepackaged, custom, and own-account software. Prepackaged software is sold or licensed in standardized form and is delivered in packages or electronic files downloaded from the Internet. Custom software is tailored to the specific application of the user and is delivered along with analysis, design, and programming services required for customization. Own-account software consists of software created for a specific application. However, only price indexes for prepackaged software hold performance constant.

Parker and Grimm (2000) present a constant quality price index for prepackaged software. This combines a hedonic model of prices for business applications software and a matched model index for spreadsheet and word processing programs developed by Oliner and Sichel (1994). Pre-

---

20. Moulton (2000) describes the eleventh comprehensive revision of NIPA and the 1999 update.

packaged software prices decline at more than 10 percent per year over the period 1962–1998. Since 1998 the BEA has relied on a matched model price index for all prepackaged software from the Producers' Price Index (PPI) program of the BLS. The BEA's prices for own-account and custom software incorporate data on programmer wage rates. Custom and own-account software prices are a weighted average of prepackaged software prices and programmer wage rates with arbitrary weights of 75 percent for programmer wage rates and 25 percent for prepackaged software.

Given market rental prices by class of asset, the implicit rental values paid by owners for the use of their property can be imputed by applying these rental rates. This method of imputation is used to estimate the rental value of owner-occupied dwellings in the U.S. national accounts. The total rental value is divided among taxes, consumption of fixed capital, interest payments, and net rent. A similar method of imputation is used for the space rental value of institutional buildings, but net rent is omitted from the imputation. The main obstacle to broader application of this method is the lack of data on market rental prices. A substantial proportion of the capital goods employed in the U.S. economy has an active rental market; most classes of structures can be rented and a rental market exists for many types of equipment, especially aircraft, trucks, construction equipment, computers, and so on. Unfortunately, very little effort has been devoted to compiling data on rental rates for either structures or equipment.

We extend the perpetual inventory method to rental prices of capital services in order to provide an alternative approach for imputation of the rental values.[21] For each type of capital we prepare perpetual inventory estimates of acquisition prices, service prices, depreciation, and revaluation. Under our assumption of geometrically declining relative efficiency of capital goods, the acquisition prices decline geometrically with vintage. The formula for the value of capital stock,

$$q_{A,t} K_t = \sum q_{A,t} (1 - \delta)^\tau A_{t-\tau},$$

is the sum of past investments weighted by relative efficiencies and evaluated at the price for acquisition of new capital goods $q_{A,t}$. Second, depreciation $q_{D,t}$ is proportional to the value of beginning-of-period capital stock:

$$q_{D,t} K_{t-1} = \delta q_{A,t} K_{t-1}.$$

Finally, revaluation $(q_{A,t} - q_{A,t-1}) K_{t-1}$ is equal to the change in the acquisition price of new capital goods multiplied by beginning-of-period capital stock.

Households and institutions and government are not subject to direct taxes. Noncorporate business is subject to personal income taxes, while corporate business is subject to both corporate and personal income taxes.

---

21. A detailed presentation of this extension of the perpetual inventory method is given by Christensen and Jorgenson (1996).

Table 1.23   **Relative proportions of capital stock by asset class and sector, 2002**

Row No.	Asset class	Corporate	Noncorporate	Households	Government	Total
1	Consumer durables			0.078		0.078
2	Nonresidential structures	0.102	0.027	0.017	0.112	0.258
3	Equipment and software	0.085	0.012	0.003	0.016	0.115
4	Residential structures	0.002	0.041	0.193	0.005	0.241
5	Nonfarm inventories	0.027	0.002		0.005	0.033
6	Farm inventories		0.003			0.003
7	Land	0.050	0.071	0.090	0.060	0.272
	Total	0.266	0.155	0.382	0.197	1.000

Businesses and households are subject to indirect taxes on the value of property. In order to take these differences in taxation into account we first allocate each class of assets among the five sectors of the U.S. domestic economy—corporations, noncorporate business, households, and institutions and government. The relative proportions of capital stock by asset class for each sector for 2002 are given in table 1.23.

For a sector not subject to either direct or indirect taxes, we can utilize the capital service price $q_{K,t}$,

$$q_{K,t} = q_{A,t-1}[r_t - \pi_t + (1 + \pi_t)\delta],$$

where r_t is the nominal rate of return and π_t is the rate of inflation in the acquisition price of new capital goods. This formula can be applied to government and nonprofit institutions by choosing an appropriate rate of return, as described below.[22]

Given the rate of return for government and nonprofit institutions, we can construct estimates of capital service prices for each class of assets held by these sectors—land held by government and institutions, residential and nonresidential structures, producer and consumer durables. Price and quantity measures of capital input by class of asset can be combined into price and quantity index numbers of capital input by government and institutions, using the chained Fisher ideal index numbers employed in the NIPAs.

Households hold consumer durables and owner-occupied dwellings that are taxed indirectly through property taxes. To incorporate property taxes into our estimates of the price and quantity of capital services we add taxes to the cost of capital, depreciation, and revaluation, obtaining the capital service price:

22. Alternative methods for imputing the rate of return to capital are reviewed by Moulton (2004). A detailed derivation of prices of capital services is given by Jorgenson and Yun (2001).

$$q_{K,t} = q_{A,t-1}[r_t - \pi_t + (1 + \pi_t)\delta + (1 - t_e)\tau_t],$$

where τ_t is the rate of property taxation and t_e is the average marginal tax rate on income from which property taxes are deductible.

The household rate of return,

$$r_t - \pi = \beta[(1 - t_e)i_t - \pi_t] + (1 - \beta)[\rho_t - \pi_t],$$

is a weighted average of the rate of interest i_t and the nominal rate of return on equity in household assets ρ_t with weights that depend on the ratio of debt to the value of household capital stock β and the average marginal individual tax rate on income from household property t_e. We set the nominal rate of return on equity equal to the corresponding rate of return for owner-occupied housing after all taxes.

Given the rate of return for households, we can construct estimates of capital service prices for each class of assets held by households—land, residential structures, and consumer durables. We employ separate effective tax rates for owner-occupied residential property, both land and structures, and for consumer durables. Price and quantity measures of capital income by class of asset are combined into price and quantity index numbers of capital income by households, using chained Fisher ideal index numbers.

Our measure of the GDP differs from the NIPAs in the treatment of durables and real estate held by households and institutions and government. We assign personal and government consumption expenditures on durables to investment rather than consumption. This leaves GDP unchanged. We add the service flow from household, institutional, and government durables to the value of output and the value of capital input. We also add the net rent component of the services of institutional and government real estate to values of both output and input.

We next consider the measurement of price and quantity of capital services for noncorporate business. The main challenge is to separate the income of unincorporated enterprises between labor and property compensation. We estimate labor compensation of the self-employed from the incomes received by comparable categories of employees.[23] Property compensation is the sum of income originating in business, other than corporate business and government enterprises and the net rent of owner-occupied dwellings, less the imputed labor compensation of proprietors and unpaid family workers, plus noncorporate consumption of fixed capital, less allowances for owner-occupied dwellings and institutional structures, and plus indirect business taxes allocated to the noncorporate sector. We also allocate the statistical discrepancy to noncorporate property compensation.

To obtain an estimate of the noncorporate rate of return we must take

---

23. Estimation of the labor compensation of the self-employed is discussed by Jorgenson, Ho, and Stiroh (2005).

into account the personal income tax. The capital service price, modified to incorporate income tax and indirect business taxes, becomes

$$q_{K,t} = \left(\frac{1 - t_e z_t - k_t + y_t}{1 - t_e}\right) q_{A,t-1}[r_t - \pi_t + (1 + \pi_t)\delta] + q_{A,t-1}\tau_t,$$

where indirect business taxes $q_{A,t-1}\tau_t$ are deducted from noncorporate property compensation before taxes as an expense, t_e is the average marginal tax rate on noncorporate property compensation, z_t is the present value of depreciation allowances on one dollar's worth of investment, k_t the investment tax credit, and $y_t = k_t u_t z_t$. The variable y_t is set equal to zero for all years but 1962 and 1963; it is used in accounting for the fact that the investment tax credit was deducted from the value of an asset for depreciation in those years. The tax credit and depreciation allowances are different from zero only for durables and structures.

The noncorporate rate of return,

$$r_t - \pi = \beta[(1 - t_e)i_t - \pi_t] + (1 - \beta)[\rho_t - \pi_t(1 - t_g)],$$

is a weighted average of the rate of interest i_t and the nominal rate of return on noncorporate assets ρ_t with weights that depend on the ratio of debt to the value of noncorporate capital stock β, the average marginal individual tax rate on income from noncorporate property t_e, and the marginal tax rate on capital gains on noncorporate assets t_g.

We multiply the capital service price by the quantity of capital services for each asset held by noncorporate business, sum over assets, and solve for the rate of return. Given data on prices of acquisition, stocks, tax rates, and replacement rates, we can estimate capital service prices for each class of assets held by the noncorporate sector. Price and quantity measures of capital input by class of asset are combined into price and quantity index numbers of capital input, using chained Fisher ideal index numbers, as before.

Finally, we consider the measurement of prices and quantities of capital services for corporate business. We measure corporate property compensation as income originating in corporate business, less compensation of employees, plus corporate consumption of fixed capital, plus business transfer payments, plus the indirect business taxes allocated to the corporate sector. To obtain an estimate of the corporate rate of return we must take into account the corporate income tax. The capital service price becomes

$$q_{K,t} = \left(\frac{1 - uz_t - k_t + y_t}{1 - u}\right) q_{A,t-1}[r_t - \pi_t + (1 + \pi_t)\delta] + q_{A,t-1}\tau_t,$$

where indirect business taxes $q_{A,t-1}\tau_t$ are deducted from corporate property compensation before taxes as an expense, u is the corporate tax rate, z_t is the present value of depreciation allowances, k_t the investment tax credit, and $y_t = k_t u_t z_t$.

The corporate rate of return,

$$r_t - \pi = \beta[(1 - u)i_t - \pi_t] + (1 - \beta)\left[\frac{\rho_t - \pi_t(1 - t_g)}{(1 - t_e)\alpha + (1 - t_g)(1 - \alpha)}\right],$$

is a weighted average of the rate of interest i_t and the nominal rate of return on corporate assets ρ_t with weights that depend on the ratio of debt to the value of corporate capital stock β, the average marginal individual tax rate on income from corporate property t_e, the marginal tax rate on capital gains on corporate equities t_g, and the dividend payout ratio α from corporate income after corporate taxes.

Our method for estimating the corporate rate of return is the same as for the noncorporate rate of return. Property compensation in the corporate sector is the sum of the value of services from residential and nonresidential structures, producer durable equipment, inventories, and land held by the sector. To estimate the rate of return in the corporate sector we require estimates of the variables that enter the value of capital services except, of course, for the rate of return. We then solve for the rate of return in terms of these variables and total property compensation. Price and quantity indexes of capital input by class of asset are combined into price and quantity indexes of capital input for the corporate sector.

We assume that the nominal rate of return is the same for all assets within a given sector. For the corporate and noncorporate sectors this rate of return is inferred from the value of property compensation, acquisition prices and stocks of capital goods, rates of replacement, and variables describing the tax structure. For households the rate of return is inferred from income from owner-occupied housing. For government, the imputed rate of return is set equal to the average of corporate, noncorporate, and household rates of return after both corporate and personal taxes. To obtain price and quantity indexes of capital income for the domestic sector we apply chained Fisher ideal index numbers to price and quantity indexes for each of the five subsectors—corporations, noncorporate business, households, institutions, and government. Price and quantity indexes of capital income for corporations, noncorporate business, households, institutions, and government, as well as the U.S. domestic economy are given for 1948–2002 in table 1.24.

We construct price and quantity index numbers for the GDI by combining indexes of labor and capital income. The weights for labor and capital are the relative shares of labor and capital income in the GDI. Price and quantity indexes of GDI for the U.S. domestic economy are given for 1948–2002 in table 1.25. Multifactor productivity, also given in table 1.25, is defined as the ratio of GDP in constant prices to GDI in constant prices.[24] Growth in multifactor productivity can be interpreted as an increase in

---

24. For further discussion of this index of multifactor productivity, see Jorgenson (2001).

Table 1.24   Domestic income and product account, capital income, 1948–2002 (constant prices of 2000)

Year	Capital income Price	Capital income Quantity	Corporate income Price	Corporate income Quantity	Noncorporate income Price	Noncorporate income Quantity	Household income Price	Household income Quantity	Government income Price	Government income Quantity	Capital income: Relative share
1948	0.268	436.8	0.333	131.6	0.171	124.5	0.325	110.9	0.175	89.7	0.402
1949	0.235	472.8	0.309	139.8	0.147	131.7	0.256	131.4	0.175	86.3	0.389
1950	0.260	506.7	0.345	147.7	0.166	139.1	0.262	151.2	0.219	83.8	0.413
1951	0.278	547.3	0.364	159.2	0.215	146.8	0.279	171.3	0.175	83.5	0.415
1952	0.272	581.8	0.337	169.6	0.211	152.2	0.279	186.6	0.195	85.9	0.408
1953	0.270	611.6	0.333	177.6	0.200	156.6	0.256	200.0	0.262	89.7	0.403
1954	0.268	639.2	0.321	184.7	0.188	160.5	0.272	212.9	0.258	93.3	0.412
1955	0.277	670.0	0.368	193.2	0.185	164.7	0.275	227.7	0.221	95.9	0.414
1956	0.274	704.1	0.357	203.4	0.161	168.6	0.292	243.9	0.221	97.8	0.405
1957	0.266	733.7	0.352	212.9	0.180	171.7	0.262	257.5	0.223	99.3	0.396
1958	0.282	756.9	0.327	219.2	0.201	175.7	0.283	268.5	0.306	101.1	0.417
1959	0.280	781.0	0.371	225.4	0.184	179.9	0.256	279.3	0.293	104.1	0.403
1960	0.293	809.4	0.357	233.7	0.173	184.1	0.296	291.3	0.331	107.4	0.411
1961	0.287	834.5	0.358	241.4	0.188	187.8	0.293	300.9	0.270	110.9	0.407
1962	0.296	863.2	0.383	250.7	0.200	192.8	0.292	310.8	0.260	114.9	0.407
1963	0.299	899.7	0.394	262.7	0.202	199.8	0.293	323.9	0.256	118.5	0.409
1964	0.316	939.5	0.410	276.0	0.216	206.5	0.303	339.5	0.299	121.7	0.416
1965	0.338	985.4	0.436	292.3	0.234	213.2	0.326	357.8	0.313	124.4	0.427
1966	0.359	1,043.2	0.440	314.0	0.275	222.1	0.350	379.7	0.330	127.5	0.433
1967	0.343	1,102.1	0.423	335.2	0.272	232.8	0.327	401.0	0.319	131.8	0.420
1968	0.350	1,158.2	0.432	354.3	0.274	242.5	0.335	423.0	0.327	136.0	0.414
1969	0.354	1,216.6	0.425	375.3	0.270	251.4	0.365	446.7	0.293	138.7	0.406
1970	0.334	1,267.6	0.396	394.3	0.291	260.5	0.347	465.7	0.210	140.4	0.386
1971	0.364	1,315.7	0.427	411.3	0.321	270.2	0.381	484.4	0.226	140.6	0.400

Year											
1972	0.404	1,389.3	0.448	436.0	0.339	288.6	0.411	513.0	0.404	140.5	0.415
1973	0.436	1,480.2	0.457	468.5	0.377	311.5	0.429	548.9	0.552	140.9	0.423
1974	0.456	1,505.6	0.469	478.3	0.392	308.2	0.432	566.9	0.679	141.2	0.415
1975	0.500	1,520.4	0.552	485.4	0.454	302.5	0.431	577.2	0.739	143.2	0.425
1976	0.545	1,586.5	0.588	512.0	0.498	313.7	0.460	602.1	0.894	146.9	0.430
1977	0.595	1,656.4	0.643	539.8	0.517	322.1	0.527	634.5	0.925	149.7	0.435
1978	0.636	1,743.1	0.682	576.1	0.560	335.5	0.563	670.5	0.989	152.4	0.434
1979	0.639	1,839.9	0.681	617.8	0.623	355.5	0.576	703.6	0.822	155.2	0.419
1980	0.627	1,925.6	0.676	659.1	0.582	372.4	0.601	726.5	0.686	158.6	0.403
1981	0.671	2,025.0	0.749	708.2	0.576	397.8	0.638	745.7	0.753	162.5	0.407
1982	0.662	2,112.7	0.734	752.0	0.480	419.6	0.662	763.3	0.847	166.4	0.401
1983	0.748	2,174.7	0.787	780.7	0.606	426.7	0.672	783.5	1.328	170.5	0.423
1984	0.812	2,292.5	0.856	827.9	0.636	452.3	0.721	826.8	1.529	175.5	0.432
1985	0.792	2,461.6	0.837	891.0	0.644	496.6	0.723	887.9	1.325	182.2	0.426
1986	0.780	2,602.4	0.806	937.2	0.694	523.5	0.748	947.2	1.057	191.6	0.422
1987	0.786	2,705.5	0.839	968.1	0.666	531.6	0.751	998.4	1.038	202.4	0.417
1988	0.831	2,806.5	0.893	999.2	0.647	541.5	0.792	1,047.6	1.230	211.5	0.421
1989	0.870	2,915.6	0.904	1,037.5	0.803	555.7	0.810	1,096.1	1.210	219.1	0.427
1990	0.881	2,992.3	0.902	1,067.4	0.867	558.2	0.827	1,131.2	1.113	227.1	0.422
1991	0.885	3,043.4	0.906	1,089.9	0.850	555.3	0.825	1,153.0	1.206	235.1	0.419
1992	0.922	3,099.5	0.917	1,116.2	0.977	554.2	0.838	1,175.5	1.272	242.3	0.421
1993	0.942	3,151.5	0.939	1,148.1	1.071	544.2	0.900	1,201.3	0.908	248.5	0.419
1994	0.990	3,200.4	1.002	1,184.7	1.148	527.8	0.917	1,229.3	0.977	253.3	0.422
1995	1.007	3,301.8	1.041	1,241.0	1.114	526.5	0.965	1,273.3	0.841	257.4	0.423
1996	1.044	3,441.4	1.077	1,312.8	1.174	533.5	0.961	1,330.2	1.042	261.9	0.431
1997	1.076	3,597.7	1.110	1,394.9	1.192	538.9	0.994	1,396.6	1.104	266.1	0.435
1998	1.036	3,817.9	1.062	1,502.5	1.091	560.1	0.991	1,484.0	1.029	270.7	0.422
1999	1.028	4,067.9	1.034	1,620.1	1.089	584.1	1.004	1,586.3	0.994	277.2	0.420
2000	1.000	4,321.6	1.000	1,738.7	1.000	606.3	1.000	1,692.5	1.000	284.2	0.411
2001	1.012	4,537.1	0.946	1,836.6	1.132	620.9	1.013	1,790.4	1.157	291.0	0.419
2002	1.021	4,709.2	0.965	1,894.1	1.211	632.6	0.994	1,887.7	1.141	298.5	0.425

Table 1.25   **Domestic income and product account, productivity, 1948–2002**
                      (constant prices of 2000)

| Year | Gross domestic product | | Gross domestic income | | Multifactor productivity |
	Price	Quantity	Price	Quantity	
1948	0.178	1,634.2	0.129	2,258.7	0.725
1949	0.171	1,674.2	0.125	2,292.6	0.732
1950	0.175	1,825.2	0.132	2,416.6	0.757
1951	0.185	1,980.1	0.140	2,609.2	0.760
1952	0.186	2,080.0	0.142	2,719.7	0.766
1953	0.188	2,181.3	0.146	2,814.3	0.775
1954	0.191	2,176.0	0.147	2,822.6	0.770
1955	0.193	2,319.8	0.153	2,930.1	0.792
1956	0.201	2,372.3	0.157	3,030.8	0.782
1957	0.203	2,427.1	0.160	3,093.0	0.786
1958	0.212	2,421.9	0.166	3,080.9	0.786
1959	0.211	2,572.0	0.170	3,185.9	0.807
1960	0.219	2,633.0	0.177	3,261.0	0.808
1961	0.218	2,700.9	0.177	3,330.9	0.811
1962	0.220	2,847.7	0.182	3,450.0	0.825
1963	0.223	2,956.9	0.186	3,537.3	0.836
1964	0.229	3,121.1	0.195	3,656.0	0.854
1965	0.236	3,303.1	0.205	3,799.1	0.870
1966	0.245	3,530.3	0.217	3,988.1	0.885
1967	0.248	3,626.7	0.219	4,118.5	0.881
1968	0.259	3,791.1	0.230	4,268.6	0.888
1969	0.272	3,909.9	0.240	4,421.1	0.884
1970	0.279	3,927.2	0.246	4,451.3	0.883
1971	0.295	4,057.0	0.265	4,516.8	0.898
1972	0.316	4,268.4	0.288	4,691.2	0.910
1973	0.338	4,511.6	0.310	4,928.6	0.915
1974	0.367	4,496.2	0.333	4,966.5	0.905
1975	0.398	4,495.4	0.362	4,941.8	0.910
1976	0.425	4,740.1	0.394	5,114.1	0.927
1977	0.455	4,974.6	0.427	5,309.2	0.937
1978	0.488	5,242.4	0.460	5,566.0	0.942
1979	0.519	5,401.8	0.483	5,804.3	0.931
1980	0.557	5,382.5	0.508	5,901.6	0.912
1981	0.607	5,500.1	0.551	6,057.4	0.908
1982	0.644	5,416.4	0.570	6,127.4	0.884
1983	0.681	5,649.0	0.615	6,256.5	0.903
1984	0.711	6,057.5	0.652	6,611.8	0.916
1985	0.722	6,337.2	0.661	6,920.1	0.916
1986	0.729	6,600.0	0.676	7,127.4	0.926
1987	0.746	6,845.6	0.690	7,395.5	0.926
1988	0.780	7,115.3	0.726	7,643.1	0.931
1989	0.806	7,365.1	0.751	7,910.7	0.931
1990	0.831	7,518.0	0.774	8,066.3	0.932
1991	0.857	7,502.9	0.796	8,076.2	0.929
1992	0.878	7,736.1	0.834	8,144.7	0.950
1993	0.892	7,943.7	0.849	8,350.5	0.951
1994	0.910	8,245.4	0.877	8,550.0	0.964
1995	0.928	8,471.2	0.893	8,798.4	0.963
1996	0.947	8,806.8	0.921	9,052.0	0.973
1997	0.966	9,220.6	0.950	9,375.2	0.984
1998	0.971	9,645.6	0.959	9,768.3	0.988
1999	0.983	10,111.7	0.978	10,168.3	0.994
2000	1.000	10,525.6	1.000	10,525.6	1.000
2001	1.027	10,670.5	1.024	10,704.1	0.997
2002	1.034	10,927.1	1.046	10,802.6	1.012

efficiency of the use of input to produce output or as a decline in the cost of input required to produce a given value of output.

1.4.6   Income and Expenditure, Domestic Capital, and Wealth Accounts

Introduction

In the previous section we have presented the Domestic Income and Product Account for the U.S. economy in constant prices. In this section we present Income and Expenditure, Domestic Capital, and Wealth Accounts in constant prices. We describe the accounts for the domestic economy in detail. The accounts for the rest of the world are identical to those generated by the BEA.

Income and Expenditures

We begin with estimates of gross saving and household and government consumption outlays in constant prices for the U.S. domestic economy. To construct price and quantity indexes of household and government expenditures, we obtain data for consumption expenditures on nondurable goods and services, excluding the services of institutional real estate, from the Domestic Income and Production Account. We evaluate consumption expenditures on market prices and combine these data with imputed values of the services of household, institutional, and government durables and the services of institutional and government real estate.

The value of consumption expenditures at market prices includes customs duties and excise and sales taxes, and excludes subsidies. We construct price and quantity indexes of consumption expenditures from the price and quantity indexes of nondurables, services, and our estimates of capital services by using chained Fisher ideal index numbers. Gross and net saving in constant prices are taken from the Domestic Capital Account, described below. Price, quantity, and tax indexes for personal and government consumption expenditures are presented in table 1.26.

The starting point for estimating price and quantity components of Domestic Capital Income is the price and quantity of capital income in the Domestic Income and Product Account. To construct price and quantity indexes of capital income our procedure is analogous to the methods we have used for the Domestic Income and Product Account. The most important innovation is in the use of a rental price formula to impute the price of capital services. Price and quantity indexes of capital income are presented in table 1.27. Similarly, prices and quantities of the different categories of labor services are combined into price and quantity indexes of labor income using chained Fisher idea index numbers. Price and quantity indexes of labor, capital, and gross income are presented in table 1.28.

The quantity index of Net Expenditures is a measure of social welfare; it consists of the quantity of current consumption and the quantity of net

Table 1.26   Income and expenditures account, expenditure, 1948–2002 (constant prices of 2000)

Year	Net expenditures		Personal consumption expenditures		Government consumption expenditures		Net saving		Effective tax rate on consumption expenditures
	Price	Quantity	Price	Quantity	Price	Quantity	Price	Quantity	
1948	0.161	1,634.4	0.176	1,014.7	0.098	401.8	0.268	166.5	0.046
1949	0.155	1,631.9	0.166	1,062.6	0.101	431.0	0.266	123.7	0.048
1950	0.159	1,806.8	0.169	1,123.7	0.110	429.5	0.263	189.1	0.046
1951	0.168	1,953.8	0.180	1,182.3	0.106	534.8	0.294	197.7	0.043
1952	0.171	2,033.3	0.183	1,239.4	0.109	624.3	0.296	175.6	0.046
1953	0.173	2,129.7	0.182	1,290.5	0.122	652.9	0.283	189.1	0.047
1954	0.177	2,087.8	0.186	1,329.4	0.124	615.3	0.297	155.2	0.045
1955	0.178	2,248.3	0.187	1,399.8	0.123	609.3	0.303	208.8	0.045
1956	0.184	2,294.3	0.193	1,465.0	0.126	612.5	0.323	194.5	0.044
1957	0.186	2,342.6	0.192	1,510.0	0.130	643.3	0.336	183.3	0.044
1958	0.196	2,308.2	0.199	1,545.8	0.149	647.5	0.333	141.3	0.046
1959	0.191	2,502.5	0.197	1,612.6	0.146	661.2	0.297	212.3	0.049
1960	0.203	2,520.1	0.207	1,658.6	0.155	668.9	0.338	190.2	0.051
1961	0.202	2,580.2	0.209	1,704.5	0.148	691.0	0.339	188.1	0.049
1962	0.204	2,737.3	0.210	1,766.1	0.150	734.9	0.341	224.7	0.050
1963	0.206	2,850.9	0.213	1,825.2	0.152	758.9	0.343	245.6	0.050
1964	0.212	3,017.2	0.217	1,924.1	0.164	774.6	0.345	277.8	0.050
1965	0.220	3,201.4	0.224	2,026.3	0.170	797.5	0.355	316.0	0.048
1966	0.229	3,406.5	0.234	2,137.5	0.179	858.8	0.362	343.1	0.043
1967	0.231	3,486.0	0.235	2,216.8	0.184	923.1	0.372	310.6	0.045
1968	0.240	3,661.2	0.243	2,331.1	0.194	964.0	0.381	327.1	0.048
1969	0.253	3,767.2	0.258	2,426.9	0.198	978.3	0.402	325.3	0.048
1970	0.260	3,737.3	0.265	2,510.5	0.199	967.4	0.433	259.7	0.050
1971	0.274	3,880.5	0.280	2,584.7	0.216	965.7	0.431	302.3	0.050

Year	(1)	(2)	(3)	(4)	(5)	(6)	(7)	(8)	(9)
1972	0.290	4,139.1	0.294	2,722.2	0.257	965.6	0.396	383.3	0.047
1973	0.319	4,292.0	0.311	2,853.2	0.295	952.5	0.494	407.0	0.048
1974	0.348	4,219.4	0.338	2,869.7	0.333	967.0	0.525	340.4	0.049
1975	0.376	4,177.3	0.359	2,938.5	0.365	988.0	0.598	257.6	0.049
1976	0.401	4,437.3	0.379	3,076.2	0.407	996.6	0.616	334.5	0.047
1977	0.433	4,631.5	0.412	3,203.8	0.432	1,016.4	0.670	369.0	0.044
1978	0.464	4,885.7	0.442	3,349.6	0.461	1,036.4	0.714	430.9	0.043
1979	0.490	5,039.4	0.475	3,458.6	0.463	1,048.7	0.752	455.0	0.042
1980	0.527	4,959.7	0.520	3,493.8	0.480	1,068.1	0.771	367.4	0.044
1981	0.575	5,044.5	0.563	3,548.3	0.527	1,086.5	0.879	377.0	0.048
1982	0.610	4,917.7	0.591	3,609.0	0.569	1,110.8	0.958	243.9	0.044
1983	0.641	5,212.0	0.614	3,765.6	0.665	1,136.5	0.844	326.3	0.044
1984	0.679	5,573.9	0.643	3,931.9	0.727	1,153.1	0.901	466.3	0.044
1985	0.692	5,787.0	0.660	4,143.1	0.718	1,210.3	0.937	430.8	0.044
1986	0.699	5,981.8	0.676	4,317.0	0.689	1,275.2	0.943	402.8	0.042
1987	0.714	6,178.2	0.695	4,494.0	0.708	1,297.7	0.921	404.5	0.041
1988	0.749	6,427.4	0.727	4,673.9	0.760	1,313.8	0.930	450.6	0.042
1989	0.777	6,644.1	0.757	4,826.9	0.781	1,337.0	0.946	486.8	0.042
1990	0.801	6,767.7	0.791	4,949.6	0.795	1,366.3	0.911	464.6	0.043
1991	0.823	6,815.5	0.815	4,999.7	0.838	1,381.7	0.843	448.7	0.046
1992	0.828	7,145.9	0.838	5,146.1	0.873	1,386.8	0.598	657.7	0.046
1993	0.868	7,107.4	0.868	5,286.6	0.828	1,384.3	0.957	458.0	0.045
1994	0.890	7,353.6	0.885	5,442.7	0.861	1,386.4	1.002	537.4	0.048
1995	0.908	7,539.8	0.911	5,593.8	0.855	1,390.0	0.995	566.1	0.046
1996	0.932	7,814.2	0.928	5,780.3	0.915	1,393.7	0.996	644.2	0.045
1997	0.956	8,153.6	0.951	5,990.9	0.943	1,417.3	1.029	743.5	0.044
1998	0.966	8,469.2	0.959	6,282.2	0.943	1,438.1	1.076	748.9	0.045
1999	0.981	8,864.5	0.978	6,582.3	0.961	1,479.6	1.043	800.5	0.043
2000	1.000	9,174.2	1.000	6,907.1	1.000	1,504.3	1.000	762.8	0.044
2001	1.031	9,206.5	1.022	7,109.7	1.055	1,547.4	1.066	554.6	0.042
2002	1.045	9,347.3	1.031	7,346.4	1.083	1,604.8	1.101	409.6	0.043

Table 1.27   Income and expenditures account, property income, 1948–2002
(constant prices of 2000)

Year	Property income Price	Property income Quantity	ROW property income Price	ROW property income Quantity	Domestic property income Price	Domestic property income Quantity
1948	0.243	497.3	0.139	63.6	0.268	436.8
1949	0.223	532.6	0.132	58.7	0.235	472.8
1950	0.248	575.9	0.149	71.5	0.260	506.7
1951	0.263	625.6	0.151	83.5	0.278	547.3
1952	0.258	671.4	0.153	99.5	0.272	581.8
1953	0.257	707.1	0.154	106.9	0.270	611.6
1954	0.255	734.5	0.157	104.4	0.268	639.2
1955	0.264	772.5	0.160	113.6	0.277	670.0
1956	0.262	810.6	0.168	117.4	0.274	704.1
1957	0.257	843.0	0.175	119.8	0.266	733.7
1958	0.272	865.9	0.181	117.9	0.282	756.9
1959	0.270	892.6	0.184	120.4	0.280	781.0
1960	0.281	932.2	0.183	135.5	0.293	809.4
1961	0.277	957.6	0.186	134.5	0.287	834.5
1962	0.285	992.7	0.192	142.3	0.296	863.2
1963	0.288	1,038.4	0.192	153.9	0.299	899.7
1964	0.303	1,085.7	0.198	162.7	0.316	939.5
1965	0.323	1,135.5	0.205	165.5	0.338	985.4
1966	0.342	1,190.1	0.212	156.3	0.359	1,043.2
1967	0.329	1,255.1	0.217	161.7	0.343	1,102.1
1968	0.337	1,326.1	0.228	180.5	0.350	1,158.2
1969	0.341	1,394.1	0.235	191.3	0.354	1,216.6
1970	0.325	1,444.0	0.249	187.4	0.334	1,267.6
1971	0.354	1,497.6	0.266	193.0	0.364	1,315.7
1972	0.391	1,573.2	0.279	192.7	0.404	1,389.3
1973	0.421	1,687.3	0.298	220.9	0.436	1,480.2
1974	0.441	1,721.7	0.318	232.6	0.456	1,505.6
1975	0.485	1,721.4	0.351	211.0	0.500	1,520.4
1976	0.528	1,801.7	0.379	227.6	0.545	1,586.5
1977	0.575	1,878.9	0.404	234.6	0.595	1,656.4
1978	0.615	1,973.9	0.434	242.1	0.636	1,743.1
1979	0.621	2,085.3	0.468	258.0	0.639	1,839.9
1980	0.616	2,176.1	0.507	261.9	0.627	1,925.6
1981	0.660	2,283.9	0.555	270.1	0.671	2,025.0
1982	0.657	2,351.7	0.594	246.1	0.662	2,112.7
1983	0.737	2,418.0	0.626	250.3	0.748	2,174.7
1984	0.797	2,551.0	0.647	266.1	0.812	2,292.5
1985	0.782	2,716.2	0.674	258.4	0.792	2,461.6
1986	0.769	2,859.1	0.654	258.7	0.780	2,602.4
1987	0.778	2,960.1	0.694	254.8	0.786	2,705.5
1988	0.822	3,079.0	0.724	273.7	0.831	2,806.5
1989	0.861	3,196.9	0.768	282.4	0.870	2,915.6
1990	0.875	3,285.4	0.807	294.6	0.881	2,992.3
1991	0.881	3,395.8	0.831	357.6	0.885	3,043.4
1992	0.914	3,420.9	0.832	323.9	0.922	3,099.5
1993	0.937	3,466.6	0.879	316.7	0.942	3,151.5
1994	0.982	3,540.0	0.900	342.7	0.990	3,200.4
1995	1.000	3,649.6	0.932	350.8	1.007	3,301.8
1996	1.036	3,793.4	0.956	354.4	1.044	3,441.4
1997	1.068	3,957.8	0.973	361.8	1.076	3,597.7
1998	1.031	4,179.6	0.973	361.9	1.036	3,817.9
1999	1.023	4,454.5	0.980	386.9	1.028	4,067.9
2000	1.000	4,718.4	1.000	396.8	1.000	4,321.6
2001	1.012	4,930.1	1.016	393.0	1.012	4,537.1
2002	1.021	5,105.1	1.011	395.9	1.021	4,709.2

Note: ROW = rest of world.

Table 1.28   **Income and expenditures account, income, 1948–2002 (constant prices of 2000)**

	Net income		Labor income		Net property income	
Year	Price	Quantity	Price	Quantity	Price	Quantity
1948	0.116	2,272.4	0.077	2,246.1	0.258	345.9
1949	0.111	2,275.6	0.080	2,184.4	0.213	368.0
1950	0.119	2,404.0	0.082	2,277.2	0.246	399.6
1951	0.126	2,604.3	0.087	2,462.3	0.261	434.4
1952	0.127	2,723.4	0.090	2,534.3	0.253	468.2
1953	0.130	2,817.8	0.094	2,596.9	0.249	493.7
1954	0.132	2,800.8	0.096	2,535.8	0.246	508.3
1955	0.137	2,913.1	0.101	2,612.7	0.256	538.3
1956	0.141	3,004.8	0.106	2,676.6	0.248	562.8
1957	0.143	3,049.0	0.111	2,683.2	0.235	585.8
1958	0.150	3,019.2	0.114	2,617.5	0.256	598.2
1959	0.153	3,128.9	0.119	2,708.2	0.249	622.0
1960	0.159	3,210.7	0.124	2,746.9	0.264	653.4
1961	0.159	3,270.4	0.125	2,787.1	0.258	670.7
1962	0.164	3,401.4	0.128	2,892.9	0.267	700.4
1963	0.169	3,488.0	0.133	2,930.2	0.271	735.9
1964	0.178	3,604.2	0.138	3,007.8	0.291	770.1
1965	0.188	3,735.4	0.144	3,105.3	0.319	803.7
1966	0.200	3,894.6	0.151	3,239.5	0.344	837.1
1967	0.201	4,000.5	0.159	3,290.1	0.323	877.3
1968	0.212	4,147.1	0.170	3,375.7	0.328	927.1
1969	0.222	4,284.0	0.183	3,463.4	0.329	970.5
1970	0.227	4,269.9	0.198	3,407.1	0.299	994.5
1971	0.246	4,320.7	0.211	3,408.0	0.332	1,032.0
1972	0.268	4,477.9	0.226	3,499.6	0.376	1,089.6
1973	0.290	4,723.9	0.242	3,640.6	0.413	1,179.8
1974	0.311	4,728.9	0.265	3,643.2	0.427	1,181.7
1975	0.338	4,646.5	0.287	3,586.6	0.467	1,156.9
1976	0.369	4,823.6	0.311	3,689.0	0.517	1,221.9
1977	0.401	5,001.7	0.335	3,813.9	0.571	1,273.8
1978	0.433	5,233.9	0.363	3,985.6	0.611	1,336.0
1979	0.453	5,448.9	0.395	4,120.0	0.597	1,409.3
1980	0.474	5,503.0	0.437	4,104.4	0.559	1,463.9
1981	0.514	5,645.2	0.478	4,144.7	0.594	1,553.9
1982	0.531	5,654.4	0.509	4,104.6	0.570	1,596.2
1983	0.579	5,768.8	0.532	4,168.0	0.682	1,644.8
1984	0.619	6,116.8	0.555	4,412.7	0.765	1,749.1
1985	0.629	6,365.0	0.580	4,530.3	0.739	1,866.4
1986	0.642	6,509.7	0.608	4,578.2	0.714	1,953.8
1987	0.658	6,712.0	0.628	4,742.8	0.720	1,995.4
1988	0.695	6,929.8	0.657	4,888.6	0.775	2,067.1
1989	0.721	7,154.8	0.674	5,046.3	0.823	2,135.0
1990	0.746	7,268.3	0.705	5,121.0	0.835	2,173.0
1991	0.769	7,296.2	0.736	5,068.4	0.837	2,243.9
1992	0.810	7,300.6	0.774	5,075.4	0.886	2,241.8
1993	0.827	7,461.5	0.787	5,232.0	0.913	2,252.4
1994	0.857	7,639.7	0.803	5,388.3	0.974	2,279.8
1995	0.874	7,837.5	0.819	5,534.9	0.993	2,332.9
1996	0.906	8,032.8	0.841	5,640.4	1.048	2,417.5
1997	0.940	8,291.5	0.867	5,799.8	1.101	2,513.0
1998	0.952	8,599.5	0.907	5,960.1	1.048	2,651.8
1999	0.974	8,924.2	0.944	6,100.0	1.039	2,827.5
2000	1.000	9,174.5	1.000	6,199.8	1.000	2,974.8
2001	1.028	9,231.4	1.033	6,162.0	1.019	3,069.9
2002	1.056	9,244.4	1.065	6,091.9	1.038	3,154.4

increments to future consumption in the current time period, as suggested by Weitzman (1976, 2003). Similarly, the quantity index of Net Income is a measure of the labor and property incomes generated by the U.S. economy. The ratio of expenditures in constant prices to income in constant prices is the Level of Living, a quantity index of welfare generated from current and future consumption in proportion to the effort required in the form of supply of labor and capital services. This must be carefully distinguished from multifactor productivity, the ratio of GDP to GDI, a measure of productive efficiency. Price and quantity indexes of Net Expenditures, Net Income and the Level of Living index are presented in table 1.29.[25]

Domestic Capital Account

The fundamental accounting identity for the Domestic Capital Account is that gross saving from the Income and Expenditures Account is equal to investment. Investment and saving are equal in current and constant prices. Investment is a chained Fisher ideal quantity index of private and government investment, evaluated at market prices. The quantities are taken from the Domestic Income and Product Account, while the prices include sales and excise taxes paid by purchasers of investment goods. Price, quantity, and tax indexes of Gross Investment are given for 1948–2002 in table 1.30.

To complete the saving side of the Domestic Capital Account in constant prices we require depreciation and the revaluation of assets in constant prices. If the decline in efficiency of capital goods is geometric, the change in wealth from period to period for a single capital good may be written

$$W_t - W_{t-1} = q_{A,t}K_t - q_{A,t-1}K_{t-1}$$
$$= q_{A,t}(K_t - K_{t-1}) + (q_{A,t} - q_{A,t-1})K_{t-1}$$
$$= q_{A,t}A_t - q_{A,t}\delta K_{t-1} + (q_{A,t} - q_{A,t-1})K_{t-1}.$$

Gross saving is represented by $q_{A,t}A_t$, which is equal to gross investment and has the same price and quantity components.

Depreciation is represented by $q_{A,t}\delta K_{t-1}$. We construct the price and quantity indexes of depreciation from the lagged stocks, K_{t-1}, with depreciation prices $q_{D,t}$ as weights. Revaluation is represented by $(q_{At} - q_{A,t-1})K_{t-1}$. We construct price and quantity indexes of revaluation from lagged capital stocks with revaluation prices $(q_{A,t} - q_{A,t-1})$ as weights. Chained Fisher ideal price and quantity index numbers of private national saving, depreciation, and revaluation for the period 1948–2002 are presented in table 1.31.

---

25. For further discussion, see Hulten (1992).

Table 1.29

Income and expenditures account, level of living, 1948–2002 (constant prices of 2000)

Year	Net expenditures		Net income		Level of living
	Price	Quantity	Price	Quantity	
1948	0.161	1,634.4	0.116	2,272.4	0.719
1949	0.155	1,631.9	0.111	2,275.6	0.717
1950	0.159	1,806.8	0.119	2,404.0	0.752
1951	0.168	1,953.8	0.126	2,604.3	0.750
1952	0.171	2,033.3	0.127	2,723.4	0.747
1953	0.173	2,129.7	0.130	2,817.8	0.756
1954	0.177	2,087.8	0.132	2,800.8	0.745
1955	0.178	2,248.3	0.137	2,913.1	0.772
1956	0.184	2,294.3	0.141	3,004.8	0.764
1957	0.186	2,342.6	0.143	3,049.0	0.768
1958	0.196	2,308.2	0.150	3,019.2	0.764
1959	0.191	2,502.5	0.153	3,128.9	0.800
1960	0.203	2,520.1	0.159	3,210.7	0.785
1961	0.202	2,580.2	0.159	3,270.4	0.789
1962	0.204	2,737.3	0.164	3,401.4	0.805
1963	0.206	2,850.9	0.169	3,488.0	0.817
1964	0.212	3,017.2	0.178	3,604.2	0.837
1965	0.220	3,201.4	0.188	3,735.4	0.857
1966	0.229	3,406.5	0.200	3,894.6	0.875
1967	0.231	3,486.0	0.201	4,000.5	0.871
1968	0.240	3,661.2	0.212	4,147.1	0.883
1969	0.253	3,767.2	0.222	4,284.0	0.879
1970	0.260	3,737.3	0.227	4,269.9	0.875
1971	0.274	3,880.5	0.246	4,320.7	0.898
1972	0.290	4,139.1	0.268	4,477.9	0.924
1973	0.319	4,292.0	0.290	4,723.9	0.909
1974	0.348	4,219.4	0.311	4,728.9	0.892
1975	0.376	4,177.3	0.338	4,646.5	0.899
1976	0.401	4,437.3	0.369	4,823.6	0.920
1977	0.433	4,631.5	0.401	5,001.7	0.926
1978	0.464	4,885.7	0.433	5,233.9	0.933
1979	0.490	5,039.4	0.453	5,448.9	0.925
1980	0.527	4,959.7	0.474	5,503.0	0.901
1981	0.575	5,044.5	0.514	5,645.2	0.894
1982	0.610	4,917.7	0.531	5,654.4	0.870
1983	0.641	5,212.0	0.579	5,768.8	0.903
1984	0.679	5,573.9	0.619	6,116.8	0.911
1985	0.692	5,787.0	0.629	6,365.0	0.909
1986	0.699	5,981.8	0.642	6,509.7	0.919
1987	0.714	6,178.2	0.658	6,712.0	0.920
1988	0.749	6,427.4	0.695	6,929.8	0.927
1989	0.777	6,644.1	0.721	7,154.8	0.929
1990	0.801	6,767.7	0.746	7,268.3	0.931
1991	0.823	6,815.5	0.769	7,296.2	0.934
1992	0.828	7,145.9	0.810	7,300.6	0.979
1993	0.868	7,107.4	0.827	7,461.5	0.953
1994	0.890	7,353.6	0.857	7,639.7	0.963
1995	0.908	7,539.8	0.874	7,837.5	0.962
1996	0.932	7,814.2	0.906	8,032.8	0.973
1997	0.956	8,153.6	0.940	8,291.5	0.983
1998	0.966	8,469.2	0.952	8,599.5	0.985
1999	0.981	8,864.5	0.974	8,924.2	0.993
2000	1.000	9,174.2	1.000	9,174.5	1.000
2001	1.031	9,206.5	1.028	9,231.4	0.997
2002	1.045	9,347.3	1.056	9,244.4	1.011

Table 1.30   Domestic capital account, investment, 1948–2002 (constant prices of 2000)

Year	Gross investment		Private investment		Government investment		Effective sales tax rate on investment expenditures
	Price	Quantity	Price	Quantity	Price	Quantity	
1948	0.243	334.4	0.252	284.3	0.174	40.7	0.046
1949	0.244	300.5	0.256	245.0	0.175	56.1	0.048
1950	0.245	383.3	0.262	327.5	0.171	57.9	0.046
1951	0.268	407.7	0.282	322.2	0.191	91.6	0.043
1952	0.270	395.4	0.283	296.6	0.195	114.2	0.046
1953	0.267	420.5	0.289	310.6	0.193	124.5	0.047
1954	0.273	396.8	0.289	296.8	0.192	117.4	0.045
1955	0.279	463.2	0.294	366.1	0.195	107.5	0.045
1956	0.294	461.1	0.305	359.1	0.213	108.0	0.044
1957	0.306	458.3	0.316	351.4	0.223	109.6	0.044
1958	0.305	422.1	0.317	320.1	0.222	119.6	0.046
1959	0.298	499.8	0.326	371.3	0.224	130.8	0.049
1960	0.316	486.3	0.327	373.7	0.222	126.8	0.051
1961	0.316	492.2	0.327	367.4	0.224	140.5	0.049
1962	0.320	537.7	0.330	409.6	0.228	145.9	0.050
1963	0.322	571.1	0.330	439.7	0.235	143.3	0.050
1964	0.325	618.9	0.333	476.3	0.237	146.1	0.050
1965	0.330	676.1	0.337	538.6	0.244	145.7	0.048
1966	0.335	726.8	0.340	586.3	0.251	158.6	0.043
1967	0.343	716.3	0.348	572.5	0.258	166.3	0.045
1968	0.354	755.4	0.362	613.7	0.268	162.1	0.048
1969	0.370	777.8	0.376	644.6	0.285	151.8	0.048
1970	0.391	729.8	0.390	608.1	0.309	141.6	0.050
1971	0.401	792.3	0.408	673.8	0.331	126.2	0.050
1972	0.399	895.3	0.423	751.2	0.364	116.9	0.047
1973	0.449	945.6	0.442	832.2	0.389	120.3	0.048
1974	0.481	902.6	0.483	770.0	0.444	126.8	0.049
1975	0.538	832.9	0.535	679.6	0.478	131.9	0.049
1976	0.564	933.4	0.565	797.7	0.495	134.0	0.047
1977	0.604	996.0	0.601	902.6	0.519	130.2	0.044
1978	0.644	1,096.4	0.646	990.6	0.553	139.3	0.043
1979	0.687	1,160.0	0.701	1,009.3	0.599	147.8	0.042
1980	0.732	1,100.3	0.764	908.5	0.660	152.1	0.044
1981	0.809	1,132.6	0.832	966.2	0.725	147.3	0.048
1982	0.861	1,099.8	0.873	867.6	0.770	146.0	0.044
1983	0.839	1,115.4	0.877	963.5	0.783	156.8	0.044
1984	0.864	1,290.5	0.883	1,203.3	0.791	176.0	0.044
1985	0.882	1,301.4	0.892	1,232.9	0.795	199.9	0.044
1986	0.893	1,325.0	0.906	1,269.0	0.796	217.5	0.042
1987	0.898	1,380.7	0.927	1,302.0	0.802	229.8	0.041
1988	0.915	1,473.6	0.947	1,346.1	0.814	228.5	0.042
1989	0.934	1,559.0	0.968	1,390.9	0.832	237.8	0.042
1990	0.934	1,585.2	0.983	1,358.8	0.852	253.1	0.043
1991	0.925	1,610.8	0.995	1,263.2	0.865	254.7	0.046
1992	0.850	1,804.6	0.996	1,353.9	0.869	256.5	0.046
1993	0.972	1,675.4	1.008	1,468.0	0.888	246.6	0.045
1994	0.998	1,799.6	1.025	1,638.1	0.911	243.0	0.048
1995	1.007	1,884.5	1.038	1,692.1	0.936	248.6	0.046
1996	1.008	2,021.4	1.031	1,835.6	0.947	258.5	0.045
1997	1.016	2,190.1	1.021	2,040.3	0.953	264.5	0.044
1998	1.025	2,277.6	1.004	2,249.8	0.959	273.7	0.045
1999	1.011	2,428.5	0.997	2,450.7	0.976	294.1	0.043
2000	1.00	2,506.5	1.000	2,598.7	1.000	304.4	0.044
2001	1.018	2,408.7	1.000	2,497.1	1.014	319.4	0.042
2002	1.018	2,343.2	0.992	2,516.3	1.026	338.6	0.043

Table 1.31 Domestic capital account, change in wealth, 1948–2002 (constant prices of 2000)

Year	Gross saving Price	Gross saving Quantity	Depreciation Price	Depreciation Quantity	Net saving Price	Net saving Quantity	Revaluation Price	Revaluation Quantity	Change in wealth Price	Change in wealth Quantity
1948	0.243	334.4	0.239	152.8	0.268	166.5	0.005	911.4	0.092	404.0
1949	0.244	300.5	0.244	166.0	0.266	123.7	0.027	951.4	0.133	565.9
1950	0.245	383.3	0.248	178.0	0.263	189.1	0.071	1,016.5	0.217	597.4
1951	0.268	407.7	0.265	193.1	0.294	197.7	0.013	1,069.7	0.116	565.9
1952	0.270	395.4	0.267	205.2	0.296	175.6	0.042	1,026.6	0.164	587.1
1953	0.267	420.5	0.273	215.6	0.283	189.1	0.009	930.8	0.110	496.5
1954	0.273	396.8	0.273	228.1	0.297	155.2	0.035	891.8	0.154	614.2
1955	0.279	463.2	0.279	236.4	0.303	208.8	0.110	916.1	0.274	599.5
1956	0.294	461.1	0.291	250.0	0.323	194.5	0.086	922.5	0.239	587.5
1957	0.306	458.3	0.303	259.6	0.336	183.3	0.035	911.8	0.155	510.7
1958	0.305	422.1	0.304	269.4	0.333	141.3	0.050	901.8	0.167	646.0
1959	0.298	499.8	0.315	273.4	0.297	212.3	0.063	878.5	0.199	600.5
1960	0.316	486.4	0.317	282.3	0.338	190.2	0.068	881.8	0.207	598.0
1961	0.316	492.2	0.317	290.5	0.339	188.1	0.084	815.1	0.229	632.0
1962	0.320	537.7	0.321	297.0	0.341	224.7	0.041	844.8	0.175	677.0
1963	0.322	571.1	0.324	308.0	0.343	245.6	-0.012	779.1	0.115	751.6
1964	0.325	618.9	0.326	321.4	0.345	277.8	0.047	816.1	0.178	849.9
1965	0.330	676.1	0.329	337.7	0.355	316.0	0.093	844.1	0.223	908.4
1966	0.335	726.8	0.331	359.3	0.362	343.1	0.066	916.5	0.200	878.8
1967	0.343	716.3	0.338	384.4	0.372	310.6	0.201	952.6	0.343	919.7
1968	0.354	755.4	0.351	405.9	0.381	327.1	0.261	915.8	0.413	895.4
1969	0.370	777.8	0.364	430.6	0.402	325.3	0.143	1,106.6	0.293	922.7
1970	0.391	729.8	0.379	455.0	0.433	259.7	0.190	1,030.5	0.347	940.9
1971	0.401	792.3	0.397	471.4	0.431	302.3	0.267	971.3	0.414	993.8
1972	0.399	895.3	0.419	490.5	0.396	383.3	0.421	858.0	0.600	938.6
1973	0.449	945.6	0.432	515.7	0.494	407.0	0.634	956.6	0.816	961.9
1974	0.481	902.6	0.468	546.9	0.525	340.4	0.485	1,126.4	0.683	1,026.0
1975	0.538	832.9	0.517	569.1	0.598	257.6				

(continued)

Table 1.31 (continued)

Year	Gross saving Price	Gross saving Quantity	Depreciation Price	Depreciation Quantity	Net saving Price	Net saving Quantity	Revaluation Price	Revaluation Quantity	Change in wealth Price	Change in wealth Quantity
1976	0.564	933.4	0.547	585.4	0.616	334.5	0.237	1,379.5	0.416	1,279.1
1977	0.604	996.0	0.579	611.0	0.670	369.0	0.837	745.2	0.992	877.9
1978	0.644	1,096.4	0.619	644.0	0.712	430.9	0.860	1,000.3	1.030	1,134.3
1979	0.687	1,160.0	0.667	682.4	0.752	455.0	1.047	1,025.9	1.208	1,172.0
1980	0.732	1,100.3	0.727	717.6	0.771	367.4	0.849	1,260.3	1.033	1,309.7
1981	0.809	1,132.6	0.791	740.0	0.879	377.0	0.511	1,647.9	0.728	1,613.4
1982	0.861	1,009.8	0.832	764.7	0.958	243.9	0.288	1,831.9	0.498	1,529.1
1983	0.839	1,115.4	0.843	783.6	0.844	326.3	0.289	1,251.6	0.476	1,339.3
1984	0.864	1,290.5	0.852	814.8	0.901	466.3	0.203	1,647.4	0.411	1,835.9
1985	0.882	1,301.4	0.861	864.1	0.937	430.8	0.417	1,364.0	0.606	1,603.3
1986	0.893	1,325.0	0.875	918.6	0.943	402.8	0.605	1,517.8	0.774	1,677.4
1987	0.898	1,380.7	0.891	973.3	0.921	404.5	0.675	1,634.0	0.833	1,771.9
1988	0.915	1,473.6	0.912	1,019.4	0.930	450.6	0.705	1,692.0	0.863	1,869.5
1989	0.934	1,559.0	0.932	1,068.2	0.946	486.8	0.605	1,745.6	0.776	1,953.9
1990	0.934	1,585.2	0.948	1,116.1	0.911	464.6	0.418	1,780.3	0.599	1,949.3
1991	0.925	1,610.8	0.963	1,155.7	0.843	448.7	0.204	1,725.2	0.387	1,886.1
1992	0.850	1,804.6	0.966	1,180.9	0.598	657.7	0.181	1,722.3	0.304	2,315.0
1993	0.972	1,675.4	0.980	1,214.7	0.957	458.0	0.535	1,849.5	0.693	2,061.4
1994	0.998	1,799.6	0.998	1,259.7	1.002	537.4	0.394	2,014.6	0.578	2,305.6
1995	1.007	1,884.5	1.014	1,315.8	0.995	566.1	0.508	1,538.3	0.669	2,009.7
1996	1.008	2,021.4	1.015	1,375.0	0.996	644.2	0.435	1,841.7	0.613	2,354.0
1997	1.016	2,190.1	1.010	1,444.3	1.029	743.5	0.340	1,377.4	0.556	2,217.9
1998	1.025	2,277.6	1.001	1,527.5	1.076	748.9	0.422	1,483.1	0.624	2,295.7
1999	1.011	2,428.5	0.997	1,626.6	1.043	800.5	0.676	1,952.9	0.787	2,737.7
2000	1.000	2,506.5	1.000	1,743.7	1.000	762.8	1.000	1,654.1	1.000	2,416.9
2001	1.018	2,408.7	1.000	1,860.5	1.066	554.6	1.012	1,541.3	1.028	2,093.0
2002	1.018	2,343.2	0.991	1,951.8	1.101	409.6	1.022	2,076.8	1.045	2,463.4

Wealth Accounts

Changes in the value of wealth from period to period can be separated between price and quantity components. Net Investment is the quantity component of the change in the value of wealth under the assumption of geometric decline in efficiency of capital goods, while revaluation is the price component. The value of wealth is

$$W_t = q_{A,t} K_t.$$

Wealth is the product of the price index $q_{A,t}$ and quantity index K_t. Acquisition prices and quantities of capital stocks can be combined into price and quantity indexes for wealth, using chained Fisher index numbers.

Our Wealth Account for the U.S. economy includes tangible assets held by businesses, households and institutions, and government and net claims on foreigners. We estimate the price and quantity of assets for each of the five sectors by applying chained Fisher ideal index numbers to price and quantity data for each class of assets held by the sector. We have constructed the price and quantity indexes of private domestic tangible assets, government tangible assets, and wealth for 1948–2002 given in table 1.32 by applying these index numbers to the price and quantity indexes for the five sectors.

1.4.7   The Sources and Uses of Economic Growth

In this section we illustrate the applications of our prototype system of national accounts for the United States. The main advantage of these prototype accounts is that they provide a framework for an integrated analysis of the U.S. economy. This framework consists of (a) an integrated production account; (b) an integrated capital and wealth account; and (c) the linking of these accounts to underlying industry, asset, and liability accounts detail. These accounts can be used for both aggregate and disaggregated analysis of such issues as the sources of economic growth, the effect of changes in the size and composition of wealth on consumption and saving, and the effect of trade deficits on wealth.

We first consider the sources of postwar U.S. economic growth. This application utilizes measures of output, input, and multifactor productivity from the Production Account presented in table 1.25. We next discuss the uses of economic growth. This draws on estimates of income, expenditures, and the level of living from the Domestic Income and Expenditures Account given in table 1.29. Finally, we present an analysis of data on investment, saving, and wealth from the Domestic Capital and Wealth Accounts in tables 1.30, 1.31, and 1.32.

The interpretation of outputs, inputs, and productivity requires the production possibility frontier introduced by Jorgenson (1996a):

$$Y(I, C) = A \cdot X(K, L)$$

Table 1.32 **Wealth, 1948–2002 (constant prices of 2000)**

Year	Wealth Price	Wealth Quantity	Private domestic tangible assets Price	Private domestic tangible assets Quantity	Government tangible assets Price	Government tangible assets Quantity
1948	0.107	7,202.7	0.118	4,158.6	0.092	2,878.3
1949	0.108	7,424.4	0.118	4,448.2	0.094	2,765.7
1950	0.111	7,893.5	0.124	4,876.6	0.093	2,758.3
1951	0.120	8,400.3	0.133	5,264.5	0.104	2,846.7
1952	0.122	8,861.0	0.134	5,582.2	0.107	2,973.6
1953	0.126	9,319.9	0.139	5,882.0	0.110	3,121.1
1954	0.127	9,710.3	0.140	6,141.4	0.111	3,241.2
1955	0.130	10,189.4	0.143	6,516.7	0.114	3,316.5
1956	0.140	10,558.4	0.153	6,840.5	0.127	3,333.6
1957	0.148	10,919.1	0.160	7,141.2	0.135	3,372.7
1958	0.151	11,222.2	0.163	7,364.8	0.138	3,441.0
1959	0.155	11,595.0	0.167	7,653.7	0.141	3,508.6
1960	0.160	11,893.8	0.172	7,920.1	0.145	3,521.4
1961	0.165	12,155.7	0.178	8,139.8	0.150	3,549.3
1962	0.171	12,550.1	0.183	8,449.3	0.156	3,617.6
1963	0.174	13,004.7	0.186	8,786.2	0.161	3,720.6
1964	0.174	13,586.7	0.185	9,166.7	0.160	3,912.9
1965	0.177	14,162.0	0.188	9,604.6	0.163	4,032.8
1966	0.183	14,822.9	0.194	10,125.4	0.169	4,151.5
1967	0.187	15,477.9	0.198	10,577.2	0.173	4,343.1
1968	0.200	15,993.5	0.212	11,050.8	0.185	4,357.9
1969	0.214	16,538.8	0.227	11,513.3	0.200	4,417.4
1970	0.224	17,103.6	0.236	11,914.0	0.215	4,567.0
1971	0.235	17,650.7	0.248	12,342.9	0.228	4,665.6
1972	0.249	18,788.9	0.261	13,340.2	0.250	4,758.4
1973	0.269	19,701.6	0.279	14,124.8	0.269	4,853.8
1974	0.300	19,277.6	0.308	13,555.4	0.308	5,015.1
1975	0.330	20,108.9	0.338	14,257.3	0.336	5,124.6
1976	0.347	20,781.6	0.358	14,807.1	0.350	5,230.4
1977	0.376	21,652.0	0.386	15,535.1	0.371	5,351.4
1978	0.415	22,529.9	0.426	16,334.9	0.403	5,409.1
1979	0.464	23,502.1	0.471	17,205.7	0.447	5,494.5
1980	0.510	24,360.7	0.518	17,813.6	0.492	5,744.8
1981	0.545	25,870.9	0.556	19,022.9	0.534	6,032.4
1982	0.567	26,480.1	0.581	19,534.5	0.559	6,119.8
1983	0.580	26,938.7	0.594	19,943.9	0.571	6,186.0
1984	0.593	28,788.4	0.609	21,790.3	0.583	6,287.0
1985	0.613	30,440.3	0.629	23,542.2	0.599	6,271.5
1986	0.641	31,165.3	0.656	24,229.2	0.624	6,413.5
1987	0.675	31,624.9	0.688	24,722.5	0.655	6,538.7
1988	0.709	32,427.9	0.723	25,481.0	0.683	6,691.5
1989	0.741	33,372.5	0.757	26,252.6	0.713	6,854.6
1990	0.762	33,075.5	0.781	26,067.9	0.738	6,788.9
1991	0.773	33,527.8	0.794	26,446.8	0.753	6,891.9
1992	0.782	33,480.3	0.806	26,469.8	0.764	6,916.3
1993	0.815	33,221.6	0.824	26,463.6	0.782	6,906.9
1994	0.843	32,710.5	0.844	26,304.4	0.803	6,854.4
1995	0.866	33,899.2	0.870	27,364.6	0.833	7,051.6
1996	0.890	34,187.2	0.889	27,747.5	0.860	7,107.0
1997	0.902	35,184.9	0.908	28,742.2	0.884	7,288.2
1998	0.921	36,874.2	0.931	30,235.7	0.913	7,525.6
1999	0.958	38,171.2	0.959	31,523.6	0.948	7,779.3
2000	1.000	39,504.6	1.000	33,046.6	1.000	8,046.6
2001	1.042	39,939.6	1.048	33,764.5	1.055	8,122.7
2002	1.096	49,950.4	1.088	35,021.8	1.107	8,428.4

Gross Domestic Product in constant prices Y consists of outputs of investment goods I and consumption goods C. These products are produced from capital services K and labor services L. These factor services are components of GDI in constant prices X and are augmented by multifactor productivity A.

The key feature of the production possibility frontier is the explicit role it provides for changes in the relative prices of investment and consumption outputs. The aggregate production function, a competing methodology, gives a single output as a function of capital and labor inputs. There is no role for separate prices of investment and consumption goods. Under the assumption that product and factor markets are in competitive equilibrium, the share-weighted growth of outputs is the sum of the share-weighted growth of inputs and growth in multifactor productivity:

$$\overline{w}_I \Delta I + \overline{w}_C \Delta \ln C = \overline{v}_K \Delta \ln K + \overline{v}_L \Delta \ln L + \Delta \ln A,$$

where $\overline{w}$ and $\overline{v}$ denote average shares of the outputs and inputs, respectively, in the value of GDP in current prices.

We calculate the average value shares for the two outputs from estimates of investment and consumption goods in current prices presented in table 1.6. The growth rates of these outputs are obtained from estimates in constant prices in table 1.20. Similarly, we calculate the average value shares for capital and labor inputs from the estimates of capital and labor services in current prices from table 1.6. The growth rates of labor input are generated from the estimates in constant prices in table 1.21 and the growth rates of capital input from constant price estimates in table 1.24. Given the accounting identity between the value of outputs and the value of inputs, the value shares of outputs and inputs sum to one.

Table 1.33 presents accounts for U.S. economic growth during the period 1948–2002 and various subperiods, following Jorgenson (2001). The earlier subperiods are divided by the business cycle peaks in 1973 and 1989. The period since 1989 is divided in 1995, the beginning of a powerful resurgence in U.S. economic growth linked to information technology. The con-

Table 1.33   **Contributions to output and growth, 1948–2002**

	1948–2002	1948–1973	1973–1989	1989–1995	1995–2002
Output					
Gross domestic product	3.52	4.06	3.06	2.33	3.64
Contribution of consumption	2.55	2.91	2.30	1.72	2.59
Contribution of investment	0.97	1.16	0.77	0.62	1.05
Growth					
Gross domestic income	2.90	3.13	2.96	1.77	2.93
Contribution of capital services	1.83	2.00	1.79	0.87	2.14
Contribution of labor services	1.07	1.13	1.17	0.90	0.79
Multifactor productivity	0.62	0.93	0.11	0.56	0.71

tribution of each output is its growth rate weighted by the relative value share. Similarly, the contribution of each input is its weighted growth rate. The contribution of multifactor productivity is the difference between growth rates of output and input.

The value shares of outputs and inputs are represented in figure 1.2. The shares of capital and labor inputs reveal little evidence of trends over the period 1948–2002. The share of investment has gradually declined, while the share of consumption has risen. Figure 1.3 depicts the contributions to U.S. economic growth by investment and consumption goods outputs and the sources of economic growth—the contributions of capital and labor services and multifactor productivity.

The graphical picture of the growth of the U.S. economy before and after 1973 reveals familiar features of the historical record. After strong output and productivity growth in the 1950s, 1960s, and early 1970s, the U.S. economy slowed markedly from 1973 through 1989. Output growth fell from 4.06 to 3.06 percent, and multifactor productivity growth declined precipitously from 0.93 to 0.11 percent. The contribution of capital input also slowed from 2.00 percent for 1948–73 to 1.79 percent for 1973–89, more than offsetting the slight increase in the labor input contribution from 1.13 to 1.17 percent. U.S. economic growth declined further from 1989 to 1995, as the contributions of capital and labor inputs slumped to 0.87 percent and 0.90 percent, counterbalancing a revival in productivity growth to 0.56 percent.

U.S. economic growth surged to 3.64 percent during the period 1995–2002. Between 1989–95 and 1995–2002 the contribution of capital input jumped by 1.27 percentage points, accounting for almost all of the increase

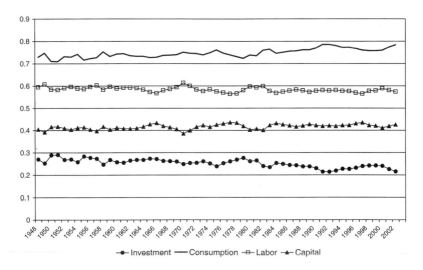

Fig. 1.2   Output and input shares

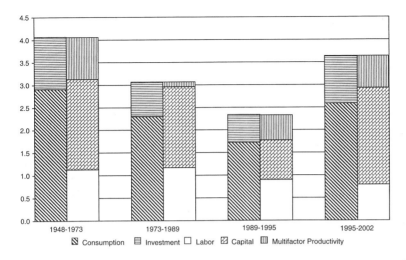

Fig. 1.3   Contributions to output and economic growth

in output growth of 1.31 percent. The contribution of capital input reflects the investment boom of the late 1990s, as businesses, households, and governments poured resources into plant and equipment, especially computers, software, and communications equipment. However, this period also includes the short and shallow recession of 2001 and the recovery of 2002. The contribution of labor input declined by 0.11 percent, while multifactor productivity growth accelerated by 0.15 percent.

Although consumption predominates in the growth of output throughout the postwar period, investment has increased in relative importance since 1995. Capital input is the most important source of economic growth for the postwar period; labor input is next in importance and multifactor productivity the least important. Productivity accounts for a little over 20 percent of postwar U.S. economic growth, while capital and labor inputs account for almost 80 percent. The contribution of capital input exceeds that of labor input, except for the period 1989–95.

The estimates of the sources of U.S. economic growth can be further decomposed to show, for example, how much of the spurt in the growth of output and productivity after 1995 was due to the increased efficiency in the production of information technology equipment and software and other investment goods. These estimates can be used to identify the proportion of growth due to increased investment and capital deepening. The accounts also show how much of the growth in labor inputs was due to growth in labor hours and the quality of labor.

Without an integrated set of production accounts, the analysis of sources of economic growth at the aggregate and industry level must rely on a mixture of BEA industry accounts estimates and BLS productivity estimates, combined with an analyst's estimates of missing information, such as labor quality growth. Different analysts can produce inconsistent results on the sources of economic growth during periods of higher or lower growth, such as the post-1973 productivity slowdown and the more recent spurt in productivity growth since 1995.[26]

We next consider the uses of economic growth, based on the measures of income, expenditures, and the level of living from the Income and Expenditures Account presented in table 1.29. The interpretation of expenditures requires a social welfare function, like the one considered by Weitzman (2003). Expenditures include personal and government consumption and represent the flow of goods and services for current consumption. Expenditures also include saving, net of depreciation, corresponding to the increment in future flows of consumption during the current period.

Economic growth creates opportunities for both present and future consumption. These opportunities are generated by expansion in the supply of capital and labor services, augmented by changes in the level of living:

$$Z(C, S) = B \cdot W(L, N),$$

where net domestic expenditures in constant prices Z consist of consumption expenditures C and saving S, net of depreciation. These expenditures are generated by net incomes in constant prices W, comprising labor incomes L and property incomes N, also net of depreciation.

The level of living B must be carefully distinguished from multifactor productivity A. An increase in the level of living implies that for given supplies of the factor services that generate labor and property incomes, the U.S. economy generates greater opportunities for present and future consumption. The share-weighted growth of expenditures is the sum of the share-weighted growth of incomes and growth in the level of living:

$$\overline{w}_C \Delta \ln C + \overline{w}_S \Delta S = \overline{v}_L \Delta \ln L + \overline{v}_N \Delta \ln N + \Delta \ln B,$$

where $\overline{w}$ and $\overline{v}$ denote average value shares for expenditures and incomes, respectively.

We calculate the average shares for the two components of expenditures—consumption and saving—from the estimates of personal consumption expenditures, government consumption expenditures, and net saving in current prices in table 1.8. The shares of labor and capital incomes are obtained from current price estimates of these incomes in the same table. We generate the growth rates of expenditures from the estimates in constant prices in table 1.26 and the growth rates of labor and property incomes from the constant price estimates in table 1.18. The level of living is given in table 1.29.

---

26. An integrated set of U.S. accounts, using common methodology and source data, will help to eliminate differences due to variations in source data and methods. This will provide an improved baseline for analysis of economic growth, extensions of the accounting system, and alternative sets of estimates.

Table 1.34   **Contributions to expenditure, 1948–2002**

Expenditure	1948–2002	1948–1973	1973–1989	1989–1995	1995–2002
Income	2.60	2.93	2.59	1.52	2.36
Contribution of labor income	1.21	1.26	1.34	1.02	0.90
Contribution of net property income	1.39	1.66	1.26	0.50	1.46
Level of living	0.63	0.93	0.14	0.59	0.71
Net expenditures	3.23	3.86	2.73	2.11	3.07
Consumption	3.00	3.38	2.69	1.93	3.25
Contribution of personal consumption	2.51	2.74	2.24	1.80	2.90
Contribution of government consumption	0.49	0.64	0.45	0.13	0.35
Net saving	0.23	0.48	0.04	0.18	−0.18

Table 1.34 presents a decomposition of the uses of economic growth for the period 1948–2002. The growth rate of expenditures is a weighted average of growth rates of personal consumption expenditures, government consumption expenditures, and net saving. The contribution of each category of expenditures is the growth rate weighted by the relative share. Similarly, the contributions of labor and property incomes are the growth rates weighted by the relative shares. The contribution of the level of living is the difference between growth rates of expenditures and incomes.

The value shares of expenditures and incomes are represented in figure 1.4. The shares of capital and labor incomes, like the shares of capital and labor inputs in the Production Account, are stationary over the period 1948–2002. The share of personal consumption expenditures has gradually risen over this period, especially after 1973, while the share of government consumption rose and fell. Net saving has steadily trended downward. Figure 1.5 shows the contributions to the growth of expenditures by supplies of capital and labor services and increases in the level of living. This figure also portrays current consumption and increments to future consumption through net saving.

The growth of net expenditures largely reflects the pattern of output growth with strong growth of expenditures during the period 1948–73, followed by a showdown after 1973, a further deceleration after 1989, and a sharp revival after 1995. The growth of expenditures for the postwar period as a whole was 3.23 percent, by comparison with output growth of 3.52 percent. However, the growth of expenditures diverged from the growth of output after 1995, rebounding by only 0.96 percent, by comparison with a jump in output of 1.31 percent.

The precipitous fall in saving has attracted a great deal of attention, for example, in the work of Gale and Sablehaus (1999) and Reinsdorf (2005). The most arresting feature of the uses of economic growth is the gradual disappearance of Net Saving. This added a healthy 0.48 percent to growth during 1948–73. The contribution of current consumption, both personal

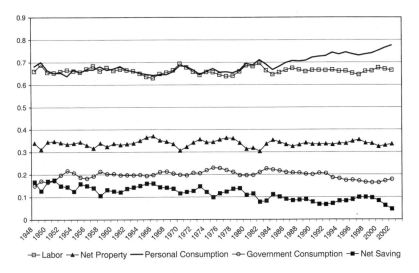

-□- Labor -▲- Net Property —— Personal Consumption -○- Government Consumption -■- Net Saving

Fig. 1.4   Income and expenditure shares

and government, declined during 1973–89, but the contribution of Net Saving nearly vanished, falling to 0.04 percent before reviving modestly to 0.18 percent from 1989 to 1995, and plunging to a negative 0.18 percent during 1995–2002. Both the investment boom of the late 1990s and the resurgence of consumption were financed by foreign borrowing.

The integration of wealth accounts can help explain the long-term decline in saving out of current income. The U.S. tax system taxes future consumption more than current consumption and provides incentives for saving in the form of capital gains for residential housing and corporate equities. The effect of the these provisions of the tax code can be seen in table 1.13, which shows the rise in the share of the annual change in wealth accounted for by revaluations versus saving out of current income from an average of 41 percent between 1950 and 1960 to 54 percent between 1995 and 2000.

We obtain further insight into the relationship between investment and saving from the Domestic Capital and Wealth Accounts presented in tables 1.30, 1.31, and 1.32. Gross Investment and Gross Saving are identical in both current and constant prices. Gross Saving is reduced by Depreciation to yield Net Saving. This is combined with Revaluation to generate the Change in Wealth. Finally, Wealth is comprised of private domestic tangible assets, government tangible assets, and the U.S. International Position. With integrated accounts and the underlying detail in the Federal Reserve Board Balance Sheets and the NIPAs we can focus on the household sector. Much of the increase in net worth was in the household sector. Between 1990 and 2000 39 percent was in equity values and mutual funds and 22 percent in residential housing.

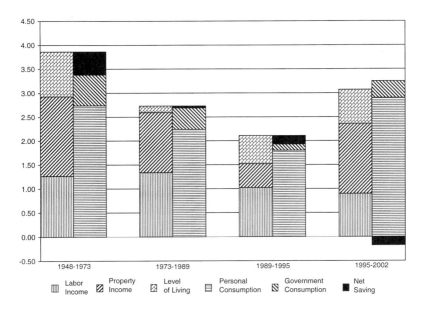

Fig. 1.5   Contributions to net expenditure and income

We calculate the average value shares of private investment, government investment, and ROW investment, the components of Gross Investment, from the estimates in current prices presented in table 1.12. The growth rates of these components are obtained from the estimates in constant prices given in table 1.30. Similarly, we calculate the average value shares of Depreciation and Net Saving from the current price estimates in table 1.13. The growth rates of these components of Gross Saving are generated from the constant price estimates in table 1.31.

One link from the Domestic Capital Account to the Domestic Wealth Account is Net Saving, a measure of change in the quantity of assets; a second link is Revaluation, a measure of change in asset prices. The two together make up the Change in Wealth presented in current prices in table 1.13, and the average value shares are obtained from this table. We calculate the growth rates of the two components of Change in Wealth from the constant price estimates in table 1.31. Finally, we provide the asset side of the Domestic Wealth Account in current prices in table 1.17. The estimates in this table are utilized in generating average value shares of the three components. Growth rates are calculated from the constant price estimates in table 1.32.

Table 1.35 presents decompositions of Gross Investment and Gross Saving. The contribution of each component is its growth rate, weighted by the relative value share. The contribution of private investment is almost the same as the growth of Gross Investment for the period 1948–2002. The contribution of government investment nearly offsets the negative contri-

Table 1.35   Contributions to investment and saving, 1948–2002

	1948–2002	1948–1973	1973–1989	1989–1995	1995–2002
Gross investment	3.61	4.16	3.13	3.16	3.11
Contribution of private investment	3.57	3.58	2.98	2.97	5.39
Contribution of government investment	0.55	0.65	0.55	0.10	0.54
Contribution of ROW investment	−0.51	−0.07	−0.41	0.09	−2.82
Saving	3.61	4.16	3.13	3.16	3.11
Contribution of net saving	0.76	1.55	0.23	0.67	−0.79
Contribution of depreciation	2.85	2.61	2.89	2.49	3.91

bution of ROW investment. Throughout the postwar period foreigners have been accumulating assets in the United States faster than the United States has been accumulating assets abroad. In fact, the contribution of ROW investment was negative in all subperiods, except 1989–95, when it was very slightly positive.

The value shares of gross investment and gross saving are presented in figure 1.6. The share of private investment has been trending upward throughout the postwar period and exceeded 100 percent after 1995. Government investment peaked in the early 1950s and has been declining gradually. ROW investment was essentially zero until the early 1980s, then dipped into negative territory until 1991, when it was positive for a single year, and then plunged deeper and deeper into the negative range through the end of the period in 2002. Net Saving has been declining as a share of Gross Saving in current prices, while Depreciation has been rising. This reflects the shift in the composition of investment toward shorter-lived assets, including information technology equipment and software.

Figure 1.7 depicts the contributions to capital formation by private investment, government investment, and ROW investment. Gross Investment dropped from 4.16 percent in 1948–73 to 3.13 percent in 1973–89. This remained essentially constant through the end of the period in 2002. However, dramatic changes in the composition of Gross Investment took place after 1995. The contribution of private investment was surprisingly stable until it soared to 5.39 percent for 1995–2002 from 2.97 percent for 1989–95. This reflects the spectacular boom in investment after 1995, powered by the surge of investment in information technology equipment and software. However, the rise in private investment was completely offset by a decline in the contribution of ROW investment, which sank from a positive 0.09 percent in 1989–95 to a negative 2.82 percent in 1995–2002.

The contribution of Net Saving has a strong negative trend, falling from 1.55 percent in 1948–73 to 0.23 percent in 1973–89, before recovering to 0.67 percent in 1989–95. Net Saving then plunged to a negative 0.79 percent in 1995–2002. By contrast the contribution of Depreciation rose grad-

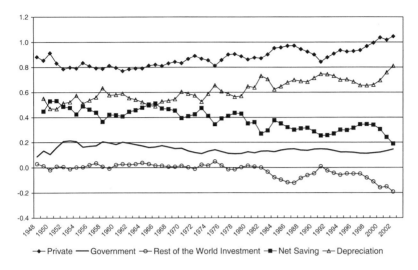

Fig. 1.6   Investment and saving shares

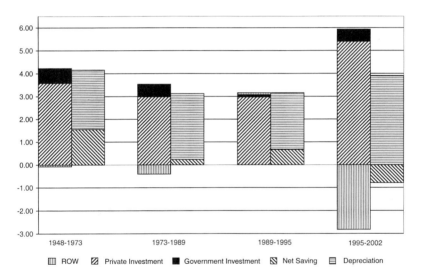

Fig. 1.7   Contributions to investment and saving

ually, reaching 3.91 percent in 1995–2002. A different perspective on Net Saving is presented in table 1.36, where the contributions of Net Saving and Revaluation are combined to generate Change in Wealth. The contribution of Revaluation has fluctuated sharply from a negative 0.13 percent in 1948–73, when asset prices were falling, to a positive 3.61 percent in 1973–89, a period of relatively rapid asset inflation that included much of the

Table 1.36   Contributions to change in wealth, 1948–2002

	1948–2002	1948–1973	1973–1989	1989–1995	1995–2002
Change in wealth	3.41	3.51	4.58	0.47	2.91
Contribution of net saving	2.11	3.65	0.97	1.61	–0.16
Contribution of revaluation	1.30	–0.13	3.61	–1.14	3.07
Wealth	3.22	4.02	3.29	0.26	2.70
Contribution of private tangible assets	2.92	3.47	2.95	0.56	2.93
Contribution of government tangible assets	0.48	0.56	0.49	0.09	0.52
Contribution of international position	–0.18	0.00	–0.15	–0.39	–0.74

1970s and 1980s. The contribution of Revaluation was a negative 1.14 percent during 1989–95, before leaping to 3.07 percent from 1995 to 2002.

Finally, table 1.36 provides a decomposition of the growth of Domestic Wealth. The growth rate of Domestic Wealth attained a postwar high of 4.02 percent during 1948–73, before declining to 3.29 percent during 1973–89. Wealth grew at only 0.26 percent during 1989–95, but recovered to 2.70 percent in 1995–2002. The contribution of the U.S. International Investment Position was essentially zero from 1948 to 1973 before moving into the negative range, ultimately declining at 0.74 percent in 1995–2002. Private tangible assets increased in relative importance throughout the period.

These integrated and consistent accounts can extend the double-entry capacity of the existing accounts to put the U.S. trade deficit in perspective. The key features are the accounting identity between national saving and investment and the trade deficit and the relationship between the trade deficit, net borrowings from abroad, and the U.S. international investment position. The extended accounts show that U.S. trade surpluses and net U.S. lending resulted in an international investment position that rose from 1.7 percent of wealth in 1948 to a peak of 3.1 percent in 1980. After that domestic demand, represented by expenditures, grew faster than supply, given by GDP, and trade surpluses turned to deficits. Net lending by the U.S. turned to net borrowing, so that by 1989 the international position was a negative 0.2 percent of U.S. wealth, falling to a negative –5.7 percent in 2002.

The integrated accounts facilitate relative comparisons of net debt to wealth that provide perspective on the magnitude of the U.S. net international position, a negative $2.6 trillion, and comparisons with external debt levels of other countries. Similarly, the NIPAs help put in perspective the trade deficit and the federal budget deficit as a percent of GDP. Currently, differences in the concepts and methods make it difficult to trace changes in the BEA's data on net exports and the U.S. International Investment Position to changes in the FRB's balance sheets.

In summary, the sources of U.S. economic growth reveal the origins of the slowdown that followed 1973 and worsened after 1989, but also the genesis of the U.S. growth resurgence after 1995. The uses of economic growth display the vanishing role of Net Saving throughout the postwar period. The investment boom and the surge in consumption of the late 1990s were financed by foreign borrowing. This is put into sharp relief by the behavior of ROW investment. Rapid accumulation of U.S. assets by foreigners is a longstanding trend that is also apparent in the deterioration in the U.S. International Investment Position. A less familiar fact, put into sharp relief by our prototype system, is the substantial fluctuations in asset prices reflected in Revaluation as a component of the Change in Wealth.

1.4.8   Summary and Conclusions

We have now completed our blueprint for a consistent and integrated system of national accounts for the United States. We have limited ourselves to national aggregates and accounts based on market transactions. The major innovation in our system of national accounts is the systematic utilization of imputed rental prices for capital assets, based on the user cost formula introduced by Jorgenson (1963). This is the key to integration of the NIPAs generated by the BEA with the BLS productivity accounts.

In order to achieve consistency between investment goods production and capital income we impute capital income to households, institutions, and governments, as well as corporations and noncorporate businesses. For residential housing we follow the BEA in imputing the rental value of owner-occupied housing from the rental value of renter-occupied housing. This imputation is based on market rental prices. We impute the rental value of consumer durables, as well as durables and real estate owned by nonprofit institutions, from market prices for the assets. We employ a similar approach for the rental value of government assets, including equipment and software, as well as government real estate.

We exclude investment in consumer durables from household consumption, but include this investment in the GDP, together with the imputed rental value of the services of the corresponding assets. We employ a similar approach for assets owned by nonprofit institutions and the government sector. As a consequence of treating investment goods production and capital income symmetrically for household, government, and business sectors, our estimate of GDP in table 1.5 is nearly 10 percent higher than the estimate of GDP given in the NIPAs.

The NIPAs present GDP in current and constant prices and GDI in current prices, while the Domestic Income and Product Account provides GDI in current and constant prices, as well as multifactor productivity, defined as the ratio of GDP in constant prices to GDI in constant prices. The Domestic Income and Product Account we have presented in table 1.6

gives the data required for the analysis of the sources of economic growth for the U.S. economy presented by Jorgenson (2001). The sources of economic growth are the contributions of labor and capital inputs and the growth of productivity.

Our blueprint continues with a consolidated Income and Expenditures Account. Income includes proceeds from the sale of factor services, plus income receipts from the rest of the world less income payments, and net current taxes and transfers from the rest of the world. Expenditures include personal and government expenditures at market prices, plus net saving from the Domestic Capital Account. Our Income and Expenditures Accounts consolidates three income and expenditures accounts from the NIPAs for household, business, and government income and expenditures. This has the advantage that payments among sectors cancel out in the consolidated account, resulting in a considerable simplification.

In order to provide data for an analysis of the disposition of income as expenditures and net saving, we present the Income and Expenditures Account in both current and constant prices in table 1.29. The uses of economic growth include personal consumption expenditures, government expenditures, and net saving. Net saving is generated in the Domestic Capital Account and the Foreign Transactions Capital Account and is equal to gross saving less depreciation. We present the level of living, defined as the ratio of Net Expenditures to Net Income. This gives current consumption and increments to future consumption in the current period as a proportion of the capital and labor services that generate the income that is required.

Our Domestic Capital Account parallels the corresponding account in the NIPAs. Investment includes private domestic investment, government investment, and expenditures on durable goods by households and nonprofit institutions, all evaluated at market prices. The Domestic Capital Account presents the change in wealth, which is equal to the sum of net saving and the revaluation of assets. This provides a necessary link between the current economic activity reflected in the Domestic Income and Product Account and the Income and Expenditures Account and the accumulation of the wealth presented in the Wealth Account. The boundaries of these accounts are consistent throughout our prototype system of national accounts.

Finally, our Wealth Account, together with the Domestic Capital Account, is consistent with the FRB flow-of-funds accounts. We consolidate the detailed accounts presented in the flow-of-funds accounts and the national balance sheets for different financial sectors. This simplifies the accounts for saving, investment, and wealth by eliminating claims among the domestic sectors, including household, government, and business sectors. We retain the Foreign Transactions Current and Capital Accounts from the NIPAs, as well as the U.S. International Position.

Appendix

The U.S. National Accounts: Guide to Data, Concepts, and Methods

Information on the availability of national accounts data, the concepts that underpin the estimates, and the methods used to develop them are spread among the agencies that produce the accounts and the international bodies that develop guides to national accounts. Below is a list of primary references for understanding the nation's economic accounts.

U.S. Resources

Bureau of Economic Analysis (BEA; www.bea.gov)

The upcoming schedule of releases for the following year is published in the December issue of the *Survey of Current Business* (SCB) and on the web site. The December issues also contain a subject guide to articles that have appeared in the SCB throughout the year, articles covering methodologies, research, and recent data releases. Articles since 1994 are available on the web site (www.bea.gov/bea/pubs.htm), and a link to the data release schedule is also available from the home page.

National accounts (www.bea.gov/bea/dn1.htm): Quarterly and annual data from the NIPAs and monthly and annual data on personal income and corporate profits are available in press releases, SCB articles, and in interactive formats on the web site, including underlying detail for selected NIPA series. Annual tangible wealth (fixed asset) data are also available in interactive table form. A brief history of the accounts can be found in an SCB article titled "GDP: One of the Great Inventions of the 20th Century," which appeared in January 2000 issue. Methodologies and source data are available from the national accounts section of the BEA web site as well as selected analytical articles and brief overviews on national accounts topics ranging from chain indexes to saving.

International accounts (www.bea.gov/bea/di1.htm): Quarterly and annual balance-of-payments (BOP) data and annual international investment position (IIP) data are available in press releases and in SCB articles. BOP interactive data and annual IIP data are accessible from the international section of the BEA web site. Methodology articles for the international accounts and other guides and articles are also available.

Regional accounts (www.bea.gov/bea/regional/data.htm): State personal income (SPI), local personal income, and GSP data and press releases are located in the regional section of the BEA web site. Separate interactive tables are available for annual SPI, quarterly SPI, annual local area income, and annual GSP. Methodology articles, recent releases, and SCB articles for the regional accounts can be accessed from the main regional page.

Industry accounts (www.bea.gov/bea/dn2.htm): Quarterly and annual GDP-by-industry data and annual and benchmark input-output (I-O) account data are accessible from the main industry page of the BEA web site. Interactive tables are available for GDP by industry, for annual I-O tables, and for benchmark I-O tables.

Federal Reserve Board (FRB; www.federalreserve.gov)

Flow-of-funds accounts (FOF): Recent quarterly and annual FOF data are available at www.federalreserve.gov/releases/z1/. Longer time series of FOF data, including access to downloadable PRN files, are located at www .federalreserve.gov/releases/z1/Current/data.htm. Within the FOF data are the balance sheet data that use the tangible asset data provided by the BEA. The *Guide to the Flow-of-Funds Accounts* provides a thorough methodology of the accounts, and part of it can be viewed online. The entire two-volume book can be ordered from the FRB.

Bureau of Labor Statistics (BLS; www.bls.gov)

Productivity accounts: The BLS publishes three productivity series. Annual and quarterly major sector productivity and annual industry productivity data are located at www.bls.gov/lpc/home.htm#overview. This main page provides links to recent releases, methodology articles, and detailed data series. Articles are also published in the *Monthly Labor Review* and are available online since 1982 (www.bls.gov/opub/mlr/mlrhome.htm). Major sector productivity estimates are constructed based on GDP data published by the BEA. Industry productivity data are estimated using basic data published by various public and private agencies. Annual multifactor productivity (MFP) data, recent releases, methodology articles, and detailed data series are available at www.bls.gov/mfp/home.htm. The MFP data series is constructed using the investment and output data provided by the BEA and the labor data collected by the BLS. The BLS *Handbook of Methods* provides a thorough guide to methodologies for BLS data series (www.bls.gov/opub/hom/homtoc_pdf.htm).

Additional Resources

System of National Accounts 1993 (SNA 1993)

SNA 1993 is an internationally recognized integrated economic accounting system. The manual and accounting project was sponsored by the

Commission of the European Communities, International Monetary Fund (IMF), Organisation for Economic Co-operation and Development, United Nations (UN), and World Bank. The complete manual can be ordered from the UN (www.un.org).

Balance of Payments Manual, 5th ed. (www.imf.org/external/np/sta/bop/biblio.htm#mg)

Published by the IMF, this manual provides international guidelines for the compilation of international accounts. The fifth edition was published in 1993.

References

Baily, Martin N., and Robert Z. Lawrence. 2001. Do we have a new e-conomy? *American Economic Review* 91 (2): 308–12.

Bureau of Economic Analysis (BEA). 1999. Fixed reproducible tangible wealth in the United States, 1925–94. Washington, DC: U.S. Government Printing Office, August.

———. 2004a. Table A: Summary National Income and Product Accounts, 2002. *Survey of Current Business* 84 (2): 37–38.

———. 2004b. National Income and Product Accounts tables. *Survey of Current Business* 84 (8): 30–166.

Bureau of Labor Statistics (BLS). 1983. *Trends in multifactor productivity, 1948–1981.* Washington, DC: U.S. Government Printing Office.

———. 1993. Labor composition and U.S. productivity growth, 1948–1990. Bureau of Labor Statistics Bulletin no. 2426. Washington, DC: U.S. Department of Labor.

———. 2003. Revisions to capital inputs for the BLS multifactor productivity measures. Available at http://www.bls.gov/web/mprcaptl.htm.

Christensen, Laurits R., and Dale W. Jorgenson. 1996. Measuring economic performance in the private sector. In *Postwar U.S. economic growth,* ed. Dale W. Jorgenson, 175–272. Cambridge, MA: MIT Press.

Congressional Budget Office. 1997. An economic model for long-run budget simulations. CBO memorandum. Washington, DC: Congressional Budget Office, July.

Corrado, Carol. 2003. Industrial production and capacity utilization: The 2002 historical and annual revision. *Federal Reserve Bulletin* 89 (April): 151–76.

Corrado, Carol, John Haltiwanger, and Daniel Sichel, eds. 2005. *Measuring capital in the new economy.* Chicago: University of Chicago Press.

Council of Economic Advisers. 1997. *Economic report of the president.* Washington, DC: U.S. Government Printing Office.

Denison, Edward F. 1967. *Why growth rates differ.* Washington, DC: Brookings Institution.

Diewert, W. Erwin. 1976. Exact and superlative index numbers. *Journal of Econometrics* 4 (2): 115–46.

———. 1978. Superlative index numbers and consistency in aggregation. *Econometrica* 46 (4): 883–900.

Doms, Mark. 2005. Communications equipment: What has happened to prices? In *Measuring capital in the new economy,* ed. C. Corrado, J. Haltiwanger, and D. Sichel, 323–62. Chicago: University of Chicago Press.

Dulberger, Ellen R. 1989. The application of a hedonic model to a quality-adjusted price index for computer processors. In *Technology and capital formation,* ed. D. Jorgenson and R. Landau, 37–76. Cambridge, MA: MIT Press.

Eisner, Robert. 1989. *The total income system of accounts.* Chicago: University of Chicago Press.

Fang, Bingsong, Xiaoli Han, Sumiye Okubo, and Ann M. Lawson. 2000. U.S. transportation satellite accounts for 1996. *Survey of Current Business* 80 (5): 14–22.

Fisher, Irving. 1922. *The making of index numbers.* Boston: Houghton-Mifflin.

Flamm, Kenneth. 1989. Technological advance and costs: Computers versus communications. In *Changing the rules: Technological change, international competition, and regulation in communications,* ed. Robert C. Crandall and Kenneth Flamm, 13–61. Washington, DC: Brookings Institution.

Fraumeni, Barbara M. 1997. The measurement of depreciation in the U.S. National Income and Product Accounts. *Survey of Current Business* 77 (7): 7–23.

Fraumeni, Barbara M., and Sumiye Okubo. 2001. Alternative treatments of consumer durables in the national accounts. Paper presented at a meeting of the Bureau of Economic Analysis Advisory Committee, May 11.

———. 2005. R&D in the National Income and Product Accounts: A first look at its effect on GDP. In *Measuring capital in the new economy,* ed. C. Corrado, J. Haltiwanger, and R. Sichel, 275–322. Chicago: University of Chicago Press.

Gale, William G., and John Sabelhaus. 1999. Perspective on the household saving rate. *Brookings Papers on Economic Activity,* Issue no. 1:181–224.

Gordon, Robert J. 1989. The postwar evolution of computer prices. In *Technology and capital formation,* ed. D. Jorgenson and R. Landau, 77–126. Cambridge, MA: MIT Press.

———. 1990. *The measurement of durable goods prices.* Chicago: University of Chicago Press.

———. 2001. Did the productivity revival spill over from manufacturing to services? Conflicting evidence from four data sources. Paper presented at the National Bureau of Economic Research Summer Institute. 27 July, Cambridge, Massachusetts.

Grimm, Bruce T. 1997. Quality adjusted price indexes for digital telephone switches. Washington, DC: Bureau of Economic Analysis. Memorandum, May.

Hall, Bronwyn H., and Robert E. Hall. 1993. The value and performance of U.S. corporations. *Brookings Papers on Economic Activity,* Issue no. 1:1–34.

Herman, Shelby W. 2000. Fixed assets and consumer durable goods for 1925–99. *Survey of Current Business* 80 (9): 19–30.

Hill, Peter. 1999. Capital stocks, capital services and depreciation. Paper presented at a meeting of the Canberra Group on Capital Stock Statistics. 8–10 November, Washington, DC.

Hulten, Charles R. 1992. Account for the wealth of nations: The net versus gross output controversy and its ramifications. *Scandinavian Journal of Economics* 94 (suppl.): 9–24.

Hulten, Charles R., and Frank C. Wykoff. 1982. The measurement of economic depreciation. In *Depreciation, inflation and the taxation of income from capital,* ed. Charles R. Hulten, 81–125. Washington, DC: Urban Institute Press.

International Monetary Fund (IMF). 1993. *Balance of payments manual.* 5th ed. Washington, DC: IMF.

Jaszi, George. 1971. Review: An economic accountant's ledger. *Survey of Current Business* 51 (7, part II): 221–25.

Jorgenson, Dale W. 1963. Capital theory and investment behavior. *American Economic Review* 53 (2): 247–59.

————. 1996a. *Postwar U.S. economic growth.* Cambridge, MA: MIT Press.

————. 1996b. Productivity and postwar U.S. economic growth. In *Postwar U.S. economic growth,* ed. Dale W. Jorgenson, 1–24. Cambridge, MA: MIT Press.

————. 2001. Information technology and the U.S. economy. *American Economic Review* 91 (1): 1–32.

Jorgenson, Dale W., and Barbara M. Fraumeni. 1996a. The accumulation of human and nonhuman capital, 1948–84. In *Postwar U.S. economic growth,* ed. D. Jorgenson, 273–332. Cambridge, MA: MIT Press.

————. 1996b. The output of the education sector. In *Postwar U.S. economic growth,* ed. D. Jorgenson, 333–70. Cambridge, MA: MIT Press.

Jorgenson, Dale W., Frank M. Gollop, and Barbara M. Fraumeni. 1987. *Productivity and U.S. economic growth.* Cambridge, MA: Harvard University Press.

Jorgenson, Dale W., Mun S. Ho, and Kevin J. Stiroh. 2005. *Information technology and the American growth resurgence.* Cambridge, MA: MIT Press.

Jorgenson, Dale W., and Kevin J. Stiroh. 2000. Raising the speed limit: U.S. economic growth in the information age. *Brookings Papers on Economic Activity,* Issue no. 1:125–211.

Jorgenson, Dale W., and Kun-Young Yun. 2001. *Lifting the burden.* Cambridge, MA: MIT Press.

Kendrick, John. 1961. *Productivity trends in the United States.* New York, National Bureau of Economic Research.

Konus, Alexander A., and S. S. Byushgens. 1926. On the problem of the purchasing power of money. *Economic Bulletin of the Conjuncture Institute* (suppl.): 151–72.

Kuznets, Simon. 1946. *National income: A summary of findings.* New York: National Bureau of Economic Research.

Landefeld, J. Steven. 2000. GDP: One of the great inventions of the 20th century. *Survey of Current Business* 80 (1): 6–14.

Landefeld, J. Steven, Carol S. Carson, Gerald F. Donahoe, Bruce T. Grimm, Stephanie L. Howell, Arnold J. Katz, Gary L. Rutledge, Timothy E. Slaper, and Eric J. Troyer. 1994. Integrated economic and environment satellite accounts. *Survey of Current Business* 74 (4): 33–49.

Landefeld, J. Steven, and Stephanie L. Howell. 1997. Accounting for nonmarketed household production within a national accounts framework. Paper presented at the Conference on Time-Use, Nonmarket Work, and Family Well-being, Bureau of Labor Statistics and MacArthur Network on the Family and the Economy. 20–21 November, Washington, DC.

Landefeld, J. Steven, and Robert P. Parker. 1997. BEA's chain indexes, time series, and measures of long-run growth. *Survey of Current Business* 77 (5): 58–68.

Landefeld, J. Steven, Obie G. Whichard, and Jeffrey H. Lowe. 1993. Alternative frameworks for U.S. international transaction. *Survey of Current Business* 73 (9): 50–61.

Meadows, Donnella H., Dennis L. Meadows, William W. Behrens, and Jorgen Randers. 1972. *The limits to growth: A report for the Club of Rome's project on the predicament of mankind.* New York: Signet.

Moulton, Brent R. 2000. Improved estimates of the National Income and Product Accounts for 1929–99: Results of the comprehensive revision. *Survey of Current Business* 80 (4): 11–17, 36–145.

————. 2001. Working with chain-type indexes: A few tricks. Paper presented at the Forecasters Club of New York. 16 June.

————. 2004. The System of National Accounts for the new economy: What should change? *Review of Income and Wealth* 50 (2): 261–78.

Nordhaus, William D. 2002. Productivity growth and the new economy. *Brookings Papers on Economic Activity,* Issue no. 2:211–65.

Nordhaus, William D., and James Tobin. 1973. Is growth obsolete? In *The measurement of economic and social performance,* ed. Milton Moss, 509–32. New York: Columbia University Press.

Office of Management and Budget. 1997. *Analytical perspectives: Budget of the United States government fiscal year 1998.* Washington, DC: U.S. Government Printing Office.

Okubo, Sumiye, and Mark A. Planting. 1998. U.S. travel and tourism satellite accounts for 1992. *Survey of Current Business* 78 (7): 8–22.

Oliner, Stephen D., and Daniel E. Sichel. 1994. Computers and output growth revisited: How big is the puzzle? *Brookings Papers on Economic Activity,* Issue no. 2:273–317.

———. 2000. The resurgence of growth in the late 1990's: Is information technology the story? *Journal of Economic Perspectives* 14 (4): 3–22.

Parker, Robert P., and Bruce T. Grimm. 2000. Recognition of business and government expenditures on software as investment: Methodology and quantitative impacts, 1959–98. Washington, DC: Bureau of Economic Analysis, November.

Reinsdorf, Marshall B. 2005. Saving, wealth, investment, and the current-account deficit. *Survey of Current Business* 85 (4): 3.

Ruggles, Richard, and Nancy D. Ruggles. 1982. Integrated economic accounts for the United States, 1947–80. *Survey of Current Business* 62 (5): 1–53.

Samuelson, Paul A. 1961. The evaluation of "social income": Capital formation and wealth. In *The theory of capital,* ed. Friedrich A. Lutz and Douglas C. Hague, 32–57. London: Macmillan.

Stiroh, Kevin. 2002. Information technology and the U.S. productivity revival: What do the industry data say? *American Economic Review* 92 (5): 1559–76.

Triplett, Jack E. 1986. The economic interpretation of hedonic methods. *Survey of Current Business* 66 (1): 36–40.

———. 1989. Price and technological change in a capital good: Survey of research on computers.

———. 2005. Performance measures for computers. In *Deconstructing the computer,* ed. Dale W. Jorgenson and Charles Wessner, 99–139. Washington, DC: National Academies Press.

Triplett, Jack E., and Barry P. Bosworth. 2004. *Productivity in the U.S. services sector: New sources of economic growth.* Washington, DC: Brookings Institution.

United Nations. 1993. *Integrated environmental and economic accounting.* Studies in Methods, Handbook of National Accounts. Series F, no. 61. New York: United Nations.

United Nations, Commission of the European Communities, International Monetary Fund, Organisation for Economic Co-operation and Development, and World Bank. 1993. *System of national accounts 1993.* Series F, no. 2, rev. 4. New York: United Nations.

Weitzman, Martin L. 1976. On the welfare significance of national product in a dynamic economy. *Quarterly Journal of Economics* 90 (364): 156–62.

———. 2003. *Income, wealth, and the maximum principle.* Cambridge, MA: Harvard University Press.

Wright, Gavin. 1990. The origins of American industrial success, 1879–1940. *American Economic Review,* September, 651–68.

2

The Architecture of the System of National Accounts
A Three-Way International Comparison of Canada, Australia, and the United Kingdom

Karen Wilson

Since the publication of *System of National Accounts 1993* (United Nations et al. 1993; hereafter SNA93) more than a decade ago there has been considerable convergence internationally in the use of the structure, scope of accounts, and measurement methods suggested in those standards. The paper begins with a brief overview of the architecture of the SNA93 standard by relating the elements of the system to their analytic roots. Based on this description of the system, three countries' application of that standard is compared. The comparison is done from two perspectives: scope (what elements of the flow of accounts are covered and how they are structured) and integration (how the various accounts are tied together when there are discrepancies and the identities do not hold).

2.1 The Development of a "System of Accounts"

The System of National Accounts (SNA) is an economic accounting structure derived from macroeconomic analysis. Its architecture is drawn from many areas of macroeconomic study. Work in the twentieth century by Richard Stone led to the development of the concept of national income, which was the earliest aggregate measure at the root of the system of accounts. Early economics was also concerned with production of commodities and the productivity concept of turning inputs into outputs and the contributions of the factors of production to changes in output. This area of analysis eventually led to the development of input-output tables

Karen Wilson is the director general of the System of National Accounts at Statistics Canada. She has a master's degree in economics and has worked in the area of national accounting and economic analysis for twenty-seven years at Statistics Canada.

by Leontief, which has heavily influenced the adoption of gross domestic product as a central variable of macroeconomic analysis. And finally, Keynes's work in developing an analytic framework to explain the dynamics of the macroeconomy following the Great Depression of the 1930s introduced many of the key macroeconomic variables—like consumption, investment, savings, and wealth—that are now focal variables in today's system of accounts. Keynes introduced the concept of "sectors" or the major decision centers and therefore transactors of the economy—households, businesses, governments, and foreign economies and their dynamic effects on the economy through their propensities to consume, save, or invest out of income that flows from the productive activity. Some time in the late 1940s and early 1950s the idea of an integrated set of accounts pulling together all of these analytic underpinnings into a system of accounts became a focus of work at the international level. By 1968, the idea came together with the publication of *A System of National Accounts* (United Nations, 1968) with major contributions by a group of experts from around the world chaired by Richard Stone of Cambridge University.

This first "system of accounts" was designed and described for its analytic content and potential uses. The need for consistent accounts was described as follows: "by providing a consistent picture of the development of an economic system, a series of national accounts are useful, indeed indispensable, in describing and analyzing economic change and so contribute to many forms of economic decision making" (United Nations 1968, 12). In addition to its analytic use, the system was also described as a "scheme for collection of economic statistics."

The system articulated the major transactions of the macroeconomy by examining activity in the economy through the production and use of incomes to the accumulation of fixed and financial assets to arrive at a closing balance for net national wealth. The fully integrated system was designed around the key macroeconomic variables: production, consumption, investment, and wealth accumulation. The various accounts were related to specific types of analysis related to research or policy management, as illustrated in table 2.1.

While the 1968 system was rich in its analytic underpinnings, the statistical infrastructure was not well developed. Since it was the early basis for a system of accounts it did not articulate the true "architecture" of the statistical system. The production boundary (the delineation between market and nonmarket production), the classification systems (industries, products, functional breakdowns), the statistical units (establishments, enterprises, institutions), and the definition of the asset boundary (produced, natural, tangible, intangible, etc.) were not fully developed.

This early system served as the foundation for the current architecture. As countries developed and applied the system and as users provided feedback on their experiences in analytic use of it, the statistical community

Table 2.1   Analytic underpinnings of the system of accounts

Supply	Opening assets		Production		Consumption		Accumulation				The rest of the world		Revaluations		Closing assets	
	1	2	3	4	5	6	7	8	9	10	11	12	13	14	15	6
1. Financial claims 2. Net assets							Studies of national wealth; analysis of productivity									
3. Commercial production 4. Noncommercial production			Input-output analysis; analysis of productivity; business cycle studies		Consumers' demand analysis; studies of government spending		Models of stock building and fixed capital formation; investment policy				Export demand analysis; studies of the "globalization" phenomenon					
5. Final consumption 6. Income and outlay			Production functions; analysis of productivity; analysis of factor shares		Distribution and redistribution of income; fiscal policy		Depreciation analysis; investment allowances				Studies of the return on foreign investment; double taxation policy				Studies of the "wealth effect" on consumption	
7. Change in stocks 8. Fixed investment 9. Financial claims 10. Capital finance	Studies of net worth				Analysis of saving behaviour		Monetary policy and liquidity preference				International finance and liquidity; long-term foreign aid policy		Studies of capital gains and losses; capital gains tax policy			
11. Current transactions 12. Capital transactions			Import demand analysis		Short-term foreign aid policy		International finance and liquidity; long-term foreign aid policy				Analysis of balance-of-trade payments					
13. Financial claims 14. Net assets							Capital revaluations									
15. Financial claims 16. Net assets							Studies of national wealth; analysis of productivity								Studies of net worth	

Note: Numbered columns correspond to Supply categories.

began to refine and articulate the statistical underpinnings of the system. An international effort in the mid- to late 1980s profited from the many experiences of countries in building economic accounts, and resulted in the set of accounts known today as SNA93.

2.2   The Architecture of SNA93—A Basis for Comparison

This section of the chapter describes the SNA93 architecture by first explaining the framework as is relates to its analytic underpinnings outlined above. The architecture of SNA93 can be broken down into three parts:

- The *central framework,* which translates the analytic view of a "system of accounts" into the basic accounting structure
- The *infrastructure,* which defines the building blocks needed to construct a fully consistent set of economic accounts
- The *integrated data system,* which is the set of accounts and tables that are central to describing the economic process

2.2.1   The Central Framework of SNA93

The central framework of SNA93 consists of the following elements:

1. *Integrated economic accounts* by institutional sector tracing production of income through to wealth accumulation for each institutional sector
2. *Supply and use of goods and services,* which traces production of commodities by industries through their use as intermediate inputs or final demand by institutional sectors
3. *Three-dimensional analysis of transactions,* which articulates all the transactions of the system from both the "real" side of the accounts (production, consumption, and investment) and the "financial" side of the same transactions (creation and deletion of financial claims and fixed assets), all by institutional sector (from whom, to whom), and which forces consistency on the system
4. *Functional analysis* of the purposes of spending by institutional sector; for example, spending by governments (health, education, defense, etc.), consumers (accommodation, food, transportation, health, etc.) and business (intermediate use and investment)
5. *Population and employment data* consistent with SNA concepts for analysis of the labor variables of the system and per capita analysis

These five elements of the framework reflect the analytic requirements of a macroeconomic data system as outlined in the earlier version of the SNA as reflected in table 2.1.

2.2.2   The Infrastructure of SNA93

In order to build this consistent data set for analysis, the architectural building blocks of the data system need to be well defined, as does the structure of the "accounts" or data sets included in the system. The important architectural elements that are the infrastructure of the system for each of the five elements of the central framework are as follows.

1. The institutional sectors and the institutional units that are aggregated to measure them are the building blocks of the integrated sequence of accounts. There are two basic institutional units: households and legal entities. Legal entities are units that are created to perform some economic function like production, in the case of enterprises, and governance and provision of public goods and services, in the case of government units. Each unit is capable of engaging in transactions with other units, of owning assets, and of incurring liabilities. The units reflect the decision centers in the economy for financing, saving, and investment. The units are grouped together into mutually exclusive sectors based on their economic objectives, functions, and behaviors. Carrying through on the examples of the units mentioned, corporations' economic function is the production of goods and services for sale on the market with an objective of gaining profit for their owners. Government institutional units are quite distinct in their function and objective. They engage in nonmarket production and also have as an economic objective the redistribution of income and wealth among institutional sectors through taxation and transfers. The main institutional sectors of the system are

    a. Nonfinancial corporations
    b. Financial corporations
    c. General governments
    d. Households
    e. Nonprofit institutions serving households
    f. Rest of the world

Sectors (a) through (e) cover the domestic economy, and (f) covers the transactions of the rest of the world with the domestic economy. The main sectors can be broken down into subsectors; for example, general government into the relevant levels of government, or financial corporations into banking, insurance, and other financial institutions.

2. The supply and use analysis articulates the production of goods and services by production units. Two important elements of the system play an important role in this part of the system: the production and asset boundaries and the valuation principles.

    a. The production boundary includes the production of all individual or collective goods and services that are supplied to institutional units other than their producer. It also includes own account production of goods that are retained by the individual unit for consumption or fixed capital formation. In the case of household units this own-account production includes production of housing services as well as own-account construction of dwellings. Any other goods produced by households for own consumption are counted only when significant. This usually means agricultural products produced and used on the farm.

b. The asset boundary defines real wealth in the system. An asset is something that is owned by a unit or units and from which economic benefits are derived over a period of time greater than one year. The benefits are often derived from use in the production process but also from holding the asset as a store of value. Financial assets and real assets that have been produced by a unit and used repeatedly in future period clearly meet the criterion. Assets that are naturally occurring (mineral deposits, forests, etc.) must be owned by an institutional unit that can exercise effective ownership rights in order to be included. Valuables are included as assets but not as capital formation.

c. Valuation of production in the supply/use framework is at basic prices, which are the prices receivable by the producer unit before taxes on those products are added, including any subsidies received. Non-market production is valued at cost when there is no market price valuation equivalent available. When production is carried forward to the sequence of accounts, the taxes on products are added in and subsidies netted out to arrive at gross domestic product (GDP) at market prices.

d. Two classification systems are at the base of this measurement: an industrial classification system (the one suggested in SNA93 is revision 3 of the International Standard Industrial Classification [ISIC Rev 3] at the two-digit level of aggregation or approximately 120 industries) and a classification of commodities (the Central Product Classification [CPC] is recommended at the three-digit level, about 300 products). The relevant statistical unit in the case of measuring output is the producer unit. This is the unit of the economy that can report on the output of products and the inputs used. The selection of the unit of statistical measure is based on homogeneous production technology, or, in SNA93 parlance, a "kind of activity unit." There are many producer units in an economy. The majority are small units producing one type of commodity. Others are part of large complex enterprises that produce many different types of products and services and participate in many industries. These enterprises are broken down into subunits called "establishments" for the statistical purpose of articulating supply and use of homogeneous products made using homogeneous production technology.

3. The three-dimensional aspect of the infrastructure is also referred to as quadruple entry book keeping. Transactions across sectors are recorded in four counterpart transactions. This ensures consistency in measuring variables across sectors and across accounts. For example, when a corpo-

ration pays income tax to the central government, the transaction is recorded simultaneously as a transfer of income from the payer, the corporate sector, and as a receipt of income by the receiver sector, the government. It is also recorded as a decrease in cash on the financial account of the corporate sector and an increase in cash by the government sector. This ensures that the closing balance on the balance sheet of each sector also reflects the transfer of income from one sector to another, thereby imposing stock-flow consistency on the system as well. This is very important for analyzing and understanding the economic process. This feature is key to ensuring that many of the types of analyses outlined in table 2.1 provide consistent results such as multifactor productivity analysis, which relates the production activity to the service flow from the stock of fixed assets.

4. Functional analyses are designed to articulate the purpose of expenditures by sector. They are designed to aid in the analysis of the objectives and functions of the institutional sectors. There are four key classifications suggested by SNA93.

a. The classification of the functions of government (COFOG) articulates fourteen key purposes of government expenditure, like health, education, and social security.

b. The classification of individual consumption by purpose (COICOP) breaks household expenditures down into 10 main purposes (with subcategories) such as housing, transportation, health, education, leisure, and so on.

c. The classification of purposes of nonprofit institutions by purpose (COPNI) articulates eight categories of nonprofit institution (NPI) outlays such as health, education, religious services, welfare services, and so on.

d. Classification of outlays of producers by purpose (COPP) breaks down the outlays of production units into classes such as research and development, repair and maintenance, employee training and welfare, and so on.

5. Employment and population data aligned with SNA concepts means having population data aligned with the national boundaries of the accounting system and definitions of the households sector. It also means aligning employment measures with the production boundary and labor input definition of the product account—key for the purposes of calculating and analyzing productivity trends. The definitions and classifications are outlined in chapter 17 of SNA93.

2.2.3   The Integrated Data System of SNA93

The Sequence Economic Accounts

The accounting model of the 1993 standard traces the transmission of income to wealth using a "sequence of accounts." The building blocks of the sequence of accounts are six major institutional sectors: households and unincorporated businesses,[1] nonprofit institutions serving households, financial corporations, nonfinancial corporations, governments, and nonresidents. The whole economic process from production of income through redistribution of income, consumption, and saving, through accumulation of fixed assets and financial assets, to the position of net worth is recorded for each institutional sector. The major macroeconomic variables are recorded or calculated as balancing items in the sequence of accounts as shown in tables 2.2 and 2.3.

The economic process of production of income, consumption, investment, and creation of wealth is reflected by the structure and the order of the sequence of accounts. Describing the economic process through a sequence of accounts imposes consistency on the data through the series of identities inherent in the system. Table 2.4 presents the main identities of the sequence of accounts.

There are three different views of the GDP aggregate, sum of value added, sum of factor incomes, and sum of final expenditures. There are two views of measuring net lending by sector, the difference of total incomes and total outlays, and the difference in transactions on assets and liabilities. The imposed consistency on the system also allows some variables to be calculated residually rather than directly; for example, savings is the residual of current incomes less consumption or current expenditure, and government deficit is the difference of total incomes and outlays of the government sector. Even detailed variables that are difficult to measure directly from administrative records or by the use of surveys can be derived. For example, inventory investment as measured by national accounting conventions is difficult to measure directly, but in a consistent set of accounts it can be arrived at residually as the difference of supply and use of a commodity. Many aspects of household wealth are also difficult to measure directly because households do not generally keep balance sheet records, but, for example, by exploiting the fundamental balance sheet identity, mortgage lending by financial institutions can be used to measure mortgage borrowing of households.

Macroeconomic analysis is greatly enhanced by the consistency of the integrated system. For example, the labor input variables can be compared to value added to analyze labor productivity trends. Debt burden of households, governments, or businesses can be measured by their debt levels from the balance sheet accounts as a ratio of their total sector income as measured in the distribution of income accounts, and at the same time

1. Unincorporated businesses are grouped with households due to the difficulty of splitting some transactions between the household and business portions. For some accounts, like the production account, it is preferable to separate the sector in two to arrive at a pure "business" sector. But for income generation and distribution accounts it is hard to delineate between the two institutional units.

Table 2.2   The sequence of economic accounts of SNA93

Production accounts: For each institutional sector (except the nonresident sector) the value of output is recorded, and intermediate consumption (goods and services used up in the transformation of inputs to outputs) is subtracted to arrive at the balancing entry for this account—value added. The sum of value added across institutional sectors is equal to the gross domestic product for the economy.

Production of income: In the course of production, the primary inputs, labor and capital, produce income. Wages, salaries, supplementary income, and gross operating surplus are recorded for each sector. The sum of the primary incomes equals value added for each sector, and the sum of all primary incomes across sectors equals gross domestic product.

Primary distribution of income: Property income is income from lending real and financial capital. Primary income is redistributed from one sector to another in this account resulting from payment of interest through financial claims or rents and royalties on use of real property. Total sector income is the sum of primary income plus net property income received. Summation across sectors (including the nonresident sector) of total primary income equals gross national income, after which subtraction of capital consumption allowances derives net national income. This is where the flow of accounts transitions from income generated by domestic production (the domestic concept) to income accruing to residents of the national territory (the national concept).

Secondary distribution of income: In this account pure transfer of incomes across sectors is recorded. Total sector income is the sum of primary income plus net property income received. After deduction of direct taxes paid and social contributions, the balancing item on primary distribution account is disposable income. In the use of income account, current expenditures are also recorded on this account as uses of income. The balancing item on this account is savings; the sum of savings across sectors is national savings. After accounting for capital consumption allowances, the result is net national savings.

Capital accumulation accounts: Net savings from the secondary distribution of income accounts are the starting point of this account as a source of funds for capital accumulation. Depreciation and net capital transfers are added to arrive at total funds available for investment. Fixed capital formation on tangible and intangible assets is recorded as the use of funds to arrive at the net lending/borrowing position of the sector. The sum of net lending/borrowing across sectors balances to zero. Also, the sum of current expenditures from the secondary distribution of income account and capital expenditures on the capital accumulation accounts less imports equals gross domestic product calculated as the sum of final expenditures.

Financial accumulation accounts: Transactions in financial assets and liabilities are recorded for each of the institutional sectors. The balance of net changes in financial assets less changes in net financial liabilities is net changes in financial assets and is equal to net lending/borrowing of the capital accumulation accounts.

Other changes in volume of assets account: This account records holding gains and losses on financial and nonfinancial assets by institutional sectors. It also records destruction of assets due to extraordinary events. Depletion and new discoveries of nonproduced assets are also part of this account. It basically records any change in asset that is not due to a "transaction."

Balance sheet accounts: Closing stocks are recorded here for financial assets and liabilities as well as tangible and intangible nonfinancial assets. Net worth is calculated as the balancing entry for the balance sheet of each institutional sector summing to national net worth across the sectors. National net worth is equal to national net wealth—the sum of the stock of all tangible and intangible fixed assets at market price.

Table 2.3   Summary of accounts and variables

Account	Key variables	Balancing entry
Production accounts	Gross domestic product, output	Value added
Production of income	Labor income, gross operating surplus	Gross domestic product
Primary distribution of income	Labor income, proprietor's income	Gross national income, national disposable income
Secondary distribution of income	Transfer income, consumption expenditures, transfers paid	Net disposable income net saving
Capital accumulation accounts	Gross fixed capital formation, capital transfers, capital consumption allowances	Net lending/borrowing
Financial accumulation accounts	Acquisitions of financial assets, incurrence of financial liabilities	Net financial investment
Other changes in volume of assets account	Revaluations of assets and liabilities, discoveries and destruction of assets	Net other changes in volume of assets
Balance sheet accounts	Gross and net capital stocks, net financial position	National net worth

interest burden ratios can be calculated as the ratio of interest paid to total income recorded in the distribution of income. The return to capital can be measured as a ratio of net operating surplus to the stock real assets. The imposition of common infrastructure (classifications and measurement principles) across all of the sequence of accounts adds explanatory power to the derived aggregates. These ratios are important in understanding the sustainability of the economic functioning of the various sectors.

The integrated system is also an audit and planning tool for the statistical system at its roots. Since the system is put together using a variety of data, both survey and administrative record based, all with varying levels of quality, aggregates derived from more than one approach will never be equal. But a high-quality statistical system will produce results that are within an acceptable range, and the inconsistency can be resolved through a balancing method. For example, SNA93 recommends that the level of GDP be derived using the value-added method or the so-called "production approach" and that the other measures be reconciled by allocating any statistical discrepancy to the lower-quality subaggregates of the income and expenditure methods. The allocation method used will depend on the relative quality of the elements of the statistical base. If the statistical discrepancies are not random but indicate bias, they are often used to identify gaps or emerging measurement issues in the statistical process. Later in the chapter examples of different balancing approaches and how the system has helped identify gaps and measurement problems will be given in the cross-country comparison.

Table 2.4   **The identities of the sequence of accounts**

Production identities

GDP = output – taxes less subsidies on products – intermediate consumption

GDP = final consumption expenditures + changes in inventories + gross fixed capital formation + acquisitions less disposals of valuables + exports of goods and services – imports of goods and services

GDP = compensation of employees + gross operating surplus of corporations + gross mixed Income + taxes less subsidies on products

Income and saving identities

Gross national income (GNI) = GDP + taxes less subsidies on production and imports (net receivable from abroad) + compensation of employees (net receivable from abroad) + property income (net receivable from abroad)

Net national income (NNI) = GNI less consumption of fixed capital

Net national disposable income (NNDI) = NNI + net taxes on income and wealth receivable from abroad + net social contributions and benefits receivable form abroad

Net saving = NNDI – final consumption expenditure + net equity of households on pension funds receivable from abroad + net capital transfers receivable

Net saving + net capital transfers = changes in net worth due to savings and capital transfers The income and savings identities apply to each institutional sector as well as to national estimates by changing the identities to net amounts receivable from other sectors.

Savings and investment identities

Net saving + net capital transfers receivable = gross fixed capital formation + changes in inventories + acquisitions less disposals of valuables and nonproduced nonfinancial assets + net lending/borrowing

Net lending (+)/borrowing (–) = net acquisitions of financial assets less net incurrence of financial liabilities

Wealth identities

Opening net worth = opening assets – opening liabilities

Changes in net worth = changes in net worth due to savings and capital transfers + changes in net worth due to other volume change in assets + changes in net worth due to holding gains or losses

Closing net worth = closing assets – closing liabilities

The "other changes in the volume of assets" account plays a big role in the stock flow consistency of the system. It can be broken down into revaluation accounts and other volume changes in assets. The revaluation account records the holding gains and losses on real and financial assets. Separating the change in wealth into components due to savings and due to holding gains and losses is central to the study of the wealth effect on the behavior of the sectors. In addition, articulating other volume changes in assets like the discovery of unknown mineral reserves or the destruction of an asset due to some catastrophic event are extremely important in the measurement of net worth and its driving factors. As will be seen later in the chapter, this account is undervalued in many national accounts systems and represents an important data gap.

Numeric examples of how the system identities work are available in the SNA93 manual and in a more recent publication by the United Nations (2004) called *National Accounts: A Practical Introduction.*

Supply and Use Tables and Input Output

In addition to the sequence of accounts outlined, the system includes goods and services accounts, supply and use tables, and symmetric input-output tables that provide detailed analysis of industries and products. The tables are, in fact, a breakdown of the production and generation of income accounts. This is the part of the system that reflects the production function at the core of structural and productivity analysis. Table 2.5 is a simplified supply and use table that demonstrates the use of identities to balance the production and the use of products in the system.

The three-way identity of arriving at GDP is tested in the table: sum of value added by industry $(5-1)$ equal to sum of incomes of primary factors of production (6) equals sum of final expenditures on domestic production $(2 + 3 + 4 - 7)$.

The supply and use identity: outputs + imports (supply 5 + 7) = intermediate consumption (by industries) + final consumption + gross fixed capital formation + exports (demand 1 + 2 + 3 + 4)

The dimensionality of the supply and use table is usually rectangular with many more products than industries. The SNA93 recommends the use of the CPC classification, which has 1,800 commodities at its five-digit level, but for countries where less detail is collected, the three-digit level could be used (about 300 product groups). ISIC Rev 3 is recommended for the industry classification. Again, the level of detail will depend on the countries' statistical system, but a reasonable breakdown is considered to be the two-digit level or more (about twenty industries).

The supply and use tables are important statistical tools in the SNA. They are used to test and monitor the quality of the data system used to feed the sequence of accounts. For example, they can be used to

1. Identify gaps, inconsistencies, and valuation problems in the data system
2. Calculate weights for the calculation of price and volume index numbers
3. Estimate variables residually that are not captured in the statistical system for reasons of response burden or expense
4. Benchmark infra-annual data and projection systems to add consistency to short-term indicators

The supply and use tables are also used to calculate symmetric input-output tables, either product by product or industry by industry. These

Table 2.5   **Simplified supply and use tables**

	Products	Industries	Rest of world	Final consumption	Gross capital formation	Total
Products		1. Intermediate consumption	2. Exports	3. Final consumption expenditure	4. Gross capital formation	Total use by product
Industries	5. Output					Total output by industry
Components of value added		6. Value added				
Rest of world	7. Imports					
Total	Total supply	Total inputs by industry				

tables convert the supply and use tables from a statistical tool to an analytic tool. Input-output tables are used to do all sorts of structural analysis and when combined with the rest of the SNA framework are used to do many types of the analyses outlined in table 2.1, which showed the analytic underpinnings of the system of accounts. These include

1. Analysis of production, input structures, and multifactor productivity
2. Analysis of the structural change of components of final demand like consumer spending and investment in fixed capital
3. Analysis of impact of changes in tax rates or tax regimes on products and production
4. Analysis of impacts of changes in regulation in the economy
5. Analysis of impact of changes in technology and/or relative price change
6. And so on

The other major advantage of a set of supply and use tables and input-output tables integrated with the rest of the system is that it provides a basis for many analytic data by-products such as satellite accounts. These are usually aggregations or classifications not readily available in either a standard product or industry classification system but are of great analytic importance. These by-products often relate to activities that cross industry and product boundaries, such as tourism, transportation, communication, or health. They also form a basis for superimposing other related data on the system, such as environmental flows to measure the impact of economy on the environment.

While supply and use data systems are the most data-intensive part of the system, they are the thread that ties the system together and have a big impact on the quality of the system in terms of both statistical integrity and analytic usefulness.

2.2.4 Functional Breakdown of Expenditures and Employment and Population Data

The last two elements of the central framework will not be described in detail here. Their purpose has already been described in the infrastructure section. Functional breakdowns add analytic depth to the purpose of expenditures in the system. For example, the purpose classification of household expenditures allows for analysis of the consumption function in the context of joint consumption (expenditures on cars and repairs grouped together) and of substitution (different modes of transportation grouped together). The alignment of population and employment data with SNA concepts facilitates many types of analysis. The employment data are essential for productivity analysis. While these data elements seem straightforward, in many statistical systems there are more than one estimate of employment—from a household survey and a business survey. Most often neither is aligned with the SNA view of hours worked or the production boundary, and work is required to create one consistent measure.

2.3 A Three-Country Comparison: Australia, Canada, and the United Kingdom

Australia, Canada, and the United Kingdom are examples of countries where the fully integrated SNA93 system has been implemented. In this section, each country's system is described to show how the system has been applied, showing to some extent how the supporting statistical system has influenced the dimensions and detail of each system.

2.3.1 Australia

The Australian System of National Accounts (ASNA) is a prime example of a system that has be designed and implemented on an integrated basis in line with SNA93—but with some differences based on what is most important to user needs and on data availability.[2] The data system is available from 1994–95 forward on a fully integrated SNA93 basis. Many parts of the system exist for longer time series.

The Production and Asset Boundaries

For the ASNA these boundaries are closely aligned with SNA93. The production boundary includes estimates of financial services for which no

2. The information in this section about the ASNA was found on the web site of the Australian Bureau of Statistics (http://www.abs.gov.au) and more specifically in two documents: *Australian National Accounts: Concepts, Sources and Methods* (Australian Bureau of Statistics 2000) and *Measuring Australia's Economy* (Australian Bureau of Statistics 2003).

explicit charge is made, the value of service of owner-occupied housing, and the service provided by homeowners in building or renovating the housing stock. No explicit estimates are made for illegal activity. This is the only exception to the SNA production boundary. The asset boundary is also largely SNA93 compliant, with the exception of the treatment of valuables, which are not as yet included as fixed assets.

Valuation Methods

The valuation methods in the ASNA are those suggested in SNA93. The accounts transactions are measured at market prices including the balance sheets. The input-output and supply and use tables use the basic price valuation as suggested in SNA93.

The ASNA Sequence of Accounts

The ASNA publishes a full sequence of accounts annually, which is a slightly modified version of the international standard. The accounts of the ASNA are as follows:

- The *gross domestic product account* records the value of production (GDP), the income from production, and the final expenditures on goods and services produced. This is a combination of the production account and production of income account of SNA93. These accounts are published by industry for GDP, by factor income type, and by final expenditure category, but not by institutional sector. This is based on the users' key demands for the three breakdowns of GDP but is less of an interest in sectoral analysis of the production account data. Volume and price measures are published based on the final expenditure approach of GDP using an annual chain-Laspeyres index formula method.
- The *income accounts* show primary and secondary income transactions, final consumption expenditures, and consumption of fixed capital. Net saving is the balancing item on this account. The ASNA income account joins the primary and secondary distribution of income accounts of SNA93 into one. These accounts are produced for four major domestic sectors: households (including nonprofit institutions serving households), financial corporations, nonfinancial corporations, and governments.
- The *capital accounts* record the net accumulation of nonfinancial assets and the financing by way of saving and capital transfers. Net lending/borrowing is the balancing item of this account. It is produced for the four domestic sectors just outlined.
- The *financial accounts* show the net acquisition of financial assets and net incurrence of financial liabilities. The balancing item is net financial position, which is equivalent to net lending/borrowing measured

in the capital accounts. This account is also recorded for the four domestic sectors of the economy.

- The *balance sheets* record the stock of assets (financial and nonfinancial) and liabilities at a point in time, and net worth is the balancing item. This account is recorded for the four domestic sectors.
- The *external account* is recorded separately from the sequence of accounts and is published according to the balance of payments manual published by the International Monetary Fund (IMF). It is fully integrated with the SNA in that common variables such as imports, exports, or interest and other income flows are equivalent in both accounts.

This sequence of accounts (missing only the other changes in volume of assets accounts) is published on a *fiscal* year basis annually with about a 150-day lag on the reference period. These are preliminary estimates until the data system matures, with all final data sources available about thirty-six months after the reference period. There are approximately twenty-four tables published that refer to the sequence of accounts, but at the same time about eighty additional tables are published that include detailed disaggregations of the many variables of the system. These include, for example, gross fixed capital formation and capital stocks by type of asset, capital consumption allowances by industry and institutional sector, household expenditure detail, and breakout of government accounts by level of government, to name just a few.

A summary version of the sequence of accounts is also published on a quarterly basis with a sixty-day lag. The quarterly sequence of accounts includes national GDP by expenditure component, projections of value added by industry, and GDP by income type. The constant price estimate of GDP is the expenditure-based GDP using an annually linked chain-Laspeyres measure. The sector accounts include a national account for current and capital accounts and income accounts for the household sector and summary income/capital accounts for the external and government sectors. The quarterly database also includes many detailed breakdowns of expenditures. The data are published on a seasonally adjusted and trend basis in addition to the original unadjusted estimates.

Supply and Use Tables and Input-Output Tables

The ASNA compiles both rectangular supply and use tables used for balancing the system and symmetrical or square industry-by-industry input output tables. The industrial classification used is the Australian and New Zealand Industrial Classification system (ANZIC), which can be concorded to ISIC Rev 3. The commodity classification used is one designed solely for the purpose of compiling input-output and supply/use tables. The input-output and supply/use tables are closely linked. They are produced as follows:

1. The first supply and use tables for any given year are compiled about twelve months after the reference period. The dimensions are some 100 industries by 150 commodity groups. This projected annual supply and use table is used to balance the production accounts of the sequence of accounts, and no statistical discrepancy is ever shown between the three measures of GDP.

2. The "preliminary" supply/use table is compiled within twenty-four months of the reference period and is based on partial benchmark data. The rest of the system is benchmarked to these preliminary data, and therefore the quarterly system is never projected for more than seven quarters.

3. The "final" supply/use tables are produced within thirty-six months of the reference period. These are based on "final" survey and administrative data, which are as complete as the statistical system can provide. The dimensions are some 109 industries by 1,100 commodity groups. The "final" version of the sequence of accounts is benchmarked to this.

4. When and only when the supply/use tables are "final," the industry-by-industry input-output tables are compiled and published. These are symmetrical tables with 109 industries. These are available about four months after the final supply and use tables or about forty months after the reference period. The particular form, industry-by-industry, and the dimensions have been chosen as the best compromise between response burden and analytic use to the tables. These include effects of changes in factor costs, productivity, and incidence of taxes on production and imports and primary input content of demand.

This particular production cycle of supply and use tables for balancing the ASNA with input-output tables available when the data become "final" takes advantage of the fully integrated design of the SNA architecture. It provides users with a consistent set of accounts, balanced with no statistical discrepancies, from the production accounts through to the capital accumulation accounts. Preliminary versions based on projected or incomplete data take advantage of input-output ratios to fill in data gaps.

The final supply/use tables are the most data-intensive part of the system, requiring respondents to fill in outputs and inputs by commodity. The input structure is collected by "establishment," which is the statistical unit based on homogeneous production technology but where full data can still be collected. This means there is primary, secondary, and ancillary production in some units, but data cannot be collected to split inputs by all types of production within an establishment. To minimize response burden and to optimize the usefulness of the data, the Australian Bureau of Statistics has designed a collection strategy that rotates industries in and out of collection on a three- or five-year basis depending on the stability of the input structure. The more rapidly evolving sectors are on the three-year cycle. For each year, about 25 percent of inputs are based on collected data as opposed to imputed or allocated input data. Since the Australian statistical system is centralized, the economic data collection is organized and oriented around the compilation of the accounts both in structure and detail and in timeliness.

Other Features of the ASNA

The integration of supply/use tables with the sequence of accounts provides a balancing tool for the sequence of accounts down to the balancing *item net lending/borrowing* of the *capital accumulation account.* Thus, the net lending/borrowing sums to zero across sectors when the external account is added in. But net lending/borrowing (net financial requirements) is also calculated from the financial accounts. Here a statistical discrepancy is shown in the financial account to equate the two balancing items. For the balance sheet, the household sector is used to balance across sectors for most instrument types due to the fact that direct balance sheet data are not generally available for households but are available for the corporate and government sectors and are collected for the external account.

In addition to the sequence of accounts, the functional breakdowns of the SNA93 architecture are available in the detailed expenditure tables of both the annual and quarterly sequence of accounts. Also, *productivity accounts* are compiled as part of the ASNA database—including the labor input as specified in SNA93.

Finally, regional or state-level production accounts are also a feature of the ASNA with some other key variables, like household and some government-sector income accounts available at the state level.

2.3.2   United Kingdom

The accounts of the United Kingdom are another example of a complete and fully integrated set of accounts.[3] The design and form of the U.K. accounts conform to the European System of Accounts (ESA95), which is a version of SNA93 written specifically for the member countries of the European Union. The ESA95 is fully consistent with SNA93. It does, however, add more precision to some aspects of SNA93 that take the form of recommendations with alternative solutions. ESA95 attempts to standardize the measurement of the SNA aggregates because they are used for the calculation of contributions to the European Union and for the monitoring of the complete European Union economy. In 1998 the United Kingdom completed a set of accounts based on the ESA95. This included completion of a longer project whereby the distributed statistical system was

---

3. The information in this section about the U.K. national accounts was found on the web site of the U.K. National Statistics Office (http://www.statistics.gov.uk) and more specifically from the following two documents: *United Kingdom National Accounts: The Blue Book 2003* (U.K. National Statistics Office 2003a) and *United Kingdom National Accounts: Concepts, Sources and Methods* (U.K. National Statistics Office 2003b).

centralized over a ten-year period. This has meant that some parts of the SNA that were previously published by other institutions are now all the responsibility of the Office of National Statistics (ONS). For example, financial accounts, balance sheets, and balance-of-payment statistics were previously published by the Bank of England.

The Production and Asset Boundaries

These boundaries are closely aligned with SNA93/ESA95 for the United Kingdom. The production boundary includes estimates of financial services for which no explicit charge is made, the value of service of owner-occupied housing. No explicit estimates are made for illegal activity, but there is extensive work done on "exhaustiveness" to account for under-reporting and data gaps. Valuation of illegal activities is being worked on at the European level by Eurostat. In employing the production boundary for households producing goods for own use, by convention, only own-account construction of housing and production of agricultural goods are included. Anything else is deemed to be insignificant.

The asset boundary is also largely SNA93 compliant, including its treatment of valuables as fixed assets. The ESA95 rule for "small tools" is employed, excluding any transactions on purchases less than 500 euros, even though it may be used in the production process for more than one year.

Valuation Methods

The valuation methods in the U.K. SNA are those suggested in SNA93 and ESA95. The sequence of accounts transactions are measured at market prices, including the balance sheets. The input-output and supply and use tables use the basic price valuation.

The U.K. Sequence of Accounts

The United Kingdom publishes a full sequence of accounts annually, which is a slightly modified version of the international standard but compliant with ESA95. The sequence of accounts as follows is produced for the four domestic sectors—nonfinancial corporations, financial corporations, governments, and households and nonprofit institutions—and the external sector wherever relevant:

- The *goods and services account* is an aggregate supply and use table constructed for each institutional sector. It records the value of output at basic prices plus imports as resources (or supply), and intermediate use, consumption, investment, government expenditure and exports of commodities as use (or demand). It presents GDP at basic prices by sector, and then by adding net taxes on products and imports it also presents GDP at market prices. Volume and price measures are published based on the "final expenditures" approach to GDP using the annual chain-Laspeyres index formula.

- The *generation of income accounts* record the uses of GDP at market prices by type of factor income.
- The *allocation of primary income accounts* show primary incomes by type as resources for each sector.
- The *secondary distribution of income account* shows the redistribution of income through transfers across sectors as sources and payments of taxes and social contributions as uses to arrive at disposable income by sector.
- The *redistribution of income in kind account* shows the income in kind produced by each sector and who it is used by sector added to the disposable income of each sector.
- The *use of income account* shows consumption spending by sector out of disposable income and the adjustment for net equity of pension funds. Net saving is the balancing item on this account.
- *The acquisition of nonfinancial capital accounts* record the net accumulation of nonfinancial assets and the financing by way of saving and capital transfers. Net lending/borrowing is the balancing item of this account. It is produced for the four domestic sectors outlined previously and net lending for the external sector.
- The *financial accounts* show the net acquisition of financial assets and net incurrence of financial liabilities. The balancing item is net financial position, which is equivalent to net lending/borrowing measured in the capital accounts. This account is also recorded for the four domestic sectors of the economy.
- The *balance sheets* record the stock of assets (financial and nonfinancial) and liabilities at a point in time, and net worth is the balancing item. This account is recorded for the four domestic sectors.

This particular view of the sequence of accounts—shown for both the *resources* and the *uses* view of each account—is the ESA95 suggested presentation. Although ESA95 suggests splitting off the nonprofit institutions serving households as a sector unto itself, this is not currently done for the U.K. accounts. The sequence of accounts is first published about six months after the reference period based on preliminary data. The accounts are revised every year for the subsequent three years.

A summary version of the sequence of accounts, with the main macro variables and sector balances with sector detail for households, governments, and the external account, is published quarterly with about a fifty-five-day lag after the reference quarter. In addition, a flash estimate of GDP is published about forty days after the reference quarter.

Detailed expenditures of households by purpose (COICOP based) and government expenditure by function (COFOG) are also available, as well as expenditure by asset type.

Input-Output and Supply/Use Tables

For the United Kingdom the supply and use tables and the input-output tables are square with the same dimensionality. The supply/use tables balance the production account for 123 industries based on the NACE Rev 1 classification system (the European industry classification system, equivalent to about ISIC level 2 industries) and 123 products based on the CPA (the European product classification system). The symmetrical input-output tables are published on a product-by-product basis for the 123 products. This dimensionality and format (product-by-product input-output tables) is based on the ESA95 recommendation of using NACE at the two-digit level and CPA at the three-digit level. Most of the published supply/use and input-output tables for European countries have roughly the same dimensionality—slightly over 100 industries and commodities—following the ESA95 recommendation.

The supply and use tables are used to balance the production account. They are produced at the time of the first full annual, about eighteen months after the reference year. This means that there are no statistical discrepancies in the sequence of accounts for all of the years for which supply/use and input-output are available. The data for the supply and use tables are based on the Annual Business Enquiry, which builds estimates for all industries while using a subsample of each industry to collect data on inputs. The data collected are summary detail (not full commodity detail; therefore, the double deflation technique is not used to calculate deflated value added by industry), but the summary detail is available for all industries.

Other Features of the U.K. SNA

The full sequence of accounts is published annually in a publication called the *Blue Book,* which covers about ten years of data (available on the internet and in a printed version). The fully integrated database exists back to 1994, but many important variables such as constant price GDP are available for longer time series.

In the *Blue Book,* the sequence of accounts is published for subsector detail as well as for the financial corporate sector and for the government sector. Transparency is a key factor in the U.K. approach to balancing and publishing of data. For the supply/use tables a series of coherence adjustments are published to show how the equality of supply and demand was achieved. When the sequence of accounts is published, these adjustments are split out by sector and published as statistical adjustments necessary to offset the balancing adjustments of the production account. This process means that no statistical discrepancies exist up to the balancing item of net lending/borrowing in the sequence of accounts—but statistical discrepancies still exist between net lending/borrowing and net financial requirements on the financial account. The whole balancing approach for the U.K. accounts is described in detail in the "Concepts, Sources, and Methods" section, also published on the National Statistical Office (NSO) web site (http://www.statistics.gov.uk).

As part of the publication of the supply and use tables, employment and capital stocks consistent with the U.K. accounts are also published on a by-industry basis for productivity analysis.

2.3.3 Canada

The Canadian System of National Accounts (CSNA) is another example of a highly integrated system of accounts based on the SNA93 standard.[4] The Canadian approach has a quarterly emphasis, the sequence of accounts being published on a quarterly basis. The supply/use and input-output tables have an important regional dimension, which is motivated in part by administrative use of the supply/use system to allocate a value-added tax system that is administered at the Canada level but harmonized with regional indirect taxes in specific regions. This administrative use means that the supply/use tables are produced on a regional basis to arrive at national supply/use tables. This imposes a cost in the form of a loss of timeliness and increased cost of data collection, as surveys are designed to produce consistent quality of value added across all regions of Canada. The Canadian system is also based on a highly centralized statistical system. The economics data system, surveys, and national accounts were designed based on the integrated framework of the 1968 system of accounts. The economic survey and administrative data collection systems have been designed and modified over the years to feed the CSNA. The CSNA is used as a quality check tool on the data collection system. The data sources are constantly monitored, and changes are applied in concert with the CSNA.

The Production and Asset Boundaries

These boundaries are closely aligned with SNA93 for Canada. The production boundary includes estimates of financial services for which there is no explicit charge and the value of service of owner-occupied housing. No imputation is made for the labor portion of own-account fixed investment by households (renovation and self home construction). Only the material portion is capitalized at present. No explicit estimates are made for illegal activity other than tobacco smuggling. Work on valuation of illegal activities is currently under review. In employing the production boundary for households producing goods for own use, by convention, only own-

---

4. The information in this section about the CSNA can be found on the Statistics Canada web site (http://www.statcan.ca/english/freepub/13-010-XIE); click on "more information" for sources and methods documents. This electronic publication is called the *Canadian Economic Accounts Quarterly Review.*

account construction of housing and production of agricultural goods are included. Anything else is deemed to be insignificant.

The asset boundary is also largely SNA93 compliant except for treatment of valuables as fixed assets. No thresholds are applied in the capitalization of fixed assets. Anything used in the production process over one year is included.

Valuation Methods

The valuation methods in the CSNA are slightly different from those suggested in SNA93. The sequence-of-accounts transactions are measured at market prices, including GDP and balance sheets, which were converted to full market value by the end of 2004 (previously measured as a mixture of market and book value). The input-output and supply and use tables use a modified basic price valuation for balancing purposes, which is a purchase price valuation by industry and product. When value added by industry is published, it is converted to the basic price concept recommended in SNA93.

The CSNA Sequence of Accounts

The CSNA publishes a full sequence of accounts quarterly, which is a slightly modified version of the international standard. The accounts of the CSNA are as follows:

- The *gross domestic product account,* which records the value of production (GDP), the income from production, and the final expenditures on goods and services produced. This is a combination of the production account and production of income accounts of SNA93. These accounts are also published monthly for value added by Industry but only in the form of chain linked value added, adjusted for inflation. No sector detail is available for the GDP account except for a business/nonbusiness split used in the production of labor and multifactor productivity estimates. Volume and price measures are published based on the final expenditure approach of GDP using the quarterly chain-linked Fisher index formula method.
- The *income and outlay accounts,* which show primary and secondary income transactions, final consumption expenditures, and consumption of fixed capital. Net saving is the balancing item on this account. The CSNA income account joins the primary and secondary distribution of income accounts of SNA93 into one. These accounts are produced for four major sectors: households (including nonprofit institutions serving households), corporations, governments, and the external sector.
- The *capital accounts,* which record the net accumulation of nonfinancial assets and the financing by way of saving and capital transfers. Net lending/borrowing is the balancing item of this account. It is produced

for the five sectors. In addition to the sectors outlined, the corporate sector is split into financial and nonfinancial corporations.

- The *financial accounts,* which show the net acquisition of financial assets and net incurrence of financial liabilities. The balancing item is net financial position, which is equivalent to net lending/borrowing measured in the capital accounts. This account is also recorded for the five sectors of the economy. In addition, financial accounts are published for thirty-five detailed subsectors.
- The *balance sheets,* which record the stock of assets (financial and nonfinancial) and liabilities at a point in time; net worth is the balancing item. This account is recorded for the five major sectors on a quarterly basis. In addition, financial accounts are published for thirty-five detailed subsectors, but only on an annual basis.

This sequence of accounts (missing only the other changes in volume of assets accounts) is published up to the financial accounts with the GDP release with about a sixty-day lag on the reference quarter. The balance sheets are published quarterly with a ninety-day lag. While the GDP account is fully reconciled with the supply/use and input-output system, the Canadian approach to balancing the sequence of accounts is different from that of other countries. As many as twelve preliminary quarters could be available before a supply/use balance is available. None of the three measures of GDP is deemed to be the most accurate in the preliminary system. The final expenditure approach and the income approach are calculated independently (at market prices) and an average is published showing a statistical discrepancy of equal and opposite sign on each account. The final expenditure approach is then deflated, and the monthly GDP deflated value added by industry at basic prices is adjusted to use the more complete information of the quarterly final expenditure approach but not entirely "reconciled." The discrepancies of the income and expenditure approach are not allocated among sectors, meaning that the net lending/borrowing of the economy across domestic sectors and the external account does not sum to zero. A separate discrepancy is also shown between the net lending/borrowing balances for the income and outlay accounts and the financial accounts. The Canadian approach is to correct data gaps and discrepancies that are specifically identifiable but to leave the basic data unadjusted to the extent that the discrepancies are not resolvable. Even after the GDP accounts have been reconciled to the supply/use tables a small discrepancy remains, as the GDP account publishes survey-based inventory change and operating surplus, which are derived residually in the supply/use system. The system then is reconciled and released on a fully consistent basis with smaller statistical discrepancies than in the preliminary years.

There is one major inconsistency in the Canadian sequence of accounts. The consumption of fixed capital recorded for corporations in the sequence of accounts is taken directly from business accounting records, measured based on a mixture of historical cost and book value. The capital stocks recorded on the balance sheet for the corporate sector are derived from a perpetual inventory model in which the stocks are valued at current replacement cost and the consumption of fixed capital inherent in the net stock value is a current value measure. In addition, a third capital stock measure is calculated for the purposes of measuring multifactor productivity. This is an area where the Canadian system needs further work to clean up the inconsistency.

Supply/Use and Input-Output Tables

As mentioned earlier, the supply/use tables are the statistical tool used to balance the production account but are also an important administrative tool used to allocate value-added tax collections between the federal and provincial governments. This determines the level of detail in terms of both geography and commodity dimensions. The supply/use tables for Canada are rectangular and balanced for 301 industries using the North American Industrial Classification System (NAICS) and 727 commodities using a product classification system unique to the Canadian input-output tables. Symmetrical input-output tables (coefficients) are published on an industry-by-industry basis for the 300 industries from the supply/use tables. The industry-by-industry configuration was chosen for the same reason as for the Australian accounts, so that no simplifying assumptions are made in going from the industry technology known from collecting data at the establishment level, as would be the case for separating secondary activities from industries to arrive at commodity-by-commodity tables.

This supply/use balancing is compiled annually for thirteen regions of Canada (provinces and territories) and forms the benchmark for GDP for the sequence of national accounts mentioned above. (The sequence of accounts is also published by province for the GDP, household, and government sectors up to net lending/borrowing.) This process, from data collection to the production of the tables, takes about three years for the preliminary version and four years for the final version. The additional detail of the Canadian system imposes an additional year in the finalizing of the sequence of the accounts relative to most other countries. Work is being done to upgrade the timeliness of this part of the system, and experimental work is also being done to produce preliminary versions of supply/use similar to those produced in Australia and the United Kingdom.

Other Features of the CSNA

Detailed breakdowns of household expenditure (COICOP) and capital expenditure are published as part of the sequence of accounts. No breakdown of government expenditure by function consistent with the CSNA is available, but one will be when Statistics Canada completes the production of government financial statistics based on the GFS2001 manual published by the IMF within the next few years.

As part of the CSNA, quarterly labor productivity data are published for the "business" sector (corporations plus unincorporated business) about ten days after the quarterly GDP release. Multifactor productivity measures are also published annually for the business sector, as are the labor and capital services data used to calculate them (consistent with the CSNA). Productivity analysis is only published for the business sector because the output of the nonbusiness sector is still only measured by deflating inputs used for nonbusiness GDP, assuming no change in productivity.

Annual data on purchasing power parities are also published as part of the CSNA based on the Organisation for Economic Co-operation and Development (OECD) benchmarks available every three years (volume indexes for GDP and prices comparisons at the GDP level and for final expenditure components). A more detailed bilateral purchasing power parity database is done for the Canada–United States comparison as demanded by the key users of the CSNA.

2.4 Summary and Conclusions

The three countries compared in this paper, Australia, Canada, and the United Kingdom, all produce a highly integrated set of accounts, which greatly facilitates consistent analysis of the economy by their domestic users and across international comparisons. Three important elements of commonality are that all three countries' systems are based on highly centralized statistical systems, all have a long track record of producing national accounts estimates, and all three countries include the balance-of-payments statistics as part of the SNA accounting system.

In each case, the balancing of the sequence of accounts is achieved using the supply/use framework as suggested in SNA93. For Australia and the United Kingdom this is a relatively new feature of the system, brought in when implementing SNA93. For Canada, the supply/use framework has been used as the official GDP benchmark of the system of accounts since 1986, and supply/use has been published annually back to 1961. Where the countries differ the most is in how the identities are used to balance the system. In both the United Kingdom and Australia, the supply and use identities are used to eliminate all discrepancies up to and including the measure of net lending/borrowing in the sequence of accounts. This is done by allocating all final demand and factor incomes in the supply/use tables and using the same estimates in other parts of the system. In Canada, the supply/use framework is based on data built from establishment-based data sources, and the institutional sector data are built from institutional unit data. The supply/use determines the level of GDP, but the variables corporate surplus and inventory change are not fully reconciled with the data from the institutional unit–based sources (this largely relates to enterprise- versus establishment-based corporate-sector data). A statistical discrepancy is shown between final expenditure-based GDP and factor income–based GDP splitting the difference between the two measures. All countries record statistical discrepancies between the net lending/borrowing and financial requirements. The advantage of leaving statistical discrepancies is in keeping track of issues in the statistical feeder system and keeping track of quality changes from preliminary to fully benchmarked estimates. This way the system of accounts can be used to monitor the quality of the statistical data used to feed it.

While each country largely follows SNA93, the application does differ across the three countries. The sequence of accounts is presented quite differently in each case—while the major analytic aggregates such as GDP, savings, investment, consumption, net lending/borrowing, and wealth are all presented. The U.K. presentation of the flow of accounts is the most akin to the SNA93 suggested presentation. Australia has a modified flow of accounts, but one consistent presentation. In Canada the parts of the sequence are all published as separate products, making it more difficult for the user to identify the integrated nature of the various products. This will be a key focus for Canada in the upcoming years in presenting the data to users in a more integrated way.

The slight differences in application of production boundary (and in likely methodology for some aspects of the accounting system) and valuation reflect what is significant for that particular economy. Some of the differences are based on the history of the accounts prior to the SNA93 standard and what the users were accustomed to as well as the data sources available. To what extent these differences affect international comparability is difficult to assess. Even areas where the apparent application of the standard is the same, methodologies or classifications of similar entities can differ. This is where international coordination plays a key role in helping to add consistency to the various systems of accounts. The adherence to ESA95 across the European Union adds discipline to the application of the standard in that ESA95 attempts to put clarity to all of the "borderline" issues related to compiling a set of accounts.

Tables 2.6 and 2.7 summarize the key features of the three-country comparison.

While a detailed comparison of the U.S. components of the national accounts has not been done as part of this chapter, the National Income and Product Accounts (NIPAs) have been compared to the SNA structure in a recent paper called "The NIPAs and the System of National Accounts" published in the December 2004 *Survey of Current Business* (Mead, Moses, and Moulton 2004). In addition, Teplin et al. (chap. 11 in this volume) presents a proposed set of integrated accounts for the United States based on the SNA93 flow of accounts and sectoring. For the countries compared in

Table 2.6   Sequence of accounts comparison

	Canada	Australia	United Kingdom
Supply and use tables	301 industry × 727 commodity Annual $t-3$	109 industry × 1,100 commodity Annual $t-3$ 100 industry × 150 commodity Preliminary $t-2$, $t-1$	123 × 123 square industry supply/use tables Preliminary and final $t-2$, $t-1$
Input/output tables	301 industry × 727 commodity Rectangular commodity Annual $t-3$	109 × 109 square industry × industry Annual $t-2$	123 × 123 square industry × industry Annual $t-2$
GDP × sector	None	5 sectors[a] Annual $t-1$	5 sectors[a] Annual $t-1$
Primary and secondary distribution of income	4 sectors[b] One joint distribution of income account Quarterly (60-day lag)	5 sectors[c] One joint distribution of income account Annual and partial quarterly (60-day lag)	5 sectors[d] Primary and secondary income distribution accounts Annual and partial quarterly (60-day lag)
Financial accounts	35 sectors Quarterly (60-day lag)	5 sectors Annual (90-day lag)	5 sectors Annual and partial quarterly
Revaluation and CVCA			
Balance sheets	35 sectors Annual (90-day lag) 5 sectors Quarterly (90-day lag)	5 sectors Annual (90-day lag)	5 sectors Annual and partial quarterly

Note: OVCA = other volume changes in assets.

[a]The sectors are households and nonprofit institutions, financial corporations, nonfinancial corporations, governments, and rest-of world.

[b]The sectors are households and nonprofit institutions, corporations, governments, and rest of world.

[c]The sectors are the same as for GDP by sector in footnote 1 above.

[d]The sectors are the same as for GDP by sector in footnote 1 above.

Table 2.7   **Boundaries and valuation comparisons**

	Canada	Australia	United Kingdom
Production boundary	FISIM Some illegal exhaustiveness	FISIM No illegal	FISIM No illegal exhaustiveness
Asset boundary	No valuables Software and E&D	No valuables Software and E&D	Valuables Software and E&D Small tools threshold
Valuation methods	GDP at basic and market price IO at purchaser price Assets at mixed market/book value	GDP at basic and market price IO at purchaser price Assets at market value	GDP at basic and market price IO at purchaser price Assets at market value
Classifications	NAICS IO products	ANZIC IO products	NACE CPA

Notes: FISIM = financial intermediation services indirectly measured; E&D = exploration and development; GDP = gross domestic product; IO = input-output; NAICS = North American Industrial Classification System; ANZIC = Australia and New Zealand Industrial Classification; NACE = the industrial classification used by the European Union member countries; CPA = the product classification used by the European Union member countries.

this study, a recent phenomenon of the corporate sectors' amassing large accumulated net lending positions (surpluses) and using those surpluses to restructure balance sheets has been a very marked trend. In the current NIPAs, no measure of corporate net lending is published in order to examine this phenomenon for the United States. Evidence appears to be emerging in the "flow of funds" accounts published by the Federal Reserve Board that this trend is also emerging in the United States. The work done in the chapter by Teplin et al. shows how net lending for U.S. corporations would be presented along with the financial accounts to explicitly show how surplus funds are used to restructure balance sheets.

In all countries included in this comparison, the users are well served by a system of national accounts that is consistent and virtually complete. The statistical systems take full advantage of using the SNA as a tool for validating and augmenting the survey and administrative data systems. This helps keep the data relevant and maintains the quality of the system.

The system of accounts was designed to facilitate the analysis of the macroeconomic process from the creation of income via production through to changes in wealth and to provide detailed information on the evolution of the economy in terms of the structure of production and spending and the uses of primary factors of production. The SNA93 has achieved the buy-in of the international community as the tool for building the statistical database.

References

Australian Bureau of Statistics. 2000. *Australian national accounts: Concepts, sources and Methods.* Canberra: Australian Bureau of Statistics.
————. 2003. *Measuring Australia's economy.* 7th ed. Canberra: Australian Bureau of Statistics.
Mead, Charles L., Karin Moses, and Brent Moulton. 2004. The NIPAs and the System of National Accounts. *Survey of Current Business* 84 (December): 17–32.
U.K. National Statistics Office. 2003a. *United Kingdom national accounts: The blue book 2003.* London: National Statistics Office.
————. 2003b. *United Kingdom national accounts: Concepts, sources and methods.* London: National Statistics Office.
United Nations. 1968. *A system of national accounts.* Studies in Methods, series F, no. 2, rev. 3. New York: United Nations.
————. 2004. *National accounts: A practical introduction; Handbook of national accounting.* New York: United Nations.
United Nations, Commission of the European Communities, International Monetary Fund, Organisation for Economic Co-operation and Development, and World Bank. 1993. *System of national accounts 1993.* Series F, no. 2, rev. 4. New York: United Nations.

3

Principles of National Accounting
For Nonmarket Accounts

William D. Nordhaus

3.1 Background and Purpose

The purpose of this essay is to sketch the major principles that might be used in the design and implementation of a set of augmented national accounts. By *augmented accounts* I mean an integrated set of accounts for both market and nonmarket economic activity. Since the major missing components of a set of augmented accounts are nonmarket in nature, I focus primarily on those activities. This note builds on the principles developed for environmental accounts in *Nature's Numbers* (Nordhaus and Kokkelenberg 2000) and fills in some of the gaps for other sectors.

Augmented accounts should be designed to follow two general principles: First, they should address the major conceptual issues by measuring income and output in ways that best correspond to net economic welfare. Second, they should include both market and nonmarket activities.

Augmented accounts are designed to illuminate that part of human economic activity that takes place outside the market place and/or outside the core national economic accounts. Some of the important areas include natural resources, unpaid work, investment in education and health, and the environment.

William D. Nordhaus is Sterling Professor of Economics at Yale University and a research associate of the National Bureau of Economic Research.

The author is grateful for comments by Katharine Abraham, Chris Mackie, and Robert Mendelsohn. This paper is an expanded version of one prepared for the National Research Council (NRC) panel "Designing Nonmarket Accounts for the United States," drawing on the lessons learned from the NRC study *Nature's Numbers: Expanding the National Economic Accounts to Include the Environment* (Nordhaus and Kokkelenberg 2000). The report of the NRC panel is contained in Abraham and Mackie (2005), but the analysis of that report is not reflected in the current analysis.

Before getting down to details, I must emphasize that, while nonmarket and environmental accounts can form an important addition to our understanding of economic activity, they are not ready for center stage. It would not be advisable to incorporate further major nonmarket activities into the core National Income and Product Accounts at this time. Nor can we sensibly recommend that the state of nonmarket accounts is more than experimental in the United States at this time. However, it would be sensible to set as a goal of the U.S. statistical system to develop satellite nonmarket accounts in different areas in the years ahead.

3.2   Fundamental Accounting Framework

The first question raised in the practical construction of any accounting system concerns the accounting framework. The natural starting point for augmented accounts, and the one that in my view will best withstand careful scrutiny, is to use the economic principles underlying the national economic accounts (called here "NEA design"). These accounts include a full set of current and capital accounts along with the accounts linking the current and capital accounts where that is possible.

The rationale for using NEA design as the jumping-off point for nonmarket accounts is based on two fundamental advantages. First, NEA design has been the subject of extensive research and practical experience for many decades. The principles of the NEA have been carefully thought out; practice has shown that they can be implemented; and they have a rough correspondence with economic welfare. Second, many questions of augmented accounts have counterparts and therefore answers in the NEA design, so they can serve as a point of departure for augmented accounts design.

Although the general principles of NEA accounting are straightforward, in fact, there are several different models, and actual practice differs among different systems.

1. One set of accounts is the national income and product accounts (NIPAs) and satellite environmental accounts of the United States. This is probably the best-known set of accounts and could usefully serve as a model. They are, however, at this time incomplete in certain respects, and nonmarket accounts should incorporate current principles.

2. There are two versions of the internationally developed System of National Accounts (SNA), the latest being 1993.[1] The major feature of the SNA is that it contains multiple sets of accounts linking production, income, consumption, accumulation, and wealth. The integrated feature of

1. The System of National Accounts, or SNA, developed under the aegis of the United Nations and other international agencies, is a set of concepts, definitions, classifications, and accounting rules. The latest SNA is from 1993 and can be found at http://esa.un.org/unsd/sna1993/introduction.asp. The United States has adopted most of the principles in the SNA.

the SNA is a goal of the U.S. accounts, is a desirable feature, and should be a key element in the development of a set of nonmarket accounts.

3. The Jorgensonian set of accounts is closely related to the SNA in developing an integrated set of accounts. The Jorgensonian accounts include nonmarket elements and an extensive set of imputations; they do not yet include a set of environmental or externality accounts.[2]

4. There are additionally several partial accounts that have been developed in different sectors. The accounts developed for natural resources and the environment have been surveyed in the Academy report *Nature's Numbers* (Nordhaus and Kokkelenberg 2000).

In considering augmented accounts design, the major issues concern the following: (a) adjustments to the NEA design that would be desirable to make augmented accounts conform more closely to a measure of economic welfare, (b) adjustments, additions, and subtractions that would be necessary to include nonmarket activities, and (c) the boundary of nonmarket accounts.

3.2.1   Adjustments Necessary to Conform to Measure of Economic Welfare

"Output" and "income" in economic accounts should, in general, be designed to measure concepts that are consistent with economic welfare. There are many areas where current NEA design does not adequately or properly reflect economic welfare. One obvious example is the focus on gross domestic product, gross domestic income, and other measures of gross output rather than net output and income. Adjusting income and output measures to a net basis is today relatively straightforward, although there are necessarily ambiguities at the margin.

Many other examples of adjustments necessary to conform to economic welfare involve the division of gross output between intermediate products and final products. For example, the U.S. NIPAs today include military expenditures in final output, while the first national accounts included only civilian output. Similar questions arise for expenditures on police, security, and pollution control, which might be classified as "defensive" rather than final expenditures.

In part, the need for rethinking the definition of output arises because nonmarket accounts might choose to tailor their design to economic welfare rather than, as in the NEA, primarily as a measure of current production and income. More important in this context is that we include

---

2. The Jorgenson set of accounts is described in Barbara Fraumeni's "The Jorgenson System of National Accounting" (1999). This overview provides a good description of the underlying philosophy. Note that the major difference between these accounts and the SNA is the extensive use of imputations of income and output from capital stocks as well as the development of extensive nonmarket accounts.

instrumental expenditures because the goods or services to which they are devoted are either nonmarket activities or imperfectly measured and are excluded from the core accounts. For example, if losses from burglary were part of the nonmarket accounts, then both those losses and home-security expenditures could be excluded from final product; then an expenditure on home security that reduced burglary losses by the same amount would be correctly treated as a zero change in net welfare. Similar issues arise with respect to pollution-control expenditures and the nonmarket impacts of pollution.

3.2.2 Adjustments, Additions, and Subtractions That Would Be Necessary to Include Nonmarket Activities

The next issue concerns the appropriate treatment of nonmarket activities. It should be noted that the accounts already include a substantial value of such activities, including owner-occupied housing and food consumed on farms. A natural principle for treating nonmarket activity is the following:

Basic principle for measuring nonmarket activity. Nonmarket goods and services should be treated as if they were produced and consumed as market activities. Under this convention, the prices of nonmarket goods and services should be imputed on the basis of the comparable market goods and services.

For example, if households gather ten pints of berries in the national forests, then the price attributed to that activity should be the price of berries of equivalent quality in that location. There may be formidable practical issues in implementing this fundamental principle, but the underlying logic is clear.

Near-Market Goods and Services

One important distinction in this regard is whether or not goods and services are "near-market." A *near-market* good or service is one that has a direct counterpart in the market (firewood, berries, owner-occupied housing, and homegrown tomatoes). Near-market goods and services obey the "third-party rule," which states that a third party could produce the good or service just as well as the party that produces the item.

Personal Goods and Services

The complementary case has no name but might be called *personal* goods and services, indicating that these items can only be produced by the consumer. Personal goods and services do not obey the third-party rule. Their prices cannot be observed because no transactions occur in markets, although behavioral traces of the valuation of personal goods can be found in household decisions. The clearest example of a personal commodity is leisure time; no one can produce leisure for me. There are no market transactions for personal goods and services, and we must rely upon imputed or implicit prices. For the case of leisure, we normally impute its value by assuming that individuals optimize their time use, which ordinarily implies that the value of leisure is the individual's after-tax marginal wage rate. (I return to this issue below.)

There are no major conceptual differences between near-market and personal goods. Rather, the implication of this distinction is the practical one that estimation of the value of personal nonmarket goods may be extremely difficult because there are no transactions and no market standards.

Public versus Private Goods

The other important distinction that will require analysis in an accounting context is between private and public goods and services (in the Samuelsonian sense). *Private* goods and services are ones that can be divided up and provided separately to different individuals, with no external benefits or costs to others. An example is bread. Ten loaves of bread can be divided up in many ways among individuals, and what one person eats cannot be eaten by others. Private goods are straightforward for economic accounting and are central to the theory behind the NEA. There are no conceptual changes that are necessary to include nonmarket private goods (either near-market or personal).

Public goods and services, by contrast, are ones whose benefits are indivisibly spread among the entire community, whether or not individuals desire to purchase them. An example is smallpox eradication. It matters not at all whether one is old or young, rich or poor, American scientist or African farmer—one will benefit from the eradication whether one wants to or not.

A major issue for nonmarket accounts, particularly environmental accounts, is the treatment of public goods (or goods with externalities). This is one area where I would suggest a revision in the treatment as compared to standard national accounting. It should be noted that public goods are already in the accounts, but there are conceptual difficulties that arise in their treatment in a complete set of accounts. There are two interesting cases: case 1, public goods where the flows are completely in the market accounts; and case 2, public goods where some of the flows are in the nonmarket sectors.

Case 1 (flows in the market sector). There are already many cases of externalities wholly in the accounts. One example is air pollution and agriculture. Suppose pollution by chemical firm A has the sole effect of reducing the production of corn of farm firm B by $100. The entire impact of the activity is in the market accounts, even though there are no market trans-actions between the two firms.

The major issue here is whether we would want to reallocate or unpack the transactions into two offsetting transactions in a process I call *external-ity disaggregation*. In this case, firm A provides an input into firm B with a value of minus $100, and firm B provides an implicit transfer or subsidy to firm A of $100. There would be no effect of this disaggregation on net out-put of the market sector, although the value added of the chemical and farming sector would change. These transactions might be illuminating in providing estimates of the size of the implicit subsidies or if the total value added of particular industries were significantly changed. It would be inter-esting to know, for example, the size and sign of the net output of the coal and tobacco industries if externality disaggregation were to take place.

Case 2 (flows cross the market boundary). The second case is more signifi-cant for overall flows and for the measurement of market output and in-come. This occurs when only part of the transactions takes place inside the market place. An example is industrial air pollution. Here, externality dis-aggregation might find that air pollution in the United States represented a minus $100 billion per year negative input from the industrial sector (power plants, etc.) into the nonmarket accounts of the household sector in damages to nonmarket activity or reduction in nonmarket output. The counterpart transaction would be a $100 billion per year implicit transfer or subsidy from the nonmarket accounts of the household sector to the in-dustrial sector.

It should be noted that an accounting analog to externality disaggrega-tion already exists in the accounts for some taxes. In these cases, the pro-ducer prices differ from the consumer prices, with the difference explicitly recognized on the income side as "taxes on production and imports less subsidies" (formerly, indirect business taxes). With externality disaggrega-tion, the balancing item would be implicit subsidies. There is also a ques-tion as to whether net output would be calculated with or without the im-plicit subsidy; this also has a parallel in the accounts in the question of whether to measure national income at market prices or factor costs.

Note that externality disaggregation in case 2 changes the value added of both the market accounts and the nonmarket accounts, while leaving unchanged the output and income of the aggregated market and nonmar-ket accounts. By contrast, proper accounting in case 1 does not change the values in any of these three major aggregates. While it is illuminating but not necessary to undertake externality disaggregation for case 1 (when the externality is confined to a particular component of the total accounts), it is definitely necessary for accurate accounting to undertake externality dis-aggregation for case 2, where the externality crosses the border between market and nonmarket sectors.

3.2.3 Border Disputes

The boundary of the market accounts is in principle clear: it involves goods and services that are transacted in markets. Probably the most difficult issue in design of augmented accounts is where to draw the border. Should they include only near-market goods? All nonmarket goods? Public goods? Global public goods? Intangible assets as well as tangible assets? The costs of crime and AIDS? The value of life, liberty, and the Constitution?

There are no clear-cut answers to these questions, but the following principles may help sort of the priorities. First, it should be emphasized that the purpose of nonmarket accounts is not to develop "accounts of everything." Rather, the purpose is to include activities that are economic in nature and those that substitute for market activities. This would suggest that unpaid work and nonmarket time devoted to research, education, and training are important targets for nonmarket accounts. Similarly, the value of "social capital" in club membership or bowling leagues would seem extremely difficult to define and measure. Second, nonmarket accounts are designed to ensure that our economic accounts are not distorted because the lines between market and nonmarket change over time. If female labor-force participation rises and moves much of female work from unpaid home production to the market, then time use is surely a candidate for inclusion to ensure that we have not overestimated per capita growth rates. Finally, some aspects of nonmarket accounts are of great relevance for policy or understanding social systems.

A closely related question involves where to begin developing nonmarket accounts. First steps will be matters of taste and interest as well as pure economic calculus. In my view, important sectors to begin are in household production, near-market sectors like forests and water, human capital, health, and pollution. These would be high on the list because they score high on the general principles listed above and because many scholars and policy-makers are interested in their contribution to total economic welfare.

3.2.4 Some Thorny Issues in Nonmarket Accounts

There are a few additional issues relating to nonmarket accounts that are worth addressing.

The Pervasive Lack of Data

Perhaps the most important single issue is the absence of *any* data on quantity, price, or total value for virtually *all* sectors of nonmarket activity. Market accounts, by contrast, have rich data on three aspects of total values: expenditures, incomes, and production.

The following paragraph from *Nature's Numbers* (Nordhaus and Kokkelenberg 2000) describes the difficulties of developing accounts based on physical data for a loaf of bread:

This section has emphasized the complexity involved in constructing environmental accounts in the absence of data on market data. Consider the problems involved in constructing accounts for a simple loaf of bread in the absence of market transactions. Doing so would require measuring and valuing a wide variety of flows of water, fertilizer, pesticides, labor, climate, and capital inputs that go into producing the wheat; the fuels, transport vehicles, emissions, weather-related delays, induced congestion, or floods involved in transportation; the molds, spores, and miscellaneous rodents and their droppings that invade the storage silos; the complex combination of human skills, equipment, and structures that go into milling the wheat; the entrepreneurship of the baker and the software in the computer-operated baking and slicing machinery; the complex chemistry and regulatory environment involved in the wrapping materials; and the evolving ecology of the distribution network.

It appears unlikely that anyone would try, and safe to conclude that no one could succeed in, describing the physical flows involved in this little loaf of bread. Fortunately, however, economic accounting does not attempt such a Herculean task. Rather, the national accounts measure all these activities by the common measuring rod of dollars. Although the dollar flows are routinely broken down into different stages—wheat, transportation, milling, baking, and distribution—one could never hope to describe the flows physically and then attach dollar values to each physical stage. Yet this is just what would be required for a full and detailed set of environmental accounts. The above comparison may give some sense of why accounting for environmental flows outside the marketplace is such a daunting task. (120–21)[3]

This example suggests that a set of nonmarket accounts will inevitably be much less detailed than the current set of market accounts and that we must be relatively modest in our aspirations in this area.

The Difficulties of Imputing Prices

The deepest practical difficulty that arises in constructing nonmarket accounts involves developing valuation for nonmarket goods, services, and assets. The problem in a nutshell is that there are no observable values or prices that are the analogs to prices the Bureau of Labor Statistics finds to write down and tabulate. The issues are least severe in valuing near-market goods, moderately severe for private but "personal" goods, and extremely severe for public goods.

In practice, values are often imputed (a) by looking at behavior that reveals consumer valuation of the commodities, (b) by unbundling the commodities and valuing component parts, or (c) by using surveys. These three techniques are exemplified by the travel-cost method, hedonic regressions or analysis, and contingent-valuation surveys, respectively. In addressing these issues, the panel in *Nature's Numbers* recommended as follows:

---

3. I have taken some editorial license to improve clarity.

Valuation methods [in environmental accounts] should rely on available market and behavioral data wherever and whenever possible. Although there are difficulties with nonbehavioral approaches such as contingent valuation, work on the development of such novel valuation techniques will be important for developing a comprehensive set of production and asset accounts. (Nordhaus and Kokkelenberg 2000, 167)

Whatever valuation technique is used, determining values for nonmarket sectors will generally be difficult and, particularly when they involve personal goods and services, may be controversial. National-income accountants generally prefer valuation techniques that have an objective behavioral component, whether in market prices or individual actions. Valuation techniques that are largely subjective and based only on survey information alone—such as contingent valuation—are difficult to validate and should be avoided where possible, but may be needed in some areas.

The Question of Consumer Surplus and the "Zero Problem"

Often, in undertaking valuations of nonmarket activities, analysts use total values rather than marginal values (prices times quantities). In other words, they sometimes include the consumer surplus along with the marginal values.[4]

Is inclusion of consumer surplus appropriate? There are two points here. First, to introduce consumer surplus in the augmented accounts would introduce a major inconsistency in the accounts because the standard national accounts are based on marginal values.

Second, using consumer surplus introduces a whole new set of decisions involving the "zero level" of different activities. For example, if we introduce the consumer surplus of water consumption, then we need to integrate the marginal surpluses (the difference between demand and cost curves) between some "zero" level and current output. But this raises the issue of the "zero" level. Is it literally zero water (in which case consumer surplus is essentially infinite)? Or the level in pre-industrial times? If the latter, should pre-industrial times relate to the 1700s, when water in the United States was plentiful? Or to the time when humans first crossed the Siberian peninsula, when ice was plentiful but water was scarce? Moreover, if we pursue consumer surplus in too many areas with low "zeroes," we will undoubtedly find ourselves with multiple infinities of output and income.

Once we travel even a few thoughts down this road, we rapidly come to the conclusion that, for purposes of measuring output and income, we should retain the standard approach of using marginal valuations in all sectors. This does not completely remove the zero problem, as I will explain in the next section, but it does ensure that we have comparability across differ-

---

4. An important example of an analysis using total values (including consumer surplus) is one valuing ecosystems. See Costanza et al. (1997).

ent accounting systems and will remove the problem of dealing with large numbers of infinitely valuable sectors.

Measurement of Natural Assets

For produced assets, there is a natural measuring rod in the number and value of the production of machines, houses, software packages, and so forth, and these can be aggregated to form capital stocks. The measurement of natural assets is not obvious. What is the value of the stock of first-growth forests, of unproved petroleum deposits, of clean air, or of breeding potential in wild fish?

One answer, but an unattractive one in this context, is the answer of the market accounts: The traditional accounts assume that the values of natural stocks are zero because their (market) production costs are zero. We clearly need to recognize that nonmarket assets have value, and that their value can be increased or decreased through human activities.

However, once we open the door to nonzero natural stock values, then the "zero problem" level arises once again. Do we measure the value of the stock relative to "zero stock" or relative to some other benchmark; and, additionally, do we value that difference using marginal or total valuations?

This question is often discussed in the context of estimates of the "value of ecosystems," which are often taken relative to their complete absence (and presumably the absence of all life). Using a total valuation system (in essence, taking the present value of consumer surpluses), ecosystems will indeed have a near-infinite value. But so would the value of human capital, technical capital, land, air, and other essential inputs, and we are back to the problem of multiple infinities of values.

To avoid the zero problem for assets, we first need to use the marginal valuation principle, whereby the value of the stock is the quantity times the marginal value. Additionally, we may want to measure the stock relative to a recent base period, the last period, or use chain indexes. These assumptions will ensure that natural and nonmarket capital are measured consistently in the income, production, and asset accounts; that they are treated consistently with market accounts; and that their size does not overwhelm the value of capital for other sectors.

One of the reasons that it is essential to prepare an integrated set of production, income, consumption, accumulation, and wealth accounts is to ensure that the definitions are consistent across the different accounts. In the integrated production and income accounts, accumulation would be the marginal valuation times the change in the stock, in which the "zero" level of the stock is clearly irrelevant.

"European" versus "American" Views on Measuring Nonreproducible Assets

Among the many thorny issues in designing augmented accounts, one interesting controversy involves the appropriate approach to measuring the value of nonreproducible assets like oil and gas reserves. Our NIPAs currently contain estimates of the production and flows of mineral products through the economy. However, changes in the stocks of valuable subsoil assets are currently omitted from the NIPAs. In its prototype satellite environmental accounts (the integrated economic and environmental satellite accounts, or IEESAs), the Bureau of Economic Analysis (BEA) prepared estimates that showed the impact of including "depletions" and "additions" to stocks of mineral resources.[5] The procedure, which I will call the "American approach," is straightforward. The BEA defined real net investment or net additions to mineral stocks as

$$(1) \qquad \text{Net investment in subsoil assets}_t = N_t = p_t(A_t - D_t),$$

where N_t = net investment in subsoil assets in prices of year 0, A_t = quantity of additions to reserves during year t, D_t = quantity of extraction or depletions during year t, and p_t = value of reserves in the ground. Current treatment of natural resources in the NIPAs omits equation (1). The main difficulty in employing the correction in equation (1) involves estimating the value of reserves in the ground, p_t.

The BEA treats mineral additions parallel with other forms of capital formation. In this respect, the U.S. accounts differ from the United Nations' System of Integrated Environmental and Economic Accounts, or SEEA, an alternative satellite accounting system proposed by the United Nations, which I will call the "European approach." In both accounting systems, depletions are treated as negative items in net investment.[6] Under SEEA, however, additions are not included as a positive item and do not appear in the production accounts as capital formation. In calculating gross domestic product (GDP), the SEEA considers as capital formation only investments in "made capital" and not mineral discoveries, treating additions as an "off-book" entry. This approach has also been used by the World Bank in its calculations of true saving.[7] Hence, under SEEA, net investment in non-renewable resources is calculated as

$$(2) \qquad \text{Net investment in subsoil assets}_t = N_t = -p_t D_t.$$

5. The BEA sketched a set of environmental and resource accounts (the IEESAs) in *Survey of Current Business,* April 1994. This research program was shut down by Congress shortly after its first publication. These accounts and the treatment above use the older convention of measuring stocks and flows as Laspeyres indexes, but there are no important differences if chain indexes are used.

6. See United Nations (1993). This study contains a description of several alternative approaches to environmental and by analog nonmarket accounting and is widely endorsed among environmentalists. It was found generally wanting by the Academy panel in *Nature's Numbers* because of analytical deficiencies. An update of this marked as "final draft" was circulated in 2003.

7. See Bolt, Matete, and Clemens (2002).

On first blush, the approach in equation (1) seems clearly appropriate because of the symmetry in treatment of additions and subtractions to the resource stock, and if required to choose between the two, equation (1) would be preferable. However, these two approaches are polar cases of a more complete theory. Both the American and the European approaches focus on a single grade of the resource, namely reserves. A more general theory would encompass at least *two* different grades of the resource, proved reserves (R_1) and unproved resources (R_2). There are two activities. The first activities are proving reserves or transforming unproved to proved reserves, which are additions (A_t); the second activities are producing output of the mineral from proved reserves, which are depletions (D_t). We can associate prices, p_t and q_t, with each of these respective quantities. In this broader conception, net output in a given year is

$$(3) \qquad N_t = p_t(A_t - D_t) - q_t A_t.$$

The first term in equation (3) is identical to the treatment in the American view in including the value of the change in proved reserves. There is, however, a second term, which reflects a correction for the depletion of unproved reserves involved in converting A_t units of unproved to proved reserves. (This could be modified to include multiple grades and prices, but the essence of the analysis would not change.)

Under the American view, there is implicitly a superabundant supply of unproved resources that can be upgraded to reserves through investment on development—somewhat akin to the vast frontier available for Americans moving west in the nineteenth century. Under this approach, q_t is zero because unproved resources are not scarce, so equation (3) becomes identical to equation (1) once the price of unproved resources is set to zero. In other words, the BEA's treatment implicitly assumes that the shadow price on unproved resources is essentially zero.

The European approach, by contrast, implicitly assumes that the stock of unproved resources is extremely limited, perhaps because virtually all the resources have been identified and proved as the frontier disappears. In this case, the shadow price on unproved resources (q_t) might be very close to that of proved resources. In the limit, if $q_t = p_t$, then equation (3) reduces to equation (2) and the SEEA approach is the appropriate treatment.

All this leads to the question of whether the shadow price of unproved reserves is likely to be closer to zero (the American approach) or to that of proved reserves (the European approach). A recent study finds that the prices of oil reserves in the United States over the 1982–2002 period have been stable, that reserve prices have averaged around 30 percent of the field price of oil, and that the price of unproved reserves appears to be much lower than those of reserves in production (Adelman and Watkins 2003). These three results are more consistent with the American approach than the European approach. Nevertheless, this is an open question that of is great importance for the correct accounting for subsoil assets.

3.3   Issues in the Use of Time-Use Data

3.3.1   Centrality of Time-Use Data

I have generally ignored specific data needs for nonmarket accounts, but I will mention one crucial area. The single most important source of data for nonmarket production and income accounts is data on how the population spends its time.

The reasoning why time use is central to nonmarket accounts is the following. Nonmarket activity consists of activities like education, recreation and other uses of leisure time, babysitting, home production of laundry and similar services, and work-related activities like commuting. The inputs into these activities consist of nonmarket and market labor, capital services, and material inputs. By far the largest component of nonmarket activity is time use. More precisely, virtually the entire value added of the nonmarket sectors comes from time inputs, while most of the nontime inputs are actually purchased in the market economy.

Consider the value of home production (such as doing the laundry) or recreation (such as golfing). The total value of such activities consists of the value of purchased market inputs (soap, washing machines, golf balls, and golf clubs) plus the value of the time spent in the activities. For example, doing the family laundry might have total value of $21, of which $20 (1 hour × $20 per hour) is the value of the time, while $1 is the cost of the soap and washing-machine services. Whatever the relative values, virtually all the nonmarket inputs are likely to be time.

The same story holds for virtually every nonmarket activity: the major nonmarket input is labor. The one important exception might be the inputs of nonmarket environmental capital (clean air, clean water, public beaches) that enter into recreation and health activities. These examples suggest that data on time use will be the most important single component of nonmarket accounts.

In this respect, it should be noted that the United States has up to now been particularly laggard with respect to generating comprehensive and periodic time use statistics. Every other major high-income country currently collects such data. Fortunately, beginning in 2003, the Bureau of Labor Statistics began the collection of a large time-use survey for the United States (the American Time Use Survey, or ATUS).[8] Starting in 2004, this survey will interview 14,000 households annually from the out-rotating

---

8. A review of the BLS time-use survey is contained at http://www.bls.gov/atus/home.htm.

panel of the Current Population Survey. As planned, it will be the only time-use survey in the world to be conducted on a continuous basis. The ATUS will be an important addition to the U.S. statistical system and a crucial ingredient in the future construction of augmented accounts.

3.3.2   Problems of Pricing Time

The problem of imputing prices for time use is usually solved by assuming that the shadow price on time is given by the price that individuals face in the labor market. Conceptually, the price is the marginal after-tax compensation, although most studies rely upon the average wage rate. Under the assumption that individuals are always able to sell hours at their after-tax wage, this puts a natural price that can be used to value leisure, nonmarket production, and other components of time use. This approach was used by Nordhaus and Tobin (1972) and is standard in most approaches to time valuation.

An alternative approach to valuation would be direct surveys of how individuals value their time. Figure 3.1 shows the results of a compilation of surveys of U.S. households as to their enjoyment of different activities. There are two striking results of this survey. The first is that there is no obvious wedge between work and nonwork that can be interpreted as a marginal wage. Indeed, working is in the middle of the pack in terms of enjoyment. Second, there is no set of activities that could be interpreted as nonwork alternatives that cluster at a preference level that can be interpreted as the nonwork alternative valued at a distinct increment above work. Rather, there seem to be a set of distinctly disliked activities—cleaning house, grocery shopping, laundry, and going to the dentist.[9]

How can we understand the results of figure 3.1 in the context of our microeconomic theories of the allocation of time?

- One possible interpretation is that the enjoyment reported in figure 3.1 pertains to average rather than marginal evaluations. For example, people might report that work is on average a highly pleasurable activity even though the last hour might be valued well below marginal nonwork hours. This interpretation is consistent with the results in another survey that second jobs are less enjoyable than "work." (Robinson and Godbey 1997, 340)[10]
- A second possible interpretation is that the underlying microeconomic theory is misspecified because most people (or most people in the survey) are unable to sell every hour on the market at the calculated post-

9. This phenomenon was noted and discussed in Juster (1985). Juster's reading of the evidence is that disequilibrium in the labor market is the most likely source of the paradox. Juster denotes the intrinsic value or enjoyment of time as "process benefits."

10. Robinson and Godbey (1997) is the most recent survey, and it ranks work between gardening and cooking or working at home.

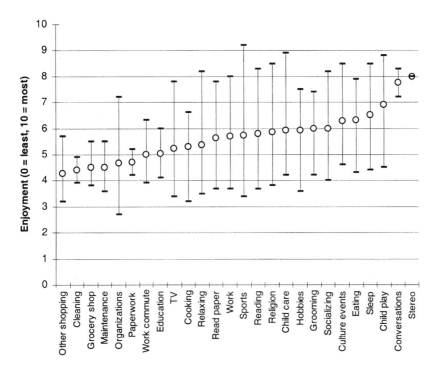

Fig. 3.1   Ranking of enjoyment of different activities

Source: Robinson and Godbey (1997, 243).

Note: The bars show the mean (as a circle) and the maxima and minima as ends of the bars for activities from five surveys over the period 1965 to 1985 with sample sizes from 133 to 2,500.

tax wage rate. For salaried workers, the marginal wage is generally zero, while waged workers often have little control of their hours on a day-to-day basis. Self-employed workers do have control of their hours, but we do not have data on their return on marginal hours. If the marginal wage is zero for a substantial number of hours, then it would be reasonable to find that enjoyment from work would not differ markedly from enjoyment from other activities.

• A third interpretation recognizes that time is a heterogeneous commodity and that there is no reason why hours should be valued at the same rate at different times of the day and different days of the year. An analog is electricity prices, which are much like time in that neither electricity nor time can be stored. Hourly electricity prices often vary by a factor of 5 during the day and varied by a factor of 50 in 1999, and there is no reason why time prices should not vary greatly as well. For individuals facing rigid schedules (for work, school, meetings, and so forth), we could easily find that marginal valuations are all over the map depending on the extent of "time crunch" or "time glut."

- A fourth possibility is that the estimates are incorrect for method-ological reasons and that work is in fact relatively unattractive. This interpretation is suggested by the survey of Kahneman, Krueger, Schkade, Schwarz, and Stone (2004; hereafter KKSSS). They use a method of evaluation that combines time-use diaries and day-after evaluation, whereas the studies shown in figure 3.1 use a "stylized" evaluation of the process value of activities. KKSSS find that the ac-tivities that have the lowest score of "enjoying myself" are, from the bottom, commuting, doing housework, and working. This finding matches quite neatly standard labor-market theories. However, these results are preliminary and use a highly nonrepresentative sample (women residing in two large Texas cities, with full-time employment and a high school education or better, after eliminating those who did not work the previous day). KKSSS's results suggest that the abstrac-tions of "work" or "taking care of children" are more pleasant than the experienced reality.

In the end, we are likely to use some variant of conventional valuations of time in terms of the average after-tax wage, particularly when we cannot measure the output of the hours, but we must recognize that this conven-tion is subject to serious reservations. This is an area ripe for serious em-pirical work, particularly as new time use data become available.

3.3.3   The Problem of Simultaneous Activities

The other major issue in applying time-use data is the treatment of si-multaneous activities. How should we classify and value time use that is devoted to multiple purposes? We frequently encounter people talking on their cell phone while walking; these are clearly two distinct and insepa-rable activities—communicating while traveling. Another example would be activities at home. We might be dog sitting, house sitting, babysitting, lis-tening to the radio, relaxing, visiting with family, and cooking dinner at the same time. I mentioned above the puzzle that work has such a high re-ported intrinsic value. Yet another possible reason is that work has positive associated activities, such as socializing. These are not isolated examples. Indeed, simultaneous time use is pervasive.

Since little time-use research to date has been economic in its orienta-tion, little attention has been given to the problem of joint production in time use. Among the approaches used to resolve the simultaneous use ques-tion are (a) designate primary and secondary activities, (b) treat activities additively so that people might have a "thirty-six-hour day," and (c) cre-ate compound activities that treat, say, babysitting and TV watching as a different commodity.

A new approach, which has firmer roots in economics, would be a "value-theoretic" approach, which allocates simultaneous activities among their components on the basis of the values of the different activities. We are always doing many things. If we are doing one thing that is useful and another thing that is useless, then the value-theoretic approach would hold that our time is devoted to the useful activity. For example, suppose I am tending for my small children, which is important, while looking at internet advertisements, which has no value. Then this approach would find that the time is spent entirely in tending for children. Valuing time devoted to simultaneously cooking mutton and washing wool socks would be similar to valuing the joint products of mutton and wool from sheep.

This approach can be illustrated by examining near-market goods and services. Suppose that during an hour I produce simultaneous babysitting services and dinner. Say that the value of babysitting services is $5 per hour and cooking services is worth $10 per hour. Then we would say that the hour was divided into twenty minutes of babysitting and forty minutes of cooking. Again, this methodology would give the same answer as traditional approaches if the first twenty minutes were babysitting and the second forty minutes were cooking. (For nonmarket activities, we would use relative utility valuations.)

One reason why the value-theoretic approach helps in considering simultaneous activities is that traditional approaches tend to emphasize the physical and locational aspects of time use. For example, if I am eating dinner and visiting with the family, the physical activity of eating will generally be classified as the principal activity and the visiting will be either ignored or classified as the secondary activity. In fact, the visiting might be the more important, and would be classified as such in the value-theoretic approach.

I will conclude with a more speculative point on treatment of simultaneous activities. As our societies are transformed from a primarily agricultural and then a manufacturing society into an information-based society, the physical aspects of time use are becoming less important. The mental, social, and psychological aspects are becoming more important. The price of brainpower is rising relative to the price of horsepower. To the extent that the traditional time-use measures are locationally and physically oriented, they will miss this transition. This point suggests that moving toward a value-theoretic approach will help us understand the evolving nature of time and employ time-use surveys accurately in economic accounts.

References

Abraham, Katharine G., and Christopher Mackie, eds. 2005. *Beyond the market: Designing nonmarket accounts for the United States.* Washington, DC: National Academies Press.

Adelman, M. A., and G. C. Watkins. 2003. Oil and natural gas reserve prices, 1982–2002. MIT Center for Energy and Environmental Policy Research. Working Paper, October.

Bolt, Katharine, Mampite Matete, and Michael Clemens. 2002. Manual for calculating adjusted net savings. Environment Department working paper. Washington, DC: World Bank, September.

Costanza, Robert, Ralph d'Arge, Rudolf de Groot, Stephen Faberk, Monica Grasso, Bruce Hannon, Karin Limburg, et al. 1997. The value of the world's ecosystem services and natural capital. *Nature* 387 (May): 253–60.

Fraumeni, Barbara F. 1999. The Jorgenson system of national accounting. In *Econometrics and the cost of capital: Essays in honor of Dale W. Jorgenson,* ed. Lawrence J. Lau, 111–42. Cambridge, MA: MIT Press.

Juster, F. Thomas. 1985. Preferences for work and leisure. In *Time, goods and well-being,* ed. F. Thomas Juster and Frank P. Stafford, 333–51. Ann Arbor, MI: Institute for Social Research.

Kahneman, Daniel, Alan B. Krueger, David A. Schkade, Norbert Schwarz, and Arthur A. Stone. 2004. A survey method for characterizing daily life experience: The day reconstruction method. *Science* 306 (December): 1776–80.

Nordhaus, William D., and Edward Kokkelenberg, eds. 2000. *Nature's numbers: Expanding the national economic accounts to include the environment.* Washington, DC: National Academy Press.

Nordhaus, William D., and James Tobin. 1972. *Is growth obsolete?* In *Fiftieth anniversary colloquium V.* New York: Columbia University Press.

Robinson, John, and Geoffrey Godbey. 1997. *Time for life: The surprising ways Americans use their time.* University Park, PA: Pennsylvania University Press.

United Nations. 1993. *Integrated environmental and economic accounting: Interim version.* Studies in Method, series F, no. 61. New York: United Nations.

A Framework for
Nonmarket Accounting

Katharine G. Abraham and Christopher Mackie

4.1 Introduction and Motivation

Since their earliest construction for the United States by Simon Kuznets in the 1930s (Kuznets 1934), concerns have been voiced that the National Income and Product Accounts (NIPAs) are incomplete. The NIPAs meet rigorous standards and enjoy broad acceptance among data users interested in tracking economic activity. They are, however, primarily market based and, by design, shed little light on production in the home or in other nonmarket situations. Further, even where activity is organized in markets, important aspects of that activity may be omitted from the NIPAs. In other cases, unpaid time inputs and associated outputs are critical to production processes but, because no market transaction is associated with their provision, they are not reflected in the accounts. One illustration is provided by estimates (LaPlante, Harrington, and Kang 2002) suggesting that the

Katharine G. Abraham is a professor of survey methodology and adjunct professor of economics at the University of Maryland and a research associate of the National Bureau of Economic Research. Christopher Mackie is a staff economist and senior study director with the Committee on National Statistics, National Academy of Sciences.

This chapter reflects the work of a National Academy of Sciences panel study on the design of nonmarket accounts. Katharine G. Abraham served as chair of the panel, and Christopher Mackie was the staff study director. The other members of the panel were David Cutler, Nancy Folbre, Barbara Fraumeni, Robert E. Hall, Daniel S. Hamermesh, Alan Krueger, Robert Michael, Henry M. Peskin, Matthew D. Shapiro, and Burton A. Weisbrod. The panel's final report recently has been published (Abraham and Mackie 2005). Although the listed authors have taken responsibility for drafting the present paper, the ideas it contains reflect the intellectual contributions of all the panel members. The paper also has benefited from the thoughtful comments of Joseph Beaulieu, William Nordhaus, Marshall Reinsdorf, participants in the Conference on Research in Income and Wealth (CRIW) Architecture for the National Accounts Conference, and two anonymous referees. Any flaws in the paper should, of course, be attributed to the listed authors.

value of in-home long-term care services provided by family and friends is greater than the value of similar market-provided services.

In other areas, the output resulting from market-based production may be incorrectly characterized or valued. There is wide agreement, for example, that the output of the education sector properly should be considered investment rather than consumption, and that its value should be assessed in terms of the returns on that investment rather than the cost of the inputs used in its production. The conventional accounts do not include the asset value of human capital production associated with education, health care and other personal investment activities. Available estimates are rough, but suggest that the value of the human capital stock may be as large as that of the physical capital stock (see Kendrick 1976, and, for a discussion in the context of analyzing economic growth, Mankiw, Romer, and Weil 1992).

Although the importance of nonmarket—but productive—endeavors has long been recognized, few attempts have been made to provide systematic information about even the most quantitatively significant of them. The state of nonmarket accounting today resembles the situation for market-based accounting in the 1920s and 1930s before the creation of the NIPAs. Economic accounting need not, and should not, extend to all nonmarket activities, but there are certain areas in which nonmarket accounts, designed to supplement the NIPAs, could make particularly important contributions. We stress the potential value of new methods of accounting for volunteer and home production efforts, education, health, and environmental improvement or degradation. The raw data pertaining to these nonmarket activities are becoming richer; it remains to be seen whether they can be effectively exploited to expand the nation's accounting of productive activities.

Extending the nation's accounting systems to better incorporate nonmarket production promises substantial benefits to policymakers and researchers. For example, researchers studying the topic of economic growth have long had to supplement data from the national accounts with external estimates of the contributions of research and development, investments in human capital, and the services of the natural environment. Economists and historians have shown that, over the last few centuries of human history, factors such as technical change, scientific inventions, and discoveries in medicine—many of which are nonmarket in character—have accounted for a very large portion of the growth in living standards. Historical trends reveal the reality that neither economic production nor contributions to social welfare take place exclusively within the market's border, but extend to many nonmarket activities.

Thus, one objective of improved nonmarket accounting is to support alternative aggregate measures of economic performance. Nonmarket accounts would enhance the ability of researchers (and the statistical agencies) to produce augmented gross domestic product (GDP) statistics and to construct appropriate price deflators needed for real output and productivity measurement. A fuller accounting of national production might lead to different conclusions regarding the level of output today relative to some earlier period, or in the United States compared with another nation.

Nonmarket accounting also would illuminate the processes whereby inputs are transformed into outputs in particular sectors. Consider, for example, the production of health. In contrast to currently constructed health *expenditure* accounts, which track market payments but do not identify the outputs in a way that is useful for measuring price change or productivity, a health account would relate health improvements—the real "good" that is produced—to medical treatments, as well as to a wide range of other inputs, including diet, the environment, exercise, and research and development. By most measures, improvements in health have outpaced increases in spending on medical care. Since medical care interacts with these interrelated factors, however, we do not know with any certainty the productivity of resources directed toward health care (Cutler and Richardson 1997; Cutler 2004). Optimally, expenditures and outcomes would be tracked so that changes in well-being associated with different actions could be monitored; in turn, this information could support better management of expenditures (both private and public) to achieve desired outcomes.

To take another example, education accounts might be designed to relate improvements in skill capital—the output—to the various inputs to the educational process. As in the health case, schooling is characterized by a mix of market and nonmarket inputs and outputs. The value of time students spend in school—the key nonmarket input—is likely to be at least comparable to the expenditures on marketed inputs. The *2003 Statistical Abstract* shows that, in 2000, school expenditures on primary and secondary education amounted to approximately $400 billion and that just over 47 million students were enrolled in primary and secondary schools. Assuming 180 days at six hours a day, plus an hour of commuting time and two hours of homework per student, students in these grades devoted more than 75 billion hours to their education. If students' time were valued at the current minimum wage of $5.15 per hour (purely for illustrative purposes), the value of unpaid student time would be almost as large as the expenditures measured in the conventional accounts.

The inherent limitation of the NIPAs—that they fail to consider the full array of the economy's productive inputs and outputs—might be less important if market and nonmarket activities trended similarly, but there is little evidence to suggest that they do. To take one frequently cited example, failing to account for the output produced within households may lead to misleading comparisons of economywide production, as conventionally measured. According to Bureau of Labor Statistics (BLS) figures, the female labor force participation rate in the United States has grown substantially, from about 34 percent in 1950 to almost 60 percent in 2000 (see http://www.bls.gov). To the extent that the entry of women into paid employment has reduced effort devoted to household production, the long-term trend in output as measured by GDP may exaggerate the true growth in national output (Landefeld and McCulla 2000). Similarly, the relatively smaller portion of total output attributable to home production in the United States as compared to many developing countries surely exaggerates its national output relative to theirs.

Perhaps less well recognized are potential problems with the measurement of national output over the business cycle. If people who lose their jobs during cyclical downturns take advantage of their absence from paid employment to increase the effort they devote to home production, the short-term decline in national output may be dampened relative to that measured by GDP. Knowing more about the level and distribution of nonmarket activity could be important for other purposes as well. Such information could, for example, change perceptions of the extent of economic inequality among U.S. households and how that has changed over time. This, in turn, could affect where welfare and poverty lines are drawn (Michael 1996).

This chapter identifies and discusses several of the key and sometimes controversial issues hinted at above relating to nonmarket accounting. One goal of this chapter is simply to remind readers of the major omissions built into our system of economic measurement. In so doing, we hope to encourage contributions by social scientists to improve the measurement of nonmarket activity and to point out new ideas and new data sources that have improved the prospects for progress. Time is the dominant input to nonmarket production, and the lack of good measures of how people spend their time has seriously handicapped work in this area. We are optimistic that the newly developed American Time Use Survey (ATUS), produced by the BLS, will spur new work to develop informative nonmarket accounts. Even a cursory glance at the first published statistics from this survey makes clear the potential importance of such an accounting—in 2003, averaging over both employed and nonemployed people, Americans age fifteen and older spent just 3.7 hours per day in market work and work-related activities, meaning that most of their time was devoted to nonmarket activities of one sort and another.

4.2   Satellite Accounts

When considering nonmarket economic activity, it is useful to think in terms of satellite accounts that report, on an experimental basis, data on selected activities not covered in conventional accounts. The core accounts have the virtues of consistency over time, hard-won comparability across countries, and solid grounding in observed market transactions. These are strong arguments for maintaining the core accounts in more or less their current form. Satellite accounts would not replace the current national accounts, but exist alongside them. They can link to the national income accounts as appropriate, but also expand into areas that the NIPAs do not cover. Further, satellite accounts can be developed, even where standards of accuracy and data quality are not up to the level of the NIPAs, without compromising the conceptual basis or technical integrity of the conventional accounts. Similarly, where no consensus yet exists regarding the best way to measure a particular aspect of nonmarket activity, satellite accounts permit experimentation with alternative methodologies. The goal is to extend the accounting of the nation's productive inputs and outputs, thereby providing a framework for examining the production functions of some difficult-to-measure nonmarket activities.

The idea of satellite accounts is not a new one. The Bureau of Economic Analysis (BEA) long has conducted research on topics beyond the scope of the conventional accounts. A representative BEA description of the role to be played by satellite accounts is as follows:

> [S]atellite accounts are frameworks designed to expand the analytical capacity of the economic accounts without overburdening them with detail or interfering with their general purpose orientation. Satellite accounts, which are meant to supplement, rather than replace, the existing accounts, organize information in an internally consistent way that suits the particular analytical focus at hand, while maintaining links to the existing accounts. In their most flexible application, they may use definitions and classifications that differ from those in the existing accounts. . . . In addition, satellite accounts typically add detail or other information, including nonmonetary information, about a particular aspect of the economy. (Bureau of Economic Analysis 1994, p. 41)

The United Nations System of National Accounts (SNA) offers a similar description:

> Satellite accounts provide a framework linked to the central accounts and which enables attention to be focused on a certain field or aspect of economic and social life in the context of national accounts; common examples are satellite accounts for the environment, or tourism, or unpaid household work. . . . Satellite accounts or systems generally stress the need to expand the analytical capacity of national accounting for selected areas of social concern in a flexible manner, without overburdening or disrupting the central system. (United Nations et al. 1993, Glossary, p. 45, and p. 489)

The accounting frameworks described in this chapter generally are harmonious with these definitions. For a number of industries and sectors with significant nonmarket components, satellite accounts hold promise for generating meaningful and useful data to inform policy and to advance research.

In considering the feasibility of nonmarket accounts, it is natural to ask how accurate and reliable measures of the relevant inputs and outputs must be in order for the construction of a nonmarket account to be worthwhile. Traditionally, the statistical agencies responsible for economic accounting—the BEA and the BLS—have set high standards of accuracy. The application of similarly rigorous standards to the production of satellite accounts is unrealistic given the inherent limitations of the underlying data. This does not mean that official statistical agencies should eschew nonmarket accounting efforts, but does imply that distinctions should be drawn between the core accounts, together with other major economic indicators, and more experimental efforts to account for important areas of nonmarket activity. Academic and private researchers may be willing to push further in their efforts to account for nonmarket activity than the official statistical agencies. The results of such private research efforts might be analogous to the monthly GDP figures currently published by a private consulting firm, using data supplied by the BEA. The BEA does not consider the data to be sufficiently reliable in all sectors to produce an official version of monthly GDP; even recognizing these data limitations, the consulting firm believes its clients will find the monthly estimates of interest and has decided to produce them.[1] We anticipate similar situations arising with nonmarket data.

4.3 Priorities for Expanded Measurement

4.3.1 The Scope of Coverage in the NIPAs

Modern national accounts include primarily goods and services that are bought and sold in market transactions.[2] The earliest national accounting effort was William Petty's 1665 attempt to estimate England's national income.[3] By modern standards, Petty's accounts, albeit based on fragmentary data, were fairly wide in scope, covering purchases in the market and imputed values for household production (Kendrick 1970, p. 285). Far narrower were the concepts of the French physiocrats, who believed that only agriculture produced a true net product, or of Adam Smith and Karl Marx, who believed that a country's productive capacity was reflected in its ability to produce material goods, excluding services.

Beginning with the writings of Alfred Marshall (1920) and A. C. Pigou (1920), the trend, in terms of a conceptual objective, was to widen the cov-

1. The business cycle dating committee of the National Bureau of Economic Research is among those making use of the monthly estimates.
2. There are many sources that provide detailed description of the components of the NIPAs and of how they are constructed. For an introduction, see Popkin (2000); further details are available on the BEA website.
3. The historical development of national income accounts has been surveyed by Kendrick (1970).

erage of national accounts to include all activities that generate "utility" or welfare, including those that take place beyond the market. Pigou wrote that national accounts should include elements that reflect economic welfare and that can "be brought directly or indirectly into relation with the measuring rod of money" (Pigou 1920, p. 11). He emphasized that the word "can" might mean anything from "can easily" to "can with mild straining" to "can with violent straining." National accounting practices in most countries lean far more toward those elements that "can easily" be measured in money terms than those that can be measured only with "violent straining."

It is important to point out that the national accounts produced by the BEA include some activities that do not involve a market transaction or produce a marketed output. Almost 15 percent of GDP ($1,559.4 billion of $10,480.8 billion in 2002) is imputed (see National Income and Product Accounts Table 7.12, Imputations in the National Income and Product Accounts, available at www.bea.gov). The most quantitatively significant imputation is that for the rental value of owner-occupied housing. That this imputation is based on assumptions that are approximately as crude as those for, say, valuing the time spent cleaning a house at the price a cleaning service would charge, suggests that the delineation between included and excluded activities is not purely the by-product of practical considerations. One reason for making an imputation for the value of owner-occupied housing is to ensure that the accounts are invariant to trends in home ownership (which has increased significantly in the past half-century). In a similar way, nonmarket accounts could improve our ability to assess trends in total output when the population shifts from unpaid or home production to market substitutes, or vice versa.

Imputations are made for other nonpriced, nonmarketed items in the NIPAs, including wages and salaries paid in kind, food and fuel consumed on farms, and the services provided by banks, insurance companies, and other financial intermediaries that are not reflected in explicit service charges. The imputations for banking services are somewhat unique. In banking, there are observable market transactions that provide an estimate of the nominal value of banking output. Imputations are necessary, however, to allocate the nominal value of unpriced services between borrowers and depositors (see Fixler, Reinsdorf, and Smith 2003, for a more complete discussion).

One key characteristic of the nonmarketed items that are covered in conventional accounting systems is that their consumption is very closely related to the sales and purchases of marketed goods and services, making the estimation reasonably straightforward. For some nonmarket items, the imputation process would be far more difficult, although these distinctions are a matter of degree. If the term "imputation" refers to any data that are not directly observable, then it is clearly the case that the development of nearly all national accounting data, whether market, near market, or non-market, involves some degree of imputation.

Finally, information relevant to many areas of nonmarket activity already is included in the national accounts. Purchases of inputs that contribute to nonmarket production often are treated as expenditures for final demand. This is true, for example, in the case of household production; spending on food, cleaning supplies, and household appliances all are counted as part of personal consumption.[4] Some of the costs borne by government and parents for children's education are included in the accounts but not the value of the time students devote to their education (on the input side), and there is no attempt to measure directly the value of the resulting human capital (on the output side). Similarly, many of the inputs to medical care are included in the accounts, but unpaid inputs of time that individuals devote to caring for themselves or family members are excluded, and the accounts shed relatively little light on the value of the health services provided or the health capital formed.

For most areas of nonmarket economic activity that merit further exploration, the accounts do not reflect the full range of inputs used in the production of the output of interest. And in no case is the value of the resulting output, whether goods and services produced for current consumption or the creation of a productive asset, measured fully and independently of the value of the inputs used in its production.

4.3.2   The Scope of Satellite Accounts

An overarching question for the architecture of nonmarket accounting is scope—where in the range of activities that could be deemed to have economic value to draw the border of inclusion. Nonmarket accounts would extend coverage of productive inputs and outputs to facets of the nation's economy that are largely nonmarket in character, but they should not include all human activities; the idea of producing an overall summary measure of total human satisfaction is futuristic at best. Instead, priority should be given to the development of experimental accounts for those areas that most closely resemble the activities represented in conventional market accounts. These experimental accounts would provide a framework for examining the production functions of some difficult to measure activities not covered—or not adequately covered—in the NIPAs. Initial work should address omissions in output measurement, somewhat narrowly defined, which implies setting a boundary that excludes activities (such as leisure or sleep) for which "prices" would be difficult, even in prin

---

4. Conceptually, it would be preferable to treat household consumer durables (such as most appliances) as capital assets since, like other capital goods, they deliver a flow of productive service over time. The fact that the BEA does not treat home production as being within the production boundary for the NIPAs is a barrier to their being treated in this fashion in the conventional accounts.

ciple, to derive from market comparisons. Additionally, the focus should be on areas where improved accounting would contribute to policymaking and science.

Satellite accounts augment information in the market-oriented economic accounts to provide a more complete picture of economic activity in key nonmarket areas. This allows the existing NIPAs, including the headline GDP measure, to continue to be constructed in a historically consistent manner. At the same time, data from mature satellite accounts could be used by researchers to construct alternative-concept measures of output or welfare. The principal reasons for having national accounts are to be able to monitor trends in the economy and to forecast the impact of alternative policy choices. This implies that satellite accounts, like the NIPAs themselves, will be most valuable to research and policy if they are produced on a regular schedule.

A wide range of productive activities are worthy of exploration for possible inclusion in a set of augmented accounts. Among the areas of top priority, we would include measurement of

- Household production
- Investments in formal education and the resulting stock of skill capital
- Investments in health and the resulting stock of health capital
- Selected activities of the nonprofit and government sectors
- Environmental assets and services

We highlight these areas for satellite accounts for several reasons, but stress that they do not represent an exhaustive set of potential accounts. Each is substantial in magnitude, so focusing attention on it should improve our understanding of the nation's total production. Several of these areas overlap the NIPAs and thus complement existing official statistics. The list of sectors also reflects a feasibility constraint. Though the construction of almost any nonmarket satellite account is likely to require controversial decisions, the list above excludes areas for which sensible approaches to quantifying and valuing inputs or outputs appear especially far from reach. We also would prioritize areas for which emerging data sources offer new opportunities.

Even within the set of areas identified here, there are differences in readiness to begin the development of new satellite accounts. At this time, accounts for household production and the environment would rest on the firmest foundations; indeed, both the BEA and other national statistical offices already have done substantial work in these areas. In the remaining areas for which we advocate development efforts—the government and nonprofit sectors, education, and health—more extensive basic research and new data collection are needed.

While we acknowledge that nonmarket production extends far beyond what we outline here, a set of accounts that included the five areas listed would go a long way toward documenting nonmarket production that contributes to social or private well-being, and would address most of the key principles generalizable to nonmarket accounting broadly.[5] Other areas of nonmarket activity are quantitatively significant and deserve further attention but, because of data limitations or the lack of a well-developed conceptual framework, are not currently good candidates for inclusion in a coordinated nonmarket accounting initiative. The component of household production associated with the creation of children and the stock of human capital these children embody is a good example. This nonmarket activity obviously has huge economic (and noneconomic) value, but defining, estimating and cataloguing the corresponding prices and quantities in an accounting framework would require knowledge we do not currently possess. Similarly, with the right kinds of data, one might envision accounting for changes in the social environment (e.g. crime and security) that affect living standards in a manner analogous to that used in satellite accounts for the physical environment. At present, however, we do not have the information that would be required to support such an account. There are important scientific and policy questions associated with underground economic production; much of this activity, however, involves market transactions, albeit illegal ones, and thus raises a rather different set of issues and challenges.

Change in the amount of leisure enjoyed by a population is also an important indicator of living standards. Fogel (1999) estimates that the average male household head enjoyed an increase in residual time for leisure activities from 1.8 hours per day in 1880 to about 5.8 hours per day in 1995. Undoubtedly the aggregate value of leisure in society is high, and could in principle be measured, but in accord with the guiding principle (articulated by William Nordhaus in chap. 3 of this volume) that "nonmarket goods and services should be treated as if they were produced and consumed as market activities . . . [and their value] imputed on the basis of the comparable market goods and services," we would recommend against committing resources to the development of a separate leisure account at this time. If the purpose of nonmarket accounts is to "include activities that are economic in nature and those that substitute for market activities" and to begin gradually expanding measurement of the society's economic output beyond that which is covered in conventional economic accounts, then priority should be given to the types of nonmarket activities that involve production in a more traditional sense. Because leisure is such a heterogeneous

5. The recent report of the National Academy of Sciences panel charged with studying the design of nonmarket accounts (Abraham and Mackie 2005) recommends the development of nonmarket satellite accounts for each of the five areas—household production, education, health, the nonprofit and government sectors, and the environment—and makes specific recommendations regarding the measurement and valuation of the relevant inputs and outputs. The report also provides further references to the relevant literature.

good, and so far removed from any kind of conventionally defined "output," we would recommend focusing attention on aspects of leisure (such as recreation or health-capital-enhancing activities) that may figure into the nonmarket accounting areas identified above.

The question of whether various activities are in scope is also contingent on the accounting objective. If the designers of an account cannot decide whether it is intended to capture changes in economic output or changes in societal welfare, the end product may be conceptually muddled. Indeed, these objectives may imply opposing valuations. The simple example of how to value time spent commuting illustrates the complication. If the goal is to measure "output," one would likely want to include the value of, say, parents' time transporting kids to school and other activities. The market cost of hiring a driver might be used to price this time, though there are other alternatives. As the amount of time driving goes up, so too does the value of this component of household production. Yet, as driving time increases, parents' welfare may actually decrease, as time is taken away from leisure and other utility-generating activities. In this case and many others, measuring output and measuring welfare are separate, though admittedly related, exercises. As a practical matter, we would recommend focusing initial efforts on a more thorough accounting of the nation's economic output.

Account designers also must be conscious of the difficulty of drawing boundaries between various related areas of nonmarket activity. Improved health, for example, may result from better medical care, better education that contributes to sounder decisions about diet and exercise, or improved air and water quality. Identifying the full set of inputs to improved health outcomes is difficult, and some of these inputs also may contribute to other desirable outputs. To take another example, additions to the stock of human capital may flow not only from investment that occurs within the formal education sector, but also from investments that occur within the home and thus might be considered a form of home production. There is no realistic alternative to considering the different areas of nonmarket activity separately, but the need to delineate the interactions and complementarities among these different areas should be recognized as work progresses.

One approach that has been used to define nonmarket output (particularly in household production applications) is Margaret Reid's (1934) third-party criterion: is the output in question something that a person could have hired someone else to produce for him? A limited-scope, consumption-oriented household production account could, with some qualifications, be developed using this criterion. For such an account, meals, clothing services, shelter services, and the custodial component of child care would be considered in scope, but fertility, studying, and exercise would not. Because of its conceptual clarity, it may be useful to construct a limited-scope household production account that conforms to the third-party criterion. In other areas, such as education and health (some of which is produced in the home), the third-party criterion is clearly inappropriate: someone else cannot engage in the activities required to enhance our cognitive skills or improve our health, but these activities produce valuable albeit nonmarketable capital outputs not adequately reflected in the existing national accounts. Nonmarket public goods, such as environmental services, also would not be captured by the third-party criterion.

Another question is whether the pleasure individuals receive from engaging in home production activities, as distinct from the quantity and value of the time they devote to production, should be included as part of the value of nonmarket production. We argue that it should not. Similarly, we would argue against counting the enjoyment experienced by those who volunteer with nonprofit organizations as a part of nonmarket production. Our view on this subject stems, in part, from a desire for consistency. The traditional accounts include the products and services produced by paid workers, but not the enjoyment they may derive from their employment, and we would preserve that distinction in accounting for home production or the output of the nonprofit sector.

There are also related questions concerning what constitutes an input to nonmarket production. In particular, how should the time devoted to consumption be treated? Enjoying a restaurant meal, for example, requires not only the meal itself, but also the time of the diner who consumes it. Should that time be counted as an input to nonmarket production? Again, we do not believe that valuing time spent in consumption is useful, at least not for the first round of nonmarket accounts; we would focus more narrowly on the quantity and value of time that is an input to the production of identifiable goods and services.

A number of other challenges arise in organizing a set of satellite accounts. Time use, for example, is a key input to nearly all areas of productive activity; specific time-use activities, such as volunteering, also may apply to more than one of the identified sectors. Nonmarket activities can be grouped by producing unit—for example, households, government, nonprofit organizations; alternatively, with some overlap and some omission, they can be thought of by industry—for example, education, health. It would be difficult to cover all major nonmarket areas while staying true to a single (delivery system or industry based) organizing principle. The interesting policy and science questions that arise seem to call for data that may be grouped along different dimensions. A consequence of adopting this approach is, of course, that satellite accounts of the type we envision cannot simply be added up to produce alternative national output or income measures.

4.4 A Conceptual Framework

Although nonmarket accounts are experimental, they should not be developed in a manner methodologically isolated from the NIPAs. Using the national accounts as the starting point offers several advantages. National accounts have been scrutinized, reflecting extensive research and policy use for many decades; the underlying principles are well tested, and practice shows they can be implemented. Additionally, many of the methodological questions about the augmented accounts have analogues and therefore answers in the national accounts (Nordhaus 2002, p. 3).

The national accounts have proven extraordinarily useful as a vehicle for monitoring and studying the evolution of the economy. They have the intentional restriction, of course, that they do not systematically incorporate nonmarket activity.[6] Given the heavy reliance of policymakers and others on the existing accounts, together with the interest researchers will have in developing augmented measures of output that are compatible with GDP, any supplemental accounts that are developed will be most useful if the information they contain is as consistent as possible with information in the NIPAs.

What specifically does this imply? The NIPAs rest on a double-entry structure that values outputs independently of inputs, and incorporates measures of quantity and price for both. One of the most important applications of the national accounts is the measurement of productivity growth, which requires these separate measures. The NIPAs use dollar prices as the metric for relative value; value outputs at their marginal rather than their total value; and derive these marginal values wherever possible from observable market transactions. Following these same practices in the nonmarket accounts would facilitate comparisons between them and the NIPAs.

The national accounts report three measures for each type of product at the most detailed level: the quantity, the price, and the dollar value. These are linked by the principle that value is price multiplied by quantity. With few exceptions, the accounts obtain data on value from primary sources, and quantity is calculated by dividing value by a measure of price. In a few cases, data on value and quantity are obtained, and price is calculated as the ratio of the two. We anticipate that similar calculations would be used in satellite accounts. In addition, a satellite account might use data on quantity together with estimates of prices to calculate value as the product of the two. This procedure seldom is necessary in the national accounts, where value generally is available from primary sources.

4.4.1   Implications of the Double-Entry Bookkeeping Approach

One of the strengths of the NIPAs is the double-entry bookkeeping used in their construction. Independent estimates of total output are developed

---

6. As discussed above, the BEA does measure services of owner-occupied housing, food consumed on farms, and certain financial services of banks and insurance companies. The BEA also measures governmental services, though they are currently measured at cost (plus depreciation of capital) and thus, from our point of view, incompletely. Work to improve the BEA's method of measuring government services is currently underway; see Fraumeni and Okubo (2005), which discusses measurement of full government services from capital.

on the basis of the dollar value of output sales, on one hand, and the dollar value of payments to factors of production, on the other. In principle, these two independently derived sums—the product side and the income side estimates of GDP—should be equal. The difference between the two estimates is the statistical discrepancy, which by construction differs from zero only because of measurement errors. In the conventional accounts, a small statistical discrepancy suggests that the value of output has been well measured, since two independent measurement methods give approximately the same answer; a larger statistical discrepancy signals the existence of measurement problems.

Interpretation of the difference between input costs and output values is somewhat less straightforward in the case of a nonmarket account. In a competitive market context, an inefficient firm—one for which the value of the resources employed exceeds the value of the output produced—eventually will be driven out of business. Competitive pressures do not operate in the same way in the nonmarket context. That households seek to optimize with respect to their allocation of time is a more tenable assumption than the alternatives, but households that fail to optimize are not driven out of business and may continue to exist indefinitely. This introduces the possibility that, depending on how it is measured, the cost of time devoted to home production could exceed or fall short of its productive value.

The conceptual equality of output values and input costs in the market accounts also reflects the convention that is employed for measuring capital costs. Revenues not spent on other costs of production are considered to be a part of the cost of capital; put differently, capital is treated as the residual claimant. An alternative approach to valuing capital services—and one that seems applicable to the nonmarket accounts—would be to use a standard measure of the flow cost of capital. Using this approach, the cost assigned to capital services could be greater or less than their productive value.

Capital-market constraints, such as those that might arise from lenders' reluctance to finance the production of assets that cannot be marketed and therefore cannot readily serve as loan collateral, may be particularly important in the nonmarket context. Absent capital market constraints, larger investments might be made. Because the amount of investment is constrained, however, the return on investments that do occur will exceed the market rate of return. Valuing nonmarket investments in a fashion that ignores this possibility—for example, valuing educational output based on the costs of the inputs employed—could lead to a figure that is less than the true value of the asset produced.

Differences in technology or scale of production between nonmarket and market production are other possible reasons for divergence between the costs of inputs and the value of output in nonmarket production. It might be more efficient, for example, to prepare ten meals rather than one;

unless they belong to a large family, however, individuals cooking at home cannot take advantage of this scale economy, and reasonable estimates of the value of resources used to produce the meal at home might exceed the market value of the restaurant meal. The transactions costs associated with traveling to dine at a restaurant, however, might still make it attractive to cook and eat at home.

Though the sum of the values of the inputs used to produce a nonmarket output may provide a poor estimate of the value of that output, this has commonly been the practice for measuring some areas of nonmarket production. It is, for example, by far the most common approach in the literature on the value of government services or of home production (see Slater and David 1998 on the former, and Holloway, Short, and Tamplin 2002 on the latter). Well-designed input-based output valuations are a clear improvement over ignoring nonmarket activity altogether. Only with an independent measure of the value of nonmarket output, however, can one hope to address many of the questions for which nonmarket accounts could be most valuable.

In sum, there is a strong argument for adapting the double-entry bookkeeping of the NIPAs for use in any satellite accounts, even if it is not operationalized in exactly the same way in the nonmarket context. For some areas—especially those such as health, where output measurement is especially difficult—input and output measurement will not develop in tandem. This should not be a deterrent to accounting efforts in these areas—a one-sided account is generally better than no account at all. For example, an input-based account for formal education based on imputed values of student time would be useful even if it did not measure the value of the output of education independently. Similarly, an accounting of volunteer labor in the economy could provide useful data for research and policy. Expanded availability of time-use data will advance efforts to identify and quantify productive inputs, and it might provide clues about how to value them.

4.4.2   Classifying Deliveries as Intermediate Output or Final Demand

Several efforts to modify or otherwise expand the national accounts have originated from the belief that misclassifications in the present accounts give a false impression of economic activity. For example, one could argue that at least some governmental activities (e.g., protection and inspection services) properly should be treated as inputs to business activity rather than as an output of the economy, as is current practice.[7] Similarly, commuting costs and other work-related consumer expenditures could be viewed as inputs to production rather than as outputs included in consumption (though it is not obvious how these costs should be assigned for

---

7. These views, as well as issues of classification more generally, are discussed in Conference on Research in Income and Wealth (1958).

use in, say, productivity measurement). Conversely, some items now classified as intermediate inputs might better be classified as output for final demand. Researchers at the BEA have recognized this issue and changed the way they classify some market production. For instance, the BEA now classifies computer software purchases by businesses as investment rather than as an intermediate expense.

As with their market counterparts, nonmarket inputs and outputs must be properly classified for use in a double-entry accounting system and to be useful for productivity analysis. Classification of market activities, much less nonmarket ones, is not always easy, but resolution of these classification issues will be a necessary step in the development of an expanded set of accounts.

4.4.3   Externalities

It would be extremely useful if satellite accounts included estimates of externalities. In this respect, satellite accounts would differ markedly from the NIPAs. An externality is an effect from the action of one individual or business that either damages or creates a benefit to others with no corresponding compensation paid or received by those who engage in the activity. The treatment of externalities is a particularly important issue for environmental accounting. The most interesting applications relate to air and water pollution, where externalities carry potentially very high values. The value of goods and services that can be produced from environmental resources are clearly linked to changes in the level of pollution; part of the impact of pollution is captured in the market accounts but part is not. A reduction in the amount of particulate emissions, for example, may result in reduced worker absence due to illness (a market effect) but also in (nonpriced) health gains. Likewise, factors affecting the state of the environment may or may not be manifest in market expenditures. The cost of catalytic converters is directly reflected in automobile prices. On the other hand, in choosing its production technology, a firm is unlikely to consider the full costs of pollution associated with different options.

The extent to which the aggregate effects of pollution are captured in the NIPAs depends on who bears the costs. As pointed out by William Nordhaus (chap. 3 in this volume), there are two relevant cases. In the first case, the entire impact of an externality flow is reflected in the market accounts, even though there is no market transaction. If a chemical firm pollutes a nearby water source, and the sole harm that arises from that action is that a farmer's crop yield (sold at market) is reduced, the flow takes place within the market. For accounting purposes, this case is a concern only if we want to disaggregate production accurately by sector—here, chemicals and agriculture. The second case, in which externalities flow across the market boundary, is more problematic. If pollution from the chemical plant affects the quality or quantity of outputs such as nonmarket recreational opportunities or the population's health, then failure to account for these effects will distort output and welfare measures. Nordhaus suggests that, to account properly for the second case, standard accounting methods in the NIPAs would need revision since externality disaggregation changes value added in both the nonmarket and the market sectors.

The relevance of this kind of information to policy is fairly obvious. Accounting data on externalities would assist policymakers charged with setting taxes or permit fees for emissions of pollutants or disposal of industrial wastes. If properly set, such taxes and fees will closely approximate the costs of the damage associated with the harmful activity, internalizing the costs and thereby encouraging socially optimal decisions about production processes. But whether or not fees and charges reflect the true positive and negative values of the air and water services provided, such as the positive value of waste disposal services or the negative value of the pollution associated with waste disposal, a society that charges firms for the right to pollute will, by conventional market measures, look different from an otherwise similar society that is laissez-faire regarding externalities.

In an accounting framework, there are two ways to handle environmental improvement or degradation that is tied with market production. We could think of pollution created by a firm in the course of its production of goods as a negatively valued output—the firm is producing goods, but also harmful emissions. We could also think of the pollution-related environmental damage as a cost of production—to produce, the firm needs workers, equipment, and the environment for waste disposal. It should be noted that pollution damage and the input of waste disposal services are not alternative measures of exactly the same thing. In fact, they are usually unequal in dollar terms and, indeed, waste disposal values can be quite high even when pollution damage is near zero, or vice versa. For this reason, environmental accounting systems should keep these concepts distinct. Valuation of degradation, as it affects nonmarket outputs (e.g., health and recreation), is difficult because the link between pollution and health is not well understood, and because valuing health increments is controversial. Nonetheless, development of such valuations clearly would have broad applications.[8]

4.4.4   Measuring Quantities

Dollar values are relatively easy to obtain for the market inputs to nonmarket production. Quantity measures for these market inputs can be constructed by applying appropriate price deflators to the nominal expenditure data. In contrast, for both nonmarket inputs and nonmarket outputs, quantity measurement often will be a necessary first step in the development of monetary valuations.

Even in the case of market inputs, complications arise. Purchases of cap-

---

8. Further discussion of environmental accounting issues can be found in Nordhaus and Kokkelenberg (1999).

ital equipment by households, for example, are treated as purchases for final consumption in the NIPAs. But measuring the inputs to household production requires a measure of the stock of consumer durables. To create such a stock estimate, one must combine information on spending over time for dishwashers, refrigerators, vacuum cleaners, washing machines, and other capital equipment used in home production with information on these items' useful lives. Although there are practical difficulties that complicate estimation of the stock of capital equipment used in home production, the basic approach is well developed.[9]

An especially important nonmarket input on which, until very recently, quantity data have been lacking is the time devoted to nonmarket production. Fortunately, the American Time Use Survey (ATUS), launched at the start of 2003 by the BLS, should go a long way toward filling this gap. The ATUS, described a bit more fully below, can be expected to provide good data on the time inputs for a range of productive household activities. These data would be even more useful if the Census Bureau were to produce regularly updated information on the distribution of demographic characteristics in the population, designed to complement the new information on time use and to support accounting efforts generally. A complete demographics database might include information on the age, gender, school enrollment status, years of education and degrees completed, occupation, household structure, immigrant status, employment status, and other characteristics of the population. Knowing about the distribution of demographic characteristics and changes in that distribution over time would, for example, help researchers determine whether observed changes in the pattern of time use reflect changes in population mix or some other factor. The demographic data to support such an effort are, for the most part, already available, largely from the Census Bureau but in some cases from the BLS, the National Center for Health Statistics, and other agencies. A determined researcher could compile these data from existing sources, but it would be very helpful if the information were assembled in a single place, adjusted to be consistent over time. The demographic database would not itself be a satellite to the existing economic accounts, but it would assist in the development and use of such satellite accounts.

The ease with which the quantity of nonmarket outputs can be measured varies widely. Relatively good data are available, for example, on the educational attainment of the working-age population. These data provide a starting point for quantifying the output of the educational sector. Changes in mortality and morbidity are similarly well documented and could provide a basis for quantifying changes in the health status of the

---

9. This is a case for which the BEA already maintains the desired data series, albeit not as a part of the core accounts. See Katz (1983) for a discussion of measuring the stock of consumer durables.

population, particularly if combined with information from a demographic account that tracked changes in population mix. In other cases, considerable creativity may be required to measure the quantities of nonmarket outputs, and doing an adequate job ultimately may require the collection of new data. Tracking air quality would require better measures of the pollutants to which the public is exposed and of the costs they impose. Tracking the output of the household sector would require data on such things as meals prepared or loads of laundry washed and dried. But, at least in principle, it is possible to see how this task might be approached.

To elaborate on the laundry example, on the input side, the accounts would tally the number of hours devoted to laundry; these hours could be valued using the wage of a domestic employee or the opportunity cost or predicted market wage of the person doing the laundry (these methods are discussed in the next section). The remaining inputs would be the capital services of the household's washing machine and dryer, together with electricity, water, detergent, and other necessary materials. Both quantities and prices would be reported. On the output side, the accounts would report the amount of laundry done and its price, estimated on the basis of what it would have cost to have the laundry cleaned commercially.[10]

4.4.5   Assigning Prices

Anyone contemplating the development of nonmarket accounts must decide how best to value inputs and outputs in the various accounts, given the absence of prices. Valuation typically involves finding market analogues for the nonmarket inputs or outputs in question. Given the distance from the market of some utility-generating activities, however, this approach is not always feasible.

How to measure the value of unpaid time devoted to nonmarket production is the central input valuation question. One possible approach is to value nonmarket time at the opportunity cost of the person performing the nonmarket activity. Another approach employed in the literature has been to value this time at market substitute prices—the wage that would be paid to a person hired to perform the task in question. The two approaches may give quite different answers if higher-wage individuals devote time to tasks for which the market wage is relatively low.

It may, at first blush, seem puzzling why anyone would choose to perform activities that compensate—in the form of either wages paid or value of nonmarket output produced—at a rate below the wage that could be earned in market employment. Further reflection makes clear that such

10. More thought needs to be given to what productivity measures mean when they are based on market replacement valuations. In the absence of direct measures of the output of nonmarket activities, one might impute using information on the relationship of outputs to inputs in market production. In such cases, productivity measures for nonmarket activities may simply recover the imputation scheme.

decisions may be entirely rational. Economic theory conceives of people making marginal choices about their allocation of time to different activities. At the point of maximum satisfaction, the marginal personal lost value associated with working for pay or to produce a valuable output should be equated to the marginal personal benefit, the wage rate, or, in the case of nonmarket production, the value of the output produced. Personal lost value equals the difference between the marginal satisfaction or enjoyment that could be derived from engaging in nonwork activities and the (presumably lesser) marginal satisfaction or enjoyment intrinsic to the work in question.

A key point in this theory is the following: even at the same moment, the time of any individual may have different marginal values reflected in different rates of compensation. The reason is that different activities may be associated with different amounts of personal lost value. A lawyer who commands \$200 per hour from corporate clients may do work at \$50 per hour for a charity. Providing the work to the charity has an offsetting personal benefit (enjoyment) absent from working for a corporation. By the same principle, highly paid individuals may choose to prepare meals at home that could have been purchased in the market at a cost far below the wages the individual could have earned by working for pay instead of cooking. The recreation component of cooking means that the marginal value of the cooking performed is lower than the wage, if there is no similar recreational value in the person's job. In both of the cases—the lawyer performing work for a charity or the highly compensated person cooking meals at home—we would overstate the cost of inputs to nonmarket activities and understate their productivity if we mistakenly used the opportunity cost wage to value the time spent in activities the individual finds enjoyable.

We turn to economic theory for guidance in attaching an appropriate replacement cost value to time spent in nonmarket activities that someone else could have been hired to perform. A production function relates the productive inputs—labor L and capital K—to output Q:

$$Q = f(bL, K)$$

Quantitatively, people's time (L) is the most important unmeasured input in nonmarket production. In the nonmarket context, we often must compare an unpaid labor input to a market replacement. People performing nonmarket tasks may be less skilled and work less hard, on average, than people doing similar work in the market for pay. In the production function for nonmarket output, b is a measure of the relative efficiency of nonmarket as compared to market labor. If our speculation is correct, b will typically be a number between zero and 1.0. An appropriate procedure for cases in which a family member performs work at home that could have been performed by someone hired in the market is to count the family member's hours as measured and to value those hours at a rate equal to the efficiency factor, b, multiplied by the market wage for someone performing the type of work in question. Thus, if a home owner chooses to reroof the house and, using the same materials and tools, takes twice as long to do a comparable job as it would have taken a professional roofer making $30 per hour, we would record all of the time the home owner spent on the task and value that time at $15 per hour. Further, we would use the same $15 per hour valuation whether the home owner earns $100 or $10 in his or her own market job. In the case of the $100 per hour person, we implicitly would be assigning the roofing task an amenity value of $85 per hour, while in the case of the $10 per hour person, we would be assigning it a disamenity value of $5 per hour.

With respect to a task that cannot be given to another person—such as studying or exercising—the appropriate price is the opportunity cost of the time. For people who work in the market, the opportunity cost may reasonably be derived from their wages; some imputation must be made for those not employed in market work. In either case, some adjustment should in principle be made for any difference in the amenities of work activities as compared to nonmarket activities.

Valuing nonmarket outputs often will be even more difficult than valuing inputs. A sensible guiding principle is to treat nonmarket goods and services as if they were produced and consumed in markets. This means that, wherever possible, the prices of nonmarket goods and services should be imputed from a market counterpart. Many youth sports organizations, for example, are operated largely by volunteers. Although a fee may be charged for participation in the activity, that fee cannot be viewed as a market price. But there are also private firms that offer opportunities for children to participate in similar recreational activities that do charge a market-determined price. Given information on the relevant output quantities—for example, numbers of children participating in a nonprofit youth sports organization's various recreational programs—the price charged for participating in similar activities offered by private firms could be used in valuing the nonprofit organization's output.

In some cases, there may be differences in quality between home-produced outputs and market outputs, just as there may be between home and market production inputs. In principle, the valuation of nonmarket outputs should take into account any differences in the quality of those outputs as compared to similar market outputs, much as we proposed for the valuation of nonmarket as compared to market labor inputs.

Even in the case of near-market goods, market and nonmarket outputs may be imperfect substitutes, complicating comparisons of their value. More difficult yet are the cases in which a nonmarket good is an asset that has no direct market counterpart and is never sold. A possible approach in these cases may be to use market prices to value the stream of output produced by the asset over time and then to treat the present value of the returns as a measure of the asset's value. This approach has a clear grounding in the standard theory that underlies the valuation of marketable capital assets and is the approach taken, for example, by Jorgenson and Fraumeni (1989, 1992) in their work on the valuation of investments in human capital. They begin by calculating the increments to earnings associated with successive increments to education. The present value of the earnings increments, cumulated over a person's productive lifetime (and assuming that education enhances the value of market and nonmarket time equally), is then used as a measure of the value of the incremental investment in human capital.

Investments in health also yield a flow of nonmarketed services over time. Improved health increases not only expected years of labor market activity, and thus labor market earnings, but also the expected number of years available in which to enjoy all that makes life rewarding. Developing a market-based measure of the value of additional years of life that may flow from health care investments is controversial, though labor market data have proven useful for this purpose. Specifically, the fact that different occupations are associated both with different risks of fatal injury and with different relative wage rates has been exploited to derive estimates of the value of an additional year of life. Such measures, while far from perfect, have the advantage of being based on real-world decisions that yield observable market outcomes, and for that reason they have appeal.

Different approaches may be necessary for the case of nonmarket outputs that are public in nature, such as crime rates and air quality. Again, however, it may be possible to develop measures of the value of these outputs on the basis of market transactions. The levels of many, if not all, of these nonmarket outputs are likely to differ across localities. People presumably will be willing to pay more to live in communities with low crime rates and good air quality than in communities that lack these attributes. The value of such positive attributes should be reflected in house prices. At least in principle, one could derive an estimate of the value of lower crime rates, better schools, or higher air quality from a hedonic model that relates house prices to these (and other) community characteristics (see Black 1999 for an interesting application).

There are a number of areas for which market valuation, or even imputations based on nonmarket analogues, are simply unavailable and impossible to obtain. Examples of these might include some aspects of social capital, such as family stability; the effect of terrorism on the population's sense of well-being; or the "existence" and "legacy" values of national monuments, such as the Grand Canyon. In these cases, any attempted valuation would have to rely on more indirect evidence. We would argue strongly that attention should be directed first to those categories of nonmarket output for which the most defensible, market-based approaches to valuation are possible.

4.4.6   Counting and Valuation Issues

The national accounts have a consistent structure for reporting prices and corresponding quantities. The two have an intimate connection, because prices form the basis for aggregating the quantities of different products. The national accounts have adopted the approach long advocated by index-number theorists—the accounts compute chain-weighted quantity indexes of groups of products by weighting the percent change of the quantity of each product by its share in the dollar value of all the products. As a result, the accounts directly support productivity calculations. Productivity growth for any group of products—including the full complement of products in GDP—is the percent growth of the aggregate quantity less the corresponding weighted growth of the inputs.

In the market economy, monetary aggregates generally are the most accessible measures of the level of activity—dollar values of sales, dollars paid as wages and salaries, and so on—and measuring quantities often is more difficult. By definition, however, nonmarket activity does not involve monetary transactions. This means that the data on monetary aggregates that form the building blocks for traditional national income accounting are simply not available. Instead, available data may consist of physical or other quantity indicators of the level of activity, such as hours of time devoted to home production, student-years of education provided, or ambient concentrations of various air pollutants.

On one side are those who argue that no nonarbitrary way exists for assigning monetary values to a heterogeneous set of nonmarket inputs or outputs, and that any such assignment unavoidably will reflect value judgments that are inappropriate for a statistical agency (see, e.g., van de Ven, Kazemier, and Keuning 2000, p. 8). The counterposition holds that, without an attempt to assign monetary values to the quantity indicators that are the basic unit of measurement for nonmarket outputs, it will be difficult for policymakers to digest and use the information. This may mean that nonmarket outputs end up being ignored, which implicitly assigns them a value of zero. Alternatively, policymakers may assign a value to the nonmarket output using subjective methods that are far less defensible than the methods that would be employed by a statistical agency. In either case, there is a good argument for measurement specialists to provide estimates based on the best possible methods, even if these are highly imperfect, rather than leaving a statistical void. Another argument for attempting to assign monetary values to quantity indicators is that the effort filters out indicators that may be of minor economic importance. One problem with purely physical accounting systems is that, useful as they may be for some research topics, they tend to be encyclopedic and difficult to comprehend. Economics can minimize biased value judgments by providing scientific guidelines for approximating prices in many cases. And with a monetary metric, the aggregation of detailed measures of output to larger, useful indexes is possible. For these reasons, nonmarket inputs and outputs should be, to the maximum extent possible, valued in dollar terms.

The usefulness of a monetary valuation approach depends on the extent and accuracy with which monetary values ultimately can be assigned to the inputs and outputs in question. In order that such assignments be as objective as possible, we favor basing these valuations wherever possible on information derived from the terms of observable market transactions or their analogues. And, even when it is difficult to base valuations on market transactions, it is important that valuation methods be reproducible by independent observers. In certain instances, assigning prices to outputs (or inputs) may be so controversial that publishing physical quantity accounts may be the best available option. Given that both price and quantity data are needed to calculate values for the conventional monetized accounts, however, it is reasonable to produce the best price and monetary estimates available, as long as sets of assumptions are clearly stated. Limiting an account to physical quantity reporting should be the exception, not the rule. We also again emphasize the desirability of giving priority to those areas of nonmarket accounting for which it is possible to draw valuations from market comparisons.

4.4.7   Marginal and Total Valuation

Economic valuation methods fall into two broad categories: the first, which tracks the framework of the national accounts, relies on prices, which reflect marginal benefits; the second considers the full amount consumers would be willing to pay for a good or service, which includes a consumer surplus to the extent that amount is greater than the price. Thus, the two approaches differ in the way benefits are measured.

In the case of a product or service sold in a competitive market, the price is set at a value that equates the cost of producing and the value of consuming the marginal unit of output. Marginal valuation omits consideration of the inframarginal benefits of goods and services. In many cases, knowing consumers' willingness to pay for first and subsequent units of a good or service does not matter for any decision. Although the public enjoys a large consumer surplus from the production of ice cream—that is, enjoyment exceeding in value the total price paid for the ice cream—there is no policy or accounting issue relating to that surplus. Productivity and other types of measurement use the marginal values revealed by the market price. The same principle applies to many of the nonmarket goods and services that would be included in satellite accounts.

One important area for which the differences between marginal and total valuations are likely to be substantial is health care. Imagine a new pill that cured sickle cell anemia and could be produced at a marginal cost of $1.00. The total value of that innovation would be enormous; the marginal valuation attached to sales of these pills would be minimal. For a health account, it would be more consistent with accounting principles to think about such cases in terms of the social profit generated by the productive activity. This requires that careful attention be given to the task of identifying and categorizing inputs and outputs. In a fully specified health account, inputs such as basic research and development (R&D), time spent in health improving activities, medical innovations—some of which are bought and sold in markets and some which are not—enter on one side; on the other (output) side, changes in health status, the valuation of which reflects some estimate of the value of a year of healthy life, must be measured and valued. Because the input and output sides are independently valued, they could, if properly measured, reveal social profits realized from research investments and other inputs. In our example, the value to society of the incremental change in health status associated with finding a cure for sickle cell anemia may well exceed the cost of its development, even taking all of the contributing inputs into account.

The potential for large social profits seems particularly relevant in the case of new products, which bring discrete changes in benefits to consumers. It has been argued that the value consumers place on new products should be reflected in properly constructed price indexes as a decline in the price level (see, for example, Hausman 1996). While there is not yet a consensus on this issue in the price index literature, we would note that deflating nominal expenditures with a price index that accounted for the value realized by the purchasers of new goods would yield an estimate of real output that included consumer surplus associated with the introduction of these goods. It is meaningless, in a national income accounting context, to estimate total value for existing products. Sometimes total value data will be needed for a cost benefit analysis, and this is fine; cost-benefit analysis and national accounts rest on different conceptual ideals and objectives.

4.5   Data for Nonmarket Accounting

One barrier to the development of satellite accounts such as we have described in this chapter has been the limitations of the data available to support quantification and valuation of covered activities. As already noted, the new ATUS will provide rich information on the most important input to nonmarket production—the time people devote to nonmarket activities. Other inputs to nonmarket production commonly are purchased in markets, meaning that the challenges associated with measuring these inputs, while not trivial, should be similar in nature to those routinely encountered in the construction of the NIPAs. Considerable work will be required to develop the data needed for independent measurement of nonmarket outputs. In this section, we briefly describe the new ATUS, then identify several other key data needs.

The data appropriate to measuring the amount of time devoted to nonmarket activities must necessarily come from recording information on people's activities away from their jobs. The vehicle for collecting such information is a time-budget survey—a study in which a large sample of individuals keeps a diary of their activities over one or several days. In a time-budget survey the activities typically are just listed descriptively together with the time spent on them, then coded into a set of categories. One of the benefits of time-budget surveys as compared to other methods of learning about how people spend their time is that time-budget surveys force the reported aggregate of time devoted to all activities to equal 1,440 minutes per day for each person.

While time use studies have periodically been funded by federal agencies, none has been designed or conducted by any part of the federal statistical system. In January 2003, the BLS began collecting time budgets as part of the monthly ATUS. Researchers and activists interested in valuing women's time in the household were the first to urge that the BLS develop a time use survey, but the data from the new survey, now operational after nearly a decade of development and testing (see Horrigan and Herz 2005), will have much wider applicability in the construction of supplemental economic accounts for the United States.

The ATUS samples are taken randomly from individuals in households that have completed their eighth month of participation in the Current Population Survey (CPS). The BLS had expected to sample roughly 2,800 households per month and to obtain a 70 percent response rate. Due to funding constraints, the number of households sampled has dropped from 2,800 per month to 1,800 per month beginning in January 2004. The response rate from the diaries taken by telephone has been just 59 percent, while from the small number taken in person (from households without telephones) it has been just 34 percent. Looking forward, actual responses thus are expected from individuals in about 1,200 households each month, with roughly 14,000 individuals expected to complete diaries each year starting in 2004.

Households are chosen based on a variety of stratifications (including race/ethnicity and presence of children of various ages), all designed to reduce the sampling variance of the statistics describing smaller subsets of the U.S. population. A crucial issue for our purposes is the classification of the respondents' verbal descriptions of activities into categories that are useful for accounting and for analysis. The basic codes are aggregated into seventeen top-level categories: Personal Care (mainly sleep); Household Activities; Caring for and Helping Household Members; Caring for and Helping Non-household Members; Work and Work-Related Activities;

Education; Consumer Purchases (e.g., food shopping); Purchasing Professional and Personal Care Services (e.g., doctors' visits); Purchasing Household Services; Obtaining Government Services and Civic Obligations; Eating and Drinking; Socializing, Relaxing, and Leisure; Sports, Exercise, and Recreation; Religious and Spiritual Activities; Volunteer Activities; Telephone Calls; and Traveling. Within each of these broad categories, there are further disaggregations. The structure of the categories appears to accord well with the construction of supplemental accounts along the lines discussed in this paper. In addition to completing the time use diaries, ATUS respondents update their CPS collected information on work behavior, demographics, earnings and (bracketed) family income.

As a large-scale and ongoing time-budget survey the ATUS is unique worldwide. Several other countries' time-budget data sets are large enough to generate reliable measures of time allocation of the sort needed to construct statistically meaningful snapshots, but no other country has time use data to support supplemental nonmarket accounts that are analogous to the NIPA accounts in being continuously updated. The annual ATUS samples are very large relative to those for other countries' time use surveys, but what makes the ATUS particularly valuable for the purposes of creating nonmarket accounts is that its information will be provided year after year.

The ATUS can be used to quantify time spent by the population in productive activities, both market and nonmarket. Some have argued that the decisions of the ATUS designers to collect only one day's time budget from each respondent and to survey only one member per household limit the value of the ATUS data. It is true that the design of the ATUS makes it less useful for certain kinds of research, such as that focused on the timing of activities or on household bargaining. These features of the survey are not, however, a major drawback when it comes to constructing time use estimates for satellite accounts.

Other aspects of the ATUS design may be more significant for the use of these data in nonmarket accounting. One relevant design feature is that the survey tracks "primary" activities, but not secondary ones; in other words, the data are coded to show people engaged in just one activity at a time. The survey does include separate questions designed to learn about time devoted to child care, which empirically is by far the most important "secondary" activity reported by respondents to other time use surveys. Still, more complete information about secondary activities could prove to be important for monitoring time devoted to productive nonmarket activities that may occur simultaneously with other tasks or pastimes. A related question is whether activities that typically require only a few minutes at a time—for example, putting a load of laundry in the washer, and then later moving it from the washer to the dryer—will be reported consistently enough to support good estimates of time devoted to them. Another limitation of the ATUS from the nonmarket accounting perspective is that data are collected only for people age fifteen and older. The exclusion of children and young teens means that other data will be needed to quantify the time spent in school or school-related pursuits, as would be required to construct an education satellite account.

Perhaps our major concern about the ATUS is the risk that the data may not be fully representative of how the average person spends his or her time. Although there is no way to know for sure until the data can be carefully examined, it seems plausible that busier individuals might simply be less likely to participate in the survey, meaning that the survey estimates could be distorted. Efforts to assess the extent of any possible bias in the survey responses—and, if necessary, to address that bias by raising response rates or making appropriate adjustments to the estimates—should be a top priority.

These comments are not, we would stress, intended as criticisms of the ATUS, which we believe represents a great leap forward with regard to accounting for the inputs to nonmarket production. We understand that there were good operational reasons for the decisions made in designing the ATUS. There was evidence, for example, that, had the survey been designed to collect time use information from multiple members of responding household on a particular day, survey response rates would have been much lower. Similarly, testing carried out during the survey development period raised serious concern that probing systematically for secondary activities in which respondents might have been engaged would have greatly increased the perceived survey response burden and thus adversely affected response rates. And the BLS is well aware of the potential for nonresponse bias and has planned research to assess its significance. Still, as work proceeds on the ATUS and on time use data collection more generally, the limitations and potential biases in the data currently being collected for nonmarket accounting purposes should be kept in mind.

A time use survey supplies data on the amounts of time that people devote to different tasks. Nonmarket accounting also requires that values (prices) be assigned to these quantity measures. For valuing time devoted to tasks that could have been performed by a third party—such as nonmarket time devoted to home production or to volunteer activities—we have argued for a replacement cost approach. If nonmarket and market labor are similarly skilled and supplied with similar intensity, the market wage paid to people hired to do the type of work in question may be a reasonable estimate of the replacement cost. In other cases, however, there may be a significant difference between the efficiency of nonmarket as compared to market labor, and in these cases observed market wages should be adjusted to account for the relative (in)efficiency of nonmarket labor. At present, however, we lack the information about market and nonmarket production function parameters that would provide an empirical basis for making such adjustments. This is another area where research and data development would be welcome.

As noted above, many nonmarket accounting applications also require information on how the demographic structure of the population is changing. Although individual researchers can compile such information through special-purpose tabulations of CPS or Census Bureau microdata, there is at present no frequently updated published source of information describing the population's basic characteristics. A well-coordinated demographic data compilation effort would have obvious value in nonmarket accounting applications—for example, constructing measures of educational attainment for an education satellite account or, in health, for determining whether changes in the observed incidence of a particular disease were attributable to changes in the age distribution of the population or some other cause. Because the raw materials needed to construct a demographic data set designed to support nonmarket accounting already exist, this should be a relatively easy data gap to fill.

In addition to labor inputs, a complete nonmarket account must include values of nonlabor inputs. Thus, for example, a home production account must include data on the capital services, materials, and energy inputs that complement unpaid labor in generating home-produced outputs. Purchases of materials used in home production already are included in the NIPAs, as consumer goods on the production side and as returns to capital, labor, and other inputs on the income side. The NIPAs also include spending on consumer durables such as refrigerators and washing machines, though the annual flow of services associated with the stock of consumer durables need not correspond especially closely on a year-by-year basis with spending on purchases of consumer durables in the same year (see Fraumeni and Okubo 2001). In accounting for household production, it is the flow of services from these durables that is relevant and for which data are required.

Finally, further research and data development are needed to solve age-old questions relating to the proper definition and measurement of output. What are the outputs of the various nonmarket activities? Zvi Griliches once observed that "in many service sectors it is not exactly clear what is being transacted, what is the output, and what services correspond to the payments made to their providers" (Griliches 1992, p. 7). This observation is especially pertinent for many of the areas of interest here which are dominated by services—and difficult services to measure, at that—such as education, health, social services, culture and the arts, and recreation.

The need for development of better measures of nonmarket outputs can be illustrated with reference to education and health. In such difficult-to-measure sectors, the value of output frequently is set equal to the aggregate value of the inputs used in its production. Accordingly, little is known about growth, quality improvements, or productivity in these sectors. In recent years, alternative approaches have been developed for estimating educational output more directly. Examples of these approaches include indicator (e.g., test-score-based) approaches, incremental earnings approaches, and housing value approaches. Similarly, for a health account, data on the population's health status, of the sort now being developed in disease state and health impairment research, hold promise of providing direct measures of the output of the health sector.

4.6 Conclusion

In this chapter, we have argued for efforts to develop a systematic accounting of nonmarket activity to complement the existing national income and product accounts. By design, the NIPAs are focused primarily on market activity and largely ignore the production of goods and services that takes place outside the market. Satellite accounts in areas such as home production, investments in education, investments in health, volunteer activity, and environmental improvements or degradation could be of enormous value in providing a more complete picture of economic growth and in promoting a better understanding of the factors that have contributed to that growth.

The existing national economic accounts have proven their value over a long period of use and refinement. Largely for that reason, we favor modeling nonmarket satellite accounting efforts on the existing national economic accounts. This means, among other things, that we favor the preservation of the double-entry bookkeeping approach that is the hallmark of the NIPAs and reliance on market transactions insofar as possible in the valuation of nonmarket inputs and outputs.

A major impediment to the development of nonmarket accounts has been the paucity of data to support their construction. Lack of suitable data undoubtedly will continue to be a constraint, but the new ATUS seems to us to justify a new round of thinking about nonmarket accounting issues. This new survey will supply key data needed to support a useful accounting of the inputs to nonmarket production. We urge researchers to continue the hard work that will be needed to develop sensible measures of the many and varied outputs associated with nonmarket economic activity.

References

Abraham, Katharine G., and Christopher Mackie, eds. 2005. *Beyond the market: Designing nonmarket accounts for the United States.* Washington, DC: National Academies Press.

Black, Sandra E. 1999. Do better schools matter? Parental valuation of elementary education. *Quarterly Journal of Economics* 114 (May): 577–99.

Bureau of Economic Analysis, U.S. Department of Commerce. 1994. A satellite account for research and development. *Survey of Current Business* 74 (November): 37–71.

Cutler, David. 2004. *Your money or your life: Strong medicine for America's health care system.* New York: Oxford University Press.

Cutler, David, and E. Richardson. 1997. Measuring the health of the United States population. *Brookings Papers on Economic Activity, Microeconomics:* 217–72.

Conference on Research in Income and Wealth. 1958. *A critique of the United States Income and Product Accounts.* A report of the National Bureau of Economic Research. Princeton, NJ: Princeton University Press.

Fixler, Dennis J., Marshall B. Reinsdorf, and George M. Smith. 2003. Measuring the services of commercial banks in the NIPAs. *Survey of Current Business* 83 (9): 33–44.

Fogel, Robert W. 1999. Catching up with the economy. *American Economic Review* 89 (March): 1–21.

Fraumeni, Barbara, and Sumiye Okubo. 2001. Alternative treatments of consumer durables in the National Accounts. Paper prepared for the BEA Advisory Committee Meeting. 11 May, Washington, DC. Available at http://www.bea.gov/bea/papers/cdinnipa.pdf.

———. 2005. R&D in the National Income and Product Accounts: A first look at its effect on GDP. In *Measuring Capital in the New Economy,* ed. Carol Corrado, John Haltiwanger, and Daniel Sichel, 275–316. Chicago: University of Chicago Press.

Griliches, Zvi. 1992. Introduction. In *Output measurement in the service sectors,* ed. Z. Griliches, 1–22. Chicago: University of Chicago Press.

Hausman, Jerry. 1996. Valuation of new goods under perfect and imperfect competition. In *The economics of new goods,* ed. T. F. Bresnahan and R. J. Gordon, 209–37. Chicago: University of Chicago Press.

Holloway, Sue, Sandra Short, and Sarah Tamplin. 2002. Household satellite account (experimental) methodology. London: United Kingdom Office for National Statistics. Available at http://www.statistics.gov.uk/hhsa/hhsa/resources/fileattachments/hhsa.pdf.

Horrigan, Michael, and Diane Herz. 2005. A study in the process of planning, designing and executing a survey program: The BLS American Time-Use Survey. In *The economics of time use data,* ed. Daniel Hamermesh and Gerard Pfann, 317–50. Amsterdam: North-Holland.

Jorgenson, Dale, and Barbara M. Fraumeni. 1989. Investment in education. *Educational Researcher* 18 (May): 35–44.

———. 1992. The output of the education sector. In *Output measurement in the service sectors,* ed. Z. Griliches, 303–38. Chicago: University of Chicago Press.

Katz, Arnold. 1983. Valuing the services of consumer durables. *Review of Income and Wealth* 29:405–77.

Kendrick, John W. 1970. The historical development of national income accounts. *History of Political Economy* 11 (Fall): 284–315.

———. 1976. *The formation and stocks of total capital.* New York: Columbia University Press for NBER.

Kuznets, Simon S. 1934. National income 1929–1932. Senate Document no. 124, 73rd Cong., 2nd sess. Washington, DC.

Landefeld, J. Steven, and Stephanie H. McCulla. 2000. Accounting for nonmarket household production within a national accounts framework. *Review of Income and Wealth* 46 (3): 289–307.

LaPlante, M. P., C. Harrington, and T. Kang. 2002. Estimating paid and unpaid hours of personal assistance services in activities of daily living provided to adults living at home. *Health Services Research* 37 (2): 397–415.

Mankiw, N. Gregory, David Romer, and David N. Weil. 1992. A contribution to the empirics of economic growth. *Quarterly Journal of Economics* 107 (May): 407–37.

Marshall, Alfred. 1920. *Principles of economics: An introductory volume.* 8th ed. London: Macmillan.

Michael, Robert. 1996. Money illusion: The importance of household time use in social policy making. *Journal of Family and Economic Issues* 17 (Winter): 245–60.

Nordhaus, William D. 2002. Principles of national accounting for nonmarket accounts. Draft document prepared for the Panel to Study the Design of Nonmarket Accounts. Yale University, Department of Economics.

Nordhaus, William D., and Edward C. Kokkelenberg, eds. 1999. *Nature's numbers: Expanding the national economic accounts to include the environment.* Washington, DC: National Academies Press.

Pigou, A. C. 1920. *The economics of welfare.* London: Macmillan.

Popkin, Joel. 2000. Data watch: The U.S. National Income and Product Accounts. *Journal of Economic Perspectives* 14 (Spring): 205–13.

Reid, Margaret. 1934. *The economics of household production.* New York: Wiley.

Slater, Courtenay M., and Martin H. David, eds. 1998. *Measuring the government sector of the U.S. accounts.* Washington, DC: National Academies Press.

United Nations, Commission of the European Communities, International Monetary Fund, Organisation for Economic Co-operation and Development, and World Bank. 1993. *System of national accounts 1993.* Series F, no. 2, rev. 4. New York: United Nations.

Van de Ven, Peter, Brugt Kazemier, and Steven Keuning. 2000. Measuring well-being with an integrated system of economic and social accounts. Paper presented at the 2000 meeting of the Sienna Group. 22–24 May, Maastrich, the Netherlands.

5

The "Architecture" of Capital Accounting
Basic Design Principles

Charles R. Hulten

"It is not reasonable for us to expect the government to produce statistics in areas where concepts are mushy and where there is little professional agreement on what is to be measured and how."
—Griliches (1994, page 14)

National income accounting would be a relatively simple matter were it not for "capital." All flows of output would then be for immediate consumption, and labor would be the sole factor of production (and relatively undifferentiated labor at that, since there would be no investments in health and education to complicate matters). The question of how the boundary between market and nonmarket activity should be defined would be one of the main issues of contention; how to measure the real output associated with intangible products like services would be another. However, both problems are essentially issues of implementation rather than of basic theory, since there is no conceptual reason to exclude the nonmarket use of economic resources from a complete set of national accounts, nor is there a controversy about the need to express inputs and outputs in both current and constant prices.

When it comes to capital, however, it is more a question of what to do than how to do it. No issue has given economic theory more trouble, from Karl Marx and the Austrian capital theorists to Keynes and the Cambridge Controversies, and the ambiguity has only gotten worse with the increased theoretical focus on Schumpeterian uncertainty, partial information, imperfect competition, and the emerging literature on the importance of intangible capital assets. This unsettled state of affairs is obviously a problem for the design of national income accounts, since, as Griliches (1994) observed, it is hard to measure something when there is a funda-

Charles R. Hulten is a professor of economics at the University of Maryland and a research associate of the National Bureau of Economic Research.

I would like to thank those who have given me valuable comments on earlier drafts of this chapter, especially Erwin Diewert and Paul Schreyer. Remaining errors are, of course, my responsibility.

mental disagreement about what exactly "it" is. This ambiguity is reflected in the current design of national accounting systems, as well as in the structure of financial accounting systems. No system currently in place achieves a complete account of capital in its many facets and dimensions.

These observations are the starting point for this chapter on the architecture of the capital accounts. To use the architectural analogy, the paper is about abstract design principles and is not a blueprint for a particular building; it is about the logically prior question of what should be done, rather than a discussion of how do it. It is inspired by Koopmans's (1947) famous injunction about the need to avoid "measurement without theory." This injunction argues that theory should guide measurement practice in order to guide the selection and definition of the variables included in the accounts and to define the boundaries, insure internal consistency among these variables, and facilitate their interpretation and subsequent use. However, while Koopmans's injunction is especially important for defining the role of capital in the national accounts, it does not specify any particular theory, and, of course, there are many candidates for this role: capital accounts can be built along Keynesian lines (as with the traditional structure of the U.S. National Income and Product Accounts [NIPAs]), or they can be broadly defined to include environmental, social, and quality-of-life indicator variables; even within the corpus of "standard economics," there are at least three ways of describing capital within the neoclassical growth model alone. No single approach can claim to be unambiguously superior for all purposes (or views of the world), since the objective of any set of accounts is to inform a particular issue, and it is the user who defines both the relevant questions and the desired method of informing the answer. However, a choice of architecture does have to be made, if for no other reason than to insure internal consistency, and this chapter describes an architecture design based on neoclassical economics. This architecture has as its foundation the familiar circular flow model of payments and commodities derived from standard supply-and-demand analysis, and it has the neoclassical theory of production and consumption as its superstructure. This architecture is implicit in contemporary accounts like the NIPAs and the United Nations' System of National Accounts (United Nations et al., 1993) though not fully realized there, and is similar to the structure outlined in the work of Christensen and Jorgenson (1969, 1970).

The circular flow model (or CFM) is organized along lines of *functional* activity (consumption and production), rather than *structural* lines (nonfinancial business, financial business, government, foreign sector, households).[1] Agents have dual roles in the accounting structure: acting as pro-

---

1. Patinkin (1973) traces the circular flow model, in its modern form, to the work of Frank Knight in the 1920s and 1930s. Earlier forms of the model can be found, according to Patinkin, but were apparently not intended as a representation of the allocation and distribution of goods and services in a complete economic system (the use to which the model is put in this paper).

ducers, they supply products for current consumption or for future consumption via investment goods, and they demand the factor inputs that are necessary for the production of goods; acting as consumers, they supply these factor inputs and demand the producers' output. The sectors are linked by markets in which the inputs and outputs are exchanged and valued according to the "laws" of supply and demand. Some of the exchanges may exist only as shadow prices outside the formal market context and therefore require imputation by the economic statistician, but this difficulty is, again, a problem of implementation and not of basic design.

Because of the complex nature of capital, the chapter starts with a minimalist description of the CFM in which there is no capital of any kind. Using this as the baseline case, the chapter then introduces various aspects of "capital" in order of increasing complexity, starting with a variant in which capital arises only from a temporal mismatch between the production and use of consumption goods, without any actual capital goods. The CFM is then expanded to allow for capital, starting with the stock of inventories and proceeding thereafter to productive capital inputs in both tangible and intangible forms. In following this sequence, it may appear as though there are many separate and distinct entities called "capital." However, a comparison of each case reveals the following unity: all aspects of capital ultimately are derived from the decision to defer current consumption in order to enhance or maintain expected future consumption.

The functional structure of the CFM also reveals the dual nature of this unified conception of "capital." From the standpoint of consumers, deferred consumption involves the diversion of current income from consumption to saving, which adds to the stock of consumer wealth and which leads, in turn, to higher income in the future and thus to higher future consumption. From the standpoint of the production sector, deferred consumption involves the diversion of resources away from consumer-good-producing industries to investment-good industries. This diversion adds to the stock of productive capital and leads, in turn, to a larger output of consumption goods in the future. This dual structure helps clarify the various linkages between producers' capital and consumers' wealth, between producers' investment and consumers' saving, and between the cost of the capital to the producer and the income from capital paid to consumers.[2]

5.1 The Basic Circular Flow Diagram

The structure of the CFM is shown in figure 5.1, which describes the flow of payments and quantities in a four-part diagram in which the production

---

2. The distinction between capital cost and capital income is particularly important for any discussion of the architecture of capital accounting, since it is largely ignored in contemporary national accounting practice. By insisting on its importance, indeed necessity, the CFM establishes its utility as an architectural model for a consistent system of national income and wealth accounts.

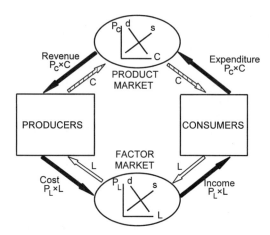

Fig. 5.1   Circular flow model without capital

activities are located on one side of a diagram and consumption is on the other side, and in which inputs are consigned to the lower half of the diagram and outputs are put in the upper part. Input and output flows are linked by "markets" in the upper and lower parts of the diagram, where the goods are transferred from one sector to the other. These bilateral exchanges are the essential feature of the CFM, and when validated by market valuations they establish the equivalence between revenue, cost, income, and expenditure. These exchanges are portrayed as a counterclockwise flow around the outer edge of figure 5.1, and they give rise to the fundamental accounting identity relating the value of output to the value of input. When consumption (C) and labor (L) are the only goods in the account, the equivalence of flows in the CFM reduces to $P^C C = P^L L$.

The ability to track the quantities of input and output over time is one of the main reasons that national accounts are constructed, since it is the flow of goods at any point in time (and not their nominal value) that is the determinant of economic well-being. The flows of consumption goods and labor input are portrayed as a clockwise inner flow around the inner edge of figure 5.1. This flow can easily be derived from the opposing flow of nominal values *in any one period* by simply normalizing all prices to equal 1 (i.e., $P^C = P^L = 1$). If these prices remain constant over time, there is no problem of intertemporal comparability and, in fact, no real need for considering prices at all. However, there is no reason to expect them to remain constant, since both productivity change and monetary inflation will cause nominal prices to change over time, both relatively and absolutely. In this case, the value flows $P^C C$ and $P^L L$ must be separated into price and quantity components in each period, using either independent estimates of price deflators or quantity indexes. The result is a time series of income and product accounts in both nominal prices,

(1a) $$P^C(t)C(t) = P^L(t)L(t),$$

and constant prices,

(1b) $$P^C(0)C(t) = A(t)P^L(0)L(t).$$

The factor $A(t)$ must be included in the constant price account in order to allow for autonomous changes in productivity over time.

There has thus far been little reference to the economic structure that gives rise to the flows of the CFM. There is, however, an implicit structure embedded in the architecture of figure 5.1 simply by virtue of its organization into sectors and markets. The flow of L into the producers' sector and the flow of C out of the sector imply a transformation of input into output, which is formalized in standard theory by the production function $C(t) = F(L[t], t)$. The t here allows for costless advances in the efficiency of production, and is the source of the term $A(t)$ in the constant-price identity, equation (1b). Similarly, the flow of C into the consumers' sector and the outflow of L implies consumer choice among competing alternatives, which is modeled in standard theory by the utility function $U(C[t], L[t])$.[3] These production and utility functions can be linked to the accounting identities in equations (1a) and (1b) using Euler's Theorem (see, for example, Hulten 2001) and also have the helpful feature that they establish natural boundaries for the flow accounts in the CFM of figure 5.1, or, indeed, for any set of accounts whose purpose is to provide a complete description of how available resources are used to satisfy economic wants. This theoretical structure suggests that any produced good that yields utility, and any input that is necessary for production, should be located within the boundaries of a complete set of economic accounts, regardless of whether they are distributed outside of formal markets.[4]

---

3. The utility function is more commonly expressed in terms of consumption and leisure, rather than hours worked—that is, as $U(C[t], H - L[t])$, where H denotes the hours available for work and leisure is thus $(H - L)$. In a multiproduct version of the CFM, each of the N types of consumer goods has its own production function and, in principle, use some of each of the M types of labor input, $C_i(t) = F - (L_{i1}[t], \ldots, L_{iM}[t], t)$; the associated utility is then $U(C_1[t], \ldots, C_N[t]; H - \Sigma_i \Sigma_j L_{ij}[t])$. For clarity, we will assume the fewest number of goods necessary for the exposition. We will also suppress the leisure term by ignoring the constant H, in order to simplify the exposition, since it does not play a central role in the capital accounts described in this paper.

4. The empirical problems associated with the development of the price deflators are often a practical constraint on the choice of accounting boundary. The problem is particularly difficult when the goods in question are intangible, where the units of measurement may be hard even to define in principle, much less to estimate accurately. Determining the appropriate deflators for nonmarket goods is also notoriously difficult. The result has been the tendency to exclude investments in human capital, research and development (R&D), and other intangibles from the accounts, along with nonmarket uses of time, despite the theoretical rationale for their inclusion.

The formulation of the accounting model in equations (1a) and (1b) makes no reference to the goods that are produced for immediate use in other industries (steel to make autos, for example). These intermediate goods are important when the aggregate economy is broken into sectors, and they introduce additional complexity into the CFM architecture. However, since these goods are produced and used up within each accounting period, they disappear in an aggregate account of the economy. Unfortunately, this can lead to the erroneous conclusion that the concept of intermediate goods is largely irrelevant in the aggregate (except, possibly, for the distinction between value added, now $P^L L$, and deliveries to final demand, $P^C C$). The deception arises because the distinction between what is an intermediate good and what is capital depends on the length of the accounting period selected. If the period is one month, a pencil is likely to be a capital good, whereas if the accounting period is one year, is it likely to be an intermediate good. A machine tool with an average economic life of twenty years is capital when the accounting period is one year but is an intermediate input when the period is a century. Since the length of the accounting period is arbitrary, capital as a productive good is itself an arbitrary accounting concept that can, in fact, be dispensed with in certain accounting models (see, for example, Hulten 1979).

5.2 Capital as Deferred Consumption

The all-consumption-labor model of the preceding section envisions a world without capital goods. Since all goods are consumed when they are produced and all input is contemporaneously generated, the magnitudes of these aggregate economic variables refer to the current accounting period, and there is no connection between periods—that is, between $C(t-1)$ and $C(t)$, or between $L(t-1)$ and $L(t)$. However, a connection may exist at the level of the *individual* agent's utility function. Since the life of most people spans multiple accounting periods, the individual utility function is more plausibly written as a function of consumption and leisure over an entire lifetime T, that is, as $U^j(C_j[1], \ldots, C_j[T]; L_j[0], \ldots, L[T])$, rather than a single period of that life. Maximization of this intertemporal utility function subject to the amount of income that can be earned in each year, $P^L(t)L_j(t)$, results in an optimal consumption plan in which desired consumption may exceed or fall short of income in any year. For example, individuals may want to shift consumption from periods of high income to others where income is lower (e.g., to years of retirement).

The opportunity for individuals to shift consumption arises if there are financial instruments that accommodate intertemporal transfers. The existence of such instruments allows individual consumers to lend or borrow part of their current income, $P^L(t)L_j(t)$, which is to say, it allows individuals to save or dissave. Since total consumption is fixed, the saving of lenders must just balance the dissaving of borrowers in every year. The income and product accounts that accommodate this consumption-shifting mechanism are an elaboration of the aggregate account in equations (1a) and (1b). When consumption shifting occurs at the individual level, an individual either saves or dissaves the amount $S_j(t)$, leading to the individual income identity

(2) $$P^C(t)C_j(t) + S_j(t) = P^L(t)L_j(t).$$

For equations (1a), (1b), and (2) to hold simultaneously, total savings across all individuals, $\Sigma_j S_j(t)$, must be zero in each year, because all goods produced within a given year must be consumed within that year.

    Moreover, individual saving or dissaving must balance over the lifetime of each person since all loans must be repaid with interest. The basic intertemporal constraint on each individual's borrowing and lending is the discounted present value of lifetime labor income, which must equal the discounted present value of lifetime consumption. Assuming that there are no bequests to future generations or inherited wealth from the past, the lifetime budget constraint at the start of economic life thus takes the form

(3) $$W_j(0) = \sum_{t=1}^{T} \frac{P^C(t)C_j(t)}{(1+r)^t} = \sum_{t=1}^{T} \frac{P^L(t)L_j(t)}{(1+r)^t}.$$

The time-discount factor $(1 + r)$ is assumed to be constant over time for simplicity of exposition. In light of equation (2), individual savings must have a zero balance over the lifetime of each person, implying that individual net worth ($NW_j[0]$) is also zero:

(4) $$NW_j(0) = \sum_{t=1}^{T} \frac{P^C(t)C_j(t)}{(1+r)^t} - \sum_{t=1}^{T} \frac{P^L(t)L_j(t)}{(1+r)^t} = \sum_{t=1}^{T} \frac{S_j(t)}{(1+r)^t} = 0.$$

This reflects the fact that all loans must be repaid out of lifetime income. Moreover, aggregate net worth *at each point in time* is zero, since the contemporaneous sum of individual net worth in each, $\Sigma_j NW_j(t)$, must reflect the condition that $\Sigma_j S_j(t)$ is zero.

    Because no net wealth is created at the economywide level of aggregation, there is no aggregate sheet balancing assets and liabilities. However, a balance sheet based on these present-value equations does exist for each individual agent, which records in each year the net consequences of all past saving and dissaving. The existence of these individual net worth positions implies that wealth, and the corresponding balance sheets, can exist even though there are no explicit capital goods and no consumption goods are actually shifted between years.

    This conclusion must be modified when an economy is open to international flows. In this case, borrowing and lending can occur across national boundaries, and there can be a nonzero net balance of claims or debits against future consumption for the residents of any one country. While the net position of all countries combined is still zero, the aggregate wealth constraint of each country is now

$$(3') \qquad W(0) = \sum_{t=1}^{T} \frac{P^C(t)C(t)}{(1+r)^t} = P^C(0)K(0) + \sum_{t=1}^{T} \frac{P^L(t)L(t)}{(1+r)^t}.$$

$P^C(0)K(0)$ is the cumulative balance of past external loans or debt (i.e., past saving or dissaving) up to the beginning of the decision interval (the "present"), measured in terms of current consumption. The aggregate net worth (and implied balance sheet) of this open economy takes the form

$$(4') \qquad NW(0) = \sum_{t=1}^{T} \frac{P^C(t)C(t)}{(1+r)^t} - \sum_{t=1}^{T} \frac{P^L(t)L(t)}{(1+r)^t} = P^C(0)K(0).$$

Net worth can be either positive or negative at any point in time, leading to the conclusion that a form of "capital" is implicit in economic activity even when there are no explicit capital goods and, indeed, even when all the consumption goods produced within a time period are also consumed (by someone) during that period.

5.3   Capital as an Inventory of Goods

A small tweak to the analysis of the preceding section gives further insights to the capital problem. The discussion of section 5.2 examined the situation in which the consumption good had to be consumed in the period it was produced but could be effectively shifted between time periods through the issuance of "paper" debt agreements among people with different preferences about the timing of their consumption. An important variant on this theme arises when the consumption good can be stored and therefore shifted directly from one period to the next. While this tweak is small, the implications are not. There is now a transfer of real goods over time, not just debt obligations, and it is thus possible to speak of a "stock of capital goods," albeit a stock composed entirely of consumption goods.

In order for an inventory of goods to be carried over from one period to the next, there must be some provision for storing the goods until they are consumed. It is natural to locate the storage activity in the production sector, given the functional classification of activity into either consumption or production and the observation that the act of storing the good can be thought of as production for future consumption. In this formulation, the production function for the consumption good must be modified to reflect the possibility that part of the current output is diverted to future use. The production function is now $C(t) + I(t) = F(L[t], t)$, where $I(t)$ is the amount of the goods sent forward to the next period. The aggregate income identity is $P^C(t)C(t) + P^C(t)I(t) = P^L(t)L(t)$.

Consumption can exceed the total quantity of the good produced during any period in this framework if there is a stock of stored consumption goods carried over from past production. This stock is equal to the addition to inventory, $I(t)$, plus any balance of unused goods left over from previous periods, $K(t-1)$, adjusted for wastage at a rate δ into the inventory goods, $K(t)$, available for consumption in the next period:

(5) $$K(t) = I(t) + (1 - \delta)K(t - 1).$$

The value of this stock in any year is determined by its replacement value, $P^C(t)K(t)$, at the current commodity price. It is also the value that the producers could capture if they were to sell their entire inventory of goods, and can thus be regarded as an *asset* of the producer sector. There is, however, an offsetting *liability* arising from the fact that producers have revenue of $P^C(t)C(t)$ from the sale of the consumption good, but have a wage obligation of $P^L(t)L(t)$. The difference, $P^L(t)L(t) - P^C(t)C(t)$, is a deferral of wages that can be thought of as the consumers' claim against the inventory stock held by the producers' sector.

One way to model this deferral is to suppose that producers issue a paper claim—for example, a debt or equity instrument—that promises to pay an amount equal to the wage deferral: $P^C(t)S(t) = P^L(t)L(t) - P^C(t)C(t)$. The $S(t)$ in this formulation is the amount of deferred consumption in units of the good and can therefore be thought of as the quantity of goods saved (an amount equal to inventory investment, $I[t]$), even though the saving takes the form of paper claims. $P^C(t)S(t)$ is the nominal value of these claims, and can be thought of as an increment to consumers' net worth. This formulation of saving in terms of claims to future consumption is evocative of the pure consumption-loan model of the preceding section: the net worth equation (4′) applies equally to the analysis of this section, since net worth is the difference in the present values of the future streams of consumption and labor in both cases; and, in both cases, net worth is equal to $P^C(t)K(t)$. The main difference between the pure consumption-loan model and the inventory model lies in the fact that the $K(t)$ in the latter represents a stock of actual goods. It is therefore possible to speak of a true balance sheet in this case, with the value of the stock on one side of the balance sheet and the wealth claims against this stock on the other.

This balance sheet exists alongside the income and product account of the circular flow model, raising the question of where to locate the balance sheet in the CFM diagram. By its very nature, the CFM portrays the flows of goods and payments into and out of the production and consumption sectors of the economy, and there is no provision for a stock of goods linking one accounting period to the next. One resolution of this problem is to append the items on the balance sheet account to the relevant sectors. The *capital stock account,* $P^C(t)K(t)$, can be attached to the producer sector and the *wealth account,* $NW(t)$, to the consumer sector. The linkage between the two stock accounts and the flows of the CFM occurs via a *saving and investment account,* in which investment in inventories, $I(t)$, flows into the capital account and the saving, $S(t)$, flows into the wealth account.

5.4   Capital as a Produced Means of Production

The capital accounts described up to this point are missing one essential thing: the entity that most people intuitively regard as "capital"—something rather solid and durable like machines and buildings. Unlike the preceding inventory case, where the capital stock is an inventory of consumption goods that has already been produced, this sort of capital is an input that is used to produce future output, and, at the same time, is itself produced. The essential analytical difference between the two cases thus lies in the structure of production. In the inventory case, the production function takes the form $C(t) + I(t) = F(L[t], t)$, with a subsidiary storage function implicit in the analysis. In the case of productive capital, the structure of production must reflect the fact that investment is a separate good with its own production function. The various equations of the preceding sections must be modified accordingly:

(6) $\qquad I(t) = F^I[L_I(t), K_I(t), t]$ and $C(t) = F^C[L_C(t), K_C(t), t]$,

with adding up conditions $L - L_I + L_C$ and $K = K_I + K_C$; the accumulation equation (5) remains $K(t) = I(t) + (1 - \delta)K(t-1)$. This structure differs from the preceding case in two regards: investment $I(t)$ and consumption $C(t)$ are now distinct goods and are not perfect substitutes as before; and the stock of capital $K(t)$ is now an intertemporal factor of production.

The difference in the structure of production between the two cases carries over to the valuation of capital goods. The unit of value associated with the inventory stock is the price of consumption goods, $P^C(t)$, which is related to the utility function. In the case of productive capital, there are two prices: one associated with the output of the investment good, $P^L(t)$, which is related to the marginal cost of producing the good, and one associated with the use of the good as an input in production, $P^K(t)$, which is related to the marginal productivity of the capital input and is the rent that the good could command for use in annual production. The two price concepts are not independent, since the willingness to pay for a unit of new capital stock must be related to the future stream of rents generated by that good, $P^K(t + \tau)$, over its economic life, N. Under the assumption that investment will continue in any year up to the point at which the cost of the last unit just equals the discounted present value of the rental income it generates:

(7) $\qquad\qquad P^I(t, 0) = \sum_{\tau=0}^{N} \frac{P^K(t + \tau, \tau)}{(1 + r)^{\tau+1}}.$

The discount rate is, again, denoted by r. We will assume for the remainder of this section that all productive capital is rented in formal markets, so

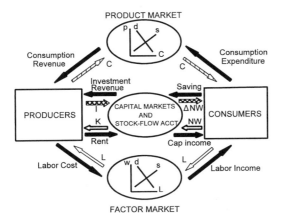

Fig. 5.2   Circular flow model with capital

that $P^K(t)$ is an observable price. The situation in which capital is producer utilized is deferred to the following section.

The circular flow diagram corresponding to the case of productive capital is shown in figure 5.2. The flows around the diagram have been adjusted to account for the output of investment goods by the producer sector and the flow of rental income out of the sector to consumers. The basic gross domestic product (GDP) identity is determined by the products of the two sectors: $P^I(t)I(t) = P^L(t)L_I(t) + P^K(t)K_I(t)$, and $P^C(t)C(t) = P^L(t)L_C(t) + P^K(t)K_C(t)$. The aggregate identity is then the sum of the two:

$$(8) \qquad P^C(t)C(t) + P^I(t)I(t) = P^L(t)L(t) + P^K(t)K(t).$$

The flows in the upper right-hand side of figure 5.2 show the product flow from the standpoint of the consumer, for whom the acquisition of the capital good is an act of saving:

$$(9) \qquad P^C(t)C(t) + P^I(t)I(t) = P^C(t)C(t) + S(t).$$

This leads to the saving account introduced in the preceding section, which now has the form $P^I(t)I(t) = S(t)$. Productive capital is stored by consumers in the producers' sector, as before. However, producers are now assumed to purchase units of new capital up to the point that marginal cost equals the discounted present value of the stream of future rents, as per equation (7). The resulting $P^I(t)I(t)$ flows into the investment account from the producer sector, and $S(t)$ flows in from the consumers' saving account, which is connected to the investment account via the financial market for debt and equity instruments. The $P^I(t)I(t)$ is added to the producers' capital account, and the $S(t)$ to the consumers' wealth account, as before. The new accounting element in the figure 5.2 variant of the CFM is the disposition of the rental payments, $P^K(t)K(t)$. They can be thought of as flowing through the rental market into a capital payment account attached to the producers' capital account, from which they flow into the consumers' capital income account in the form of the return to the debt and equity instruments held in the wealth account.

The analogue to the balance sheet equation, equation (4') above, is derived from the expanded income identity by taking present values. In the current case, it takes the form

$$(10) \qquad NW(0) = \sum_{t=1}^{\infty} \frac{P^C(t)C(t)}{(1+r)^t} - \sum_{t=1}^{\infty} \frac{P^L(t)L(t)}{(1+r)^t}$$

$$= \sum_{t=1}^{\infty} \frac{P^K(t)K(t)}{(1+r)^t} - \sum_{t=1}^{\infty} \frac{P^I(t)I(t)}{(1+r)^t} = P^I(0)K(0).$$

The last equality above follows because the terms involving $K(t)$ and $I(t)$ cancel out except for the value of the initial endowment of capital carried forward from the past. This is, of course, exactly the same result previously obtained for inventory capital and for net foreign debt. The income and wealth accounts in the case of productive capital are thus an extension of the accounts described in the preceding sections, revealing that the architecture of the accounts is not fundamentally changed when the concept of capital is extended to include capital as a produced means of production.

5.5   Producer-Operated Fixed Capital

Accounting for fixed assets would still be relatively easy if only they were rented in active markets. All the prices in the income and product accounts would correspond to observed data based on actual market transactions. Unfortunately, this is not the way capital markets normally operate. Only a small fraction of the productive capital stock flows through a formal rental market, so there is thus no explicit rental price $P^K(t)$, nor is there a rental flow $P^K(t)K(t)$, for the national accountant to observe. The lower left "cost" branch in figure 5.2 is therefore an empirical void, and, as a result, current accounting practice has traditionally ignored this cost branch and has thereby lost sight of the structure of the circular flow model.[5] Fortunately, this situation is beginning to change.

The absence of formal rental markets unquestionably creates a serious empirical challenge to the task of implementing the full CFM, but economic theory provides a way of using the observable aggregate data to impute the unobserved rental price. The solution is based on the user cost of

---

5. The user-cost was introduced by Jorgenson (1963) and has been an established part of applied capital and growth theory since then, but its diffusion into accounting practice has been slow. The surveys by Diewert (1976) and Hulten (1990) provide overviews of this theory with further details.

capital approach, pioneered by Jorgenson (1963) and Hall and Jorgenson (1967), in which the asset pricing equation (7) is solved to yield an expression for the implicit rental price:

(11) $$P^K(t) = \{r(t) - \rho(t) + [1 + \rho(t)]\delta\} P^I(t).$$

This expression is the user cost for a new asset without provision for taxes or other complications. It is the opportunity cost that the producer-user of the capital must recover in each year, and it is equivalent to the rental price of capital. Estimates of the user cost can be constructed for each type of asset if the elements on the right-hand side of equation (11) are measurable: the rate of asset price revaluation, $\rho(t)$, the rate of economic depreciation, δ, the rate of return, $r(t)$, and the acquisition price of the asset, $P^I(t)$. The result is an imputed value of the rental price for each type of capital.

Estimation of the components of the user cost imputation varies in the degree of difficulty. Data on the acquisition price of the asset of tangible capital, $P^I(t)$, are readily obtainable, yielding estimates of asset price revaluation, $\rho(t)$. Estimation of the rate of economic depreciation, δ, presents the greatest difficulties, and is discussed in a separate section below. Estimating the rate of return, $r(t)$, is also a difficult issue (see Schreyer 2004 for a recent discussion of this problem). One approach is to base the estimate of $r(t)$ on the rate of interest used to finance the acquisition of the capital good, under the assumption that arbitrage will drive the rate of return into line with this interest rate. Another option is to use a weighted average of the return to debt and corporate equity. The use of an ex ante measure of $r(t)$ in one form or another has the virtue of tying the user cost to the financial costs that investors face when contemplating the acquisition of a capital good. On the other hand, there is no guarantee that the investor's decision was in fact based on any particular financial rate of return. The presence of risk and liquidity constraints might cause the investor to use a higher rate of discount in assessing the costs and benefits implicit in the asset pricing equation (7). Moreover, there is no guarantee that any ex ante measure of $r(t)$ will lead to an imputed estimate of $P^K(t)$ that satisfies the requirement that the value of input should equal the value of output in the fundamental income and product accounting identity, equation (8).

Jorgenson and Griliches (1967) and Christensen and Jorgenson (1969, 1970) develop an alternative approach to imputing the user cost based on an ex post rate of return to capital that insures that the right-hand side of equation (8) equals the left-hand side. The first step in this procedure is to estimate the total payment to capital input, $\Pi(t)$, by measuring the residual revenue not paid out as labor income—that is, $\Pi(t) = P^C(t)C(t) + P^I(t)I(t) - P^L(t)L(t)$. This expression is also equal to $P^K(t)K(t)$ given the basic accounting identity, which results in

(12) $$\Pi(t) = P^K(t)K(t) = \{r(t) - \rho(t) + [1 + \rho(t)]\delta\} P^I(t)K(t),$$

when the user cost formula is inserted in place of $P^K(t)$. Once the other elements on the right-hand side of equation (12) have been estimated, equation (12) can be solved to yield an estimate of $r(t)$.[6] As a bonus, Berndt and Fuss (1986) show that this ex post rate of return can be interpreted as a Marshallian quasi-rent that embodies a correction for changes in capital utilization. On the negative side, this procedure assumes that all the relevant capital has been accounted for in equation (12) and that there are no other sources of rent (an issue taken up in greater detail below). An empirical difficulty also arises because this procedure can lead to the imputation of negative user costs during periods of high asset-price inflation.

5.6   Producer-Constructed Fixed Capital

The preceding section explored the implications for national income and wealth accounting of indirect ownership, where the problem was the absence of an explicit rental price. A further problem arises when capital stock is not only producer operated but also producer constructed. When capital assets are constructed and used by their operators, not only is there no market rental price $P^K(t)$ to estimate, but there is no observable market transactions on the value of the asset acquired this way (i.e., on the implied $P^I(t)I(t)$). The cost of constructing this type of asset can sometimes be determined, but a firm's internal construction costs may not always equal the value of the asset it constructs, due to lumpiness and other factors. Moreover, even when they are equal a problem still arises because there is no price deflator, $P^I(t)$, with which to isolate the real quantity of the investment, $I(t)$.

The problem of self-construction is of limited quantitative significance for business tangible capital, arising mainly in the case of certain types of maintenance and repair. However, it is the dominant situation for investment in business intangibles like research and development, computer software developed within firms, human competencies, and product marketing. Many items in these categories are firm specific, in the sense that they are of value only (or mainly) to the firm that makes them, and also because firm-specific expertise is required for their production. Other items, like research and development (R&D), may also have a value outside the firm but are closely held because of appropriability problems. All share the feature that it is almost impossible to define the units of measurement in

---

6. When there are multiple types of productive capital, with different user costs, the analogue of equation (12) is

$$\Pi(t) = \sum_{i=1}^{N} P_i^K(t)K_i(t) = \sum_{i=1}^{N} \{r(t) - \rho_i(t) + [1 + \rho_i(t)]\delta_i\} P_i^I(t)K_i(t).$$

As with a single asset, once all of the other elements on the right-hand side of this equation have been estimated, it can be solved to yield an estimate of the common $r(t)$.

which the quantity, $I(t)$, might be measured in principle, much less observed in practice. Indeed, their very presence may be a matter of some dispute because they have no tangible embodiment. Expenditures on intangible capital are thus potentially subject to manipulation by firms seeking to "improve" balance sheets and income statements. As a result, accountants at both micro and macro levels have historically been reluctant to treat them as capital expenditures, though this is beginning to change at the macro level with the capitalization of software expenditures in the NIPAs and the move toward a satellite account for research and development.

The fact that this type of expenditure presents measurement difficulties has no direct bearing on the question of whether or not the expenditure should be treated as capital. This is a matter of the intrinsic nature of the good in question and, specifically, whether or not a current expenditure is made in order to increase future consumption (or to prevent a decrease in future consumption). If it passes this test, standard intertemporal economic theory unambiguously implies that it should be regarded as saving and treated as capital (Corrado, Hulten, and Sichel, 2005). When applied to specific cases, this rule suggests that those maintenance and repair expenditures made with the expectation that they will prevent a reduction of consumption in the future should largely be treated as capital. R&D spending is also capital formation under this rule, as are many other intangible business expenditures made with the intention of increasing future output and thus potential consumption. Outside the business sector, the opportunity cost of delaying entry into the labor force in order to acquire additional education should be treated as an investment in human capital, as should many health-related expenditures.[7]

5.7 Depreciation and Obsolescence

The problem of economic depreciation has troubled the field of national accounting for many years and therefore deserves special attention.[8] The essential characteristic of depreciable assets is that they are "used up" in the process of production through wear and tear, causing the productive efficiency of an asset to erode as it ages. This erosion was dealt with in equation (5) above by the simplifying assumption that it occurs at a constant rate δ. A more general specification, which includes this simple case, de-

---

7. Corrado, Hulten, and Sichel (2005) find that more than one trillion dollars of business intangibles are currently excluded from U.S. investment spending each year, a sum approximately equal to the amount business spends annually on tangible fixed capital. Jorgenson and Fraumeni (1989, 1992) also argue that large amounts of human capital spending are ignored by current practice.

8. A full account of this history is beyond the scope of this chapter, as is the algebraic derivation of the link between asset deterioration, depreciation, and asset valuation. More complete accounts can be found in Hulten and Wykoff (1981, 1996) and Triplett (1996), and a mathematical formulation of the issues is provided in Hulten (1990).

fines the stock of capital as the sum of all surviving past investments weighted by their remaining productive efficiency, ϕ_i:[9]

$$(13) \qquad K(t) = \phi_0 I(t) + \phi_1 I(t-1) + \ldots + \phi_N I(t-N)$$

The relative efficiency terms, ϕ_i, of this stock accumulation equation decline over time until they become zero at the time, N, when the asset is finally retired from service (the stock accumulation equation of the preceding sections assumes the special case $\phi_i = [1-\delta]^i$).

The decline in the ϕ_i weights leads, ceteris paribus, to a decline in the quantity of capital services. This, in turn, leads to a decline in the value of the capital asset, partly because of the loss in productivity before retirement and partly because each year that passes moves the asset closer to the end of its productive life, thus shortening the remaining stream of income in the asset valuation equation (7) above. The decline in value is termed "economic depreciation" and is conceptually distinct from deterioration ($\Delta\phi_i$), though it should be noted that when depreciation follows a geometric pattern, the rates of depreciation and deterioration are identical (i.e., $\Delta\phi_i/\phi_i = \delta$). Given equation (7), economic depreciation $\delta(t)$ can be shown to be the partial derivative of the asset's price, $P^I(t, s)$, with respect to age, s, while asset revaluation (the term $\rho[t]$ in the user cost expression, equation [11]) is the partial derivative of price with respect to time. Under certain assumptions, an estimate of the pure age effect can be obtained by measuring the price differential between two similar assets of different ages at the same point in time. This is the basis for the Hulten-Wykoff measures of economic depreciation embodied in the U.S. national accounts.[10]

This analysis has the following implications for the measurement of income and wealth. The depreciation portion of the annual gross return to capital (i.e., the δ term in the user cost) must be considered to be the cost associated with maintaining the value of the original investment intact, and not as income to the owner. This principle implies that the gross value of the goods emanating from the production side of the CFM is equal to the net income accruing to the consumer sector plus depreciation, and not net income alone. This does not disturb the equality of the circular flow of

9. The relative efficiency terms, ϕ_i, are actually the marginal rate of technical substitution between a new asset and an asset of age i. The relative efficiency of a new asset is therefore one (i.e., $\phi_0 = 1$). The ϕ's are assumed to be constants in order to make the model empirically operational, but they could be allowed to vary according to economic conditions in a more general model (see, for example, Jorgenson 1973 or Hulten 1990).

10. It is worth noting that the depreciation experience of a single asset is not necessarily the same as the average experience of the whole cohort of similar assets that were put in place in the same year, and it is the whole cohort of assets that matters for national accounting purposes. The members of the cohort will generally be retired at different ages, and if the retirement pattern is normally distributed, the average rate of depreciation for the cohort will be close to the geometric rate (Hulten and Wykoff 1981). This result seems to contradict the intuition that a physical asset like a chair retains most of its productive value up the point that it is retired from service (the one-hoss shay model), but this intuition is flawed by the fallacy of composition.

payments, since the flows in the top quadrants of the CFM are the gross value of goods produced and purchased, and they are equal to the flow of gross payments from producers to consumers in the bottom quadrants. However, the difference between net and gross income suggests that there may be two separate measures of total economic activity, one appropriate to the production side of the CFM, the other to the consumer side, and that GDP is not necessarily the appropriate indicator of annual output's contribution to intertemporal utility.

This idea is rigorously developed in Weitzman (1976), who shows that the optimal solution to the problem of maximizing the intertemporal utility function is $C(t) + p(t)\Delta K(t)$, where $p(t)$ is the investment good price relative to the price of consumption. This expression is Haig-Simon income, consumption plus change in net worth, but it is also equal to factor income less depreciation as well as to net domestic product (Hulten 1992). The Weitzman result can be interpreted as implying that net domestic product (NDP) is a better measure of aggregate economic activity than gross domestic product (GDP), but the CFM makes clear that both are important. The production functions on the supply side of the CFM represent a transformation of labor and capital inputs into gross output—the output that actually leaves the factory doors. No one has ever seen, or can ever see, a unit of physical output net of depreciation leave a factory because it simply does not exist. GDP is the appropriate concept for studying the parameters of the production function and how the productivity of the inputs changes over time. On the other hand, NDP is the appropriate concept for studying consumer welfare, since, as Weitzman puts it, NDP "is a proxy for the present discounted value of future consumption" (p. 156). This dichotomy points to the utility of the CFM as a way of classifying economic activity: once the issue of net versus gross output is framed in the context of the CFM, both concepts are seen to be important for their respective realms of economic activity. Moreover, the failure of accountants to maintain a clear view of the CFM architecture contributes to confusions like the net versus gross output debate.

Technological obsolescence is another aspect of asset valuation, and it greatly complicates the asset valuation model and has been the source of much confusion recently. This phenomenon occurs when improvements in technology are embodied in the design of new capital goods. These higher-quality assets are often quite different from the older assets against which they compete (e.g., jet versus propeller-driven aircraft) and are, in principle, a separate type of capital that should be accorded its own production function. Unfortunately, the data requirements of this approach are so great that they render it nonoperational.[11] However, Hall (1968) shows that the

---

11. If each new technological vintage of, say, machine tools were treated as part of a separate production process, data on output, labor, and material input would have to be collected on a machine-by-machine basis. It is a major undertaking to assemble consistent production

embodied technical change model can be made empirically operational by assuming that differences in quality between old and new assets can be expressed as a difference in the effective quantity of the capital services that they represent. In terms of the preceding formulation in which quality differentials were absent, the relative efficiency parameters for new assets, ϕ_0, is no longer constrained to equal one, but now increases over time at the rate of embodied technical change, λ. The efficiency function of *new* assets evolves, accordingly, as $\phi_{t,0} = (1 + \lambda) \phi_{t-1,0}$. The efficiency function of existing assets of age s in year t takes the form $\phi_{t,s}$ and the vintage of that asset is denoted by $v = t - s$. This $\phi_{t,s}$ pattern is assumed to decline due to wear and tear alone, but not because of the arrival of new capital (thus, $\phi_{t+1,s+1} = [1 - \delta]\phi_{t,s}$, when deterioration proceeds at a constant rate). The capital accumulation analogue to equation (13) for this case has the form

$$(13')\qquad K(t) = \phi_{t,0}I(t) + \phi_{t,1}I(t-1) + \ldots + \phi_{t,N}I(t-N).$$

The essential feature of this approach is to characterize embodied technical change as an increase in the effective quantity of new capital, which is then added to the quantity of older capital adjusted for deterioration.[12]

On the other hand, the *value* of older vintages of capital is driven down by the arrival of new capital even if their own productivity has not changed, because the value of the marginal product of older capital falls even if the marginal product itself is not affected: the superior efficiency of new capital translates into a fall in output price in competitive markets, which in turn lowers the marginal revenue earned by existing capital. In this framework, the price of older assets now evolves according to three factors: the rate of embodied technical change, λ, the average rate of wear and tear, δ, and the average revaluation effect, ρ.

When economic depreciation is defined as the partial derivative of asset price with respect to age, it becomes apparent that depreciation includes the combined effects of wear and tear *and* the obsolescence. Since the measures of economic depreciation currently in the U.S. NIPAs are derived from the Hulten-Wykoff price-based estimates, these measures must be interpreted as the combined effects of δ and λ. The Hall (1968) result shows that these two effects cannot be separated, given used price data alone, but in another paper, Hall (1971) shows that the technique of price hedonics can be used to resolve the identification problem—that is, to provide separate estimates of the parameters δ and λ, as well as ρ. These separate esti-

---

data at an establishment level of detail, and it is hard to expect that these data could be uniquely disaggregated to the level of individual machines.

12. This is not the only way to introduce embodied technical change into the capital accumulation model. An alternative approach would allow for an acceleration in the retirement of older vintages when the *expected* rate of embodied technical change accelerates. This is a more realistic approach, but it is also more complicated and is generally beyond the capacity of existing data to implement.

mates can then be used to split price-based estimates of economic depreciation into its components. The results can, in turn, be employed separately to measure the quantity of capital stock on the producer side of the CFM using the modified accumulation equation (13′), while, at the same time, the same estimates can be used to measure the change in the value of that capital.

5.8 The "Nonzero-Rent Economy"

The accounting architecture described in the preceding sections has two levels: a foundation based on the circular flow of goods and payments, and a superstructure based on the application of economic theory. The first is rather general, but the latter employs specific assumptions about technology and preferences and about the valuation of the stocks and flows, assumptions that Hall (2001) collectively terms the "zero-rent economy." That economy is characterized by competitive markets, constant returns to scale, and the possibility that all factors can be freely adjusted in the long run. There are thus no economic rents in that economy, leading to the income identity, equation (12), connecting the total gross return to capital assets, $\Sigma P_i^K K_i$, and the flow of income to consumers generated by the assets. This is one of the main assumptions of the accounting models of Jorgenson and Griliches (1967) and Christensen and Jorgenson (1969, 1970).

These identities require a different interpretation in an economy with economic rents generated by monopoly power, intramarginal efficiency rents, persistent disequilibrium, imperfect information, or uncertainty. In this more realistic world, some of the income thought to accrue to the collection of capital assets, $\Sigma P_i^K K_i$, is in reality a return to entrepreneurship or to the owners of the firm. Any attempt to impose the zero-rent-economy rules in this world results in a biased estimate of the return to the specific capital assets included in the analysis. Moreover, there is a potential disconnect between the value of capital stock and the amount of wealth. However, this does not mean that the use of theory, per se, is at fault, but rather that it is important to use the right theory. Nor does it mean that the zero-rent model is irrelevant. Given the difficulty of adapting models of imperfect competition, Schumpetarian entrepreneurship, and uncertainty to national income accounting problems, the zero-rent model is a logical and important step along the way toward Koopmans's vision of measurement with theory.

5.9 Summary and Conclusion

This chapter has discussed the design principles of a set of income and product accounts based on the circular flow model of payments and goods. While these flows encompass much more that just capital, the CFM has been shown to be a useful framework for sorting out just what is meant by the term "capital." In particular, the clear division on the CFM between the consumer and business sectors reveals the dual nature of capital: on one hand, it is a stock of inventories and productive assets held by producers, and, on the other hand, it is simultaneously a stock of wealth held by consumers. Moreover, by approaching the problem of capital in gradual stages, it has become clear that capital in its most primitive form originates with the decision by consumers to defer consumption, and that this aspect carries over to capital in all its forms.

These are general architectural principles. The analysis of capital within the context of the CFM also yields insights into specific accounting practices. First, these general principles suggest a criterion for determining what is and is not capital: if an expenditure is made with the intention of increasing future rather than current consumption, then it should be treated as capital. This rule clearly applies to most R&D and many other intangible expenditures, most of which are not treated as capital under prevailing practice. This situation is beginning to change, and the CFM analysis suggests that this trend needs to be sustained.

Second, the structure of the CFM also calls attention to the need for a full accounting for the cost of capital in the lower left-hand branch of the model. This part of the model is an integral part of the production account associated with the business sector of the CFM, but it is largely missing from conventional national accounts like the NIPAs and the System of National Accounts. Extending these accounts to include a full production sector is currently under consideration, and the analysis in this paper strongly supports the adoption of this approach.

Third, division of the CFM into two functional sectors helps resolve the debate over gross versus net product as a measure of aggregate output. The clear answer is that both measures are relevant statistics of an aggregate economy. Gross output (GDP) is the natural measure to apply to the producer sector, because the production functions of that sector transform input into output that is gross of depreciation. On the other hand, net output (NDP) is the more appropriate indicator of consumer welfare, both current and future. Many researchers have, in the past, lost sight of the circular flow organization of the economy and used net output in their analysis of productivity.

Fourth, the division of the CFM into production and consumption sectors helps resolve the question of asset assignment. This issue has arisen in the debate occasioned by the proposed revisions to the SNA. The CFM suggests that assets rented under very long-term leases or under sales-lease-back arrangements, or that have split ownership, should be accorded the same treatment as other assets: as productive capital, they should be assigned to the industry of the producer sector in which they are used to produce output. The ownership of the asset should then be traced through the process of financial intermediation to wealth accounts of the ultimate owners in the consumer sector.

The CFM, with its emphasis on production and consumption as separate economic activities, provides a useful architecture for sorting out many accounting problems associated with "capital." It also provides a flexible infrastructure for incorporating theoretical developments that improve the value of the accounts to the various user communities. Moving current accounting practice toward the CFM structure should be a central goal of the field of national income and wealth accounting.

References

Berndt, Ernest R., and Melvyn A. Fuss. 1986. Productivity measurement with adjustments for variations in capacity utilization and other forms of temporary equilibrium. *Journal of Econometrics* 33:7–29.

Christensen, Laurits R., and Dale W. Jorgenson. 1969. The measurement of U.S. real capital input, 1929–1967. *Review of Income and Wealth* 15 (December): 293–320.

———. 1970. U.S. real product and real factor input, 1929–1969. *Review of Income and Wealth* 16 (March): 19–50.

Corrado, Carol, Charles Hulten, and Daniel Sichel. 2005. Measuring capital and technology: An expanded framework. In *Measuring capital in the new economy,* ed. Carol Corrado, John Haltiwanger, and Daniel Sichel, 11–41. Chicago: University of Chicago Press.

Diewert, W. Erwin. 1976. Aggregation problems in the measurement of capital. In *The measurement of capital,* ed. Dan Usher, 433–528. Chicago: University of Chicago Press.

Griliches, Zvi. 1994. Productivity, R&D, and the data constraint. *American Economic Review* 84:1–23.

Hall, Robert E. 1968. Technical change and capital from the point of view of the dual. *Review of Economic Studies* 35:34–46.

———. 1971. The measurement of quality change from vintage price data. In *Price indexes and quality change,* ed. Zvi Griliches, 240–71. Cambridge: Harvard University Press.

———. 2001. The stock market and capital accumulation. *American Economic Review* 91:1185–1202.

Hall, Robert E., and Dale W. Jorgenson. 1967. Tax policy and investment behavior. *American Economic Review* 57:391–414.

Hulten, Charles R. 1979. On the "importance" of productivity change. *American Economic Review* 69:126–36.

———. 1990. The measurement of capital. In *Fifty years of economic measurement: The jubilee of the Conference on Research in Income and Wealth,* ed. Ernst R. Berndt and Jack E. Triplett, 119–52. Chicago: University of Chicago Press.

———. 1992. Accounting for the wealth of nations: The net versus gross output controversy and its ramifications. *Scandinavian Journal of Economics* 94 (suppl.): S9–S24.

———. 2001. Total factor productivity: A short biography. In *New developments in productivity analysis,* ed. Charles R. Hulten, Edwin R. Dean, and Michael J. Harper, 1–47. Chicago: University of Chicago Press.

Hulten, Charles R., and Frank C. Wykoff. 1981. The estimation of economic depreciation using vintage asset prices. *Journal of Econometrics* 15:367–96.

———. 1996. Issues in the measurement of economic depreciation. *Economic Inquiry* 34 (1): 10–23.

Jorgenson, Dale W. 1963. Capital theory and investment behavior. *American Economic Review* 53 (2): 247–59.

———. 1973. The economic theory of replacement and depreciation. In *Econometrics and economic theory,* ed. W. Sellykaerts. New York: MacMillan.

Jorgenson, Dale W., and Barbara M. Fraumeni. 1989. The accumulation of human and nonhuman capital, 1948–84. In *The measurement of saving, investment, and wealth,* ed. Robert E. Lipsey and Helen Stone Tice, 119–52. Chicago: University of Chicago Press.

———. 1992. The output of the education sector. In *Output measurement in the service sectors,* ed. Zvi Griliches, 303–41. Chicago: University of Chicago Press.

Jorgenson, Dale W., and Zvi Griliches. 1967. The explanation of productivity change. *Review of Economic Studies* 34 (July): 349–83.

Koopmans, Tjalling. 1947. Measurement without theory. *Review of Economic Statistics* 29 (3): 161–72.

Patinkin, Don. 1973. In search of the "wheel of wealth": On the origins of Frank Knights circular flow diagram. *American Economic Review* 63 (5): 1037–46.

Schreyer, Paul. 2004. Measuring multi-factor productivity when rates of return are exogenous. Paper presented at the Social Sciences and Humanities Research Council (SSHRC) International Conference on Index Number Theory and the Measurement of Price and Productivity. 30 June–3 July, Vancouver, Canada.

Triplett, Jack E. 1996. Depreciation in production analysis and economic accounts. *Economic Inquiry* 34 (January): 93–115.

United Nations. Commission of the European Communities, International Monetary Fund, Organisation for Economic Co-operation and Development, and World Bank. 1993. *System of national accounts 1993.* Series F, no. 2, rev. 4. New York: United Nations.

Weitzman, Martin L. 1976. On the welfare significance of national product in a dynamic economy. *Quarterly Journal of Economics* 90:156–62.

6

Integrating Industry and National Economic Accounts
First Steps and Future Improvements

Ann M. Lawson, Brian C. Moyer, Sumiye Okubo, and
Mark A. Planting

6.1 Introduction

As part of its continuing efforts to improve the system of economic
accounts, the Bureau of Economic Analysis (BEA) has begun a series of
strategic initiatives to ultimately integrate the gross domestic product
(GDP)–by-industry, annual input-output (I-O), and benchmark I-O programs within the industry accounts, as well as to integrate the industry accounts with the National Income and Product Accounts (NIPAs).[1] Full
achievement of this goal will require several years of effort by the BEA, as
well as the continuing participation and cooperation by other statistical
agencies, particularly the Bureau of the Census and the Bureau of Labor
Statistics (BLS), to further enhance source data. In the interim, the BEA

Ann M. Lawson is chief of the Industry Economics Division at the Bureau of Economic
Analysis. Brian C. Moyer is the deputy chief of the National Income and Wealth Division at
the Bureau of Economic Analysis. Sumiye Okubo is associate director for Industry Accounts
at the Bureau of Economic Analysis. Mark A. Planting is the chief of industry studies in the
Industry Economics Division at the Bureau of Economic Analysis.

The authors wish to acknowledge Matthew Atkinson, Mahnaz Fahim-Nader, Jiemin Guo,
Karen Horowitz, Sherlene K. S. Lum, George Smith, and all other staff of the Industry Accounts Directorate at the Bureau of Economic Analysis, who made significant contributions
directly and indirectly to the development of this paper. We thank Jack Triplett, Eric Bartelsman, and other participants of the NBER/CRIW conference in April 2004 for their many
helpful comments on the direction of this research.

1. In addition, it is the BEA's long-run goal to integrate the industry accounts and NIPAs
with related regional accounts, namely gross state product (GSP) by industry and regional
I-O multiplier estimates. Consistency between the annual I-O accounts and the GDP-by-
industry accounts will improve the quality of the GSP accounts, and any increase in timeliness of the GDP-by-industry estimates will be reflected in more speedy delivery of the GSP
estimates. Consistent and better measures of value added would also potentially strengthen
the links between the GSP accounts and the regional I-O multiplier estimates.

has moved forward with integrating two out of three of its industry programs—specifically the merging of the GDP-by-industry accounts with the annual I-O accounts. Initial results of this effort were released in June 2004 as part of BEA's five-year comprehensive revision.

The integration of the GDP-by-industry accounts with the annual I-O accounts is the most recent in a series of improvements to the industry accounts. These improvements include the following: resuming the publication of the annual I-O accounts; accelerating the release of the annual I-O accounts to within three years after the end of the reference year; expanding the GDP-by-industry accounts to include gross output and intermediate inputs for all industries; developing an accelerated set of GDP-by-industry accounts that are available with a lag of four months after the end of the reference year; and continuing to work closely with the Bureau of the Census on new initiatives to improve the quality and the timeliness of the source data used to prepare the industry accounts.[2]

With these improvements to the industry accounts in place, as well as with the general improvements made to the quality of industry source data, the BEA is ready to integrate the annual I-O accounts and the GDP-by-industry accounts as a first step toward full integration.[3] For purposes of the current paper, this integration is being referred to as "partial integration" and is the first tangible result of the initiative to reach the BEA's data users.

This partial integration could have been achieved through a variety of methods. For example, many countries produce integrated annual I-O accounts and GDP-by-industry accounts by assuming that the industry ratios of intermediate inputs to gross output do not change from the most recent set of benchmark I-O accounts. With this assumption, they then use these ratios to estimate a time series of value added by industry from the annual source data on gross output by industry. The BEA has taken a very different approach in developing its integration methodology because of the richness of the source data that are available in the United States. For example, the Bureau of the Census, the BLS, and the Internal Revenue Service (IRS) provide data that can be used to estimate value added by industry in various ways. However, the quality of these source data varies by data series and by industry, particularly in terms of their relative coverage and definitional consistency. As a result, the BEA has developed a method that ranks the available source data based on measures of coverage and consistency, among other factors, and then estimates a balanced set of annual

2. For an overview of the accounts see Lawson (2000); for a presentation on the resumed annual I-O accounts see Lawson, Okubo, and Planting (2000); for the presentation of the expanded GDP-by-industry accounts see Lum, Moyer, and Yuskavage (2000); and for a discussion of the accelerated GDP-by-industry estimates see Yuskavage (2002).
3. For a discussion on integrating the industry accounts, see Yuskavage (2000).

I-O accounts and GDP-by-industry accounts that incorporate the resulting weighted average of these source data. In this manner, the BEA's integrated annual I-O accounts and GDP-by-industry accounts will provide a more consistent and a more accurate set of estimates.

For full integration of the industry accounts, the measure and level of value added by industry for the industry accounts will be based on the benchmark I-O accounts, beginning with the 2002 accounts. These accounts are prepared for years of the quinquennial economic census and are currently used to establish the measure and level of final expenditures by use category contributing to GDP in the NIPAs. Annual updates of the integrated industry accounts would be based on less comprehensive survey and administrative record data available in nonbenchmark years. For full integration, the measures of value added by industry would be independent of the NIPA measures of gross domestic income (GDI) and would provide a "feedback" loop to the NIPAs that would improve the estimates of the commodity composition of GDP final expenditures.[4] To achieve this ambitious goal, the BEA is working cooperatively with the Census Bureau, BLS, and other statistical agencies to make the necessary improvements to the quality and coverage of the underlying source data, particularly for information on industry expenses.

This chapter has five sections and three appendices. The first section is this introduction. The second section describes in greater detail the partial integration being achieved in the short run. The third section presents the BEA's vision for full integration in the long run, including some of the major requirements for achieving this goal as well as the major benefits. The fourth section describes the methodology developed for the partial integration of the annual industry accounts. The last section outlines the future steps required to reach the goal of full integration. The appendices include an expanded description of the probability-based method used to develop a weighted-average estimate of each industry's gross operating surplus; a detailed description of the new balancing procedure developed for automating production of the annual I-O tables; and a statement of the computation method used to estimate chain-type price and quantity indexes in the GDP-by-industry accounts.

Highlights of the partial integration methodology are as follows:

---

4. The BEA currently uses two approaches to measure GDP: the expenditures approach and the income approach. The expenditures approach measures GDP as the sum of consumption spending, investment spending, government expenditures, and exports minus imports. The income approach measures GDP as the sum of compensation of employees; taxes on production and imports, less subsidies; and gross operating surplus. These approaches allow maximum use of up-to-date, high-quality economic indicators from the Bureau of the Census, the IRS, and the BLS to produce timely, reliable measures of the economy's current performance.

- It allows the BEA to incorporate the most timely and highest-quality source data available into both the annual I-O accounts and the GDP-by-industry accounts.
- The quality of the annual industry accounts is improved because the accounts are prepared within a balanced I-O framework; that is, all the components of the accounts are in agreement within a balanced row-and-column framework.
- The annual I-O accounts and the GDP-by-industry accounts are now released concurrently and present fully consistent measures of gross output, intermediate inputs, and value added by industry.
- The annual I-O accounts are available within one year after the end of the reference year or two years earlier than previously.
- The annual I-O accounts are now presented as a consistent time series; as a consequence, the annual I-O accounts are more useful for analyses of trends over time.

6.2   Partial Integration: The First Step

The BEA prepares two sets of national industry accounts: the I-O accounts, which consist of the benchmark I-O accounts and the annual I-O accounts, and the GDP-by-industry accounts. Both the I-O accounts and the GDP-by-industry accounts present measures of gross output, intermediate inputs, and value added by industry; however, they are often inconsistent because of the use of different methodologies, classification frameworks, and source data. These inconsistencies are frustrating to data users, who would like to be able to combine the richness of information from each for their own applications. The goal of partial integration is to eliminate these inconsistencies, as well as to improve the accuracy of the combined accounts by drawing on their relative strengths in methodologies and source data. In this section, the traditional I-O and GDP-by-industry methodologies are reviewed and the comparative advantages of each are examined in the context of an integrated methodology that produces both sets of accounts.

6.2.1   The Traditional I-O Accounts Methodology

The I-O accounts present a detailed picture of how industries interact to provide inputs to, and use output from, each other to produce the nation's GDP. The I-O accounts consist of benchmark I-O accounts and annual I-O accounts. The benchmark I-O accounts are prepared every five years and are based on data from the quinquennial economic census covering most businesses.[5] The annual I-O accounts update the most recent benchmark I-O accounts, and, although they are more timely than the benchmark

---

5. For more information, see Lawson et al. (2002).

I-O accounts, they are generally less detailed because they rely on annual data based on smaller sample surveys.[6] At present, the I-O accounts are prepared only in current dollars.[7]

Both the benchmark and the annual I-O accounts are prepared within a balanced row-and-column framework that is presented in two tables: a "make" table and a "use" table. The make table shows the commodities that are produced by each industry, and the use table shows the commodities that are used in industry production and that are consumed by final users. In the use table, the columns consist of industries and final uses (figure 6.1). The column total for an industry is its gross output (consisting of sales or receipts, other operating income, commodity taxes, and inventory change). The rows in the use table consist of commodities and value added. The commodities are the goods and services that are produced by industries or imported and that are consumed either by industries in their production processes or by final users. The commodities consumed by industries in the production process are referred to as intermediate inputs (consisting of energy, materials, and purchased services). Value added in the I-O accounts is computed as a residual—that is, as gross output less intermediate inputs by industry. In concept, this residual, which represents the sum of the costs incurred and the incomes earned in production, consists of compensation of employees, gross operating surplus, and taxes on production and imports, less subsidies.[8] GDP equals valued added summed over all industries, and it also equals final uses summed over all commodities.

The I-O accounts have traditionally served two major purposes, both of which have focused on information about the use of commodities and which have supported the BEA's NIPAs. First, the accounts have provided the NIPAs with best-level estimates of the commodities that comprise final expenditures for GDP in benchmark years. Second, they provide the NIPAs with information to split estimates of commodities produced annually into their business (intermediate) and final consumer components—information that is critical for estimating GDP final expenditures in nonbenchmark years. Because of their importance in determining the levels of GDP in the NIPAs, the I-O accounts have traditionally focused more on the

6. For more information, see Lawson, Okubo, and Planting (2000) and Planting and Kuhbach (2001).

7. The BEA is beginning research to explore the feasibility of preparing real (inflation-adjusted) I-O accounts.

8. Previously, these costs and incomes were classified as either compensation of employees, property-type income, or indirect business tax and nontax liability. These new classifications are consistent with the aggregations introduced as part of the comprehensive NIPA revision; see Moulton and Seskin for more information. Specifically, all the nontax liabilities except special assessments are removed from indirect business tax and nontax liability, and the remainder of this category is renamed "taxes on production and imports"; the nontax liabilities except special assessments are added to property-type income; subsidies are removed from property-type income, and the remainder of this category is renamed "gross operating surplus"; and subsidies are netted against the value of taxes on production and imports.

		Industries																				Final Uses							
		Agriculture, forestry, fishing, and hunting	Mining	Utilities	Construction	Manufacturing	Wholesale trade	Retail trade	Transportation and warehousing	Information	Finance and insurance	Real estate, rental, and leasing	Professional and technical services	Management of companies and enterprises	Administrative and waste management services	Educational services	Health care and social assistance	Arts, entertainment, and recreation	Accommodation and food services	Other services except government	Government	Total Intermediate use	Personal consumption expendiutres	Private fixed investment	Change in business inventories	Exports of goods and services	Imports of goods and services	Government consumption expenditures and gross investment	GDP	Total Commodity Output
Commodities	Agriculture, forestry, fishing, & hunting																													
	Mining																													
	Utilities																													
	Construction																													
	Manufactured products																													
	Wholesale Trade																													
	Retail trade																													
	Transportation and warehousing																													
	Information																													
	Finance and insurance																													
	Real estate, rental, and leasing																													
	Professional and technical services																													
	Management of companies and enterprises																													
	Administrative and waste management services																													
	Educational services																													
	Health care and social assistance																													
	Arts, entertainment, and recreation																													
	Accommodation and food services																													
	Other services except government																													
	Government																													
	Other inputs /1/																													
	Total intermediate inputs																													
Value Added	Compensation of employees																													
	Taxes on production and imports, less subsidies																													
	Gross operating surplus																													
	Total																													
Total Industry Output																														

Total commodity output

Total industry output

1. Includes noncomparable imports, scrap, used goods, inventory valuation adjustment, and rest-of-the-world adjustment.
GDP: Gross domestic product

Fig. 6.1 Use table: Commodities used by industries and final uses

commodity composition of the economy and less on the measures of value added by industry.

6.2.2 The Traditional GDP-by-Industry Accounts Methodology

In contrast to the I-O accounts, the GDP-by-industry accounts have traditionally focused on the industry composition of the U.S. economy and the relative performance of these industries as reflected in their measures of value added. The GDP-by-industry accounts are particularly suited for time series analysis of changes in industry shares of GDP and contributions to GDP growth. They provide annual estimates of gross output, of intermediate inputs, and of value added by industry and the corresponding price and quantity indexes.[9]

The GDP-by-industry accounts use a different estimating approach than that used for the I-O accounts. They measure value added by industry as the sum of the costs incurred and the incomes earned in production. Value added by industry is estimated as the sum of the industry distributions of compensation of employees, gross operating surplus, and taxes on production and imports, less subsidies (figure 6.2). In the GDP-by-industry accounts, total intermediate inputs by industry are measured as a residual—that is, total intermediate inputs equal gross output less value added for an industry.

The GDP-by-industry estimates are based on data from three primary sources. Gross output by industry is based on establishment-based annual survey data from the Bureau of the Census that are used to extrapolate best-level estimates from the most recent set of benchmark I-O accounts. The measures of value added by industry are derived from the industry distributions of the components of GDI from the NIPAs, which, in turn, are based on establishment-based data from the BLS and on enterprise-based annual tax return and administrative record data from the IRS.

Real measures of gross output and intermediate inputs by industry are estimated by deflating with detailed price indexes. Price indexes and quantity indexes are derived for each industry's gross output, of intermediate inputs, and of value added.

6.2.3 Combining the Two Methodologies

The primary strength of the I-O methodology is the balanced row-and-column framework in which the detailed estimates of gross output and intermediate inputs by industry are prepared; this framework allows for a simultaneous look at both the economy's industries and commodities. The primary strength of the GDP-by-industry accounts methodology is the direct approach to estimating a time series of value added by industry from high-quality source income data. The methodology for partial integration

---

9. For more information, see Lum, Moyer, and Yuskavage (2000).

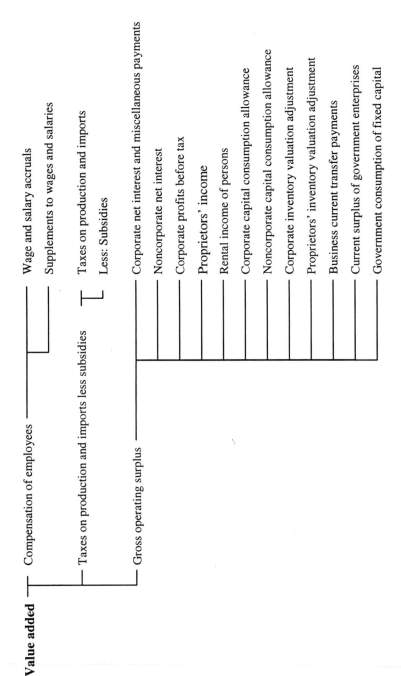

Fig. 6.2 Components of GDI-based value added by industry
Source: U.S. Bureau of Economic Analysis.

incorporates the relative strengths of both. It yields a new and improved set of annual I-O accounts and GDP-by-industry accounts that are prepared within a balanced framework and that incorporate the most timely and highest-quality source data available. It also ensures the consistency of the estimates of gross output, of intermediate inputs, and of value added by industry across the two sets of accounts.

The strength of using a balanced I-O framework is demonstrated by again referring to figure 6.1. A balanced use table ensures that the industry estimates of the I-O accounts (the column totals) are in balance with the commodity estimates of the I-O accounts (the row totals).[10] This framework tracks all of the detailed input and output flows in the economy and guarantees that each commodity that is produced is either consumed by industries as an intermediate input or is consumed by final users. An imbalance in the use table—for example, too little, or too much, supply of a commodity after intermediate inputs by industry and final uses have been accounted for—flags an inconsistency in the data. Therefore, a balanced framework provides a "consistency check" of the use table. No comparable procedure to balance industries and commodities exists for the GDP-by-industry accounts.

The strength of the GDP-by-industry methodology is that the estimates of value added by industry are derived directly from high-quality source data, so these measures generally provide better estimates of value added for industries relative to the I-O estimates. Nonetheless, several factors can affect the quality of the GDP-by-industry estimates for specific industries. For example, gross operating surplus, one component of value added by industry, includes several items—such as corporate profits before tax, corporate net interest, and corporate capital consumption allowances—that are based on corporate tax return data from the IRS. Because the consolidated tax return data of an enterprise may account for activities by several establishments classified in different industries, the BEA must convert these enterprise- or company-based data to an establishment or plant basis. The conversion can introduce errors because it is based on employment data for establishments that are cross-classified by enterprise, and because it is based on relationships from an economic census year that are likely to change over time. In addition, proprietors' income, another component of gross operating surplus, can introduce errors because the industry distributions of proprietors' income are based on incomplete source data. Industries with large shares of value added from proprietors' income are regarded as having lower-quality estimates.[11]

---

10. The I-O framework also includes a balanced make table, which requires that the different commodities produced by industries are consistent with total commodity and industry outputs for the economy.

11. Proprietors' income is defined here to equal the sum of NIPA estimates for proprietors' income without inventory valuation adjustment (IVA) and capital consumption adjustment

The GDP-by-industry measures of value added may be of a higher or lower quality than those from the benchmark I-O accounts, depending on the data used. For an industry with high-quality data on gross output and intermediate inputs, the measure of value added from the benchmark I-O accounts may be superior, particularly when the GDP-by-industry measure includes a large enterprise-establishment adjustment or a substantial amount of proprietors' income. Alternatively, for an industry with a small enterprise-establishment adjustment and a negligible amount of proprietors' income, the GDP-by-industry measure may be superior, particularly if the coverage of intermediate inputs in the quinquennial economic census is small for the benchmark I-O measure. For the 1997 benchmark I-O accounts, less than half of all intermediate inputs were covered by the economic census; for many industries, this results in lower-quality measures of value added. In contrast, for nonbenchmark years, the GDP-by-industry accounts always provide the preferred measures of value added, because estimates of intermediate inputs in the annual I-O accounts are currently based on very sparse data and are unable to yield high-quality measures of value added by industry.[12]

The advantages of a partial integration methodology, however, go beyond incorporating the best methods and source data from each methodology. Because the annual I-O accounts are estimated concurrently with the GDP-by-industry accounts, they are released on an accelerated schedule. The 2002 annual I-O table, published in June 2004, was released eighteen months rather than thirty-six months after the end of the reference year. In addition, in the fall of 2004, the annual I-O accounts adopted the revision schedule of the NIPAs; at that time, the revised tables for 2001 and 2002 and new tables for 2003 were released. The revised I-O estimates that are consistent with the annually revised NIPA estimates provide users with yet another level of consistency. Finally, the partial integration methodology imposes a time series consistency on the annual I-O tables, making the tables more useful for analyses of trends over time.

A further advantage of the partial integration methodology is a "feedback loop" to the NIPAs that is demonstrated by examining the relationships among the national accounts (figure 6.3). Before the integration of

---

(CCAdj), proprietors' net interest, proprietors' capital consumption allowance, and proprietors' IVA. The NIPA adjustment to nonfarm proprietors' income without IVA and CCAdj for misreporting on income tax returns is shown in NIPA table 7.14, "Relation of Nonfarm Proprietors' Income in the National Income and Product Accounts to Corresponding Measures as Published by the Internal Revenue Service."

12. The Bureau of the Census has recently undertaken initiatives to improve the coverage of intermediate inputs by industry in several of its annual surveys. For example, the Annual Survey of Manufactures has expanded its coverage of expenses to include purchased services by industry, and the Service Annual Survey has initiated the collection of data on expenses by industry.

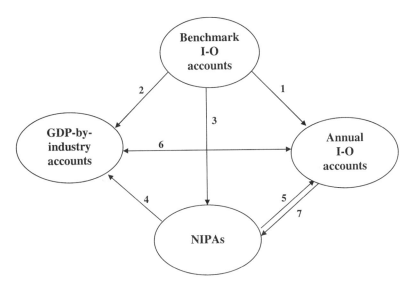

Fig. 6.3   Relationships among national economic accounts
Source: U.S. Bureau of Economic Analysis.
Notes: GDP = gross domestic product; I-O = input-output; NIPAs = National Income and Product Accounts

the annual I-O accounts and the GDP-by-industry accounts, the benchmark I-O accounts provided the following: a starting point for updating the annual I-O accounts (arrow 1), the best-level estimates of gross output to the GDP-by-industry accounts (arrow 2), and the best-level estimates and commodity splits of GDP to the NIPAs (arrow 3). The NIPAs provided estimates of GDI by industry to the GDP-by-industry accounts (arrow 4) and information on the annual composition of GDP to the annual I-O accounts (arrow 5). The partial integration results in an exchange of information between the annual I-O accounts and the GDP-by-industry accounts (arrow 6), and it also provides a feedback loop to the NIPAs (arrow 7). Because the integrated industry accounts will be prepared within a balanced framework, they will provide annual estimates of the commodity composition of GDP final expenditures that could potentially be used to improve the NIPA measures of GDP.

6.3   Full Integration: The Long-Run Goal

Integration of the annual I-O accounts and the GDP-by-industry accounts is only the first step, although a very important one, toward the BEA's long-run goal to fully integrate all components of its industry accounts, including the benchmark I-O accounts, and to integrate the industry accounts with the NIPAs. Although full integration is dependent upon continued costly investments by the federal statistical agencies to improve the coverage and consistency of their economic data, the benefits are significant in providing higher-quality information to data users. With more consistent and comprehensive data on industry inputs, the benchmark I-O accounts would provide the best measures of value added by industry for benchmark years. With updated annual information on intermediate inputs by industry, the annual I-O accounts and the GDP-by-industry accounts would provide annual updates of value added by industry that would be independent of the NIPA measures of GDP. With full integration, BEA would have a production-based measure of GDP that would provide new information to the NIPAs through the feedback loop discussed earlier (figure 6.3). That is to say, it could provide valuable insights into imbalances between the BEA's primary measure of GDP based on the final expenditures approach and its alternative measure based on income—that is, GDI.

The BEA views the underlying framework now being implemented for partial integration as able to accommodate the requirements for full integration. That being said, however, for full integration, the data needed to populate much of this framework are presently missing, particularly consistent and comprehensive data on intermediate inputs for industries. For example, less than half of the intermediate input estimates in the 1997 benchmark I-O accounts were based on high-quality, consistent data collected by the Bureau of the Census; estimates for the balance were based on fragmented information from trade associations, company annual reports, anecdotal information, and prior benchmark I-O accounts. To be reliable, a production-based estimate of GDP requires an expansion by the Census Bureau in its coverage of business expenses from less than half to 100 percent. The methods developed by the BEA to achieve partial integration in the short run are not an adequate substitute for these improvements to source data in the long run, if the goals of full integration are to be realized. To acquire this information, the BEA is working collaboratively with other statistical agencies, particularly the Bureau of the Census, to expand information collected both for its annual surveys and for its quinquennial economic census, beginning with that for 2002.

Full integration also implies greater consistency in the data provided by different statistical agencies. For example, the quality of the BEA's industry estimates can be affected by inconsistencies in the sampling frames used by the statistical agencies, as well as differences in classification and data collection and tabulation practices. Table 6.1 compares estimates of nonagricultural payroll data collected by the Bureau of the Census with wage and salary data collected by the BLS for selected industries in 1992. Industries for which comparable information was not available are excluded from the table. The comparison shows that the estimates differ by 5 percent

Table 6.1   **Comparison of Bureau of Labor Statistics (BLS) and census nonagricultural payroll data for selected private industries, 1992 (millions of dollars unless otherwise noted)**

Industry description	BLS	Census	BLS less Census	Absolute percent difference
Total	2,046,864	2,020,570	26,294	1.3
Industries with absolute difference of 10 percent or more				
Membership organizations	15,458	10,188	5,270	34.1
Tobacco products	2,103	2,534	−431	20.5
Miscellaneous repair services	8,263	9,849	−1,586	19.2
Health services	236,388	278,598	−42,210	17.9
Pipelines, except natural gas	975	821	154	15.8
Motor freight transportation and warehousing	35,536	41,070	−5,534	15.6
Leather and leather products	2,320	1,973	347	15.0
Security and commodity brokers and dealers	39,908	34,390	5,518	13.8
Oil and gas extraction	15,539	13,933	1,606	10.3
Insurance agents, brokers, and services	21,327	19,123	2,204	10.3
Nondepository credit institutions	15,007	16,509	−1,502	10.0
Industries with absolute difference of 5 to less than 10 percent				
Real estate	29,634	26,817	2,817	9.5
Textile mill products	14,801	13,531	1,270	8.6
Transportation services	8,959	8,225	734	8.2
Water transportation	5,949	5,481	468	7.9
Industrial machinery and equipment	69,749	64,588	5,161	7.4
Social services	27,508	25,565	1,943	7.1
Retail trade	268,207	249,328	18,879	7.0
Holding and other investment offices	10,313	9,626	687	6.7
Transportation equipment	74,475	69,706	4,769	6.4
Paper and allied products	24,542	23,079	1,463	6.0
Amusement and recreation services	20,816	19,612	1,204	5.8
Motion pictures	9,611	10,160	−549	5.7
Stone, clay, and glass products	15,283	14,441	842	5.5
Wholesale trade	199,687	188,780	10,907	5.5
Industries with absolute difference of less than 5 percent				
Primary metal industries	24,612	23,483	1,129	4.6
Lumber and wood products	15,345	14,669	676	4.4
Petroleum and coal products	7,568	7,246	322	4.2
Local and interurban passenger transportation	5,624	5,394	230	4.1
Rubber and miscellaneous plastics products	24,058	25,028	−970	4.0
Food and kindred products	44,712	43,032	1,680	3.8
Automotive repair, services, and parking	17,207	16,597	610	3.5
Depository institutions	59,464	57,479	1,985	3.3
Fabricated metal products	39,745	40,929	−1,184	3.0
Construction	122,135	118,600	3,535	2.9
Electric, gas, and sanitary services	40,683	39,623	1,060	2.6
Electronic and other electric equipment	52,057	50,812	1,245	2.4
Communications	48,908	47,742	1,166	2.4
Chemicals and allied products	47,911	46,835	1,076	2.2
Insurance carriers	49,457	50,559	−1,102	2.2

(continued)

Table 6.1 (continued)

Industry description	BLS	Census	BLS less Census	Absolute percent difference
Instruments and related products	35,932	36,613	−681	1.9
Apparel and other textile products	16,792	16,506	286	1.7
Legal services	40,480	39,995	485	1.2
Nonmetallic minerals, except fuels	3,291	3,265	26	0.8
Printing and publishing	43,655	43,926	−271	0.6
Business services	115,010	114,446	564	0.5
Furniture and fixtures	10,650	10,678	−28	0.3
Miscellaneous manufacturing industries	9,210	9,189	21	0.2

Note: Several industries are excluded because of differences in coverage or nondisclosure issues. These industries include metal mining, coal mining, air transportation, hotels and other lodging places, personal services, educational services, museums, art galleries and botanical gardens, membership organizations, engineering, and accounting services.

or more for about half of these industries. Although these differences do not directly affect measures of total value added, they can potentially affect the reliability of the BEA's estimates of the labor-capital splits of industry value added. The BEA envisions that it will be able to further enhance the consistency and quality of its fully integrated accounts because data-sharing initiatives should reveal the sources of these and other similar differences in source data from the various federal statistical agencies. In the case cited, the consistency between its measures of gross output by industry and compensation of employees by industry would be improved if payroll-by-industry data prepared by the Bureau of the Census and the wages and salaries data prepared by the BLS were brought into agreement by the source agencies.

At the earliest, full integration could not be attained until the 2008–10 time frame, which is when expanded data from the 2002 Economic Census will be fully incorporated into the BEA's economic accounts, beginning with the release of the 2002 benchmark I-O accounts in 2007. If limited data sharing by statistical agencies is also made viable in the interim, the BEA will be able to better identify the sources of the differences in data from other agencies such as those identified in the example presented above for the BLS and Census Bureau data. The major benefit of such data sharing would be to enhance the consistency and quality of the BEA's fully integrated economic accounts.

6.4 The Partial Integration Methodology

The methodology, including the source data and the estimating procedures that will be used for the partial integration of the annual I-O accounts and the GDP-by-industry accounts, is discussed in this section.[13] The methodology is described in a sequence of five steps: (1) establishing a level of detail for both industries and commodities; (2) revising the previously published 1997 benchmark I-O accounts that will serve as a reference point for the integrated accounts; (3) developing a 1998–2002 time series for the annual estimates of value added by industry; (4) updating and balancing the annual I-O accounts for 1998–2002, incorporating the revised 1997 benchmark I-O accounts from step 2 and the 1998–2002 estimates of value added by industry from step 3; and (5) preparing price and quantity indexes for the GDP-by-industry accounts for 1998–2002.

6.4.1 Step 1: Level of Industry and Commodity Detail

The first step in integrating the annual I-O accounts and the GDP-by-industry accounts is to establish the level of detail that can be used for both sets of accounts. Table 6.2 shows this detail and the corresponding 1997 North American Industry Classification System (NAICS) industry codes. Table 6.2 no longer shows a statistical discrepancy that has traditionally appeared as an industry in the GDP-by-industry accounts. This reflects the use of a balanced framework that requires consistency between GDP measured in terms of final expenditures and in terms of value added or income. In addition, table 6.2 does not include an industry for the inventory valuation adjustment, which has traditionally been shown in the I-O accounts. In the integrated accounts, the inventory valuation adjustment is treated as a secondary product produced by industries and included in their gross output, as well as a separate commodity going to final demand. The level of detail shown in table 6.2 applies to both industries and commodities and serves as the publication level of detail. Most of the estimation procedures, however, are applied at a finer level of industry and commodity detail in order to ensure the best estimates at the publication level.

6.4.2 Step 2: Revised 1997 Benchmark I-O Accounts

The second step in the partial integration process is to revise the previously published 1997 benchmark I-O accounts, because it must provide the relationships and levels for integrating the annual I-O accounts and GDP-by-industry accounts. The necessary revisions are from two sources. First, the 1997 benchmark I-O accounts must be modified to incorporate the definitional, methodological, and statistical changes from the 2003 comprehensive revision of the NIPAs. Incorporating these changes ensures that the integrated accounts for 1998–2002 are consistent with the levels and composition of GDP in the NIPAs. The major NIPA changes and their effects on the 1997 benchmark I-O accounts are summarized in table 6.3.

Second, after the NIPA revisions are incorporated, the level and the

---

13. See Moyer, Planting, Fahim-Nader, et al. (2004) and Moyer, Planting, Kern, et al. (2004).

Table 6.2   **Industries and commodities in the integrated accounts**

1997 NAICS industries	1997 NAICS codes
Private industries	
Agriculture, forestry, fishing, and hunting	11
Farms	111, 112
Forestry, fishing, and related activities	113, 114, 115
Mining	21
Oil and gas extraction	211
Mining, except oil and gas	212
Support activities for mining	213
Utilities	22
Construction	23
Manufacturing	31, 32, 33
Durable goods	33, 321, 327
Wood products	321
Nonmetallic mineral products	327
Primary metals	331
Fabricated metal products	332
Machinery	333
Computer and electronic products	334
Electrical equipment, appliances, and components	335
Motor vehicle, bodies and trailers, and parts	3361, 3362, 3363
Other transportation equipment	3364, 3365, 3366, 3369
Furniture and related products	337
Miscellaneous manufacturing	339
Nondurable goods	31, 32 (except 321 and 327)
Food and beverage and tobacco products	311, 312
Textile mills and textile product mills	313, 314
Apparel and leather and allied products	315, 316
Paper products	322
Printing and related support activities	323
Petroleum and coal products	324
Chemical products	325
Plastics and rubber products	326
Wholesale trade	42
Retail trade	44, 45
Transportation and warehousing	48, 49
Air transportation	481
Rail transportation	482
Water transportation	483
Truck transportation	484
Transit and ground passenger transportation	485
Pipeline transportation	486
Other transportation and support activities	487, 488, 492
Warehousing and storage	493
Information	51
Publishing industries (includes software)	511
Motion picture and sound recording industries	512

Table 6.2 (continued)

1997 NAICS industries	1997 NAICS codes
Broadcasting and telecommunications	513
Information and data processing services	514
Finance and insurance	52
Federal Reserve banks, credit intermediation, and related activities	521, 522
Securities, commodity contracts, and investments	523
Insurance carriers and related activities	524
Funds, trusts, and other financial vehicles	525
Real estate and rental and leasing	53
Real estate	531
Rental and leasing services and lessors of intangible assets	532, 533
Professional, scientific, and technical services	54
Legal services	5411
Computer systems design and related services	5415
Miscellaneous professional, scientific, and technical services	5412–5414, 5416–5419
Management of companies and enterprises	55
Administrative and waste management services	56
Administrative and support services	561
Waste management and remediation services	562
Educational services	61
Health care and social assistance	62
Ambulatory health care services	621
Hospitals and nursing and residential care facilities	622, 623
Social assistance	624
Arts, entertainment, and recreation	71
Performing arts, spectator sports, museums, and related activities	711, 712
Amusements, gambling, and recreation industries	713
Accommodation and food services	72
Accommodation	721
Food services and drinking places	722
Other services, except government	81
Government	
Government total	92
Federal	n.a.
General government	n.a.
Government enterprises	n.a.
State and local	n.a.
General government	n.a.
Government enterprises	n.a.

Note: n.a. = not applicable.

Table 6.3   NIPA changes incorporated into the 1997 benchmark input-output accounts

NIPA changes	I-O components affected
Recognize the implicit services provided by property and casualty insurance companies and provide a more appropriate treatment of insured losses.	Industry and commodity gross output for insurance carriers and related activities; intermediate inputs and gross operating surplus for all industries; final uses.
Allocate a portion of the implicit services of commercial banks to borrowers.	Industry and commodity gross output for Federal Reserve banks, credit intermediation and related activities; intermediate inputs and gross operating surplus for all industries; final uses.
Redefine change in private farm inventories to include farm materials and supplies.	Intermediate inputs and gross operating surplus for the farms industry; change in private inventories.
Reclassify Indian tribal government activities from the private sector to the state and local government sector.	Gross output, intermediate inputs, and value added for the amusements, gambling, and recreation; accommodation; and state and local government enterprises industries; state and local general government.
Reclassify military grants-in-kind as exports.	Federal general government; exports.
Recognize explicitly the services produced by general government and treat government purchases of goods and services as intermediate inputs.	Gross output and intermediate inputs for the state and local general government and Federal general government industries.
Reclassify business nontax liability as current transfer payments to government and as rent and royalties to government.	Taxes on production and imports, less subsidies and gross operating surplus for all industries; gross output for the rental and leasing services and lessors of intangible assets industry; purchases of the rental and leasing services and lessors of intangible assets commodity by selected industries.

Note: NIPAs = national income and product accounts; I-O = input-output. For details of NIPA changes, see Moulton and Seskin (2003).

composition of value added for each industry must be further modified on the basis of information from both the I-O accounts and the GDP-by-industry accounts.[14] As discussed above, value added by industry in the I-O accounts is computed as the difference between gross output and intermediate inputs by industry, and value added by industry in the GDP-by-industry accounts is computed from the industry distributions of GDI from the NIPAs. In general, these two measures of value added for an industry will differ (see the first two columns of table 6.4).[15]

14. The GDP-by-industry value added that is based on the NIPA GDI estimates will also incorporate the results from the 2003 comprehensive NIPA revision.

15. Research indicates that the magnitude and sign of these differences vary across industries and across time. For example, using data for 1992, Yuskavage (2000) finds that the

Figure 6.4 shows a matrix that demonstrates how the quality of the value added by industry estimates varies across the benchmark I-O accounts and the GDP-by-industry accounts. For example, both the benchmark I-O accounts and the GDP-by-industry accounts provide good measures of value added for the health care industry because of the near-complete coverage of gross output and intermediate inputs by the economic census and the relatively small amount of redistributions of income resulting from enterprise-establishment adjustments. On the other hand, both sets of accounts provide poor measures for the construction industry because of incomplete coverage in the economic census and because of large lower-quality, enterprise-establishment adjustments. For many industries, the quality of industry value added is mixed. Mining value added, for example, is good in the benchmark I-O accounts because of near-complete industry coverage, yet poor in the GDP-by-industry accounts because of relatively very large enterprise-establishment adjustments. The partial integration methodology draws the best information from both sets of accounts into a single "combined" estimate of value added for each industry. These combined measures are then incorporated into the 1997 benchmark I-O accounts.[16]

The combined value added for an industry is an average with weights determined by criteria that reflect the relative quality of value added from the two sets of accounts. In general, these criteria are based on the quality of the source data used for each. The criteria for the benchmark I-O accounts include the following:

- the percent of intermediate inputs by industry that are covered by source data from the quinquennial economic census
- the percent of an industry's total gross output that is accounted for by the quinquennial economic census.

The criteria for the GDP-by-industry accounts include the following:

- the quality and the size of adjustments used to convert the enterprise-based, profit-type income data to an establishment basis
- the percent of an industry's value added that is accounted for by proprietors' income

---

property-type income for the manufacturing sector is, on average, lower in the GDP-by-industry accounts than in the benchmark I-O accounts. However, more recent research, using data for 1997, finds that the reverse is true; for the manufacturing sector, the gross operating surplus from the GDP-by-industry accounts is, on average, larger than the gross operating surplus from benchmark I-O accounts. The BEA is continuing its research into the sources of these differences.

16. The estimates of "compensation of employees" and "taxes on production and imports, less subsidies" in the revised 1997 benchmark I-O accounts are consistent with those published in the NIPAs. For census-covered industries, the compensation in the previously published 1997 benchmark I-O accounts was based on the 1997 Economic Census. See Lawson et al. (2002), p. 31.

Table 6.4   **1997 industry value added estimates**

Industry	Revised benchmark I-O accounts	GDP-by-industry accounts	Combined
Farms	88,142	88,142	88,142
Forestry, fishing, and related activities	21,110	23,771	22,595
Oil and gas extraction	48,084	59,236	52,902
Mining, except oil and gas	25,869	27,854	26,414
Support activities for mining	11,941	18,439	13,333
Utilities	162,264	180,852	180,289
Construction	310,029	346,223	337,558
Wood products	26,207	30,666	28,008
Nonmetallic mineral products	40,720	37,829	40,708
Primary metals	43,799	51,214	48,337
Fabricated metal products	114,396	102,625	108,119
Machinery	104,664	88,649	98,164
Computer and electronic products	178,019	144,110	154,403
Electrical equipment, appliances, and components	41,230	79,140	45,596
Motor vehicle, bodies and trailers, and parts	93,396	117,083	103,195
Other transportation equipment	55,538	52,444	54,418
Furniture and related products	28,181	25,568	27,060
Miscellaneous manufacturing	47,861	47,793	47,729
Food and beverage and tobacco products	158,928	130,224	135,357
Textile mills and textile product mills	26,012	27,829	26,996
Apparel and leather and allied products	28,918	26,249	27,186
Paper products	51,046	51,354	51,484
Printing and related support activities	42,725	47,362	44,667
Petroleum and coal products	22,595	67,926	27,116
Chemical products	149,879	150,776	150,846
Plastics and rubber products	62,402	49,828	60,704
Wholesale trade	487,913	531,865	521,250
Retail trade	517,499	588,270	574,192
Air transportation	45,285	55,017	49,457
Rail transportation	23,133	22,590	23,030
Water transportation	7,162	6,273	6,510
Truck transportation	87,016	76,343	80,524
Transit and ground passenger transportation	17,090	12,164	12,978
Pipeline transportation	9,227	8,095	8,774
Other transportation and support activities	50,523	59,586	55,032
Warehousing and storage	19,014	20,003	19,549
Publishing industries (includes software)	114,475	65,572	87,457
Motion picture and sound recording industries	25,272	22,899	24,298
Broadcasting and telecommunications	196,395	212,151	208,862
Information and data processing services	30,418	18,550	27,189
Federal Reserve banks, credit intermediation, and related activities	274,457	251,974	259,541
Securities, commodity contracts, and investments	107,598	131,109	119,470
Insurance carriers and related activities	175,610	217,464	206,566
Funds, trusts, and other financial vehicles	9,957	9,882	9,965
Real estate	944,801	886,560	908,544
Rental and leasing services and lessors of intangible assets	118,401	74,444	89,854

Table 6.4   (continued)

Industry	Revised benchmark I-O accounts	GDP by industry accounts	Combined
Legal services	111,052	119,435	114,460
Computer systems design and related services	69,536	87,477	78,642
Miscellaneous professional, scientific, and technical services	343,445	308,416	325,057
Management of companies and enterprises	145,665	145,665	145,665
Administrative and support services	228,861	197,921	211,363
Waste management and remediation services	22,618	20,339	21,372
Educational services	63,371	61,295	62,240
Ambulatory health care services	267,784	261,920	267,232
Hospitals and nursing and residential care facilities	205,830	199,526	203,543
Social assistance	38,834	43,181	40,065
Performing arts, spectator sports, museums, and related activities	30,050	34,717	32,911
Amusements, gambling, and recreation industries	45,180	37,667	41,133
Accommodation	75,769	71,018	74,689
Food services and drinking places	151,890	133,183	141,062
Other services, except government	206,147	185,476	197,403

For both the benchmark I-O accounts and the GDP-by-industry accounts, these criteria, along with expert analyst judgment, are applied at the industry level shown in table 6.2 in order to identify point estimates and estimates of variance for each industry's measure of value added.[17] These point estimates and estimates of variance are used to develop a probability distribution of value added for each industry from each set of accounts. Each probability distribution represents a measure of the likelihood that the "true" value added takes on a particular value, given the information available. The distributions are then combined to produce a measure of value added for each industry. Essentially, the combined measure is an average of the two point estimates with the weights being determined by the relative variances—that is, a point estimate with a smaller variance receives a larger weight. Appendix A provides technical details on the procedures used.

Figure 6.5 gives an example of this process for the educational services industry. The point estimate of value added is $63.4 billion from the revised 1997 benchmark I-O accounts and $61.3 billion from the GDP-by-

17. The estimates are prepared at this level of detail because the industry distributions of GDI are available at this level. These estimates are allocated to more detailed industries when the revised benchmark I-O table is balanced. Source data for 1997 were not available on the 1997 NAICS basis for all of the components of GDI. For selected components, the BEA converted data from the 1987 Standard Industrial Classification (SIC) basis to the 1997 NAICS basis.

Benchmark Value Added

	Good Benchmark data/ good GDP-by-industry data e.g., Health care	Good Benchmark data/ poor GDP-by-industry data e.g., Mining
GDP-by-Industry Value Added	Poor Benchmark data/ Good GDP-by-industry data e.g., Transportation/ Warehousing	Poor Benchmark data/ poor GDP-by-industry data e.g. Construction

Fig. 6.4   Merging information for setting value-added levels
Source: U.S. Bureau of Economic Analysis.

industry accounts. The benchmark I-O value-added estimate reflects only a limited amount of information on this industry's gross output and intermediate inputs, because most establishments classified in this industry are out of the scope of the quinquennial economic census. Therefore, the information used to prepare the I-O estimates was drawn from a variety of sources, including trade association data. The quality of these data is not as high as data from the economic census. In contrast, the GDP-by-industry value-added estimate reflects relatively complete data, based on the industry distributions of GDI from the NIPAs. Nevertheless, examining the two quality criteria for the GDP-by-industry accounts reveals that proprietors' income for this industry is about 3 percent of total value added and that the amount of adjustment required to convert enterprise-based profit-type income data to an establishment basis is about 1 percent. This implies that the combined estimate should be close, but not equal to, the GDP-by-industry point estimate.

A more formal analysis of the educational services industry is shown in figure 6.5, which includes the related probability distributions for each of the two point estimates. Note that the GDP-by-industry distribution is more peaked (smaller variance) than the distribution from the I-O accounts (larger variance). The smaller variance reflects a relatively good GDP-by-industry estimate; the larger variance for the benchmark I-O accounts reflects a relatively lower-quality estimate. As expected, the combined estimate of $62.2 billion is closer to the GDP-by-industry estimate than to the I-O estimate; the GDP-by-industry estimate is given a weight of about 57 percent, while the I-O estimate is given a weight of about 43 percent. Because more information is used to make this combined estimate, its overall quality is higher than that for either of the individual estimates, as shown by their distributions in figure 6.5. A complete list of the

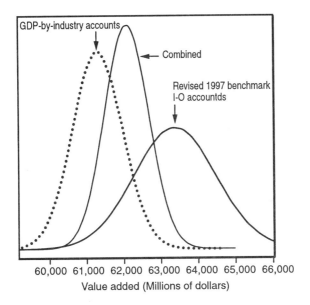

Fig. 6.5   Probability distributions of value added for educational services
Source: U.S. Bureau of Economic Analysis.

combined estimates of value added by industry is shown in the third column of table 6.4.

After the two sets of revisions have been made to the 1997 benchmark I-O accounts, it is then balanced. For this balancing, each industry's gross output and new measure of value added are fixed, and its total of intermediate inputs is allowed to adjust to the difference. Balancing ensures that the use of commodities equals their supply, the sum of each industry's value added and intermediate inputs equals its gross output, and the sum of final uses equals published GDP. The revised and balanced 1997 benchmark I-O accounts then provide a starting point for preparing the integrated accounts for 1998–2002.

6.4.3   Step 3: A Time Series of Value Added for 1998–2002

A time series of value added by industry is prepared by extrapolating the revised 1997 benchmark I-O estimates of value added by industry forward to 1998–2002, using the GDI-based measure of value added from the GDP-by-industry accounts as the extrapolator for each industry. The integrated industry accounts for 1998–2002 are presented on the 1997 NAICS basis.[18] The components of GDI that compose value added by industry and

18. On November 9, 2005, the BEA published the NAICS-based GDP-by-industry estimates for years 1947–86.

information on the major source data and on the industrial distribution for each component are shown in table 6.5.

As discussed above, the quality of the GDI-based measures of value added depends on a number of factors, including the size of adjustments required to convert enterprise-based, profit-type GDI data to an establishment basis and the size of proprietors' income. Nonetheless, they are preferred as growth indicators when compared with those from the annual I-O residual methodology because of the scarcity of annual data on intermediate inputs for credible measures of value added.

After extrapolating the revised 1997 benchmark I-O level of value added forward with the GDI-based measure for each industry, the resulting sum of value added across industries will not necessarily sum to GDP in a given year—part of the difference being the statistical discrepancy and the other part being extrapolation errors.[19] This procedure allocates this difference in two steps. In the first step, expert analyst judgment is used to adjust some industries with known measurement problems. In the second step, the remaining difference is distributed across industries in proportion to the industries' value added.

6.4.4   Step 4: Updated and Balanced Annual I-O Accounts for 1998–2002

Five tasks must be completed sequentially to update and balance each of the five annual I-O tables for 1998–2002. These tasks are (a) estimating gross output for each industry and commodity; (b) estimating the commodity composition of intermediate inputs for each industry; (c) estimating the domestic supply for each commodity; (d) incorporating estimates of commodities used for personal consumption, for gross private fixed investment, and for government consumption and investment as part of GDP final-demand expenditures; and (e) balancing the use of commodities with available supply and the output of industries with necessary inputs for production.

Industry and Commodity Gross Output

For most industries and commodities, annual source data are available to estimate current-year industry and commodity gross output. The data sources used are shown in table 6.6. Manufacturing, trade, and most service industry estimates are based on annual survey data from the Bureau of the Census. Agriculture, insurance, and government enterprise estimates, as well as transportation, utilities, finance, and real estate estimates,

---

19. The BEA also investigated using gross output by industry as an extrapolator for the revised 1997 benchmark I-O value added. This procedure—which assumes industry input-output ratios are constant over time—was not adopted, because tests on historical data showed that it yields larger discrepancies between the sum of extrapolated value added and GDP relative to GDI extrapolation.

Table 6.5   Principal source data for value-added extrapolators

		Industrial distribution	
Component of gross domestic income	Major source data	Distribution available in source data	Data or assumption used if distribution by establishment is not available in source data
Compensation of employees, paid			
Wages and salary accruals[a]	BLS tabulations of wages and salaries of employees covered by state UI programs and OPM data on wages and salaries of Federal Government employees.	Establishment	
Supplements to wages and salaries			
Employer contributions for employee pension and insurance funds	DOL tabulations of IRS data (Form 5500) on pension plans, HHS data from the Medical Expenditure Panel Survey on health insurance, and trade association data for other types.	None[b]	BLS employer cost index and UI tabulations.
Employer contributions for government social insurance	Federal budget data.	None	Social Security Administration and BLS tabulations.
Taxes on production and imports less subsidies			
Taxes on production and imports	Federal budget data and Census Bureau data on state and local governments.	None	Property taxes are based on BEA capital stock distribution.
Subsidies	Federal budget data and Census Bureau data on state and local governments.	None	Payments are assigned to the industries being supported.

(continued)

Table 6.5 (continued)

Component of gross domestic income	Major source data	Distribution available in source data	Industrial distribution — Data or assumption used if distribution by establishment is not available in source data
	Gross operating surplus		
Private enterprises			
Net interest and miscellaneous payments, domestic industries			
Corporate	IRS tabulations of data from corporate tax returns (Form 1120 series), FFIEC Call Report data on commercial banks, trade association data on life insurance companies.	Company	Census Bureau company-establishment employment matrix.
Noncorporate	IRS tabulations of tax return data from sole proprietorships (Form 1040 Schedule C) and partnerships (Form 1065), FRB flow-of-funds-account data on residential mortgages.	Company	Assumed to be equivalent to an establishment distribution.
Business current transfer payments (net)	IRS tabulations of data from corporate tax returns (Form 1120 series), trade association data for property-casualty insurance net settlements and for other types.	Company	Industry-specific payments are assigned to those industries; others are based on IRS company industry distribution.
Proprietors' income with IVA and without CCAdj			
Farm	USDA farm income statistics.	Establishment	
Nonfarm			
Proprietors' income without IVA and CCAdj	IRS tabulations of tax return data from sole proprietorships (Form 1040 Schedule C) and partnerships (Form 1065).	Company	Assumed to be equivalent to an establishment distribution.
IVA	BLS prices and IRS inventory data.	Establishment	

		Type of agency	
Rental income of persons without CCAdj	Census Bureau data on housing units and rents from the American Housing Survey, HMDA data on residential mortgages, and IRS tabulations of data from individual tax returns (Form 1040).	Establishment	
Corporate profits before tax with IVA and without CCAdj, domestic industries			
Corporate profits before tax without IVA and CCAdj	IRS tabulations of data from corporate tax returns (Form 1120 series) and regulatory agencies and public financial reports data.	Company	Census Bureau company-establishment employment matrix.
IVA	BLS prices and IRS inventory data	Establishment	
Capital consumption allowances			
Corporate	IRS tabulations of data from corporate tax returns (Form 1120 series).	Company	Census Bureau company-establishment employment matrix.
Noncorporate	IRS tabulations of tax return data from sole proprietorships (Form 1040 Schedule C) and partnerships (Form 1065).	Company	Assumed to be equivalent to an establishment distribution.
Current surplus of government enterprises	Federal budget data and Census Bureau data on state and local governments.	Establishment	
Consumption of fixed capital			
Households and institutions[c]	BEA capital stock estimates.	Establishment	
Government	BEA capital stock estimates.	Type of agency	

Notes: BEA = Bureau of Economic Analysis; BLS = Bureau of Labor Statistics; CCAdj = Capital consumption adjustment; DOL = Department of Labor; FFIEC = Federal Financial Institutions Examination Council; FRB = Federal Reserve Board of Governors; HCFA = Health Care Financing Administration; HHS = Department of Health and Human Services; HMDA = Home Mortgage Disclosure Act; IRS = Internal Revenue Service; IVA = Inventory valuation adjustment; OPM = Office of Personnel Management; UI = Unemployment insurance; USDA = U.S. Department of Agriculture.

[a]Includes wage and salary disbursements to the rest of the world and excludes wages and salaries received from the rest of the world.

[b]A company-based industrial distribution for pension plans is available in the source data.

[c]Consists of owner-occupied housing and nonprofit institutions primarily serving households.

Table 6.6   **Principal sources of data for industry and commodity output and prices**

Industry and commodity	Source data for extrapolator	Source data for price index
Agriculture, forestry, fishing and hunting		
Farms	USDA cash receipts from marketing and inventory change	USDA prices received by farmers; PPI
Forestry, fishing, and related activities	For forestry, Census Bureau shipments; for fishing, NOAA value of fish landings; for related activities, NIPA estimates	PPI; NOAA; NIPA deflator
Mining		
Oil and gas extraction	DOE quantity produced and prices	For crude petroleum and natural gas, IPD from DOE; for natural gas liquids, PPI
Mining, except oil and gas	DOE quantity produced and average price for uranium and coal; USGS quantity and price data for all others	IPD from DOE and USGS
Support activities for mining	DOE, USGS, and trade sources for quantity produced and prices	IPD from DOE, USGS and trade sources; for exploration, PPI
Utilities		
Electric utilities	EIA	PPI
Natural gas	EIA quantity and price data	PPI
Water, sewage, and other systems	PCE	CPI
Construction		
For the Department of Defense	DOD expenditures data	DOD prices for military construction; cost indexes from trade sources and government agencies for other construction
For state and local highways	Census Bureau data from the ASGF	Cost indexes from government agencies
For private electric and gas utilities	Federal regulatory agencies and trade sources expenditures data	Cost indexes from trade sources and government agencies
For farms, excluding residential	USDA expenditures data	Trade sources cost index; Census Bureau price deflator for new single-family houses under construction
For other nonresidential	Census Bureau data on value of construction put in place	Trade sources and government agency cost indexes; Census Bureau price index for new single-family houses under construction; BEA quality-adjusted price indexes for factories, office buildings, warehouses, and schools

Industry	Source	Method
For other residential	Census Bureau data on value of construction put in place	Census Bureau price index for new single-family houses under construction; BEA price index for multifamily construction
Manufacturing	Census Bureau data on shipments and inventory change	PPI; quality-adjusted price indexes for computers, photocopying equipment, digital telephone switching equipment, and LAN equipment; BEA price indexes based on DOD prices paid for military equipment
Wholesale trade	Census Bureau ATS data	Sales price by kind-of-business computed from PPI
Retail trade	Census Bureau ARTS data	Sales price by kind-of-business computed from CPI
Transportation and warehousing		
Air transportation	BTS Air Carrier Financial Statistics	IPD for total passenger-related revenues and passenger miles from DOT; IPD for total freight-, mail-, and express-related revenues and ton miles from DOT; wages and salaries per employee from BLS
Rail transportation	Amtrak and trade sources	PPI
Water transportation	Army Corps of Engineers; trade sources	PPI for freight; for passengers, CPI
Truck transportation	Census Bureau SAS	PPI
Transit and ground passenger transportation	PCE; BTS	For taxicabs, intercity buses, and other local transit, PCE price index; for school buses, BLS data on wages and salaries per employee
Pipeline transportation	Trade sources	PPI
Other transportation and support activities	PCE	For sightseeing, PCE price index; for other transportation and support activities, PCE price indexes and PPI
Warehousing and Storage	Census Bureau SAS	PPI
Information		
Publishing industries (includes software)	Census Bureau SAS	BEA price indexes for prepackaged and custom software for software publishers; for all other publishing industries, PPI

(continued)

Table 6.6 (continued)

Industry and commodity	Source data for extrapolator	Source data for price index
Motion picture and sound recording industries	Census Bureau SAS	PCE price indexes
Broadcasting and telecommunications	Census Bureau SAS	For cable networks, programming, and telecommunications, PPI; for radio and television broadcasting, network receipts, and all other telecommunications, composite price index of PPIs
Information and data processing services	Census Bureau SAS	For information services, PCE price indexes; for data processing services, PPI
Finance and insurance		
Federal Reserve banks, credit intermediation, and related activities	FDIC; FRB; NIPA imputed service charges; NCUA; and other private agencies	PCE price indexes; other government data
Securities, commodity contracts, investments	SEC FOCUS Report	PCE price indexes
Insurance carriers and related activities	Trade sources for insurance carriers; BEA estimates for property and casualty insurance; for all other insurance, PCE; for insurance agents, brokers, and services, IRS tabulations of business tax returns	For health and life insurance, PCE price indexes; for property and casualty insurance, PPI; for agents, brokers, and services, composite price index based on trade sources data and PCE price indexes
Funds, trusts, and other financial vehicles	NIPA imputed service charges for other financial institutions; EBSA data on pension funds	IPD from NIPA imputed service charges; composite price index based on PCE price indexes; PPI data; BLS data on wages and salaries per full-time employee
Real estate and rental and leasing		
Real estate	For residential dwellings and real estate agents and managers, NIPA housing data; for nonresidential dwellings, IRS tabulations of business tax returns; NIPA rental value of buildings owned by nonprofits	For nonfarm residential dwellings, NIPA price index; for nonresidential dwellings, PPI; for real estate managers and agents, PPI and trade sources; IPD for nonprofit and farm residential dwellings

Industry	Source	Price index
Rental and leasing services and lessors of intangible assets	For rental and leasing services, Census Bureau SAS; for royalties, IRS tabulations of business tax returns	For automotive equipment rental, PPI; for other rental services, PCE price indexes; for royalties, PCE price index and IPD from DOE and PPI
Professional, scientific, and technical services		
Legal services	Census Bureau SAS	PPI
Computer systems design and related services	Census Bureau SAS	BEA price indexes for prepackaged and custom software
Miscellaneous professional, scientific and technical services	Census Bureau SAS	PPI; BLS wages and salaries per full-time employee
Management of companies and enterprises	BLS wages and salaries	BLS wages and salaries per full-time employee
Administrative and waste management services		
Administrative and support services	Census Bureau SAS	BLS wages and salaries per full-time employee; PCE price indexes; PPI
Waste management and remediation services	Census Bureau SAS	CPI
Educational services	PCE	PCE price index based on trade sources
Health care and social assistance		
Ambulatory health care services	Census Bureau SAS	PPI; PCE price indexes
Hospitals and nursing and residential care facilities	Census Bureau SAS	PCE price indexes
Social assistance	Census Bureau SAS	PCE price indexes
Arts, entertainment, and recreation		
Performing arts, spectator sports, museums, and related activities	Census Bureau SAS	PCE price indexes

(continued)

Table 6.6 (continued)

Industry and commodity	Source data for extrapolator	Source data for price index
Amusements, gambling, and recreation industries	Census Bureau SAS	PCE price indexes
Accommodation and food services		
Accommodation	Census Bureau ARTS	For hotels and motels, PPI; PCE price index
Food services and drinking places	Census Bureau ARTS	CPI
Other services except government	For religious, labor, and political organizations, PCE; for other services, Census Bureau SAS; for private households, BEA compensation of employees	CPI; BLS data on wages and salaries per full-time employee; PCE price indexes
Government		
Federal		
General government	NIPA estimates	NIPA price indexes
Government enterprises	USPS receipts; for electric utilities, DOE; other government data	For USPS and electric utilities, PPI; for all others, PCE price index and NIPA price indexes
State and local		
General government	NIPA estimates	NIPA price indexes
Government enterprises	For electric utilities, DOE data; for other enterprises, BEA data on revenue by type	PPI

Notes: ARTS = Annual Retail Trade Survey, Census Bureau; ASGF = Annual Survey of Government Finances, Census Bureau; ATS = Annual Trade Survey, Census Bureau; BEA = Bureau of Economic Analysis; BLS = Bureau of Labor Statistics; BTS = Bureau of Transportation Statistics; CPI = Consumer Price Index, BLS; DOC = Department of Commerce; DOD = Department of Defense; DOE = Department of Energy; DOT = Department of Transportation; EBSA = Employee Benefits Security Administration; EIA = Energy Information Administration; FDIC = Federal Deposit Insurance Corporation; FOCUS = Financial and Operational Combined Uniform Single Report, SEC; FRB = Federal Reserve Board of Governors; IPD = Implicit price deflator; IRS = Internal Revenue Service; NCUA = National Credit Union Association; NIPA = National income and product accounts, BEA; NOAA = National Oceanic and Atmospheric Administration; PCE = Personal consumption expenditures, BEA; PPI = Producer Price Index, BLS; SAS = Service Annual Survey; SEC = Securities and Exchange Commission; USDA = U.S. Department of Agriculture; USGS = U.S. Geological Survey, Office of Minerals; USPS = U.S. Postal Service.

are primarily based on data from other government statistical agencies and private sources. For those industries and commodities for which annual source data are not available at the 1997 benchmark I-O level of detail, more aggregated source data are used as extrapolators.

Intermediate Inputs to Industries

Industry inputs are estimated in three steps. First, for domestic inputs, each industry's current-year output is valued in terms of the previous year's prices, using an industry price index that is calculated—in a Fisher index-number formula—as a weighted average of the price indexes for commodities produced by the industry. Estimates of inputs from foreign sources are revalued using import price indexes. For commodities for which a price index is unavailable, an aggregate price index is applied to multiple commodities. The data sources used to prepare these indexes are shown in table 6.6.

Second, each industry's current-year output, valued in the prices for the previous year, is multiplied by the previous year's direct requirements coefficient for the same industry. The initial set of coefficients used are from the revised 1997 benchmark I-O accounts. The result of this multiplication yields current-year intermediate inputs valued in the prices of the previous year.[20] At this point, the composition of an industry's inputs per dollar of output (valued in the prices of the previous year) is unchanged from that of the previous year. To adjust for changes in relative prices, the results are reflated to current-year prices, using the commodity price indexes.

Finally, commodity taxes, transportation costs, and trade margins for each intermediate input are estimated. Commodity taxes are added to increase the value of intermediate inputs from basic prices to producers' prices, and transportation costs and trade margins are added to increase the value further to purchasers' prices.[21] Estimates for commodity taxes and total transportation costs and margins are developed as part of the annual estimates of commodity gross output and are distributed to transactions using 1997 benchmark I-O relationships.

Domestic Supply

The domestic supply is estimated. The domestic supply of each commodity is the total value of goods and services available for consumption as intermediate inputs by industries or for final use as personal consumption, private fixed investment, and government consumption and gross investment. It is calculated as domestic commodity output, plus government sales, and imports less exports and change in private inventories. Imports and exports are based on foreign trade statistics from the Bureau of the

20. A direct requirements coefficient represents the amount of a commodity required by an industry to produce a dollar of the industry's output.

21. The basic price is the price received by the producer for goods sold; it excludes the taxes collected by the producer from purchasers, as well as transportation costs and trade margins.

Census and on the BEA's international transactions accounts. Changes in private inventories are from the NIPAs, and the commodity composition of inventories held by industries is based on relationships from the revised 1997 benchmark I-O accounts.

Commodity Composition of Final Uses Excluding Imports and Exports and Changes in Private Inventories

The annual estimates of the major expenditure components of final uses for personal consumption, private fixed investment, and government consumption and gross investment are obtained directly from the NIPAs. The initial commodity compositions of these components are estimated using relationships from the revised 1997 benchmark I-O accounts.

Balancing the Use Table

Finally, commodities and industries are brought into balance using a biproportional adjustment procedure. This procedure sequentially adjusts rows and columns to equal the estimated output control totals. The adjustments are made iteratively until the use of each commodity equals its domestic supply, the sum of value added and intermediate inputs for each industry equals its gross output, and final-demand expenditures equal levels in the NIPAs. Unlike many I-O balancing systems, the system employed for the annual I-O tables takes advantage of the very detailed relationships included in the 1997 benchmark I-O accounts and balances in both producers' and purchasers' prices. The system balances approximately 3,000 rows and 1,200 columns while maintaining information on transportation costs and margins for each transaction. Appendix B provides a more detailed discussion of the techniques used for this balancing.

The annual I-O accounts are finalized for 1998–2002 after the results have been reviewed and verified. The measures of gross output, intermediate inputs, and value added by industry are then incorporated into the GDP-by-industry accounts.

6.4.5   Step 5: Price and Quantity Indexes for the GDP-by-Industry Accounts

Price and quantity indexes for the GDP-by-industry accounts are prepared in two steps. First, price and quantity indexes for gross output and intermediate inputs are prepared for each industry. Second, information on gross output by industry is combined with information on intermediate inputs by industry to derive price and quantity indexes for value added by industry, using the double-deflation procedure.

Indexes for Gross Output and Intermediate Inputs by Industry

Price and quantity indexes for gross output by industry are derived by separately deflating each commodity produced by an industry and included in its gross output. Information on the commodities produced by industries is obtained from annual I-O make tables. Price and quantity indexes for intermediate inputs are estimated by deflating the commodities used by industries from the annual I-O use tables. The commodity price indexes used for this deflation are listed in table 6.6. When a commodity price index is based on more than one detailed price index, a Fisher index-number formula is used to prepare the composite index. Appendix C, "Computing Chain-Type Price and Quantity Indexes in the GDP-by-Industry Accounts," shows the Fisher index-number formulas that are used to prepare the price and quantity indexes for gross output and intermediate inputs by industry.

Indexes for Value Added by Industry

Price and quantity indexes for value added by industry are calculated using the double-deflation method. In the double-deflation method, separate estimates of gross output and intermediate inputs by industry are combined in a Fisher index-number formula in order to generate price and quantity indexes for value added by industry (see appendix C). This method is preferred for computing price and quantity indexes for value added by industry because it requires the fewest assumptions about the relationships among gross outputs.

6.5   Future Research

There are several areas of research that must be addressed in order to achieve the BEA's long-run goal of full integration of the accounts. The most important of these are the following:

- Additional evaluation of the coverage, quality, and consistency of data from different sources for the purpose of improving the BEA's industry accounts overall and its estimates of value added by industry specifically. This includes working cooperatively with other statistical agencies for the purpose of collecting additional data as well as expanding data-sharing initiatives to address differences across alternative data sources.
- Related research to determine the underlying reasons for the discrepancies that existed between the GDP-by-industry and I-O levels of value added prior to setting a "combined" level for the integrated accounts. The fact that these discrepancies were clearly evident prior to the integration indicates underlying inconsistencies in source data and methodologies that need to be explored further. This research will also require working cooperatively with the statistical agencies providing the source data.
- Continued research to develop new methods and data sources that improve measures of gross operating surplus and direct measures of value added by industry that are consistent with establishment-based

definitions for industries. This is in contrast to the method of estimating value added as a residual resulting from intermediate purchases being subtracted from gross output. Although this method results in consistent estimates, it also picks up statistical errors that do not have anything to do with value added.

- Development of additional procedures to incorporate new data from the 2002 Economic Census and annual surveys of intermediate inputs by industry into the BEA's industry accounts on a more accelerated basis, including techniques for evaluating "best-level" estimates as compared to "best-change" estimates.
- Development of new processes and procedures for incorporating information from the production-based approach of measuring GDP into the NIPAs on a timely basis.
- Extension of the NAICS-based industry accounts backward for years prior to 1998.[22] Research is needed to develop current-dollar annual I-O tables for years prior to 1998.

Appendix A

Estimating the "Combined" Level of Value Added by Industry

This appendix describes the procedure used to determine the "combined" estimates of value added by industry that are incorporated into the revised 1997 benchmark I-O accounts. The procedure allows for the best information from both the I-O accounts and the GDP-by-industry accounts to be used in determining the combined estimates. This is accomplished by preparing a weighted average of the two independent measures of value added where the weights reflect the relative quality of the two measures. For each of the sixty-one industries presented in table 6.4, a weighted average is given by

$$\text{Combined}_i = b_{i,\text{I-O}}(\text{I-O}_i) + b_{i,\text{GDP by Industry}}(\text{GDP by Industry}_i),$$

where (I-O$_i$) is industry i's point estimate of value added from the benchmark I-O accounts and (GDP by Industry$_i$) is industry i's point estimate from the GDP-by-industry accounts. $b_{i,\text{I-O}}$ and $b_{i,\text{GDP by Industry}}$ are the weights for the benchmark I-O accounts and the GDP-by-industry accounts, respectively.

In this linear combination, the weights are a simple function of the rela-

---

22. In November 2004 and November 2005, the BEA published the NAICS-based GDP-by-industry accounts for the periods 1987–97 and 1947–86, respectively. See Yuskavage and Pho (2004) and Yuskavage and Fahim-Nader (2005).

tive precision of each point estimate. A modeling framework is developed to estimate the precision of each industry's value-added estimator. The precision of each point estimate is summarized using two measures. First, an ordinal quality ranking of industries is developed for both the benchmark I-O accounts and the GDP-by-industry accounts. Second, an approximate 95 percent confidence interval for each point estimate is determined by evaluating the uncertainty in the underlying source data. Implicit in both the ordinal ranking and the confidence intervals are the quality criteria outlined in section 6.4.2 (step 2) of the main text. A review of these criteria suggests that a significant amount of expert analyst judgment is incorporated into this framework.

Two practical considerations constrained the modeling framework finally selected by the BEA for estimating weights. First, the overall objective is to obtain the most accurate weighted average feasible from the information currently available. Second, the model must not be overly sensitive to misspecifications of the 95 percent confidence intervals.

The chosen model requires the following assumptions:

1. Information about each benchmark I-O and GDP-by-industry value-added estimate can be effectively summarized by estimating the mean and standard deviation of a normal distribution. (This assumption implies that the standard deviation accurately summarizes the uncertainty associated with each estimator.)

2. The relative quality of the estimates from the benchmark I-O accounts and the GDP-by-industry accounts can be evaluated based on their ratios of point estimate to standard deviation.

3. The point estimate–standard deviation ratios for all industries can be represented by an ordered vector with elements sampled from a beta distribution.

The steps for estimating each industry's standard deviation are as follows (for illustrative purposes, only the benchmark I-O accounts are discussed but the process is performed on the GDP-by-industry accounts as well):

1. For the benchmark I-O accounts, set candidate values for the two parameters of the beta distribution as a starting point. This distribution is evaluated as a candidate for characterizing the underlying distribution of point estimate–standard deviation ratios for all industries in the benchmark I-O accounts.

2. Sample sixty-one values from the distribution from step 1.

3. Rank order the sixty-one values from step 2 and assign one to each benchmark industry based on its ordinal ranking.

4. For each industry, use the assigned point estimate–standard deviation ratio and the known point estimate to determine the implied standard

deviation—that is, solve the following equation for industry i's standard deviation.

$$\text{Error Metric}_i = \frac{\text{Standard Deviation}_i}{\text{Point Estimate}_i}$$

5. Repeat this process many times (on average, about 5,000 times), storing the implied standard deviations of the industry estimators from each repetition.

6. Compute the average of the sampled standard deviations for each industry using the results from step 5; use this average to develop a 95 percent confidence interval based on the *normal* distribution—that is,

$$N(\text{Point Estimate}_i, \text{Average Standard Deviation}).$$

7. Compare the upper and lower bounds of the confidence interval estimated in step 6 with the original 95 percent confidence interval estimated for the benchmark I-O accounts.

8. Repeat steps 1 through 7 with all candidate beta parameters. Find the beta parameters that minimize the sum of squared deviations between the 95 percent confidence intervals from the benchmark I-O accounts and those from step 6.

9. After estimating the beta parameters from step 8, follow steps 2 through 6 to estimate the standard deviation for each of the 61 industries in the benchmark I-O accounts.

This procedure approximates the estimator variance for each benchmark I-O and GDP-by-industry value-added estimate. The estimator variance estimates are used to determine the weights for the combined estimates. Estimators with smaller variances are given greater weight; that is to say, the following weights are used to estimate the combined level of value added for each industry:

$$b_{i,\text{I-O}} = \frac{\sigma^2_{i,\text{GDP by Industry}}}{\sigma^2_{i,\text{GDP by Industry}} + \sigma^2_{i,\text{I-O}}} \text{ and } b_{i,\text{GDP by Industry}} = \frac{\sigma^2_{i,\text{I-O}}}{\sigma^2_{i,\text{GDP by Industry}} + \sigma^2_{i,\text{I-O}}}$$

Appendix B

New Updating and Balancing Processes for the BEA's Annual I-O Tables

Since 1999, when the BEA reinstated its annual I-O program beginning with the release of accounts for 1996, the BEA has had among its many goals that of releasing annual I-O tables on a schedule synchronized with that for the

GDP-by-industry accounts. To achieve this goal implies regularly providing a time series of annual I-O tables with those for the most recent years being updated and revised through the standard advance, preliminary, and final iterations—a potentially very resource-intensive process.

The five broad tasks required to produce annual I-O tables were identified and discussed in the main body of this chapter (see section 6.4.4). In evaluating likely prospects for increased automation, the BEA focused on the last task, "balancing the use table," which has tended to be very labor intensive because of the BEA's extensive use of hand adjustments for the process. This appendix summarizes the results of the BEA's research in this area and describes the changes being incorporated into the current balancing procedures for the 1998–2002 annual I-O accounts.[23]

The appendix is divided into three sections. The first section describes the BEA's new balancing procedure. The second section describes the different tests that the BEA performed on this procedure before it was adopted. The third section provides summary remarks.

Expanded Automation of Balancing Procedures

The BEA has developed a new set of automated procedures for balancing its time series of integrated annual I-O tables for 1998 to 2002. Consistent with the research results, the new balancing procedures

- are based on a biproportional adjustment process;
- balance the I-O table in producers' and purchasers' prices simultaneously;
- incorporate more exogenous data; and
- process the tables at the most detailed level of data feasible.

The new procedures generally begin with an I-O use table that has been updated, following steps 1 through 4 described in the main body of this chapter. The I-O use table matrix is then balanced in both basic prices and purchasers' prices. (The purchasers' price equals the basic price plus commodity taxes, transportation costs, and margin costs.) This process allocates transportation costs and margin costs to industries and final uses as functions of how the commodities are moved by the economy's transportation system (rail, truck, water, air, pipeline, and gas pipeline) and through its distribution channels (wholesale trade and retail trade). In the use table, these costs are summed for each industry and shown as separate commodity purchases.

The new balancing procedures require fifteen matrices, each of which must be balanced internally while maintaining the different relationships

---

23. For further information on this research, see Planting and Guo (2004). The complete paper can also be obtained from the BEA's web site at http://www.bea.gov/bea/papers/Timeliness.pdf.

specified among matrices. The following matrices are prepared: a matrix with commodities valued in basic prices and one in purchasers' prices; one for commodity taxes; one for each of the six transportation modes (rail, truck, water, air, oil pipe, and gas pipe); one for wholesale trade margin; one for retail trade margin; and two matrices for taxes by each type of margin (see figure 6.B1). The transportation and wholesale trade matrices are of the same dimensions as those for producers' and purchasers' prices. The retail trade matrix is a single vector with one margin total for all consuming industries and final users. The matrix valued in basic prices is related to that valued in purchasers' prices through the taxes, transportation, and trade matrices. A cell in the purchasers' value matrix equals the corresponding cell in the basic value matrix plus the cells in the taxes, transportation, and trade matrices; conversely, a cell in the basic value matrix equals the corresponding cell in the purchasers' value matrix less those in the taxes, transportation, and trade matrices.

Control totals are identified for each matrix. The basic price, tax, transportation, and trade matrices are two-dimensional and have separate control totals for each row or commodity. The retail trade margin matrices are one-dimensional and have single control totals for the margin, sales tax, and other retail tax. The purchasers' price matrix is two-dimensional and is the sum of producers' price inputs plus transportation and trade margin costs; it has column control totals for each industry and final use category.

Detailed NIPA estimates, in purchasers' prices, are used as controls for the different types of final uses. These detailed data provide the basis for expanding estimates of personal consumption expenditures from 1 to 210 categories; gross private fixed investment from 1 to 33; structures, from 1 to 26; and government expenditures and investment from 6 to 136. Elements that remain constant or fixed in all matrices include exports, imports, changes in business inventories, and other negative cells.

Balancing the fifteen matrices is complex and requires several steps and iterations. Beginning first with the rows, adjustment factors are calculated, equaling the row control less the sum of the fixed cells in the row, divided by the sum of the new cells less the fixed cells. These adjustment factors are applied to the row cells that are not fixed in each matrix. The purchasers' price matrix is then calculated as the sum of the twelve other matrices. To balance the columns, adjustment factors are again calculated, this time equaling the column control less the sum of the fixed cells in the column, divided by the sum of the column cells less the fixed cells. These factors are then applied to the column cells that are not fixed in each matrix. The cells in the basic price matrix are then calculated as the difference between the purchasers' price and the sum of the twelve other matrices.

After a set number of iterations, and when the cells are close to being balanced in both basic and purchasers' values, then the taxes, transportation, and trade matrices are forced to also balance to their respective row

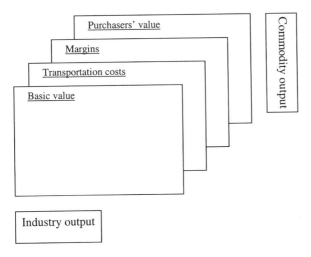

Fig. 6.B1   Relationship between basic value and purchasers' value matrices in the new balancing model

control totals. The balancing of the taxes, transportation, and trade matrices is delayed until the matrices valued in basic and purchasers' prices are approximately balanced in order to maintain the initial tax rates, transportation cost rates, and trade margin rates as long as possible.

Tests on the New Procedures

The BEA tested both the new balancing procedures and an alternative, more highly automated set of procedures, referred to as a "basic model," using an old work file with 1997 detailed data. Results were then compared to the published 1997 annual I-O use table. Unlike the new procedures, which balance multiple matrices, the basic model balances the table in producers' prices only. To evaluate the results from the two approaches, a set of tests were designed to answer the following questions:

- Does balancing in both producers' and purchasers' prices improve results? Most I-O tables are balanced in producers' prices (basic model). However, balancing in producers' prices ignores the detailed estimates of final use expenditures from the NIPAs, which are valued in purchasers' prices as well as the relationships between transportation and margin costs and the use of goods. It is hypothesized that valuing in purchasers' prices and using detailed data from the NIPAs improve the reliability of the balancing model.
- Does the addition of known estimates of value added for industries improve results? Value added makes up a significant portion of each industry's input structure. It is hypothesized that providing estimates

of value added for industries significantly reduces necessary adjustments and improves overall results. (Value added is determined endogenously as a residual for the basic model.)

- Does greater industry and commodity detail improve the results? The more aggregated the table, the more diverse the mix of products grouped together as a single commodity and the more diverse the market. Conversely, the more disaggregated the table, the more specialized commodities are to different markets. It is hypothesized that using more detail at the working level improves the initial distributions of commodities to users and, consequently, also improves the reliability of the balancing model.

To answer these questions, the BEA designed twelve tests that could be used to compare results from the new procedures with those from the basic model. Each version of a use table was balanced, using both the new adjustment process and the basic adjustment process. For the balancing, each was run through forty iterations. Each final use table was then collapsed to the summary level and compared to the published 1997 annual I-O use table.

The measure used for comparing results is the direct coefficient—that is, the amount of a commodity required by an industry to produce a dollar of output. The fewer the differences in direct coefficients between the balanced tables and the published 1997 annual table, the better the balancing model. Our comparisons were limited to the larger cells of the use table, that is, to direct coefficients with underlying intermediate values of $100 million or greater in producers' prices, and to those cells with absolute value difference (published less the balanced direct coefficient) of greater than 0.01 for direct coefficients.

Table 6B.1 provides the major test results. Overall, large coefficient differences decreased from 11.7 percent for the basic model, balanced at the publication level of data and using value added calculated as a residual, to 5.8 percent for the new model, balanced at the source data level and using independent, fixed value-added estimates. The major conclusions from the tests are as follows:

- Results from the new balancing procedures are better than those from the basic model.
- Working with more detail data improves results.
- The addition of known value-added estimates improves results.
- The new balancing procedures result in only 5.8 percent of the direct coefficients changing by more than 0.01 with an absolute average change of 0.029.

Conclusions

One of the BEA's goals has been to develop the capability for producing I-O tables that are more current but are not extremely resource intensive to produce. Research to this end has resulted in the BEA's development of

Table 6B.1   Large coefficient differences from the new balancing model compared
with those from the basic balancing model

Model	Balancing level	Value added	Percent of cells with large coefficient differences	Mean absolute value of coefficient difference
Basic	Detailed publication level	Residual	11.7	0.027
		Fixed	9.8	0.025
	Source data level	Residual	8.3	0.030
		Fixed	6.5	0.028
New	Detailed publication level	Residual	7.3	0.032
		Fixed	9.6	0.027
	Source data level	Residual	7.3	0.033
		Fixed	5.8	0.029

Note: Large coefficient differences are defined as those greater than 0.01 from the same cell in the published 1997 input-output use table.

new automated procedures for balancing its use tables. From the test results examined, it is concluded that the best results are obtained when balancing in both purchasers' and basic prices. The test results also show that providing fixed estimates of value added and working at the detailed source data level both improve final results. However, although the new procedures produce use tables that are fairly comparable to the published table, the remaining differences are still important. Additional research is needed to evaluate these remaining coefficient differences and their causes.

Appendix C

Computing Chain-Type Price and Quantity Indexes in the GDP-by-Industry Accounts

The computation of the chain-type Fisher price and quantity indexes for gross output, intermediate inputs, and value added for an industry or an aggregate is summarized below. The value-added price index for an industry represents the price of its primary factors of production—that is, it represents the price of capital and labor used in the production of gross output. Similarly, the value-added quantity index for an industry represents the quantity of capital and labor used in the production of gross output.

Chain-Type Price Indexes

In the notation, $LP_{t-1,t}$ refers to the Laspeyres price relative for the years $t - 1$ and t; $PP_{t-1,t}$ refers to the Paasche price relative; $FP_{t-1,t}$ refers to the

Fisher price relative; and CP_t refers to the Fisher chain-type price index. The superscript GO refers to gross output, II refers to intermediate inputs, and VA refers to value added; p refers to detailed prices, and q refers to quantities.

Laspeyres price relatives for gross output, intermediate inputs, and value added, respectively, are

$$LP^{GO}_{t-1,t} = \frac{\sum p^{GO}_t q^{GO}_{t-1}}{\sum p^{GO}_{t-1} q^{GO}_{t-1}},$$

$$LP^{\Pi}_{t-1,t} = \frac{\sum p^{\Pi}_t q^{\Pi}_{t-1}}{\sum p^{\Pi}_{t-1} q^{\Pi}_{t-1}}, \text{ and}$$

$$LP^{VA}_{t-1,t} = \frac{\left(\sum p^{GO}_t q^{GO}_{t-1}\right) - \left(\sum p^{\Pi}_t q^{\Pi}_{t-1}\right)}{\left(\sum p^{GO}_{t-1} q^{GO}_{t-1}\right) - \left(\sum p^{\Pi}_{t-1} q^{\Pi}_{t-1}\right)}.$$

Paasche price relatives for gross output, intermediate inputs, and value added are

$$PP^{GO}_{t-1,t} = \frac{\sum p^{GO}_t q^{GO}_t}{\sum p^{GO}_{t-1} q^{GO}_t},$$

$$PP^{\Pi}_{t-1,t} = \frac{\sum p^{\Pi}_t q^{\Pi}_t}{\sum p^{\Pi}_{t-1} q^{\Pi}_t}, \text{ and}$$

$$PP^{VA}_{t-1,t} = \frac{\left(\sum p^{GO}_t q^{GO}_t\right) - \left(\sum p^{\Pi}_t q^{\Pi}_t\right)}{\left(\sum p^{GO}_{t-1} q^{GO}_t\right) - \left(\sum p^{\Pi}_{t-1} q^{\Pi}_t\right)}.$$

Fisher price relatives for gross output, intermediate inputs, and value added are

$$FP^{GO}_{t-1,t} = \sqrt{LP^{GO}_{t-1,t} \times PP^{GO}_{t-1,t}},$$

$$FP^{\Pi}_{t-1,t} = \sqrt{LP^{\Pi}_{t-1,t} \times PP^{\Pi}_{t-1,t}}, \text{ and}$$

$$FP^{VA}_{t-1,t} = \sqrt{LP^{VA}_{t-1,t} \times PP^{VA}_{t-1,t}},$$

Fisher chain-type price indexes for gross output, intermediate inputs, and value added for years after the reference year are

$$CP^{GO}_t = CP^{GO}_{t-1} \times FP^{GO}_{t-1,t},$$

$$CP^{\Pi}_t = CP^{\Pi}_{t-1} \times FP^{\Pi}_{t-1,t}, \text{ and}$$

$$CP^{VA}_t = CP^{VA}_{t-1} \times FP^{VA}_{t-1,t}.$$

In the reference year (2000 for this comprehensive revision),

$$CP_t^{GO} = CP_t^{\Pi} = CP_t^{VA} = 100.$$

Chain-Type Quantity Indexes

In the notation, $LQ_{t-1,t}$ refers to the Laspeyres quantity relative for the years $t-1$ and t; $PQ_{t-1,t}$ refers to the Paasche quantity relative; $FQ_{t-1,t}$ refers to the Fisher quantity relative; and CQ_t refers to the Fisher chain-type quantity index. The superscript GO refers to gross output, Π refers to intermediate inputs, and VA refers to value added; p refers to detailed prices, and q refers to quantities.

Laspeyres quantity relatives for gross output, intermediate inputs, and value added, respectively, are

$$LQ_{t-1,t}^{GO} = \frac{\sum p_{t-1}^{GO} q_t^{GO}}{\sum p_{t-1}^{GO} q_{t-1}^{GO}},$$

$$LQ_{t-1,t}^{\Pi} = \frac{\sum p_{t-1}^{\Pi} q_t^{\Pi}}{\sum p_{t-1}^{\Pi} q_{t-1}^{\Pi}}, \text{ and}$$

$$LQ_{t-1,t}^{VA} = \frac{\left(\sum p_{t-1}^{GO} q_t^{GO}\right) - \left(\sum p_{t-1}^{\Pi} q_t^{\Pi}\right)}{\left(\sum p_{t-1}^{GO} q_{t-1}^{GO}\right) - \left(\sum p_{t-1}^{\Pi} q_{t-1}^{\Pi}\right)}.$$

Paasche quantity relatives for gross output, intermediate inputs, and value added are

$$PQ_{t-1,t}^{GO} = \frac{\sum p_t^{GO} q_t^{GO}}{\sum p_t^{GO} q_{t-1}^{GO}},$$

$$PQ_{t-1,t}^{\Pi} = \frac{\sum p_t^{\Pi} q_t^{\Pi}}{\sum p_t^{\Pi} q_{t-1}^{\Pi}}, \text{ and}$$

$$PQ_{t-1,t}^{VA} = \frac{\left(\sum p_t^{GO} q_t^{GO}\right) - \left(\sum p_t^{\Pi} q_t^{\Pi}\right)}{\left(\sum p_t^{GO} q_{t-1}^{GO}\right) - \left(\sum p_t^{\Pi} q_{t-1}^{\Pi}\right)}.$$

Fisher quantity relatives for gross output, intermediate inputs, and value added are

$$FQ_{t-1,t}^{GO} = \sqrt{LQ_{t-1,t}^{GO} \times PQ_{t-1,t}^{GO}},$$

$$FQ_{t-1,t}^{\Pi} = \sqrt{LQ_{t-1,t}^{\Pi} \times PQ_{t-1,t}^{\Pi}}, \text{ and}$$

$$FQ_{t-1,t}^{VA} = \sqrt{LQ_{t-1,t}^{VA} \times PQ_{t-1,t}^{VA}},$$

Fisher chain-type quantity indexes for gross output, intermediate inputs, and value added for years after the reference year are

$$CQ_t^{GO} = CQ_{t-1}^{GO} \times FQ_{t-1,t}^{GO},$$

$$CQ_t^{\Pi} = CQ_{t-1}^{\Pi} \times FQ_{t-1,t}^{\Pi}, \text{ and}$$

$$CQ_t^{VA} = CQ_{t-1}^{VA} \times FQ_{t-1,t}^{VA}.$$

In the reference year (2000 for this comprehensive revision),

$$CQ_t^{GO} = CQ_t^{\Pi} = CQ_t^{VA} = 100.$$

References

Lawson, Ann M. 2000. Current and future directions for the U.S. industry accounts. Paper presented at the thirteenth International Conference on Input-Output Techniques. 21–25 August, Macerata, Italy. Available at http://www.bea.gov/bea/papers/usindacc.pdf

Lawson, Ann M., Kurt S. Bersani, Mahnaz Fahim-Nader, and Jiemin Guo. 2002. Benchmark input-output accounts of the United States, 1997. *Survey of Current Business* 82 (December): 19–109. Available at http://www.bea.gov/bea/articles/2002/12December/1202I-OAccounts2.pdf

Lawson, Ann M., Sumiye O. Okubo, and Mark A. Planting. 2000. Annual input-output accounts of the United States, 1996. *Survey of Current Business* 80 (January): 37–86. Available at http://www.bea.gov/bea/articles/national/inputout/2000/0100io.pdf

Lum, Sherlene K. S., Brian C. Moyer, and Robert E. Yuskavage. 2000. Improved estimates of gross product by industry for 1947–98. *Survey of Current Business* 80 (June): 24–54. Available at http://www.bea.gov/bea/articles/National/niparel/2000/0600gpi.pdf

Moulton, Brent R., and Eugene P. Seskin. 2003. Preview of the 2003 comprehensive revision of the National Income and Product Accounts: Changes in definitions and classifications. *Survey of Current Business* 83 (June): 17–34. Available at http://www.bea.gov/bea/articles/2003/06June/0603NIPArevs.pdf

Moyer, Brian C., Mark A. Planting, Mahnaz Fahim-Nader, and Sherlene K. S. Lum. 2004. Preview of the comprehensive revision of the annual industry accounts. *Survey of Current Business* 84 (March): 38–51. Available at http://www.bea.gov/bea/articles/2004/03March/0304IndustryAcctsV3.pdf

Moyer, Brian C., Mark A. Planting, Paul V. Kern, and Abigail Kish. 2004. Improved annual industry accounts for 1998–2003. *Survey of Current Business* 84 (June): 21–57. Available at http://www.bea.gov/bea/articles/2004/06June/0604GDP_Industry.pdf

Planting, Mark A., and Jiemin Guo. 2004. Increasing the timeliness of U.S. annual I-O accounts. *Economic Systems Research* 16 (2): 157–67. Available at http://www.bea.gov/bea/papers/Timeliness.pdf

Planting, Mark A., and Peter D. Kuhbach. 2001. Annual input-output accounts of the U.S. economy, 1998. *Survey of Current Business* 81 (December): 41–70. Available at http://www.bea.gov/bea/articles/2001/12december/1201io98.pdf

Yuskavage, Robert E. 2000. Priorities for industry accounts at BEA. Paper presented at a meeting of the BEA Advisory Committee. 17 November, Washington, DC. Available at http://www.bea.gov/bea/papers/priority.pdf

Yuskavage, Robert E. 2002. Gross domestic product by industry: A progress report on accelerated estimates. *Survey of Current Business* 82 (June): 19–27. Available at http://www.bea.gov/bea/articles/2002/06June/0602GDPbyIndy.pdf

Yuskavage, Robert E., and Mahnaz Fahim-Nader. 2005. Gross domestic product by industry for 1947–86, new estimates on the North American industry classification system. *Survey of Current Business* 85 (December), forthcoming.

Yuskavage, Robert E., and Yvon H. Pho. 2004. Gross domestic product by industry for 1987–2000, new estimates on the North American industry classification system. *Survey of Current Business* 84 (November): 33–53. Available at http://www.bea.gov/bea/articles/2004/11November/1104GDP_by_Indy.pdf

7

Aggregation Issues in Integrating and Accelerating the BEA's Accounts
Improved Methods for Calculating GDP by Industry

Brian C. Moyer, Marshall B. Reinsdorf, and
Robert E. Yuskavage

The gross domestic product (GDP)–by-industry accounts prepared by the
Bureau of Economic Analysis (BEA) are frequently used to study structural change and sources of growth in the U.S. economy, to compare U.S.
industrial performance with that of other countries, and to assess the contributions of industries and sectors to aggregate productivity growth. By
providing annual estimates of nominal and real gross output, intermediate
inputs, and value added for sixty-six industries, these accounts allow researchers to understand changes over time in the relative importance of industries. The nominal (current-dollar) value added estimates provide measures of industry size relative to GDP, and the real value added estimates
provide measures of industry contributions to real GDP growth.

Aggregate measures of real GDP growth obtained from the GDP-by-
industry accounts, however, often differ from the featured measure of real
GDP growth obtained from the National Income and Product Accounts
(NIPAs). Because these differences have raised concerns among researchers about the consistency of the industry and national economic accounts, the BEA is working on a more complete integration of these accounts that would reduce or eliminate existing discrepancies. The BEA is
also investigating whether changes in methodology can reduce discrepancies between the sum of the industry contributions and real GDP growth
from the NIPAs. One of our most important findings is that the same "exact contributions" formula used to calculate the contributions of final

Brian C. Moyer is the deputy chief of the National Income and Wealth Division at the Bureau of Economic Analysis. Marshall B. Reinsdorf is a research economist at the Bureau of
Economic Analysis. Robert E. Yuskavage is a senior economist in the Office of the Director
at the Bureau of Economic Analysis.

expenditures to real GDP growth in the NIPAs can also be used to calculate industry contributions based on value added.

In this paper, we describe some of the causes of discrepancies between estimates based on the GDP-by-industry accounts and estimates based on the NIPAs, and we identify several options for bringing the BEA's aggregate real output measures into closer alignment. We investigate reasons for the differences between the growth of real GDP and the sum of the industry contributions to real growth, including the treatment of the statistical discrepancy, differences in the data sources and methods used for the expenditures and industry (production) approaches to measuring GDP, deflation and aggregation methods, and the contributions formula itself. Reasons for the nominal statistical discrepancy are beyond the scope of this chapter.

This chapter also tests the feasibility of short-run and long-run options for bringing the aggregate real output measures into closer alignment using newly developed data sets. This research is one of the goals in the BEA's multiyear strategic plan for better integrating the industry and national accounts. Possible options, which are described in the last section of the chapter, include partial or full integration of the different approaches to measuring GDP, modifications to the contributions formula, and changes in presentation of the estimates. This chapter also identifies improvements in source data that are needed to achieve more highly integrated national and industry economic accounts.

An important conclusion from this chapter is that differences in source data, combined with differences in methodology, account for most of the difference in aggregate real output growth rates; very little of the difference is attributable to the treatment of the statistical discrepancy, differences in aggregation methods, or the contributions formula. In fact, this chapter demonstrates that with consistent data, the Fisher Ideal aggregation procedure used by the BEA to measure real GDP yields the same estimate when real GDP is obtained by aggregating value added across industries as when real GDP is measured by aggregating final uses of commodities. Thus, two major approaches to measuring real GDP—the "expenditures" approach used in the NIPAs and the "production" or "industry" approach used in the industry accounts—give the same answer under certain conditions. This result also leads to the finding that the NIPA "exact contributions" formula can also be used for GDP by industry. Although these results imply that some sources of discrepancy could be eliminated, accomplishing this would require improvements in industry source data to go along with the more integrated estimation framework.

The remainder of the chapter is presented in four sections. Section 7.1 provides background on the GDP-by-industry accounts and the magnitude of the existing discrepancies. Section 7.2 describes the sources of the existing discrepancies for nominal shares and real contributions. These factors include methodology and source data, deflation and aggregation procedures, the treatment of the statistical discrepancy, and the current contributions formula. Section 7.3 presents the empirical results, including tests of the relative importance of the factors described above. This section also describes how the research data sets were developed and the ways they were used to evaluate the various sources of difference. Section 7.4 is a summary and conclusion that describes possible solutions to the discrepancies, options for implementation, and directions for future research on integration of the industry and national accounts.

7.1 Discrepancies between the Industry and National Accounts

The industry estimates of nominal value added from the GDP-by-industry accounts are largely derived from the income-side industry estimates in the NIPAs. The total for gross domestic income (GDI) in the NIPAs, however, differs from the featured expenditure-based estimate of GDP by an amount known as the statistical discrepancy. Therefore, to balance GDP by industry summed over all industries with the expenditure-based estimate of GDP in the NIPAs, the industry estimates include the statistical discrepancy as a separate "industry."

As a result of the statistical discrepancy, industry shares of nominal GDP rarely sum to unity, and in recent years the statistical discrepancy has occasionally exceeded 1 percent of GDP in absolute value. Furthermore, for several reasons real output for all industries combined from the GDP-by-industry accounts usually differs from the product-side estimate of real GDP; indeed, in some years the growth rates differ by several tenths of a percentage point. This is a major reason why the published industry contributions to real GDP growth do not necessarily sum to the growth in real GDP. These discrepancies cause problems for researchers who are using the real value added by industry estimates for studying industry performance and contributions to productivity growth. (For a recent example, see Faruqui et al. 2003.)

To illustrate the magnitude of the problem, table 7.1 presents the published shares of nominal GDP and contributions to real GDP growth for industry groups and higher-level aggregates for 1999–2001.[1] The industry groups shown are aggregates of the more detailed, generally two-digit Standard Industrial Classification (SIC) industries found in the regularly published GDP-by-industry accounts. The higher-level aggregates include

1. Revised estimates of GDP by industry that are consistent with the 2003 NIPA comprehensive revision and that are classified on the 1997 North American Industry Classification System (NAICS) basis were released June 17, 2004. These revised estimates were not available for use in this chapter.

Table 7.1   Industry group shares of GDP and contributions to real GDP growth, 1999–2001

Industry group	Shares			Contributions		
	1999	2000	2001	1999	2000	2001
Gross domestic product	100.0	100.0	100.0	4.1	3.8	0.3
Private industries[a]	87.6	87.6	87.3	4.21	3.42	0.34
Private goods-producing industries	23.1	22.9	21.6	1.06	0.83	−0.96
Agriculture, forestry, and fishing	1.4	1.4	1.4	0.09	0.11	−0.02
Mining	1.1	1.4	1.1	−0.05	−0.13	0.06
Construction	4.6	4.7	4.8	0.23	0.13	−0.08
Manufacturing	16.0	15.5	14.1	0.78	0.75	−0.93
Durable goods	9.2	9.0	8.1	0.60	0.92	−0.47
Nondurable goods	6.8	6.5	6.1	0.19	−0.15	−0.46
Private services-producing industries	64.9	66.0	66.8	3.23	3.54	1.15
Transportation and public utilities	8.3	8.2	8.1	0.60	0.56	−0.01
Transportation	3.3	3.2	3.0	0.14	0.17	−0.14
Communications	2.8	2.8	2.9	0.28	0.34	0.35
Electric, gas, and sanitary services	2.3	2.2	2.2	0.18	0.05	−0.20
Wholesale trade	7.0	7.1	6.8	0.47	0.41	−0.01
Retail trade	9.0	9.0	9.2	0.52	0.67	0.42
Finance, insurance, and real estate	19.4	20.1	20.6	0.79	1.21	0.56
Services	21.3	21.5	22.1	0.85	0.69	0.20
Government	12.4	12.4	12.7	0.16	0.33	0.21
Not allocated by industry	−0.4	−1.3	−1.2	−0.35	−1.00	−0.18
Statistical discrepancy	−0.4	−1.3	−1.2	−0.08	−0.94	0.14
Other	n.a.	n.a.	n.a.	−0.27	−0.05	−0.32

Note: n.a. = not applicable.
[a]Includes the statistical discrepancy.

private industries, private goods-producing industries, private services-producing industries, and government. Table 7.1 also presents shares and contributions that are "not allocated by industry," which consist of the statistical discrepancy and "other" amounts not allocated by industry.[2] Since the statistical discrepancy was negative in each year, industry group contributions sum to more than 100 percent of GDP.

For shares of nominal GDP, the amount "not allocated by industry" consists only of the statistical discrepancy. For contributions to real GDP growth, however, the amount "not allocated by industry" represents the combined effects of the real statistical discrepancy and other factors, such as differences in source data, methodology, aggregation procedures, and the contributions formula itself. These other factors account for some of

2. For a more detailed description of the amounts not allocated by industry, see the box entitled "Nonadditivity of Chained Dollars and 'Not Allocated by Industry' in the GDP-by-Industry Accounts," in McCahill and Moyer (2002).

the difference between real GDP growth and the sum of the industry contributions. The statistical discrepancy made an unusually large contribution to real GDP growth in 2000 (–0.94 percentage points) because of the large increase in the nominal statistical discrepancy between 1999 and 2000. In 1999, other factors contributed –0.27 percentage points, primarily reflecting faster growth in real GDP by industry for "all industries" than in the published real GDP growth from the NIPAs.

7.2   Sources of Discrepancies

This section describes the factors that contribute to the existing discrepancies for shares of nominal GDP and for contributions to real GDP growth. These sources of discrepancies include methodology and source data, deflation and aggregation procedures, the treatment of the statistical discrepancy, and the contributions formula used by the BEA at the time the industry estimates were prepared. Each of these sources of difference is described separately.

7.2.1   Methodology and Source Data

Different methodologies can lead to different estimates of aggregate output levels and growth rates, as well as different estimates of the shares and contributions to growth of the components of aggregate output. The BEA currently uses two approaches, the expenditures approach and the income approach, to measure GDP. The expenditures approach measures GDP as the sum of final uses of goods and services, which consist of personal consumption expenditures, gross private domestic investment, net exports of goods and services, and government consumption expenditures and gross investment. This approach provides a good framework for measuring real GDP because it relies on detailed current-dollar data that can be deflated by price indexes to compute quantity indexes. The income approach measures GDP as the sum of the costs incurred and incomes earned in production, including compensation of employees, gross operating surplus such as corporate profits, proprietors' income, capital consumption allowances, and net interest, and other charges against GDP such as taxes on production and imports.

In addition to the expenditures and income approaches, the 1993 *System of National Accounts* (United Nations et al. 1993; hereafter SNA93) identifies the *production approach* (also known as the *industry approach*) as a third way to measure GDP. In the production approach, GDP is calculated as the sum over all industries—including government—of gross output (sales) less intermediate inputs (purchases). With this method, real GDP can be computed using the double-deflation method as the difference between real gross output and real intermediate inputs for all industries. Although the BEA does not use this approach to measure GDP, a variant of it is used for preparing the estimates of real value added by industry in the GDP-by-industry accounts.[3]

Figure 7.1 is a diagram of a highly aggregated input-output (I-O) "use table" that can illustrate the three different approaches to measuring GDP.[4] Industries, final uses, and total commodity output are the major column descriptions, and commodities, value added, and total industry output are the major row descriptions. Because total commodity output equals total industry output, and because the same value of total intermediate uses is subtracted from both measures of gross output, final uses summed over all commodities equals value added summed over all industries. The expenditures approach to measuring GDP is the equivalent of summing final uses over each of the subcategories (e.g., personal consumption expenditures) and each of the commodities (e.g., manufacturing). This is shown in the shaded column. The incomes approach to measuring GDP is the equivalent of summing each of the value-added components (such as "compensation") over all industries. The production approach is equivalent to summing each industry's total value added over all industries. This is shown in the shaded row.

In concept, these three approaches yield the same measure of GDP, but in practice they generally differ because they use source data that are not entirely consistent. The source data for implementing the expenditures approach are derived largely from Census Bureau business surveys, but allocations of some commodities between final uses and intermediate uses are often based on the benchmark I-O accounts for economic census years. The source data for the incomes approach are largely derived from administrative records such as business tax returns. Census Bureau business surveys also provide source data that could be used to measure gross output in the production approach, but the allocations between intermediate uses and value added would be more reliant on the I-O accounts than are the estimates of final demand under the expenditures approach. While the production approach could be used to measure both nominal and real GDP, major improvements would first be needed in the source data for gross output for selected industries, price indexes, and intermediate inputs, especially purchased services. The BEA has not attempted to prepare independent measures of GDP using the production approach.

In the BEA's GDP-by-industry accounts, a variety of data sources are used to measure outputs and inputs for a given industry. For most industries, gross output is based on annual survey data collected by the Bureau of the Census, compensation of employees is based largely on data

3. The input-output (I-O) accounts compute nominal value added by industry using the production approach, but the total over all industries in the I-O accounts is benchmarked to the final expenditures estimate of GDP.

4. For a description of the BEA's benchmark I-O accounts, see Lawson et al. (2002).

	INDUSTRIES										FINAL USES (GDP)							TOTAL COMMODITY OUTPUT
	Agriculture	Mining	Construction	Manufacturing	Transportation	Trade	Finance	Services	Other	Total Intermediate Use	PCE	PFI	CBI	X	M	GOVT	GDP	
COMMODITIES Agriculture																		
Minerals																		
Construction																		
Manufacturing																		
Transportation																		
Trade																		
Finance																		
Services																		
Other																		
Noncomparable imports																		
Total Intermediate inputs																		
VALUE ADDED Compensation																		
IBT																		
Other value added																		
Total																		
TOTAL INDUSTRY OUTPUT																		

Abbreviations: PCE–personal consumption expenditures; PFI–private fixed investment; CBI–change in business inventories; IBT–indirect business taxes.

Fig. 7.1   Input-output use table

collected by the Bureau of Labor Statistics, and gross operating surplus is based largely on data reported on business income tax returns filed with the Internal Revenue Service. Because the same data-reporting unit can be classified in different industries by different statistical agencies, inconsistencies often arise in the tabulated data, even at the two-digit SIC level. In addition, data are reported on corporate tax returns on a consolidated company basis rather than on an establishment basis. The BEA converts the company-based estimates of corporate profits, corporate net interest, and corporate capital consumption allowances to establishment-based estimates using data on the employment of corporations. (See Yuskavage 2000 for a more detailed description and a discussion of the impact of these issues.)

7.2.2 Deflation and Aggregation Procedures

Theoretical Overview

The use table shown in figure 7.1 is part of an integrated estimation framework in the I-O accounts that yields both a production approach estimate of real GDP and an expenditures approach estimate of real GDP. The other components of this estimation framework are the make table and the deflators for the commodities shown in the make table and the use table. The make table shows the value of each primary or secondary commodity produced by each industry, while the use table shows the use of each commodity as an intermediate input by each industry. To estimate real GDP using either the production approach or the expenditures approach, the current-dollar values in the make and use tables—which are measured at producers' prices—must be deflated by indexes of producers' prices for each commodity.[5]

In the absence of data inconsistencies, the production approach estimate of nominal GDP calculated from the make and use tables agrees with the expenditures approach estimate because the two approaches differ only in the order in which they combine the elements of the make and use tables. The production approach first aggregates over commodities within each industry, and then aggregates over industries. Letting V_{cit} represent the production of commodity c by industry i in year t from the make table, the industry's gross output g_{it} equals

$$(1) \qquad\qquad g_{it} = \sum_c V_{cit}.$$

Letting U_{cit} represent the use of commodity c by industry i in year t from the use table, for industry i in year t the total use of intermediate inputs m_{it} equals

5. Use tables but not make tables are also available valued at purchasers' prices.

(2)
$$m_{it} = \sum_c U_{cit}.$$

The production approach estimate of nominal GDP is, then,

(3)
$$TVA_t = \sum_i (g_{it} - m_{it})$$
$$= \sum_i VA_{it},$$

where VA_{it} represents value added of industry i in period t and TVA is total value added for the economy.

The expenditures approach first aggregates commodity gross output net of intermediate uses over industries to obtain the final use of each commodity in GDP, and then sums over all commodities. Final uses e_{ct} of commodity c are

(4)
$$e_{ct} = \sum_i (V_{cit} - U_{cit}).$$

The expenditures approach estimate of nominal GDP is then

(5)
$$GDP_t = \sum_c e_{ct}.$$

The production approach estimate of real GDP obtained using the double-deflation method (i.e., real gross output minus real intermediate inputs) will also agree with the expenditures approach estimate of real GDP, provided that the deflator for any commodity is the same wherever that commodity is used. (This assumption is more likely to hold if commodities and their deflators are defined at a high level of detail). Real GDP growth is defined as the growth rate of a Fisher index calculated from Laspeyres and Paasche constant-dollar estimates of GDP growth.

To calculate a Laspeyres constant-dollar estimate of GDP in time t, we first deflate each V_{cit} and each U_{cit} by r_{ct}, the deflator from time $t-1$ to time t for commodity c. To obtain the production approach Laspeyres index, we then use these deflated values in equations (1) through (3), and to obtain the expenditures approach Laspeyres index we use these values in equations (4) and (5). The equivalence of the production and expenditures approaches then follows from the fact that they both combine the same elements of the deflated make and use table to compute the numerator of the Laspeyres index.

Similarly, to obtain the Paasche constant-dollar estimates of GDP for time t, we reflate each $V_{ci,t-1}$ and each $U_{ci,t-1}$ by r_{ct} and then apply equations (1) through (3) for the production approach or equations (4) and (5) for the expenditures approach. The order of addition of the elements of the make and use tables is again the only difference between the expenditures approach and the production approach; in particular, both approaches compute the denominator of the Paasche index as the same combination of the entries in the reflated make and use tables. Whether the production approach or the expenditures approach is used therefore has no effect on the Laspeyres and Paasche indexes on which the Fisher index depends.

Since—given the assumptions of consistent data and uniform deflators—real GDP growth is the same measured by the production approach as it is measured by the expenditures approach, use of double deflation does not itself cause a discrepancy between the measure of real GDP from the industry accounts and the measure of real GDP from the NIPAs. In theory, a decomposition of real GDP into industry contributions that add up exactly to the NIPA measure requires only a way to identify the contribution of each industry to a Fisher index aggregate of industries.

Using expenditures on final uses for weighting purposes, the Laspeyres price index for GDP is defined as

$$
(6) \qquad L^P = \frac{\sum_c e_{ct-1} r_{ct}}{\sum_c e_{ct-1}}.
$$

Similarly, the Paasche price index is

$$
(7) \qquad P^P = \frac{\sum_c e_{ct}}{\sum_c \dfrac{e_{ct}}{r_{ct}}}.
$$

The Fisher price index F^P is defined as the geometric mean of L^P and P^P. Finally, the Fisher quantity index may be defined as the expenditures change deflated by the Fisher price index. Hence, the change in real GDP at time t equals the change in nominal GDP deflated by F^P:

$$
(8) \qquad F^Q = \frac{GDP_t}{GDP_{t-1}} \frac{1}{F^P}.
$$

The following proposition shows how to express F^Q as the change in the sum over commodities of final uses, and also as the change in the sum over industries of value added. The method, which is based on van IJzeren's (1952) additive decomposition of the Fisher index, requires both deflated make and use tables from period t and reflated make and use tables from period $t - 1$. Each deflated or reflated make or use table effectively holds prices constant at an average of their level in period $t - 1$ and their deflated level in period t, where F^P is taken to be the appropriate deflator. Exactly additive commodity contributions to the change in real GDP are implied by the final uses of commodities measured at these constant prices, and exactly additive industry contributions are implied by the constant-price measures of value added.

PROPOSITION 1: *Define h_{ct} as the harmonic mean of r_{ct} and F^P, the Fisher price index for the expenditure-approach estimate of GDP:*

(9)
$$h_{ct} \equiv \frac{2}{\dfrac{1}{r_{ct}} + \dfrac{1}{F^P}}.$$

Also, define a_{ct} as the arithmetic mean of r_{ct}/F^P and 1:

(10)
$$a_{ct} \equiv \frac{\dfrac{r_{ct}}{F^P} + 1}{2}.$$

Then: (a) the Fisher estimate of real GDP equals

(11)
$$F^Q = \frac{\sum_c \dfrac{e_{ct}}{h_{ct}}}{\sum_c e_{ct-1} a_{ct}};$$

(b) the additive contribution C_γ of the arbitrary commodity γ to the change in F^Q is

(12)
$$C_\gamma = \frac{\dfrac{e_{\gamma t}}{h_{\gamma t}} - e_{\gamma t-1} a_{\gamma t}}{\sum_c e_{ct-1} a_{ct}};$$

and (c) the additive contribution $\hat{C}_j$ of the arbitrary industry j to the change in F^Q is

(13)
$$\hat{C}_j = \frac{\sum_c \dfrac{V_{cjt}}{h_{ct}} - \sum_c \dfrac{U_{cjt}}{h_{ct}} - \left(\sum_c V_{cjt-1} a_{ct} - \sum_c U_{cjt-1} a_{ct} \right)}{\sum_i \left(\sum_c V_{cit-1} a_{ct} - \sum_c U_{cit-1} a_{ct} \right)}.$$

PROOF: To prove part (a), note that by equation (6),

(14)
$$\sum_c e_{ct-1} a_{ct} = GDP_{t-1} \frac{\dfrac{L^P}{F^P} + 1}{2}.$$

From equation (7),

(15)
$$\sum_c \frac{e_{ct}}{h_{ct}} = GDP_t \frac{\dfrac{1}{P^P} + \dfrac{1}{F^P}}{2}.$$

Therefore,

$$(16) \quad \frac{\sum_c \dfrac{e_{ct}}{h_{ct}}}{\sum_c e_{ct-1} a_{ct}} = \frac{\text{GDP}_t}{\text{GDP}_{t-1}} \cdot \frac{\dfrac{1}{P^P} + \dfrac{1}{F^P}}{\dfrac{L^P}{F^P} + 1}$$

$$= \frac{\text{GDP}_t}{\text{GDP}_{t-1}} \cdot \frac{P^P + F^P}{P^P F^P \left(\dfrac{L^P}{F^P} + 1 \right)}$$

$$= \frac{\text{GDP}_t}{\text{GDP}_{t-1}} \cdot \frac{P^P + F^P}{F^P (P^P + F^P)}$$

$$= F^Q.$$

Part (b) of Proposition 1 is an immediate corollary of part (a). Substituting from equation (4) for e_{ct} in part (a) of proposition 1 then rearranging yields the equation in part (c).

Using Proposition 1, we deflate all the entries for each commodity c in the use and make tables for period t by h_{ct} and we reflate all the entries for commodity c in the use and make tables for period $t-1$ by a_{ct}. Summed over industries, these adjusted use and make tables yield the *commodity* contributions to change of Proposition 1:

$$(17) \quad C_\gamma = \frac{\left(\sum_i V_{\gamma it} - \sum_i U_{\gamma it} \right)/h_{\gamma t} - \left(\sum_i V_{\gamma it-1} - \sum_i U_{\gamma it-1} \right) a_{\gamma t}}{\sum_c \left(\sum_i V_{cit-1} - \sum_i U_{cit-1} \right) a_{ct}}.$$

When the adjusted entries in the make and use tables are instead summed over commodities to obtain adjusted values of VA_{it}, they provide exact *industry* contributions to the change in a production approach estimate of real GDP, $\hat{C}_i$.

Note that the formula for contributions to change has the price index for the aggregate to be decomposed, F^P, as one of its arguments. This dependence on the price index of the aggregate to be decomposed means that the relative sizes of contributions can change if the definition of the aggregate is altered. The contributions to change in real GDP depend on F^P because they value quantity changes for commodities based on a price vector that is a weighted average of time t prices and time $t-1$ prices, where the weight given the time t prices is inversely proportional to F^P.

Differences between Theory and Practice

In the NIPAs, real GDP is computed using a Fisher index that is calculated from Laspeyres and Paasche constant-dollar estimates of GDP. Detailed components of nominal final expenditures valued in purchasers' prices are deflated primarily with purchasers' price indexes, such as the consumer price index for components of personal consumption expenditures. Constant-dollar estimates are summed over all final expenditure components in a single-stage procedure to obtain the Laspeyres and Paasche estimates.

In the GDP-by-industry accounts, the double-deflation method is used to calculate an industry's real value added as the difference between real gross output and real intermediate inputs. Because Fisher indexes lack the property of *consistency in aggregation,* Fisher measures of value added must be computed from separate Laspeyres and Paasche measures of gross output and intermediate inputs, not from Fisher measures of output and inputs.[6] The Fisher index for real value added in an industry is therefore calculated as the geometric mean of one value-added index based on Laspeyres double-deflation and another index based on Paasche double-deflation.

Real value added for "all industries"—the production approach estimate of real GDP available from the BEA—is an aggregate Fisher quantity index for sixty-two private industries and four types of government. Yuskavage (1996, p. 142) explains how the aggregate Fisher index is calculated. Separate Laspeyres and Paasche indexes are computed for the aggregate of all industries, resulting in two sets of estimates of economywide real gross output and economywide real intermediate inputs. Next, Laspeyres and Paasche indexes of aggregate value added are computed by subtracting economywide intermediate inputs from economywide gross output, then averaged to obtain the aggregate Fisher index.

The agreement that exists in theory between the expenditures approach estimate of real GDP and the production approach estimate is difficult to achieve in practice because of inconsistencies in source data and in deflators constructed from different kinds of prices. Even within the fully integrated framework of the I-O accounts, estimates must be balanced in constant prices as well as in current prices. This balancing process often raises thorny practical issues because of the need to reconcile underlying inconsistencies in both nominal values and price indexes. Agreement between the currently used expenditures approach estimate of real GDP from the NIPAs and the production approach estimate from the GDP-by-industry accounts is likewise very difficult to achieve because the source data used for the two approaches are not completely consistent.[7]

Nevertheless, differences in the quality and detail of available source data most likely render the NIPA expenditures approach more accurate for

---

6. An index number formula is consistent in aggregation if calculating lower-level aggregates using the formula and then combining these lower-level aggregates into a top-level aggregate using that same formula yields the same result as using the formula just once to calculate the top-level aggregate directly from the detailed components (Vartia 1976, p. 124). The Fisher formula is not consistent in aggregation, although Diewert (1978) shows that it is approximately consistent in aggregation.

7. Similar data inconsistencies cause problems for those countries that try to combine both approaches.

measuring GDP than an integrated expenditures/production approach might be. In particular, for many commodities the NIPAs can use data that directly measure narrow categories of final expenditures, eliminating the need to rely on I-O relationships for deriving final uses from total commodity supply.[8] Also, in the NIPAs the components of final expenditures and the price indexes used to compute real GDP are generally quite detailed, but in the industry accounts consistent and detailed data on commodity output and prices are available just for the manufacturing industries; for other kinds of industries, output data are often not detailed or not completely consistent. For intermediate inputs, detail is quite extensive and consistent across industries, but these data are not as timely as the data on the components of gross output.

The use of less detailed and less timely data in parts of the GDP-by-industry accounts is not the only source of difference in real estimates. Price indexes also differ because the GDP-by-industry accounts use producers' price, while the NIPAs use purchasers' prices, which include wholesale and retail trade margins and transport costs. Price indexes used for deflation in the NIPAs, such as components of the Bureau of Labor Statistics (BLS) consumer price index (CPI) and the BLS export and import price indexes, generally reflect purchaser price concepts and thus can be used directly.[9] These differences in deflation procedures mean that F^P in the GDP-by-industry accounts—which plays a critical role in the contributions formulas of Proposition 1—can be expected to deviate slightly from the price index for GDP in the NIPAs.

Another kind of discrepancy in the published GDP-by-industry accounts is that the published industry contributions to change in real GDP generally do not sum to even the (unpublished) production approach estimate of real GDP growth. Calculating industry contributions to the production approach estimate of real GDP is a difficult problem because Fisher indexes are not consistent in aggregation. This means that the total over all industries of the Fisher index estimate of real value added in each industry is algebraically different from the production approach estimate of real GDP. Hence, an industry's contribution cannot be calculated simply by dividing its real value added by the production approach estimate of real GDP. The difference between the sum of the published industry contributions and the actual change in NIPA real GDP is known as the amount "not allocated by industry" (NAI). Data inconsistencies—including the statistical discrepancy—contribute to the NAI residual, but with the for-

8. For some commodities, however, such as restaurant meals and beverages and air passenger transportation, an assumption must be made that relationships between total supply and final uses have not changed since the latest benchmark I-O accounts.

9. However, producer price indexes are used for some items, such as some business investment in equipment.

mula that had been used to compute contributions to change, this residual would exist even in the absence of data inconsistencies.

A formula for contributions to change that would eliminate the NAI residual in the absence of data inconsistencies, however, is given by equation (13). This formula extends the approach that the NIPAs use for contributions to change in a Fisher index to a new application, double deflation, an idea that was suggested by Dumagan (2002). (For additional background on the NIPA formula for contributions to change in real GDP, see Reinsdorf, Diewert, and Ehemann 2002.) To use equation (13) in practice, however, requires some algebraic manipulation because the GDP-by-industry accounts currently do not include complete make and use tables. (Make and use tables were scheduled to become available in June 2004 in data sets that "partially integrate" the GDP-by-industry accounts and the I-O accounts.) The appendix shows how to express $\check{C}_i$ as a function of data that are available in the GDP-by-industry accounts, in particular, Laspeyres and Paasche indexes for industry gross output and intermediate inputs.

7.2.3 Statistical Discrepancy

The statistical discrepancy is defined as current-dollar GDP less GDI. It is recorded in the NIPAs as an "income" component that reconciles the income side with the product side of the accounts. It arises because the two sides are estimated using independent and imperfect data. For the GDP-by-industry estimates, which are derived from the income side of the accounts, the statistical discrepancy is treated as an industry, such that nominal GDP by industry sums to nominal GDP. This balancing role for the statistical discrepancy in GDP by industry carries over directly from its balancing role in the NIPAs. The real statistical discrepancy is computed by deflating the nominal (current-dollar) statistical discrepancy with the implicit price deflator (IPD) for the business sector in GDP. This choice for a deflator reflects the BEA's view that the source data inconsistencies underlying the statistical discrepancy are most likely located in a broad spectrum of private business-sector industries. Otherwise, assumptions would need to be made about which industries are most likely affected by this discrepancy.

One of the most important uses of the nominal GDP-by-industry estimates is to calculate an industry's share of nominal GDP. These shares can be used to determine the relative size of an industry at a point in time, and how relative sizes are changing over time. A nonzero statistical discrepancy clouds the interpretation of these shares because some portion of GDP is not accounted for in the value added of a specific industry. The statistical discrepancy indicates that the nominal value added for at least one industry is either too high or too low, relative to the final expenditures estimate of GDP. This problem is compounded when the statistical discrepancy is large and volatile, as it has been for recent years. Estimates of industry contributions to real GDP growth are also affected to the extent that the estimates of nominal value added growth are in error. In addition, because the statistical discrepancy is treated as an industry, it is included in the calculation of real value added for "all industries."

7.2.4   Contributions Formula

The formula that had been used for the published industry contributions to real GDP change is a Laspeyres approximation. This formula computes an industry's contribution to the growth in an aggregate as the industry's weighted growth rate, with the weight equal to the industry's share of aggregate nominal value added in the first period. Aside from its computational simplicity, this formula avoids complications associated with including the statistical discrepancy as an industry. This discrepancy can change sign from one year to the next, making the use of the exact contributions formula very difficult. While the current contributions formula provides a close approximation to the exact contributions, it does not capture changes in shares between periods, and is not consistent with the procedure used to compute the Fisher quantity indexes for value added. Section 7.2.2 demonstrates, however, that exactly the same contributions formula used for the NIPAs can be used for GDP by industry if the statistical discrepancy is not present and if source data inconsistencies are minimized, resulting in close agreement in aggregate growth rates.

7.3   Empirical Results

This section presents the empirical results, including tests of the relative importance of the factors described above. This section also describes the data sets that were developed for this research and how these data sets were used to evaluate the various sources of difference. The empirical work was designed to assess the relative importance of several of the sources of difference described above. These results are presented in three subsections: on methodology and aggregation procedures, on source data consistency (including the role of the statistical discrepancy), and on the contributions formula.

7.3.1   Methodology and Aggregation Procedures

One possible reason for the observed differences in aggregate growth rates and contributions is the use of different estimation methodologies and aggregation procedures. Both the published GDP-by-industry accounts and the NIPAs use Fisher aggregation procedures, but the estimation frameworks are quite different. As a result, even if source data inconsistencies could be entirely eliminated, and if the same contributions formulas were used, aggregation over the existing GDP-by-industry variant of the production approach might not yield the same results as the NIPA final expenditures approach. A previous section has demonstrated, however, that consistent source data used in a consistent framework should yield the same aggregate indexes.

In order to test the impact of these possible sources of difference, an experimental "conceptually ideal" database was developed from the published annual I-O accounts for 1998 and 1999. Nominal make and use tables were prepared at the summary level for ninety-five commodities and industries, and composite Fisher price indexes were computed for each commodity from detail underlying the GDP-by-industry accounts. As a result, the same price index was used to deflate a commodity regardless of whether it was consumed in final uses or intermediate uses. In addition, current-dollar source data were consistent among total supply, intermediate use, and final use because of the use of balanced use and make tables. The 1999 tables were expressed in 1998 prices, and the 1998 tables were expressed in 1999 prices in order to compute the necessary Laspeyres and Paasche quantity indexes for value added over industries and final uses over commodities.

The assumption of a single homogeneous price index for all uses of a commodity is convenient for this experiment, but it raises a question about the consistency of the aggregate constant-price estimates when prices vary. In other words, would the aggregate equality between final uses and value added still hold if either producers' prices or purchasers' prices varied among different intermediate and final uses? Variation in producers' prices may arise for several reasons, including price discrimination, regional differences, or unobserved heterogeneity in the commodity itself. Variation in purchasers' prices may arise due to differences in transport costs, trade margins, and product taxes for different users. Achieving consistency between the approaches while including price variation in the model will require more complex procedures than the ones developed for this paper. Separate price indexes for each cell in the use table are generally not available for either producers or purchasers. In the experiment described above, the estimates were derived in constant producers' prices for both intermediate and final uses, using separate (but unvarying) price indexes for producers' value, transport costs, and trade margins. A worthwhile extension, however, would be to decompose the current-price use table into separate layers for each of the valuation components, with separate deflators for each component. Recent work at the BEA on developing integrated industry accounts may allow this approach to be tested in the future.

In this experimental database, real growth rates are the same using both the expenditures and production approaches to measuring GDP (4.0 percent). Industry value-added contributions based on the production approach sum exactly to real GDP growth using the exact Fisher formula. Table 7.2 shows the exact contributions to change calculated from the con-

Table 7.2   Fisher exact contributions to change in real GDP by commodity final use and by industry value added, 1999

	Commodity final use	Industry value added
Agriculture	0.0	0.1
Mining	−0.1	0.0
Construction	0.3	0.0
Manufacturing	0.6	0.4
Transportation, communication, and utilities	0.4	0.3
Trade	1.0	1.2
Finance, insurance, and real estate	0.9	0.9
Services	1.0	1.1
Government	0.2	0.2
Inventory valuation adjustment (IVA)	−0.3	−0.3
Noncomparable imports and used goods	−0.1	n.a.
Total	4.0	4.0

Note: n.a. = not applicable.

stant-price make and use tables for 1998 and 1999. Note that the price indexes used for these calculations are experimental and may differ substantially from the price indexes used for the published estimates of real value added by industry and industry contributions to real GDP growth. Differences between the results in table 7.2 and the published estimates reflect other effects besides the use of the Fisher exact contributions formula.

By construction, the sum of the industry value-added contributions to change in real GDP equals the sum of the commodity final use contributions. Table 7.2, however, demonstrates that contributions can differ substantially between the commodity and the industry. Differences between commodity and industry contributions primarily reflect differential changes in the use of a commodity as an intermediate input and changes in an industry's use of intermediate inputs in its production process. For example, the construction commodity contributed much more to real GDP growth than the construction industry because an increased portion of the maintenance and repair construction commodity went to final uses in 1999, but little change took place in the construction industry's use of intermediate inputs. Also, the contribution to growth of manufacturing industries was below the contribution of manufactured commodities because the industries used relatively more intermediate inputs in 1999 but less of the production was used for intermediate purposes. On the other hand, mining commodities make a negative contribution to growth while the industry had a small positive contribution because of rising petroleum imports in 1999, which are a subtraction from final uses.

7.3.2   Source Data Consistency

As described above, one possible reason for differences in real growth rates between GDP from the NIPAs and "all industries" from the industry accounts is the use of data from different sources within the industry accounts, along with the presence of the statistical discrepancy. For most industries, gross output is based on annual survey data collected by the Bureau of the Census, compensation of employees is based largely on data collected by the BLS, and gross operating surplus is based largely on data reported on business income tax returns filed with the Internal Revenue Service. These different data sources can lead to inconsistent industry value-added estimates.

For this research, the BEA developed experimental industry time series of nominal and real gross output, intermediate inputs, and value added for 1992–2001 for sixty-five industries.[10] These estimates were consistent with the levels of both value added and gross output by industry from the 1992 benchmark I-O accounts, which do not include a statistical discrepancy. (This database was also used in research to test the feasibility of "partial integration" of the BEA's industry accounts.) After first adjusting the levels in the 1992 benchmark I-O accounts to incorporate the definitions and conventions from the NIPAs and the GDP-by-industry accounts, nominal value-added estimates were extrapolated annually using the published components of GDP by industry for compensation of employees, gross operating surplus, and taxes on production and imports. The nominal statistical discrepancy was allocated to each private nonfarm industry in proportion to its unadjusted gross operating surplus. The sum of these estimates over all industries was constrained to match nominal GDP from the NIPAs in each year. Nominal gross output estimates were also benchmarked to the 1992 I-O accounts, and nominal intermediate inputs were obtained as a residual. Value-added quantity indexes were obtained for each industry using a modified double-deflation procedure that utilized the existing published chain-type price indexes for gross output and for intermediate inputs.

Aggregate "integrated" real value-added quantity indexes were computed for industry groups and for "all industries" using Fisher aggregation. Annual growth rates for "all industries" for the period 1993–2001 were compared with real growth rates for GDP and for "all industries" from the published GDP-by-industry accounts. The results are shown in table 7.3. Relative to GDP, the mean error for the "integrated" estimates for 1993–2001 is smaller than that for the "published" estimates (0.03 percentage points vs. 0.08 percentage points). The mean absolute error is about the same (0.19 points vs. 0.18 points). These results suggest that reducing the source data inconsistencies within the industry accounts would slightly reduce the differences in real growth rates between NIPA GDP and "all industries." It is important to note, however, that the adjustments to improve consistency that were made for this research database are not as

10. These estimates were prepared by Abigail Kish of the BEA's Industry Economics Division. They do not incorporate the comprehensive revision of the annual industry accounts that was released on June 17, 2004.

Table 7.3   Annual percent changes in aggregate real output measures

Year	NIPA GDP (1)	All industries		All industries less NIPA	
		Published GDP by industry (2)	Integrated GDP by industry (3)	Published (4)	Integrated (5)
1993	2.65	2.35	2.36	−0.31	−0.30
1994	4.04	3.90	3.87	−0.14	−0.17
1995	2.67	2.67	2.53	0.01	−0.14
1996	3.57	3.82	3.84	0.25	0.27
1997	4.43	4.78	4.70	0.35	0.27
1998	4.28	4.28	4.17	−0.00	−0.11
1999	4.11	4.37	4.33	0.25	0.22
2000	3.75	3.75	3.72	−0.01	−0.03
2001	0.25	0.55	0.50	0.30	0.25
Averages					
1992–2001	3.30	3.38	3.33	0.078	0.029
1992–2000	3.69	3.74	3.69	0.049	0.001
1995–2000	4.03	4.20	4.15	0.168	0.123
Mean error				0.078	0.029
Mean absolute error				0.179	0.194

extensive as those that would be made in a formal "partial integration" methodology. As a result, these findings may understate the gain from using more consistent source data.

The BEA released the first results of its new partial integration methodology in late June 2004. (See Moyer, Planting, Fahim-Nader, et al. 2004 for background on the new methodology.) While those estimates were not available for use in this paper, selected preliminary results suggest that the more extensive adjustments that were made to improve consistency did have a significant effect on reducing aggregate real growth rate differences. The new integrated estimates—which incorporate the NIPA comprehensive revision released in December 2003–were prepared on the NAICS basis rather the SIC basis, and are available only for the years 1998–2002 using the regular methodology. (Estimates for 2003 are based on an abbreviated methodology designed to achieve more timely release.)

Differences between estimates of real GDP growth from the revised NIPAs and estimates for "all industries" from the integrated industry accounts are smaller on average than in the previously published estimates for 1998–2001. (See Moyer, Planting, Kern, et al. 2004 for these results.) Another measure of the effect of integration comes from revised estimates that were prepared on the "unintegrated" SIC basis for the years 1998–2000. For both 1999 and 2000, real growth for "all industries" was much closer to real GDP growth from the NIPAs using the integrated estimates rather than the "unintegrated" estimates.

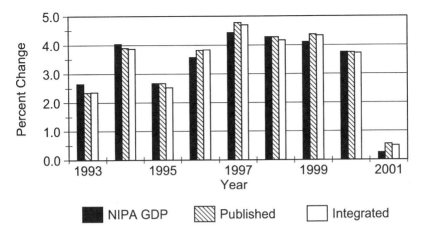

Fig. 7.2   NIPA versus all industries, published versus integrated GDP by industry

Figure 7.2 presents the annual percent change for NIPA GDP, published GDP by industry for all industries, and integrated GDP by industry for all industries. It is clear that most of the improvement resulting from use of the integrated estimates took place after 1996.

7.3.3   Contributions Formula

Table 7.4 presents the differences in industry contributions to real GDP growth for 1999–2001 caused by using a Laspeyres approximation rather than the Fisher exact contributions formula.[11] The format of this table is the same as table 7.1, which presented the published contributions of industry groups to real GDP growth. The NAI amount consists of the statistical discrepancy and other factors, including the contributions formula. Exact contributions were calculated using the Laspeyres and Paasche quantity and price indexes underlying the published Fisher indexes.

The differences are generally quite small for 1999–2001; all industry group differences round to less than 0.1 percentage points. The largest difference was for durable goods manufacturing in 2000, where the Laspeyres approximation exceeded the Fisher exact contribution by 0.03 percentage points (0.92 vs. 0.89). While the BEA's use of the Laspeyres approximation does not appear to have a significant impact on the computed contributions for individual industry groups, it can play a role in explaining differences between the sum of the industry group contributions and real GDP growth. For example, in 2000 the residual NAI amount due to factors other than the statistical discrepancy was moved farther away from zero using the Laspeyres approximation; it changed from 0.01 points using the exact

11. Erich Strassner of the Industry Economics Division computed the Fisher exact contributions.

Table 7.4   Differences in industry group contributions to real GDP growth:
                  Laspeyres approximation less Fisher exact

Industry group	Difference in contribution (percentage points)		
	1999	2000	2001
Gross domestic product	0.00	0.00	0.00
Private industries	0.01	0.00	0.00
Private goods-producing industries	0.00	0.00	−0.00
Agriculture, forestry, and fishing	0.00	0.00	0.00
Mining	0.00	0.02	0.00
Construction	−0.01	−0.00	0.00
Manufacturing	0.01	0.01	−0.01
Durable goods	0.01	0.03	−0.01
Nondurable goods	0.00	−0.00	0.00
Private services-producing industries	0.00	0.00	0.00
Transportation and public utilities	0.01	0.01	−0.00
Transportation	0.00	0.00	−0.00
Communications	0.00	0.01	0.02
Electric, gas, and sanitary services	0.01	0.00	0.01
Wholesale trade	0.00	0.00	−0.00
Retail trade	0.00	0.01	0.00
Finance, insurance, and real estate	0.00	−0.01	−0.00
Services	−0.01	−0.01	−0.00
Government	−0.00	−0.00	−0.00
Not allocated by industry	−0.02	−0.06	0.02
Statistical discrepancy	−0.00	−0.00	−0.00
Other	−0.02	−0.06	−0.02

formula to −0.05 points using the approximation, a difference of −0.06 points. Somewhat larger improvements would be expected for more detailed industries and for time periods with large changes in relative prices.

7.4   Summary and Conclusion

This chapter identifies the major sources of difference between annual estimates of real GDP growth from the NIPAs and real GDP by industry for "all industries," and provides indications of their empirical magnitudes. The difference in aggregate real output measures is important because it is one of the reasons that the published industry contributions do not sum to the growth in real GDP, clouding our understanding of how specific industries and sectors are contributing to economic growth and productivity. The principal finding of this chapter is that differences in the quality, consistency, and detail of the source data—in combination with differences in methodology—are the major factor contributing to the discrepancy. The treatment of the statistical discrepancy and the specification of the contributions formula each make small contributions. Consistent source data used in a consistent conceptual framework—such as an I-O make and use table—would result in no aggregate discrepancy, and the same contributions formula used for the NIPAs could also be used for GDP by industry.

For resolving the aggregate inconsistencies, the BEA should consider and evaluate both short-run and long-run solutions. The most promising short-run option is a partial integration methodology of the kind that was evaluated for the comprehensive revision scheduled for release in June 2004. More consistent source data within the industry accounts—including elimination of the statistical discrepancy—should reduce aggregate real growth rate differences in most years. The Fisher exact contributions formula could then be introduced as part of this partial integration. Other short-run solutions that are feasible are not as desirable because they would distort the relative differences in industry real growth rates. One such option is to adjust specific industry value-added quantity indexes so that the growth for "all industries" matches real GDP growth; this adjustment would be consistent with the current methodology that constrains aggregate nominal industry growth to match nominal GDP growth by including the statistical discrepancy as an "industry." Another short-run option would be to treat the real statistical discrepancy as a balancing item for real GDP in much the same way that it is now treated on the nominal side (Dumagan 2002, p. 9).

The most appealing long-run solution to the problem of inconsistent estimates is full integration of the industry and expenditures accounts using consistent source data in a consistent framework such as balanced annual I-O accounts, along with the Fisher exact contributions formula. This chapter has shown that consistent data used in such a framework yields aggregate real output measures that are the same. This solution depends, however, on major improvements in the source data for gross output, final uses, and intermediate uses. Such improvements in source data would also improve industry and sector estimates along with reducing discrepancies in aggregate output measures. Although the Census Bureau has several new initiatives designed to move toward this goal for the 2002 economic census, and the BLS continues to expand and improve service-sector producer price indexes, implementation of this solution is realistically years away.

As a first step toward long-run integration of the industry and expenditures accounts, the BEA has begun research to develop procedures to estimate annual controls for final-expenditures categories using an I-O framework. Because these controls will be based on I-O methodology and on I-O source data, they are likely to differ from the corresponding final-expenditures estimates in the NIPAs. An analysis of these differences is expected to show how annual information from the industry accounts can be used to improve the estimates of final expenditures in the NIPAs and how final-expenditures data can be used to improve the estimates of value added by industry. While this approach will not achieve the benefits of full integration, it—along with improvements in source data—may move the estimates into closer alignment and further reduce aggregate discrepancies.

Appendix

From equation (13) in the main text:

$$\hat{C}_j + 1 = \frac{\sum_c (V_{cjt} - U_{cjt})/h_{ct}}{\sum_i \sum_c (V_{cit-1} - U_{cit-1})a_{ct}}.$$

Recall that VA_{it} denotes nominal value added, and that $2a_{ct} = r_c/F^P + 1$. Let L^P denote the Laspeyres price index for the value added of industry i. Then we can define the constant-price industry share as:

$$\bar{s}_{it} = \frac{\sum_c (V_{cit-1} - U_{cit-1})a_{ct}}{\sum_j \sum_c (V_{cjt-1} - U_{cjt-1})a_{ct}}$$

$$= \frac{VA_{it-1}(1 + L_i^P/F^P)}{\sum_j VA_{jt-1}(1 + L_j^P/F^P)}.$$

Recall that $2/h_{ct} = 1/r_{ct} + 1/F^P$. Let P_i^P denote the Paasche price index for the value added of industry i, let L_i^Q denote the Laspeyres quantity index, and let P_i^Q denote the Paasche quantity index. For industry i:

$$\hat{C}_i + 1 = \bar{s}_{it}\frac{\sum_c (V_{cjt} - U_{cjt})/h_{ct}}{\sum_c (V_{cit-1} - U_{cit-1})a_{ct}},$$

where

$$\frac{\sum_c (V_{cjt} - U_{cjt})/h_{ct}}{\sum_c (V_{cit-1} - U_{cit-1})a_{ct}} = \frac{VA_{it}(1/P_i^P + 1/F^P)}{VA_{it-1}(1 + L_i^P/F^P)}$$

$$= \frac{L_i^Q + L_i^P P_i^Q/F^P}{1 + L_i^P/F^P}$$

$$= \frac{F^P L_i^Q + L_i^P P_i^Q}{F^P + L_i^P}.$$

References

Dumagan, Jesus C. 2002. Exact income-side contributions to percent change in GDP. U.S. Department of Commerce. Mimeograph, August.

Diewert, Erwin W. 1978. Superlative index numbers and consistency in aggregation. *Econometrica* 46 (4): 883–900. Repr. in *Essays in index number theory,* Vol. 1, ed. W. E. Diewert and A. O. Nakamura, 253–73, Amsterdam: North Holland, 1993.

Faruqui, Umar, Wulong Gu, Mustapha Kaci, Mireille Laroch, and Jean-Pierre Maynard. 2003. Differences in productivity growth: Canadian-U.S. business sectors, 1987–2000. *Monthly Labor Review* 126 (4): 16–29.

Lawson, Ann M., Kurt S. Bersani, Mahnaz Fahim-Nader, and Jiemin Guo. 2002. Benchmark input-output accounts of the United States, 1997. *Survey of Current Business* 82 (December): 19–109.

McCahill, Robert J., and Brian C. Moyer. 2002. Gross domestic product by industry for 1999–2001. *Survey of Current Business* 82 (November): 23–41.

Moyer, Brian C., Mark A. Planting, Mahnaz Fahim-Nader, and Sherlene K. S. Lum. 2004. Preview of the comprehensive revision of the annual industry accounts. *Survey of Current Business* 84 (March): 38–51.

Moyer, Brian C., Mark A. Planting, Paul V. Kern, and Abigail Kish. 2004. Improved annual industry accounts for 1998–2003. *Survey of Current Business* 84 (June): 21–57.

Reinsdorf, Marshall B., W. Erwin Diewert, and Christian Ehemann. 2002. Additive decompositions for Fisher, Törnqvist and geometric mean indexes. *Journal of Economic and Social Measurement* 28:51–61.

United Nations, Commission of the European Communities, International Monetary Fund, Organisation for Economic Co-operation and Development, and World Bank. 1993. *System of national accounts 1993.* Series F, no. 2, rev. 4. New York: United Nations.

van IJzeren, J. 1952. Over de plausibiliteit van Fisher's Ideale Indices [On the plausibility of Fisher's Ideal Indices]. *Statistische en Econometrische Onderzoekingen* 7 (2): 104–15.

Vartia, Y. O. 1976. Ideal log-change index numbers. *Scandinavian Journal of Statistics* 3:121–26.

Yuskavage, Robert E. 1996. Gross product by industry, 1959–94. *Survey of Current Business* 82 (August): 133–55.

———. 2000. Priorities for industry accounts at BEA. Paper presented at a meeting of the BEA Advisory Committee, November 17. Available at http://www.bea/gov/bea/papers/

Comment   W. Erwin Diewert

Introduction

Moyer, Reinsdorf, and Yuskavage address a number of important and interesting issues in their chapter. They first review the fact that (nominal) GDP can in theory be calculated in three equivalent ways:

W. Erwin Diewert is a professor of economics at the University of British Columbia and a research associate of the National Bureau of Economic Research.

- By summing final demand expenditures
- By summing value added[1] over all industries
- By summing over all sources of income received

However, the authors go beyond this well-known fact[2] and show that under certain conditions, *real GDP that is constructed by aggregating over the components of final demand is exactly equal to real GDP that is constructed by aggregating over the components of each industry's gross outputs less intermediate inputs,* provided that the Laspeyres, Paasche, or Fisher (1922) ideal formula is used in order to construct the real quantity aggregates.[3] This index number equivalence result is the most important result in the chapter.[4]

When the BEA calculates the rate of growth of GDP using a chained Fisher ideal index, it also provides a sources of growth decomposition; that is, it provides an additive decomposition of the overall growth rate into a number of subcomponents or contributions of the subcomponents to the overall growth rate. Thus, the growth contributions of $C + I + G + X - M$ add up to the overall growth of GDP.[5] However, many analysts are interested in the contributions to overall GDP growth of *particular industries* as opposed to the contributions of particular components of final demand. The index number equivalence result derived by Moyer, Reinsdorf, and Yuskavage means that if their conditions for the result to hold are satisfied, *then industry contributions to growth can be calculated that will exactly add up to total GDP growth,* provided that the Fisher formula is used.

What are the authors' conditions for the equivalence result to hold? Some of the more important conditions are

- Accurate industry value data on gross outputs and intermediate inputs that sum up to the components of final demand in value terms must be available for the two periods in the index number comparison.
- For each commodity produced or used as an intermediate input in the

1. Value added is defined as the value of gross outputs produced over the reference period minus the value of intermediate inputs used during the period. An intermediate input is defined as an input that has been produced by some other domestic or foreign producer.

2. See, for example, Hicks (1952).

3. When calculating Fisher, Laspeyres, or Paasche price or quantity indexes of value added for an industry, all prices are entered as positive numbers but the corresponding quantities are positive or negative numbers depending on whether the particular commodity is being produced as an output (entered as a positive quantity) or being used as an input (entered as a negative quantity).

4. Their result is generalized somewhat in Reinsdorf and Yuskavage (2004).

5. The particular Fisher decomposition formula being used by the BEA is due originally to Van Ijzeren (1987, 6). This decomposition was also derived by Dikhanov (1997), Moulton and Seskin (1999, 16), and Ehemann, Katz, and Moulton (2002). An alternative additive decomposition for the Fisher index was obtained by Diewert (2002) and Reinsdorf, Diewert, and Ehemann (2002). This second decomposition has an economic interpretation; see Diewert (2002). However, the two decompositions approximate each other fairly closely; see Reinsdorf, Diewert, and Ehemann (2002).

economy, the price faced by final demanders and by suppliers of that commodity must be the same for all demanders and suppliers.
- Commodity taxes are small enough in magnitude that they can be ignored.

The authors note that in practice, the first condition listed above is not satisfied for various reasons. We will not focus our discussion on this particular assumption. However, in the next section, we will attempt to find a counterpart to the Moyer, Reinsdorf, and Yuskavage equivalence result when commodity prices are *not* constant across demanders and suppliers of a particular commodity. In the upcoming section, we assume that there are no commodity taxes to worry about, but in the following section we again attempt to find a counterpart to the authors' equivalence result when there are commodity taxes on final outputs and possibly also on intermediate inputs. The final section concludes by looking at some of the implications of our results for statistical agencies and their data collection and presentation strategies.

Input-Output Accounts with No Commodity Taxes

In this section, we will address some of the problems associated with the construction of input-output tables for an economy, in both real and nominal terms. We will defer the problems that the existence of commodity taxes causes until the next section. However, in the present section, we will allow for a complication that makes the construction of input output tables somewhat difficult and that is the existence of *transportation margins*. The problem occurs when real input-output tables are constructed. Moyer, Reinsdorf, and Yuskavage note that the industry method for constructing real GDP will coincide with the usual final-demand method for constructing real GDP, provided that the deflator for any commodity is the same wherever that commodity is used or produced. In fact, in their empirical work, they make use of this assumption since independent deflators for all of the cells of the use and make matrices are generally not available and hence final demand deflators or selected gross output deflators are used as proxy deflators throughout the input-output tables. However, when an industry produces a commodity, its selling price will be less than the purchase price for the same commodity from final and intermediate demanders of the good, due to the costs of shipping the good from the factory gate to the geographic location of the purchasing unit. In addition, there may be various marketing and selling costs that need to be added to the manufacturer's factory gate price.

In the present section, we will address the problem of accounting for transportation margins in the simplest possible model of industry structure where there will be one industry (industry M) that produces a good (commodity 1), one industry (industry S) that produces a service (commodity 2), and one industry (industry T) that transports the good to final demanders[6] or to the service industry.[7] The transportation service will be regarded as commodity 3. We assume that the service output does not require transportation inputs to be delivered to purchasers of services.

Table 7C.1 combines the make and use matrices for the value flows in this highly simplified economy into a single input-output table. The industry M, S, and T columns list the sales of goods and services (plus signs are associated with sales) and the purchases of intermediate inputs (minus signs are associated with purchases) for each of the three inputs. The *final demand column* gives the total of the industry sales less industry intermediate input purchases for rows 1 to 4 over the three industries in the economy. Row 5 in table 7C.1 sums all of the transactions in the industry M, S, and T columns and thus is equal to *industry value added* (the value of gross outputs produced less the value of intermediate inputs used by the industry). The entry in row 5 of the final demand column is nominal GDP, and it is equal to both the sum of the final demands above it and to the sum of the industry M, S, and T value added along the last row of the table.

Rows 1 to 3 of table 7C.1 lists the transactions involving the manufactured good, commodity 1. We will explain these transactions and the associated notation row by row. In the industry M row 1 entry, we list the value of manufactured goods sold to the service sector, $p_1^{MS}q_1^{MS}$, where q_1^{MS} is the number of units sold to the service sector and p_1^{MS} is the average sales price.[8] Also in the industry M row 1 entry, we list the value of manufactured goods sold to the final demand sector, $p_1^{MF}q_1^{MF}$, where q_1^{MF} is the number of units sold to the final demand sector and p_1^{MS} is the corresponding average sales price. Note that p_1^{MS} will usually not equal p_1^{MF}; that is, for a variety of reasons, the average selling price of the manufactured good to the two sectors that demand the good will usually be different.[9] Now $p_1^{MS}q_1^{MS} + p_1^{MF}q_1^{MF}$ is the total revenue received by industry M during the period under consideration, but it will not be the total cost paid by the receiving sectors due to the existence of transport costs. Thus in row 1 of table 7C.1, we show the transportation industry as purchasing the goods from industry M, which explains the entry $-p_1^{MS}q_1^{MS} - p_1^{MF} q_1^{MF}$. The sum of the row 1 entries across the three entries is 0, and so the row 1 entry for the final demand column is left empty and corresponds to a 0 entry. Turning now to the row 2 entries,

---

6. In this highly simplified model, we will have only one final demand sector and we neglect the problems posed by imported goods and services. The transportation industry can be thought of as an aggregate of the transportation, advertising, wholesaling, and retailing industries.

7. Service industries generally require some materials in order to produce their outputs.

8. Hence this price will be a unit value price over all sales of commodity 1 to the service sector.

9. Even if there is no price discrimination on the part of industry M at any point in time, the price of good 1 will usually vary over the reference period, and hence if the proportion of daily sales varies between the two sectors, the corresponding period average prices for the two sectors will be different.

Table 7C.1   Detailed input-output table in current dollars with no taxes

Row No.	Industry M	Industry S	Industry T	Final demand
1	$p_1^{MS}q_1^{MS} + p_1^{MF}q_1^{MF}$		$-p_1^{MS}q_1^{MS} - p_1^{MF}q_1^{MF}$	
2			$(p_1^{MF} + p_3^{MF})q_1^{MF}$	$(p_1^{MF} + p_3^{MF})q_1^{MF}$
3		$-(p_1^{MS} + p_3^{MS})q_1^{MS}$	$(p_1^{MS} + p_3^{MS})q_1^{MS}$	
4	$-p_2^{SM}q_2^{SM}$	$p_2^{SM} + q_2^{SM} + p_2^{SF}q_2^{SF}$		$p_2^{SF}q_2^{SF}$
5	$p_1^{MS} + q_1^{MS} + p_1^{MF}q_1^{MF}$ $-p_2^{SM}q_2^{SM}$	$p_2^{SM}q_2^{SM} + p_2^{SF}q_2^{SF}$ $-(p_1^{MS}+ p_3^{MS})q_1^{MS}$	$p_3^{MF}q_1^{MF} + p_3^{MS}q_1^{MS}$	$(p_1^{MF} + p_3^{MF})q_1^{MF}$ $+ p_2^{SF}q_2^{SF}$

Note: Blank cells signify a 0 entry.

the industry T row 2 entry shows the transportation industry selling commodity 1 to the final demand sector and getting the revenue $(p_1^{MF} + p_3^{MF})q_1^{MF}$ for this sale. This revenue consists of the initial cost of the goods delivered at the manufacturer's gate, $p_1^{MF}q_1^{MF}$, plus revenue received by the transportation sector for delivering good 1 from the manufacturing plant to the final demand sector, $p_3^{MF}q_1^{MF}$. Thus we are measuring the quantity of transportation services in terms of the number of goods delivered to the final demand sector, q_1^{MF}, and the corresponding average delivery price is p_3^{MF}, which can be interpreted as a transportation markup or margin rate.[10] Turning now to the row 3 entries, the industry T row 3 entry shows the transportation industry selling commodity 1 to the service sector and getting the revenue $(p_1^{MS} + p_3^{MS})q_1^{MS}$ for this sale. This revenue consists of the initial cost of the goods delivered at the manufacturer's gate, $p_1^{MS}q_1^{MS}$, plus revenue received by the transportation sector for delivering good 1 from the manufacturing plant to the service sector, $p_3^{MS}q_1^{MS}$. Thus we are measuring the quantity of transportation services in terms of the number of goods delivered to the services sector, q_1^{MS}, and the corresponding average delivery price is p_3^{MS}, which again can be interpreted as a transportation markup or margin rate. There is no reason to expect the transportation margin rates p_3^{MS} and p_3^{MF} to be identical since the costs of delivery to the two purchasing sectors could be very different.

Row 4 of table 7C.1 lists the transactions involving services, commodity 2. The industry S row 4 entry, $p_2^{SM}q_2^{SM} + p_2^{SF}q_2^{SF}$, lists the value of services output delivered to the manufacturing industry, $p_2^{SM}q_2^{SM}$, plus the value of services output delivered to the final demand sector, $p_2^{SF}q_2^{SF}$. The quantities delivered to the two sectors are q_2^{SM} and q_2^{SF}, and the corresponding average prices are p_2^{SM} and p_2^{SF}. As usual, there is no reason to expect that these two service prices should be identical. The term $-p_2^{SM}q_2^{SM}$ appears in row 4 of the

---

10. Actually, p_3^{MF} should be interpreted more broadly as a combination of transport costs and selling costs, which would include retailing and wholesaling margins.

industry M column, since this represents the cost of services to the M sector. Similarly, the term $^{SF}_2 q^{SF}_2$ appears in row 4 of the final demand column, since this represents the value of services delivered to the final demand sector, and this amount is also equal to the sum of the M, S, and T entries for row 4.

Note that every transaction listed in rows 1–4 of table 7C.1 has a separate purchaser and seller, and so the principles of double-entry bookkeeping are respected in this table.[11]

The entries in row 5 for the M, S, and T columns are the simple sums of the entries in rows 1–4 for each column and are equal to the corresponding industry value added. Thus, the industry M value added is equal to $p^{MS}_1 Q^{MS}_1$ + $p^{MF}_1 q^{MF}_1 - p^{SM}_2 q^{SM}_2$, the value of manufacturing output at factory gate prices less purchases of services. The industry S value added is equal to $p^{SM}_2 q^{SM}_2 + p^{SF}_2 q^{SF}_2 - (p^{MS}_1 + p^{MS}_3)q^{MS}_1$, the value of services output less the value of materials purchases but at prices that include the transportation margins. The industry T value added is equal to $p^{MF}_3 q^{MF}_1 + p^{MS}_3 q^{MS}_1$, which is the product of the transportation margin rate times the amount shipped, summed over the deliveries of transport services to the final demand sector, $p^{MF}_3 q^{MF}_1$, and to the services sector, $p^{MS}_3 q^{MS}_1$. Finally, the entry in row 5 of the last column is equal to both the sum of industry value added over industries or to the sum of commodity final demands, $(p^{MF}_1 + p^{MF}_3)q^{MF}_1 + p^{SF}_2 q^{SF}_2$. Note that the final demand price for the good (commodity 1) is $p^{MF}_1 + p^{MF}_3$, which is equal to industry M's factory gate price, p^{MF}_1, plus the transportation margin rate, p^{MF}_3, that is, the final demand price for the good has imbedded in it transportation (and other selling) costs.

Looking at table 7C.1, it can be seen that there are three ways that we could calculate a Laspeyres quantity index of net outputs for the economy that the table represents:

- Look at the nonzero cells in the 4 × 3 matrix of input output values of outputs and inputs for the economy represented by rows 1–4 and columns M, S, and T and sum up these nonzero cells into ten distinct $p_n q_n$ transactions.
- Look at the row 5, column M, S, and T entries for the industry value added components and sum up these cells into eight distinct transactions.
- Look at rows 1–4 of the final demand column and sum up the nonzero cells into two distinct $p_n q_n$ transactions.[12]

---

11. Our notation is unfortunately much more complicated than the notation that is typically used in explaining input-output tables because we do not assume that each commodity trades across demanders and suppliers at the same price. Thus, our notation distinguishes three superscripts or subscripts instead of the usual two: we require two superscripts to distinguish the selling and purchasing sectors and one additional subscript to distinguish the commodity involved in each transaction. This type of setup was used in Diewert (2004b).

12. The first $p_n q_n$ is $(p^{MF}_1 + p^{MF}_3)q^{MF}_1$ and the second $p_n q_n$ is $p^{SF}_2 q^{SF}_2$.

Denote the ten-dimensional $\mathbf{p}$ and $\mathbf{q}$ vectors that correspond to the first detailed cell method of aggregating over commodities listed above as $\mathbf{p}^{IO}$ and $\mathbf{q}^{IO}$ respectively, denote the eight-dimensional $\mathbf{p}$ and $\mathbf{q}$ vectors that correspond to the second value-added method of aggregating over commodities listed above as $\mathbf{p}^{VA}$ and $\mathbf{q}^{VA}$ respectively and denote the two-dimensional $\mathbf{p}$ and $\mathbf{q}$ vectors that correspond to the third aggregation over final demand components method of aggregating over commodities listed above as $\mathbf{p}^{FD}$ and $\mathbf{q}^{FD}$ respectively.[13] Add a superscript t to denote these vectors evaluated at the data pertaining to period t. Then it is obvious that the inner products of each of these three period-t price and quantity vectors are all equal since they are each equal to period-t nominal GDP; that is, we have

(1) $$\mathbf{p}^{IOt} \cdot \mathbf{q}^{IOt} = \mathbf{p}^{VAt} \cdot \mathbf{q}^{VAt} = \mathbf{p}^{FDt} \cdot \mathbf{q}^{FDt}; \quad t = 0, 1.$$

What is not immediately obvious is that the inner products of the three sets of price and quantity vectors are also equal if the price vectors are evaluated at the prices of one period and the corresponding quantity vectors are evaluated at the quantities of another period; that is, we also have, for periods 0 and 1, the following equalities:[14]

(2) $$\mathbf{p}^{IO1} \cdot \mathbf{q}^{IO0} = \mathbf{p}^{VA1} \cdot \mathbf{q}^{VA0} = \mathbf{p}^{FD1} \cdot \mathbf{q}^{FD0}$$

(3) $$\mathbf{p}^{IO0} \cdot \mathbf{q}^{IO1} = \mathbf{p}^{VA0} \text{ dot } \mathbf{q}^{VA1} = \mathbf{p}^{FD0} \cdot \mathbf{q}^{FD1}$$

Laspeyres and Paasche quantity indexes that compare the quantities of period 1 to those of period 0 can be defined as follows:

(4) $$Q_L^{IO}(\mathbf{p}^{IO0}, \mathbf{p}^{IO1}, \mathbf{q}^{IO0}, \mathbf{q}^{IO1}) \equiv \frac{p^{IO0} \cdot q^{IO1}}{p^{IO0} \cdot q^{IO0}};$$

$$Q_L^{VA}(\mathbf{p}^{VA0}, \mathbf{p}^{VA1}, \mathbf{q}^{VA0}, \mathbf{q}^{VA1}) \equiv \frac{p^{VA0} \cdot q^{VA1}}{p^{VA0} \cdot q^{VA0}};$$

$$Q_L^{FD}(\mathbf{p}^{FD0}, \mathbf{p}^{FD1}, \mathbf{q}^{FD0}, \mathbf{q}^{FD1}) \equiv \frac{p^{FD0} \cdot q^{FD1}}{p^{FD0} \cdot q^{FD0}};$$

(5) $$Q_P^{IO}(\mathbf{p}^{IO0}, \mathbf{p}^{IO1}, \mathbf{q}^{IO0}, \mathbf{q}^{IO1}) \equiv \frac{p^{IO1} \cdot q^{IO1}}{p^{IO1} \cdot q^{IO0}};$$

$$Q_P^{VA}(\mathbf{p}^{VA0}, \mathbf{p}^{VA1}, \mathbf{q}^{VA0}, \mathbf{q}^{VA1}) \equiv \frac{p^{VA1} \cdot q^{VA1}}{p^{VA1} \cdot q^{VA0}};$$

$$Q_P^{FD}(\mathbf{p}^{FD0}, \mathbf{p}^{FD1}, \mathbf{q}^{FD0}, \mathbf{q}^{FD1}) \equiv \frac{p^{FD1} \cdot q^{FD1}}{p^{FD1} \cdot q^{FD0}}.$$

13. All prices are positive, but if a quantity is an input it is given a negative sign.
14. The proof follows by a set of straightforward computations.

Using equations (1) and (3) and the definitions in equation (4), it can be seen that all three Laspeyres indexes of real output are equal; that is, we have

$$(6) \qquad Q_L^{IO}(\mathbf{p}^{IO0}, \mathbf{p}^{IO1}, \mathbf{q}^{IO0}, \mathbf{q}^{IO1}) = Q_L^{VA}(\mathbf{p}^{VA0}, \mathbf{p}^{VA1}, \mathbf{q}^{VA0}, \mathbf{q}^{VA1})$$
$$= Q_L^{FD}(\mathbf{p}^{FD0}, \mathbf{p}^{FD1}, \mathbf{q}^{FD0}, \mathbf{q}^{FD1}).$$

Using equations (1) and (2) and the definitions in equation (5), it can be seen that all three Paasche indexes of real output are equal; that is, we have

$$(7) \qquad Q_P^{IO}(\mathbf{p}^{IO0}, \mathbf{p}^{IO1}, \mathbf{q}^{IO0}, \mathbf{q}^{IO1}) = Q_P^{VA}(\mathbf{p}^{VA0}, \mathbf{p}^{VA1}, \mathbf{q}^{VA0}, \mathbf{q}^{VA1})$$
$$= Q_P^{FD}(\mathbf{p}^{FD0}, \mathbf{p}^{FD1}, \mathbf{q}^{FD0}, \mathbf{q}^{FD1}).$$

Since a Fisher ideal quantity index is the square root of the product of a Laspeyres and Paasche quantity index, it can be seen that equations (6) and (7) imply that all three Fisher quantity indexes, constructed by aggregating over input-output table cells or by aggregating over industry value added components or by aggregating over final demand components, are equal; that is, we have

$$(8) \qquad Q_F^{IO}(\mathbf{p}^{IO0}, \mathbf{p}^{IO1}, \mathbf{q}^{IO0}, \mathbf{q}^{IO1}) = Q_F^{VA}(\mathbf{p}^{VA0}, \mathbf{p}^{VA1}, \mathbf{q}^{VA0}, \mathbf{q}^{VA1})$$
$$= Q_F^{FD}(\mathbf{p}^{FD0}, \mathbf{p}^{FD1}, \mathbf{q}^{FD0}, \mathbf{q}^{FD1}).$$

The above results extend to more complex input-output frameworks provided that all transactions between each pair of sectors in the model are accounted for in the model. Thus, we have extended the results of Moyer, Reinsdorf, and Yuskavage to input-output models where prices are not constant across industries.[15]

It is well known that the Laspeyres and Paasche quantity indexes are consistent in aggregation. Thus, if we construct Laspeyres indexes of real value added by industry in the first stage of aggregation and then use the resulting industry prices and quantities as inputs into a second stage of Laspeyres aggregation, then the resulting two-stage Laspeyres quantity index is equal to the corresponding single-stage index, $Q_L^{IO}(\mathbf{p}^{IO0}, \mathbf{p}^{IO1}, \mathbf{q}^{IO0}, \mathbf{q}^{IO1})$. Similarly, if we construct Paasche indexes of real value added by industry in the first stage of aggregation and then use the resulting industry prices and quantities as inputs into a second stage of Paasche aggregation, then the resulting two-stage Paasche quantity index is equal to the corresponding single-stage index, $Q_P^{IO}(\mathbf{p}^{IO0}, \mathbf{p}^{IO1}, \mathbf{q}^{IO0}, \mathbf{q}^{IO1})$. Unfortunately, the corresponding result does not hold for the Fisher index. However, the two-stage Fisher quantity index usually will be quite close to the corresponding single-stage index, $Q_F^{IO}(\mathbf{p}^{IO0}, \mathbf{p}^{IO1}, \mathbf{q}^{IO0}, \mathbf{q}^{IO1})$.[16]

15. The exact index number results in equation (8) were also derived by Diewert (2004b, 497–507) in an input-output model with no commodity taxes but with transportation margins and hence unequal prices.
16. See Diewert (1978, 889).

Table 7C.2   **Consolidated current-dollar table with transportation detail**

Row No.	Industry M	Industry S	Industry T	Final demand
1	$p_1^{MS}q_1^{MS} + p_1^{MF}q_1^{MF}$	$-p_1^{MS}q_1^{MS}$		$p_1^{MF}q_1^{MF}$
2	$-p_2^{SM}q_2^{SM}$	$p_2^{SM}q_2^{SM} + p_2^{SF}q_1^{SF}$		$p_2^{SF}q_2^{SF}$
3		$-p_3^{MS}q_1^{MS}$	$p_3^{MS}q_1^{MS} + p_3^{MF}q_1^{MF}$	$p_3^{MF}q_1^{MF}$

We are not quite through with table 7C.1. In the remainder of this section, we provide some consolidations of the entries in table 7C.1 and derive some alternative input output tables that could be useful in applications.

Table 7C.2 represents a consolidation of the information presented in table 7C.1. First, we sum the entries in rows 1 to 3 of table 7C.1 for each industry column. Recall that the entries in rows 1 to 3 represent the transactions involving the output of industry M. Second, we separate out from the sum of the entries over rows 1–3 all of the transactions involving the transportation price p_3 and put these entries in a separate row, which is row 3 in table 7C.2. The sum of the row 1–3 entries in table 7C.1 less row 3 in table 7C.2 is row 1 in table 7C.2. Row 2 in table 7C.2 is equal to row 4 in table 7C.1 and gives the allocation of the service commodity across sectors.

Table 7C.2 resembles a traditional input-output table. Rows 1 to 3 correspond to transactions involving commodities 1–3, respectively, and each industry gross output is divided between deliveries to the other industries and to the final demand sector. Thus the industry M row 1 entry in table 7C.2 gives the value of goods production delivered to the service sector, $p_1^{MS}q_1^{MS}$, plus the value delivered to the final demand sector, $p_1^{MF}q_1^{MF}$. Note that these deliveries are at the prices actually received by industry M; that is, transportation and selling margins are excluded. Similarly, the industry S row 2 entry gives the value of services production delivered to the goods sector, $p_2^{SM}q_2^{SM}$, plus the value delivered to the final demand sector, $p_2^{SF}q_2^{SF}$. Finally, the industry T row 3 entry gives the value of transportation (and selling) services delivered to the services sector, $p_3^{MS}q_3^{MS}$, plus the value delivered to the final demand sector, $p_3^{MS}q_3^{MF}$. If we summed the entries in rows 1–3 for each column in table 7C.2, we would obtain row 5 in table 7C.1, which gives the value added for columns M, S, and T and GDP for the last column. Thus, the new table 7C.2 does not change any of the industry value added aggregates listed in the last row of table 7C.1.

Although table 7C.2 looks a lot simpler than table 7C.1, there is a cost to working with table 7C.2 compared to table 7C.1. In table 7C.1, there were two components of final demand, $(p_1^{MS} + p_3^{MF})q_1^{MF}$, and $p_2^{SF}q_2^{SF}$. These two components are deliveries to final demand of goods at final demand prices (which include transportation margins) and deliveries of services to final demand. In table 7C.2, the old goods deliveries to final demand component is broken up into two separate components, $p_1^{MF}q_1^{MF}$ (deliveries of goods to final demand at factory gate prices), and $p_3^{MF}q_1^{MF}$, the transport costs of shipping the goods from the factory gate to the final demander. Thus, table 7C.2 requires that information on transportation margins be available; that is, information on both producer prices and margins be available whereas GDP could be evaluated using the last column in table 7C.1, which required information only on final demand prices.[17]

Looking at table 7C.2, it can be seen that it is unlikely that commodity prices are constant along the components of each row. This is unfortunate since it means that *in order to construct accurate productivity statistics for each industry, it generally will be necessary to construct separate price deflators for each nonzero cell in the input-output tables.*

Table 7C.2 allows us yet another way that real GDP for the economy can be constructed. For this fourth method for constructing Laspeyres, Paasche, and Fisher output indexes for the economy, we could use the nine nonzero p_nq_n values that appear in the nonzero components of rows 1–3 and the M, S, and T columns of table 7C.2 and use the corresponding p and q vectors of dimension 9 as inputs into the Laspeyres, Paasche, and Fisher quantity index formulae. It is easy to extend the string of equations (6), (7), and (8) to cover these new indexes. Thus we have a fourth method for constructing a Fisher output index that will give the same answer as the previous three methods.

The *real* input-output table that corresponds to the *nominal value* input-output table 7C.2 is table 7C.3.

The entries in row 1 of table 7C.3 are straightforward: the total production of goods by industry M, $q_1^{MS} + q_1^{MF}$, is allocated to the intermediate input use by industry S (q_1^{MS}) and to the final demand sector (q_1^{MF}). Similarly, the entries row 2 of table 7C.3 are straightforward: the total production of services by industry S, $q_2^{MS} + q_2^{SF}$, is allocated to the intermediate input use by industry M (q_2^{SM}) and to the final demand sector (q_2^{SF}). However, the entries in row 3 of table 7C.3 are a bit surprising in that they are essentially the same as the entries in row 1. This is due to the fact that we have measured transportation services in quantity units that are equal to the number of units of the manufactured good that are delivered to each sector.

We conclude this section by providing a further consolidation of the nominal input-output table 7C.2. Thus in table 7C.4, we aggregate the transportation industry with the goods industry and add the entries in row 3 of table 7C.2 to the corresponding entries in row 1; that is, we aggregate the transportation commodity with the corresponding good commodity that is being transported.

Row 1 in table 7C.4 allocates the good across the service industry and the final demand sector. Thus, the value of goods output produced by industry

---

17. Of course, in order to evaluate *all* of the cells in the input output tables represented by tables 7C.1 or 7C.2, we would require information on transportation margins in any case.

Table 7C.3   Consolidated constant-dollar table with transportation detail

Row No.	Industry M	Industry S	Industry T	Final demand
1	$q_1^{MS} + q_1^{MF}$	$-q_1^{MS}$		q_1^{MF}
2	$-q_2^{SM}$	$q_2^{SM} + q_2^{SF}$		q_2^{SF}
3		$-q_1^{MS}$	$q_1^{MS} + q_1^{MF}$	q_1^{MF}

Table 7C.4   Consolidated current-dollar table with no transportation detail

Row No.	Industry M + T	Industry S	Final demand
1	$(p_1^{MS} + p_3^{MS})q_1^{MS}$ $+ (p_1^{MF} + p_3^{MF})q_1^{MF}$	$-(p_1^{MS} + p_3^{MS})q_1^{MS}$	$(p_1^{MF} + p_3^{MF})q_1^{MF}$
2	$-p_2^{SM}q_2^{SM}$	$p_2^{SM}q_2^{SM} + p_2^{SF}q_2^{SF}$	$p_2^{SF}q_2^{SF}$
3	$(p_1^{MS} + p_3^{MS})q_1^{MS}$ $+ (p_1^{MF} + p_3^{MF})q_1^{MF} - p_2^{SM}q_2^{SM}$	$p_2^{SM}q_2^{SM} + p_2^{SF}q_2^{SF}$ $- (p_1^{MS} + p_3^{MS})q_1^{MS}$	$(p_1^{MF} + p_3^{MF})q_1^{MF} + p_2^{SF}q_2^{SF}$

M + T is $(p_1^{MS} + p_3^{MS})q_1^{MS} + (p_1^{MF} + p_3^{MF})q_1^{MF}$ and hence purchasers' prices are used in valuing these outputs. The value of deliveries to the services and final demand sectors are (including transportation margins) $(p_1^{MS} + p_3^{MS})q_1^{MS}$ and $(p_1^{MF} + p_3^{MF})q_1^{MF}$ respectively. The row 2 entries in table 7C.4, which allocate the service-sector outputs across demanders, are the same as the row 2 entries in table 7C.2. Row 3 in table 7C.4 gives the sum of the entries in rows 1 and 2 for each column. Thus the row 3, column (1) entry gives the value added of the combined goods producing and transportation industries while the row 3, industry S entry gives the value added for the services industry. The final demand entry in row 3 of table 7C.4 is the nominal value of GDP, as usual.

Looking at table 7C.4, it can be seen that it is unlikely that commodity prices are constant along the components of each row. Again, this is unfortunate since it means that *in order to construct accurate productivity statistics for each industry, it generally will be necessary to construct separate price deflators for each nonzero cell in the input-output tables.*

Table 7C.4 allows us yet another way that real GDP for the economy can be constructed. For this fifth method for constructing Laspeyres, Paasche, and Fisher output indexes for the economy, we could use the six nonzero $p_n q_n$ values that appear in rows 1 and 2 and columns (1) and (2) of table 7C.4 and use the corresponding **p** and **q** vectors of dimension 6 as inputs into the Laspeyres, Paasche, and Fisher quantity index formulae. It is easy to extend the string of equations (6), (7), and (8) to cover these new indexes. Thus we have a fifth method for constructing a Fisher output index that will give the same answer as the previous four methods.

The organization of production statistics that is represented by table

7C.4 is convenient for some purposes, in that outputs are valued consistently at final demand prices. However, it has the disadvantage that the transportation, retailing, and wholesaling industries have disappeared, which means that these margins have to be imputed to the goods-producing industries. Moreover, the primary inputs that are used by the transportation, retailing, and wholesaling industries would also have to be allocated to goods-producing industries. It is unlikely that users of industry production statistics would welcome these changes. Thus we conclude that organizing production statistics according to the layout in table 7C.2 would be preferable for most purposes.

In the following section, we introduce commodity taxes into our highly simplified model of the industrial structure of the economy.

Input-Output Tables When There are Commodity Taxes

Although governments in the United States do not impose very large commodity taxes on production as compared to many European countries, U.S. commodity taxes are large enough so that they cannot be ignored.

We return to the production model that corresponds to table 7C.1 in the previous section but we now assume that there is the possibility of a commodity tax falling on the output of each industry. In order to minimize notational complexities, we assume that each producing industry collects these commodity taxes and remits them to the appropriate level of government. Thus industry M collects the tax revenue $t_1^{MS}q_1^{MS}$ on its sales of goods to industry S and the tax revenue $t_1^{MF}q_1^{MF}$ on its sales to the final demand sector so that t_1^{MS} and t_1^{MF} are the specific tax rates that are applicable (across all levels of government) on sales of goods to the service industry and to the final demand sector respectively.[18] Similarly, industry S collects the tax revenue $t_2^{SM}q_2^{SM}$ on its sales of services to industry M and the tax revenue $t_2^{SF}q_2^{SF}$ on its sales to the final demand sector. Finally, industry T collects the tax revenue $t_3^{MS}q_1^{MS}$ on its sales of transportation services to industry S and the tax revenue $t_3^{MF}q_1^{MF}$ on its sales of transportation services to the final demand sector.

We now add the commodity taxes collected by each industry to the old industry revenues that appeared in table 7C.1. Thus the old revenue received by industry M listed in row 1 of table 7C.1, $p_1^{MS}q_1^{MS} + p_1^{MF}q_1^{MF}$, is replaced by $(p_1^{MS} + t_1^{MS})q_1^{MS} + (p_1^{MF} + t_1^{MF})q_1^{MF}$ in row 1 of table 7C.5. Similarly, the old revenue received by industry S listed in row 4 of table 7C.1, $p_2^{SM}q_2^{SM} + p_2^{SF}q_2^{SF}$, is replaced by $(p_2^{SM} + t_2^{SM})q_2^{SM} + (p_2^{SF} + t_2^{SF})q_2^{SF}$ in row 4 of

18. Ad valorem tax rates can readily be converted into specific taxes that are collected for each unit sold. Usually, tax rates are lower for sales to industry purchasers compared to sales to final demand, but this is not always the case since exports are generally taxed at zero rates. In any case, usually t_1^{MS} will not be equal to t_1^{MF}. If sales to a particular sector are not taxed, then simply set the corresponding tax rate equal to zero. Product-specific subsidies can be treated as negative commodity taxes.

Table 7C.5 **Detailed input-output table in current dollars with commodity taxes**

Row No.	Industry M	Industry S	Industry T	Final demand
1	$(p_1^{MS}+ t_1^{MS})q_1^{MS}$ $+ (p_1^{MF} + t_1^{MF})q_1^{MF}$		$-(p_1^{MS} + t_1^{MS})q_1^{MS}$ $-(p_1^{MF} + t_1^{MF})q_1^{MF}$	
2			$(p_1^{MF} + t_1^{MF})q_1^{MF}$ $+ (p_3^{MF} + t_3^{MF}) q_1^{MF}$	$(p_1^{MF} + t_1^{MF})q_1^{MF}$ $+ (p_3^{MF} + t_3^{MF}) q_1^{MF}$
3		$-(p_1^{MS} + t_1^{MS})q_1^{MS}$ $-(p_3^{MS} + t_3^{MS})q_1^{MS}$	$(p_1^{MS} + t_1^{MS})q_1^{MS}$ $+ (p_3^{MS} + t_3^{MS})q_1^{MS}$	
4	$-(p_2^{SM} + t_2^{SM})q_2^{SM}$	$(p_2^{SM} + t_2^{SM})q_2^{SM}$ $+ (p_2^{SF} + t_2^{SF})q_2^{SF}$		$(p_2^{SF} + t_2^{SF})q_2^{SF}$
5	$-t_1^{MS}q_1^{MS} - t_1^{MF}q_1^{MF}$	$-t_2^{SM}q_2^{SM} - t_2^{SF}q_2^{SF}$	$-t_3^{MF}q_1^{MF} - t_3^{MS}q_1^{MS}$	
6	$p_1^{MS}q_1^{MS} + p_1^{MF}q_1^{MF}$ $-p_2^{SM}q_2^{SM} - t_2^{SM}q_2^{SM}$	$p_2^{SM}q_2^{SM} + p_2^{SF}q_2^{SF}$ $-(p_1^{MS} + t_1^{MS})q_1^{MS}$ $-(p_3^{MS} + t_3^{MS}) q_1^{MS}$	$p_3^{MF}q_1^{MF} + p_3^{MS}q_1^{MS}$	$(p_1^{MF} + t_1^{MF})q_1^{MF}$ $+ (p_3^{MF} + t_3^{MF})q_1^{MF}$ $+ (p_2^{SF} + t_2^{SF})q_2^{SF}$

table 7C.5. The old revenue received by industry T for its deliveries of goods shipped to the final demand sector listed in row 2 of table 7C.1, $(p_1^{MF} + p_3^{MF})q_1^{MF}$, is replaced by $(p_1^{MF} + t_1^{MF})q_1^{MF} + (p_3^{MF} + t_3^{MF})q_1^{MF}$ in row 2 of table 7C.5. The term $(p_1^{MF} + t_1^{MF})q_1^{MF}$ is equal to $p_1^{MF}q_1^{MF}$ (the revenue that the manufacturer gets for its sales of goods to the final demand sector) plus $t_1^{MF}q_1^{MF}$ (the amount of commodity taxes collected by the manufacturing sector on its sales of goods to the final demand sector). The term $(p_3^{MF} + t_3^{MF})q_1^{MF}$ reflects the additional charges that final demanders of the good pay for delivery of the good to the final demand sector, and this term is equal to the sum of $p_3^{MF}q_1^{MF}$ (the transportation sector's revenue for shipping goods to the final demand sector) plus $t_3^{MF}q_1^{MF}$ (the amount of taxes collected by the transportation sector that fall on shipping services to the final demand sector). Finally, the old revenue received by industry T for its deliveries of goods shipped to the services sector listed in row 3 of table 7C.1, $(p_1^{MS} + p_3^{MS})q_1^{MS}$, is replaced by $(p_1^{MS} + t_1^{MS})q_1^{MS} + (p_3^{MS} + t_3^{MS})q_1^{MS}$ in row 3 of table 7C.5. The term $(p_1^{MS} + t_1^{MS})q_1^{MS}$ is equal to $p_1^{MS}q_1^{MS}$ (the revenue that the manufacturer gets for its sales of goods to the services sector) plus $t_1^{MS}q_1^{MS}$ (the amount of commodity taxes collected by the manufacturing sector on its sales of goods to the services sector). The term $(p_3^{MS} + t_3^{MS})q_1^{MS}$ reflects the additional charges that service sector demanders of the good pay for delivery of the good to the service sector, and this term is equal to the sum of $p_3^{MS}q_1^{MS}$ (the transportation sector's revenue for shipping goods to the services sector) plus $t_3^{MS}q_1^{MS}$ (the amount of taxes collected by the transportation sector that fall on shipping services to the services sector). With the addition of the commodity tax terms, it can be seen that the first four rows of table 7C.5 are exact counterparts to the first four rows of table 7C.1.

Row 5 in table 7C.5 is a new row that has been added to the rows of table 7C.1, and it lists (with negative signs) the commodity tax revenues raised by the industry on its sales of products to final demand and other industries. These tax payments to the government are costs and hence are listed with negative signs.

The cells in row 6 of table 7C.5 are the sums down each column of the entries in rows 1 to 5. Thus the entries in row 6 list the *value added* of each industry for industries M, S, and T.[19] The row 6 entry for the final demand sector is simply the sum of final demand purchases for goods, including all tax and transportation margins, $(p_1^{MF} + t_1^{MF} + p_3^{MF} + t_3^{MF})q_1^{MF}$, plus final demand purchases of services, including indirect taxes on services, $(p_2^{SF} + t_2^{SF})q_2^{SF}$.

We now come to an important difference between table 7C.1 and table 7C.5: the sum of the industry M, S, and T value added (the entries along row 6 of table 7C.5) is no longer equal to the sum of the final demands down rows 1 to 4 of the final demand column: we need to add the commodity tax payments made by the three industries to the industry value-added sum in order to get the sum of final demands at final demand prices. It is worth spelling out this equality in some detail. Thus, define the industry M, S, and T value added, v^M, v^S, and v^T respectively, as follows:

$$(9) \qquad v^M \equiv p_1^{MS}q_1^{MS} + p_1^{MF}q_1^{MF} - p_2^{SM}q_2^{SM} - t_2^{SM}q_2^{SM};$$

$$(10) \qquad v^S \equiv p_2^{SM}q_2^{SM} + p_2^{SF}q_2^{SF} - (p_1^{MS} + t_1^{MS})q_1^{MS} - (p_3^{MS} + t_3^{MS})q_1^{MS};$$

$$(11) \qquad v^T \equiv p_3^{MF}q_1^{MF} + p_3^{MS}q_1^{MS}.$$

Notice that for each industry, outputs are valued at producer prices that exclude the commodity taxes collected by the industry but intermediate inputs are valued at prices that the industry faces; that is, the intermediate input prices include the commodity taxes paid by the supplying industries. In summary, the prices for outputs and intermediate inputs that are in the definitions in equations (9)–(11) are the prices actually faced by the respective

---

19. Note that our definition of industry value added is the value of outputs sold at purchasers' prices less the value of intermediate inputs at purchasers' prices less commodity taxes collected for the government by that industry. The usual definition of industry value added does not net off industry commodity tax remittances to the government; that is, the usual definition of value added does not subtract off row 5 but rather adds these commodity tax remittances to primary input payments. The problem with this latter treatment of industry commodity tax payments is that it does not provide a suitable framework for measuring industry productivity growth performance. Thus, our suggested treatment of indirect commodity taxes in an accounting framework that is suitable for productivity analysis follows the example set by Jorgenson and Griliches (1972), who advocated the following treatment of indirect taxes: "In our original estimates, we used gross product at market prices; we now employ gross product from the producers' point of view, which includes indirect taxes levied on factor outlay, but excludes indirect taxes levied on output" (85). Put another way, commodity tax payments to the government cannot readily be regarded as a payment for the services of a primary input.

industry. This is the set of prices that is best suited to a set of productivity accounts.[20] Finally, define the value of final demands, v^F, and the value of commodity taxes, v^τ, as follows:

(12) $$v^F \equiv (p_1^{MF} + t_1^{MF} + p_3^{MF} + t_3^{MF})q_1^{MF} + (p_2^{SF} + t_2^{SF})q_2^{SF};$$

(13) $$v^\tau \equiv t_1^{MS}q_1^{MS} + t_1^{MF}q_1^{MF} + t_2^{SM}q_2^{SM} + t_2^{SF}q_2^{SF} + t_3^{MF}q_1^{MF} + t_3^{MS}q_1^{MS}.$$

Using the definitions in equations (9) to (13), it is straightforward to verify that the following identity holds:

(14) $$v^M + v^S + v^T = v^F - v^\tau;$$

that is, the sum of industry M, S, and T value added equals GDP (or the value of final demands at purchasers' prices) less the value of commodity taxes that fall on outputs and intermediate inputs.

In addition to adding row 5 (the industry commodity tax payments to the government) to the rows of table 7C.1, table 7C.5 has another important difference compared to table 7C.1: the principles of double-entry bookkeeping are not respected in the present version of table 7C.5. The problem is that the industry tax payments listed in row 5 of table 7C.5 are not transferred to another column in the table. However, this deficiency could be corrected by creating a government "industry" column where the industry tax payments could be received. A more complete model of the economy would decompose final demand into a government sector as well as the other traditional $C + I + X - M$ final demand sectors.

Table 7C.6 is the counterpart to table 7C.2 in the previous section and it represents a consolidation of the information presented in table 7C.5. The industry M, row 1 entry in table 7C.6 is the sum of the row 1 and row 5 entries in table 7C.5 (this consolidation nets out the commodity taxes on the manufacturing output) and the industry M, row 2 entry in table 7C.6 is equal to the industry M, row 4 entry in table 7C.5 (the services intermediate input allocation to industry M remains unchanged). The industry S, row 3 entry in table 7C.5 is split between rows 1 and 3 in table 7C.5 (this splits the total intermediate input cost for industry S into a goods component and a transportation component). The industry S, row 2 entry in table 7C.6 is equal to the sum of the industry S, rows 4 and 5 entries in table 5 (this consolidation nets out the commodity taxes on the service sector outputs). The industry T, row 3 entry in table 7C.6 is the sum of rows 1–5 for industry T in table 7C.5. The table 7C.5 final demand entry for row 2 is split into goods and transportation services components, which are allocated to rows 1 and 3 of table 7C.6. The final demand for services entry in row 4 of table 7C.5 is switched to row 2 of the final demand column in table 7C.6.

---

20. As noted earlier, these are the prices that were recommended by Jorgenson and Griliches (1972, 85) for productivity accounts.

Table 7C.6   **Consolidated input-output table in current dollars with commodity taxes**

R	Industry M	Industry S	Industry T	Final Demand
1	$p_1^{MS}q_1^{MS} + p_1^{MF}q_1^{MF}$	$-(p_1^{MS} + t_1^{MS})q_1^{MS}$		$(p_1^{MF} + t_1^{MF})q_1^{MF}$
2	$-(p_2^{SM} + t_2^{SM})q_2^{SM}$	$p_2^{SM}q_2^{SM} + p_2^{SF}q_2^{SF}$		$(p_2^{SF} + t_2^{SF})q_2^{SF}$
3		$-(p_3^{MS} + t_3^{MS})q_1^{MS}$	$p_3^{MF}q_1^{MF} + p_3^{MS}q_1^{MS}$	$(p_3^{MF} + t_3^{MF})q_1^{MF}$

Thus, row 1 of table 7C.6 allocates the production of goods across the sectors of the economy, row 2 allocates the flow of services and row 3 allocates the flow of transportation services. If we summed down each column of table 7C.6, we would obtain the value added of industry M, v^M defined by equation (9), the value added of industry S, v^S defined by equation (10), the value added of industry T, v^T defined by equation (11), and (nominal) GDP, v^F defined by equation (12). The constant-dollar input-output table that corresponds to the nominal input-output table 7C.6 is still table 7C.3 in the previous section.

Looking at table 7C.6, it can be seen that the existence of commodity tax wedges means it is unlikely that commodity prices are constant along the components of each row. Again, this is unfortunate since it means that *in order to construct accurate productivity statistics for each industry, it generally will be necessary to construct separate price deflators for each nonzero cell in the input-output tables.*

We conclude this section by again seeing if we can obtain a counterpart to the Moyer, Reinsdorf, and Yuskavage exact index number result in this more complicated model where there are commodity tax wedges. Looking at the identity in equation (14), it can be seen that since nominal GDP is not equal to the sum of industry value added, if the value of commodity tax revenue v^T is not equal to zero, we will not be able to get an exact result unless we add a government commodity tax revenue "industry" to the M, S, and T industries. Thus, we now define the value added of the commodity tax "industry" as v^τ, and we rewrite the identity in equation (14) as follows:

$$(15) \qquad v^F = v^M + v^S + v^T + v^\tau.$$

Now we can repeat the analysis in the previous section with a few obvious modifications. Thus, looking at equation (15) and table 7C.6, it can be seen that there are three ways that we could calculate a Laspeyres GDP quantity index for the economy that the table represents:

- Look at the nonzero cells in the 3×3 matrix of input-output values of outputs and inputs for the economy represented by rows 1–3 and columns M, S, and T of table 7C.6 and sum up these nonzero cells into nine distinct $p_n q_n$ transactions. Add to these nine $p_n q_n$ transactions the six $t_n q_n$ tax transactions that are defined by the right-hand side of equation (13), which gives us fifteen distinct price $\times$ quantity transactions in all.

- Look at the row 5, column M, S, and T entries for the industry value-added components listed in table 7C.5 and sum up these cells into eight distinct $p_n q_n$ transactions. Add to these eight $p_n q_n$ transactions the six $t_n q_n$ tax transactions that are defined by the right-hand side of equation (13), which gives us fourteen distinct price times quantity transactions in all.

- Look at rows 1–3 of the final demand column in table 7C.6 and sum up the nonzero cells into two distinct $p_n q_n$ transactions.[21]

Denote the fifteen-dimensional $\mathbf{p}$ and $\mathbf{q}$ vectors that correspond to the first detailed cell method of aggregating over commodities listed above as p^{IO} and q^{IO} respectively, denote the fourteen-dimensional $\mathbf{p}$ and $\mathbf{q}$ vectors that correspond to the second value-added method of aggregating over commodities listed above as p^{VA} and q^{VA} respectively, and denote the two-dimensional $\mathbf{p}$ and $\mathbf{q}$ vectors that correspond to the third aggregation over final demand components method of aggregating over commodities listed above as p^{FD} and q^{FD} respectively. Add a superscript t to denote these vectors evaluated at the data pertaining to period t. Then it is obvious that the inner products of each of these three period-t price and quantity vectors are all equal since they are each equal to period-t nominal GDP; that is, we have

$$(16) \qquad \mathbf{p}^{IOt} \cdot \mathbf{q}^{IOt} = \mathbf{p}^{VAt} \cdot \mathbf{q}^{VAt} = \mathbf{p}^{FDt} \cdot \mathbf{q}^{FDt}; \quad t = 0, 1.$$

Now the rest of the analysis can proceed as in the previous section; see equations (2)–(8) and repeat this analysis in the present context. As in the second section, it can be shown that all three Fisher quantity indexes, constructed by aggregating over input-output table cells or by aggregating over industry value-added components or by aggregating over final demand components, are equal; that is, we have

$$(16) \qquad Q_F^{IO}(\mathbf{p}^{IO0}, \mathbf{p}^{IO1}, \mathbf{q}^{IO0}, \mathbf{q}^{IO1}) = Q_F^{VA}(\mathbf{p}^{VA0}, \mathbf{p}^{VA1}, \mathbf{q}^{VA0}, \mathbf{q}^{VA1})$$

$$= Q_F^{FD}(\mathbf{p}^{FD0}, \mathbf{p}^{FD1}, \mathbf{q}^{FD0}, \mathbf{q}^{FD1}).$$

Thus, we have extended the results of Moyer, Reinsdorf, and Yuskavage to input output models where commodity tax distortions are present.[22] The usual BEA Fisher contributions to growth methodology can be used in order to decompose overall GDP growth into industry growth contributions plus a commodity tax change contribution (this is the contribution to GDP growth of the artificial commodity tax industry).

---

21. The first $p_n q_n$ is $(p_1^{MF} + t_1^{MF} + p_3^{MF} + t_3^{MF})q_1^{MF}$ and the second $p_n q_n$ is $(p_2^{SF} + t_2^{SF})q_2^{SF}$.
22. Results analogous to equation (16) were derived by Diewert (2004a, 479–84) under more restrictive assumptions; that is, each sector was assumed to face the same vector of commodity prices except for the commodity tax distortions.

Conclusion

There are a number of important implications that emerge from the above discussion:

- With appropriate adjustments for commodity taxes, a Fisher index of value added growth by industry can be used to construct an independent estimate of real GDP growth.
- The existence of transportation and selling margins and commodity taxes means that the assumption that a *single* price deflator can be used for productivity measurement purposes to deflate all of the value cells long the row of an input-output table is likely to be a very rough approximation at best. In principle, each nonzero cell in a nominal input output table will require its own separate deflator.[23]
- The existence of commodity taxes that fall within the production sector poses special problems for statistical agencies. These taxes need to be identified by cell position in the input-output tables instead of just reported as a single sum for the industry as is done at present.

The last point requires a bit more explanation. Looking at table 7C.6, it can be seen that row 2 entry for industry M is $-(p_2^{SM} + t_2^{SM})q_2^{SM}$, which is (minus) the value of service intermediate inputs used by industry M, including the commodity tax portion, $t_2^{SM}q_2^{SM}$. Similarly, the row 1 entry for industry S is $-(p_1^{MS} + t_1^{MS})q_1^{MS}$, which is minus the value of materials intermediate inputs used by industry S, including the commodity tax portion, $t_1^{MS}q_1^{MS}$. The row 3 entry for industry S is $-(p_3^{MS} + t_3^{MS})q_1^{MS}$, which is (minus) the value of transportation services purchased by industry S, including the commodity tax on transport services, $t_3^{MS}q_1^{MS}$. It can be shown that the existence of these commodity tax distortions on intermediate input purchases by the private production sector leads to a loss of overall productive efficiency. Thus, even though industry M and industry S are operating efficiently so that they are on the frontiers of their production possibilities sets, the consolidated production sector is not operating efficiently. The explanation for this phenomenon was given by Gerard Debreu (1951, 285):[24] there is a loss of systemwide output (or waste, to use Debreu's term) due to the imperfection of economic organization; that is, different production units, while techni-

---

23. In the very simple model considered in the previous two sections, there was no aggregation bias in each cell of the various input-output tables that were constructed. However, in a real-life input-output table, we will not be able to classify commodities down to a very fine level of detail. Hence, there will be a mix of related commodity transactions in each cell of an empirical input-output table. Due to the differing mixes of micro commodities in each cell, it can be seen that each cell will require its own deflator and moreover, the entries along any row of the resulting deflated real input-output table will not in general add up to the corresponding total in the final demand column. Thus, forcing constant-dollar input-output tables to add up along rows will generally impose errors on the data.

24. See also Diamond and Mirrlees (1971).

cally efficient, face different prices for the same input or output, and this causes net outputs aggregated across production units to fall below what is attainable if the economic system as a whole were efficient. In other words, a condition for systemwide efficiency is that all production units face the same price for each separate input or output that is produced by the economy as a whole. Thus, the existence of commodity taxes that fall on intermediate inputs causes producers to face different prices for the same commodity, and if production functions exhibit some substitutability, then producers will be induced to jointly supply an inefficient economywide net output vector. The overall size of the loss of productive efficiency depends on the magnitudes of elasticities of substitution and on the size of the commodity tax distortions, t_2^{SM}, t_1^{MS}, and t_3^{MS}.[25] In order to obtain empirical estimates of this loss of productive efficiency, it is necessary to estimate production functions or dual cost or profit functions for each industry in the economy. Thus, for the economy represented by table 7C.6, it would be necessary to estimate three sectoral production functions (or their dual equivalents), and hence a time series of the price quantity data in each cell of the input-output table would need to be collected. For the econometric estimation, it would not be necessary for the statistical agency to provide information on the tax wedges; that is, only prices that include the tax wedges (along with the associated quantities) would need to be provided by the statistical agency.[26] However, in order to *calculate* the loss of productive efficiency induced by the tax wedges, t_2^{SM}, t_1^{MS}, and t_3^{MS}, the statistical agency would have to provide information on the size of these wedges.

The loss of productive efficiency due to the existence of taxes that fall within the production sector of the economy is of course not the total loss of efficiency that can be attributed to indirect tax wedges: there are additional losses of efficiency that are due to the taxes that fall on the components of final demand. Thus if we look down the three rows of the final demand column in table 7C.6, we see that each final demand price has a tax wedge included in it: t_1^{MF} is the final demand tax wedge for commodity 1 (the good), t_1^{SF} is the final demand tax wedge for commodity 2 (the service), and t_3^{MF} is the final demand tax wedge for commodity 3 (the transport service).[27] Each of these three tax wedges creates some additional losses of overall efficiency in the economy. In order to obtain empirical estimates of these efficiency losses or excess burdens, it will be necessary to estimate household preferences in addition to the production functions mentioned

25. To the accuracy of a second-order approximation, the size of the loss will grow quadratically in the tax rates t_2^{SM}, t_1^{MS} and t_3^{MS}; see Diewert (1983, 171).

26. For examples of econometric studies that estimate sectoral production functions or their dual equivalents, see Jorgenson (1998) or Diewert and Lawrence (1994, 2002).

27. Note that these three tax rates plus the three that appeared as taxes on intermediate inputs in the input-output table 7C.6 add up to the six commodity tax wedges in our model of the economy.

in the previous paragraph. For econometric estimation purposes, it is sufficient for the statistical agency to provide final demand prices and quantities demanded where the prices include the commodity tax wedges; that is, only the total prices, including commodity taxes, are required for econometric estimation. However, in order to calculate the deadweight loss generated by these commodity taxes, it will be necessary to have estimates of the tax wedges; that is, tax researchers will require estimates of t_1^{MF}, t_2^{SF}, and t_3^{MF}.[28] This information is required not only so that total excess burdens can be estimated but also so that *marginal excess burdens* of each tax can be estimated. The marginal excess burden of a tax rate is an estimate of the efficiency loss generated by a small increase in the tax rate divided by the extra revenue that the increase in the tax rate generates. If reasonably accurate information on marginal excess burdens could be made available to policymakers, this information would be very valuable in evaluating the consequences of either increasing or decreasing existing tax rates.[29] However, as indicated in this paragraph and the preceding one, it will not be possible to calculate estimates of these marginal excess burdens unless the statistical agency makes available information on the tax wedges and the associated quantities for each major indirect tax in the economy.

Thus, for purposes of modeling the effects of indirect commodity taxes, our conclusion is that the new architecture for an expanded set of U.S. accounts that is outlined in Jorgenson and Landefeld (2004) is not quite adequate to meet the needs of taxation economists. In addition to the tables that are presented in Jorgenson and Landefeld, we need an additional table that gives tax rates and the associated quantities (or revenues) for each cell where the tax appears. In terms of table 7C.6, we need not only price and quantity information for each of the nonzero cells in the table, but also price and quantity information for the six tax revenue flows in our model, namely t and q information for the tax flows $t_1^{MS} q_1^{MS}$, $t_1^{MF} q_1^{MF}$, $t_2^{SM} q_2^{SM}$, $t_2^{SF} q_2^{SF}$, $t_3^{MF} q_1^{MF}$, and $t_3^{MS} q_1^{MS}$. An additional benefit of making this information available is that this information is also required in order to reconcile the industry productivity accounts with the economy's final demand GDP accounts.

References

Debreu, G. 1951. The coefficient of resource utilization. *Econometrica* 19:273–92.
Diamond, P. A., and J. A. Mirrlees. 1971. Optimal taxation and public production I–II. *American Economic Review* 61:8–27, 261–78.
Diewert, W. E. 1978. Superlative index numbers and consistency in aggregation. *Econometrica* 46:883–900.

28. For additional material on measuring deadweight losses, see Diewert (1981, 1983).
29. For examples of studies that estimate marginal excess burdens, see Jorgenson and Yun (2001) or Diewert and Lawrence (1994, 1995, 2002).

———. 1981. The measurement of deadweight loss revisited. *Econometrica* 49: 1225–44.

———. 1983. The measurement of waste within the production sector of an open economy. *Scandinavian Journal of Economics* 85 (2): 159–79.

———. 2002. The quadratic approximation lemma and decompositions of superlative indexes. *Journal of Economic and Social Measurement* 28:63–88.

———. 2004a. Aggregation issues. In *Producer price index manual: Theory and practice,* ed. P. Armknecht, 463–84. Washington, DC: International Monetary Fund.

———. 2004b. Price indices using an artificial data set. In *Producer price index manual: Theory and practice,* ed. P. Armknecht, 495–507. Washington, DC: International Monetary Fund.

Diewert, W. E., and D. A. Lawrence. 1994. *The marginal costs of taxation in New Zealand.* Canberra, New Zealand: Swan Consultants.

———. 1995. New Zealand's excess burden of tax. *Agenda: A Journal of Policy Analysis and Reform* 2 (1): 27–34.

———. 2002. The deadweight costs of capital taxation in Australia. In *Efficiency in the public sector,* ed. Kevin J. Fox, 103–67. Boston: Kluwer Academic Publishers.

Dikhanov, Y. 1997. The sensitivity of PPP-based income estimates to choice of aggregation procedures. Washington, DC: World Bank, International Economics Department. Mimeograph, January.

Ehemann, C., A. J. Katz, and B. R. Moulton. 2002. The chain-additivity issue and the U.S. National Accounts. *Journal of Economic and Social Measurement* 28: 37–49.

Fisher, I. 1922. *The making of index numbers.* Boston: Houghton-Mifflin.

Hicks, J. 1952. *The social framework: An introduction to economics.* Oxford, UK: Clarendon Press.

Jorgenson, D. W. 1998. *Growth.* Vol. 1, *General equilibrium modeling.* Cambridge, MA: MIT Press.

Jorgenson, D. W., and Z. Griliches. 1972. Issues in growth accounting: A reply to Edward F. Denison. *Survey of Current Business* 52 (5, part II): 65–94.

Jorgenson, D. W., and K.-Y. Yun. 2001. *Investment.* Vol. 3, *Lifting the burden: Tax reform, the cost of capital and U.S. economic growth.* Cambridge, MA: MIT Press.

Moulton, B. R., and E. P. Seskin. 1999. A preview of the 1999 comprehensive revision of the National Income and Product Accounts. *Survey of Current Business* 79 (October): 6–17.

Reinsdorf, M. B., W. E. Diewert, and C. Ehemann. 2002. Additive decompositions for the Fisher, Törnqvist and geometric mean indexes. *Journal of Economic and Social Measurement* 28:51–61.

Reinsdorf, M., and R. Yuskavage. 2004. Exact industry contributions to labor productivity change. Paper presented at the Social Sciences and Humanities Research Council SSHRC International Conference on Index Number Theory and the Measurement of Prices and Productivity. 1 July, Vancouver, Canada.

United Nations, Commission of the European Committees, International Monetary Fund, Organisation for Economic Co-operation and Development, and World Bank. 1993. *System of national accounts 1993.* Series F, no. 2, rev. 4. New York: United Nations.

Van IJzeren. 1987. Bias in international index numbers: A mathematical elucidation. PhD diss., Hungarian Academy of Sciences.

Integrating Expenditure and Income Data
What to Do with the Statistical Discrepancy?

J. Joseph Beaulieu and Eric J. Bartelsman

A man with one watch knows what time it is:
A man with two watches is never quite sure.
—French Proverb

8.1 Introduction

The Bureau of Economic Analysis (BEA) publishes two measures of domestic output. The better-known measure, gross domestic product (GDP), is the sum of private and government consumption and investment (including inventory investment) and net exports. A second measure, gross domestic income (GDI), is the sum of factor and nonfactor payments paid to input providers; these payments include compensation, profits and profit-like income, production and import taxes (formerly known as indirect business taxes), and the consumption of fixed capital. GDP and GDI conceptually measure the same thing, but because the two are calculated using imperfect source data, the two measures differ by what is called the statistical discrepancy.

Historically, the level of the statistical discrepancy has been small relative to GDP or GDI. As shown in panel A of figure 8.1, the absolute value of the statistical discrepancy as a fraction of the average of nominal GDP and nominal GDI peaked at 2.1 percent in 1993. From 1977 to 2001, the fraction averaged 0.8 percent with a standard deviation of 0.9 percent.

Nonetheless, different movements in real GDP and in real GDI can be economically meaningful. Panel B of figure 8.1 plots the average annual

J. Joseph Beaulieu, formerly a member of the staff of the Board of Governors of the Federal Reserve, is now an economist for BrevanHoward, Inc. Eric J. Bartelsman is a professor of economics at the Vrije Universiteit Amsterdam, and Fellow of the Tinbergen Institute.

The authors thank the discussant, Bart van Ark, other participants of the Conference on Research in Income and Wealth (CRIW) conference for their comments, and Michael Harper and Brian Moyer for their detailed and insightful suggestions for revision. This paper represents the authors' own views and not those of the Board of Governors of the Federal Reserve System or its staff.

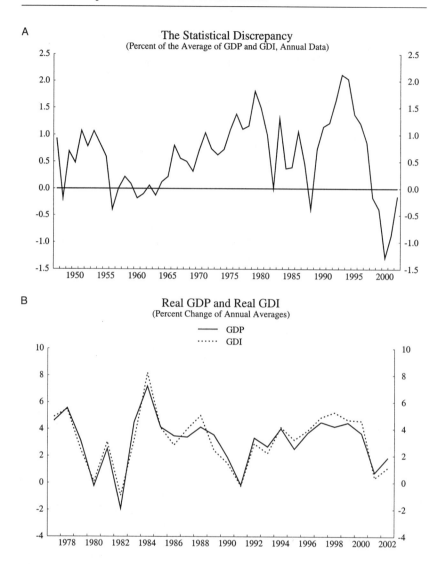

Fig. 8.1

growth rates of real GDP and GDI. Although the movements of the two appear to coincide from year to year, between 1994 and 2000, real GDI grew on average 1/2 percentage point (annual rate) faster than real GDP, which is sizable when compared to the average growth rate of the two series of 4.1 percent.

The recent difference in the growth rates of the two measures of domestic product has been a problem for policymakers. The two measures imply different paths for productivity and potential output, which are important for planning purposes. Many analysts have pointed to the rapid rate of growth of GDI as being more consistent with the expected productivity gains from investment in high-tech equipment. Problems for analysts are especially acute when they need to combine data from the expenditure and income accounts, such as when modeling the components of national saving or projecting tax receipts. Indeed, the Congressional Budget Office (CBO) points to the large swing in the statistical discrepancy as a substantial hindrance in its ability to forecast tax revenue in the past few years (CBO 2003). The statistical discrepancy also leads to inconsistencies when analyzing particular types of income as a share of GDP.

Finally, the existence of the statistical discrepancy is a problem for researchers trying to reconcile their estimates of productivity trends by industry using data measured on the income side with aggregate estimates of productivity trends that are based on product-side measures. Bartelsman and Beaulieu (2004), Bosworth and Triplett (2003), and Nordhaus (2000) use the BEA's GDP-by-industry data (2003 or earlier) to model industry-level productivity. These data aggregate to GDI, making it hard to compare their results to the BLS's measure of productivity in the nonfarm business sector, which equals GDP less the value added from a few select sectors.[1]

Several researchers have speculated on the data deficiencies that have led to the statistical discrepancy. GDP may be mismeasured because estimating the consumption of services is difficult (Council of Economic Advisers 1997; Moulton 2000) or exports are underreported (Moulton 2000). GDI may be mismeasured because purging income of capital gains, which do not represent current production, is hard (Baker 1998; Moulton 2000), because stock options and other nontraditional forms of compensation show up in the compensation statistics without an offset in the profits data (Baker 1998; Moulton 2000), or because measures of proprietors' income have to be adjusted for underreporting in the tax return data. These adjustments to proprietors' income are based on an outdated and discontinued study (Council of Economic Advisers 1997). Many of these explanations appear to be confirmed by Klein and Makino (2000), who find that the statistical discrepancy is inversely related to profits and proprietors' income and positively related to government spending and exports.[2]

---

1. Despite what one may infer from the name "gross domestic product by industry," the industry estimates in this data set aggregate to GDI. A balancing item is included in this data set, but this discrepancy is not allocated across industries; see Yuskavage and Strassner (2003). The BEA has recently altered its methodology to produce industry data, and its latest estimates of these data now aggregate to GDP; see Lawson et al. (chap. 6 in this volume).

2. Recall the convention that more GDP relative to GDI leads to a more positive statistical discrepancy; more GDI leads to a more negative discrepancy.

The BEA prefers GDP as its measure of domestic output. Parker and Seskin (1997) write:

> [The BEA] considers the source data underlying the estimates of GDP to be more accurate. For example, most of the annual source data used for estimating GDP are based on complete enumerations, such as the Federal Government budget data, or are regularly adjusted to complete enumerations, such as the quinquennial economic censuses and census of governments. . . . For GDI, only the annual tabulations of employment tax returns and Federal Government budget data are complete enumerations, and only farm proprietors' income and State and local government budget data are regularly adjusted to complete enumerations. For most of the remaining components of GDI, the annual source data are tabulations of samples of income tax returns.

This view is reflected in the presentation of the NIPAs. The BEA presents only GDP-related data in its summary tables, and in its decomposition of national income it portrays the statistical discrepancy as if it were all an error in the measurement of income vis-à-vis GDP. A few years ago, the BLS appeared to adopt this view when it switched its definition of nonfarm business output in its Productivity and Cost release from one based on GDI to one based on GDP, as described in Dean, Harper, and Otto (1995).

Others, however, have argued that GDI has more desirable properties, at least at certain points in time. The Council of Economic Advisers (1997) found that the behavior of Okun's law, the sharp jump in personal tax payments, and the behavior of the real product wage were more consistent with the faster-growing GDI measure of output in the mid-1990s, as measured at that time. During that same period, Greenspan (2004) observed that the rapid rise in measured labor and capital income, along with quiescent price inflation, suggested that productivity was increasing briskly. These productivity gains were apparent in the income-side measure, but not in the product-side measure of domestic output. Based on their time-series properties, Weale (1992) argued that GDI should be weighted almost twice as much as GDP in an optimal combination of the two measures into a single output series.

The paper presents two sets of exercises. One is to conduct a "forensic" examination of the statistical discrepancy by allocating the statistical discrepancy across industries; perhaps we can lessen the size of the aggregate discrepancy through focused, improved measurement at the industry level. Next, we present some metrics that allow us to evaluate a sequence of data sets created under varying assumptions regarding the quality of the underlying data sources. Optimizing on these metrics should provide one, best, coherent data set to conduct further research.

The structure of the paper is as follows. In section 8.2 we describe the underlying source data, the manipulations to the data undertaken to make the sources consistent in classifications and definitions, and the method used to integrate the varying source data. In section 8.3, we compare estimates of value added by industry from a consistent data set controlled to GDP data with value added by industry from a consistent data set controlled to GDI data to calculate statistical discrepancies by industry. Two sets of estimates of deliveries to final demand by industry also yield statistical discrepancies by industry. Similarly, we compare our two sets of estimates of final demand by major expenditure category. It appears that the mismeasurement of deliveries to final demand and value added in a few problem industries explains most of the broad movements in the aggregate discrepancy. In the following section, we discuss the metrics used to find an optimal combination of the GDP and GDI data to create an integrated data set. These metrics are based on standard economic arguments. We find that a mixture of data that do not aggregate either to GDP or to GDI appears to generate a data set that yields the best results. The fifth section concludes.

8.2   Methodology and Data

The main goal of the chapter is to construct and compare *consistent, integrated data sets* of the U.S. economy. We take "data set" to mean detailed information on the gross output, value added, final demand expenditures, and use of intermediate inputs by industry. We define a "consistent" data set to be one where the underlying components are based on the same definitions and industry classifications. And by "integrated," we mean that, despite the numerous data sources employed, the estimates conform to the accounting identities linking production, income, and expenditures.

Integration is not a unique transformation of the data, so different assumptions and methods to enforce integration can yield different estimates. We have built into our integration technique "tuning parameters" that summarize the specific assumptions that we use to obtain unique estimates. Adjusting these "tuning parameters" allows us to obtain different consistent, integrated data sets. In section 8.3, we compare two data sets based on polar assumptions: one integrates the data assuming that detailed GDP expenditures are correct; the other case assumes that income by industry (summing to GDI) is correct. In section 8.4, we estimate numerous data sets by varying the tuning parameters between the polar cases to compare their performance on predefined criteria.

It should be noted that the integration exercises are carried out on nominal data and that any comparisons made in real terms are based on the same deflators applied to either side of the comparison. Issues concerning how price and quantities can be consistently aggregated are considered in Moyer, Reinsdorf, and Yuskavage (chap. 7 in this volume).

The rest of this section describes the data and method employed to conduct our analysis. The first subsection illustrates our input-output system that defines the components of our data set. The second subsection describes the sources of our initial estimates of these components and the manipulations we made to make them consistent. The final subsection describes the methodology used to integrate the source data to satisfy the constraints in our input-output system.

8.2.1   Our Input-Output System

The input-output system that describes the data set used in this study is shown in figure 8.2. Domestic industries, represented as the first N rows of the table, produce gross output (vector $\mathbf{Y}$) and deliver it to final demand (matrix $\mathbf{F}$) or to other domestic industries, (matrix $\mathbf{I}$), which use it as intermediate inputs in their production processes. The fact that the sum of each industry's deliveries to final demand and to other industries equals its gross output is called the *gross output identity*. The value added of an industry equals its gross output less the sum of its use of intermediate inputs (*value added identity*). The sum across industries of deliveries to final demand equals GDP (*GDP identity*), and the sum of value added across industries equals GDI (*GDI identity*). The *reconciliation identity* that integrates the system is that GDP equals GDI.

The first N rows of the system represent flows of goods from domestic industries. In order to simplify the exposition of our analysis, we account for the flows of imported goods in a nonstandard fashion: imported goods that are used in the production process of domestic industries or that are delivered to final domestic purchasers are the product of a separate industry,

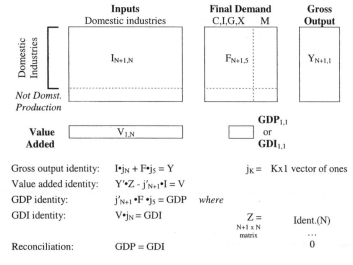

Fig. 8.2   **Input-output system**

called *Not Domestic Production,* which is the last row of the upper blocks. Deliveries of imports to domestic industries or to domestic purchasers are positive entries in the input-output system. The final demand category, imports, has an offsetting negative entry, so that the gross output of imports is zero. Note that, by definition, domestic industries do not deliver any output to the final demand category imports, and so the first N rows of the import column contain zeros.

In addition, used and secondhand goods and scrap show up in the input-output accounts. They are used as intermediates to the production process and are either delivered to or supplied by the final demand categories. They do not represent new production, so, like imports, their gross output equals zero. Negative entries represent net suppliers of the goods; positive entries represent net users. For example, businesses scrap some of their equipment each year, so the final expenditure category, business fixed investment, is a net supplier of used and secondhand goods and scrap. These commodity flows are also included in the pseudoindustry Not Domestic Production.

8.2.2 Developing a Consistent Initial Data Set

In order to conduct our analysis, we need to populate the elements of the input-output system with initial values using consistent definitions. As described below, these initial values come from different published sources that do not match precisely in terms of definitions, accounting conventions, basis for data collection, or product and industry classifications. The GDP and GDI data for the years 1977 through 2001 come from the recently released benchmark National Income and Product Account (NIPA) data. Other data were adapted or created from the latest published data source from the BEA.

Value Added by Industry

Value added for farms, private households, and owner-occupied housing comes directly from the NIPAs. Value added for owner-occupied housing was subtracted out of the real estate industry and placed in its own industry (before further aggregation). For other industries, estimates of value added by industry are sourced from the BEA's 2003 GDP-by-industry data set. Pre-1987 data were concorded to the 1987 Standard Industrial Classification (SIC) as in Bartelsman and Beaulieu (2004). All of the income components were adjusted proportionately so that they sum to the latest aggregate estimates.

Value added in the real estate industry was also adjusted to exclude the imputed rental value of capital equipment and structures owned by nonprofit institutions. Instead, this imputed income was distributed to industries according to estimates of the compensation paid by nonprofit institutions by industry, as estimated in Bartelsman and Beaulieu (2004). Redistributing this income is useful because the final expenditures on many of the products produced by nonprofit institutions are not identified as to whether they were produced in the nonprofit sector or in the business sector, so these expenditures will not show up as coming from the real estate sector.

In putting together its GDP-by-industry data set, the BEA had to adjust some of its source data to put the data set consistently on an establishment basis. In particular, the original information on corporate profits, nonfarm proprietors' income, net interest paid, and capital consumption allowances is measured on a firm basis (U.S. Bureau of Economic Analysis 2001, pp. M21–M22). Other data, such as gross output and compensation paid, are measured on an establishment basis. The same income components collected on these two bases for the same industry will differ when firms in that industry have extensive operations in different lines of work. Data collected at the establishment level will split a multiestablishment firm into different industries, but data collected on a firm basis will put all of the firm's operations into one industry. For its GDP-by-industry data set (2003), the BEA adjusted the source data to put all of it on an establishment basis using a cross-classification table. But these are difficult adjustments to make, and this adjustment could be a source of error in allocating domestic data among industries. The finance industry is one where the distinction between firm and establishment data is particularly important (see Bartelsman and Beaulieu 2004).

Deliveries to Final Demand by Industry

No published data on deliveries to final demand by industry exist, so estimates based on detailed NIPA expenditure and input-output data had to be developed. First, detailed NIPA data on all expenditures, except software investment, construction, and inventory investment, were allocated to the input-output tables' commodity classification system. These mappings are called "bridge tables," the construction of which is described in detail below. The second step involves dividing final expenditures between domestically produced and imported commodities. Third, estimates of deliveries of commodities were converted to deliveries by industries. The domestic production of each commodity is converted to an industry basis using the 1987 and 1992 make tables, and these industries are then aggregated to the definitions in appendix table 8A.1. Imports of all commodities are aggregated into one industry, called Not Domestic Production.

The method used to estimate the bridge tables differs by expenditure category. For personal consumption and equipment investment (including residential equipment), detailed bridge tables were published by the BEA for 1987 and 1992. These bridge tables include the fraction of expenditures due to transportation and trade margins; these margins are treated as a separate commodity delivered to the specific expenditure category. For exports, imports, and government expenditures, bridge tables were created by assigning commodities to specific NIPA categories using the 1987 and 1992 use tables to estimate specific proportions. For exports and imports of goods, NIPA expenditures were disaggregated to more detailed census categories using information in the Bureau of the Census report on international trade in goods and services; input-output (I-O) commodities were assigned to these more detailed census categories. Export margins for wholesale trade and goods transportation were allocated across expenditure categories in the same proportion as total margins to all goods exports as shown in the use tables.

Bridge tables for government consumption were built by first assigning the consumption of fixed capital and the compensation paid to general government employees, excluding own-account investment to the general government industry. Compensation paid to employees for own-account investment is treated with other government investment. Commodities with positive values in the I-O use tables were assigned to government purchases of intermediate durables, nondurables, and services, depending on the commodity's characteristics. Commodities with negative values in the I-O use table were assigned to government sales.[3] Netting out government sales from intermediate purchases yields government consumption excluding its own value added. The NIPA data on federal nondefense, nondurable consumption were augmented with data from the Energy Information Agency to account for purchases and sales from the Strategic Petroleum Reserve. As with trade, margins were distributed to all expenditure categories in fixed proportions.

Bridge tables for government investment were created by first splitting own-account investment into equipment and structures using pre-revision data on compensation paid to force-account construction. Own-account investment originates from the general government. The remaining investment in structures was assigned to the construction industry, and the remaining investment in equipment was split among commodities using relative proportions in the 1987 and 1992 I-O use tables.

Imports are different from other expenditure categories in that all imports are counted as coming from one industry. However, it is necessary to allocate a fraction of imports to the domestic final purchases categories and the rest to intermediate inputs to domestic production in order to estimate the fraction of each commodity delivered to final demand that was produced domestically versus imported. This split was done by assuming that the fraction of an imported commodity delivered to final demand categories versus to domestic industries is the same as that observed in the I-O use tables. The rest of final demand is then assumed to be produced domestically.

The production of each commodity was then converted to an industry basis using the 1987 and 1992 I-O make tables. We assumed that the pro-

---

3. The NIPAs provide more detail on intermediate purchases for federal defense and the sales by state and local governments that are used to refine these assignments.

portion of each commodity that was produced by the I-O industry was the same as indicated in the make tables. Using 1987 and 1992 data produces two estimates. For the years 1987 and before we used the estimates based on the 1987 tables; for the years 1992 and after we used the estimates based on the 1992 tables. For the years in between, we used a weighted average of the two, where the weights are based on the distance from each benchmark year. These industry estimates were then aggregated to the industry definitions as in appendix table 8A.1.

Residential and nonresidential investment in structures by industry had to be estimated in a different manner than would follow from the published I-O tables. Some expenditure categories were assigned directly to specific industries: drilling and exploration to mining, mobile homes to the appropriate manufacturing industry, and commissions to real estate.

The I-O tables appear to suggest that the remainder of investment in structures originates in the construction industry, but this is not correct. For construction, the I-O tables make an exception to the rule that production is classified according to the primary output of an establishment. Instead, the tables classify all construction regardless of the primary output of an establishment to the construction industry, a classification scheme known as activity based. Most of the rest of the input-output data are essentially organized on an establishment basis.[4] Figure 8.3 illustrates the problem with mixing establishment-based classifications and activity-based classifications: domestic investment in structures, excluding government own-account investment in structures exceeds the BEA's estimate of gross output in the construction industry. Consequently, we have to estimate how much of private structures investment originates in the construction industry versus other industries.

The value of deliveries to final demand by the construction industry was calculated as a fraction of the BEA's estimate of gross output. This equals the interpolated values of one minus the ratio of receipts for maintenance and repair to total sales in the Censuses of Construction (1977, 1982, 1987, 1992, and 1997).

The remainder of investment in structures was assigned to other industries based on their share of employment of construction workers in 2001 (from the BLS occupational survey) times the BEA's estimate of the real wealth stock of structures by industry. Including the real wealth stock allows the indicators used to allocate the estimate of force-account construction to vary over time.

Software investment was allocated across industries by first splitting in-

4. Farms and real estate services are the other industries in the input-output tables that are defined on an activity basis instead of an establishment basis. The farm industry, however, is consistently treated in the NIPAs. All royalty income, regardless of its origination, is counted in the real estate industry, but this is the same treatment in the GDP-by-industry data. Thus, adjustments are not necessary to improve the consistency of these industry estimates.

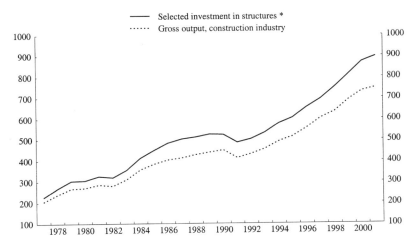

Fig. 8.3   Measures of construction activity (billions of dollars)

Note: Selected investment in structures excludes investment in mining and exploration, manufactured homes, commissions, and government own-account investment.

vestment into two components: own account and purchased software using the BEA's detailed new investment-by-industry data. Own-account investment was then allocated across industries using these data. Purchased software was distributed to industries using the 1987 and 1992 make tables; 98 percent of the production of purchased software in 1992 was assigned to the data-processing services industry, SIC 737.

Inventory investment was allocated to industries based on published NIPA data. Farm inventories were assigned to farms. Manufacturing inventory investment was allocated among manufacturing industries using book value data from the Annual Survey of Manufacturers (ASM). ASM data reported on a NAICS basis or on the 1977 SIC were concorded to the 1987 SIC using available concordances. Wholesale and retail trade inventories were simply assigned to the trade industry. The remainder of inventory investment was allocated among other industries using data from the Sources of Income (Department of Treasury) for 1995–97. Shares for other years were assumed to equal either the 1995 or 1997 value.

Table 8.1 describes how well our bridge tables translate the available detailed NIPA expenditure data into deliveries to final demand by industry. As shown in the first row, personal consumption expenditures (PCEs) were $3,100.2 billion in 1987. The BEA breaks up total PCE into 141 categories, such as sporting equipment, sugar and sweets purchased for off-premise consumption, and spending on theater and opera performances. On average, each of the 141 detailed categories was divided among 6.1 industries. One quarter of PCE was in expenditure categories that were allocated all to just one industry. Another 22.5 percent of PCE was in categories where over

Table 8.1 Splitting NIPA expenditure categories (1987) across 26 industries

	Billions of 1987 $	Number of expenditures categories	Industries per expenditure category	Dominant industry's share of expenditure category						Standard Deviation[a]
				100%	95–100%	85–95%	75–85%	50–75%	Under 50%	
Personal Consumption	3,100.2	141	6.1	24.9	22.5	5.2	8.1	28.7	10.6	2.4
Equipment Investment	326.7	27	11.5	8.8	0.0	16.0	51.8	17.9	5.5	6.7
Software Investment	29.0	1	23.0	0.0	0.0	0.0	0.0	100.0	0.0	11.1
Structures Investment	402.1	5	5.8	3.3	1.3	6.1	0.0	89.3	0.0	10.0
General Government	591.2	1	1.0	100.0	0.0	0.0	0.0	0.0	0.0	0.0
Other Government	408.4	39	7.2	18.8	15.8	0.7	5.0	12.1	47.7	5.6
Exports, Goods	257.5	124[b]	8.3	0.0	8.6	33.9	18.8	27.3	11.4	2.4
Exports, Services	106.4	7	5.6	29.8	18.0	9.6	0.0	42.6	0.0	7.1
Imports, Goods	−414.8	128[b]	5.5	58.1	27.2	2.3	3.0	9.5	0.0	3.0
Imports, Services	−94.4	7	4.4	48.9	12.2	0.0	0.0	20.1	18.8	9.9
Inventory Investment[c]	27.1	4	6.8	53.8	0.0	0.0	18.2	0.0		57.6
GDP	4,739.5	484	6.9	26.4	14.5	7.0	9.9	30.4	11.8	3.3

[a]Average standard deviation of deliveries by industry to these major expenditure categories assuming a 10 percent standard deviation in the bridge tables. Deliveries by industry are subsequently calculated by controlling the bridge tables to the actual values of the detailed expenditure categories.
[b]NIPA expenditure categories are divided into more categories using data from the monthly report on international trade in goods and services.
[c]Dominant industry's share calculated using absolute values instead of actual values. Standard deviation calculated using normal, additive errors.

95 percent of the category was allocated to one industry (fifth column). Only 10.6 percent of PCE was in categories that were so diffuse that the largest industry did not account for half of the category (ninth column).

The bridge tables contain a lot of structure that constrains how relative errors in the bridge tables can affect our estimates of deliveries to final demand by industry. For example, the value added of the general government, which the BEA publishes, maps to only one industry, and so, conditional on this published value, this category cannot contribute to an error in our estimates. To take another example, PCE radio and television repair services are estimated to be produced by three industries—personal services, business services, and machinery manufacturing—with personal services accounting for 95 percent of final demand. As a result, for this category of consumption, a large relative error in the bridge table for business services and machinery manufacturing can have only a small effect on the estimated deliveries of personal services.

To see how errors in the bridge table can translate into variation in our estimates of deliveries to final demand by industry, we performed the following experiment. We multiplied the cell values in our 1987 bridge tables by lognormally distributed errors so that the standard deviation of the cell values was 10 percent, and then we recontrolled the bridge tables so that the sum across industries equaled the published values of the detailed expenditure categories. We then recalculated the implied deliveries to final demand. We repeated this procedure 2,500 times. As shown in the last column of the table, a 10 percent random error in the bridge tables translates to only an average variation of deliveries by industry to PCE of 2.4 percent.

Other major categories are not measured as well. For equipment investment a 10 percent error in the bridge table leads to an average standard deviation of 6.7 percent in deliveries to final demand by industry. This weaker performance is probably due to the poorer precision in the equipment investment bridge table. On average, there are 11.5 industries per category, and three-quarters of equipment investment is spread among categories where the dominant industry accounts for less than 75 percent spending. For all of GDP, a 10 percent error in the bridge tables translates to a 3.3 percent error in deliveries to final demand by industry.

Gross Output by Industry

Estimates of gross output by industry come mainly from the published GDP-by-industry data, except for farms, owner-occupied housing, general government, and households, which are available or easily estimated from NIPA data. In a few early years, the estimate of value added by the legal services industry was higher than the estimate of gross output. To allow our analysis to proceed, we boosted the value of gross output so that it exceeds value added by at least 5 percent, a figure consistent with the 1987 I-O use table.

Intermediate Inputs

The starting point for constructing the intermediate block of the consistent data set is the use table from the published BEA benchmark I-O data. Unlike the vectors and matrices for gross output, deliveries to final demand, and value added, the initial values for the intermediate block, $\mathbf{I}$, are calculated only for the base years 1982, 1987, and 1992. Initial values for other years are developed iteratively using results from the balancing routine described in the next subsection.

Initial values for the base years were calculated twice and then averaged to get one estimate. The first estimate allocates the vector of gross output less deliveries to final demand $(\mathbf{Y} - \mathbf{F})$ across the columns of $\mathbf{I}$ in proportion to the values observed in the 1982, 1987, or 1992 use tables. The second estimate allocates the vector of gross output less value added $(\mathbf{Y}' - \mathbf{V})$ across the rows of $\mathbf{I}$, also in proportion to the values observed in the corresponding use tables. These two estimates, one of which can be thought of as consistent with the expenditure-side data, the other as consistent with the income-side data, are then combined by taking a geometric average of the two values cell by cell.

The resulting benchmark-year initial estimates of $\mathbf{I}$ are adjusted to subtract out the intermediate value of software purchases, which are now counted as final demand (see Bartelsman and Beaulieu 2004), and adjusted to allocate own-account construction to the appropriate industries. Further, the values in the columns from the use table for transportation margins and distribution margins are entered as intermediate purchases by the industry purchasing the relevant input and as sales to other industries by the "margin industries," such as water and rail transport or retail trade.

8.2.3   Integrating the Data

The consistent I-O data set populated with initial values is adjusted, or integrated, so that the various constraints in the input-output system are satisfied with cell values "close" to the initial estimates. Specifically, we choose values for each element in the I-O system to minimize the weighted sum of squares of the difference with its initial estimate subject to the linear constraints. The inverse of the weights equals the absolute value of the cell times a "tuning" parameter; these tuning parameters are what we use to control the integration process. The closer the tuning parameter is to zero, the more we restrict the final estimate to lie close to the initial estimate. If the tuning parameter equals zero, the value of the cell is not adjusted. This solution technique is a straightforward generalization of the least squares method first proposed by Stone, Champernowne, and Meade (1942).

Formally, denote the initial estimates of each element of the vectors and matrices of the I-O system with a bar. We solve

$$(1) \quad \min_{\{Y_t, F_t, V_t, I_t\}} \sum_{i=1}^{I} \frac{1}{\sigma^Y |\overline{Y}_{it}|} (Y_{it} - \overline{Y}_{it})^2 + \sum_{i=1}^{I} \frac{1}{\sigma^F |\overline{F}_{it}|} (F_{it} - \overline{F}_{it})^2$$

$$+ \sum_{i=1}^{I} \frac{1}{\sigma^V |\overline{V}_{it}|} (V_{it} - \overline{V}_{it})^2$$

$$+ \sum_{i=1}^{I} \sum_{j=1}^{I} \frac{1}{\sigma^I |\overline{I}_{ijt}|} (I_{ijt} - \overline{I}_{ijt})^2$$

$$\text{s.t.} \quad Y_{it} = F_{it} + \sum_{j=1}^{I} I_{ijt}$$

$$Y_{jt} = V_{jt} + \sum_{i=1}^{I} I_{ijt},$$

where σ denotes preset tuning parameters, i denotes row, j denotes column, and t denotes time. If σ equals zero, then the weight becomes a Lagrange multiplier and the fact that the cell value equals its initial value becomes another restriction in the minimization problem.

As indicated in equation (1), because the inverse of the weights are proportional to the initial values, initial values that are equal to zero are restricted to remain zero. In our application we restrict the values of σ to be the same for all elements of the same vector or matrix. For example, all values of σ for the value-added vector are equal to σ^V, with one exception, which is described in the next section. One could also allow these parameters to differ across industries, for instance, if there was some idea that some industries were measured better than others, but we do not pursue this angle. Finally, it should be obvious from equation (1) that only the relative values of σ matter; doubling all of them does not change the solution. Thus, we standardize the parameters by setting $\sigma^I = 1$. Furthermore, to focus our analysis we only consider $\sigma^Y = 0$; this leaves a pair of tuning parameters $\{\sigma^F, \sigma^V\}$ to vary.

Other solution techniques have been used for similar problems. In particular, a popular routine is the so-called RAS iterative solution. Although Leontief in 1941 had already suggested a biproportional form for the relationship between the values taken by an I-O matrix at different points of time it became popular after it was used in R. A. Stone's Cambridge Growth Project in the early 1960s. It then became familiar under the name "RAS technique." In the traditional RAS or biproportional balancing method used for integration, differences between "control" totals and the sum of unadjusted data in one dimension are iteratively applied to proportionally adjust data in the other dimension until both restrictions are satisfied within a prescribed tolerance level.

The starting point of the algorithm is a given matrix **A** with semipositive rows and columns and strictly positive vectors **u** and **v**. One first multiplies each row by a scalar that will make the row sum equal the row constraint. Next one multiplies each column of the resulting matrix $\mathbf{A}^1$ by a scalar that will make its sum equal its constraint. This gives matrix $\mathbf{A}^2$, which serves as starting point for the next iteration. In general the process can be described as follows:

$$\mathbf{A}^{2t+1} = \hat{\mathbf{r}}^{t+1}\mathbf{A}^{2t}$$

$$\mathbf{A}^{2t+2} = \mathbf{A}^{2t+1}\hat{\mathbf{s}}^{t+1} = \hat{\mathbf{r}}^{t+1}\mathbf{A}^{2t}\hat{\mathbf{s}}^{t+1}$$

$$\hat{\mathbf{r}}^{t+1} = \frac{\mathbf{u}_i}{\sum_{j=1}^{n} a_{ij}^{2t}}$$

$$\hat{\mathbf{s}}^{t+1} = \frac{\mathbf{v}_j}{\sum_{i=1}^{m} a_{ij}^{2t+1}},$$

where $\hat{\mathbf{r}}$ and $\hat{\mathbf{s}}$ indicate a matrix with diagonal elements $\mathbf{r}_i$ such that $\mathbf{r}_i = \mathbf{u}_i / \Sigma\, a_{ij}$.

Bacharach (1970) established the existence of a solution to the RAS process under weak conditions and the uniqueness of the solution unconditionally. Also, for the first time stochastic elements (specification errors) were introduced. It is further shown that this RAS method is equivalent to a minimization problem with as solution the biproportional estimates r and s.

Bishop, Fienberg, and Holland (1975) present a methodology that is developed specifically for the analysis of categorical (qualitative) data in multidimensional contingency tables. Although they focus on maximum likelihood estimation and log-linear models, elements of the development and statistical properties of the RAS method are discussed. They discuss both complete and incomplete tables (including iterative proportional fitting of log-linear models) and pay special attention to marginal homogeneity and symmetry.

Unlike our technique, the iterative RAS method does not have a natural role for tuning parameters.[5] In addition, a problem with the RAS method arises when the controls do not sum to the same total; in practice, one or both of the controls are adjusted to coincide before the RAS procedure is

---

5. The iterative RAS solution is the solution of a minimization problem subject to the biproportional constraint, where instead of minimizing quadratic differences, the entropy kernel is used. Schneider and Zenios (1990) credit a Russian mathematician Bregman for this result, although the fact that the first-order conditions for the minimization problem yield the RAS iterative solution is not difficult to illustrate; see, for example, Günlük-Şenesen and Bates (1988). One could therefore weight the entropy kernel to allow for tuning parameters, though this would complicate the iterative technique to arrive at a solution. Bartelsman and Beaulieu (2003) explore some of the implications of the choice of balancing technique; see also Schneider and Zenios.

applied. In our method, the "controls" are not adjusted before minimization; instead, our routine adjusts the controls simultaneously with the other estimates as specified by the tuning parameters.

As noted in the previous subsection, our estimation procedure is dynamic in that our initial estimates of $\overline{\mathbf{I}}_t$ depend on the final results for other years when $t \neq 1982, 1987, 1992$. We first estimate the system for 1982 and then move backward in time to 1977 and forward in time to 1986, using the final estimate of $\mathbf{I}_{t \pm 1}$ as a basis for $\overline{\mathbf{I}}_t$. Specifically, $\overline{\mathbf{I}}_t$ is calculated by adapting $\mathbf{I}_{t \pm 1}$ for demand changes in the various columns by multiplying each cell of $\mathbf{I}_{t \pm 1}$ by the ratio of real gross output of column j in period t to real output of j in period $t \pm 1$. The matrix $\mathbf{I}_{t \pm 1}$ is also adapted for price changes in the various rows by multiplying each cell by the ratio of the gross output deflators for row i in period t to the output deflator in period $t \pm 1$. The same process is repeated starting in 1987 for the years 1983–91 and starting in 1992 for the years 1988–2001. This produces two sets of estimates, in current dollars, for 1983–86 and for 1988–91; these estimates are averaged to obtain one series of $\overline{\mathbf{I}}_t$ for 1977–2001.

8.3   Results Controlled to the GDP or GDI Data

Equation (1) was first estimated under two sets of tuning parameters. The first set, $\{\sigma^F = 0; \sigma^V = 1\}$,[6] means that we controlled the estimates to the expenditure-side data, and it leads to estimates of industry value added and deliveries to final demand that add to GDP. We allow the initial income-side value-added estimates to inform our final estimates, but with $\sigma^V = \sigma^I = 1$ the routine treats the estimates of value added symmetrically with the initial estimates of $\mathbf{I}$. The second set of tuning parameters, $\{\sigma^F = 1; \sigma^V = 0\}$, implies that we controlled the estimates to the income-side data; it leads to estimates of industry value added and deliveries to final demand that sum to GDI. In both cases, $\sigma^V_{MISC} = \sigma^V_{MISC} = 0$ because the income and gross output of these industries are already integrated between the expenditure and income accounts. Early experiments with the estimation procedure gave estimates for the Not Domestic Production industry that tended to drift. With both negative and positive values for deliveries of this series tied down only to sum to zero, the estimates of this industry can be volatile. As a result, $\sigma^V_{NDP} = \sigma^F_{NDP} = 0.00001$ if it otherwise is not equal to zero. Thus, we allow only small differences from the initial estimates for this industry, and it means that our estimate for the statistical discrepancy for imports essentially equals zero.

Figure 8.4 plots the difference of the two estimates for each industry's deliveries to final demand in the left-hand panels and the difference of the two estimates for each industry's value added in the right-hand panels. Using

6. Recall that in all of our estimates $\sigma^V = 0$ and $\sigma^I = 1$.

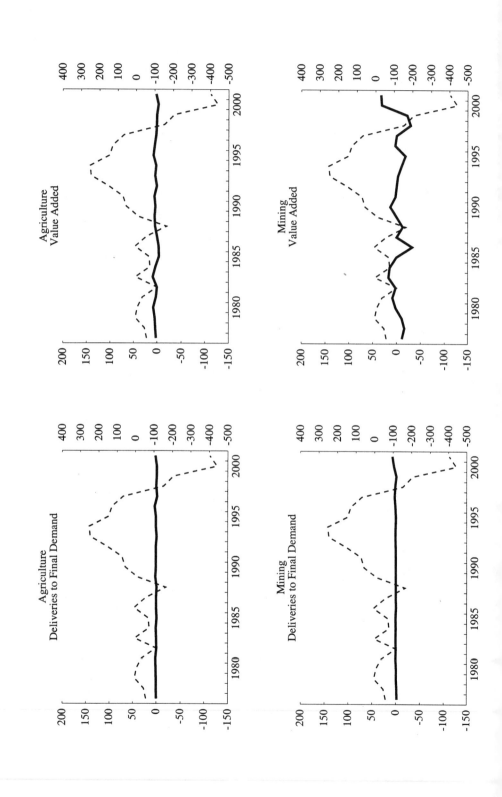

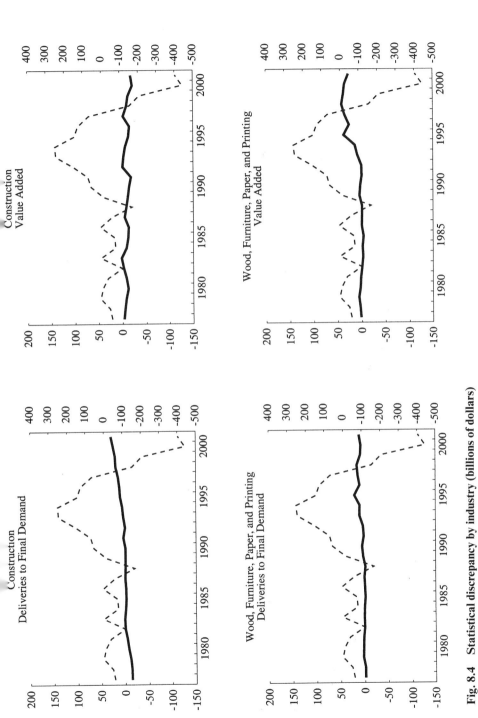

Fig. 8.4 Statistical discrepancy by industry (billions of dollars)

Note: Industry discrepancy is shown by the solid line; aggregate discrepancy is shown by the dashed line.

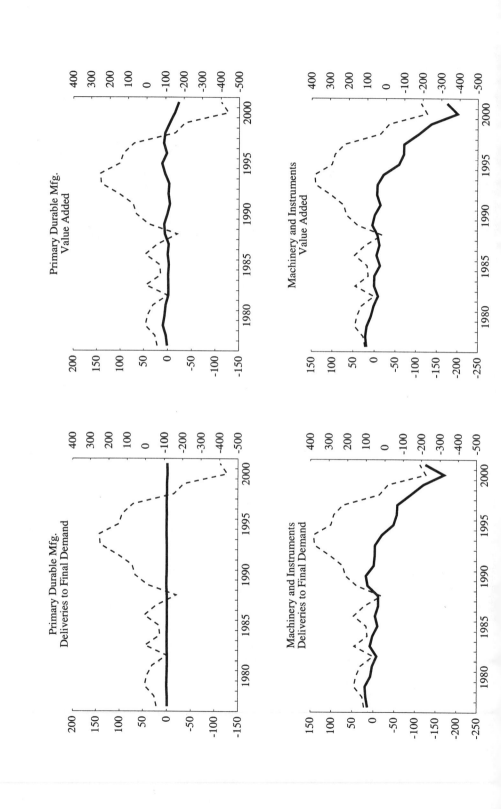

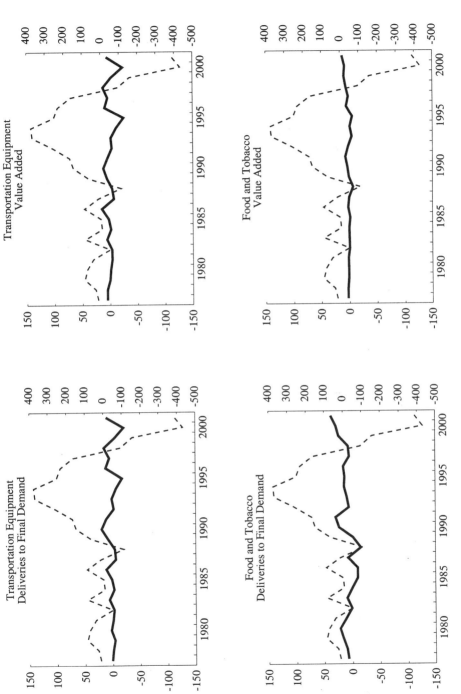

Fig. 8.4   (cont.)

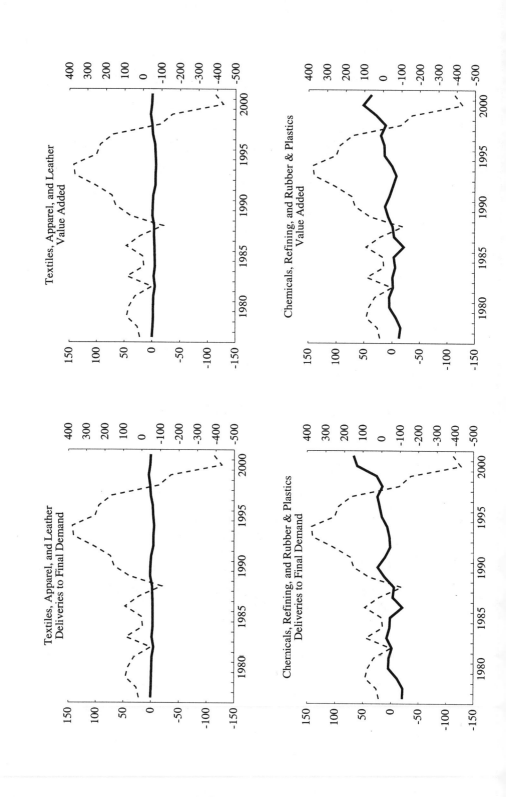

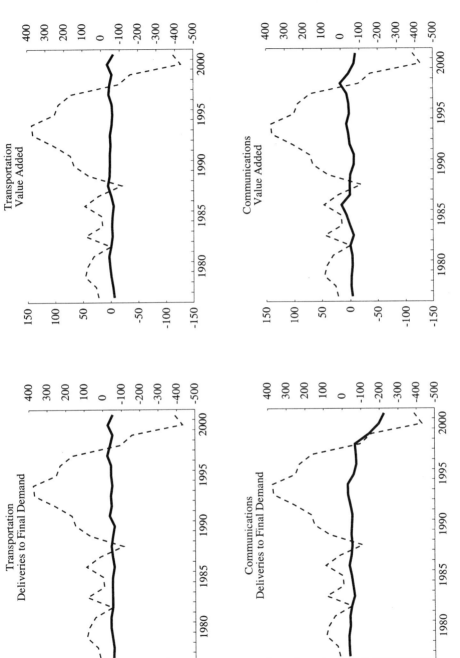

Fig. 8.4 (cont.)

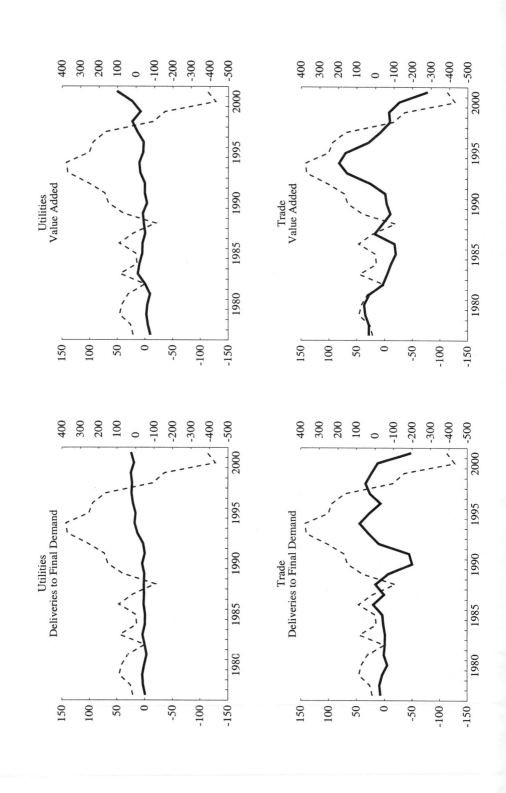

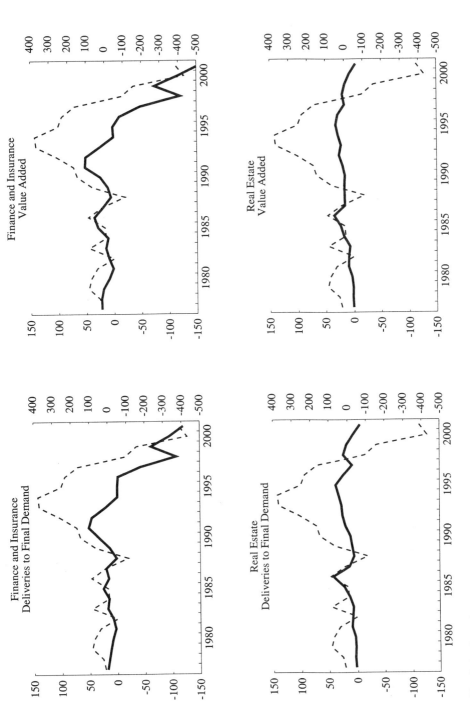

Fig. 8.4 (cont.)

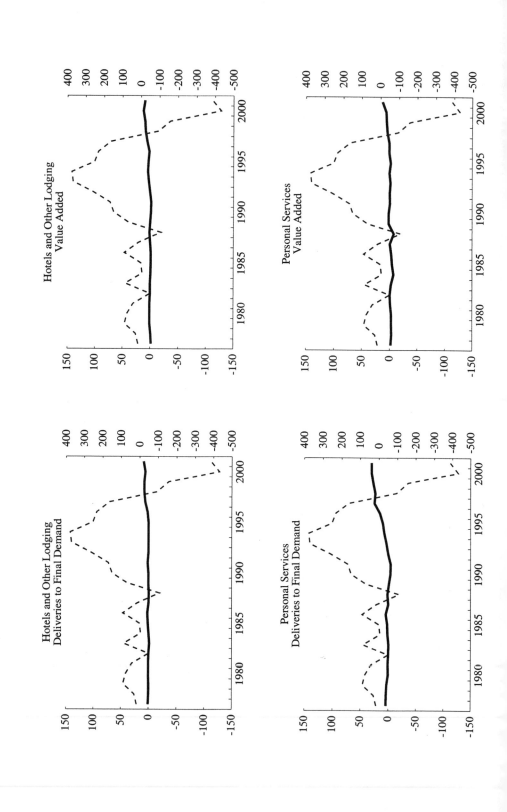

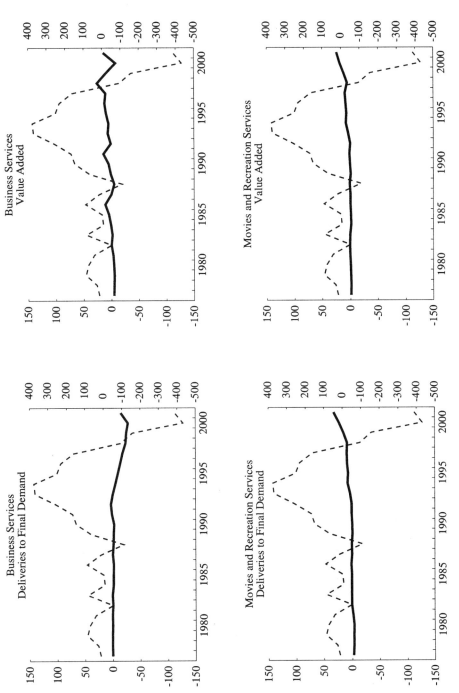

Fig. 8.4 (cont.)

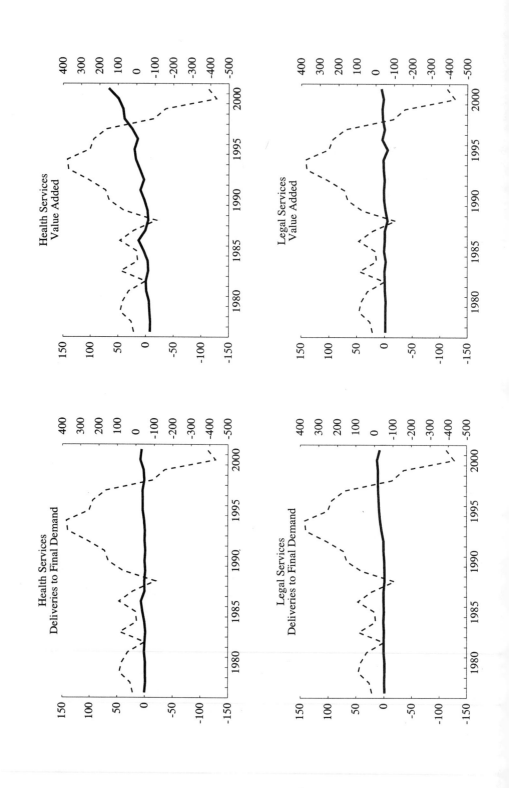

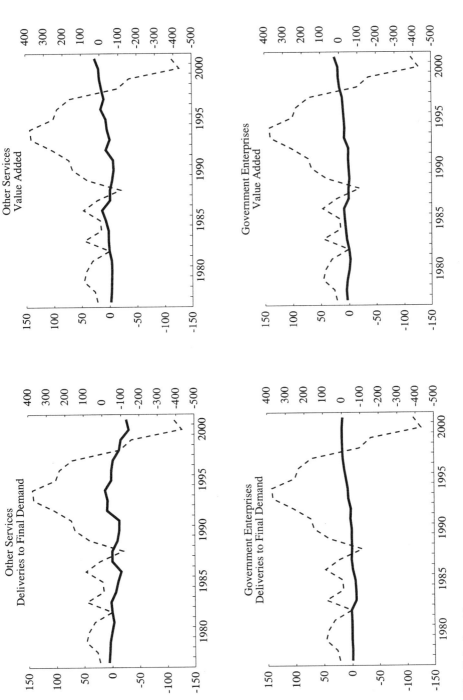

Fig. 8.4   (cont.)

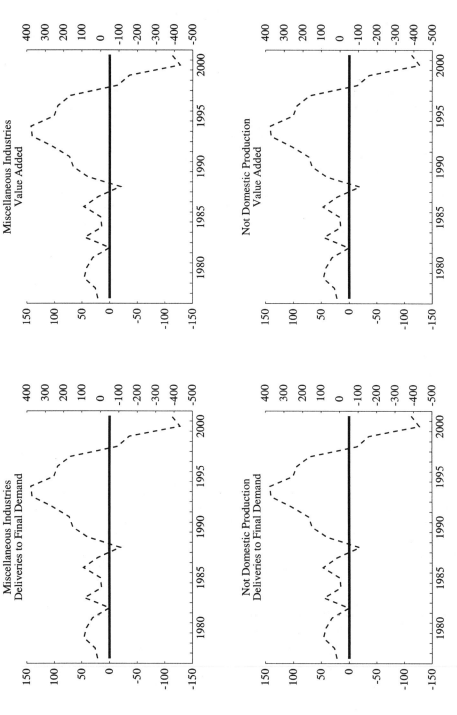

Fig. 8.4 (cont.)

the convention used in the definition of the overall discrepancy, the figure plots the difference in the first measure, which aggregates to GDP, less the second measure, which aggregates to GDI. Each of these differences can be considered statistical discrepancies by industry. The economywide statistical discrepancy is also plotted in all of the panels.

For most industries, the industry discrepancies are small relative to the overall discrepancy. Three industries, however, stand out: Machinery and Instruments, Trade, and Finance and Insurance, where the pattern of deliveries to final demand and value added appear to move with the total discrepancy. Indeed, as shown in figure 8.5, the difference in value added of the combination of these three "problem" industries, moved up in the early 1990s and dropped sharply subsequently, more so than the total discrepancy. The coincidence with the discrepancy in deliveries to final demand is not as sharp. The difference in deliveries to final demand of the problem industries remained flat in the first half of the 1990s, but, like value added, the difference dropped sharply after 1996.

The fact that these three industries—Machinery and Instruments, Trade, and Finance and Insurance—show up as problem industries is not surprising. The Machinery and Instruments industry has evolved significantly over the last twenty-five years as productivity growth in high-tech industries has been substantial. Profit swings have been significant, and the adjustment of industry profits from a firm basis to an establishment basis is probably difficult. The semiconductor industry is particularly challenging as several firms have become "fabless." These firms develop products but contract out their production to overseas fabrication plants. Morgan Stanley estimates that about 15 percent of the industry's worldwide revenue is derived from products outsourced to different firms (Edelstone et al. 2003); much of this figure represents U.S. firms contracting with overseas foundries. Morgan Stanley expects this share to double by 2010.

The difficulties with the Trade industry likely relate to the accounting for margins on products sold. To the extent that these differences represent margins on domestic products, there is a corresponding offset in the difference between the two measures in the domestic industries producing the output. If this is the reason for the discrepancy in the trade sector, then it cannot be a source for the economywide discrepancy. On the other hand, if the differences arise from different margins on imported products, difficulties in tracing these products from imports to deliveries to domestic purchasers could be a source of the overall discrepancy.

Finance and Insurance is clearly an industry fraught with measurement difficulties. A good deal of banking services is not explicitly charged for. Banks offer services like "free checking" to its customers because it can make money by lending the balances that customers leave in their accounts; customers choose to deposit their money in banks instead of lending it at higher rates to take advantage of the convenience of checking. The BEA has

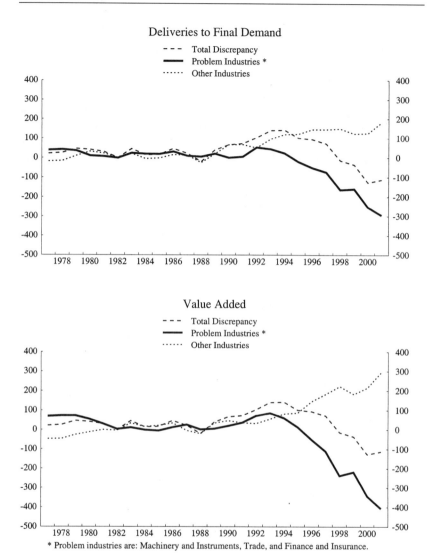

Fig. 8.5 Statistical discrepancy of problem industries (billions of dollars)
Note: Problem industries are Machinery and Instruments, Trade, and Finance and Insurance.

made substantial improvements to its estimation of imputed bank service charges in PCE and government consumption to account for these services (Fixler, Reinsdorf, and Smith 2003); however, the division of these services between final demand and intermediate inputs to business is probably still imprecise. The accounting for insurance services is likewise difficult. The same issue of imputed intermediation services arises in insurance. Moreover, the true value of insurance services is not realized only when claims are paid; there is a continual flow of services. Over the long run, the difference in premiums received less claims paid equals the services provided. How to estimate the evolution of these services over time is a thorny problem; the BEA has also improved its measures of deliveries to final demand of property-casualty insurance in the latest revision (Chen and Fixler 2003). On the income side, adjusting for capital gains has to be more difficult in the Finance and Insurance industry than in any other. Another complication may be the allocation of profits of large firms, such as GE, General Motors, and Ford, with establishments that operate in finance and in manufacturing.

A few other industries show some important differences that are not related to the overall discrepancy. Since 1995, deliveries to final demand of Chemicals, Refining, and Rubber and Plastics controlled to expenditure-side aggregates has risen sharply relative to estimated deliveries controlled to income-side aggregates, while for Communications the opposite is true. Over the same period, the value-added statistical discrepancy in Mining and in Health Services has increased rapidly, helping to offset some of the sharp decline in the statistical discrepancy of the problem industries.

Figure 8.6 plots the difference in the estimates of total deliveries to final demand by major expenditure categories. As is evident in the chart, essentially all of the run-up in the aggregate discrepancy in the first half of the 1990s occurred in PCE; much of the subsequent decline in the aggregate is also reflected in PCE. At the same time, however, the statistical discrepancy in private fixed investment also has trended down because of problems in the Machinery and Instruments industry. In 2001, there is an anomalous jump in the discrepancy in private fixed investment. Most of this is also in the Machinery and Instruments industry, but about $10 billion of this jump comes from Business Services, which includes software makers. As such, the post-Y2K slowdown in high-tech shows up more strongly in the data set controlled to income measures than in the data set controlled to expenditure measures.

8.4   Optimal Combination of the Data

In contrast to the exercise in the previous section, we now consider tuning parameters chosen to allow both value added by industry and final demand data to deviate from their initial estimates. The exercise is to search for a set of tuning parameters that provides an optimal result with respect to metrics based on desirable economic properties. The economic properties that we consider concern

- the equalization of returns to capital,
- the orthogonality of total factor productivity shocks, and
- the stability of the intermediate block.

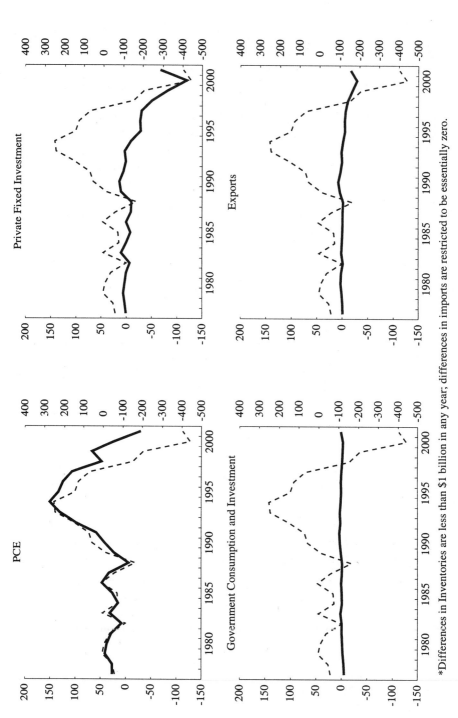

Fig. 8.6 Statistical discrepancy by expenditure category (billions of dollars)

Notes: Expenditure category discrepancy is shown by the solid line; aggregate discrepancy is shown by the dashed line. Differences in inventories are

*Differences in Inventories are less than $1 billion in any year; differences in imports are restricted to be essentially zero.

Our strategy is to estimate a series of consistent, integrated data sets under different assumptions for the tuning parameters $\{\sigma^F, \sigma^V\}$. For the I-O systems integrated under a particular set of tuning parameters, we calculate a statistic to evaluate the performance of the estimates with respect to each of the three economic properties. The I-O system with the statistics closest to their theoretical values is considered optimal.

While the descriptions of the exercises below start by providing some intuitive explanations for the desirable economic properties, they do not derive the desired properties explicitly from first principles. Instead, the exercises are meant to exhibit that methodological choices made to construct economic data from underlying statistics may be grounded in economic theory. Further, the exercises are conducted using readily available data. In the descriptions some suggestions are made for improvements in the empirical application in future research.

8.4.1 Equalization of Returns to Capital

The idea that returns to capital should be equalized across industries is straightforward. Simple arbitrage requires industries with below-average returns to sell their capital to industries with above-average returns to take advantage of the more profitable activity. Of course, if capital cannot be changed instantaneously because of adjustment costs, a putty-clay technology, or the quasi-fixity of capital, then the simple arbitrage argument breaks down. The fact that we do not estimate equalized capital returns under any calculation suggests that something more than data mismeasurement is needed to explain cross-sectional variation in capital returns. Nonetheless, data mismeasurement probably widens the distribution of returns; estimates that minimize the variation are indicative of an optimal combination of the expenditure-side and income-side data with respect to this metric.

To measure the performance of each integrated estimate, we calculate the return to capital for each year. We exclude Government Enterprises, Miscellaneous Industries, and Not Domestic Production from consideration because there is no presumption of profit-maximizing behavior in these industries. For each year we calculate the variance of returns across industries and then average the variance over the 1977–2001 period.

The return to capital is defined as capital income divided by an estimate of the wealth stock. Capital income equals value added less compensation paid to all types of labor less noncapital taxes on production and imports plus government subsidies. These data come from Bartelsman and Beaulieu (2004) as adapted from the GDP-by-industry data. Compensation is adjusted to include an imputation for the labor income of the self-employed; as measured in the NIPAs this income is counted in proprietors' income.[7] Noncapital production taxes are composed mostly of sales taxes.

---

7. The BLS makes the same adjustment in its productivity and cost estimates.

Simply plugging in the data on compensation, taxes, and subsidies assumes that these components of income paid are not mismeasured. The compensation data, at least to employees, is probably better measured than profits, interest, and proprietors' income; nonetheless, the idea that all of the mismeasurement of income resides in capital income is simply a maintained hypothesis that is not pursued further.

Estimates of the wealth stock are calculated based on detailed BEA estimates of investment by industry and by asset type. Wealth stocks were calculated using the appropriate formula (Hulten 1990) that is consistent with the age-efficiency schedule used in Bartelsman and Beaulieu (2004). The BEA investment data are adjusted for each input-output estimate of total investment to the extent that estimated deliveries to private fixed investment differs from the original estimate in the NIPAs on which the detailed BEA data are based.

In future work this exercise could be improved upon in three directions. The most difficult improvement would to provide some indicator of differences across industries in intangible investments that are not captured in the official data. Clearly, high implied rates of return—for example, in the movies and recreational services sector—could reflect returns to intangibles. A proxy for the cross-industry variation in intangible investment could be constructed based on expenditures on R&D and advertising. Next, the risk premium required may vary across industries, reflecting both differences in the time-series variation of returns, and differences in creditworthiness of firms in the industry. A proxy for this could be computed by looking at average bond yields and equity returns of publicly traded firms by industry, and by assessing the share of industry output that is provided by publicly traded firms, other corporations, and the noncorporate sector.

Finally, a third method could improve the rate of return in our exercise, now computed for each industry by dividing capital income with the wealth stock. The implied rate of return that equates the sum across asset types of the user cost times the stock of each asset to the total capital income differs from our crude measure because it takes into account differences across industries and asset types in depreciation rates, expected capital gains, and taxes.

8.4.2   Orthogonality of Innovations to Total Factor Productivity

The idea that variation in GDP is driven by productivity shocks that are common across industries is a central tenant of real business-cycle theories. Opponents to this theory have generally held that the size of the aggregate shock required to generate business cycle variation is implausibly large; candidate sources for such aggregate shocks, such as the weather, appear to amount to little. Simply adding up idiosyncratic shocks leads to an aggregate productivity shock that does not equal exactly zero, but because of the law of large numbers the aggregate is too small unless the sector-specific shocks are large.[8]

Inherent in the counterargument to real business cycle models is that industry total factor productivity (TFP) growth rates should be uncorrelated. With measurement error, however, TFP growth rates can be correlated, even if they are orthogonal in reality. The measurement error can be correlated if it involves an allocation error of a fixed aggregate across industries. If the measurement error affects industries differently and this is somehow related to the business cycle—perhaps due to whether the product is a good or service—mismeasurement can also generate a correlation.

Economists have tested whether there is a common factor to industry productivity shocks (Lebow 1990; Forini and Reichlin 1998). In this exercise we do the opposite: we assume that this common factor is small and look for what combination of data produces a set of TFP growth rates that are as close to orthogonal as possible. To measure the orthogonality of TFP growth rates, we model the TFP growth rates as a linear function of a reduced number of principal components. The sum of the largest handful of standardized eigenvalues is a measure of the percent of the variation explained by the corresponding principal components; the smaller this measure, the more uncorrelated the TFP growth rates are.[9]

Industry TFP measures are calculated by modeling real gross output as a function of capital services, labor hours, and real intermediate inputs, using the usual Divisia formulation. Deflators for gross output come from the BEA's GDP-by-industry data set, as adopted in Bartelsman and Beaulieu (2004). The same gross output deflators are used to generate a deflator for intermediate input usage. Industry data on hours and capital services also come from Bartelsman and Beaulieu, although capital services built from investment flows are adjusted for differences in estimated aggregate deliveries to business fixed investment, as in subsection 8.4.1.

8.4.3   Stability of Intermediate Block

The idea that the coefficients of an I-O table should be stable is common in the literature. After all, the coefficients represent the structure and technology of an economy that evolve slowly due to "technical progress, exhaustion of natural resources, or variation in consumers' tastes"; the stability of the structure of the economy stands in contrast to final demand,

---

8. Horvath (2000) shows that the law of large numbers has to be augmented by the I-O structure of the economy. If the I-O table is sparse, then the law of large numbers applies at a much slower rate than is commonly presumed.

9. The fact that we compare twenty-one series with twenty-four years of data makes the measurement of orthogonality difficult. If the number of years in our data set was large relative to the number of series, we could choose a simpler measure, such as the determinant of the cross-correlation matrix.

which is less stable (Leontief 1953). Immediately, the question arises whether the stability of I-O coefficients should be measured using nominal data or real estimates (see Sawyer 1992 and references therein), and whether the values in the intermediate block should be constant with respect to the gross output of the supplying industries or the gross output of the demanding industries. De Mesnard (2002) uses the relative stability of the cells of the intermediate block divided by supplying industries versus those divided by demanding industries as a measure of whether an industry is "supply oriented" or "demand oriented."

For each estimate of the I-O system, we make four different calculations: two use nominal data, and two use real data, which are calculated by dividing the rows of the I-O table by the gross output deflators from Bartelsman and Beaulieu (2004). When using deflated measures, we ignore the obvious complications of taking ratios of chain-aggregated deflated data (Whelan 2000). Let $\mathbf{D(Y)}$ denote a square matrix with the gross output vector $\mathbf{Y}$ along the main diagonal and zeros otherwise. $\mathbf{I}$ is the intermediate block. Define allocation and technical coefficients thus:

$$\text{Allocation coefficients: } \mathbf{A}_t = \mathbf{D(Y}_t)^{-1} \cdot \mathbf{I}_t$$

$$\text{Technical coefficients: } \mathbf{T}_t = \mathbf{I}_t \cdot \mathbf{D(Y}_t)^{-1}.$$

We then take the standard deviation of each cell of $\mathbf{A}_t$ and $\mathbf{T}_t$ across time and then collapse this matrix into a single statistic by taking a weighted average of the standard deviations of each cell, where the weights equal the average of the absolute value of the cells of $\mathbf{I}$ over time.

8.4.4 Results

Figure 8.7 plots the results of these exercises. On the bottom axis of each panel are the values of $\{\sigma^F, \sigma^V\}$, displayed as σ^F on top of σ^V. Two other integrated I-O systems were calculated, denoted as $\{0, \infty\}$ and $\{\infty, 0\}$. The first system, $\{0, \infty\}$, is calculated by sweeping the vector $\mathbf{Y}\text{-}\mathbf{F}$ across the columns of the initial estimates of $\mathbf{I}$ without any reference to the initial values of $\mathbf{V}$; the value of $\mathbf{V}$ is calculated as a residual according to the value added identity. The second system, $\{\infty, 0\}$, is calculated by sweeping the vector $\mathbf{Y}'\text{-}\mathbf{V}$ across the rows of the initial estimates of $\mathbf{I}$, ignoring the initial values of $\mathbf{F}$; the resulting value of $\mathbf{F}$ is calculated using the gross output identity.[10]

The upper left panel plots the average cross-sectional standard deviation of the return to capital. Except for the estimate $\{0, \infty\}$, this measure of variation in the return to capital lies in the range 37.3 to 43.3. The minimum at 37.38 is at $\{.7, .3\}$, but 37.44 at $\{0, .5\}$ is also fairly close to the minimum. None of the data sets controlled to the GDI data ($\sigma^V = 0$) perform relatively well on this score.

---

10. Using the notation above, where $\mathbf{j}$ is a vector of ones that conforms to ($\bar{\mathbf{I}}$): $\mathbf{I}\{0, \infty\} = \mathbf{D}(\bar{\mathbf{Y}} - \bar{\mathbf{F}}) \cdot \mathbf{D}(\bar{\mathbf{I}}\mathbf{j})^{-1} \cdot \bar{\mathbf{I}}$ and $\mathbf{I}\{\infty, 0\} = \bar{\mathbf{I}} \cdot \mathbf{D}(\bar{\mathbf{I}}'\mathbf{j})^{-1} \cdot \mathbf{D}(\bar{\mathbf{Y}} - \bar{\mathbf{Y}}')$.

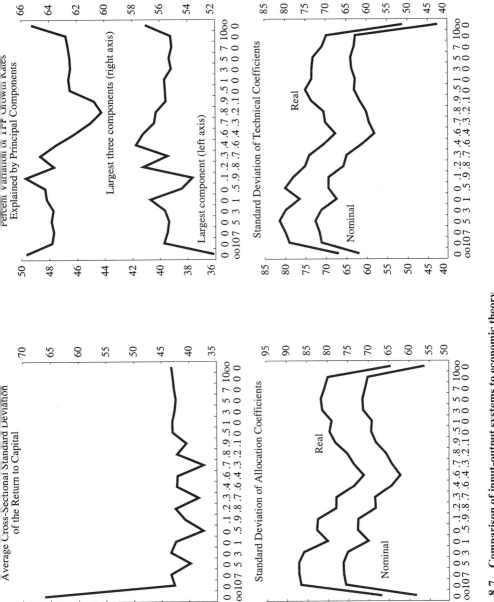

Fig. 8.7   Comparison of input-output systems to economic theory

Notes: Bottom axis shows tuning parameter for final demand (top row) and for value added (bottom row).

The upper right panel plots the percent of the variation of TFP growth rates explained by the largest principal component and by the largest three components. One principal component explains somewhere between 36 and 41 percent of the cross-sectional variation of TFP growth rates, with $\{0, \infty\}$ proving to be the least explainable among the integrated data sets calculated. However, using only one component to measure orthogonality is probably too restrictive, and we also present results using the three largest principal components. On this measure $\{0, \infty\}$ performs the worst, while $\{.8, .2\}$ at 60.25 percent has the least amount of variation explained by three principal components. Raising the number of components to four or five does not change this result, while adding even more components yields statistics that vary little across data sets.

The bottom two panels present results on the stability of the I-O coefficients. The bottom left panel plots the standard deviations of the real and nominal allocation coefficients; the bottom right panel plots the same for the technical coefficients. Excluding the tails, $\{0, \infty\}$ and $\{\infty, 0\}$, the data set with the most stable coefficients is $\{.6, .4\}$, with other data sets that roughly evenly mix the expenditure and income-side data also performing relatively well. The fact that the $\{0, \infty\}$ and $\{\infty, 0\}$ estimates produce the least variation in the standard deviation of real technical coefficients is essentially by construction because the calculation of the initial values of $\mathbf{I}$ are developed under the assumption that the real technical coefficients are constant. The stability of the nominal technical coefficients and the nominal and real allocation coefficients also benefit by this construction.

Taking the results together, the differences across data sets are not large, and some of the results do not smoothly vary when the data sets are ordered by tuning parameters. Nonetheless, they appear to point in a consistent direction: data sets constructed by mixing the information from the expenditure side and income side without controlling the aggregate to equal GDP or GDI yields estimates that perform well on all three criteria. The results also seem to favor a small bias towards the income-side data, a result that echoes Weale (1992).

8.5   Conclusion

In this chapter we employ industry estimates of deliveries to final demand and value added to investigate possible sources of the statistical discrepancy. We find that the expenditure-side data and the income-side data imply two different paths for the production of goods and services from the Machinery and Instruments, Trade, and Finance and Insurance industries that appear to be related to the statistical discrepancy. Important for the measurement of recent movements in productivity, there is an anomalous shortfall in 2001 in the change in private fixed investment implied from the income-side data relative to that measured from the expenditure-side data, due to mismeasurement in sectors that include the high-tech industries. At a minimum, it might be useful to push on the source data for these industries to see if some improvement in data collection could help reconcile these discrepancies.

Our analysis also uncovered some other possible discrepancies that warrant some attention, even if they are not consistently related to the aggregate discrepancy. There are some important differences in our two sets of estimates of deliveries to final demand in the Chemicals, Refining, and Rubber and Plastics industry and in the Communications industry. There are also some significant differences in the estimates of value added in the Mining and Health Services industries.

Viewed differently, most of the statistical discrepancy shows up in PCE, but problems in the Machinery and Instruments industry also affect the statistical discrepancy in private fixed investment.

As a necessary step of this analysis we produced a consistent, integrated set of estimates of industry gross output, deliveries to final demand, intermediates used, and value added. We also produced a series of estimates and offered some means to judge how they should be combined. Some combination of the expenditure-side and income-side data should be employed, perhaps weighted more to the GDI data than to the GDP data.

We could not have written this paper if the BEA had not produced the wealth and the variety of the data that it does. Besides all of the information provided in the NIPAs, the GDP-by-industry data, and the published I-O tables, the importance of various estimates that the BEA makes available on its web site for researchers, such as the tables on underlying expenditure detail and the estimates of investment by industry and by asset type should not be overlooked. Of course, there would be no point in writing this paper if the BEA did not publish two estimates of domestic product; some countries only produce one estimate by balancing the information from expenditure-side and income-side data. If the BEA published only one estimate of domestic product, then only the BEA could have done the forensic analysis in this paper.

Even though "the man with two watches is never quite sure what time it is," the man with one watch may not realize that his watch has slowed or even stopped. An English version of this proverb that we have seen starts with "It's possible to own too much . . ."; as economists we know this cannot be true—especially with respect to data. Policymakers found important clues in the income-side measures of the transition of the economy when the production of and investment in high-tech goods pushed the growth rate of potential GDP higher (Jorgenson and Stiroh 2000).

As part of its strategic plan, the BEA has now published integrated value added I-O accounts with GDP-by-industry accounts. These integrated data add to GDP (Lawson et al., chap. 6 in this volume); they supplant the former GDP-by-industry data that add to GDI. While a published, consistent, integrated data set that relates gross output, value added, and deliveries to final demand by industry is certainly useful, it comes at a cost. The new GDP-by-industry data are inconsistent with the prior data because the data now aggregate to GDP instead of GDI.

It is easy to recommend that others find resources in their budgets to provide additional data. Fortunately, the BEA already publishes a lot of the data that would be needed to develop a set of industry estimates of value added that add to GDI. In section 6 of the NIPAs—Income and Employment by Industry—the BEA provides data on the various components of income paid by industry. As discussed earlier, the problem with using these data directly is that some of the data are organized on a firm basis, instead of an establishment basis. However, if the BEA were to make available on its web site the factors that it uses to convert the data on a firm basis to an establishment basis—something the BEA will have to develop in-house anyway in order to prepare its integrated accounts—the research community could develop a second, consistent data set in real time that could be used to monitor and investigate future data discrepancies.

Appendix

Table 8A.1

Industry	SIC 87	Description
Agriculture	01–09	Farms, agricultural services, forestry, fishing, hunting, and trapping
Mining	10–14	Metal mining, coal mining, oil and gas extraction, and mineral mining
Construction	15–17	Construction
Wood, furniture, paper, and printing	24–27	Manufacturers of lumber and wood, furniture, paper, and printing
Primary durable manufacturing	32–34	Stone, clay and glass, primary metal, and fabricated metal manufacturing
Machinery and instruments	35–36, 38–39	Machinery, electrical machinery, instruments, and miscellaneous manufacturing. This industry includes computers, communications equipment, and semiconductors.
Transportation equipment	37	Motor vehicles and parts, aircraft and parts, and other transportation equipment
Food and tobacco	20–21	Food and beverages and tobacco manufacturing
Textiles, apparel, and leather	22–23, 31	Textiles, apparel, and leather manufacturing
Chemicals, refining, and rubber and plastics	28–30	Chemicals, petroleum refining, and rubber and plastics manufacturing
Transportation	40–42, 44–47	Trucking, water, rail, and air transport, warehousing, pipelines (except natural gas), and transportation services
Communications	48	Telephone and telegraph, radio and television, and other communications services
Utilities	49pt.	Electrical, natural gas, and water and sanitary services utilities. It excludes government enterprises such as TVA and Bonneville.
Trade	50–59	Wholesale and retail trade
Finance and insurance	60–64, 67	Depository and nondepository institutions, securities dealers and brokers, insurance carriers and agents, and holding companies
Real estate	65	Real estate, excluding imputations for owner-occupied housing and the rental value of nonprofits' capital[a]
Hotels and other lodging	70	Hotels and other lodging
Personal services	72, 75–76	Personal services, automotive repair services and parking, and miscellaneous repair services
Business services	73	Business services, including software and data processing
Movies and recreation services	78–79	Motion pictures, and amusement and recreation services
Health services	80	Health services
Legal services	81	Legal services
Other services	82–84, 86–87, 89	Social services, museums, membership organizations, engineering, accounting, research and management services, and miscellaneous services
Government enterprises	43, 49pt, other	Federal, state, and local government enterprises, including the postal service, TVA, and Bonneville Power
Miscellaneous industries	88, other	Private households, owner-occupied housing, and general government
Not domestic production	—	Imports, used and secondhand goods, and scrap

[a]The rental value of nonprofits' capital equipment and structures was distributed to other industries according to estimates of nonprofit activity in those industries.

References

Bacharach, Michael. 1970. *Biproportional matrices and input-output change.* Cambridge, UK: Cambridge University Press.

Baker, Dean. 1998. The new economy does not lurk in the statistical discrepancy. Challenge 41 (4): 5–13.

Bartelsman, Eric J., and J. Joseph Beaulieu. 2003. Techniques to reconcile data with linear constraints. Washington, DC: Board of Governors of the Federal Reserve System. Mimeograph, January.

———. 2004. A consistent accounting of U.S. productivity growth. FEDS Working Paper no. 2004-55. Washington, DC: Board of Governors of the Federal Reserve System, October.

Bishop, Y. M., S. E. Fienberg, and P. W. Holland. 1975. *Discrete multivariate analysis: Theory and practice.* Cambridge, MA: MIT Press.

Bosworth, Barry P., and Jack E. Triplett. 2003. Services productivity in the United States: Griliches' services volume revisited. Washington, DC: The Brookings Institution. Mimeograph, September. Available at http://www.brookings.org/views/papers/bosworth/20030919.htm.

Chen, Baoline, and Dennis J. Fixler. 2003. Measuring the services of property-casualty insurance in the NIPAs: Changes in concepts and methods. *Survey of Current Business* 83 (10): 10–25.

Congressional Budget Office (CBO). 2003. CBO's economic forecasting record: An evaluation of the economic forecasts CBO made from January 1976 through January 2001. Available at http://www.cbo.gov/showdoc.cfm?index=4639&sequence=0.

Council of Economic Advisers. 1997. Economic report of the president. Washington, DC: Government Printing Office.

De Mesnard, Louis. 2002. Forecast output coincidence and biproportion: Two criteria to determine the orientation of an economy; Comparison for France (1980–1997). *Applied Economics* 34:2085–91.

Dean, Edwin R., Michael J. Harper, and Phyllis F. Otto. 1995. Improvements to the quarterly productivity measures. *Monthly Labor Review* 118 (10): 27–32.

Edelstone, Marc, Louis Gerhardy, Harlan Sur, Steven Pelayo, and Jay Iyer. 2003. Transition to 300-mm wafers should drive secular changes. Equity research. New York: Morgan Stanley, December.

Fixler, Dennis J., Marshall B. Reinsdorf, and George M. Smith. 2003. Measuring the services of commercial banks in the NIPAs: Changes in concepts and methods. *Survey of Current Business* 83 (9): 33–44.

Forini, Mario, and Lucrezia Reichlin. 1998. Let's get real: A factor analytic approach to disaggregated business cycle dynamics. *Review of Economic Studies* 65 (3): 453–73.

Greenspan, Alan. 2004. Risk and uncertainty in monetary policy. Remarks at the meeting of the American Economic Association. 3 January, San Diego, California.

Günlük-Şenesen, G., and J. M. Bates. 1988. Some experiments with methods of adjusting unbalanced data matrices. *Journal of the Royal Statistical Society* Series A (*Statistics in Society*) 151 (3): 473–90.

Horvath, Michael. 2000. Sectoral shocks and aggregate fluctuations. *Journal of Monetary Economics* 45:69–106.

Hulten, Charles R. 1990. The measurement of capital. In *Fifty years of economic measurement studies in income and wealth,* ed. Ernst R. Berndt and Jack E. Triplett, 119–52. Chicago: University of Chicago Press.

Jorgenson, Dale W., and Kevin J. Stiroh. 2000. Raising the speed limit: U.S. economic growth in the information age. *Brookings Papers on Economic Activity,* Issue no. 1:125–211.

Klein, L. R., and J. Makino. 2000. Economic interpretations of the statistical discrepancy. *Journal of Economic and Social Measurement* 26 (1): 11–29.

Lebow, David E. 1990. The covariability of productivity shocks across industries. Board of Governors of the Federal Reserve System, Economic Activity Section, Working Paper no. 104. Washington, DC: Federal Reserve.

Leontief, Wassily. 1953. *Studies in the structure of the American economy: Theoretical and empirical explorations in input-output analysis.* New York: Oxford University Press.

Moulton, Brent R. 2000. Getting the 21st century right: What's underway? *American Economic Review: Papers and Proceedings* 90 (2): 253–58.

Nordhaus, William D. 2000. New data and output concepts for understanding productivity trends. Cowles Foundation Discussion Paper no. 1286. New Haven, CT: Yale University, November. Available at http://cowles.econ.yale.edu/P/ab/a12/a1286.htm

Parker, Robert P., and Eugene P. Seskin. 1997. The statistical discrepancy. *Survey of Current Business* 77 (8): 19.

Sawyer, John A. 1992. Forecasting with input-output matrices: Are the coefficients stationary? *Economic Systems Research* 4 (4): 325–48.

Schneider, M. H., and S. A. Zenios. 1990. A comparative study of algorithms for matrix balancing. *Operations Research* 38:439–55.

Stone, Richard, D. G. Champernowne, and J. E. Meade. 1942. The precision of national income estimates. *Review of Economic Studies* 9 (2): 111–25.

U.S. Bureau of Economic Analysis. 2001. A guide to the NIPAs. Washington, DC: Bureau of Economic Analysis, Department of Commerce. Available at http://www.bea.doc.gov/bea/an/nipaguid.htm

Weale, Martin. 1992. Estimation of data measured with error and subject to linear restrictions. *Journal of Applied Econometrics* 7 (2): 167–74.

Whelan, Karl. 2000. A guide to the use of chain aggregated NIPA data. FEDS Working Paper no. 2000-35. Washington, DC: Board of Governors of the Federal Reserve System, June.

Yuskavage, Robert E., and Erich H. Strassner. 2003. Gross domestic product by industry for 2002. *Survey of Current Business* 83 (5): 7–14.

An Integrated BEA/BLS Production Account
A First Step and Theoretical Considerations

Barbara M. Fraumeni, Michael J. Harper,
Susan G. Powers, and Robert E. Yuskavage

9.1 Introduction

This paper takes the first steps toward shedding light on similarities and differences between output measures produced by the Bureau of Economic Analysis (BEA) and the Bureau of Labor Statistics (BLS). The BEA, the BLS, and the Census Bureau (the Census) work together as partners in the U.S. statistical system to provide a complete picture of U.S. economic activity. The Census collects data on nominal output measures such as sales, shipments, inventories, and investment. The BLS collects data on prices, employment, wages and salaries, and other compensation components. The BEA uses the data collected by the BLS, the Census, and others to construct nominal and real output measures for the economy as a whole (gross domestic product [GDP]), by sector, by industry, and by state, as well as to construct measures of investment, capital stock and income components. The BLS uses its own data, as well as data provided by the BEA, the Census, and others, to estimate productivity.

The BLS productivity statistics, the BEA National Income and Product Accounts (NIPAs), and the BEA industry accounts have evolved over time to meet particular needs. The BLS primarily seeks to achieve maximum reliability in its various measures of productivity and can focus on those in-

Barbara M. Fraumeni was the chief economist of the Bureau of Economic Analysis (BEA) at the time that this chapter was written and is presently professor and chair of the PhD program in public policy at the Muskie School of Public Service, University of Southern Maine. Michael J. Harper is chief of the Division of Productivity Research and Program Development of the Bureau of Labor Statistics (BLS), Susan G. Powers is a research economist at the BLS, and Robert E. Yuskavage is a senior economist at the BEA. The views expressed in this paper are those of the authors and do not necessarily reflect the policies of the BEA or of the BLS or the views of other staff members.

dustries for which measures are quite robust. The BEA strives to provide complete and consistent coverage of the entire economy in the NIPAs. Each agency thus publishes a variety of measures, and each follows procedures that balance a variety of customer requirements. These include the need for timely release of detailed information, for long historical time series, to use the best data sources, and to use assumptions that are consistent with economic theory. In addition, each agency's programs have unique needs, such as the need for national accounting measures that aggregate consistently and the need for productivity statistics that match the coverage of input and output data.

The growth and improvement in each agency's programs, coupled with differences in purpose, have led to cases of overlapping and sometimes different measures for the same industry or sector, both between and within the BEA and BLS.[1] In theory, consistency is possible, but source data fall far short of what would be required. This deficiency is bridged by different assumptions in different measurement programs, leading to inconsistencies. While the agencies have worked hard to avoid duplicative efforts and differences in measures, the competing customer requirements have tended to frustrate efforts to eradicate differences. The differing purposes sometimes lead to differences in definition (such as value added or gross output), coverage (government is omitted from featured aggregate productivity data because output is based on inputs), or methodology (index number formulas used in each program have evolved progressively but sporadically[2]). Differences also arise from choices among alternative and inconsistent sources of underlying data, especially at detailed industry lev-

---

1. Differences between the BEA and BLS data have led some researchers to construct their own sets of measures, particularly for studying the "new economy" of the late 1990s. For example, Jorgenson (2003) uses a hybrid of BEA and BLS data to construct estimates of productivity. Results of these studies have sometimes differed significantly, depending partly on data sources and the level of detail provided, leading to differing interpretations of the sources of productivity growth. This is even true at the business-sector level. Since 1996, following consultation with the BEA, the BLS has used the product side of the NIPAs rather than the income side for measuring business and nonfarm business-sector productivity. Use of income instead of product-side measures can lead to a different attribution of productivity to industries, as Nordhaus (2002) showed. Triplett and Bosworth have documented how productivity estimates may differ significantly for broad sectors (Triplett and Bosworth 2004) and for individual industries (Bosworth 2003a, 2003b) depending upon whether BEA or BLS data are used. These differences can hinder integrated analysis of the sources of productivity growth, and leave researchers to either choose one set of estimates over the other, or to develop their own estimates.

2. In 1983, the BLS introduced use of a superlative index formula, the Tornqvist index to aggregate components of its multifactor productivity accounts. This choice was made because analysts of production functions and productivity typically used that measure. In 1996, the BEA introduced a Fisher index-number formula to aggregate components of the NIPAs. This choice was made because Fisher price and quantity indexes consistently decompose the nominal change in GDP. Research has consistently shown that the choice between these two superlative price and quantity index formulations makes little difference in practice. We do not discuss this difference further in this chapter.

els. Until the recent NIPA comprehensive revision, moreover, the BEA and BLS defined the business sector differently to suit their particular needs.

The goal of this chapter is to make progress toward improving the accuracy and usefulness of both the BEA and BLS data by taking advantage of the best features of both data sets and to increase the consistency and integration of these data sets. Ultimate success will require continuing efforts aimed at identifying differences, understanding their nature, documenting them, and eliminating them where possible. This goal is part of a broader objective of the BEA to better integrate data sets. For example, the Lawson et al. chapter and the Teplin et al. chapter (chaps. 6 and 11, respectively, in this volume) are other contributions toward this objective.

The chapter begins in section 9.2 by examining the theoretical foundation for a production account that can be used to analyze productivity. It goes on to present an illustrative production account at the major sector level, detailing the relationship between GDP and the major sector estimates to help clarify how the BEA and BLS data relate to each other. While the 1993 System of National Accounts (SNA) includes a production account in its recommendations for economic accounts, it is not one that can be used to construct multifactor productivity (MFP) estimates, primarily because of the absence of a capital services measure.[3] A production account suitable for MFP analysis, however, was constructed by Jorgenson, Gollop, and Fraumeni (1987; hereafter JGF), and it provides the framework for the account presented here.

Next, section 9.3 uses the production account framework to reveal the relationship between GDP and the major-sector estimates. Aggregate production account tables are presented that illustrate how existing BEA and BLS accounts could be better harmonized, thereby providing a crosswalk between the two that could facilitate comprehensive, integrated analysis of growth and productivity. The illustrative set of integrated production accounts, which are presented in nominal and real (1996) dollars, are based on aggregate BEA and BLS data and detailed data underlying the BLS estimates of major-sector MFP. Estimates for private business and for private nonfarm business are the published BLS series.

After presenting the illustrative aggregate integrated production account, in section 9.4 the chapter begins the task of developing a crosswalk between BEA and BLS data by documenting the types of industry output measures produced by each agency, describing the major source data and conceptual and methodological differences, and comparing output measures for both broad and detailed industries. All analysis is undertaken using information that was available in early 2003 before the NIPA comprehensive revision, and that was classified according to the Standard Industrial Classification (SIC) system. Documentation of the existing differ-

3. See Hulten (1995).

ences is the most challenging task undertaken. This analysis does not fully reconcile the differences, but it is a first step toward explaining differences in output measures and in productivity estimates constructed from BEA and BLS data. The final section summarizes and looks to possible future efforts.

9.2   A General Formulation of Production Accounts

Production accounts that are suitable for studies of economic growth, productivity, and structural change match outputs with the inputs used to produce them, typically at both the aggregate and the industry levels and frequently for large-sector subaggregates. These accounts must consist of both nominal and real accounts. Aggregation over the cells of the real account is performed using index number formulas with weights from the nominal account. The general formulation, which is presented in matrix form, is an elaboration and refinement of the type of production account proposed by JGF. It is general enough to examine issues related to the scope of the accounts, such as which inputs and outputs to exclude in moving from the aggregate level to a large-sector subaggregate. None of the production accounts that underlie the BLS productivity measures use this general formulation because the large database needed to implement it is unavailable and constructing that database would require many assumptions and additional resources. Accordingly, the following discussion indicates where current practice significantly departs from the general formulation.

9.2.1   The Nominal Production Account

Valuing Intermediate Input: Flows of Commodities between Industries

Assume that there are m "commodities" made in an economy or a large sector of an economy. Each "commodity" represents some category of goods or service that is sold for some value. In this model, the categories would ideally be "fine enough" that each represents a homogeneous commodity. Of course, due to data limitations, real-world accounts must settle for "as fine as possible." Suppose further that there are n industries and that each industry uses labor, capital, and purchased commodities (both domestically and foreign produced) to create one or more commodities of its own. Each establishment is assumed to be classified to an industry by its "primary" product—the commodity accounting for the largest share of its sales. Other commodities produced by establishments in an industry are considered "secondary" products. Let

$VM_{i,j}$ = the value of the ith commodity made by the jth industry, and

$VU_{i,k}$ = the value of the ith domestically produced commodity used by the kth industry.

In the context of the total economy, the matrix **VU** is the core of an input-output "use" table. Each row describes the disposition of a commodity type, while each column describes commodities used by an industry. The matrix **VM** corresponds to a complete "make" table. In the United States, benchmark "make and use" tables are created once every five years by the BEA, when data from the economic censuses are collected. In these years, fairly extensive data are collected on the values of commodities by type that are made and used by each establishment, particularly in manufacturing. These tables, supplemented with other data, are used by the BEA to benchmark GDP and other important series.

In this general formulation, a key matrix of the nominal production account, which is similar to the "use" table but has a separate row for each commodity produced by each given industry, is

$VN_{i,j,k}$ = value of the ith type of commodity made by the jth industry and used by the kth industry.

VN is depicted in figure 9.1. A row is reserved for each i, j combination that is nonzero at any point in time. In the example shown the first industry ($j = 1$) produces two commodities: commodities 1 ($i = 1$) and 2 ($i = 2$), and the second industry ($j = 2$) produces three commodities: commodities 2 ($i = 2$), 4 ($i = 4$), and 5 ($i = 5$). **VN** records the values of the commodities used by each industry both by the industry source and by the type of commodity. **VN** resembles a "use" table, but contains the additional information on secondary products needed to rearrange the rows and to group inputs by producing industry instead of by commodity.[4] While doing that, **VN** also represents all of the information on the commodity mix of inputs obtained from each industry, which ideally would be available for creating the real production account in order to define deflation of industry inputs in terms of commodity price indexes.[5]

Like the use table, the new table, **VN**, excludes capital goods, produced in one industry and sold to a second industry, as inputs to the second. As in national accounting, production accounts treat capital goods as final outputs of the economy that enter the "capital stock" and provide input "services" in subsequent periods.

VN is a matrix that allows the accounting structure to be readily adapted to construction of different aggregate sectors, such as the "total economy" or the "private business" sector (section 9.2.3). **VN** is a matrix of intrasec-

4. Currently the type of data needed to track commodities in this kind of detail is not available. However, the BEA has developed alternative tables showing commodities used by each industry, on the one hand, and the industry origins of commodities on the other. The assumptions involved in moving secondary products to get from one type of table to the other are explored by Guo, Lawson, and Planting (2002).

5. The detailed information to measure each cell of **VN** is not available, but existing BEA and BLS real industry output measures make assumptions that effectively estimate this information. For example, the single price index available for a commodity group is applied to all commodities of that type, regardless of industry source.

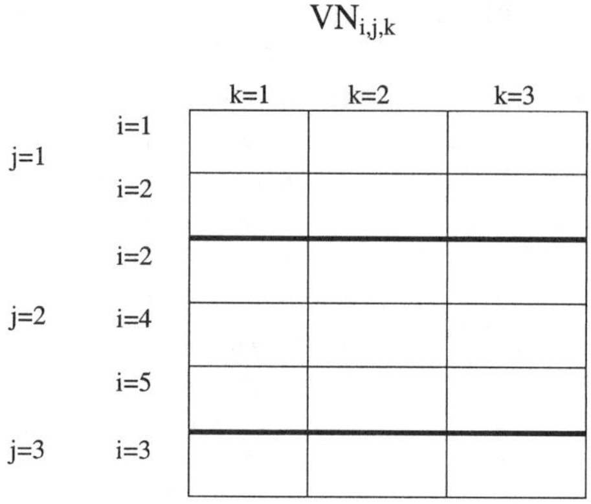

$$VN_{i,j,k}$$

Fig. 9.1   Matrix of flows of intermediate inputs between industries

Note: This is a schematic of the matrix (**VN**) of intrasectoral sales (from *j* to *k*) of commodities (*i*).

toral transactions; that is, it includes only transactions in intermediate inputs that are traded among industries in the sector being analyzed. For example, purchases from businesses by governments or nonprofit institutions, which are intrasectoral transactions for the total economy, would move outside of **VN** when private business is analyzed.

Value of Sector Output and Costs of Factor Input

Assume that each commodity made is sold either to another industry within the sector for use as an intermediate input or is sold outside of the sector, including to industries and sectors outside the sector and to final uses such as personal consumption or investment. As with a "use" table, we can append a column, **VS**, just to the right of **VN** (see figure 9.2), indicating the value of outputs that are sold outside of the sector being analyzed:

$VS_{i,j}$ = value of sales outside the sector of the *i*th commodity made in the *j*th industry.

In addition, "sectoral output" will be defined as the total output sold outside of the sector being analyzed,[6] and defined as $VS_T = \sum_{i=1}^{m} \sum_{j=1}^{n} VS_{i,j}$, where *m* is the number of commodities and *n* is the number of industries. (VS_T is not depicted in figure 9.2, but it would be the sum of all cells of $VS_{i,j}$.) The sum of $VN_{i,j,k}$ and $VS_{i,j}$ is depicted in figure 9.2 as a vector of length $i \times j$ totaling the value of each commodity type made by each industry:

6. Section 9.4 of this chapter will present industry "gross output" $VY_{i,j}^G$ and "sectoral output" $VY_{i,j}^S$ measures. The BEA and BLS refer to output as gross output and sectoral output, respectively, to distinguish these constructs from value added, a convention adopted in this chapter. Gross output includes intrasectoral sales; sectoral output excludes intrasectoral sales.

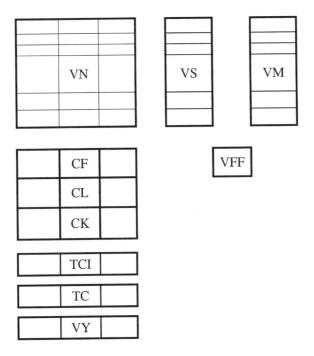

Fig. 9.2   The nominal production account

$$\sum_{k=1}^{n} \mathbf{VN}_{i,j,k} + \mathbf{VS}_{i,j} = \mathbf{VM}_{i,j}.$$

This matrix, $\mathbf{VM}_{i,j}$, corresponds to the total industry output column of a typical make table, with more detail added as there is a separate entry for how much of each commodity is made in each industry.

This matrix is appended to the far right of figure 9.2. Next, the total value of industry output, $\mathbf{VY}_j$, for each industry, j, is the total value of all of the commodities it makes:

$$\mathbf{VY}_j = \sum_{i=1}^{m} \mathbf{VM}_{i,j} = \sum_{i=1}^{m}\left(\sum_{k=1}^{n} \mathbf{VN}_{i,j,k} + \mathbf{VS}_{i,j}\right).$$

Note that $\mathbf{VY}$ is grouped by making industry, j, not by using industry, k. The vector $\mathbf{VY}$ is too small to be appended as a column. However, it does have the right dimension to be appended as a row. It is placed at the far bottom, below $\mathbf{VN}$, where its usefulness will become apparent shortly.

In figure 9.2 rows are appended immediately below the intrasectoral transactions table, $\mathbf{VN}$, indicating costs of primary factors used by industry k:[7]

---

7. In table 9.1 these are called labor compensation and costs of capital services, respectively.

$\mathbf{CL}_k$ = labor costs of the kth industry

$\mathbf{CK}_k$ = capital costs of the kth industry.

Capital costs, $\mathbf{CK}$, are the implicit costs of using the capital stock in the current period, and not the costs for purchasing capital goods; that is, they are not investments. Capital stock itself is not represented in this matrix model. Industries add to the capital stock (investments, a part of final uses) and derive services from the existing capital stock. Investment as a delivery to outside of the sector is part of $\mathbf{VS}$, and capital input rentals are treated as coming from outside of the sector.[8]

Next we define the total cost of all inputs, $\mathbf{TCI}_k$, to include the intrasectoral purchases of materials and services and also the expenses for the "primary" factors of capital and labor,

$$\mathbf{TCI}_k = \sum_{i=1}^{m} \sum_{j=1}^{n} \mathbf{VN}_{i,j,k} + \mathbf{CL}_k + \mathbf{CK}_k.$$

Then $\mathbf{TCI}$ is appended to $\mathbf{VN}$ as a row, just below $\mathbf{CL}$ and $\mathbf{CK}$, but just above the final row, $\mathbf{VY}$ (see figure 9.2). Factor costs include some indirect business taxes assigned to a specific factor cost, such as business property taxes and business motor vehicle licenses. Total costs, $\mathbf{TC}_k$, is defined to include any other indirect business taxes less subsidies, $\mathbf{SUB}_k$, less subsidies that are not assigned to any specific factor of production, $\mathbf{OIBT}_k$; that is,

$$\mathbf{TC}_k = \mathbf{TCI}_k + -(\mathbf{SUB}_k - \mathbf{OIBT}_k).$$

A fundamental of cost accounting is that profits are the difference between revenues and costs. Similarly, national accounts fully account for revenues in terms of costs and profits. The nominal production account will adopt this treatment, imposing an identity between the value of each industry k's output, $\mathbf{VY}_k$, and total costs, $\mathbf{TC}_k$. In practice, the assumption is imposed either by identifying capital costs with "residual property income":

$$\mathbf{CK}_k = \mathbf{VY}_k - \mathbf{CL}_k - \sum_{i=1}^{m} \sum_{j=1}^{n} \mathbf{VN}_{i,j,k} - \mathbf{OIBT}_k + \mathbf{SUB}_k,$$

or by measuring the value of output in terms of total factor outlays and indirect taxes:

$$\mathbf{VY}_k = \mathbf{CK}_k + \mathbf{CL}_k + \sum_{i=1}^{m} \sum_{j=1}^{n} \mathbf{VN}_{i,j,k} + \mathbf{OIBT}_k - \mathbf{SUB}_k.$$

8. A firm usually owns its own capital, in which case capital services are treated as flowing in from outside the sector (from the capital stock) similar to labor services. For cases where a firm in one industry leases an asset to another firm with an operating lease, capital services are treated as an input ($\mathbf{CK}$) to the leasing industry and then are recorded in $\mathbf{VN}$ or $\mathbf{VS}$ as a flow of intermediate services from the leasing industry to the using industry. The BEA classifies an asset as being in the possession of the lessee (user) for capital leases and in the possession of the lessor for operating leases.

The residual property income method is used by national accountants for industries that sell products in markets, allowing **VY** to be measured in terms of revenues. This method was introduced into productivity work by Jorgenson and Griliches (1967; hereafter JG), who identified this residual measure of capital costs with the implicit rents of capital. In long-run competitive equilibrium, firms presumably earn a fair return to investments. Under these conditions, profits can be regarded as part of the cost of capital, along with interest, depreciation, and taxes.

Output is valued in terms of factor costs by national accountants for industries and sectors, such as governments and nonprofit institutions, that do not sell in markets. This requires an explicit estimate of capital costs. The accounting procedures prescribed in the 1993 System of National Accounts (United Nations et al. 1993; hereafter SNA93) for government "product" reflect only labor costs, omitting capital costs. The U.S. BEA and others in the international community have recently included estimates of capital consumption (depreciation), along with labor costs, in government product estimates. JG showed that the rental cost for capital will include both depreciation and returns to the initial investment. While we cannot directly measure returns to government capital, government investments do compete for funds with private investments. Moulton (2004) has suggested the further step of including some empirical estimate of real returns to government capital in government product.

Imports in the Nominal Production Account

Each row of an input-output "use" table records the disposition of a given type of commodity. In addition to the intermediate transactions table, **VU**, there are appended columns indicating specific "final uses." Among the final use columns, one column, $\mathbf{VF}_i$, records imports of each type of commodity, with negative entries. With this negative import entry, total commodity output, the sum across a row, is equal to domestic output, and the sum of all final uses is equal to GDP. The single-column treatment of imports does not distinguish how much of the imports went to intermediate uses and how much went to final uses. It is unnecessary to distinguish this when computing GDP because GDP is a measure of domestic product and excludes all intermediates inputs.

In a production account used for productivity measurement it is desirable to match outputs with all inputs, regardless of their source, at each level of aggregation. An architecture that is ideal for productivity measurement would keep inputs and outputs separate, and would not adopt the treatment of imported intermediates as an offset to output, even though this simplification is suitable for measuring product. Imported final commodities should be excluded from sector output, since they are not made inside the sector, but ideally imported intermediate inputs would be included in sector output.

The production account specifications being developed here follow the treatment of imported intermediates proposed by Gollop (1981). First, the intermediate transactions matrix, **VN**, which includes only transactions that are internal to the sector, includes only intermediate inputs obtained from domestic sources. The nominal production account treats the value of imported intermediate inputs as input costs (**CF**) rather than as offsets to the value of output (**VF**). In the production account, each type of imported commodity has its own row, indicating the disposition of the imported portion of that commodity:

$\mathbf{CF}_{i,k}$ = cost of imported commodities of the ith type used by the kth industry.

These rows are not a part of **VN** but are appended below **VN** in figure 9.2, similar to the rows for labor costs (**CL**) and capital costs (**CK**), which are also inputs purchased from outside the sector. The block of commodity rows for imports, **CF**, is very similar to the blocks of commodity rows for each industry inside the sector, which describe the uses of each type of commodity coming from a given industry source.[9] Imported final products are, of course, excluded from **VS**. In figure 9.2 a small "import" box, $\mathbf{VFF}_i$, is appended that records deliveries of final imported products of type i to domestic final consumption. The entries of **VFF** would be positive but would be omitted in the calculation of sector output by adding up **VS**. For an economy open to trade, sector output includes exports and excludes imported final products. GDP excludes intermediate inputs whether the economy is open or closed, so GDP = $\mathbf{VS}_T - \Sigma_{i=1}^m \Sigma_{k=1}^n \mathbf{CF}_{i,k}$.[10] Industry gross output, however, includes imported intermediate inputs.

Finally, to inject this treatment into the full model, the formula equating the value of industry output with the cost of factor outlays, presented earlier, needs to be modified to reflect the cost of imported intermediate inputs:

$$\mathbf{TCL}_k = \sum_{i=1}^m \sum_{j=1}^n \mathbf{VN}_{i,j,k} + \mathbf{CF}_k + \mathbf{CL}_k + \mathbf{CK}_k, \text{ in order to preserve the identity,}$$

$$\mathbf{TC}_k = \mathbf{VY}_k.$$

---

9. It should be noted that the data currently being collected are insufficient to estimate these new rows.

10. The BLS business, nonfarm business, private business, and private nonfarm business output measures are net of all intermediates including imported intermediates, so, strictly speaking, they are product measures. Gullickson and Harper (1999) pointed out the difference between the BLS MFP measures, and measures based on the sector output concept, as are specified in section 9.2.2, would be tiny. If imported intermediates were included in outputs, they would also need to be included in inputs. They would enter output and input with the same weight, and would approximately offset each other.

9.2.2   The Real Production Account

Real Industry Outputs and Inputs and Their Prices

In this section, vectors and arrays of growth rate functions are described that parallel the elements of the nominal production account. Each element of the account ($\mathbf{VN}_{i,j,k}$, $\mathbf{VS}_{i,j}$, $\mathbf{CL}_k$, $\mathbf{CF}_k$, and $\mathbf{CK}_k$) is considered to be a function of time rather than an observation for a single period. These functions would be continuous and differentiable in the context of a continuous model, while, for application to discrete data, these are time series. Bold italics are used to refer to the growth rate of a variable: for example, $\mathbf{Z} = d \ln z/dt = (dz/dt)/z$ in continuous time, while, for example with a discrete Tornqvist index formulation, $\mathbf{Z}$ would refer to $\ln(Z_t) - \ln(Z_{t-1})$. Next, for any element Z it is assumed that either the value of Z, VZ, or the cost of Z, CZ, is equal to the product of a real quantity (Z without prefix) and a price (PZ). VZ or CZ = $Z \cdot$ PZ. In growth rates, the decomposition is $\mathbf{VZ} = \mathbf{Z} + \mathbf{PZ}$ or $\mathbf{CZ} = \mathbf{Z} + \mathbf{PZ}$.

Price and quantity are defined in line with normal conventions in national accounting and productivity measurement. Time series information on value or cost usually are available for some level of cell detail. Typically we have price indexes for commodities and quantity information for hours worked and capital stock.[11] Prices and quantities may both exist for some cells, but in order to ensure the value-price-quantity relationship price or quantity must be chosen, and the other (price or quantity) is then implicitly determined to ensure that price times quantity equals value. This can also be thought of in terms of growth rates. We define the following terms:

$PN_{i,j,k}$ = the growth rate of the price of the ith commodity made in industry j and used by the kth industry,

$PS_{i,j}$ = the growth rate of price for sales of the ith commodity sold outside the sector,

QL_k = the growth rate of labor hours in the kth industry,

$PF_{i,k}$ = the growth rate of the price for the ith imported commodity paid by the kth industry, and

QK_k = the growth rate of the stock of capital inputs to the kth industry.

---

11. We will just note that, in the productivity work of Jorgenson, Gollop, and Fraumeni (1987) and of BLS (2002), labor and capital inputs, for each industry, are constructed from detailed "types," such as workers with different amounts of education and stocks of high tech assets, other equipment, and buildings. Prices and quantities are estimated for each component and then superlative aggregation procedures are used. This is entirely symmetric with the approach that will be spelled out shortly (in the second subsection of 9.2.2) for aggregating heterogeneous intermediate inputs and heterogeneous outputs.

The growth rate of the other component is determined either by deflating the value with the commodity price or by determining the unit cost of the input; that is,

$N_{i,j,k} = VN_{i,j,k} - PN_{i,j,k}$ (intermediate outputs/inputs),

$S_{i,j} = VS_{i,j} - PS_{i,j}$ (industry outputs of the commodity delivered outside the sector),

$PL_k = CL_k - L_k$ (average compensation per hour),

$F_{i,k} = CF_{i,k} - PF_{i,k}$ (imported intermediate input), and

$PK_k = CK_k - K_k$ (capital rental price).

Industry Accounting: Aggregation of Real Inputs and Real Outputs, and MFP

The solution to the standard economic index number problem is to use values to add up heterogeneous quantities, such as apples and oranges. Having estimated the values and the quantity and price trends for numerous detailed cells representing heterogeneous outputs and inputs, it is now easy to spell out the various real aggregations needed to complete the real production account.

The growth rate of total input, I_k, for industry k is derived using weights from column k of the nominal production account together with corresponding quantity growth rate functions:

$$I_k = \left(\frac{CL_k}{TCI_k}\right)L_k + \sum_{i=1}^{m}\left(\frac{CF_{i,k}}{TCI_k}\right)F_{i,k} + \left(\frac{CK_k}{TCI_k}\right)K_k + \sum_{i=1}^{m}\sum_{j=1}^{n}\left(\frac{VN_{i,j,k}}{TCI_k}\right)N_{i,j,k}.$$

This formula defines the growth rate of the input function at a specific point in time.[12] Similarly, the industry's real output is aggregated in conformity with a model of joint production. Aggregation is in growth rate form in terms of the commodities the industry makes, aggregated using revenue share weights:

$$Y_j = \sum_{i=1}^{m}\left\{\left[\sum_{k=1}^{n}\left(\frac{VN_{i,j,k}}{VY_j}\right)N_{i,j,k}\right] + \left(\frac{VS_{i,j}}{VY_j}\right)S_{i,j}\right\}.$$

It is worth emphasizing that, for implementation with discrete data, it is very important to have consistent categories of industries at successive observations. The growth rate of MFP in industry k (MFP_k) is defined in terms of its inputs and its output (matched with itself, industry k, not industry j):

---

12. The line integral of this function over time is a Divisia index. A discrete Tornqvist index can be formulated using weights that are arithmetic averages of shares in the two periods being compared. While the formula is a bit harder to describe, it is easy to compute a Fisher ideal index from the same information.

$$MFP_k = Y_k - I_k.$$

Sectoral Accounting: Aggregation across Industries

The macroeconomics literature of the 1950s and 1960s emphasized aggregate production models that described the generation of GDP from a few aggregate factors of production. Such a model can provide a formal framework[13] within which we can consider how best to define inputs and outputs to measure a sector's productivity. Real sectoral output for an economy or sector is the total of outputs, delivered by each industry, that are sold outside of the economy or sector. When the joint production model is applied to the sector, the sector is viewed as if it were a firm choosing an output mix, and then it can be shown that aggregation should be done using revenue share weights:

$$S_T = \sum_{k=1}^{m}\left(\frac{\text{VS}_k}{\text{VS}_T}\right)S_k.$$

An aggregate production model can also be used to rationalize aggregation of each type of input across industries, again using industry shares in total cost:

$$L_T = \sum_{k=1}^{n}\left(\frac{\text{CL}_k}{\text{CL}_T}\right)L_k \quad \text{where } \text{CL}_T = \sum_{k=1}^{n}\text{CL}_k,$$

$$F_T = \sum_{i=1}^{m}\sum_{k=1}^{n}\left(\frac{\text{CF}_{i,k}}{\text{CF}_T}\right)F_j \quad \text{where } \text{CF}_T = \sum_{i=1}^{m}\sum_{k=1}^{n}\text{CF}_{i,k}, \text{ and}$$

$$K_T = \sum_{k=1}^{n}\left(\frac{\text{CK}_k}{\text{CK}_T}\right)K_k \quad \text{where } \text{CK}_T = \sum_{k=1}^{n}\text{CK}_k.$$

We then aggregate these inputs across types of input to get a measure of the "sectoral input"—that is, the input to the economy or sector from outside sources:

$$I_T = \left(\frac{\text{CL}_T}{\text{TCI}_T}\right)L_T + \left(\frac{\text{CF}_T}{\text{TCI}_T}\right)F_T + \left(\frac{\text{CK}_T}{\text{TCI}_T}\right)K_T,$$

$$\text{where } \text{TCI}_T = \text{CL}_T + \text{CF}_T + \text{CK}_T.$$

Based on these we obtain a measure of aggregate MFP:

13. A central element of these models is an aggregate production function. This function describes the production of the economy as if it were operated as a single giant firm. To measure productivity in this tradition, one applies the joint production model to the final outputs and primary inputs of the economy while assuming their prices are exogenously determined. The optimum flows of intermediates are not explicitly modeled, but rather presumed to be efficiently determined inside the economy. (Gullickson and Harper [1999] described this as treating the intermediates as if they were inside the firm's "black box.")

$$MFP_T = S_T - I_T.$$

Note that GDP differs from sectoral output in that it excludes imported intermediate inputs. MFP_T treats imported intermediate inputs as an additional input rather than an exclusion from output.[14]

The Relationship of Industry and Aggregate Productivity Measures

Evsey Domar's (1961) key result was to show the relationship of this measure to the industry MFP trends:

$$MFP_T = \sum_{j=1}^{n} \left(\frac{VY_j}{VS_T} \right) MFP_j.$$

The individual terms in this sum represent individual industry contributions to aggregate MFP. Now the sum of these weights exceeds 1.00:

$$\sum_{j=1}^{n} \left(\frac{VY_j}{VS_T} \right) = 1.00 + \sum_{j=1}^{n} \sum_{i=1}^{m} \frac{VN_{i,j,k}}{VS_T}.$$

This may seem counterintuitive, but intermediate transactions contribute to aggregate productivity by allowing productivity gains in successive industries to augment one another.[15]

However, Domar effectively assumed that the value of output equals the total cost of factor inputs. In the BLS aggregate MFP work and in section 9.3.1 of this chapter, business, property taxes, and business motor vehicle fees are assigned to capital costs, but other indirect business taxes are not assigned to any specific factor of production. Subsidies are also unassigned to input factors, and are included in TC with a negative sign. Production theory would recommend this treatment for taxes and subsidies that do not affect firms' costs for specific factors. The treatment parallels that of the BLS MFP work. In this context,

$$MFP_T = \sum_{j=1}^{n} \left(\frac{VY_j}{VS_T} \right) MFP_j - \sum_{j=1}^{n} \left(\frac{OIBT_j - SUB_j}{VS_T} \right) I_j$$

$$= \sum_{j=1}^{n} \left(\frac{VY_j}{VS_T} \right) S_j - \sum_{j=1}^{n} \left(\frac{VY_j + OIBT_j - SUB_j}{VS_T} \right) I_j$$

14. For its business and nonfarm business-sector MFP measures, BLS output is derived from GDP without restoring F, and, in calculating MFP, this is compared to inputs of capital and labor. While the BLS does not employ the sectoral treatment of imported intermediates (F), the MFP measures are almost the same as if it did. For the sectoral treatment, F would need to be restored to output and included with inputs using the same weight, and as a consequence it would lower the MFP trend just slightly.

15. For example, suppose there is a 1 percent MFP increase in the leather industry and a 1 percent MFP increase in the shoe industry. Further suppose that shoes are the only final good in an economy and that leather represents half the cost of making shoes. Then the economy experiences a 1.5 percent productivity gain as the result of productivity advances in both industries.

Note that if all $OIBT_j - SUB_j = 0$, then Domar's equation holds. While perhaps inappropriate, this could be ensured by assigning all of **OIBT** and **SUB** to specific factors' costs. However, if the sum $IBT_j - SUB_j$ is positive, and if inputs are growing, then the aggregate MFP trend will be slightly lower than the Domar-weighted average of industry MFP trends.[16] Also note that any other circumstance causing measured factor input costs to differ from the measured value of output in this model, such as a statistical discrepancy, will act like **OIBT** – **SUB** in affecting the relationship between industry and aggregate.[17]

9.2.3 Adapting the Account to Different Large Sectors: Total Economy and Business

As indicated in section 9.1, the BEA measures GDP for the "total" economy, while the largest subset of the economy for which the BLS measures MFP is the private business sector.[18] Private business output excludes the following activities from GDP: general government, government enterprises, private households, nonprofit institutions, and the rental value of owner occupied dwellings. The BLS excludes these activities from productivity measures because in most cases inadequate data exists to construct output estimates independently of input costs.[19] The BEA includes these activities in GDP because its goal is to measure all current production in the United States.

The alterations to the nominal production account for the total economy needed to convert the account to one for one of its subsectors, such as business, are described next. The alterations described can be applied to the problem of how to remove an industry or activity from any larger sector's production account. The technique could be applied to removal of a sequence of industries or activities, such as governments and nonprofit institutions, or it could be reversed to understand how to enlarge the sector, perhaps to include selected household activities. The alterations are de-

16. If **OIBT** – **SUB** is typically 7 percent pro rata on the value of industry output, then for each additional percent of input growth, the industry must produce 1.07 percent more output to pay for it. The BLS aggregate MFP measures would exclude the extra .07 percent. In terms of production theory, the .07 is treated as a scale effect that is excluded from the measure of the production function shift, MFP.

17. Note that the BLS has not used the Domar equation to attribute productivity to industries in its publications. However, Gullickson and Harper (2002) did use the Domar equation, in its original form, to compare their exploratory nonmanufacturing industry multifactor productivity estimates to the published BLS aggregate measures.

18. In a later section the relationship between BEA GDP and BEA/BLS private business-sector output is discussed. The BLS's quarterly labor productivity measures refer to the business sector that includes government enterprises.

19. The output values for general government, nonprofit institutions, and rental housing are estimated by identifying them with factor costs. The value of government enterprise output is measured in terms of revenues, but revenues scarcely account for labor costs because capital is heavily subsidized. The prices used to deflate all five types of product are formulated, at least partly, in terms of input costs.

signed to create a complete production account for both sector and sub-sector, that is, to use the same general equations for measuring real inputs, outputs, and productivity that were developed in sections 9.2.1 and 9.2.2.

The alterations treat the industry, M, being removed from the sector as exogenous to the remaining subsector. First the row and column associated with industry M are removed from the matrix $\mathbf{VN}$. When the column (industry M's costs) is removed from $\mathbf{VN}$, the labor and capital inputs purchased by M will vanish from the account altogether, as depicted in figure 9.3. However, the intermediate inputs purchased by industry M ($\mathbf{VN}_{i,j,M}$) become sector outputs of the remaining subsector. The column of the larger sector's outputs, $\mathbf{VS}$, is replaced with a column of the subsector's outputs, $\mathbf{VSX}$, where $\mathbf{VSX}_{i,j} = \mathbf{VS}_{i,j} + \mathbf{VN}_{i,j,M}$ (for all $j \neq m$). The output rows associated with industry M, $\mathbf{VN}_{i,M,k}$, are removed from $\mathbf{VN}$ but are appended below as rows of commodity costs, similar to the treatment of imports. A block of exogenous cost rows, $C_{i,M,k}$, one for each commodity i

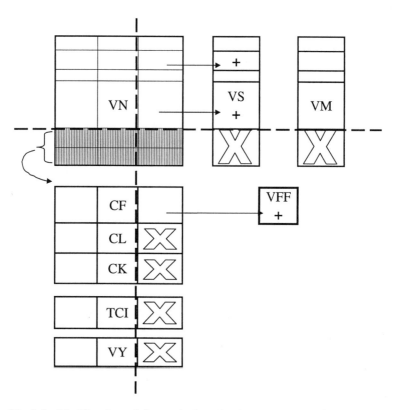

Fig. 9.3   Modifications of the nominal production account to address a subsector, such as the business sector of the total economy

that industry M produces, is created to show which industries k are buying the commodities. The flexible scope of this formulation of production accounts will facilitate determining how to treat various outputs and inputs as emphasis shifts from the total economy to a major subsector, such as private nonfarm business or manufacturing.

9.3   Illustrative Integrated Production Account

The U.S. statistical system is largely decentralized. Production data come from three statistical agencies—the BEA, the BLS, and the Census—as well as from other sources. Accordingly, constructing an integrated aggregate production account requires an interagency joint effort, which the BEA and BLS have undertaken. Most of the aggregate production data are either compiled by the BLS or are compiled by BEA and then used by BLS for its MFP estimates. This section first discusses the productivity-related estimates produced by the BEA and BLS, and the source data underlying those estimates. It then presents the illustrative aggregate production account and briefly analyzes the components of this account.

9.3.1   An Aggregate Production Account

Table 9.1 presents the illustrative aggregate production account for 1996.[20] This account shows the relationship between GDP and the two major sectors for which the BLS provides estimates of MFP: the private business sector and the private nonfarm business sector. Estimates are in billions of dollars; since 1996 is the base year the nominal dollar value is equal to the real value for that year.

The historical data presented in this section and in the rest of the chapter were considered current by both the BEA and the BLS between April 8, 2003, and September 17, 2003. They predate the BEA comprehensive revision to the NIPAs of December 2003 and the corresponding revision to the BLS Productivity and Cost series. The industry data presented in section 9.4 are all on an SIC basis and predate the switching of any of the BEA or BLS industry output and productivity series to the North American Industrial Classification System (NAICS). Some of the detailed industry data have become available on a NAICS basis since the cutoff for this chapter.[21]

The data time series for all entries in the table, with the exception of two

20. Note: In table 9.1, MFP refers to BLS Private Business and Private Nonfarm Business MFP. The BLS MFP data, the BEA NIPA data, and the BEA GDP-by-industry data are no longer on the web because more recent versions have become available; however, the data are listed in the appendix.

21. BEA's GDP-by-industry estimates classified on a NAICS basis are available back to 1987 at http://www.bea.gov/bea/dn2/gdpbyind_data.htm. The BLS's industry output and labor productivity estimates classified on a NAICS basis are available back to 1987 at http://www.bls.gov/lpc/iprdata1.htm.

Table 9.1   **Aggregate production account, 1996 (billions of dollars)**

1. *Gross domestic product (NIPA table 1.7, line 1)*	7813.2
2. −Households and institutions (NIPA table 1.7, line 7)	348.6
2a. Private households (NIPA table 1.7, line 8)	12.0
2b. +Nonprofit institutions serving individuals (NIPA table 1.7, line 9)	336.5
3. −General government (NIPA table 1.7, line 10)	908.7
4. =*Gross domestic business product (NIPA table 1.7, line 2)*	6556.0
5. −Owner-occupied housing (NIPA table 8.21, line 172)	487.1
6. −Rental value of nonresidential assets owned and used by nonprofit institutions serving individuals (NIPA table 8.21, line 173)	49.8
7. =*BEA/BLS business sector output*	6019.0
8. −Government enterprises	111.8
8a. Federal (BEA GDP by Industry table, line 80)	54.9
8b. State and local (BEA GDP by Industry table, line 83)	56.9
9. =*BEA/BLS private business sector output*	5907.2
9a. Statistical and other discrepancies	32.7
9b. +BLS total factor costs plus taxes (MFP table PB1a, current dollar output)	5874.5
9b-ii. BLS cost of capital services (MFP table PB1a, capital income)	1839.8
9b-ii. BLS labor compensation (MFP table PB1a)	3600.7
9b-iii. Indirect business taxes, less portion assigned to capital services, plus subsidies	434.0
10. −Farms (NIPA table 1.7, line 6)	92.2
11. +Farm space rent for owner-occupied housing (NIPA table 8.21, line 114)	5.8
12. Farm intermediate inputs for owner-occupied housing (NIPA table 8.21, line 114)	1.0
13. =*BEA/BLS private nonfarm business sector output*	5819.8
13a. Statistical and other discrepancies	32.7
13b. +BLS total factor costs plus taxes (MFP table NFB1a, current dollar output)	5787.1
13b-i. BLS cost of capital services (MFP table NFB1a, capital income)	1776.1
13b-ii. BLS labor compensation (MFP table NFB1a, labor compensation)	3570.8
13b-iii. Indirect business taxes, less portion assigned to capital services, plus subsidies	440.2

repeated entries, are listed in the data appendix.[22] First, there are two entries labeled "Statistical and Other Discrepancies" (lines 9a and 13a). These entries are at most .1 different from the NIPA statistical discrepancy shown in NIPA table 1.9, line 15. The "other" discrepancy results from the fact that the major-sector MFP estimates are calculated from the bottom up (i.e., from more detailed industry data), while the estimates shown in this table are calculated from the top down (i.e., starting with GDP). As a result, rounding differences between these two approaches are included. Second, there are two entries labeled "Indirect Business Taxes, Less Portion Assigned to Capital Services, Plus Subsidies" (lines 9b-iii and 13b-iii).

Before the December 2003 NIPA comprehensive revision, the BEA defined business product differently than the BLS. This chapter—including table 9.1—uses pre-2003 NIPA comprehensive revision data and defini-

22. All table entries labeled "NIPA" are available from the BEA web site.

tions for MFP estimates. Incorporation of the 2003 comprehensive revision data will not be completed until late 2005. The BLS excludes from business product (line 7) all production by households, nonprofit institutions serving individuals, and general government.[23] Before the comprehensive revision, the BEA included owner-occupied housing (line 5) and the rental value of nonresidential assets owned and used by nonprofit institutions serving persons (line 6) in business product (line 4).[24] Adopting the BLS definition of business product was a strategic decision by the BEA to harmonize the BEA and BLS accounts to facilitate their use.

The most highly aggregated sector for which the BLS estimates MFP is the private business sector, because of the previously noted difficulty of estimating output independently of inputs for the household, nonprofit institutions, and government sectors. Government enterprise product (line 8) from BEA's GDP-by-industry accounts program is deducted from business-sector output to arrive at private business-sector output (line 9). The details under lines 9 and 13 are the input side of the production account for the two major sectors for which the BLS prepares estimates of MFP on an annual basis. Lines 10 through 12 deduct farms from the private business sector to arrive at private nonfarm business-sector output. Farm owner-occupied housing in line 5 excludes intermediate inputs; farms in line 10 include owner-occupied housing and exclude intermediate inputs; and farm space rent for owner-occupied housing in line 11 includes intermediate inputs. The adjustments in lines 11–12 therefore ensure that nothing is subtracted twice and that intermediate inputs are excluded from output.

For many years the BLS has estimated both capital and labor inputs (lines 9b-i and 9b-ii, and lines 13b-i and 13b-ii, respectively) within a production account. The possibility of constructing capital services as a measure of capital input for inclusion in a revised SNA is being discussed for inclusion in international guidelines.[25] The BLS already estimates capital services and was one of the first statistical agencies in the world to do so. The GDP-by-industry accounts program of the BEA provides nominal estimates of labor compensation, property-type income, and indirect business tax and nontax liability by industry. From these estimates, the BLS determines the allocation of proprietor's income between capital and labor income in order to derive nominal capital services using the methodology described above in section 9.2.1. In addition, the BLS determines the amount of indirect business taxes (e.g., business property taxes and business motor vehicle licenses) to be allocated to capital services as shown in table 9.1.

---

23. Nonprofit institutions serving business are included in business product by both the BEA and BLS; this is a small number.

24. See Moulton and Seskin (2003), p. 29.

25. Discussions are taking place at the meetings of Canberra II, which is a continuation of Canberra I. The latter worked to produce a capital manual as a companion piece to SNA 1993. See OECD (2001) and United Nations et al. (1993).

9.3.2 Major Components of the Illustrative Aggregate Production Account

Table 9.2 shows the nominal shares of GDP and the real growth rates for selected components and major sectors (shown in italic) of the illustrative aggregate production account. Although the identifying labels such as "BEA/BLS" are continued from table 9.1, the BEA and BLS estimates may differ. In addition, not all of the components are available for all years 1948–2001, and in some cases 1996 dollar estimates are not directly available for any year on the BEA or BLS web site.[26] Between 1948–73 and 1973–90, the nominal shares of the major sectors (shown in italic) in GDP decreased. This reflects the fact that the nominal share of the GDP components that are excluded from the private business sector increased during 1973–90. For nonprofit institutions serving individuals and owner-occupied housing, the shares continued to rise between 1973–90 and 1990–95, but then are nearly constant. For general government, the share decreased over each of the last three subperiods shown. The government enterprise share varies little over time.

The share of the private nonfarm business sector in GDP declined less than the shares of the other major sectors during 1973–90 and was larger in 2000–2001 than in 1948–73. This is because the farm share of GDP decreased from 6.1 percent in 1948–73 to 0.8 percent in 2000–2001, which offset the increases in the other excluded components. The drop in the farms share is very significant from 1948–73 to 1973–90. While the farms share continued to decline at a rapid rate between 1990–95, 1995–2000, and 2000–2001, the share had become so small that it no longer had much impact on the private nonfarm business share. The share of the private business sector in GDP continued to decline between 1973–90 and 1990–95, but it then returned to the 1973–90 level.

The real growth rates of the major sectors are very similar, differing by at most .2. For the period as a whole and the middle subperiods—1973–90, 1990–95, and 1995–2000—the real rates of growth of the major sectors are higher than the real growth rate of GDP. This is largely because of the lower real growth rates of the two government components. The real growth rates for these components are always below that of GDP with the exception of general government for 2000–2001. In 1948–73, the real growth rates of the major sectors are very similar to that for GDP; in 2000–2001 they are negative while real GDP grew slightly. Nonprofit institutions serving individuals, general government, and owner-occupied housing all grew significantly faster than the major sectors in 2000–2001; these sectors bolstered the growth of real GDP relative to the major sectors. The real growth rate of nonprofit institutions serving individuals is consistently strong compared

26. Implicit deflators were calculated in several cases from figures available on the BEA or BLS web sites.

Table 9.2   Major components of the aggregate production account nominal shares and real growth rates

	1948–2001		1948–1973		1973–1990		1990–1995		1995–2000		2000–2001	
	Share of GDP	Growth rate (%)	Share of GDP	Growth rate (%)	Share of GDP	Growth rate (%)	Share of GDP	Growth rate (%)	Share of GDP	Growth rate (%)	Share of GDP	Growth rate (%)
BEA gross domestic product	1.000	3.4	1.000	4.0	1.000	2.9	1.000	2.4	1.000	4.0	1.000	0.3
Nonprofit institutions serving individuals	0.028	3.9	0.020	4.6	0.033	3.6	0.041	3.3	0.043	2.7	0.043	3.1
General government	0.107	2.1	0.118	3.0	0.129	1.6	0.122	0.3	0.115	1.1	0.112	2.1
BEA gross domestic business product	0.859	3.6	0.856	4.1	0.835Â	3.1	0.835	2.7	0.841	4.5	0.844	−0.1
Owner-occupied housing	0.048	3.9	0.042	2.8	0.057	6.3	0.063	2.8	0.063	3.1	0.064	1.7
BEA/BLS business-sector output	0.807	3.6	0.811	4.0	0.772	3.1	0.766	2.8	0.772	4.7	0.774	−0.2
Government enterprises	0.012	2.2	0.012	3.2	0.014	1.3	0.015	−0.05	0.014	3.4	0.014	−0.9
BEA/BLS private business-sector output	0.795	3.6	0.799	4.0	0.758	3.1	0.752	2.8	0.758	4.7	0.760	−0.2
Farms	0.047	2.2	0.061	1.1	0.025	3.3	0.012	0.3	0.009	7.1	0.008	−5.1
BEA/BLS private nonfarm business-sector output	0.750	3.6	0.741	4.2	0.734	3.1	0.741	2.8	0.749	4.6	0.753	−0.1

Note: Shares of GDP are computed as the average of the shares for the first and last years of the period.

to that for GDP, except in 1995–2000. Owner-occupied housing real growth rates show no consistent pattern. The real growth rate for farms is the highest of any sector in 1995–2000, but the lowest of any sector in 2000–2001.

9.3.3 BLS Major-Sector MFP Accounts

Table 9.3 focuses on nominal shares and real growth rates for the detailed components of the BLS major-sector MFP accounts. The rates of MFP change are also given.

As expected, the capital services share of nominal output is always about one-third and that of labor input is about two-thirds, but there is some variation in the shares across major sectors and across time. The capital services share is always slightly lower for the private nonfarm business sector than for the private business sector. The trends are similar for the major sectors including and excluding farms. Between 1948–73 and 1973–90 the shares are essentially stable; they increase significantly between 1973–90 and 1990–95, then drop into the second half of the nineties, followed by a more significant drop between 1995–2000 and 2000–2001. The labor input shares are simply a reflection of the capital services shares as the nominal shares always sum to 1.0.

The capital services and labor input real growth rates for private nonfarm business are always equal to or above those for private business. The subperiod differences between the capital services real growth rates of private business and private nonfarm business are equal to or greater than the difference between the labor input real growth rates of these major sectors except in 1948–73. The labor input growth rate difference of .5 in 1948–73 is a very significant difference as it represents a 50 percent increase of the private nonfarm business rate over that for private business. Aside from this subperiod, the difference is no greater than .1 percentage point. Finally, the capital services real growth rate for the periods shown is always greater than the labor input real growth rate for both major sectors.

The rate of MFP change shows trends and relationships documented elsewhere by the BLS and others.[27] The drop between 1948–73 and 1973–90 is often called the "productivity slowdown." The resurgence in 1995–2000 occurs in the subperiod associated with the new economy and is often called the "productivity revival." The negative MFP change in 2000–2001 may be a reflection of the recession dated as beginning in March 2001. In every subperiod, MFP change for the private business sector is equal to, or greater than, that for the private nonfarm business sector, reflecting ongoing strong productivity growth in the farm sector.

---

27. The rate of MFP change is equal to the growth rate of output minus a weighted growth rate of inputs. The weights are computed from the BLS Factor Cost of Capital Services and BLS Labor Compensation time series (e.g., in table 9.1 lines 9b-i and 9b-ii, and 13b-i and 13b-ii). Accordingly, the statistical and other discrepancies (e.g., lines 9a and 13a in table 9.1) and Indirect Business Taxes, Less Portion Assigned to Capital Services, Plus Subsidies (e.g., lines 9b-iii and 13b-iii) do not enter into the calculation.

Table 9.3   BLS private business and private nonfarm business sectors (inputs and rates of multifactor productivity change nominal shares and real growth rates)

	1948–2001		1948–1973		1973–1990		1990–1995		1995–2000		2000–2001	
	Share of sector	Growth rate (%)	Share of sector	Growth rate (%)	Share of sector	Growth rate (%)	Share of sector	Growth rate (%)	Share of sector	Growth rate (%)	Share of sector	Growth rate (%)
BEA/BLS private business-sector output	n.a.	3.6	n.a.	4.0	n.a.	3.1	n.a.	2.8	n.a.	4.7	n.a.	−0.2
BLS private business-sector input	n.a.	2.2	n.a.	1.8	n.a.	2.6	n.a.	2.1	n.a.	3.3	n.a.	0.9
BLS capital services	0.320	3.9	0.319	3.7	0.318	4.1	0.328	2.8	0.324	5.3	0.315	4.1
BLS labor input	0.680	1.4	0.681	1.0	0.682	1.9	0.672	1.9	0.676	2.4	0.685	−0.5
BLS rate of multifactor Productivity change	n.a.	1.3	n.a.	2.1	n.a.	0.5	n.a.	0.6	n.a.	1.3	n.a.	−1.0
BEA/BLS private nonfarm business-sector output	n.a.	3.6	n.a.	4.2	n.a.	3.1	n.a.	2.8	n.a.	4.6	n.a.	−0.1
BLS private nonfarm business-sector input	n.a.	2.5	n.a.	2.2	n.a.	2.7	n.a.	2.2	n.a.	3.5	n.a.	1.0
BLS capital services	0.315	4.1	0.306	4.0	0.305	4.4	0.321	2.9	0.319	5.5	0.311	4.1
BLS labor input	0.685	1.7	0.694	1.5	0.695	2.0	0.679	1.9	0.681	2.5	0.689	−0.5
BLS rate of multifactor productivity change	n.a.	1.1	n.a.	1.9	n.a.	0.3	n.a.	0.6	n.a.	1.1	n.a.	−1.0

	1990–1995	1995–2000	1995–2000 less 1990–1995
BEA industry accounts	2.61	5.27	2.67
BLS nonfarm business	2.71	4.63	1.92
Industry accounts less BLS	−0.11	0.64	0.75
Statistical discrepancy	0.05	0.46	0.41
Definition and coverage	0.09	0.04	−0.05
Deflation procedures	−0.25	0.14	0.39

Note: n.a. = not available.

9.4   Comparison of BEA and BLS Output Measures for Sectors and Industries

The BEA and BLS both provide output measures for broad sectors of the economy and for industries that are widely used to study economic growth, productivity, and structural change. Although these output measures are fairly consistent with one another and usually tell similar stories about trends in economic growth, there are some differences. The BEA and BLS have worked closely to achieve consistency. For example, when the BEA introduced annually chained indexes to the NIPAs in 1996, the BLS—after close consultation between the agencies—began to base its productivity measures for the business and nonfarm business sectors on estimates from the product side of the NIPAs.[28] Also around the same time the BEA and BLS worked closely to develop a common set of output price indexes for all manufacturing industries.[29] Each year, the BLS sends the BEA a table of price deflator series for every five-digit product class in manufacturing. While progress has been made, differences remain, especially outside of manufacturing.

Differences in output measures reflect differences in definition, coverage, and methodology that are primarily due to different purposes for the measures. For example, the BEA strives to provide complete and consistent coverage of the entire economy in the NIPAs, whereas the BLS primarily seeks maximum reliability in its various measures of productivity. These differing goals are not necessarily inconsistent with one another, since both require reliable output measures, but they can lead to differences in definition and coverage as well as in methodology. A part of the differences, especially at detailed industry levels, reflects different choices for underlying source data and aggregation techniques. This section describes the key sources of difference among the output measures for major sectors, for broad manufacturing industry groups, and for selected detailed industries in both manufacturing and nonmanufacturing.

The focus in this section of the chapter is on sources of difference in output measures, as it is a useful starting point for comparisons. Tables 9.4 through 9.11 compare growth rates of the BEA and BLS output measures. Most tables present average annual growth rates for 1990–95 and for 1995–2000, and the annual growth rate for 2001, the latest year for which most of the output measures are available. Because of the interest in the acceleration of productivity growth after 1995, and because of the sharp slowdown in growth in 2001, most tables also present the acceleration in average annual output growth between 1990–95 and 1995–2000.

---

28. The product side differs from the income side of the NIPAs by the statistical discrepancy.

29. The BEA and BLS also met in 2001 to discuss reducing differences for nonmanufacturing industries.

Table 9.4   **Real output for major sectors (average annual growth rates; %)**

Program/Measure	1990–1995 (1)	1995–2000 (2)	2000–2001 (3)	1995–2000 less 1990–1995 (2) – (1)
BEA NIPAs				
GDP	2.38	4.03	0.25	1.65
GDI (excludes SD)	2.41	4.38	0.11	1.96
Nonfarm business[a]	2.68	4.47	−0.06	1.79
Nonfarm business less housing	2.74	4.72	−0.09	1.98
BLS				
Nonfarm business[b]	2.71	4.63	−0.07	1.92
Private nonfarm business[b]	2.79	4.64	−0.08	1.86
BEA industry accounts				
All industries	2.22	4.20	0.55	1.97
All industries less SD	2.26	4.55	0.41	2.29
Nonfarm business[c]	2.56	4.85	0.45	2.28
Nonfarm business less SD[c]	2.61	5.27	0.27	2.67
Private nonfarm business[c]	2.62	4.86	0.47	2.24
Private nonfarm business less SD[c]	2.67	5.31	0.29	2.64

[a]Includes all housing.

[b]Includes tenant-occupied housing only.

[c]Excludes all housing.

9.4.1   Major Sectors

Tables 9.4 and 9.5 present real and nominal output measures for the entire economy and for major sectors such as nonfarm business and private nonfarm business. These measures are drawn from the BEA's NIPAs, from the BLS major-sector productivity measurement program, and from the BEA's GDP-by-industry accounts. In the NIPAs, real gross domestic income (GDI) accelerates much faster than real GDP in the 1995–2000 period (1.96 vs. 1.65 percentage points) because GDI excludes the statistical discrepancy, which became increasingly negative during the latter part of the 1990s. In the nonfarm business sector, the BEA's NIPA measure accelerates more slowly than the BLS measure (1.79 vs. 1.92 points) because the BEA includes both owner-occupied and tenant-occupied housing services, whereas the BLS includes only tenant-occupied housing.[30] The BEA's measure for nonfarm business less housing accelerates 1.98 points.

Turning to the BEA industry accounts, it is important to note that the value-added output of "All industries" is conceptually equivalent to GDP measured as the sum of final expenditures, and that nominal value-added for "All industries" equals nominal GDP from the NIPAs. As a result, nominal growth rates and their acceleration (or deceleration) are identical

30. Nonfarm owner-occupied housing accounted for 7.5 percent of BEA nonfarm business output in 1996.

Table 9.5   Nominal output for major sectors (average annual growth rates; %)

Program/Measure	1990–1995 (1)	1995–2000 (2)	2000–2001 (3)	1995–2000 less 1990–1995 (2) – (1)
BEA NIPAs				
GDP	4.98	5.83	2.62	0.85
GDI (excludes SD)	5.02	6.18	2.47	1.16
Nonfarm business[a]	5.13	6.12	2.05	0.99
Nonfarm less housing	5.14	6.22	1.82	1.08
BLS				
Nonfarm business[b]	5.13	6.13	1.86	1.00
Private nonfarm business[b]	5.13	6.17	1.81	1.04
BEA industry accounts				
All industries	4.98	5.83	2.62	0.85
All industries less SD	5.02	6.18	2.47	1.16
Nonfarm business[c]	5.22	6.19	2.11	0.97
Nonfarm business less SD[c]	5.26	6.63	1.93	1.37
Private nonfarm business[c]	5.21	6.22	2.07	1.01
Private nonfarm business less SD[c]	5.26	6.67	1.89	1.42

[a]Includes all housing.
[b]Includes tenant-occupied housing only. Nominal measure derived from BEA data.
[c]Excludes all housing.

for "All industries" and for NIPA GDP. (See table 9.5.) Real growth rates can differ substantially, however, because of differences in the source data and deflation procedures used for the two measures. Real output for "All Industries" accelerates much faster than GDP (1.97 points vs. 1.65 points). The faster acceleration for "All industries" represents the combined effects of slower growth in the 1990–95 period and faster growth in the 1995–2000 period.

A difference of comparable magnitude arises between nonfarm business output computed from the BEA's industry accounts and the BLS measure. Although the industry-based measure of nonfarm business is not published by the BEA, some analysts compute it from the published GDP-by-industry data in order to determine industry contributions to nonfarm business growth. Measures that are computed from the BEA's industry accounts data are not exactly equivalent to the BLS measure, however, because tenant-occupied housing services cannot be separately identified in the BEA data; as a result, most analysts exclude all nonfarm housing services. In addition, the industry accounts measure includes nonprofit institutions serving persons, which are excluded from the NIPA and BLS measures.[31]

31. BLS business-sector output excludes the compensation of employees of nonprofit institutions serving persons (line 2b in table 9.1) and the rental value of nonresidential assets

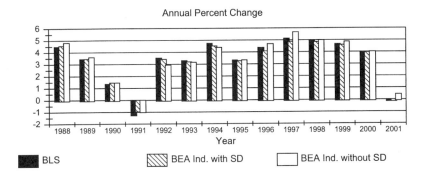

Fig. 9.4   Real nonfarm business output

These institutions are embedded in the source data for several industries and cannot be identified separately. Finally, and perhaps most important for recent periods, some analysts exclude the statistical discrepancy from the industry accounts data in order to construct a pure income-side measure, which further widens the gap in real growth rates.

Figure 9.4 shows the annual percent change in selected real output series for nonfarm business output from 1988 to 2001. Annual changes in the BLS series and the BEA industry accounts series with the statistical discrepancy match very closely over the entire period. Changes in the BEA industry accounts series *without* the statistical discrepancy match the other two series closely in some years, but are usually different. Faster growth is most evident in 1997 and 2001.

Acceleration in the BEA industry accounts measure for nonfarm business *excluding* the statistical discrepancy exceeds the BLS nonfarm business measure by 0.75 points (table 9.4: 2.67 vs. 1.92). The exclusion of the statistical discrepancy and differences in deflation procedures contribute roughly equal amounts (0.4 points) to the difference. Differences in definition and coverage (i.e., nonprofit institutions and tenant-occupied housing) are small and on balance reduce the overall difference. The bottom panel of table 9.3 above summarizes an approximate accounting for the sources of difference in average real growth rates and their acceleration (all in percentage points) during the 1990s.

Most of the difference in the acceleration of real output growth is due to the faster growth in the BEA industry accounts measure during 1995–2000 (0.64 points), which is largely due to the exclusion of the statistical discrepancy (0.46 points). Differences in deflation procedures result in slower growth in the industry accounts deflator, which contribute 0.14 points. In

owned and used by nonprofit institutions serving individuals (line 6 in table 9.1). BEA business-sector output excludes only the compensation of employees of these institutions.

the 1990–95 period, the BEA industry accounts measure grows slower than the BLS measure. This slower growth is more than accounted for by the differences in deflation procedures, which contributed –0.25 points because of faster growth in the industry accounts deflator.

Differences in deflation procedures between the measures reflect differences in source data, deflation level of detail, and aggregation methods. Real GDP and NIPA/BLS nonfarm business output are quantity indexes derived by Fisher aggregation over the detailed types of deflated final expenditures. The value-added quantity indexes from BEA's industry accounts are computed using the double-deflation method and Fisher aggregation over the relevant group of industries. The statistical discrepancy is deflated with the BEA's business-sector price index. Compared with the NIPA price indexes, implicit price deflators for "All Industries" and for nonfarm business from the industry accounts increase faster in the 1990–95 period and slower in the 1995–2000 period.

9.4.2   Manufacturing Sectors

Tables 9.6 and 9.7 compare real and nominal output growth rates for all manufacturing, durable goods, and nondurable goods. Both tables include the BLS sectoral output measures and the BEA measures for gross output and value added. Table 9.6 also includes the Federal Reserve Board's Industrial Production Index (IPI), which is used in the BLS labor productivity program for quarterly and recent period output estimates. For all of manufacturing, both the BLS sectoral output measure, which excludes intrasectoral transactions, and the BEA gross output measure, which includes intrasectoral transactions and other adjustments, accelerate much less than BLS private nonfarm business. Acceleration is slightly less in the BLS measure than in the BEA measure (1.00 vs. 1.15).

Comparable results also are obtained for the durable goods and nondurable goods subaggregates, with durable goods accelerating more than 2 percentage points and nondurable goods decelerating slightly, according to both measures. Acceleration in the BEA value added measure for manufacturing, which excludes intermediate inputs such as energy, materials, and purchased services, is quite similar to the other measures, but the differences are larger for the subgroups. Durable goods accelerates faster and nondurable goods decelerates faster than in the other output measures. Acceleration in the IPI is much higher (2.67 points on the SIC basis) for manufacturing, primarily because of a much faster acceleration for durable goods.[32] Deceleration for nondurable goods in the IPI is similar to that in the BLS and BEA measures.

Figure 9.5 presents selected series for real manufacturing output from 1987 to 2001. The BLS sectoral output series and the BEA gross output

---

32. The IPI is provided on both the SIC basis and the NAICS basis for total manufacturing. Durable goods and nondurable goods are provided only on the NAICS basis.

Table 9.6   **Real output for manufacturing (average annual growth rates; %)**

Program/Measure	1990–1995 (1)	1995–2000 (2)	2000–2001 (3)	1995–2000 less 1990–1995 (2) – (1)
BLS				
Sectoral output, all manufacturing	3.11	4.11	–4.83	1.00
Durable goods	3.89	6.37	–6.29	2.48
Nondurable goods	2.28	1.51	–3.13	–0.78
BEA				
Gross output, all manufacturing	3.09	4.24	–6.71	1.15
Durable goods	4.47	6.72	–8.93	2.25
Nondurable goods	1.57	1.31	–4.07	–0.26
Value added, all manufacturing	3.11	4.30	–6.00	1.18
Durable goods	4.09	7.87	–5.19	3.79
Nondurable goods	1.86	–0.44	–7.12	–2.29
FRB IPI				
Manufacturing (SIC)	3.25	5.92	–4.07	2.67
Manufacturing (NAICS)	3.49	6.04	–4.14	2.55
Durable goods (NAICS)	4.88	9.55	–4.98	4.67
Nondurable goods (NAICS)	1.76	1.36	–3.01	–0.40

Table 9.7   **Nominal output for manufacturing (average annual growth rates; %)**

Program/Measure	1990–1995 (1)	1995–2000 (2)	2000–2001[a] (3)	1995–2000 less 1990–1995 (2) – (1)
BLS				
Sectoral output, all manufacturing	4.10	3.99	n.a.	–0.11
Durable goods	4.79	4.23	n.a.	–0.56
Nondurable goods	3.52	3.60	n.a.	0.08
BEA				
Gross output, all manufacturing	4.30	3.75	–7.62	–0.55
Durable goods	5.31	4.19	–11.21	–1.12
Nondurable goods	3.21	3.23	–3.28	0.02
Value added, all manufacturing	4.38	3.35	–6.40	–1.02
Durable goods	4.47	3.96	–8.30	–0.50
Nondurable goods	4.26	2.54	–3.74	–1.72

Note: Nominal estimates are not available for the FRB IPI.

[a]BLS estimates for 2001 are not available.

(GO) series track one another very closely over the entire period. The IPI series follows the BLS and BEA series very closely through 1997, but then begins to grow faster than the other series after 1997. This divergence is primarily due to much faster growth for durable goods in the FRB series.

Table 9.7 provides some insight into the impact of the definitional and coverage differences between the BEA and BLS output measures, because

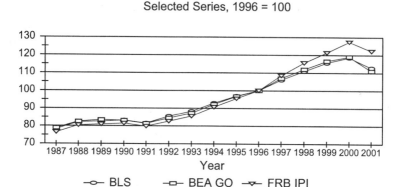

Selected Series, 1996 = 100

Fig. 9.5   Real manufacturing output

nominal estimates are not affected by differences in deflation and aggregation procedures. While differences in levels are not shown here, it is important to note that the nominal value of manufacturing BLS sectoral production, BEA gross output, and BEA value added differ significantly. This is not surprising, given the difference in the sectoral, gross, and value-added output concepts and their respective treatments of intermediates. In recent years, the BLS value of manufacturing sectoral production has averaged about 64 percent of BEA gross output and about 177 percent of BEA value added. Despite these important differences in the definition of output that affect levels, nominal growth rates and their acceleration are quite consistent, especially between BLS sectoral output and BEA gross output. The small differences in nominal growth rates sometimes lead to small differences in real growth rates. The BEA and BLS have minimized the impact of differences in deflation procedures in the manufacturing sector by the use of a common database of product prices and by sharing some of the detailed components of nominal gross output.

9.4.3   Detailed Industry Comparisons

To further understand the magnitude and sources of differences among the output measures, the BEA and BLS detailed industry output series were compared and the sources of their differences were explored in some depth. As noted above, differences may arise among output measures either because of differences in the choice of output concept or because of differences in measurement techniques. Empirical implementation of an output measure requires numerous decisions, including choices of source data, extrapolation techniques, aggregation methods, deflation procedures, and possible adjustments to match concepts and correct for data limitations.[33]

---

33. See appendix table 9B.1 for a description of differences among the output series.

The selection of the output concept and the decisions regarding empirical measurement are driven both by the purpose for the output measure and by underlying data limitations.

For the detailed industry comparisons, output measures from the BEA industry accounts GDP-by-industry program, the BLS Office of Productivity and Technology industry productivity program, and the BLS Office of Productivity and Technology major-sector productivity program (Gullickson-Harper output measures) were compared for those SIC two-digit industries where more than one output measure is available.[34] In those industries with large differences, BEA and BLS output measures were further examined to assess whether the disparity results from differences in data sources, deflation methods, agency-specific adjustments, or the output concept. For selected industry groups, sufficient data are available to relate differences in output measures at the SIC two-digit level to differences in output measures for the underlying three- and four-digit level industries.

Overview of Comparisons

Comparisons were made among the real and nominal output growth rates of various BEA and BLS output measures for selected industries. These measures include published and unpublished BEA gross output measures Y^{G}_{BEA-P} and Y^{G}_{BEA-U}, published BLS sectoral output measures $Y^{S}_{BLS-M-P}$, unpublished BLS gross output measures $Y^{G}_{BLS-M-U}$, and published and unpublished BLS sectoral output measures $Y^{S}_{BLS-I-P}$ and $Y^{S}_{BLS-I-U}$.[35]

---

34. The BEA gross output measures in this comparison are drawn from the BEA industry accounts GDP-by-industry program rather than the BEA input-output program. The BLS Office of Productivity and Technology industry productivity program produces sectoral output measures for SIC three- and four-digit industries for use in production of industry productivity measures. The SIC-based industry productivity program sectoral output measures were published or unpublished, depending on the quality of the measure, although all were available upon request. Starting with the 2003 data, all NAICS-based four-digit and above data from the industry productivity program are published. The BLS Office of Productivity and Technology major-sector productivity program produces published sectoral output measures for SIC two-digit manufacturing industries and unpublished gross output measures for selected SIC two-digit nonmanufacturing industries. These measures are presented and discussed in Gullickson (1995) and Gullickson and Harper (1999, 2002). The BEA and BLS output measures used in this paper were considered current by both BEA and BLS between April 8 and September 17, 2003.

35. In this chapter, a variety of output measures produced by the BEA and BLS are compared. For comparison purposes, these data sets may in some cases be aggregated or disaggregated to levels that the agencies do not publish. The following notation has been developed in order to be clear at all times about which data set is being discussed, which type of output concept is involved, and whether the data are published:

$$Y^{\text{Output concept, Aggregation Level}}_{\text{Agency, Program, Status}}$$

where Output Concept indicates gross (G) or sectoral (S) output concepts; Aggregation Level indicates the SIC level of aggregation (two, three, or four-digit); Agency indicates BEA or BLS; Program indicates the BLS major-sector productivity program (M) or the BLS industry productivity program (I); and Status indicates whether the measure is published (P) or unpublished (U).

Value added measures were not included among the comparisons because BLS does not prepare such measures, and BEA prepares value added measures only at the SIC two-digit level.

For any two output measures, differences in the real and nominal output growth rates were assessed using two different approaches. The first approach calculated the difference in the acceleration of the average annual growth rate in the 1995–2000 period compared to the 1990–95 period. This difference in acceleration reflects differences in the change in the growth rate trends of the output measures between these two time periods. The second approach examined how closely the average annual growth rates of any two output series are correlated. The correlation coefficient, computed for the annual growth rates of the output series from 1988 to 2000, reflects the degree of consistency in the annual movements of the output measures over this time period.

To identify the sources of the differences among the output series, a series of comparisons were made. Current-dollar output series were compared to determine the role of differences in underlying data sources; constant and current-dollar output series were compared to determine the role of differences in price indexes and deflation methods; adjusted and unadjusted constant-dollar output estimates were compared to determine the impact of agency-specific adjustments; and related gross and sectoral output series were compared to determine the role of differences in output concept. In addition, an effort was made to document the raw data sources, adjustments, price indexes, deflation methods, aggregation methods, and other procedures used to prepare each series. Differences found among output series at the more aggregate two-digit level were further explored where data permit by examining differences in the underlying three- and four-digit industry output data. This case-study approach allows differences among output measures for SIC two-digit industries to be traced to the underlying three- and four-digit industry levels, where data permit. Appendix table 9B.2 summarizes the availability of the BEA and BLS output series by SIC two-, three-, and four-digit industry.[36]

SIC Two-Digit Manufacturing Industry Differences

Detailed manufacturing industry measures produced by both the BEA and the BLS are generally based on Census current-dollar data for the value of shipments, inventory change, and value of resales. Constant-dollar output series are developed by each agency using similar price indexes and

36. For example, SIC two-digit industries where comparisons among two or more of the BEA and BLS output series are possible include SICs 10, 12, 13, 14, 20–39, 40, 41, 42, 44, 45, 46, 47, 48, 49, 62, 63, 64, 67, 70, 72, 75, 78, 79, 80, and 82. SIC three-digit industries where comparisons are possible include all three-digit industries in the manufacturing industry groups 20–39 and in 43, 50, and 51; and selected three-digit industries in industry groups 10, 14, 48, 52, 53, 54, 55, 56, 58, 72, 75, and 78. SIC four-digit industry comparisons are possible for all four-digit industries in the manufacturing industry groups 20–39 and in 43 and 58; and for selected four-digit industries in industry groups 10, 57, 59, and 72.

deflation procedures, according to a 1997 memorandum of agreement between the BEA and the BLS. Although the published BEA SIC two-digit measures reflect a gross output concept, and the published BLS measures are based on a sectoral output concept, the measures are quite similar as a result of the common data source and price index agreement.

Three output measures as described below were compared for the SIC two-digit manufacturing industries. Y^{G-2}_{BEA-P} is a gross output measure for SIC two-digit industries that includes adjustments to correspond to NIPA definitions.[37] $Y^{S-2}_{BLS-M-P}$ is a sectoral output measure for SIC two-digit industries that was developed by the BLS for use in measuring MFP in manufacturing industries. The sectoral output concept excludes sales of intermediate products and services between establishments within a particular sector (intrasectoral transactions). $Y^{S-2}_{BLS-I-U}$ is a measure constructed for this chapter. It is a sectoral output measure for SIC two-digit industries, constructed by Tornqvist aggregation of BLS SIC three-digit sectoral output measures.[38] This output measure, while constructed based on SIC three-digit sectoral output measures, is not adjusted for additional intrasectoral transactions at the SIC two-digit level, and also does not reflect many of the adjustments which are made to the Y^{G-2}_{BEA-P} output measure.[39]

Comparisons of real output growth rates were made among these three output measures for selected SIC two-digit manufacturing industries. Eight of the twenty SIC two-digit manufacturing industries, SICs 20, 21, 27, 29, 31, 35, 38, and 39, were selected for further review based on fairly subjective criteria concerning differences in growth rate acceleeration and consistency of annual growth rates. Each of these industries has either an acceleration difference of 0.90 points or more or a correlation coefficient of 0.85 or less, for some combination of two of the three measures.[40] Based on these criteria and the results of the comparisons described in table 9.8, these industries were flagged for further exploration.[41]

---

37. BEA published gross output is measured as the value of shipments plus inventory changes less the cost of resales, plus misreporting and coverage adjustments, plus adjustments for own-account production of software, own-account construction work, and commodity (sales) taxes. Adjustments for inventory change and cost of resales are made only for goods-producing industries.

38. The sectoral measure for SIC two-digit industries is constructed by Tornqvist aggregation of BLS SIC three-digit sectoral output measures and contains no additional adjustments. The BLS sectoral output measures for SIC three-digit industries are measured as the value of shipments plus inventory changes, less resales and intra-industry shipments.

39. NAICS three-digit sectoral output measures that exclude all intrasectoral transfers are now available from the BLS industry productivity program.

40. The eight industries are SIC 20, Food and Kindred Products; SIC 21, Tobacco Products; SIC 27, Printing, Publishing, and Allied Industries; SIC 29, Petroleum Refining and Related Industries; SIC 31, Leather and Leather Products; SIC 35, Industrial and Commercial Machinery and Computer Equipment; SIC 38, Measuring, Analyzing, and Controlling Instruments; Photographic, Medical, and Optical Goods; Watches and Clocks; and SIC 39, Miscellaneous Manufacturing Industries.

41. It is useful to note that SIC 21, Tobacco Products, and SIC 31, Leather and Leather Products, are particularly small industries as measured by either employment or value added.

Table 9.8 Comparison of real output measures: Selected SIC 2-digit industries

SIC 2-digit industry	Output series	Average annual growth rate		Acceleration (2) − (1)	Output measure comparisons	Difference in acceleration	Correlation coefficient
		1990–1995 (1)	1995–2000 (2)				
SIC 20, Food and Kindred Products	Y^{G-2}_{BEA-P}	1.95	1.23	−0.72	$Y^{G-2}_{BEA-P}/Y^{S-2}_{BLS-I-U}$	−0.03	0.979
	$Y^{S-2}_{BLS-I-U}$	1.96	1.27	−0.69	$Y^{G-2}_{BEA-P}/Y^{S-2}_{BLS-M-P}$	0.94	0.640
	$Y^{S-2}_{BLS-M-P}$	2.67	1.02	−1.66	$Y^{S-2}_{BLS-I-U}/Y^{S-2}_{BLS-M-P}$	0.96	0.687
SIC 21, Tobacco Products	Y^{G-2}_{BEA-P}	0.33	−2.62	−2.95	$Y^{G-2}_{BEA-P}/Y^{S-2}_{BLS-I-U}$	0.66	0.996
	$Y^{S-2}_{BLS-I-U}$	0.82	−2.78	−3.61	$Y^{G-2}_{BEA-P}/Y^{S-2}_{BLS-M-U}$	0.95	0.977
	$Y^{S-2}_{BLS-M-U}$	0.70	−3.20	−3.89	$Y^{S-2}_{BLS-I-U}/Y^{S-2}_{BLS-M-U}$	−0.26	0.991
SIC 27, Printing, Publishing, and Allied Industries	Y^{G-2}_{BEA-P}	−0.47	1.22	1.69	$Y^{G-2}_{BEA-P}/Y^{S-2}_{BLS-I-U}$	−1.51	0.769
	$Y^{S-2}_{BLS-I-U}$	−0.42	2.77	3.20	$Y^{G-2}_{BEA-P}/Y^{S-2}_{BLS-M-P}$	0.41	0.904
	$Y^{S-2}_{BLS-M-P}$	−0.10	1.18	1.28	$Y^{S-2}_{BLS-I-U}/Y^{S-2}_{BLS-M-P}$	1.92	0.727
SIC 29, Petroleum Refining and Related Industries	Y^{G-2}_{BEA-P}	0.81	1.08	0.27	$Y^{G-2}_{BEA-P}/Y^{S-2}_{BLS-I-U}$	−0.11	−0.044
	$Y^{S-2}_{BLS-I-U}$	1.20	1.58	0.39	$Y^{G-2}_{BEA-P}/Y^{S-2}_{BLS-M-P}$	−0.35	−0.127
	$Y^{S-2}_{BLS-M-P}$	0.88	1.51	0.63	$Y^{S-2}_{BLS-I-U}/Y^{S-2}_{BLS-M-P}$	−0.24	0.988
SIC 31, Leather and Leather Products	Y^{G-2}_{BEA-P}	−1.97	−1.59	0.38	$Y^{G-2}_{BEA-P}/Y^{S-2}_{BLS-I-U}$	−1.14	0.949
	$Y^{S-2}_{BLS-I-U}$	−2.67	−1.15	1.52	$Y^{G-2}_{BEA-P}/Y^{S-2}_{BLS-M-U}$	−1.23	0.923
	$Y^{S-2}_{BLS-M-U}$	−3.14	−1.53	1.60	$Y^{S-2}_{BLS-I-U}/Y^{S-2}_{BLS-M-U}$	−0.08	0.969
SIC 35, Industrial and Commercial Machinery and Computer Equipment	Y^{G-2}_{BEA-P}	8.44	9.38	0.94	$Y^{G-2}_{BEA-P}/Y^{S-2}_{BLS-I-U}$	−1.09	0.991
	$Y^{S-2}_{BLS-I-U}$	8.02	10.05	2.03	$Y^{G-2}_{BEA-P}/Y^{S-2}_{BLS-M-P}$	−1.15	0.976
	$Y^{S-2}_{BLS-M-P}$	7.94	10.03	2.09	$Y^{S-2}_{BLS-I-U}/Y^{S-2}_{BLS-M-P}$	−0.06	0.985
SIC 38, Measuring, Analyzing, and Controlling Instruments; Photographic, Medical, and Optical Goods; Watches and Clocks	Y^{G-2}_{BEA-P}	1.05	3.20	2.15	$Y^{G-2}_{BEA-P}/Y^{S-2}_{BLS-I-U}$	−0.39	0.916
	$Y^{S-2}_{BLS-I-U}$	0.87	3.41	2.54	$Y^{G-2}_{BEA-P}/Y^{S-2}_{BLS-M-P}$	−0.62	0.597
	$Y^{S-2}_{BLS-M-P}$	1.27	4.04	2.77	$Y^{S-2}_{BLS-I-U}/Y^{S-2}_{BLS-M-P}$	−0.23	0.701
SIC 39, Miscellaneous Manufacturing Industries	Y^{G-2}_{BEA-P}	1.44	3.22	1.78	$Y^{G-2}_{BEA-P}/Y^{S-2}_{BLS-I-U}$	0.96	0.954
	$Y^{S-2}_{BLS-I-U}$	2.00	2.82	0.81	$Y^{G-2}_{BEA-P}/Y^{S-2}_{BLS-M-P}$	0.94	0.867
	$Y^{S-2}_{BLS-M-P}$	2.02	2.85	0.83	$Y^{S-2}_{BLS-I-U}/Y^{S-2}_{BLS-M-P}$	−0.02	0.842

Note: For SIC 21, Tobacco Products, and SIC 31, Leather and Leather Products, BLS output measures are unpublished because the output data for these industries is considered unreliable.

As seen in table 9.8, comparing the $Y_{\text{BEA-P}}^{\text{G-2}}$ and the $Y_{\text{BLS-M-P}}^{\text{S-2}}$ output measures, acceleration rate differences for SICs 20, 21, 31, 35, and 39 ranged from .94 points to –1.23 points.[42] Annual movements in these two output measures also differ for SICs 20, 29, 38, and 39. For the $Y_{\text{BEA-P}}^{\text{G-2}}$ and the $Y_{\text{BLS-IU}}^{\text{S-2}}$ output measures, acceleration rate differences for SICs 27, 31, 35, and 39 range from .96 points to –1.51 points, and the correlation coefficients for SICs 27 and 29 are low. For the two BLS measures, $Y_{\text{BLS-I-U}}^{\text{S-2}}$ and $Y_{\text{BLS-M-P}}^{\text{S-2}}$, acceleration rates differ for SICs 20 and 27 by .96 points and 1.92 points, respectively, and correlation coefficients are low for SICs 20, 27, 38, and 39.

SIC Two-Digit Nonmanufacturing Industry Differences

Although the nonmanufacturing sector accounts for about 80 percent of nonfarm business output excluding housing, data quality and industry detail are generally much less than for the manufacturing sector, and the BEA and BLS output measures accordingly are not as comparable as in manufacturing. The nonmanufacturing sector is a broad collection of diverse industries that includes goods-producing industries such as mining and construction and all of the services-producing industries. The BEA provides complete coverage of the nonmanufacturing sector at approximately the two-digit SIC level, whereas the BLS industry productivity program provides output and labor productivity measures for a wide variety of selected industries for which data quality is high and reliable labor productivity estimates can be prepared.[43] As a result of the differences in objectives and priorities, coverage by the BLS varies considerably across the nonmanufacturing sector.

Table 9.9 provides insight into the extent of coverage by the BLS industry productivity program by comparing the 1996 receipts of industries for which the BLS provides productivity measures to the BEA's published 1996 gross output. For each nonmanufacturing industry group, column (1) shows the sum of the BEA-derived receipts for those detailed industries for which BLS currently provides labor productivity measures. Column (2) shows the published BEA gross output measure for the industry group, and the third column shows column (1) as a percentage of column (2).[44] Farms,

42. BLS output and productivity measures for SIC 21, Tobacco Products, and SIC 31, Leather and Leather products, are unpublished because the output data for these industries are considered unreliable.

43. The BLS also provides SIC two-digit output and productivity measures for a broad range of industries for selected years in Gullickson and Harper (2002). These measures are prepared by the BLS major-sector productivity program. For SIC two-digit industries in the nonmanufacturing sector, these measures are considered unpublished and unofficial.

44. BEA gross output includes commodity taxes, own-account production, and adjustments for misreporting and coverage that are included at the publication level, but that are not included in the detailed industry receipts measures. As a result, the percentage in column (3) will always be less than 100 percent, even when all of the detailed industries in a group are covered by the BLS.

Table 9.9   **Receipts of industries covered by BLS compared with BEA gross output for nonmanufacturing industry groups, 1996 (billions of dollars)**

Industry group	Receipts of BLS industries in industry group[a] (1)	Published BEA industry gross output (2)	Receipts as percent of BEA gross output (1)/(2)
Nonmanufacturing, total	3622.1	7826.9	46.3
Agriculture excl. farms	0.0	55.8	0.0
Mining	178.1	186.6	95.4
Metal mining	8.7	12.6	68.7
Coal mining	25.3	27.1	93.3
Oil and gas extraction	127.6	129.8	98.2
Nonmetallic minerals	16.5	17.0	97.1
Construction	0.0	554.5	0.0
Transportation	351.5	477.9	73.6
Railroad transportation	39.2	40.7	96.3
Local passenger transit	0.0	24.2	0.0
Trucking and warehousing	189.6	213.8	88.7
Water transportation	0.0	36.4	0.0
Transportation by air	115.3	117.3	98.3
Pipelines, excl. natural gas	7.4	7.8	94.5
Transportation services	0.0	37.7	0.0
Communications	318.0	348.7	91.2
Telephone and telegraph	240.5	270.0	89.1
Radio and television	77.5	78.8	98.4
Electricity, gas, and sanitary services	308.0	336.2	91.6
Wholesale trade	672.9	789.8	85.2
Retail trade	951.8	1070.9	88.9
FIRE less nonfarm housing	339.4	1499.3	22.6
Depository institutions	339.4	342.7	99.1
Nondepository Institutions	0.0	108.4	0.0
Security and communication brokers	0.0	169.3	0.0
Insurance carriers	0.0	261.5	0.0
Insurance agents and brokers	0.0	74.0	0.0
Real estate excl. housing	0.0	520.4	0.0
Holding and investment offices	0.0	23.1	0.0
Services less households	502.4	2507.3	20.0
Hotels and lodging	95.6	106.5	89.8
Personal services	83.3	84.6	98.5
Business services	214.8	510.6	42.1
Auto repair and services	101.6	124.3	81.7
Miscellaneous repair services	0.0	46.4	0.0
Motion pictures	7.1	56.8	12.6
Amusement and recreation services	0.0	110.7	0.0
Health services	0.0	688.0	0.0
Legal services	0.0	134.1	0.0
Educational services	0.0	103.8	0.0
Social services	0.0	98.7	0.0
Membership organizations	0.0	96.2	0.0
Other services	0.0	346.6	0.0

[a]Sum of BEA detailed receipts estimates for those industries covered by BLS.

nonfarm housing services, private households, and government are excluded for comparability with the nonfarm business sector.

For all of nonmanufacturing, receipts of industries covered by the BLS industry productivity program accounted for nearly one-half of gross output in 1996. Industry groups with complete or nearly complete coverage by the BLS include mining, communications, wholesale trade, retail trade, and electric, gas, and sanitary services. Industry groups with partial coverage include transportation and services. The BLS does not provide any output measures for agriculture and construction, and provides a measure only for commercial banks (part of depository institutions) in the finance, insurance, and real estate (FIRE) group. Within the services group, the BLS provides complete or nearly complete coverage for hotels and lodging places, personal services, and auto repair and services. No output measures are provided for industries with a large nonprofit component, such as health services, educational services, social services, and membership organizations.

BEA and BLS real output measures were compared for SIC two-digit nonmanufacturing industries when two or more output measures were available.[45] These measures include a published BEA gross output measure, Y^{G-2}_{BEA-P}, an unpublished BLS gross output measure, $Y^{G-2}_{BLS-M-U}$, and an unpublished BLS sectoral output measure, $Y^{S-2}_{BLS-I-U}$. As with manufacturing, trend growth rates by industry for 1990–95 and 1995–2000 were compared and differences in acceleration between these two time periods were calculated. Correlation coefficients were are also calculated among the output series.

Given the greater differences in data sources and methods for the BEA and BLS output measures for SIC two-digit nonmanufacturing industries, it is unsurprising that these measures differ from one another to a much greater extent and for a higher proportion of the industries than in manufacturing. Of the twenty-two SIC two-digit nonmanufacturing industries examined, sixteen display acceleration differences that exceed 0.90 points for some combination of two of the three measures. As seen in table 9.10, for the Y^{G-2}_{BEA-P} and the $Y^{G-2}_{BLS-M-U}$ output measures, differences in acceleration rates exceed the cutoff for SICs 10, 13, 41, 42, 44, 45, 46, 48, 49, 62, 63, 64, 72, 78, 79, and 82. Among these sixteen industries, acceleration differences

45. These industries include SIC 10, Metal Mining; SIC 12, Coal Mining; SIC 13, Oil and Gas Extraction; SIC 14, Mining and Quarrying of Nonmetallic Minerals, Except Fuels; SIC 40, Railroad Transportation; SIC 41, Local and Suburban Transit and Interurban Highway Passenger Transportation; SIC 42, Motor Freight Transportation and Warehousing; SIC 44, Water Transportation; SIC 45, Transportation by Air; SIC 46, Pipelines, Except Natural Gas; SIC 47, Transportation Services; SIC 48, Communications; SIC 49, Electric, Gas, and Sanitary Services; SIC 62, Security and Commodity Brokers, Dealers, Exchanges, and Services; SIC 63, Insurance Carriers; SIC 64, Insured Agents, Brokers, and Service; SIC 70, Hotels, Rooming Houses, Camps, and Other Lodging Places; SIC 72, Personal Services; SIC 75, Automotive Repair, Services, and Parking; SIC 78, Motion Pictures; SIC 79, Amusement and Recreation Services; SIC 80, Health Services; and SIC 82, Educational Services.

Table 9.10   Comparison of real output measures: SIC 2-digit nonmanufacturing industries

SIC 2-digit industry	Output measures	Average annual growth rate (1990–1995) (1)	Average annual growth rate (1995–2000) (2)	Acceleration (2) – (1)	Output measure comparisons	Difference in acceleration	Correlation coefficient
SIC 10, Metal Mining	Y^{G-2}_{BEA-P}	2.08	−0.48	−2.57	$Y^{G-2}_{BEA-P}/Y^{S-2}_{BLS-I-U}$	n.a.	n.a.
	$Y^{S-2}_{BLS-I-U}$	n.a.	n.a.	n.a.	$Y^{G-2}_{BEA-P}/Y^{G-2}_{BLS-M-U}$	−1.52	0.93
	$Y^{G-2}_{BLS-M-U}$	1.69	0.65	−1.04	$Y^{S-2}_{BLS-I-U}/Y^{G-2}_{BLS-M-U}$	n.a.	n.a.
SIC 12, Coal Mining	Y^{G-2}_{BEA-P}	0.50	0.58	0.08	$Y^{G-2}_{BEA-P}/Y^{S-2}_{BLS-I-U}$	−0.37	0.98
	$Y^{S-2}_{BLS-I-U}$	−0.91	−0.45	0.46	$Y^{G-2}_{BEA-P}/Y^{G-2}_{BLS-M-U}$	n.a.	n.a.
	$Y^{G-2}_{BLS-M-U}$	n.a.	n.a.	n.a.	$Y^{S-2}_{BLS-I-U}/Y^{G-2}_{BLS-M-U}$	n.a.	n.a.
SIC 13, Oil and Gas Extraction	Y^{G-2}_{BEA-P}	−0.40	0.74	1.14	$Y^{G-2}_{BEA-P}/Y^{S-2}_{BLS-I-U}$	1.15	0.68
	$Y^{S-2}_{BLS-I-U}$	−0.75	−0.75	−0.01	$Y^{G-2}_{BEA-P}/Y^{G-2}_{BLS-M-U}$	−1.09	0.92
	$Y^{G-2}_{BLS-M-U}$	−1.12	1.12	2.24	$Y^{S-2}_{BLS-I-U}/Y^{G-2}_{BLS-M-U}$	−2.24	0.70
SIC 14, Mining and Quarrying of Nonmetallic Minerals, Except Fuels	Y^{G-2}_{BEA-P}	1.14	2.10	0.96	$Y^{G-2}_{BEA-P}/Y^{S-2}_{BLS-I-U}$	−0.05	0.97
	$Y^{S-2}_{BLS-I-U}$	0.14	1.15	1.01	$Y^{G-2}_{BEA-P}/Y^{G-2}_{BLS-M-U}$	−0.10	0.83
	$Y^{G-2}_{BLS-M-U}$	1.61	2.67	1.06	$Y^{S-2}_{BLS-I-U}/Y^{G-2}_{BLS-M-U}$	−0.05	0.82
SIC 40, Railroad Transportation	Y^{G-2}_{BEA-P}	3.39	0.67	−2.72	$Y^{G-2}_{BEA-P}/Y^{S-2}_{BLS-I-U}$	n.a.	n.a.
	$Y^{S-2}_{BLS-I-U}$	n.a.	n.a.	n.a.	$Y^{G-2}_{BEA-P}/Y^{G-2}_{BLS-M-U}$	−0.47	0.64
	$Y^{G-2}_{BLS-M-U}$	1.63	−0.62	−2.25	$Y^{S-2}_{BLS-I-U}/Y^{G-2}_{BLS-M-U}$	n.a.	n.a.
SIC 41, Local and Suburban Transit and Interurban Highway Passenger Transportation	Y^{G-2}_{BEA-P}	0.54	2.36	1.82	$Y^{G-2}_{BEA-P}/Y^{S-2}_{BLS-I-U}$	n.a.	n.a.
	$Y^{S-2}_{BLS-I-U}$	n.a.	n.a.	n.a.	$Y^{G-2}_{BEA-P}/Y^{G-2}_{BLS-M-U}$	2.18	0.75
	$Y^{G-2}_{BLS-M-U}$	1.59	1.22	−0.36	$Y^{S-2}_{BLS-I-U}/Y^{G-2}_{BLS-M-U}$	n.a.	n.a.
SIC 42, Motor Freight Transportation and Warehousing	Y^{G-2}_{BEA-P}	4.89	4.06	−0.82	$Y^{G-2}_{BEA-P}/Y^{S-2}_{BLS-I-U}$	n.a.	n.a.
	$Y^{S-2}_{BLS-I-U}$	n.a.	n.a.	n.a.	$Y^{G-2}_{BEA-P}/Y^{G-2}_{BLS-M-U}$	−0.97	0.54
	$Y^{G-2}_{BLS-M-U}$	4.48	4.63	0.15	$Y^{S-2}_{BLS-I-U}/Y^{G-2}_{BLS-M-U}$	n.a.	n.a.

SIC	Variable				Ratio		
SIC 43, United States Postal Service	Y^{G-2}_{BEA-P}	n.a.	n.a.	n.a.	$Y^{G-2}_{BEA-P}/Y^{S-2}_{BLS-I-U}$	n.a.	n.a.
	$Y^{S-2}_{BLS-I-U}$	1.45	2.37	0.93	$Y^{G-2}_{BEA-P}/Y^{G-2}_{BLS-M-U}$	n.a.	n.a.
	$Y^{G-2}_{BLS-M-U}$	n.a.	n.a.	n.a.	$Y^{S-2}_{BLS-I-U}/Y^{G-2}_{BLS-M-U}$	n.a.	n.a.
SIC 44, Water Transportation	Y^{G-2}_{BEA-P}	2.39	4.72	2.33	$Y^{G-2}_{BEA-P}/Y^{S-2}_{BLS-I-U}$	n.a.	n.a.
	$Y^{S-2}_{BLS-I-U}$	n.a.	n.a.	n.a.	$Y^{G-2}_{BEA-P}/Y^{G-2}_{BLS-M-U}$	5.25	0.54
	$Y^{G-2}_{BLS-M-U}$	2.40	-0.52	-2.92	$Y^{S-2}_{BLS-I-U}/Y^{G-2}_{BLS-M-U}$	n.a.	n.a.
SIC 45, Transportation by Air	Y^{G-2}_{BEA-P}	3.14	5.39	2.25	$Y^{G-2}_{BEA-P}/Y^{S-2}_{BLS-I-U}$	n.a.	n.a.
	$Y^{S-2}_{BLS-I-U}$	n.a.	n.a.	n.a.	$Y^{G-2}_{BEA-P}/Y^{G-2}_{BLS-M-U}$	4.61	0.40
	$Y^{G-2}_{BLS-M-U}$	3.84	1.48	-2.36	$Y^{S-2}_{BLS-I-U}/Y^{G-2}_{BLS-M-U}$	n.a.	n.a.
SIC 46, Pipelines, Except Natural Gas	Y^{G-2}_{BEA-P}	-5.39	0.14	5.52	$Y^{G-2}_{BEA-P}/Y^{S-2}_{BLS-I-U}$	n.a.	n.a.
	$Y^{S-2}_{BLS-I-U}$	n.a.	n.a.	n.a.	$Y^{G-2}_{BEA-P}/Y^{G-2}_{BLS-M-U}$	7.17	0.62
	$Y^{G-2}_{BLS-M-U}$	-1.39	-3.04	-1.65	$Y^{S-2}_{BLS-I-U}/Y^{G-2}_{BLS-M-U}$	n.a.	n.a.
SIC 47, Transportation Services	Y^{G-2}_{BEA-P}	4.78	6.21	1.43	$Y^{G-2}_{BEA-P}/Y^{S-2}_{BLS-I-U}$	n.a.	n.a.
	$Y^{S-2}_{BLS-I-U}$	n.a.	n.a.	n.a.	$Y^{G-2}_{BEA-P}/Y^{G-2}_{BLS-M-U}$	0.16	0.56
	$Y^{G-2}_{BLS-M-U}$	4.48	5.75	1.26	$Y^{S-2}_{BLS-I-U}/Y^{G-2}_{BLS-M-U}$	n.a.	n.a.
SIC 48, Communications	Y^{G-2}_{BEA-P}	5.55	11.38	5.83	$Y^{G-2}_{BEA-P}/Y^{S-2}_{BLS-I-U}$	n.a.	n.a.
	$Y^{S-2}_{BLS-I-U}$	n.a.	n.a.	n.a.	$Y^{G-2}_{BEA-P}/Y^{G-2}_{BLS-M-U}$	3.53	0.70
	$Y^{G-2}_{BLS-M-U}$	4.38	6.67	2.30	$Y^{S-2}_{BLS-I-U}/Y^{G-2}_{BLS-M-U}$	n.a.	n.a.
SIC 49, Electric, Gas, and Sanitary Services	Y^{G-2}_{BEA-P}	1.96	1.48	-0.48	$Y^{G-2}_{BEA-P}/Y^{S-2}_{BLS-I-U}$	n.a.	n.a.
	$Y^{S-2}_{BLS-I-U}$	n.a.	n.a.	n.a.	$Y^{G-2}_{BEA-P}/Y^{G-2}_{BLS-M-U}$	-1.97	0.11
	$Y^{G-2}_{BLS-M-U}$	0.14	1.63	1.49	$Y^{S-2}_{BLS-I-U}/Y^{G-2}_{BLS-M-U}$	n.a.	n.a.
SIC 50, Wholesale Trade: Durable Goods	Y^{G-2}_{BEA-P}	n.a.	n.a.	n.a.	$Y^{G-2}_{BEA-P}/Y^{S-2}_{BLS-I-U}$	n.a.	n.a.
	$Y^{S-2}_{BLS-I-U}$	5.56	8.57	3.01	$Y^{G-2}_{BEA-P}/Y^{G-2}_{BLS-M-U}$	n.a.	n.a.
	$Y^{G-2}_{BLS-M-U}$	n.a.	n.a.	n.a.	$Y^{S-2}_{BLS-I-U}/Y^{G-2}_{BLS-M-U}$	n.a.	n.a.
SIC 51, Wholesale Trade: Nondurable Goods	Y^{G-2}_{BEA-P}	n.a.	n.a.	n.a.	$Y^{G-2}_{BEA-P}/Y^{S-2}_{BLS-I-U}$	n.a.	n.a.
	$Y^{S-2}_{BLS-I-U}$	1.05	2.29	1.24	$Y^{G-2}_{BEA-P}/Y^{G-2}_{BLS-M-U}$	n.a.	n.a.
	$Y^{G-2}_{BLS-M-U}$	n.a.	n.a.	n.a.	$Y^{S-2}_{BLS-I-U}/Y^{G-2}_{BLS-M-U}$	n.a.	n.a.

(continued)

Table 9.10   (continued)

SIC 2-digit industry	Output measures	Average annual growth rate (1990–1995) (1)	Average annual growth rate (1995–2000) (2)	Acceleration (2) − (1)	Output measure comparisons	Difference in acceleration	Correlation coefficient
SIC 60, Depository Institutions	$Y^{G\text{-}2}_{BEA\text{-}P}$	1.31	2.93	1.63	$Y^{G\text{-}2}_{BEA\text{-}P}/Y^{S\text{-}2}_{BLS\text{-}I\text{-}U}$	n.a.	n.a.
	$Y^{S\text{-}2}_{BLS\text{-}I\text{-}U}$	n.a.	n.a.	n.a.	$Y^{G\text{-}2}_{BEA\text{-}P}/Y^{G\text{-}2}_{BLS\text{-}M\text{-}U}$	n.a.	n.a.
	$Y^{G\text{-}2}_{BLS\text{-}M\text{-}U}$	n.a.	n.a.	n.a.	$Y^{S\text{-}2}_{BLS\text{-}I\text{-}U}/Y^{G\text{-}2}_{BLS\text{-}M\text{-}U}$	n.a.	n.a.
SIC 61, Nondepository Credit Institutions	$Y^{G\text{-}2}_{BEA\text{-}P}$	9.49	12.27	2.78	$Y^{G\text{-}2}_{BEA\text{-}P}/Y^{S\text{-}2}_{BLS\text{-}I\text{-}U}$	n.a.	n.a.
	$Y^{S\text{-}2}_{BLS\text{-}I\text{-}U}$	n.a.	n.a.	n.a.	$Y^{G\text{-}2}_{BEA\text{-}P}/Y^{G\text{-}2}_{BLS\text{-}M\text{-}U}$	n.a.	n.a.
	$Y^{G\text{-}2}_{BLS\text{-}M\text{-}U}$	n.a.	n.a.	n.a.	$Y^{S\text{-}2}_{BLS\text{-}I\text{-}U}/Y^{G\text{-}2}_{BLS\text{-}M\text{-}U}$	n.a.	n.a.
SIC 62, Security and Commodity Brokers, Dealers, Exchanges, and Services	$Y^{G\text{-}2}_{BEA\text{-}P}$	16.11	23.35	7.24	$Y^{G\text{-}2}_{BEA\text{-}P}/Y^{S\text{-}2}_{BLS\text{-}I\text{-}U}$	n.a.	n.a.
	$Y^{S\text{-}2}_{BLS\text{-}I\text{-}U}$	n.a.	n.a.	n.a.	$Y^{G\text{-}2}_{BEA\text{-}P}/Y^{G\text{-}2}_{BLS\text{-}M\text{-}U}$	-1.24	0.80
	$Y^{G\text{-}2}_{BLS\text{-}M\text{-}U}$	13.54	22.02	8.48	$Y^{S\text{-}2}_{BLS\text{-}I\text{-}U}/Y^{G\text{-}2}_{BLS\text{-}M\text{-}U}$	n.a.	n.a.
SIC 63, Insurance Carriers	$Y^{G\text{-}2}_{BEA\text{-}P}$	-0.15	-1.53	-1.38	$Y^{G\text{-}2}_{BEA\text{-}P}/Y^{S\text{-}2}_{BLS\text{-}I\text{-}U}$	n.a.	n.a.
	$Y^{S\text{-}2}_{BLS\text{-}I\text{-}U}$	n.a.	n.a.	n.a.	$Y^{G\text{-}2}_{BEA\text{-}P}/Y^{G\text{-}2}_{BLS\text{-}M\text{-}U}$	-1.15	0.72
	$Y^{G\text{-}2}_{BLS\text{-}M\text{-}U}$	0.87	0.64	-0.23	$Y^{S\text{-}2}_{BLS\text{-}I\text{-}U}/Y^{G\text{-}2}_{BLS\text{-}M\text{-}U}$	n.a.	n.a.
SIC 64, Insurance Agents, Brokers, and Service	$Y^{G\text{-}2}_{BEA\text{-}P}$	-2.67	4.07	6.74	$Y^{G\text{-}2}_{BEA\text{-}P}/Y^{S\text{-}2}_{BLS\text{-}I\text{-}U}$	n.a.	n.a.
	$Y^{S\text{-}2}_{BLS\text{-}I\text{-}U}$	n.a.	n.a.	n.a.	$Y^{G\text{-}2}_{BEA\text{-}P}/Y^{G\text{-}2}_{BLS\text{-}M\text{-}U}$	2.30	-0.11
	$Y^{G\text{-}2}_{BLS\text{-}M\text{-}U}$	-0.41	4.03	4.44	$Y^{S\text{-}2}_{BLS\text{-}I\text{-}U}/Y^{G\text{-}2}_{BLS\text{-}M\text{-}U}$	n.a.	n.a.
SIC 65, Real Estate	$Y^{G\text{-}2}_{BEA\text{-}P}$	2.28	3.18	0.90	$Y^{G\text{-}2}_{BEA\text{-}P}/Y^{S\text{-}2}_{BLS\text{-}I\text{-}U}$	n.a.	n.a.
	$Y^{S\text{-}2}_{BLS\text{-}I\text{-}U}$	n.a.	n.a.	n.a.	$Y^{G\text{-}2}_{BEA\text{-}P}/Y^{G\text{-}2}_{BLS\text{-}M\text{-}U}$	n.a.	n.a.
	$Y^{G\text{-}2}_{BLS\text{-}M\text{-}U}$	n.a.	n.a.	n.a.	$Y^{S\text{-}2}_{BLS\text{-}I\text{-}U}/Y^{G\text{-}2}_{BLS\text{-}M\text{-}U}$	n.a.	n.a.
SIC 67, Holding and Other Investment Offices	$Y^{G\text{-}2}_{BEA\text{-}P}$	1.35	7.85	6.50	$Y^{G\text{-}2}_{BEA\text{-}P}/Y^{S\text{-}2}_{BLS\text{-}I\text{-}U}$	n.a.	n.a.
	$Y^{S\text{-}2}_{BLS\text{-}I\text{-}U}$	n.a.	n.a.	n.a.	$Y^{G\text{-}2}_{BEA\text{-}P}/Y^{G\text{-}2}_{BLS\text{-}M\text{-}U}$	n.a.	n.a.
	$Y^{G\text{-}2}_{BLS\text{-}M\text{-}U}$	n.a.	n.a.	n.a.	$Y^{S\text{-}2}_{BLS\text{-}I\text{-}U}/Y^{G\text{-}2}_{BLS\text{-}M\text{-}U}$	n.a.	n.a.

SIC 70, Hotels, Rooming Houses, Camps, and Other Lodging Places	Y^{G-2}_{BEA-P}	2.62	3.19	0.57	$Y^{G-2}_{BEA-P}/Y^{S-2}_{BLS-I-U}$	n.a.	n.a.
	$Y^{S-2}_{BLS-I-U}$	n.a.	n.a.	n.a.	$Y^{G-2}_{BEA-P}/Y^{G-2}_{BLS-M-U}$	0.08	0.93
	$Y^{G-2}_{BLS-M-U}$	2.27	2.76	0.49	$Y^{S-2}_{BLS-I-U}/Y^{G-2}_{BLS-M-U}$	n.a.	n.a.
SIC 72, Personal Services	Y^{G-2}_{BEA-P}	2.45	2.71	0.26	$Y^{G-2}_{BEA-P}/Y^{S-2}_{BLS-I-U}$	-1.20	0.95
	$Y^{S-2}_{BLS-I-U}$	1.44	2.89	1.45	$Y^{G-2}_{BEA-P}/Y^{G-2}_{BLS-M-U}$	-1.97	0.90
	$Y^{G-2}_{BLS-M-U}$	1.33	3.56	2.23	$Y^{S-2}_{BLS-I-U}/Y^{G-2}_{BLS-M-U}$	-0.78	0.97
SIC 73, Business Services	Y^{G-2}_{BEA-P}	6.76	11.10	4.34	$Y^{G-2}_{BEA-P}/Y^{S-2}_{BLS-I-U}$	n.a.	n.a.
	$Y^{S-2}_{BLS-I-U}$	n.a.	n.a.	n.a.	$Y^{G-2}_{BEA-P}/Y^{G-2}_{BLS-M-U}$	n.a.	n.a.
	$Y^{G-2}_{BLS-M-U}$	n.a.	n.a.	n.a.	$Y^{S-2}_{BLS-I-U}/Y^{G-2}_{BLS-M-U}$	n.a.	n.a.
SIC 75, Automotive Repair, Services, and Parking	Y^{G-2}_{BEA-P}	2.98	4.09	1.12	$Y^{G-2}_{BEA-P}/Y^{S-2}_{BLS-I-U}$	n.a.	n.a.
	$Y^{S-2}_{BLS-I-U}$	n.a.	n.a.	n.a.	$Y^{G-2}_{BEA-P}/Y^{G-2}_{BLS-M-U}$	0.33	0.84
	$Y^{G-2}_{BLS-M-U}$	4.40	5.18	0.79	$Y^{S-2}_{BLS-I-U}/Y^{G-2}_{BLS-M-U}$	n.a.	n.a.
SIC 76, Miscellaneous Repair Services	Y^{G-2}_{BEA-P}	2.11	0.96	-1.15	$Y^{G-2}_{BEA-P}/Y^{S-2}_{BLS-I-U}$	n.a.	n.a.
	$Y^{S-2}_{BLS-I-U}$	n.a.	n.a.	n.a.	$Y^{G-2}_{BEA-P}/Y^{G-2}_{BLS-M-U}$	n.a.	n.a.
	$Y^{G-2}_{BLS-M-U}$	n.a.	n.a.	n.a.	$Y^{S-2}_{BLS-I-U}/Y^{G-2}_{BLS-M-U}$	n.a.	n.a.
SIC 78, Motion Pictures	Y^{G-2}_{BEA-P}	3.89	2.95	-0.94	$Y^{G-2}_{BEA-P}/Y^{S-2}_{BLS-I-U}$	n.a.	n.a.
	$Y^{S-2}_{BLS-I-U}$	n.a.	n.a.	n.a.	$Y^{G-2}_{BEA-P}/Y^{G-2}_{BLS-M-U}$	-2.78	0.46
	$Y^{G-2}_{BLS-M-U}$	4.74	6.58	1.83	$Y^{S-2}_{BLS-I-U}/Y^{G-2}_{BLS-M-U}$	n.a.	n.a.
SIC 79, Amusement and Recreation Services	Y^{G-2}_{BEA-P}	6.74	3.87	-2.86	$Y^{G-2}_{BEA-P}/Y^{S-2}_{BLS-I-U}$	n.a.	n.a.
	$Y^{S-2}_{BLS-I-U}$	n.a.	n.a.	n.a.	$Y^{G-2}_{BEA-P}/Y^{G-2}_{BLS-M-U}$	-3.80	0.34
	$Y^{G-2}_{BLS-M-U}$	5.85	6.79	0.94	$Y^{S-2}_{BLS-I-U}/Y^{G-2}_{BLS-M-U}$	n.a.	n.a.
SIC 80, Health Services	Y^{G-2}_{BEA-P}	2.32	2.57	0.25	$Y^{G-2}_{BEA-P}/Y^{S-2}_{BLS-I-U}$	n.a.	n.a.
	$Y^{S-2}_{BLS-I-U}$	n.a.	n.a.	n.a.	$Y^{G-2}_{BEA-P}/Y^{G-2}_{BLS-M-U}$	-0.27	0.91
	$Y^{G-2}_{BLS-M-U}$	2.66	3.18	0.52	$Y^{S-2}_{BLS-I-U}/Y^{G-2}_{BLS-M-U}$	n.a.	n.a.
SIC 81, Legal Services	Y^{G-2}_{BEA-P}	-0.66	2.86	3.52	$Y^{G-2}_{BEA-P}/Y^{S-2}_{BLS-I-U}$	n.a.	n.a.
	$Y^{S-2}_{BLS-I-U}$	n.a.	n.a.	n.a.	$Y^{G-2}_{BEA-P}/Y^{G-2}_{BLS-M-U}$	n.a.	n.a.
	$Y^{G-2}_{BLS-M-U}$	n.a.	n.a.	n.a.	$Y^{S-2}_{BLS-I-U}/Y^{G-2}_{BLS-M-U}$	n.a.	n.a.

(continued)

Table 9.10 (continued)

SIC 2-digit industry	Output measures	Average annual growth rate (1990–1995) (1)	Average annual growth rate (1995–2000) (2)	Acceleration (2) − (1)	Output measure comparisons	Difference in acceleration	Correlation coefficient
SIC 82, Educational Services	$Y^{G\text{-}2}_{BEA\text{-}P}$	2.86	2.75	−0.11	$Y^{G\text{-}2}_{BEA\text{-}P}/Y^{S\text{-}2}_{BLS\text{-}I\text{-}U}$	n.a.	n.a.
	$Y^{S\text{-}2}_{BLS\text{-}I\text{-}U}$	n.a.	n.a.	n.a.	$Y^{G\text{-}2}_{BEA\text{-}P}/Y^{G\text{-}2}_{BLS\text{-}M\text{-}U}$	−3.44	0.58
	$Y^{G\text{-}2}_{BLS\text{-}M\text{-}U}$	0.35	3.68	3.33	$Y^{S\text{-}2}_{BLS\text{-}I\text{-}U}/Y^{G\text{-}2}_{BLS\text{-}M\text{-}U}$	n.a.	n.a.
SIC 83, Social Services	$Y^{G\text{-}2}_{BEA\text{-}P}$	4.15	5.01	0.87	$Y^{G\text{-}2}_{BEA\text{-}P}/Y^{S\text{-}2}_{BLS\text{-}I\text{-}U}$	n.a.	n.a.
	$Y^{S\text{-}2}_{BLS\text{-}I\text{-}U}$	n.a.	n.a.	n.a.	$Y^{G\text{-}2}_{BEA\text{-}P}/Y^{G\text{-}2}_{BLS\text{-}M\text{-}U}$	n.a.	n.a.
	$Y^{G\text{-}2}_{BLS\text{-}M\text{-}U}$	n.a.	n.a.	n.a.	$Y^{S\text{-}2}_{BLS\text{-}I\text{-}U}/Y^{G\text{-}2}_{BLS\text{-}M\text{-}U}$	n.a.	n.a.
SIC 86, Membership Organizations	$Y^{G\text{-}2}_{BEA\text{-}P}$	3.21	1.05	−2.15	$Y^{G\text{-}2}_{BEA\text{-}P}/Y^{S\text{-}2}_{BLS\text{-}I\text{-}U}$	n.a.	n.a.
	$Y^{S\text{-}2}_{BLS\text{-}I\text{-}U}$	n.a.	n.a.	n.a.	$Y^{G\text{-}2}_{BEA\text{-}P}/Y^{G\text{-}2}_{BLS\text{-}M\text{-}U}$	n.a.	n.a.
	$Y^{G\text{-}2}_{BLS\text{-}M\text{-}U}$	n.a.	n.a.	n.a.	$Y^{S\text{-}2}_{BLS\text{-}I\text{-}U}/Y^{G\text{-}2}_{BLS\text{-}M\text{-}U}$	n.a.	n.a.
SIC 88, Private Households	$Y^{G\text{-}2}_{BEA\text{-}P}$	1.43	−0.42	−1.84	$Y^{G\text{-}2}_{BEA\text{-}P}/Y^{S\text{-}2}_{BLS\text{-}I\text{-}U}$	n.a.	n.a.
	$Y^{S\text{-}2}_{BLS\text{-}I\text{-}U}$	n.a.	n.a.	n.a.	$Y^{G\text{-}2}_{BEA\text{-}P}/Y^{G\text{-}2}_{BLS\text{-}M\text{-}U}$	n.a.	n.a.
	$Y^{G\text{-}2}_{BLS\text{-}M\text{-}U}$	n.a.	n.a.	n.a.	$Y^{S\text{-}2}_{BLS\text{-}I\text{-}U}/Y^{G\text{-}2}_{BLS\text{-}M\text{-}U}$	n.a.	n.a.

Notes: n.a. = not available. Output data are not available for the following: SIC 01, Agricultural Production Crops; SIC 02, Agricultural Production, Livestock, and Animal Specialties; SIC 07, Agricultural Services; SIC 08, Forestry; SIC 09, Fishing, Hunting and Trapping; SIC 15, Building Construction, General Contractors, and Operative Builders; SIC 16, Heavy Construction Other Than Building Construction; SIC 17, Construction, Special Trade Contractors; SIC 84, Museums, Art Galleries, and Botanical and Zoological Gardens; SIC 87, Engineering, Accounting, Research, Management, and Related Services; SIC 91, Executive, Legislative, and General Government, Except Finance; SIC 92, Justice, Public Order, and Safety; SIC 93, Public Finance, Taxation, and Monetary Policy; SIC 94, Administration of Human Resource Programs; SIC 95, Administration of Environmental Quality and Housing; SIC 96, Administration of Economic Programs; SIC 97, National Security and International Affairs; SIC 99, Nonclassifiable Establishments.

range from .9 points to 2.0 points for seven industries; from 2.0 points to 3.0 points for three industries; from 3.0 points to 4.0 points for three industries; and from 4.0 points to more than 7.0 points for three industries. The largest differences in acceleration rates were found in the transportation industries and in the pipelines except natural gas industry.

Based on the correlation coefficient criteria for consistency in annual changes, the $Y^{\text{G-2}}_{\text{BEA-P}}$ and $Y^{\text{G-2}}_{\text{BLS-M-U}}$ nonmanufacturing output measures differ in annual movements for SICs 14, 40, 41, 42, 44, 45, 46, 47, 48, 49, 62, 63, 64, 75, 78, 79, and 82. The $Y^{\text{G-2}}_{\text{BEA-P}}$ measure and the $Y^{\text{S-2}}_{\text{BLS-I-U}}$ measure were compared only for SICs 12, 13, 14, and 72 at the SIC two-digit level, with acceleration differences greater than .90 in SIC 13 and 72 as well as differences in annual movements in SIC 13. The $Y^{\text{G-2}}_{\text{BLS-M-U}}$ and the $Y^{\text{S-2}}_{\text{BLS-I-U}}$ measures were compared for SICs 13, 14, and 72 as well, indicating differences in acceleration and annual movements for SIC 13. Based on these results, BEA and BLS output measures for SICs 10, 13, 41, 42, 44, 45, 46, 48, 49, 62, 63, 64, 72, 78, 79, and 82 were flagged for further examination.

Sources of Differences

BEA and BLS real output measures for SIC two-digit industries 12, 14, 22, 23, 24, 25, 26, 28, 30, 32, 33, 34, 36, 37, 70, 75, and 80 have very similar trend growth rates and annual movements in growth rates.[46] However, according to these criteria, BEA and BLS output measures for SICs 10, 13, 20, 21, 27, 29, 31, 35, 38, 39, 40, 41, 42, 44, 45, 46, 47, 48, 49, 62, 63, 64, 72, 78, 79, and 82 differ significantly. Possible explanations for differences among these output measures include differences in source data, deflation methods, adjustments to the source data, and differences in output concept.

Source data. Source data differences were examined by comparing trend growth rates and correlations for available current-dollar measures. Source data are most likely fundamentally different when current-dollar trend growth rates differ across output measures and the correlation of current-dollar annual growth rates is low. Among the twenty-six industries identified above with significant differences in real output growth rates, nineteen exhibit similar differences in their current-dollar growth rates. As shown in appendix table 9B.3, these nineteen industries are SICs 10, 13, 20, 21, 27, 38, 41, 44, 45, 46, 47, 48, 49, 62, 63, 64, 78, 79, and 82. Of these industries, SICs 20, 38, 63, and 64 have acceleration differences less than .90 points, but two or more of the output measures have correlation coefficients less than .85. Of the remaining industries, acceleration differences range from .90 points to 2.0 points in SICs 27, 48, and 49; from 2.0 points to 3.0 points in SICs 41 and 82; from 3.0 points to 4.0 points in SICs 21, 45, 78, and 79;

---

46. The more detailed three- and four-digit industries in each of these industry groups have not been compared.

and from 4.0 points to more than 12.0 points in SICs 10, 13, 44, 46, 47, and 62. For each of these industries, correlation coefficients between two or more output measures are, in most instances, considerably less than .85. Current-dollar output series for SICs 29, 31, 35, 39, 40, 42, and 72 appear to be similar across available output measures.

Price indexes and deflation methods. Differences in price indexes and deflation methods were examined by comparing differences between constant and current-dollar trend growth rates across output series. Differences in price indexes or deflation methods are suspected when the difference between the constant and current-dollar trend growth rates varies widely across output measures. As shown in table 9B.3, fifteen industries (SICs 10, 13, 21, 40, 42, 44, 46, 47, 48, 49, 62, 63, 64, 78, and 82) exhibit differences of more than .90 points in the acceleration rates of the constant dollar and current-dollar output series, which suggests differences due to price index choice or deflation methods. Among these industries, differences in constant-dollar and current-dollar acceleration rates range from .9 points to 2.0 points for SICs 40, 42, 44, 46, 48, 63, and 82; from 2.0 points to 3.0 points for SIC 64; from 3.0 points to 4.0 points for SICs 13, 21, 49, and 62; and from 4.0 points to 7.0 points for SICs 10, 47, and 78. Output series for SICs 20, 27, 29, 31, 35, 38, 39, 41, 45, 72, and 79 appear to use similar price indexes and deflation methods.

Data adjustments. The impact of BEA adjustments to underlying source data was examined by comparing trend growth rates and their acceleration using both the published BEA output measures and the unadjusted BEA output measures for those SIC two-digit industries where both are available.[47] As shown in table 9.11, industries for which BEA adjustments appear to have an important effect on the trend growth rates for 1990–95 and 1995–2000 include SIC 21, Tobacco Products; SIC 31, Leather and Leather Products; SIC 35, Industrial and Commercial Machinery and Computer Equipment; SIC 39, Miscellaneous Manufacturing Industries; and SIC 46, Pipelines, Except Natural Gas. For SIC 21, the BEA adjustment results in a small but increased difference in acceleration between the Y^{G-2}_{BEA-P} measure and the $Y^{S-2}_{BLS-I-U}$. For SICs 31, 35, 39, and 46, the BEA adjustments appear to widen the difference in acceleration rate between the Y^{G-2}_{BEA-P} measure and the $Y^{S-2}_{BLS-I-U}$ and $Y^{G-2}_{BLS-M-U}$ measures.

Output concept. The impact of using a sectoral output concept rather than a gross output concept was examined by computing the correlation of the $Y^{S-2}_{BLS-M-P}$ output measure with the underlying gross (value of production) output series for the each of the SIC two-digit manufacturing industries.

47. SICs 20–39, 46, and 64.

Table 9.11 Comparisons of BEA adjusted (Y_{BEA-P}^{G-2}) and unadjusted (Y_{BEA-U}^{G-2}) output measures (constant-dollar annual percent change in output series)

SIC 2-digit industry	Acceleration rate (1990–1995, 1995–2000)		Y_{BEA-P}^{G-2} (adjusted) vs. $Y_{BLS-I-U}^{S-2}$		Y_{BEA-U}^{G-2} (unadjusted) vs. $Y_{BLS-I-U}^{S-2}$		Y_{BEA-P}^{G-2} (adjusted) vs. $Y_{BLS-M-P}^{S-2}$ (or, for SIC 46, $Y_{BLS-M-U}^{G-2}$)		Y_{BEA-U}^{G-2} (unadjusted) vs. $Y_{BLS-M-P}^{S-2}$ (or, for SIC 46, $Y_{BLS-M-U}^{G-2}$)	
	Y_{BEA-P}^{G-2} (adjusted)	Y_{BEA-U}^{G-2} (unadjusted)	Difference in acceleration rates	Correlation coefficient	Difference in acceleration rates	Correlation coefficient	Difference in acceleration rates	Correlation coefficient	Difference in acceleration rates	Correlation coefficient
SIC 21, Tobacco products	−2.95	−3.84	0.66	0.996	−0.23	1.000	0.95	0.977	0.06	0.988
SIC 31, Leather and leather products	0.38	1.1	−1.14	0.949	−0.42	0.995	−1.23	0.923	−0.50	0.959
SIC 35, Industrial and commercial machinery and computer equipment	0.94	1.91	−1.09	0.991	−0.12	0.993	−1.15	0.976	−0.18	0.985
SIC 39, Miscellaneous manufacturing industries	1.78	0.96	0.96	0.954	0.15	0.957	0.94	0.867	0.13	0.831
SIC 46, Pipelines, except natural gas	5.52	2.93	n.a.	n.a.	n.a.	n.a.	7.17	0.617	4.58	0.151

Note: Data required for comparisons is unavailable in SICs 02, 07, 08, 09, 10, 12, 13, 14, 15, 16, 17, 37, 40, 41, 42, 43, 44, 45, 47, 48, 49, 50, 51, 52, 53, 54, 55, 56, 57, 58, 59, 61, 61, 62, 63, 65, 70, 72, 73, 75, 76, 78, 79, 80, 82, 83, 84, 86, 87, 88, 91, 92, 93, 94, 95, 96, 97, and 99.

Only SICs 21 and 23 had correlation coefficients below .97, with $R = .85$ and .64 respectively. This particular difference in output concept thus appears to have only a minimal role in explaining differences in real growth rates among output series for any given industry group.

Case Studies

For some of the SIC two-digit industries with significant differences in output measures, the differences at the two-digit level could be traced to the more detailed three- and four-digit industries.[48] Sufficient detailed industry output data are available for industry group 10, Metal Mining; 20, Food and Kindred Products; 21, Tobacco Products; 27, Printing, Publishing, and Allied Industries; 29, Petroleum Refining; 31, Leather and Leather Products; 35, Industrial and Commercial Machinery and Computer Equipment; 38, Measuring, Analyzing, and Controlling Instruments; Photographic, Medical, and Optical Goods; and Watches and Clocks; 39, Miscellaneous Manufacturing; 48, Communications; 72, Personal Services; and 78, Motion Pictures. Among these industry groups, case studies were conducted for SICs 10, 27, 29, 31, 35, 38, 48, and 72. Data for these industry groups are summarized in table 9B.3. By comparing the underlying BEA and BLS SIC three- or four-digit industry data in each of these two-digit industries, we can determine if differences in output measurement at the three- and four-digit level are contributing to the higher-level differences.

Metal Mining (SIC 10). In this industry group, the underlying four-digit industries overwhelmingly exhibit differences in output behavior. At the two-digit level, the Y^{G-2}_{BEA-P} and $Y^{G-2}_{BLS-M-U}$ constant- and current-dollar output series differ significantly. As seen in table 9B.4, at a four-digit level, Y^{G-4}_{BEA-U} and $Y^{S-4}_{BLS-I-P,U}$ output series are available for five of the nine four-digit industries, and for four of these industries the Y^{G-4}_{BEA-U} and $Y^{S-4}_{BLS-I-P,U}$ real output series have differences in acceleration ranging from -1.28 points to 7.54 points. The annual percent changes of the nominal Y^{G-4}_{BEA-U} and $Y^{S-4}_{BLS-I-P,U}$ output are highly correlated for each of the four-digit industries, although current-dollar trend growth rates for 1011, 1041, and 1044 differ, particularly for 1990–95.

Printing, Publishing, and Allied Industries (SIC 27). The Y^{G-2}_{BEA-P} and $Y^{S-2}_{BLS-I-U}$ real output series exhibit differences in acceleration of -1.51 points and a correlation coefficient of .769. Of the eight underlying three-digit industries, three have differences in acceleration among the Y^{G-3}_{BEA-U} and $Y^{S-3}_{BLS-I-P}$ real output series ranging from -2.09 points to -5.70 points, and a fourth has a correlation coefficient of .269 between the Y^{G-3}_{BEA-U} and $Y^{S-3}_{BLS-I-P}$ real output series. Four of the fourteen SIC four-digit industries in this

---

48. Because SIC three- and four-digit output measures are not available from the BLS major-sector program, the comparisons are limited to industries where the BEA and BLS industry productivity program output measures are both available.

group have low correlations between the annual percent change rates for the real output measures Y^{G-4}_{BEA-U} and $Y^{S-4}_{BLS-I-P}$. Particularly noticeable is SIC 2771, Greeting Cards, with a correlation of .269.

Petroleum Refining and Related Industries (SIC 29). This industry is included primarily because of the extremely low correlation coefficients between the Y^{G-2}_{BEA-P} and $Y^{S-2}_{BLS-I-P}$ output series (–.044) and the Y^{G-2}_{BEA-P} and $Y^{S-2}_{BLS-M-P}$ output series (–.013). Looking at the constant-dollar output series for the three three-digit industries in this group shows that SIC 291, Petroleum Refining, also has a very low negative correlation (–.130) between the Y^{G-3}_{BEA-U} and $Y^{S-3}_{BLS-I-P}$ output series. BEA and BLS current-dollar data series are highly correlated in each of these industries.[49]

Leather and Leather Products (SIC 31). Both the $Y^{S-2}_{BLS-I-U}$ and $Y^{S-2}_{BLS-M-P}$ output series appear to differ from the Y^{G-2}_{BEA-P} output series. Of the seven underlying three-digit industries, four have differences in acceleration ranging from 1.24 points to –8.77 points using the Y^{G-3}_{BEA-U} and $Y^{S-3}_{BLS-I-U,P}$ output series, and one of these four (SIC 313) has a correlation coefficient of .611 between these two output series. Current-dollar data series for these output measures are highly correlated in six of the seven three-digit industries, with a correlation coefficient of .625 for SIC 313.

Industrial and Commercial Machinery and Computer Equipment (SIC 35). For this industry, both the $Y^{S-2}_{BLS-I-U}$ and $Y^{S-2}_{BLS-M-P}$ series have an acceleration rate about 1 percentage point greater than the Y^{G-2}_{BEA-P} output series. For the nine three-digit industries in this group, the Y^{G-3}_{BEA-U} and $Y^{S-3}_{BLS-I-P}$ real output series appear to be quite close, with one exception. SIC 357, Computer and Office Equipment, which exhibits a rather large acceleration between the 1990–95 and 1995–2000 time periods, has an acceleration difference of –2.87 points between the Y^{G-3}_{BEA-U} and $Y^{S-3}_{BLS-I-P}$ real output series, although the series are highly correlated. This may in part reflect BEA adjustments to underlying data.

Measuring, Analyzing and Controlling Instruments; Photographic, Medical and Optical Goods; Watches and Clocks (SIC 38). This industry exhibits differences in output series at the two-digit level primarily because of the low correlation between the Y^{G-2}_{BEA-P} and $Y^{S-2}_{BLS-M-P}$ series (.597), and the $Y^{S-2}_{BLS-I-U}$ and $Y^{S-2}_{BLS-M-P}$ series (.701). The trend growth rates of these series for 1990–95 and 1995–2000 are fairly similar. The current-dollar data series for each of these SIC 38 output measures also are very poorly correlated. Of the six three-digit industries in this group, SIC 381, Search, Detection, Navigation, Guidance, Aeronautical and Nautical has a difference in acceleration for the Y^{G-3}_{BEA-U} and $Y^{S-3}_{BLS-I-P}$ constant-dollar output measures of –1.09 points, and SIC 387, Watches, Clocks, and Clockwork-Operated Devices, has a differences in acceleration for the Y^{G-3}_{BEA-U} and $Y^{S-3}_{BLS-I-U}$ constant-

---

49. It should be noted that the $Y^{S-3}_{BLS-I-p}$ measure is a physical quantity measure, as compared to the Y^{G-3}_{BEA-U} measure, which is developed using Census value of shipments data.

dollar output measures of 5.61 points. However, the real and nominal annual percent change in output series are highly correlated at the SIC three-digit level.

Communications (SIC 48). The two-digit output series are found to differ based both on differences in acceleration between the Y^{G-2}_{BEA-P} and $Y^{G-2}_{BLS-M-U}$ output series, and a correlation coefficient of .70. Selected data are available for this industry at a three-digit level, including SIC 483, Radio and Television Broadcasting Stations, and SIC 484, Cable and Other Pay Television Stations. Y^{G-3}_{BEA-U} and $Y^{S-3}_{BLS-I-P}$ constant-dollar output series for both of these industries differ as indicated both by differences in acceleration and low correlation between the output series. In SIC 483, the Y^{G-3}_{BEA-U} and $Y^{S-3}_{BLS-I-P}$ measures have a difference in acceleration of –1.21 points, and a correlation coefficient of .73. In SIC 484, the Y^{G-3}_{BEA-U} and $Y^{S-3}_{BLS-I-P}$ measures have a difference in acceleration of –1.70 points and a correlation coefficient of .47. In SICs 483 and 484, the correlation coefficients for annual percent change in the current-dollar output series for the Y^{G-3}_{BEA-U} and $Y^{S-3}_{BLS-I-P}$ measures are .392 and .494 respectively, suggesting that differences exist in the underlying data.

SIC Four-Digit Industry Differences

In addition to comparisons of the Y^{G-2}_{BEA-P}, $Y^{S-2}_{BLS-I-U}$, and $Y^{S-2}_{BLS-M-P}$ output measures for the SIC two-digit manufacturing industries, we have compared BEA and BLS SIC four-digit industry real output measures for all industries where both measures are available. The BEA measures for the four-digit industries, Y^{G-4}_{BEA-U} are either the unadjusted gross output measures, based primarily on Census annual survey data[50] and benchmarked to the input-output accounts (nonmanufacturing), or the unadjusted shipments-based output measures (manufacturing). The BLS measures for the four-digit industries, $Y^{S-4}_{BLS-I-U,P}$, are BLS sectoral output measures, which are generally based on the quinquennial Census and annual survey data from the Bureau of the Census. Less commonly, in some industries these measures are based on physical quantity data. Where both output measures are available, differences in acceleration rates were computed for the 1990–95 and 1995–2000 time periods. For 128 of the 458 SIC four-digit industries compared, or roughly 28 percent of the industries, differences in acceleration rates of greater than 1.0 points were found to exist between the Y^{G-4}_{BEA-U} and the $Y^{S-4}_{BLS-I-U,P}$ output measures.

Summary of Detailed Industry Differences

While BEA and BLS output measures for detailed manufacturing industries are quite similar, it may be important to address some differences

---

50. While these measures generally are based on the Census annual survey data, they may also involve data from a variety of other sources.

in current-dollar source data and agency-specific adjustments in order to improve consistency among these measures. For the majority of nonmanufacturing industries, BEA and BLS output measures differ significantly, primarily because of differences in underlying data sources, price index choices, and deflation methods. However, these differences can be readily addressed. An effort to understand the sources of differences among the BEA and BLS nonmanufacturing output measures, at all levels, is highly recommended and has potentially large benefits for data users. Where appropriate, given the purposes of the measures, greater consistency among measures can be achieved. Finally, reasons for remaining differences among the output measures should be documented and described.

9.5 Summary

This chapter takes some initial steps toward the goal of constructing complete integrated production accounts for the U.S. economy. These steps include the provision of a description of an ideal framework, the construction of an illustrative integrated aggregate level account, and an extensive examination of the various industry output measures that have been published by the BEA and the BLS.

This chapter spells out a more ambitious framework for a "production account' than that presented in earlier national accounting literature. The framework is intended to describe, from the ground up, the process of assembling data to account for growth along the lines of JGF. The framework starts with data on industry production of commodities and on interindustry flows (both in nominal terms), similar to those available in an input-output system, and with data on commodity prices. The production account describes deflation and Divisia or superlative aggregation. This leads to measures of real input, real output, and productivity.

The chapter also presents an integrated aggregate production account for the U.S. private business and private nonfarm business sectors. It shows how line items from the BEA's national accounts are used in moving from total economy nominal GDP to business sector nominal output and how that, in turn, consists of components such as labor compensation, property income, indirect taxes, subsidies, and statistical discrepancy. For the business sectors, the chapter also presents real output, published by the BEA, and real inputs and MFP as published by BLS.

Finally, it describes the most comprehensive effort to date to document, present, and compare the various measures of industry output available from the BEA and BLS. The chapter describes which measures are available, provides information on how they are put together by the agencies, and where possible compares the measures empirically. Several comparisons are made to assess whether the differences that exist are due to differences in nominal output (differences in data sources), differences in concept, differences in adjustments to data, or differences in deflation. In the future, the results of these comparisons may be used by the two agencies to construct crosswalks between series and, wherever warranted, to reduce the differences. The comparisons are in the form of spreadsheets, and these materials will be made available to the research community.

This paper represents an important collaborative first step between the BEA and BLS. Future efforts will focus on further explaining and documenting differences in BEA and BLS measures with a goal of improving the accuracy of these accounts. This improvement will be achieved by capturing the best features of both data sets, harmonizing and integrating the measures when appropriate, and increasing understanding of the remaining differences to facilitate economic research, in particular that focusing on economic growth and productivity. In some cases the BEA and BLS measures differ because the primary purpose for which the measures are constructed dictates differences in methodology. For example, the BEA estimates benchmark input-output accounts every five years. Because input-output conventions call for the trade sector to be a margin sector, the BEA follows that convention. The BLS, on the other hand, estimates trade productivity, defining sectoral output in terms of sales volume. In other cases methodological differences are a product of decisions made where the BEA methodology would have been acceptable to the BLS (and vice versa) if methodologies had been coordinated across agencies. In these cases, the BEA and BLS intend to coordinate methodologies after they have been jointly reviewed by the relevant staff. Going forward, the transition to NAICS and any attempt to estimate historical time series on a NAICS basis represent an important opportunity for cross-agency methodology coordination.

Appendix A

Table 9A.1   **BLS time series: Private business (MFP table PB1a, PB1b, and PB4b)**

	Time series associated with table 1 (billions of dollars)			Index time series associated with table 3 (1996 = 100.0)				
	Line 9b	Line 9b-ii	Line 9b-i					
Year	Current dollar output	Labor compensation	Cost of capital services	Real output	Labor input	Capital services	Combined input quantity	Multifactor productivity
1948	225.5	142.4	68.8	18.6	51.1	17.2	36.1	51.6
1949	218.3	137.0	66.2	18.6	49.4	17.6	35.6	52.2
1950	243.0	149.9	76.7	20.5	50.3	18.3	36.5	56.0
1951	276.6	171.1	87.7	21.8	52.1	19.3	38.0	57.3
1952	288.6	181.3	87.5	22.2	52.2	19.9	38.5	57.8
1953	303.9	194.4	88.2	23.2	53.2	20.5	39.3	59.1
1954	301.9	193.2	87.7	23.0	51.7	20.9	38.8	59.2
1955	331.4	206.5	102.2	24.9	53.7	21.6	40.2	62.0
1956	352.1	223.6	104.2	25.4	54.6	22.3	41.1	61.7
1957	367.7	234.6	108.3	25.8	53.9	23.0	41.1	62.6
1958	366.3	233.1	107.9	25.3	51.6	23.4	40.1	62.9
1959	400.3	251.7	121.0	27.1	53.7	23.9	41.6	65.1
1960	413.6	262.4	121.0	27.5	54.0	24.6	42.1	65.5
1961	424.6	268.8	125.2	28.1	53.3	25.1	42.0	66.9
1962	455.6	286.9	136.8	29.9	54.8	25.8	43.2	69.3
1963	479.9	299.5	147.1	31.3	55.2	26.7	43.8	71.4
1964	514.4	321.8	156.9	33.3	56.2	27.6	44.9	74.2
1965	559.0	346.3	174.7	35.6	58.0	28.9	46.5	76.6
1966	608.2	381.3	187.5	38.1	59.5	30.5	48.2	78.9
1967	638.4	403.3	193.0	38.8	59.4	32.3	49.1	79.0
1968	697.1	440.9	209.0	40.7	60.3	33.7	50.3	81.1
1969	752.3	483.2	217.4	42.0	62.1	35.5	52.1	80.6
1970	780.9	508.5	216.5	42.0	61.0	37.1	52.2	80.5
1971	842.0	539.1	240.7	43.6	60.5	38.7	52.5	83.0
1972	931.2	594.3	272.0	46.5	62.6	40.3	54.5	85.5
1973	1050.8	673.6	306.7	49.8	64.8	42.6	56.8	87.8
1974	1132.1	735.5	319.5	49.0	65.2	44.9	57.9	84.6
1975	1222.0	771.9	368.9	48.5	62.4	46.6	56.8	85.4
1976	1367.9	868.2	414.0	51.9	64.2	48.1	58.5	88.6
1977	1540.7	972.4	467.4	54.8	66.8	50.0	60.9	90.0
1978	1757.3	1115.3	524.7	58.2	70.2	52.2	63.9	91.2
1979	1959.2	1262.4	568.5	60.2	72.4	54.8	66.2	90.8
1980	2117.8	1374.0	602.1	59.4	71.9	57.6	67.0	88.8
1981	2382.8	1510.8	705.1	61.0	73.0	60.5	68.7	88.9
1982	2468.6	1576.6	739.9	59.3	71.7	63.0	68.8	86.2
1983	2643.6	1673.4	799.1	62.5	73.4	65.0	70.5	88.6
1984	2992.3	1867.1	934.5	68.1	77.7	68.1	74.4	91.5
1985	3205.2	2010.8	983.8	71.0	79.6	71.3	76.8	92.4
1986	3344.3	2134.1	990.0	73.6	80.4	74.4	78.4	93.9

(continued)

Table 9A.1 (continued)

Year	Line 9b Current dollar output	Line 9b-ii Labor compensation	Line 9b-i Cost of capital services	Real output	Labor input	Capital services	Combined input quantity	Multifactor productivity
1987	3591.9	2274.7	1088.3	76.3	83.1	76.9	81.0	94.2
1988	3906.9	2461.9	1212.6	79.6	86.3	79.2	83.9	94.8
1989	4132.8	2606.3	1273.6	82.4	88.8	81.6	86.4	95.3
1990	4329.9	2750.1	1317.4	83.6	89.4	83.8	87.5	95.5
1991	4432.0	2800.7	1328.8	82.6	88.3	85.7	87.4	94.5
1992	4661.3	2956.9	1381.2	85.7	89.3	87.5	88.7	96.7
1993	4897.5	3101.3	1451.3	88.5	91.8	89.7	91.1	97.1
1994	5239.6	3265.5	1602.6	92.8	95.6	92.5	94.6	98.2
1995	5541.7	3430.6	1700.8	95.8	98.0	96.0	97.3	98.4
1996	5874.5	3600.7	1839.8	100.0	100.0	100.0	100.0	100.0
1997	6299.3	3830.0	1973.2	105.2	103.5	104.9	104.0	101.2
1998	6729.2	4149.7	2043.6	110.5	106.1	111.3	107.9	102.5
1999	7121.6	4446.1	2154.8	115.7	109.0	117.9	111.9	103.4
2000	7624.2	4819.4	2222.6	120.4	110.1	124.5	114.7	105.0
2001	7748.8	4899.9	2255.5	120.2	109.5	129.6	115.7	103.9

(Time series associated with table 1, billions of dollars. Index time series associated with table 3, 1996 = 100.0.)

Table 9A.2   **BLS time series: Private nonfarm business (MFP table NFB1a, NFB1b, and NFB4b)**

Year	Line 13b Current dollar output	Line 13b-ii Labor compensation	Line 13b-i Cost of capital services	Real output	Labor input	Capital services	Combined input quantity	Multifactor productivity
1948	203.2	128.6	60.2	18.0	44.1	15.2	31.8	56.4
1949	200.6	126.3	59.1	17.9	42.2	15.6	31.2	57.6
1950	224.1	139.0	68.6	19.7	43.7	16.2	32.3	61.1
1951	254.7	159.6	77.2	21.3	45.8	17.1	33.9	62.7
1952	267.6	170.7	77.0	21.8	46.6	17.7	34.7	62.7
1953	285.0	184.9	78.6	22.7	48.1	18.2	35.8	63.5
1954	283.5	183.9	78.5	22.4	46.7	18.7	35.3	63.5
1955	314.0	198.4	92.7	24.4	48.6	19.3	36.7	66.5
1956	334.8	215.6	94.5	24.9	49.9	20.1	37.8	65.9
1957	350.6	226.7	98.2	25.4	49.8	20.7	38.1	66.6
1958	347.2	224.6	96.4	24.9	47.7	21.1	37.2	66.8
1959	382.8	243.9	110.7	26.7	49.9	21.6	38.7	69.1
1960	395.2	254.7	109.5	27.2	50.1	22.3	39.2	69.4

(Time series associated with table 1, billions of dollars. Index time series associated with table 3, 1996 = 100.0.)

Table 9A.2   (continued)

	Time series associated with table 1 (billions of dollars)			Index time series associated with table 3 (1996 = 100.0)				
	Line 13b	Line 13b-ii	Line 13b-i					
Year	Current dollar output	Labor compensation	Cost of capital services	Real output	Labor input	Capital services	Combined input quantity	Multifactor productivity
1961	405.9	260.5	113.4	27.7	49.9	22.9	39.3	70.5
1962	436.9	278.2	125.1	29.6	51.5	23.6	40.6	73.0
1963	461.0	291.2	135.0	31.0	52.1	24.4	41.4	75.0
1964	496.6	313.5	145.6	33.1	53.4	25.4	42.6	77.8
1965	538.7	336.9	161.7	35.5	55.4	26.6	44.3	80.0
1966	587.0	371.2	173.5	38.0	57.2	28.3	46.2	82.3
1967	618.0	394.2	178.9	38.7	57.1	30.0	47.0	82.2
1968	676.2	431.6	194.4	40.8	58.2	31.4	48.3	84.4
1969	729.1	473.3	200.8	42.0	60.1	33.1	50.2	83.6
1970	756.8	497.9	199.8	41.9	59.3	34.8	50.5	83.1
1971	816.2	528.4	222.9	43.6	58.9	36.3	50.9	85.6
1972	901.0	582.5	250.1	46.6	60.9	38.1	52.8	88.2
1973	1003.6	657.2	273.4	50.0	63.3	40.3	55.2	90.7
1974	1087.4	720.5	289.3	49.2	63.7	42.6	56.3	87.4
1975	1175.9	756.4	337.6	48.4	60.9	44.3	55.2	87.6
1976	1324.3	853.0	384.9	51.9	62.8	45.9	57.0	91.1
1977	1496.5	957.4	436.5	54.9	65.4	47.7	59.3	92.4
1978	1705.7	1099.4	486.6	58.4	68.8	49.9	62.3	93.7
1979	1898.2	1244.3	524.5	60.3	71.1	52.6	64.8	93.1
1980	2065.3	1357.8	564.8	59.6	70.7	55.4	65.5	91.0
1981	2316.8	1493.6	654.8	60.8	71.7	58.4	67.2	90.5
1982	2407.4	1559.2	693.9	59.0	70.6	61.0	67.4	87.5
1983	2598.4	1658.5	761.3	62.8	72.3	63.3	69.3	90.6
1984	2927.7	1849.9	880.1	68.1	76.7	66.4	73.3	93.0
1985	3141.9	1993.9	931.3	70.8	78.8	69.8	75.8	93.4
1986	3285.2	2117.6	937.9	73.5	79.8	73.0	77.6	94.8
1987	3530.4	2257.1	1030.9	76.2	82.5	75.8	80.3	94.9
1988	3846.7	2442.2	1160.5	79.7	85.9	78.3	83.4	95.6
1989	4060.3	2584.3	1213.9	82.4	88.5	80.8	86.0	95.8
1990	4254.3	2725.4	1259.0	83.5	89.2	83.2	87.2	95.8
1991	4362.8	2777.3	1276.2	82.5	87.9	85.1	87.0	94.8
1992	4584.9	2932.7	1321.4	85.5	89.0	87.0	88.4	96.7
1993	4828.3	3076.1	1396.0	88.4	91.8	89.4	91.0	97.2
1994	5160.3	3237.3	1545.1	92.6	95.4	92.2	94.3	98.2
1995	5473.1	3404.0	1652.8	95.8	97.8	95.8	97.2	98.6
1996	5787.1	3570.8	1776.1	100.0	100.0	100.0	100.0	100.0
1997	6216.1	3800.4	1913.2	105.1	103.6	105.1	104.1	101.0
1998	6654.0	4120.6	1986.5	110.5	106.4	111.7	108.1	102.2
1999	7052.0	4415.7	2097.3	115.7	109.5	118.5	112.4	102.9
2000	7552.3	4789.7	2161.0	120.2	110.6	125.4	115.2	104.4
2001	7674.3	4866.4	2197.0	120.1	110.1	130.5	116.3	103.3

Table 9A.3   BEA nominal time series associated with table 1 (billions of dollars)

	Table 1							
	Line 1	Line 2	Line 2a	Line 2b	Line 3	Line 4	Line 6	Line 7
	NIPA table 1.7						NIPA table 8.21	
	Line 1	Line 7	Line 8	Line 9	Line 10	Line 2	Line 172	Line 173
Year	Gross domestic product	Households and institutions	Private households	NPIs serving individuals	General government	Gross domestic business product	Owner-occupied housing	Rental value of nonresidential assets owned and used by NPIs serving individuals
1948	269.6	5.6	2.4	3.2	27.3	236.6	8.4	0.8
1949	267.7	5.9	2.4	3.6	28.4	233.3	9.4	0.8
1950	294.5	6.5	2.6	3.9	28.7	259.1	10.6	0.9
1951	339.5	6.9	2.7	4.3	35.8	296.8	12.2	1.0
1952	358.6	7.2	2.6	4.6	40.5	310.9	14.0	1.1
1953	379.9	7.8	2.7	5.1	42.2	329.9	15.9	1.1
1954	381.1	8.1	2.6	5.5	43.5	329.4	17.7	1.2
1955	415.2	9.1	3.1	6.1	45.9	360.2	19.3	1.3
1956	438.0	9.9	3.3	6.6	49.2	378.9	21.0	1.4
1957	461.5	10.6	3.3	7.3	52.6	398.3	22.8	1.6
1958	467.9	11.5	3.5	8.0	55.9	400.5	24.8	1.6
1959	507.4	12.4	3.6	8.9	58.4	436.6	26.9	1.6
1960	527.4	13.9	3.8	10.1	62.1	451.3	29.2	1.8
1961	545.7	14.5	3.7	10.7	66.1	465.1	31.2	1.9
1962	586.5	15.6	3.8	11.8	70.9	500.0	33.6	2.0
1963	618.7	16.7	3.8	12.8	75.7	526.3	35.6	2.2
1964	664.4	17.9	3.9	14.0	81.3	565.2	37.6	2.4
1965	720.1	19.3	4.0	15.3	86.8	613.9	40.1	2.6
1966	789.3	21.3	4.0	17.2	97.0	671.0	42.8	2.9
1967	834.1	23.4	4.2	19.2	107.3	703.4	45.6	3.2
1968	911.5	26.1	4.4	21.7	119.3	766.1	48.4	3.6

1969	985.3	29.5	4.4	25.0	130.5	825.4	52.3	4.0
1970	1039.7	32.4	4.5	27.9	144.2	863.1	56.1	4.5
1971	1128.6	35.6	4.6	31.0	157.3	935.7	61.5	5.0
1972	1240.4	38.9	4.6	34.3	171.5	1030.0	66.7	5.5
1973	1385.5	43.0	4.8	38.2	185.7	1156.8	72.8	6.3
1974	1501.0	47.1	4.6	42.6	203.4	1250.5	79.8	7.3
1975	1635.2	52.0	4.6	47.3	226.4	1356.8	86.5	8.4
1976	1823.9	57.1	5.4	51.6	245.3	1521.6	94.5	9.1
1977	2031.4	62.4	5.9	56.4	266.2	1702.8	103.7	9.9
1978	2295.9	69.7	6.5	63.2	288.9	1937.3	117.5	11.2
1979	2566.4	77.3	6.4	70.9	314.2	2174.9	134.6	12.7
1980	2795.6	87.1	6.1	81.0	349.7	2358.8	157.4	14.6
1981	3131.3	97.6	6.2	91.4	386.5	2647.3	179.6	16.8
1982	3259.2	108.2	6.3	102.0	421.2	2729.8	196.5	19.0
1983	3534.9	119.2	6.3	112.9	447.7	2968.1	209.2	20.7
1984	3932.7	131.2	7.3	123.9	487.7	3313.9	228.1	22.2
1985	4213.0	141.0	7.3	133.6	525.3	3546.8	246.0	24.1
1986	4452.9	153.7	7.7	146.0	558.2	3740.9	263.3	25.7
1987	4742.5	173.3	7.7	165.6	593.1	3976.0	284.7	28.1
1988	5108.3	195.1	8.3	186.8	632.0	4281.2	311.3	30.8
1989	5489.1	214.6	8.9	205.7	673.6	4600.9	338.1	33.6
1990	5803.2	237.9	9.4	228.6	723.3	4842.0	362.2	36.1
1991	5986.2	257.5	9.1	248.4	766.3	4962.4	381.0	38.9
1992	6318.9	279.5	10.1	269.4	797.3	5242.1	398.2	41.8
1993	6642.3	297.0	10.7	286.3	827.3	5518.0	413.8	45.4
1994	7054.3	313.3	11.1	302.2	854.5	5886.6	439.7	45.7
1995	7400.5	330.3	11.9	318.4	880.1	6190.1	464.4	48.1
1996	7813.2	348.6	12.0	336.5	908.7	6556.0	487.1	49.8
1997	8318.4	363.2	12.0	351.2	944.6	7010.5	509.1	52.2
1998	8781.5	383.8	14.0	369.8	979.8	7418.0	541.0	55.2
1999	9274.3	403.1	12.7	390.4	1023.5	7847.7	581.9	55.2
2000	9824.6	431.1	13.6	417.5	1082.1	8311.4	621.5	58.7
2001	10082.2	459.6	11.9	447.7	1139.8	8482.7	648.5	61.2

(continued)

Table 9A.3   (continued)

Table 1

	Line 8a	Line 8b	Line 10	Line 11	Line 12
	GDP by industry		NIPA table 1.7	NIPA table 8.21	
				Line 114	Line 117
	Line 80	Line 83	Line 6	Farm space rent for owner-occupied housing	Farm intermediate inputs for owner-occupied housing
			Farms		
1948	1.4	1.4	23.3	1.4	0.4
1949	1.5	1.6	18.7	1.3	0.3
1950	1.3	1.7	19.9	1.4	0.3
1951	1.3	1.9	22.9	1.5	0.4
1952	2.0	2.1	22.1	1.6	0.4
1953	2.1	2.3	20.1	1.6	0.4
1954	2.4	2.4	19.5	1.6	0.4
1955	2.5	2.7	18.6	1.6	0.4
1956	2.4	2.9	18.4	1.6	0.4
1957	2.7	3.0	18.3	1.7	0.4
1958	2.9	3.1	20.5	1.7	0.4
1959	3.2	3.6	18.9	1.8	0.5
1960	3.4	4.0	19.8	1.9	0.5
1961	3.4	4.1	20.1	2.0	0.6
1962	3.6	4.5	20.2	2.0	0.6
1963	4.2	4.9	20.4	2.1	0.6
1964	4.4	5.2	19.3	2.2	0.7
1965	4.7	5.5	21.9	2.3	0.7
1966	4.9	5.8	22.9	2.4	0.7
1967	5.3	6.0	22.2	2.5	0.7
1968	6.2	6.5	22.7	2.6	0.8
1969	6.7	7.1	25.2	2.8	0.7
1970	7.1	7.7	26.2	3.0	0.8

Year					
1971	7.7	8.2	28.1	3.2	0.9
1972	9.0	8.9	32.6	3.4	1.0
1973	9.0	9.9	49.8	3.5	1.0
1974	10.8	10.5	47.4	3.6	1.0
1975	10.8	11.5	48.8	3.7	1.0
1976	13.5	12.0	46.4	3.8	1.0
1977	14.1	12.7	47.2	4.0	1.0
1978	16.2	14.0	54.7	4.3	1.1
1979	17.9	14.7	64.5	4.5	1.1
1980	19.4	15.7	56.1	4.7	1.1
1981	24.0	16.6	69.9	4.9	1.0
1982	25.0	18.3	65.1	4.7	0.8
1983	26.3	21.3	49.2	4.7	0.8
1984	27.8	25.0	68.5	4.7	0.8
1985	31.1	28.7	67.1	4.6	0.8
1986	32.5	31.3	63.0	4.5	0.7
1987	34.5	33.5	65.1	4.6	1.0
1988	37.4	37.0	63.8	4.5	0.8
1989	39.5	40.5	76.2	4.6	0.9
1990	40.4	42.8	79.6	4.8	0.8
1991	46.5	44.3	73.2	4.9	0.9
1992	51.1	46.0	80.5	5.0	1.0
1993	49.2	48.2	73.6	5.2	0.9
1994	52.2	50.9	83.6	5.5	1.1
1995	55.5	53.9	73.2	5.6	1.0
1996	54.9	56.9	92.2	5.8	1.0
1997	59.2	60.9	88.3	6.1	1.0
1998	61.3	62.2	80.6	6.4	1.0
1999	62.2	65.6	75.2	6.8	1.0
2000	66.1	69.4	77.8	7.2	1.2
2001	63.4	78.1	80.6	7.6	1.4

Note: The GDP-by-industry data are from http://www.bea.gov/bea/dn2/gpo.htm, the zip files Gpo72sic.xls and Gpo87sic.xls.

Appendix B

Table 9B.1   Comparison of output measures: Concept of measurement methods

	BEA published gross output ($Y_{BEA\text{-}P}^{G}$)	BEA unpublished unadjusted gross output for nonmanufacturing detailed industries ($Y_{BEA\text{-}U}^{G\text{-}2,3,4}$)	BEA unpublished sum of shipments output series for detailed manufacturing industries ($Y_{BEA\text{-}U}^{SS\text{-}2,3}$)	BEA published value added output series ($Y_{BEA\text{-}P}^{VA}$)
Output concept	Gross output is the market value of an industry's production including commodity taxes. Gross output is measured as value of shipments plus inventory changes less cost of resales plus misreporting and coverage adjustments, plus adjustments for own-account production of software, own-account construction work, and commodity (sales) taxes. Adjustments for inventory change and cost of resales are made only for goods-producing industries.	For nonmanufacturing industries, unadjusted gross output is usually measured as receipts or sales. For wholesale trade and retail trade, gross output is measured as sales minus the cost of goods sold (margin).	Sum of shipments is a narrower concept than gross output, computed as an intermediate step in the calculation of BEA's published gross output measure.	Value added output is the difference between gross output and the cost of raw materials and other inputs (intermediate inputs), which are used up in production.
Industry coverage	All industries, private industries, goods-producing industries, services-producing industries, SIC divisions, and selected 2-digit major groups of industries. Data are available for all 2-digit manufacturing industries with the exception of 37. Instead of 37, data are available at the more detailed level for 371 and 372-9. Data are available for numerous 2-digit nonmanufacturing industries, including SIC 10, 12, 13, 14, 40, 41, 42, 44, 45, 46, 47, 48, 49, 60, 61, 62, 63, 64, 65, 67, 70, 72, 73, 75, 76, 78, 79, 80, 81, 82, 83, 86, and 88.	Data are available for selected SIC 2-, 3-, and 4-digit nonmanufacturing industries.	SIC 2-digit major groups, 3-digit industry groups, and 4-digit industries.	All industries, private industries, goods-producing industries, services-producing industries, SIC divisions, and selected 2-digit major groups of industries. Data are available for all 2-digit manufacturing industries with the exception of 37. Instead of 37, data are available at the more detailed level for 371 and 372-9. Data are available for numerous 2-digit non-manufacturing industries, including SIC 10, 12, 13, 14, 40, 41, 42, 44, 45, 46, 47, 48, 49, 60, 61, 62, 63, 64, 65, 67, 70, 72, 73, 75, 76, 78, 79, 80, 81, 82, 83, 86, and 88

Industry classification	Data for 1977–86 are on a 1972 SIC basis. Data for 1988–2001 are on a 1987 SIC basis. For 1987, both the 1972 and 1987 SIC basis is available.	Data for 1977–86 are on a 1972 SIC basis. Data for 1988–2001 are on a 1987 SIC basis. For 1987, both the 1972 and 1987 SIC basis is available.	Data for 1977–86 are on a 1972 SIC basis. Data for 1988–2001 are on a 1987 SIC basis. For 1987, both the 1972 and 1987 SIC basis is available.	Data for 1947–86 are on a 1972 SIC basis. Data for 1988–2001 are on a 1987 SIC basis. For 1987, both the 1972 and 1987 SIC basis is available.
Source data	The gross output data series are developed by additional adjustments to the unadjusted or "raw" data series ($Y^{G\text{-}2}_{BEA\text{-}U}$ and $Y^{SS\text{-}2}_{BEA\text{-}U}$) created for the detailed industries. Additional adjustments are made for cost of resales, misreporting and coverage adjustments, own-account production of software, own-account construction work, and commodity (sales) taxes.	Current dollar estimates are obtained from BEA's benchmark input-output accounts for 1977, 1982, 1987, and 1992. For nonbenchmark years, current dollar estimates are developed by interpolating annual series between benchmark levels and by extrapolating from the most recent benchmark. Annual interpolator and extrapolator series are developed from various sources, including BEA's NIPAs, Census Bureau annual surveys, other government surveys, and trade sources.	Census Bureau Annual Survey of Manufactures: Statistics for Industry Groups and Industries (Value of Estimated Shipments Data).	Current-dollar estimates are largely based on the components of gross domestic income from the NIPAs. Value added is the sum of compensation of employees, property-type income, and indirect business taxes and nontax liabilities.
Deflation procedure	Deflation is generally done with price indexes obtained from the BLS, the NIPAs, and trade sources. Deflation takes place at the most detailed component level possible.	Deflation is generally done with price indexes obtained from the BLS, the NIPAs, and trade sources.	Primary product, secondary product, and miscellaneous receipt deflators are largely derived from the BLS's Producer Price Indexes, but also BEA's deflators for computers, selected semiconductor products, telephone switching equipment, local area network equipment, and government purchases. In the computation of these quantity and price indexes, the 4-digit industry shipments are first decomposed into their components: primary products, secondary products, and miscellaneous receipts. Each component is then deflated separately before applying the chain-type index formulas.	Double-deflation is used in most cases.

(continued)

	BEA published gross output (Y^G_{BEA-P})	BEA unpublished unadjusted gross output for nonmanufacturing detailed industries ($Y^{G-2,3,4}_{BEA-U}$)	BEA unpublished sum of shipments output series for detailed manufacturing industries ($Y^{SS-2,3,4}_{BEA-U}$)	BEA published value added output series (Y^{VA}_{BEA-P})	BLS published sectoral output series for manufacturing industries ($Y^{S-1,2}_{BLS-P}$)	BLS unpublished gross ouput series for nonmanufacturing industries (Y^{G-2}_{BLS-U})	BLS unpublished sectoral output series for SIC 2-digit manufacturing industries (Y^{S-2}_{BLS-U})	BLS published sectoral output series for detailed industries ($Y^{S-3,4}_{BLS-P}$)
Aggregation methods	Fisher Index	Laspeyres Index	Fisher Index	Fisher Double-Deflation Index				
Data available	Current-dollar output data are available for 1977–2001. Chain-type quantity and price indexes (1996 = 100) are available for 1977–2001. Data are available on the BEA web site, www.bea.gov.	Current-dollar receipts data are available for 1977–2001. Constant-dollar output data are available for 1977–86 in 1987 dollars and for 1988–2001 in 1996 dollars. Constant (1987) dollar and constant (1996) dollar estimates are available for 1987. Data are available on the BEA web site, www.bea.gov.	Current-dollar shipments data are available for 1977–2001. Chain-type quantity and price indexes with 1987 = 100 are available for 1977–86 and chain type quantity and price indexes with 1996 = 100 are available for 1988–2001. Chain-type quantity and price indexes with both 1987 = 100 and 1996 = 100 are available for 1987. Data are available on the BEA web site, www.bea.gov.	Current-dollar output data are available for 1947–2001. Chain-type quantity and price indexes (1996 = 100) are available for 1977–2001. Chain-dollar data are also available. Data are available on the BEA web site, www.bea.gov.				
Output concept					Sectoral output is the value of shipments plus inventory changes, less intra-industry shipments. This sectoral output series is measured by BLS as the deflated value of shipments plus inventory change, plus federal excise taxes. Federal excise taxes are added so that production will be shown at market value.	Gross output is the market value of an industry's production, including commodity taxes.	Sectoral output is the value of shipments plus inventory changes, less resales and intra-industry shipments. The constant dollar output series is constructed for comparison purposes only, by Tornqvist aggregation of BLS SIC 3-digit sectoral real output measures. Note that this measure does not include adjustments to remove intrasectoral transactions at the SIC 2-digit level.	Sectoral output is the value of shipments plus inventory changes, less resales and intra-industry shipments.

Industry coverage	SIC 1-digit manufacturing division and 20 SIC 2-digit manufacturing industries.	Selected SIC 2-digit nonmanufacturing industries, including SIC 10, 13, 14, 40, 41, 42, 44, 45, 46, 47, 48, 49, 62, 63, 64, 70, 72, 75, 78, 79, 80, and 82.	20 SIC 2-digit manufacturing industries	SIC 3- and 4-digit industries, including over 190 3-digit industries and over 335 4-digit industries. All SIC 3- and 4-digit manufacturing and wholesale and retail trade industries are covered.
Industry classification	Data for 1947–2000 are available on a 1987 SIC basis.	Data for 1947, 1958, 1963, and 1967–2000 is available on a 1987 SIC basis.	Data for 1987–2000 are available on a 1987 SIC basis.	Data for 1987–2000 are available on a 1987 SIC basis.
Source data	Receipts, value of shipments, inventory change and cost of materials data are obtained from the Bureau of the Census for 4-digit establishment groups in manufacturing.	Gross output measures are developed based on BLS OEP data on gross output and output price series. Values of production and output measures are constructed by interpolation between input-output tables, using interpolator series from the best available sources. The input-output benchmarks used by OEP are those presently part of their growth model (i.e., the 1977, 1982, and 1987 benchmarks). Earlier tables for 1963, 1967, and 1972 were conformed to the 1987 SIC by Harper and Gullickson. The employment projections series on output were also adjusted to conform with the 1992 I/O table published by BEA. This output measure was originally developed with a five year periodicity, 1947–97 (47, 58, 63, 67, 72, 77, 82, 87, 92, 97). The output measure was updated to annual periodicity using OEP I/O tables, October, 2002. Output is developed from BEA input-output tables, adjusted by BLS.	A real output series was constructed for comparison purposes only by Tornqvist aggregation of the BLS real sectoral output series for SIC 3-digit manufacturing industries.	Industry output indexes are prepared from basic data published by various public and private agencies, using the greatest level of detail available. Bureau of the Census quinquennial survey data and other Census Survey data are used extensively in developing output statistics for manufacturing, trade, and services industries. The U.S. Geological Survey compiles most of the information for the mining and cement industries. Other important government sources include the U.S. Departments of Energy, Agriculture, Transportation, and Housing and Urban Development, and the Federal Railroad Administration, the Federal Reserve Board, and the Federal Deposit Insurance Corporation. In addition, a wide range of industry trade sources are used to provide detailed data.

(continued)

Table 9B.1   (continued)

	BLS published sectoral output series for manufacturing industries ($Y^{S-1,2}_{BLS-P}$)	BLS unpublished gross ouput series for nonmanufacturing industries (Y^{G-2}_{BLS-U})	BLS unpublished sectoral output series for SIC 2-digit manufacturing industries (Y^{S-2}_{BLS-U})	BLS published sectoral output series for detailed industries ($Y^{S-3,4}_{BLS-P}$)
Deflation procedure	Deflation is done at the 5-digit product code level by BEA using primarily BLS producer price indexes. In some instances, 5-digit price estimates developed by BEA are used. Four-digit industry real output is aggregated by BEA from the 5-digit indexes, and then BLS Tornqvist aggregates from the 4-digit to the 2-digit level.	Deflation is done using price measures obtained from the OEP. The price data rely heavily on the detail of the industry sector price indexes, the producer price indexes, and the consumer price indexes prepared and published by BLS.	None	Deflation is done at the 5-digit product code level using BLS Producer Price Indexes. For a small number of product classes, such as selected electronic products, price deflators developed by BEA, are used. In a few other product classes, a weighted deflator is specifically developed.
Aggregation methods	Constant-dollar output at the SIC 2-digit level is computed as a Tornqvist Index of the 4-digit industry data.	Constant-dollar output at the SIC 2-digit level is computed as a Tornqvist Index of the 3-digit industry data.	Constant-dollar output at the SIC 2-digit level is computed as a Tornqvist Index of the BLS real sectoral output for the SIC 3-digit manufacturing industries.	Constant-dollar output at the SIC 4-digit level is computed as a Tornqvist Index of the 5-digit product class data.
Data available	Current- and constant-dollar output data are available annually for 1947–2000. Data are available on the BLS web site, www.bls.gov	Current- and constant-dollar output data are available for 1947, 1958, 1963, and annually for 1967–2000. Data are available upon request from the authors.	Current- and constant-dollar output data are available annually for 1987–2000. Data are constructed for comparison purposes only and are available from the authors.	Current- and constant-dollar output data are available annually for all industries, for 1987–2000. For selected industries, data extend back as far as 1947. Data are available on the BLS web site, www.bls.gov.

Notes: BEA = Bureau of Economic Analysis; BLS = Bureau of Labor Statistics; NIPAs = National Income and Product Accounts; OEP = Office of Employment Projections; I/O = input-ouput.

Table 9B.2   BEA and BLS output measure availability for detailed industries, 1987–2001

SIC industry	SIC 2-digit output measures available	SIC 2-digit output measures available		SIC 3-digit output measure comparisons possible	SIC 4-digit output measure comparisons possible
		BEA only or BLS only	BEA and BLS Series		
01, Agricultural Production Crops	n.a.			No	No
02, Agricultural Production Livestock and Animal Specialties	n.a.			No	No
07, Agricultural Services	n.a.			No	No
08, Forestry		$Y^{G\text{-}2}_{BEA\text{-}U}$		No	No
09, Fishing, Hunting and Trapping	n.a.			No	No
10, Metal Mining			$Y^{G\text{-}2}_{BEA\text{-}P}$ $Y^{G\text{-}2}_{BLS\text{-}M\text{-}U}$	Selected industries	Selected industries
12, Coal Mining			$Y^{G\text{-}2}_{BEA\text{-}P}$ $Y^{S\text{-}2}_{BLS\text{-}I\text{-}U}$	No	No
13, Oil and Gas Extraction			$Y^{G\text{-}2}_{BEA\text{-}P}$ $Y^{G\text{-}2}_{BLS\text{-}M\text{-}U}$ $Y^{S\text{-}2}_{BLS\text{-}I\text{-}U}$	No	No
14, Mining and Quarrying of Nonmetallic Minerals, Except Fuels			$Y^{G\text{-}2}_{BEA\text{-}P}$ $Y^{G\text{-}2}_{BLS\text{-}M\text{-}U}$ $Y^{S\text{-}2}_{BLS\text{-}I\text{-}U}$	Selected industries	No
15, Building Construction General Contractors and Operative Builders	n.a.			No	No
16, Heavy Construction Other Than Building Construction Contractors	n.a.			No	No
17, Construction Special Trade Contractors	n.a.			No	No
20, Food and Kindred Products			$Y^{G\text{-}2}_{BEA\text{-}P}$ $Y^{G\text{-}2}_{BEA\text{-}U}$ $Y^{S\text{-}2}_{BLS\text{-}M\text{-}P}$ $Y^{S\text{-}2}_{BLS\text{-}I\text{-}U}$	All industries	All industries

(continued)

SIC industry	SIC 2-digit output measures available		SIC 3-digit output measure comparisons possible	SIC 4-digit output measure comparisons possible
	SIC 2-digit output measures available			
	BEA only or BLS only	BEA and BLS Series		
21, *Tobacco Products*		$Y^{G\text{-}2}_{BEA\text{-}P}$ $Y^{G\text{-}2}_{BEA\text{-}U}$ $Y^{S\text{-}2}_{BLS\text{-}M\text{-}P}$ $Y^{S\text{-}2}_{BLS\text{-}I\text{-}U}$	All industries	All industries
22, Textile Mill Products		$Y^{G\text{-}2}_{BEA\text{-}P}$ $Y^{G\text{-}2}_{BEA\text{-}U}$ $Y^{S\text{-}2}_{BLS\text{-}M\text{-}P}$ $Y^{S\text{-}2}_{BLS\text{-}I\text{-}U}$	All industries	All industries
23, Apparel and Other Finished Products Made From Fabrics and Similar Materials		$Y^{G\text{-}2}_{BEA\text{-}P}$, $Y^{G\text{-}2}_{BEA\text{-}U}$, $Y^{S\text{-}2}_{BLS\text{-}M\text{-}P}$, and $Y^{S\text{-}2}_{BLS\text{-}I\text{-}U}$	All industries	All industries
24, Lumber and Wood Products, Except Furniture		$Y^{G\text{-}2}_{BEA\text{-}P}$ $Y^{G\text{-}2}_{BEA\text{-}U}$ $Y^{S\text{-}2}_{BLS\text{-}M\text{-}P}$ $Y^{S\text{-}2}_{BLS\text{-}I\text{-}U}$	All industries	All industries
25, Furniture and Fixtures		$Y^{G\text{-}2}_{BEA\text{-}P}$ $Y^{G\text{-}2}_{BEA\text{-}U}$ $Y^{S\text{-}2}_{BLS\text{-}M\text{-}P}$ $Y^{S\text{-}2}_{BLS\text{-}I\text{-}U}$	All industries	All industries
26, Paper and Allied Products		$Y^{G\text{-}2}_{BEA\text{-}P}$ $Y^{G\text{-}2}_{BEA\text{-}U}$ $Y^{S\text{-}2}_{BLS\text{-}M\text{-}P}$ $Y^{S\text{-}2}_{BLS\text{-}I\text{-}U}$	All industries	All industries

27, Printing, Publishing, and Allied Industries	$Y^{G\text{-}2}_{BEA\text{-}P}$ $Y^{G\text{-}2}_{BEA\text{-}U}$ $Y^{S\text{-}2}_{BLS\text{-}M\text{-}P}$ $Y^{S\text{-}2}_{BLS\text{-}I\text{-}U}$	All industries	All industries
28, Chemicals and Allied Products	$Y^{G\text{-}2}_{BEA\text{-}P}$ $Y^{G\text{-}2}_{BEA\text{-}U}$ $Y^{S\text{-}2}_{BLS\text{-}M\text{-}P}$ $Y^{S\text{-}2}_{BLS\text{-}I\text{-}U}$	All industries	All industries
29, Petroleum Refining and Related Industries	$Y^{G\text{-}2}_{BEA\text{-}P}$ $Y^{G\text{-}2}_{BEA\text{-}U}$ $Y^{S\text{-}2}_{BLS\text{-}M\text{-}P}$ $Y^{S\text{-}2}_{BLS\text{-}I\text{-}U}$	All industries	All industries
30, Rubber and Miscellaneous Plastics Products	$Y^{G\text{-}2}_{BEA\text{-}P}$ $Y^{G\text{-}2}_{BEA\text{-}U}$ $Y^{S\text{-}2}_{BLS\text{-}M\text{-}P}$ $Y^{S\text{-}2}_{BLS\text{-}I\text{-}U}$	All industries	All industries
31, Leather and Leather Products	$Y^{G\text{-}2}_{BEA\text{-}P}$ $Y^{G\text{-}2}_{BEA\text{-}U}$ $Y^{S\text{-}2}_{BLS\text{-}M\text{-}P}$ $Y^{S\text{-}2}_{BLS\text{-}I\text{-}U}$	All industries	All industries
32, Stone, Clay, Glass, and Concrete Products	$Y^{G\text{-}2}_{BEA\text{-}P}$ $Y^{G\text{-}2}_{BEA\text{-}U}$ $Y^{S\text{-}2}_{BLS\text{-}M\text{-}P}$ $Y^{S\text{-}2}_{BLS\text{-}I\text{-}U}$	All industries	All industries
33, Primary Metal Industries	$Y^{G\text{-}2}_{BEA\text{-}P}$ $Y^{G\text{-}2}_{BEA\text{-}U}$ $Y^{S\text{-}2}_{BLS\text{-}M\text{-}P}$ $Y^{S\text{-}2}_{BLS\text{-}I\text{-}U}$	All industries	All industries
34, Fabricated Metal Products, Except Machinery and Transportation Equipment	$Y^{G\text{-}2}_{BEA\text{-}P}$ $Y^{G\text{-}2}_{BEA\text{-}U}$ $Y^{S\text{-}2}_{BLS\text{-}M\text{-}P}$ $Y^{S\text{-}2}_{BLS\text{-}I\text{-}U}$	All industries	All industries

(continued)

Table 9B.2 (continued)

SIC industry	SIC 2-digit output measures available			SIC 3-digit output measure comparisons possible	SIC 4-digit output measure comparisons possible
	SIC 2-digit output measures available	BEA only or BLS only	BEA and BLS Series		
35, *Industrial and Commercial Machinery and Computer Equipment*			Y^{G-2}_{BEA-P} Y^{G-2}_{BEA-U} $Y^{S-2}_{BLS-M-P}$ $Y^{S-2}_{BLS-I-U}$	All industries	All industries
36, Electronic and Other Electrical Equipment and Components, Except Computer Equipment			Y^{G-2}_{BEA-P} Y^{G-2}_{BEA-U} $Y^{S-2}_{BLS-M-P}$ $Y^{S-2}_{BLS-I-U}$	All industries	All industries
37, Transportation Equipment			Y^{G-2}_{BEA-P} Y^{G-2}_{BEA-U} $Y^{S-2}_{BLS-M-P}$ $Y^{S-2}_{BLS-I-U}$	All industries	All industries
38, *Measuring, Analyzing, and Controlling Instruments; Photographic, Medical and Optical Goods; Watches and Clocks*			Y^{G-2}_{BEA-P} Y^{G-2}_{BEA-U} $Y^{S-2}_{BLS-M-P}$ $Y^{S-2}_{BLS-I-U}$	All industries	All industries
39, *Miscellaneous Manufacturing Industries*			Y^{G-2}_{BEA-P} Y^{G-2}_{BEA-U} $Y^{S-2}_{BLS-M-P}$ $Y^{S-2}_{BLS-I-U}$	All industries	All industries
40, *Railroad Transportation*			Y^{G-2}_{BEA-P} $Y^{G-2}_{BLS-M-U}$	No	No
41, *Local and Suburban Transit and Interurban Highway Passenger Transportation*			Y^{G-2}_{BEA-P} $Y^{G-2}_{BLS-M-U}$	No	No

Industry				
42, Motor Freight Transportation and Warehousing		Y^{G-2}_{BEA-P} $Y^{G-2}_{BLS-M-U}$	No	No
43, United States Postal Service	$Y^{S-2}_{BLS-I-U}$		All industries (**431** with 4311)	All industries (**431** with 4311)
44, Water Transportation		Y^{G-2}_{BEA-P} $Y^{G-2}_{BLS-M-U}$	No	No
45, Transportation By Air		Y^{G-2}_{BEA-P} $Y^{G-2}_{BLS-M-U}$	No	No
46, Pipelines, Except Natural Gas		Y^{G-2}_{BEA-P} Y^{G-2}_{BEA-U} $Y^{G-2}_{BLS-M-U}$	No	No
47, Transportation Services		Y^{G-2}_{BEA-P} $Y^{G-2}_{BLS-M-U}$	Selected industries	No
48, Communications		Y^{G-2}_{BEA-P} $Y^{G-2}_{BLS-M-U}$	No	No
49, Electric, Gas, and Sanitary Services		Y^{G-2}_{BEA-P} $Y^{G-2}_{BLS-M-U}$	No	No
50, Wholesale Trade-Durable Goods	$Y^{S-2}_{BLS-I-U}$		All industries	No
51, Wholesale Trade-Nondurable Goods	$Y^{S-2}_{BLS-I-U}$		All industries	No
52, Building Materials, Hardware, Garden Supply, and Mobile Home Dealers	$Y^{S-2}_{BLS-I-U}$		Selected industries	No
53, General Merchandise Stores	$Y^{S-2}_{BLS-I-U}$		Selected industries	No
54, Food Stores	$Y^{S-2}_{BLS-I-U}$		Selected industries	No
55, Automotive Dealers and Gasoline Service Stations	$Y^{S-2}_{BLS-I-U}$		Selected industries	No
56, Apparel and Accessory Stores	$Y^{S-2}_{BLS-I-U}$		Selected industries	Selected industries
57, Home Furniture, Furnishings, and Equipment Stores	$Y^{S-2}_{BLS-I-U}$		No	Selected industries
58, Eating and Drinking Places	$Y^{S-2}_{BLS-I-U}$		No	All industries
59, Miscellaneous Retail	$Y^{S-2}_{BLS-I-U}$		Selected industries	Selected industries

(continued)

Table 9B.2   (continued)

SIC industry	SIC 2-digit output measures available	SIC 2-digit output measures available		SIC 3-digit output measure comparisons possible	SIC 4-digit output measure comparisons possible
		BEA only or BLS only	BEA and BLS Series		
60, Depository Institutions		Y^{G-2}_{BEA-P}		No	No
61, Non-depository Credit Institutions		Y^{G-2}_{BEA-P}		No	No
62, Security and Commodity Brokers, Dealers, Exchanges, and Services			Y^{G-2}_{BEA-P} $Y^{G-2}_{BLS-M-U}$	No	No
63, Insurance Carriers			Y^{G-2}_{BEA-P} $Y^{G-2}_{BLS-M-U}$	No	No
64, Insurance Agents, Brokers and Service			Y^{G-2}_{BEA-P} Y^{G-2}_{BEA-U} $Y^{G-2}_{BLS-M-U}$	No	No
65, Real Estate		Y^{G-2}_{BEA-P}		No	No
67, Holding and Other Investment Offices		Y^{G-2}_{BEA-P} Y^{G-2}_{BEA-U}		No	No
70, Hotels, Rooming Houses, Camps, and Other Lodging Places			Y^{G-2}_{BEA-P} $Y^{G-2}_{BLS-M-U}$	No	No
72, *Personal Services*			Y^{G-2}_{BEA-P} $Y^{G-2}_{BLS-M-U}$ $Y^{S-2}_{BLS-I-U}$	Selected industries	Selected industries
73, Business Services		Y^{G-2}_{BEA-P}		No	No
75, Automotive Repair, Services, and Parking			Y^{G-2}_{BEA-P} $Y^{G-2}_{BLS-M-U}$	Selected industries	No
76, Miscellaneous Repair Services		Y^{G-2}_{BEA-P}		No	No
78, *Motion Pictures*			Y^{G-2}_{BEA-P} $Y^{G-2}_{BLS-M-U}$	Selected industries	No

Industry					
79, Amusement and Recreation Services			Y^{G-2}_{BEA-P} $Y^{G-2}_{BLS-M-U}$	No	No
80, Health Services			Y^{G-2}_{BEA-P} $Y^{G-2}_{BLS-M-U}$	No	No
81, Legal Services		Y^{G-2}_{BEA-P}		No	No
82, Educational Services			Y^{G-2}_{BEA-U} Y^{G-2}_{BEA-P} $Y^{G-2}_{BLS-M-U}$	No	No
83, Social Services		Y^{G-2}_{BEA-P}		No	No
84, Museums, Art Galleries, and Botanical and Zoological Gardens	n.a.			No	No
86, Membership Organizations		$^{G-2}y_{BEA-P}$		No	No
87, Engineering, Accounting, Research, Management and Related Services	n.a.			No	No
88, Private Households	n.a.			No	No
91, Executive, Legislative, And General Government, Except Finance	n.a.			No	No
92, Justice, Public Order, And Safety	n.a.			No	No
93, Public Finance, Taxation, And Monetary Policy	n.a.			No	No
94, Administration Of Human Resource Programs	n.a.			No	No
95, Administration Of Environmental Quality And Housing Programs	n.a.			No	No
96, Administration Of Economic Programs	n.a.			No	No
97, National Security And International Affairs	n.a.			No	No
99, Nonclassifiable Establishments	n.a.			No	No

Note: Italic type indicates industries with SIC 2-digit output measure differences and ***bold italic*** indicates such industries with case studies completed.

Table 9B.3   Constant and current U.S. dollar trends, selected industries

SIC Industry	Output measure	Constant $ 1990–1995	Constant $ 1995–2000	Current $ 1990–1995	Current $ 1995–2000	Constant $ less current $ 1990–1995	Constant $ less current $ 1995–2000	Acceleration, constant $	Acceleration, current $	Difference in constant and current $ acceleration (for each measure)	Output measure comparisons	Correlation coefficient: Annual percent change in constant dollar output measures	Correlation coefficient: Annual percent change in current dollar output measures
10, Metal Mining	Y^{G-2}_{BEA-P}	2.08	-0.48	2.72	-5.62	-0.64	5.14	-2.56	-8.34	5.78	Y^{G-2}_{BEA-P} and $Y^{G-2}_{BLS-M-U}$	0.927	0.83
	$Y^{G-2}_{BLS-M-U}$	1.69	0.65	2.5	0.89	-0.81	-0.24	-1.04	-1.61	0.57			
1011, Iron Ores	Y^{G-4}_{BEA-U}	3.21	0.18	3.84	-1.55	-0.62	1.73	-3.03	-5.39	2.35	Y^{G-4}_{BEA-U} and $Y^{S-4}_{BLS-I-U}$	0.960	0.915
	$Y^{S-4}_{BLS-I-U}$	1.88	0.13	0.40	-1.70	1.48	1.83	-1.75	-2.10	0.35			
1021, Copper Ores	Y^{G-4}_{BEA-U}	2.39	-5.43	4.79	-13.58	-2.41	81.5	-7.81	-18.37	10.56	Y^{G-4}_{BEA-U} and $Y^{S-4}_{BLS-I-P}$	0.87	0.987
	$Y^{S-4}_{BLS-I-P}$	2.86	-4.90	5.18	-12.43	-2.32	7.52	-7.77	-17.60	9.84			
1031, Lead and Zinc Ores	Y^{G-4}_{BEA-U}	1.61	5.24	-3.60	5.30	5.21	-0.05	3.64	8.89	-5.26	Y^{G-4}_{BEA-U} and $Y^{S-4}_{BLS-I-U}$	0.77	0.985
	$Y^{S-4}_{BLS-I-U}$	8.81	4.91	-3.59	5.53	12.39	-0.62	-3.90	9.11	-13.01			
1041, Gold Ores	Y^{G-4}_{BEA-U}	2.75	2.17	2.89	-4.25	-0.14	6.43	-0.58	-7.15	6.57	Y^{G-4}_{BEA-U} and $Y^{S-4}_{BLS-I-P}$	0.98	0.987
	$Y^{S-4}_{BLS-I-P}$	1.29	2.08	1.64	-4.24	-0.35	6.32	0.79	-5.89	6.68			
1044, Silver Ores	Y^{G-4}_{BEA-U}	-8.53	3.54	-7.11	2.96	-1.42	0.58	12.07	10.07	2.00	Y^{G-4}_{BEA-U} and $Y^{S-4}_{BLS-I-U}$	0.77	0.921
	$Y^{S-4}_{BLS-I-U}$	-4.83	2.53	-4.65	2.91	-0.17	-0.38	7.36	7.57	-0.21			
1061, Ferroalloy Ores, Except Vanadium								No BEA or BLS output series available.					
1081, Metal Mining Services								Only a single series (Y^{G-4}_{BEA-U}) is available.					
1094, Uranium–Radium–Vanadium Ores								Only a single series (Y^{G-4}_{BEA-U}) is available.					
1099, Miscellaneous Metal Ores, NEC								Only a single series (Y^{G-4}_{BEA-U}) is available.					
13, Oil and Gas Extraction	Y^{G-2}_{BEA-P}	-0.4	0.74	-3.81	13.84	3.41	-13.1	1.14	17.65	-16.51	Y^{G-2}_{BEA-P} and $Y^{S-2}_{BLS-I-U}$	0.684	0.980
	$Y^{S-2}_{BLS-I-U}$	-0.75	-0.75	-5.28	14.88	4.53	-15.63	0	20.16	-20.16	Y^{G-2}_{BEA-P} and $Y^{G-2}_{BLS-M-U}$	0.919	0.770
	$Y^{G-2}_{BLS-M-U}$	-1.12	1.12	-4.65	2.89	3.53	-1.77	2.24	7.54	-5.30	$Y^{S-2}_{BLS-I-U}$ and $Y^{G-2}_{BLS-M-U}$	0.697	0.710
20, Food and Kindred Products	Y^{G-2}_{BEA-P}	1.95	1.23	2.84	2.09	-0.89	-0.86	-0.72	-0.75	0.03	Y^{G-2}_{BEA-P} and $Y^{S-2}_{BLS-I-U}$	0.979	0.990
	$Y^{S-2}_{BLS-I-U}$	1.96	1.27	2.81	1.98	-0.85	-0.71	-0.69	-0.83	0.14	Y^{G-2}_{BEA-P} and $Y^{G-2}_{BLS-M-U}$	0.640	0.740
	$Y^{G-2}_{BLS-M-U}$	2.67	1.02	3.48	1.88	-0.81	-0.86	-1.65	-1.6	-0.05	$Y^{S-2}_{BLS-I-U}$ and $Y^{G-2}_{BLS-M-U}$	0.687	0.760

Industry	Variable										Correlation pair		
21, Tobacco Products	Y^{G-2}_{BEA-P}	0.33	−2.62	2.74	7.87	−2.41	−10.49	−2.95	5.13	−8.06	Y^{G-2}_{BEA-P} and $Y^{S-2}_{BLS-I-U}$	0.996	0.980
	$Y^{S-2}_{BLS-I-U}$	0.82	−2.78	2.09	8.3	−1.27	−11.08	−3.6	6.21	−9.81	Y^{G-2}_{BEA-P} and $Y^{G-2}_{BLS-M-U}$	0.977	0.810
	$Y^{G-2}_{BLS-M-U}$	0.7	−3.2	2.19	4.46	−1.49	−7.66	−3.9	2.27	−6.17	$Y^{S-2}_{BLS-I-U}$ and $Y^{G-2}_{BLS-M-U}$	0.991	0.890
27, Printing, Publishing, and Allied Industries	Y^{G-2}_{BEA-P}	−0.47	1.22	3.17	3.89	−3.64	−2.67	1.69	0.72	0.97	Y^{G-2}_{BEA-P} and $Y^{S-2}_{BLS-I-U}$	0.769	0.699
	$Y^{S-2}_{BLS-I-U}$	−0.42	2.77	3.31	5.51	−3.73	−2.74	3.19	2.2	0.99	Y^{S-2}_{BEA-P} and $Y^{G-2}_{BLS-M-U}$	0.904	0.883
	$Y^{G-2}_{BLS-M-U}$	−0.1	1.18	3.54	3.79	−3.64	−2.61	1.28	0.25	1.03	$Y^{S-2}_{BLS-I-U}$ and $Y^{S-3}_{BLS-I-P}$	0.727	0.660
271, Newspapers: Publishing, or Publishing and Printing	Y^{G-3}_{BEA-U}	−3.79	0.19	1.38	4.47	−5.17	−4.26	3.97	3.09	0.88	Y^{G-3}_{BEA-U} and $Y^{S-3}_{BLS-I-P}$	0.907	0.818
	$Y^{S-3}_{BLS-I-P}$	−3.86	2.20	1.37	6.50	−5.23	−4.30	6.06	5.13	0.93			
272, Periodicals: Publishing, or Publishing and Printing	Y^{G-3}_{BEA-U}	−0.71	3.71	2.74	6.60	−3.45	−3.43	3.88	3.86	0.02	Y^{G-3}_{BEA-U} and $Y^{S-3}_{BLS-I-P}$	0.692	0.689
	$Y^{S-3}_{BLS-I-P}$	−1.15	7.39	2.73	11.13	−3.88	−3.74	8.55	8.40	0.15			
273, Books	Y^{G-3}_{BEA-U}	1.64	0.12	5.52	2.78	−3.88	−2.66	−1.52	−2.74	1.22	Y^{G-3}_{BEA-U} and $Y^{S-3}_{BLS-I-P}$	0.891	0.877
	$Y^{S-3}_{BLS-I-P}$	1.80	1.25	5.52	4.07	−3.72	−2.82	−0.55	−1.45	0.90			
274, Miscellaneous Publishing	Y^{G-3}_{BEA-U}	1.27	2.46	5.90	6.46	−4.63	−4.00	1.19	0.56	0.63	Y^{G-3}_{BEA-U} and $Y^{S-3}_{BLS-I-P}$	0.888	0.877
	$Y^{S-3}_{BLS-I-P}$	1.20	8.09	5.78	12.40	−4.58	−4.31	6.89	6.62	0.27			
275, Commercial Printing	Y^{G-3}_{BEA-U}	1.50	1.83	3.88	3.23	−2.38	−1.40	0.33	−0.65	0.98	Y^{G-3}_{BEA-U} and $Y^{S-3}_{BLS-I-P}$	0.995	0.998
	$Y^{S-3}_{BLS-I-P}$	1.47	1.94	3.91	3.28	−2.44	−1.34	0.47	−0.63	1.10			
276, Manifold Business Forms	Y^{G-3}_{BEA-U}	−5.58	−3.52	−0.12	−1.25	−5.46	−2.27	2.06	−1.13	3.19	Y^{G-3}_{BEA-U} and $Y^{S-3}_{BLS-I-P}$	0.994	0.996
	$Y^{S-3}_{BLS-I-P}$	−5.74	−3.60	−0.10	−1.53	−5.64	−2.07	2.14	−1.43	3.57			
277, Greeting Cards	Y^{G-3}_{BEA-U}	−0.54	1.05	4.38	3.77	−4.92	−2.72	1.59	−0.61	2.20	Y^{G-3}_{BEA-U} and $Y^{S-3}_{BLS-I-P}$	0.269	0.196
	$Y^{S-3}_{BLS-I-P}$	−1.14	0.88	4.02	3.55	−5.16	−2.67	2.02	−0.47	2.49			
278, Blankbooks, Looseleaf Binders and Bookbinding	Y^{G-3}_{BEA-U}	1.73	0.23	5.52	1.65	−3.79	−1.42	−1.50	−3.87	2.37	Y^{G-3}_{BEA-U} and $Y^{S-3}_{BLS-I-P}$	0.994	0.994
	$Y^{S-3}_{BLS-I-P}$	1.59	0.11	5.41	1.52	−3.82	−1.41	−1.48	−3.89	2.41			
279, Service Industries for the Printing Trade	Y^{G-3}_{BEA-U}	0.03	−2.24	0.86	−1.46	−0.83	−0.78	−2.27	−2.32	0.05	Y^{G-3}_{BEA-U} and $Y^{S-3}_{BLS-I-P}$	0.998	0.998
	$Y^{S-3}_{BLS-I-P}$	0.00	−2.12	0.85	−1.48	−0.85	−0.64	−2.12	−2.33	0.21			
29, Petroleum Refining and Related Industries	Y^{G-2}_{BEA-P}	0.81	1.08	−2.53	8.88	3.34	−7.8	0.27	11.41	−11.14	Y^{G-2}_{BEA-P} and $Y^{S-2}_{BLS-I-U}$	−0.044	0.997
	$Y^{S-2}_{BLS-I-U}$	1.2	1.58	−2.86	9.27	4.06	−7.69	0.38	12.13	−11.75	Y^{G-2}_{BEA-P} and $Y^{G-2}_{BLS-M-U}$	−0.013	0.994
	$Y^{G-2}_{BLS-M-U}$	0.88	1.51	−2.76	9.2	3.64	−7.69	0.63	11.96	−11.33	$Y^{S-2}_{BLS-I-U}$ and $Y^{G-2}_{BLS-M-U}$	0.988	0.992
291, Petroleum Refining	Y^{G-3}_{BEA-U}	0.63	1.20	−3.19	9.47	3.82	−8.26	0.57	12.66	−12.08	Y^{G-3}_{BEA-U} and $Y^{S-3}_{BLS-I-P}$	−0.130	0.998
	$Y^{S-3}_{BLS-I-P}$	1.15	1.57	−3.38	9.73	4.52	−8.17	0.42	13.11	−12.69			
295, Asphalt Paving and Roofing Materials	Y^{G-3}_{BEA-U}	1.95	2.96	2.74	5.75	−0.79	−2.79	1.01	3.01	−2.00	Y^{G-3}_{BEA-U} and $Y^{S-3}_{BLS-I-P}$	0.997	0.997
	$Y^{S-3}_{BLS-I-P}$	1.96	2.87	2.71	5.93	−0.76	−3.06	0.91	3.21	−2.30			
299, Miscellaneous Products of Petroleum and Coal	Y^{G-3}_{BEA-U}	1.11	0.69	3.05	2.70	−1.93	−2.01	−0.43	−0.35	−0.08	Y^{G-3}_{BEA-U} and $Y^{S-3}_{BLS-I-P}$	0.984	0.982
	$Y^{S-3}_{BLS-I-P}$	0.94	0.58	2.91	2.58	−1.96	−2.00	−0.36	−0.33	−0.03			
31, Leather and Leather Products	Y^{G-2}_{BEA-P}	−1.97	−1.59	−0.13	−1.42	−1.84	−0.17	0.38	−1.29	1.67	Y^{G-2}_{BEA-P} and $Y^{S-2}_{BLS-I-U}$	0.949	0.953
	$Y^{S-2}_{BLS-I-U}$	−2.67	−1.15	−0.85	−0.92	−1.82	−0.23	1.52	−0.07	1.59	Y^{G-2}_{BEA-P} and $Y^{G-2}_{BLS-M-U}$	0.923	0.915
	$Y^{G-2}_{BLS-M-U}$	−3.14	−1.53	−1.28	−1.31	−1.86	−0.22	1.61	−0.03	1.64	$Y^{S-2}_{BLS-I-U}$ and $Y^{G-2}_{BLS-M-U}$	0.969	0.951

(continued)

Table 9B.3 (continued)

SIC Industry	Output measure	Constant $ 1990–1995	Constant $ 1995–2000	Current $ 1990–1995	Current $ 1995–2000	Constant $ less current $ 1990–1995	Constant $ less current $ 1995–2000	Acceleration, constant $	Acceleration, current $	Difference in constant and current $ acceleration (for each measure)	Output measure comparisons	Correlation coefficient: Annual percent change in constant dollar output measures	Correlation coefficient: Annual percent change in current dollar output measures
311, Leather Tanning and Finishing	Y^{G-3}_{BEA-U}	4.22	0.13	6.02	-1.07	-1.80	1.20	-4.09	-7.10	3.01	Y^{G-3}_{BEA-U} and $Y^{S-3}_{BLS-I-U}$	0.984	0.984
	$Y^{S-3}_{BLS-I-U}$	3.41	1.65	5.15	0.58	-1.74	1.07	-1.76	-4.57	2.81			
313, Boot and Shoe Cut Stock and Findings	Y^{G-3}_{BEA-U}	-8.30	-8.63	-6.71	-7.89	-1.59	-0.74	-0.33	-1.18	0.85	Y^{G-3}_{BEA-U} and $Y^{S-3}_{BLS-I-U}$	0.611	0.625
	$Y^{S-3}_{BLS-I-U}$	-8.14	0.30	-6.64	1.10	-1.50	-0.80	8.44	7.75	0.69			
314, Footwear, Except Rubber	Y^{G-3}_{BEA-U}	-3.28	-5.49	-1.29	-4.70	-1.99	-0.79	-2.21	-3.41	1.20	Y^{G-3}_{BEA-U} and $Y^{S-3}_{BLS-I-P}$	0.984	0.985
	$Y^{S-3}_{BLS-I-P}$	-3.62	-7.07	-1.65	-6.44	-1.97	-0.63	-3.45	-4.79	1.34			
315, Leather Gloves and Mittens	Y^{G-3}_{BEA-U}	-7.49	5.54	-5.21	7.15	-2.28	-1.61	13.03	12.36	0.67	Y^{G-3}_{BEA-U} and $Y^{S-3}_{BLS-I-U}$	0.992	0.992
	$Y^{S-3}_{BLS-I-U}$	-7.95	5.71	-5.84	7.22	-2.11	-1.51	13.66	13.06	0.60			
316, Luggage	Y^{G-3}_{BEA-U}	-4.50	5.53	-3.48	6.48	-1.02	-0.95	10.03	9.96	0.07	Y^{G-3}_{BEA-U} and $Y^{S-3}_{BLS-I-U}$	0.971	0.975
	$Y^{S-3}_{BLS-I-U}$	-4.00	4.75	-2.87	5.99	-1.13	-1.24	8.75	8.85	-0.10			
317, Handbags and Other Leather Goods	Y^{G-3}_{BEA-U}	-7.35	-1.27	-6.61	-0.94	-0.74	-0.33	6.08	5.66	0.42	Y^{G-3}_{BEA-U} and $Y^{S-3}_{BLS-I-U}$	0.996	0.996
	$Y^{S-3}_{BLS-I-U}$	-7.40	-0.91	-6.61	-0.54	-0.79	-0.37	6.49	6.07	0.42			
319, Leather Goods, NEC	Y^{G-3}_{BEA-U}	-8.75	7.86	-7.39	9.94	-1.36	-2.08	16.61	17.33	-0.72	Y^{G-3}_{BEA-U} and $Y^{S-3}_{BLS-I-U}$	0.994	0.995
	$Y^{S-3}_{BLS-I-U}$	-8.63	7.13	-7.23	9.14	-1.40	-2.01	15.76	16.38	-0.62			
35, Industrial and Commercial Machinery and Computer Equipment	Y^{G-2}_{BEA-P}	8.44	9.38	6.66	3.6	1.78	5.78	0.94	-3.06	4.00	Y^{G-2}_{BEA-P} and $Y^{S-2}_{BLS-I-U}$	0.991	0.989
	$Y^{S-2}_{BLS-I-U}$	8.02	10.05	6.61	4.12	1.41	5.93	2.03	-2.49	4.52	Y^{G-2}_{BEA-P} and $Y^{G-2}_{BLS-M-U}$	0.976	0.975
	$Y^{G-2}_{BLS-M-U}$	7.84	10.03	6.21	4.12	1.63	5.91	2.19	-2.09	4.28	$Y^{S-2}_{BLS-I-U}$ and $Y^{G-2}_{BLS-M-U}$	0.985	0.986
351, Engines and Turbines	Y^{G-3}_{BEA-U}	3.62	4.41	6.00	5.28	-2.38	-0.87	0.79	-0.72	1.51	Y^{G-3}_{BEA-U} and $Y^{S-3}_{BLS-I-P}$	0.955	0.939
	$Y^{S-3}_{BLS-I-P}$	3.40	2.35	5.48	5.72	-2.08	-3.37	-1.05	0.23	-1.28			
352, Farm and Garden Machinery and Equipment	Y^{G-3}_{BEA-U}	2.14	-0.85	4.48	0.42	-2.34	-1.27	-2.99	-4.06	1.07	Y^{G-3}_{BEA-U} and $Y^{S-3}_{BLS-I-P}$	0.993	0.992
	$Y^{S-3}_{BLS-I-P}$	2.13	-0.87	4.43	0.41	-2.30	-1.28	-3.00	-4.02	1.02			
353, Construction, Mining, and Materials Handling	Y^{G-3}_{BEA-U}	2.49	3.75	4.50	5.43	-2.01	-1.68	1.26	0.92	0.34	Y^{G-3}_{BEA-U} and $Y^{S-3}_{BLS-I-P}$	0.991	0.990
	$Y^{S-3}_{BLS-I-P}$	2.73	3.83	4.75	5.43	-2.02	-1.60	1.10	0.68	0.42			
354, Metalworking Machinery and Equipment	Y^{G-3}_{BEA-U}	3.41	1.46	6.01	2.89	-2.60	-1.43	-1.95	-3.12	1.17	Y^{G-3}_{BEA-U} and $Y^{S-3}_{BLS-I-P}$	0.991	0.990
	$Y^{S-3}_{BLS-I-P}$	3.75	1.11	6.42	2.59	-2.67	-1.48	-2.64	-3.83	1.19			

Table (continued — no column headers on this page)

Industry	Series	1	2	3	4	5	6	7	8	9
355, Special Industrial Machinery, Except Metalworking	$Y^{G\text{-}3}_{BEA\text{-}U}$	5.83	5.39	8.48	7.07	−2.65	−1.68	−0.44	−1.42	0.98
	$Y^{S\text{-}3}_{BLS\text{-}I\text{-}P}$	6.31	5.11	9.08	6.90	−2.77	−1.79	−1.20	−2.18	0.98
356, General Industrial Machinery and Equipment	$Y^{G\text{-}3}_{BEA\text{-}U}$	2.36	1.29	5.21	3.16	−2.85	−1.87	−1.07	−2.05	0.98
	$Y^{S\text{-}3}_{BLS\text{-}I\text{-}P}$	2.36	1.11	5.30	3.01	−2.94	−1.90	−1.25	−2.29	1.04
357, Computer and Office Equipment	$Y^{G\text{-}3}_{BEA\text{-}U}$	21.89	32.38	6.94	4.09	14.95	28.29	10.49	−2.85	13.34
	$Y^{S\text{-}3}_{BLS\text{-}I\text{-}P}$	22.55	35.91	7.43	4.27	15.12	31.64	13.36	−3.16	16.52
358, Refrigeration and Service Industry Machinery	$Y^{G\text{-}3}_{BEA\text{-}U}$	5.10	2.61	6.72	3.54	−1.62	−0.93	−2.49	−3.18	0.69
	$Y^{S\text{-}3}_{BLS\text{-}I\text{-}P}$	5.31	2.72	7.05	3.72	−1.74	−1.00	−2.59	−3.33	0.74
359, Miscellaneous Industrial and Commercial	$Y^{G\text{-}3}_{BEA\text{-}U}$	6.80	2.56	8.09	3.72	−1.29	−1.16	−4.24	−4.38	0.14
	$Y^{S\text{-}3}_{BLS\text{-}I\text{-}P}$	6.73	2.49	8.10	3.69	−1.37	−1.20	−4.24	−4.41	0.17
38, Measuring, Analyzing, and Controlling Instruments, Photographic and Optical Goods, Watches and Clocks	$Y^{G\text{-}2}_{BEA\text{-}P}$	1.05	3.20	2.58	3.43	−1.53	−0.23	2.15	0.85	1.30
	$Y^{S\text{-}2}_{BLS\text{-}I\text{-}U}$	0.87	3.41	2.29	3.58	−1.42	−0.17	2.54	1.29	1.25
	$Y^{G\text{-}2}_{BLS\text{-}M\text{-}U}$	1.27	4.04	2.71	4.08	−1.44	−0.04	2.77	1.37	1.40
381, Search, Detection, Navigation, Guidance, Aeronautical, and Nautical	$Y^{G\text{-}3}_{BEA\text{-}U}$	−5.25	−0.11	−3.69	0.34	−1.56	−0.45	5.14	4.02	1.12
	$Y^{S\text{-}3}_{BLS\text{-}I\text{-}P}$	−5.52	0.71	−4.03	1.16	−1.49	−0.45	6.23	5.19	1.04
382, Laboratory Apparatus and Analytical, Optical	$Y^{G\text{-}3}_{BEA\text{-}U}$	4.29	2.74	6.28	3.54	−1.99	−0.80	−1.55	−2.74	1.19
	$Y^{S\text{-}3}_{BLS\text{-}I\text{-}P}$	4.32	2.52	6.26	3.41	−1.94	−0.89	−1.80	−2.86	1.06
384, Surgical Medical and Dental Instruments	$Y^{G\text{-}3}_{BEA\text{-}U}$	3.97	6.98	5.95	6.97	−1.98	0.01	3.01	1.02	1.99
	$Y^{S\text{-}3}_{BLS\text{-}I\text{-}P}$	3.85	6.73	5.89	6.97	−2.04	−0.24	2.88	1.08	1.80
385, Ophthalmic Goods	$Y^{G\text{-}3}_{BEA\text{-}U}$	3.90	7.73	5.57	7.00	−1.67	0.73	3.83	1.42	2.41
	$Y^{S\text{-}3}_{BLS\text{-}I\text{-}P}$	3.45	7.50	5.13	6.81	−1.68	0.69	4.05	1.68	2.37
386, Photographic Equipment and Supplies	$Y^{G\text{-}3}_{BEA\text{-}U}$	0.72	0.75	0.58	−0.18	0.14	0.93	0.03	−0.76	0.79
	$Y^{S\text{-}3}_{BLS\text{-}I\text{-}P}$	0.84	1.39	0.39	−0.64	0.45	2.03	0.55	−1.03	1.58
387, Watches, Clocks, Clockwork Operated Devices	$Y^{G\text{-}3}_{BEA\text{-}U}$	−9.33	5.51	−7.74	6.16	−1.59	−0.65	14.84	13.91	0.93
	$Y^{S\text{-}3}_{BLS\text{-}I\text{-}P}$	−6.57	2.67	−7.11	3.44	0.54	−0.77	9.24	10.55	−1.31
39, Miscellaneous Manufacturing	$Y^{G\text{-}2}_{BEA\text{-}P}$	1.44	3.22	3.52	4.13	−2.08	−0.91	1.78	0.61	1.17
	$Y^{S\text{-}2}_{BLS\text{-}I\text{-}U}$	2.00	2.82	4.01	3.63	−2.01	−0.81	0.82	−0.38	1.20
	$Y^{G\text{-}2}_{BLS\text{-}M\text{-}U}$	2.02	2.85	4.02	3.64	−2	−0.79	0.83	−0.38	1.21
40, Railroad Transportation	$Y^{G\text{-}2}_{BEA\text{-}P}$	3.39	0.67	3.18	1.26	0.21	−0.59	−2.72	−1.92	−0.80
	$Y^{G\text{-}2}_{BLS\text{-}M\text{-}U}$	1.63	−0.62	2.41	−0.02	−0.78	−0.6	−2.25	−2.43	0.18
41, Local and Suburban Transit and Interurban Highway Passenger Transportation	$Y^{G\text{-}2}_{BEA\text{-}P}$	0.54	2.36	3.71	4.64	−3.17	−2.28	1.82	0.93	0.89
	$Y^{G\text{-}2}_{BLS\text{-}M\text{-}U}$	1.59	1.22	5.09	3.73	−3.5	−2.51	−0.37	−1.36	0.99

Correlation pair		
$Y^{G\text{-}3}_{BEA\text{-}U}$ and $Y^{S\text{-}3}_{BLS\text{-}I\text{-}P}$	0.994	0.993
$Y^{G\text{-}3}_{BEA\text{-}U}$ and $Y^{S\text{-}3}_{BLS\text{-}I\text{-}P}$	0.993	0.992
$Y^{G\text{-}3}_{BEA\text{-}U}$ and $Y^{S\text{-}3}_{BLS\text{-}I\text{-}P}$	0.990	0.981
$Y^{G\text{-}3}_{BEA\text{-}U}$ and $Y^{S\text{-}3}_{BLS\text{-}I\text{-}P}$	0.994	0.993
$Y^{G\text{-}3}_{BEA\text{-}U}$ and $Y^{S\text{-}3}_{BLS\text{-}I\text{-}P}$	0.995	0.995
$Y^{G\text{-}2}_{BEA\text{-}P}$ and $Y^{S\text{-}2}_{BLS\text{-}I\text{-}U}$	0.916	0.160
$Y^{G\text{-}2}_{BEA\text{-}P}$ and $Y^{G\text{-}2}_{BLS\text{-}M\text{-}U}$	0.597	0.054
$Y^{S\text{-}2}_{BLS\text{-}I\text{-}U}$ and $Y^{G\text{-}2}_{BLS\text{-}M\text{-}U}$	0.701	0.657
$Y^{G\text{-}3}_{BEA\text{-}U}$ and $Y^{S\text{-}3}_{BLS\text{-}I\text{-}P}$	0.973	0.957
$Y^{G\text{-}3}_{BEA\text{-}U}$ and $Y^{S\text{-}3}_{BLS\text{-}I\text{-}P}$	0.990	0.985
$Y^{G\text{-}3}_{BEA\text{-}U}$ and $Y^{S\text{-}3}_{BLS\text{-}I\text{-}P}$	0.987	0.989
$Y^{G\text{-}3}_{BEA\text{-}U}$ and $Y^{S\text{-}3}_{BLS\text{-}I\text{-}P}$	0.972	0.973
$Y^{G\text{-}3}_{BEA\text{-}U}$ and $Y^{S\text{-}3}_{BLS\text{-}I\text{-}P}$	0.920	0.960
$Y^{G\text{-}3}_{BEA\text{-}U}$ and $Y^{S\text{-}3}_{BLS\text{-}I\text{-}P}$	0.880	0.913
$Y^{G\text{-}2}_{BEA\text{-}P}$ and $Y^{S\text{-}2}_{BLS\text{-}I\text{-}U}$	0.954	0.947
$Y^{G\text{-}2}_{BEA\text{-}P}$ and $Y^{G\text{-}2}_{BLS\text{-}M\text{-}U}$	0.867	0.863
$Y^{S\text{-}2}_{BLS\text{-}I\text{-}U}$ and $Y^{G\text{-}2}_{BLS\text{-}M\text{-}U}$	0.842	0.838
$Y^{G\text{-}2}_{BEA\text{-}P}$ and $Y^{G\text{-}2}_{BLS\text{-}M\text{-}U}$	0.638	0.970
$Y^{G\text{-}2}_{BEA\text{-}P}$ and $Y^{G\text{-}2}_{BLS\text{-}M\text{-}U}$	0.747	0.090

(continued)

Table 9B.3   (continued)

SIC Industry	Output measure	Constant $ 1990–1995	Constant $ 1995–2000	Current $ 1990–1995	Current $ 1995–2000	Constant $ less current $ 1990–1995	Constant $ less current $ 1995–2000	Acceleration, constant $	Acceleration, current $	Difference in constant and current $ acceleration (for each measure)	Output measure comparisons	Correlation coefficient: Annual percent change in constant dollar output measures	Correlation coefficient: Annual percent change in current dollar output measures
42, Motor Freight Transportation and Warehousing	Y^{G-2}_{BEA-P}	4.89	4.06	5.56	7.14	-0.67	-3.08	-0.83	1.58	-2.41	Y^{G-2}_{BEA-P} and $Y^{G-2}_{BLS-M-U}$	0.536	0.980
	$Y^{G-2}_{BLS-M-U}$	4.48	4.63	5.14	6.80	-0.66	-2.17	0.15	1.66	-1.51			
44, Water Transportation	Y^{G-2}_{BEA-P}	2.39	4.72	3.76	7.07	-1.37	-2.35	2.33	3.31	-0.98	Y^{G-2}_{BEA-P} and $Y^{G-2}_{BLS-M-U}$	0.544	0.280
	$Y^{G-2}_{BLS-M-U}$	2.40	-0.52	4.98	1.71	-2.58	-2.23	-2.92	-3.27	0.35			
45, Transportation by Air	Y^{G-2}_{BEA-P}	3.14	5.39	4.27	6.90	-1.13	-1.51	2.25	2.63	-0.38	Y^{G-2}_{BEA-P} and $Y^{G-2}_{BLS-M-U}$	0.399	0.360
	$Y^{G-2}_{BLS-M-U}$	3.84	1.48	4.41	3.11	-0.57	-1.63	-2.36	-1.3	-1.06			
46, Pipelines, Except Natural Gas	Y^{G-2}_{BEA-P}	-5.39	0.14	-3.00	-0.85	-2.39	0.99	5.53	2.15	3.38	Y^{G-2}_{BEA-P} and $Y^{G-2}_{BLS-M-U}$	0.617	0.670
	$Y^{G-2}_{BLS-M-U}$	-1.39	-3.04	1.53	-4.99	-2.92	1.95	-1.65	-6.52	4.87			
47, Transportation Services	Y^{G-2}_{BEA-P}	4.78	6.21	6.77	7.80	-1.99	-1.59	1.43	1.03	0.40	Y^{G-2}_{BEA-P} and $Y^{G-2}_{BLS-M-U}$	0.557	0.560
	$Y^{G-2}_{BLS-M-U}$	4.48	5.75	5.59	2.45	-1.11	3.3	1.27	-3.14	4.41			
48, Communications	Y^{G-2}_{BEA-P}	5.55	11.38	6.77	11.09	-1.22	0.29	5.83	4.32	1.51	Y^{G-2}_{BEA-P} and $Y^{G-2}_{BLS-M-U}$	0.701	0.760
	$Y^{G-2}_{BLS-M-U}$	4.38	6.67	6.06	8.61	-1.68	-1.94	2.29	2.55	-0.26			
481, Telephone Communications										Only a single series ($Y^{S-3}_{BLS-I-P}$) is available.			
482 Telegraph and Other Message Communications										No BEA or BLS output series available.			
483 Radio and Television Broadcasting Stations	Y^{G-3}_{BEA-U}	0.08	-0.06	2.65	8.13	-2.57	-8.19	-0.14	5.48	-5.62	Y^{G-3}_{BEA-U} and $Y^{S-3}_{BLS-I-P}$	0.733	0.392
	$Y^{S-3}_{BLS-I-P}$	1.13	2.19	4.14	-0.05	-3.01	2.24	1.06	-4.19	5.25			
484 Cable and Other Pay Television Stations	Y^{G-3}_{BEA-U}	5.38	8.93	10.42	13.48	-5.04	-4.55	3.55	3.07	0.48	Y^{G-3}_{BEA-U} and $Y^{S-3}_{BLS-I-P}$	0.470	0.494
	$Y^{S-3}_{BLS-M-U}$	2.96	8.21	7.92	13.55	-4.96	-5.34	5.25	5.62	-0.37			
489, Communications Services, NEC										No BEA or BLS output series available.			
49, Electric, Gas and Sanitary Services	Y^{G-2}_{BEA-P}	1.96	1.48	3.49	4.40	-1.53	-2.92	-0.48	0.91	-1.39	Y^{G-2}_{BEA-P} and $Y^{G-2}_{BLS-M-U}$	0.108	0.650
	$Y^{G-2}_{BLS-M-U}$	0.14	1.63	2.36	2.20	-2.22	-0.57	1.49	-0.16	1.65			

Industry	Series										Correlation	Corr.
62, Security and Commodity Brokers, Dealers, Exchanges, and Services	Y^{G-2}_{BEA-P}	16.11	23.35	17.11	19.02	−1.00	4.33	7.24	1.91	5.33	Y^{G-2}_{BEA-P} and $Y^{G-2}_{BLS-M-U}$	0.800 / 0.760
	$Y^{G-2}_{BLS-M-U}$	13.54	22.02	10.55	17.21	2.99	4.81	8.48	6.66	1.82		
63, Insurance Carriers	Y^{G-2}_{BEA-P}	−0.15	−1.53	7.10	3.11	−7.25	−4.64	−1.38	−3.90	2.61	Y^{G-2}_{BEA-P} and $Y^{G-2}_{BLS-M-U}$	0.718 / 0.790
	$Y^{G-2}_{BLS-M-U}$	0.87	0.64	8.74	4.56	−7.87	−3.92	−0.23	−4.18	3.95		
64, Insurance Agents, Brokers, and Service	Y^{G-2}_{BEA-P}	−2.67	4.07	3.91	7.91	−6.58	−3.84	6.74	4	2.74	Y^{G-2}_{BEA-P} and $Y^{G-2}_{BLS-M-U}$	−0.114 / 0.040
	$Y^{G-2}_{BLS-M-U}$	−0.41	4.03	1.17	4.93	−1.58	−0.9	4.44	3.76	0.68		
72, Personal Services	Y^{G-2}_{BEA-P}	2.45	2.71	5.56	5.44	−3.11	−2.73	0.26	−0.12	0.38	Y^{G-2}_{BEA-P} and $Y^{S-2}_{BLS-I-U}$	0.946 / 0.930
	$Y^{S-2}_{BLS-I-U}$	1.44	2.89	5.00	6.02	−3.56	−3.13	1.45	1.02	0.43	Y^{G-2}_{BEA-P} and $Y^{G-2}_{BLS-M-U}$	0.900 / 0.880
	$Y^{G-2}_{BLS-M-U}$	1.33	3.56	4.48	6.32	−3.15	−2.76	2.23	1.84	0.39	$Y^{S-2}_{BLS-I-U}$ and $Y^{G-2}_{BLS-M-U}$	0.965 / 0.960
721, Laundry, Cleaning, and Garment Services	Y^{G-3}_{BEA-U}	1.16	2.78	3.84	4.88	−2.68	−2.10	1.62	1.04	0.58	Y^{G-3}_{BEA-U} and $Y^{S-3}_{BLS-I-P}$	0.975 / 0.986
	$Y^{S-3}_{BLS-I-P}$	0.82	2.85	3.61	5.00	−2.79	−2.15	2.03	1.39	0.64		
722, Photographic Studios, Portrait	Y^{G-3}_{BEA-U}	5.32	0.85	8.48	2.62	−3.16	−1.77	−4.47	−5.87	1.40	Y^{G-3}_{BEA-U} and $Y^{S-3}_{BLS-I-P}$	0.975 / 0.972
	$Y^{S-3}_{BLS-I-P}$	5.54	1.49	8.71	3.17	−3.17	−1.68	−4.05	−5.54	1.49		
723, Beauty Shops	Y^{G-3}_{BEA-U}	2.69	3.06	5.05	6.29	−2.36	−3.23	0.37	1.24	−0.87	Y^{G-3}_{BEA-U} and $Y^{S-3}_{BLS-I-P}$	0.989 / 0.987
	$Y^{S-3}_{BLS-I-P}$	2.63	3.16	4.99	6.39	−2.36	−3.23	0.53	1.40	−0.87		
724, Barber Shops	Y^{G-3}_{BEA-U}	−0.06	1.28	2.93	4.53	−2.99	−3.25	1.34	1.59	−0.25	Y^{G-3}_{BEA-U} and $Y^{S-3}_{BLS-I-P}$	0.934 / 0.934
	$Y^{S-3}_{BLS-I-P}$	−0.71	1.61	2.26	4.88	−2.97	−3.27	2.32	2.63	−0.31		
725, Shoe Repair Shops and Shoeshine Parlors		Only a single series (Y^{G-3}_{BEA-U}) is available.										
726, Funeral Service and Crematories	Y^{G-3}_{BEA-U}	1.76	−0.13	7.09	3.87	−5.33	−4.00	−1.89	−3.21	1.32	Y^{G-3}_{BEA-U} and $Y^{S-3}_{BLS-I-P}$	0.941 / 0.959
	$Y^{S-3}_{BLS-I-P}$	1.39	−0.58	6.70	3.40	−5.31	−3.98	−1.97	−3.30	1.33		
729, Miscellaneous Personal Services		Only a single series ($Y^{G-3}_{BLS-I-U}$) is available.										
78, Motion Pictures	Y^{G-2}_{BEA-P}	3.89	2.95	6.54	6.72	−2.65	−3.77	−0.94	0.18	−1.12	Y^{G-2}_{BEA-P} and $Y^{G-2}_{BLS-M-U}$	0.458 / 0.700
	$Y^{G-2}_{BLS-M-U}$	4.74	6.58	7.40	4.24	−2.66	2.34	1.84	−3.16	5.00		
79, Amusement and Recreation Services	Y^{G-2}_{BEA-P}	6.74	3.87	10.03	7.62	−3.29	−3.75	−2.87	−2.41	−0.46	Y^{G-2}_{BEA-P} and $Y^{G-2}_{BLS-M-U}$	0.337 / 0.340
	$Y^{G-2}_{BLS-M-U}$	5.85	6.79	8.89	10.20	−3.04	−3.41	0.94	1.31	−0.37		
82, Educational Services	Y^{G-2}_{BEA-P}	2.86	2.75	6.19	6.48	−3.33	−3.73	−0.11	0.29	−0.40	Y^{G-2}_{BEA-P} and $Y^{G-2}_{BLS-M-U}$	0.584 / 0.570
	$Y^{G-2}_{BLS-M-U}$	0.35	3.68	4.90	7.38	−4.55	−3.7	3.33	2.48	0.85		

Notes: NEC = not elsewhere classified. SIC 2-digit industry current dollar data: BEA, published (adjusted) current dollar gross output series GOC from BEA file GPO87SIC; BLS industry program, sum of nominal value of production for 3-digit groups for manufacturing, and nominal value of production data for 2-digit nonmanufacturing industries; BLS major sector program, value of production series. For 3- and 4-digit industries: BEA, value of shipments data for manufacturing and unadjusted gross output data from GO8701 for nonmanufacturing; BLS industry program, benchmark value of production data.

Table 9B.4   Comparison of real output series: Selected SIC 3- and 4-digit industries

SIC 4-digit industry	Output series	Average annual growth rate		Acceleration (2) – (1)	Output series comparisons	Difference in acceleration	Correlation coefficient
		1990–1995 (1)	1995–2000 (2)				
SIC 4-digit industries in major group 10, Metal Mining Industries							
1011, Iron Ores	Y^{G-4}_{BEA-U}	3.21	0.18	-3.03	Y^{G-4}_{BEA-U} and $Y^{S-4}_{BLS-I-U}$	-1.28	0.960
	$Y^{S-4}_{BLS-I-U}$	1.88	0.13	-1.75			
1021, Copper Ores	Y^{G-4}_{BEA-U}	2.39	-5.43	-7.81	Y^{G-4}_{BEA-U} and $Y^{S-4}_{BLS-I-P}$	-0.04	0.872
	$Y^{S-4}_{BLS-I-P}$	2.86	-4.90	-7.77			
1031, Lead and Zinc Ores	Y^{G-4}_{BEA-U}	1.61	5.24	3.64	Y^{G-4}_{BEA-U} and $Y^{S-4}_{BLS-I-U}$	7.54	0.768
	$Y^{S-4}_{BLS-I-U}$	8.81	4.91	-3.90			
1041, Gold Ores	Y^{G-4}_{BEA-U}	2.75	2.17	-0.58	Y^{G-4}_{BEA-U} and $Y^{S-4}_{BLS-I-P}$	-1.36	0.982
	$Y^{S-4}_{BLS-I-P}$	1.29	2.08	0.79			
1044, Silver Ores	Y^{G-4}_{BEA-U}	-8.53	3.54	12.07	Y^{G-4}_{BEA-U} and $Y^{S-4}_{BLS-I-U}$	4.71	0.767
	$Y^{S-4}_{BLS-I-U}$	-4.83	2.53	7.36			
1061, Ferroalloy Ores, Except Vanadium				No BEA or BLS output series available.			
1081, Metal Mining Services				Only a single series (Y^{G-4}_{BEA-U}) is available.			
1094, Uranium-Radium-Vanadium Ores				Only a single series (Y^{G-4}_{BEA-U}) is available.			
1099, Miscellaneous Metal Ores, NEC				Only a single series (Y^{G-4}_{BEA-U}) is available.			
SIC 4-digit industries in major group 27, Printing, Publishing and Allied Industries							
2711 Newspapers: Publishing, or Publishing and Printing	Y^{G-4}_{BEA-U}	-3.79	0.19	3.97	Y^{G-4}_{BEA-U} and $Y^{S-4}_{BLS-I-P}$	-2.09	0.907
	$Y^{S-4}_{BLS-I-P}$	-3.86	2.20	6.06			
2721, Periodicals: Publishing or Publishing and Printing	Y^{G-4}_{BEA-U}	-0.71	3.17	3.88	Y^{G-4}_{BEA-U} and $Y^{S-4}_{BLS-I-P}$	-4.66	0.692
	$Y^{S-4}_{BLS-I-P}$	-1.15	7.39	8.55			
2731 Books: Publishing, or Publishing and Printing	Y^{G-4}_{BEA-U}	1.56	-0.31	-1.87	Y^{G-4}_{BEA-U} and $Y^{S-4}_{BLS-I-P}$	-1.14	0.895
	$Y^{S-4}_{BLS-I-P}$	1.84	1.11	-0.73			
2732 Book Printing	Y^{G-4}_{BEA-U}	1.98	1.85	-0.13	Y^{G-4}_{BEA-U} and $Y^{S-4}_{BLS-I-P}$	-0.32	0.973
	$Y^{S-4}_{BLS-I-P}$	1.62	1.81	0.19			
2741 Miscellaneous Publishing	Y^{G-4}_{BEA-U}	1.27	2.46	1.19	Y^{G-4}_{BEA-U} and $Y^{S-4}_{BLS-I-P}$	-5.70	0.888
	$Y^{S-4}_{BLS-I-P}$	1.20	8.09	6.89			

Industry	Series					
2752 Commercial Printing, Lithographic	Y^{G-4}_{BEA-U} and $Y^{S-4}_{BLS-I-P}$	1.75	2.41	0.66	-0.07	0.997
		1.72	2.45	0.73		
2754 Commercial Printing, Gravure	Y^{G-4}_{BEA-U} and $Y^{S-4}_{BLS-I-P}$	1.93	-0.40	-2.33	0.75	0.975
		2.71	-0.37	-3.08		
2759 Commercial Printing, NEC	Y^{G-4}_{BEA-U} and $Y^{S-4}_{BLS-I-P}$	0.51	0.10	-0.41	-0.63	0.997
		0.24	0.46	0.22		
2761 Manifold Business Forms	Y^{G-4}_{BEA-U} and $Y^{S-4}_{BLS-I-P}$	-5.58	-3.52	2.05	-0.08	0.994
		-5.74	-3.60	2.13		
2771 Greeting Cards	Y^{G-4}_{BEA-U} and $Y^{S-4}_{BLS-I-P}$	-0.54	1.05	1.58	-0.43	0.269
		-1.14	0.88	2.02		
2782 Blankbooks, Looseleaf Binders and Devices	Y^{G-4}_{BEA-U} and $Y^{S-4}_{BLS-I-P}$	2.42	-1.52	-3.94	-0.08	0.993
		2.22	-1.64	-3.86		
2789 Bookbinding and Related Work	Y^{G-4}_{BEA-U} and $Y^{S-4}_{BLS-I-P}$	-0.03	4.89	4.92	0.44	0.994
		0.06	4.54	4.48		
2791 Typesetting	Y^{G-4}_{BEA-U} and $Y^{S-4}_{BLS-I-P}$	-4.85	4.48	9.32	-0.01	0.999
		-4.95	4.39	9.34		
2796 Platemaking and Related Services	Y^{G-4}_{BEA-U} and $Y^{S-4}_{BLS-I-P}$	3.03	-6.39	-9.42	-0.25	0.999
		3.03	-6.15	-9.18		

SIC 3-digit industries in major group 29, Petroleum Refining and Related Industries

Industry	Series					
291 Petroleum Refining	Y^{G-3}_{BEA-U} and $Y^{S-3}_{BLS-I-P}$	0.63	1.20	0.57	0.15	-0.130
		1.15	1.57	0.42		
295, Asphalt Paving and Roofing Materials	Y^{G-3}_{BEA-U} and $Y^{S-3}_{BLS-I-P}$	1.95	2.96	1.01	0.10	0.997
		1.96	2.87	0.91		
299, Miscellaneous Products of Petroleum and Coal	Y^{G-3}_{BEA-U} and $Y^{S-3}_{BLS-I-P}$	1.11	0.69	-0.43	-0.06	0.984
		0.94	0.58	-0.36		

SIC 3-digit industries in major group 31, Leather and Leather Products

Industry	Series					
311, Leather Tanning and Finishing	Y^{G-3}_{BEA-U} and $Y^{S-3}_{BLS-I-U}$	4.22	0.13	-4.09	-2.33	0.984
		3.41	1.65	-1.76		
313, Boot and Shoe Cut Stock and Findings	Y^{G-3}_{BEA-U} and $Y^{S-3}_{BLS-I-U}$	-8.30	-8.63	-0.33	-8.77	0.611
		-8.14	0.30	8.44		

(continued)

Table 9B.4   (continued)

SIC 4-digit industry	Output series	Average annual growth rate 1990–1995 (1)	Average annual growth rate 1995–2000 (2)	Acceleration (2) − (1)	Output series comparisons	Difference in acceleration	Correlation coefficient
314, Footwear, Except Rubber	Y^{G-3}_{BEA-U}	−3.28	−5.49	−2.21	Y^{G-3}_{BEA-U} and $Y^{S-3}_{BLS-I-P}$	1.24	0.984
	$Y^{S-3}_{BLS-I-P}$	−3.62	−7.07	−3.45			
315, Leather Gloves and Mittens	Y^{G-3}_{BEA-U}	−7.49	5.54	13.03	Y^{G-3}_{BEA-U} and $Y^{S-3}_{BLS-I-U}$	−0.63	0.992
	$Y^{S-3}_{BLS-I-U}$	−7.95	5.71	13.66			
316, Luggage	Y^{G-3}_{BEA-U}	−4.50	5.53	10.03	Y^{G-3}_{BEA-U} and $Y^{S-3}_{BLS-I-U}$	1.28	0.971
	$Y^{S-3}_{BLS-I-U}$	−4.00	4.75	8.75			
317, Handbags and Other Leather Goods	Y^{G-3}_{BEA-U}	−7.35	−1.27	6.08	Y^{G-3}_{BEA-U} and $Y^{S-3}_{BLS-I-U}$	−0.41	0.996
	$Y^{S-3}_{BLS-I-U}$	−7.40	−0.91	6.49			
319, Leather Goods, NEC	Y^{G-3}_{BEA-U}	−8.75	7.86	16.62	Y^{G-3}_{BEA-U} and $Y^{S-3}_{BLS-I-U}$	0.86	0.994
	$Y^{S-3}_{BLS-I-U}$	−8.63	7.13	15.75			
SIC 3-digit industries in major group 35, Industrial and Commercial Machinery and Computer Equipment							
351, Engines and Turbines	Y^{G-3}_{BEA-U}	3.62	4.41	0.78	Y^{G-3}_{BEA-U} and $Y^{S-3}_{BLS-I-P}$	−0.94	0.955
	$Y^{S-3}_{BLS-I-P}$	3.13	4.86	1.73			
352, Farm and Garden Machinery and Equipment	Y^{G-3}_{BEA-U}	2.14	−0.85	−2.99	Y^{G-3}_{BEA-U} and $Y^{S-3}_{BLS-I-P}$	0.00	0.993
	$Y^{S-3}_{BLS-I-P}$	2.13	−0.87	−3.00			
353, Construction, Mining, and Materials Handling	Y^{G-3}_{BEA-U}	2.49	3.75	1.26	Y^{G-3}_{BEA-U} and $Y^{S-3}_{BLS-I-P}$	0.16	0.991
	$Y^{S-3}_{BLS-I-P}$	2.73	3.83	1.10			
354, Metalworking Machinery and Equipment	Y^{G-3}_{BEA-U}	3.41	1.46	−1.95	Y^{G-3}_{BEA-U} and $Y^{S-3}_{BLS-I-P}$	0.69	0.991
	$Y^{S-3}_{BLS-I-P}$	3.75	1.11	−2.64			
355, Special Industry Machinery, Except Metalworking	Y^{G-3}_{BEA-U}	5.83	5.39	−0.43	Y^{G-3}_{BEA-U} and $Y^{S-3}_{BLS-I-P}$	0.76	0.994
	$Y^{S-3}_{BLS-I-P}$	6.31	5.11	−1.20			
356, General Industrial Machinery and Equipment	Y^{G-3}_{BEA-U}	2.36	1.29	−1.07	Y^{G-3}_{BEA-U} and $Y^{S-3}_{BLS-I-P}$	0.18	0.993
	$Y^{S-3}_{BLS-I-P}$	2.36	1.11	−1.25			
357, Computer and Office Equipment	Y^{G-3}_{BEA-U}	21.89	32.38	10.48	Y^{G-3}_{BEA-U} and $Y^{S-3}_{BLS-I-P}$	−2.87	0.990
	$Y^{S-3}_{BLS-I-P}$	22.55	35.91	13.35			

Industry	Series				Comparison		
358, Refrigeration and Service Industry Machinery	Y^{G-3}_{BEA-U}	5.10	2.61	-2.49	Y^{G-3}_{BEA-U} and $Y^{S-3}_{BLS-I-P}$	0.09	0.994
	$Y^{S-3}_{BLS-I-P}$	5.31	2.72	-2.59			
359, Miscellaneous Industrial and Commercial	Y^{G-3}_{BEA-U}	6.80	2.56	-4.24	Y^{G-3}_{BEA-U} and $Y^{S-3}_{BLS-I-P}$	0.00	0.995
	$Y^{S-3}_{BLS-I-P}$	6.73	2.49	-4.24			

SIC 3-digit industries in major group 38, Measuring, Analyzing, and Controlling Instruments, Photographic, Medical and Optical Goods, Watches and Clocks

Industry	Series				Comparison		
381, Search, Detection, Navigation, Guidance, Aeronautical, and Nautical	Y^{G-3}_{BEA-U}	-5.25	-0.11	5.14	Y^{G-3}_{BEA-U} and $Y^{S-3}_{BLS-I-P}$	-1.09	0.973
	$Y^{S-3}_{BLS-I-P}$	-5.52	0.71	6.23			
382, Laboratory Apparatus and Analytical, Optical	Y^{G-3}_{BEA-U}	4.29	2.74	-1.55	Y^{G-3}_{BEA-U} and $Y^{S-3}_{BLS-I-P}$	0.26	0.990
	$Y^{S-3}_{BLS-I-P}$	4.32	2.52	-1.81			
384, Surgical Medical and Dental Instruments	Y^{G-3}_{BEA-U}	3.97	6.98	3.00	Y^{G-3}_{BEA-U} and $Y^{S-3}_{BLS-I-P}$	0.12	0.987
	$Y^{S-3}_{BLS-I-P}$	3.85	6.73	2.88			
385, Opthalmic Goods	Y^{G-3}_{BEA-U}	3.90	7.73	3.84	Y^{G-3}_{BEA-U} and $Y^{S-3}_{BLS-I-P}$	-0.21	0.972
	$Y^{S-3}_{BLS-I-P}$	3.45	7.50	4.05			
386, Photographic Equipment and Supplies	Y^{G-3}_{BEA-U}	0.72	0.75	0.03	Y^{G-3}_{BEA-U} and $Y^{S-3}_{BLS-I-P}$	-0.52	0.920
	$Y^{S-3}_{BLS-I-P}$	0.84	1.39	0.55			
387, Watches, Clocks, Clockwork Operated Devices	Y^{G-3}_{BEA-U}	-9.33	5.51	14.85	Y^{G-3}_{BEA-U} and $Y^{S-3}_{BLS-I-U}$	5.61	0.880
	$Y^{S-3}_{BLS-I-P}$	-6.57	2.67	9.24			

SIC 3-digit industries in major group 48, Communications

Industry	Series				Comparison		
481, Telephone Communications					Only a single series (YS-3BLS-I-P) is available.		
482, Telegraph and Other Message Communications					No BEA or BLS output series available.		
483, Radio and Television Broadcasting Stations	Y^{G-3}_{BEA-U}	0.08	-0.06	-0.14	Y^{G-3}_{BEA-U} and $Y^{S-3}_{BLS-I-P}$	-1.21	0.733
	$Y^{S-3}_{BLS-I-P}$	1.13	2.19	1.06			
484, Cable and Other Pay Television Stations	Y^{G-3}_{BEA-U}	5.38	8.93	3.55	Y^{G-3}_{BEA-U} and $Y^{S-3}_{BLS-I-P}$	-1.70	0.470
	$Y^{S-3}_{BLS-I-P}$	2.96	8.21	5.25			
489, Communications Services, NEC					No BEA or BLS output series available.		

References

Bosworth, Barry P. 2003a. Output and productivity growth in the communications industry, chapter IIb. Draft. Productivity in Services Industries: Trends and Measurement Issues, Summary of What We Have Learned from the Brookings Economic Measurement Workshops Economic Measurement Workshop. Washington, DC: Brookings Institution, November 21.

———. 2003b. Output and productivity in the transportation sector, chapter IIa. Draft. Productivity in Services Industries: Trends and Measurement Issues, Summary of What We Have Learned from the Brookings Economic Measurement Workshops Economic Measurement Workshop. Washington, DC: Brookings Institution, November 21.

Bureau of Labor Statistics (BLS). 2002. Multifactor productivity trends in manufacturing, 2000. News release. Washington, DC: BLS, August 29.

Domar, Evsey D. 1961. On the measurement of technological change. *Economic Journal* 71 (284): 709–29.

Gollop, Frank M. 1981. Growth accounting in an open economy. Paper presented at conference on Current Issues in Productivity. April, Newark, New Jersey.

Gullickson, William. 1995. Measurement of productivity growth in U.S. manufacturing. *Monthly Labor Review* 118 (7): 13–27.

Gullickson, William, and Michael J. Harper. 1999. Possible measurement bias in aggregate productivity growth. *Monthly Labor Review* 122 (2): 47–67.

———. 2002. Bias in aggregate productivity trends revisited. *Monthly Labor Review* 125 (3): 32–40.

Guo, Jiemin, Ann M. Lawson, and Mark A. Planting. 2002. From make-use to symmetric I-O tables: An assessment of alternative technology assumptions. Paper presented at the fourteenth international conference on Input-Output Techniques. 10–15 October, Montreal, Canada.

Hulten, Charles R. 1995. Capital and wealth in the revised SNA. In *The new system of national accounts,* ed. J. W. Kendrick, 149–81. Boston: Kluwer Academic.

Jorgenson, Dale W. 2003. Economic growth in the information age. National Bureau of Economic Research, Conference on Research in Income and Wealth. Hard-to-Measure Goods and Services: Essays in Memory of Zvi Griliches Conference. 19 September, Bethesda, MD.

Jorgenson, Dale W., Frank M. Gollop, and Barbara M. Fraumeni. 1987. *Productivity and U.S. economic growth.* Cambridge, MA: Harvard University Press.

Jorgenson, Dale W., and Zvi Griliches. 1967. The expansion of productivity change. *Review of Economic Studies* 34 (99): 249–83.

Moulton, Brent R. 2004. The System of National Accounts for the new economy: What should change? *Review of Income and Wealth* 50 (2): 261–78.

Moulton, Brent R., and Eugene P. Seskin. 2003. Preview of the 2003 comprehensive revision of the National Income and Product Accounts: Changes in definitions and classifications. *Survey of Current Business* 83 (June): 17–34.

Nordhaus, William D. 2002. Productivity growth and the new economy. *Brookings Papers on Economic Activity,* Issue no. 2:211–65.

Organisation for Economic Co-operation and Development (OECD). 2001. *Measuring capital: OECD manual; Measurement of capital stocks, consumption of fixed capital and capital services.* Paris: OECD.

Triplett, Jack E., and Barry P. Bosworth. 2004. *Productivity in the U.S. services sector: New sources of economic growth.* Washington, DC: Brookings Institution Press.

United Nations, Commission of the European Communities, International Monetary Fund, Organisation for Economic Co-operation and Development, and World Bank. 1993. *System of National Accounts 1993*. Series F, no. 2, rev. 4. New York: United Nations.

Comment   Carol Corrado

The empirical analysis of the sources of economic growth requires consistent measures of outputs and inputs. The requirement is important because the rate of change in productivity is usually estimated residually from measures of outputs and inputs. This paper focuses on the definition and construction of the output measures used to estimate productivity. Because the BEA and BLS each publish apparently similar, but statistically different, major sector and industry-level output measures, a major goal of this chapter is to take some steps to document and understand these differences.

The chapter first reviews the theoretically ideal production account, that is, one that includes capital services so that the account can be used to construct estimates of multifactor productivity. The authors show how the theoretical account can be adapted for a major sector, which reveals the relationship between GDP and the output of the major sector. They also illuminate the role of imports and show how reconciling items in economic accounts (certain taxes and subsidies) should be treated to calculate capital income as required for productivity measurement. Using elements currently published by both the BEA and BLS, the chapter then illustrates an empirical production account for the nonfarm business sector and presents the BLS multifactor productivity (MFP) estimates derived from the account.

Thus, the U.S. national accounts, viewed broadly across the agencies, already contain a cornerstone of the new architecture, a production account for (something close to) GDP in current and constant prices. The new architecture also calls for a production account for GDI in current and constant prices and suggests that both be extended to the industry level. The theoretical framework laid out in the chapter shows how aggregate output and productivity can be built from industry-level data, an approach that is conceptually consistent with GDP as measured in benchmark input-output accounts. Other chapters in this volume indicate the BEA's plans for more timely integration of its industry and input-output accounts, and thus the theoretical section of this paper illustrates how productivity measurement fits into this longer range scheme.

Carol Corrado is chief of the Industrial Output section in the Division of Research and Statistics at the Federal Reserve Board.

The paper's empirical results pertain to two themes in the recent productivity literature. First, many productivity analysts noted that the difference between GDP and GDI in the mid- to late 1990s was significant and affected estimates of the trend in aggregate productivity. The chapter documents and explains the statistical sources of these GDP-GDI differences. Second, productivity researchers have long pointed to conflicts in the industry-level data issued by various programs of the federal government. Accordingly, the paper documents and analyzes the sources of differences among available industry output measures during the 1990s.

With regard to statistical integration, the contribution and relevance of the two empirical exercises in the paper are different: the aggregate results, though important, are not new to the literature,[1] whereas the industry results represent an important first step in work to create consistent industry-level production accounts common to the two agencies. Moreover, the authors do *not* suggest that aggregate differences between GDP and GDI should be eliminated (as have some observers), but they are clear that the ultimate goal of their industry-level analysis is "reducing differences" among the myriad BEA and BLS industry output measures and "capturing the best in both data sets." I concur with this emphasis.

Aggregate Measures

The official aggregate productivity statistics are derived from expenditure-based GDP, but researchers and analysts also look at productivity derived from GDI. The paper provides a useful accounting for the sources of the difference in the growth rates of these alternative measures, reminding us of just how much alternative measures of the same or similar concept can differ.[2] The authors show that the step-up in real nonfarm business output in the late 1990s could have been as much as 2.7 percentage points—or it could have been 3/4 percentage point less! This statistical uncertainty flows through to the residually measured productivity figures and is especially large relative to the typical rates of change in MFP.

Despite the statistical imprecision suggested by the differences between GDP and GDI, macroeconomists and policymakers have been well served by the availability of official MFP estimates. Moreover, it is probably fair to say that this group of users views the consistency of the aggregate productivity data with GDP (rather than GDI) as a plus. Such users also recognize, however, that input-output relationships are held fixed in GDP for long periods, and that the income and tax data used in GDI, though not

1. See the references cited in footnote 1 of the chapter and Moyer, Reinsdorf, and Yuskavage.
2. With the 2003 comprehensive revision of the NIPAs, the BEA took an important step toward integrating the output data reported by both agencies by adopting the BLS definition of business-sector output. The empirical analysis in this paper pertains to the earlier data in which coverage and definitional differences also created inconsistencies.

without problems of their own, provide an additional perspective that often proves valuable. An important example is the pickup in productivity in the mid-1990s: productivity measures based on initial estimates of GDI showed an acceleration before the official measures based on GDP. All told, therefore, the occasional large size of discrepancies between alternative output measures is informative for aggregate analysis.

Industry Measures

Researchers seeking to attribute economic growth by industry have used industry-level data from the BEA, BLS, or a hybrid of both. Because these data often differ significantly, the choice can affect the resulting attribution of productivity to individual industries. A key contribution of this chapter thus is table 9B.1. The table summarizes the definitions and estimating methods employed in eight (*yes, eight!*) separate BEA or BLS programs that compile and/or issue industry output measures; that a ninth program, at the BLS, is not included in the comparisons is a drawback of the chapter. That said, related contributions are table 9B.2, which reports the availability of measures for detailed industries by program, and the discussion in section 9.4 of the results of comparing the alternative detailed measures. Much of this section of the chapter provides comparisons of alternative industry concepts and aggregates, which might be expected to differ. However, the results for detailed industries spotlight the actual statistical differences and issues.

Economic accountants and productivity estimators use the same basic data to compile different concepts and different aggregates to meet the analytical needs of their users. Table 9B.1 shows that detailed industry data on gross output (or gross receipts or gross margins, depending on the industry) in current and constant dollars are the basic building blocks of all output and productivity measures. The users of the data compiled in the industry programs at the BEA and BLS, as well as users of the IPI, issued by the Federal Reserve Board (FRB), need to know the role of differences in the basic building blocks used in each program. For example, differences in the price deflators for semiconductors and communications equipment explain virtually all of the difference between the FRB measure and the other measures shown in table 9.6, whereas differences in the treatment of oil pipeline company revenue explains some of the discrepancy between the BEA and BLS measures, and so on. The chapter would be stronger if it contained more of this concrete information. Importantly, though, when the authors narrow their BEA and BLS comparisons to detailed industry output data, they find that the rate of change in real output in the late 1990s was relatively different for only 28 percent of comparable SIC four-digit industries (128 out of 458). All manufacturing industries and nearly half of nonmanufacturing (in terms of gross receipts) were available for comparison (table 9.9).

The statistical agencies should collaborate so that, inasmuch as it is possible, their programs begin with common source data for detailed industries. The results quoted above suggest that developing a common industry-level database for real output is doable and that the agencies should work toward that end. The definitions and concepts used in this work should be as close as possible to those used in primary data collection. For example, the concept for gross output (or gross margins or receipts) should conform to the definitions used by the Census Bureau because they are the primary source for comprehensive data on the value of output by detailed industry; the BEA's definitional adjustments to Census gross output (the addition of own-account construction and own-account production of software to Census gross output) would be part of the data and documentation it provides to its users.

The industry output data issued by the Census Bureau, as well as the raw data on prices and inputs to production from other sources, periodically need to be adjusted for changes in classification systems, shortfalls in coverage, and the like. The various agencies often go their own ways in this work although, in the mid-1990s, a collaborative effort involving staff of the BEA, Census, and Federal Reserve developed adjustments for "drift" in the annual surveys of manufacturing between the periodic censuses; prior to that effort, time-series inconsistency in the Census Bureau's manufacturing data often caused confusion among users of the various data sets on manufacturing activity. The results in this paper suggest that the development of common source data and adjustments for nonmanufacturing output, and the resolution of issues with selected price deflators, are important next steps in the integration of the industry data systems issued by BEA and BLS

The Integration of the Canadian Productivity Accounts within the System of National Accounts
Current Status and Challenges Ahead

John R. Baldwin and Tarek M. Harchaoui

10.1 Introduction

Statistical agencies succeed when public debate moves beyond arguments over the value that should be attached to a statistic to discussions about what the value of the statistic implies for policy purposes. If political debate concerns itself with whether productivity growth is just 0.5 percent or as high as 4.0 percent, it is less likely to focus on what policy challenges are posed by the level of productivity growth.

Productivity measures are often used as key economic indicators for evaluating relative performance across industries, across countries, and over time. Unfortunately, debates about productivity all too often revolve around what the growth in productivity actually is. Part of this problem arises because some statistical systems produce conflicting estimates of productivity growth. Integrated systems of national accounts (SNAs) reduce these problems. This paper describes how the integration of the Canadian Productivity Accounts (CPA) into the Canadian System of National Accounts (CSNA) is used to provide a coherent and consistent set of productivity estimates.

The publication of productivity measures is an important activity of the CPA. Statistics Canada's productivity program has evolved over the years,

John R. Baldwin is director of the Micro Economics Analysis Division of Statistics Canada, the division responsible for productivity estimates at Statistics Canada, and is associated with the Conference on Research in Income and Wealth (CRIW). Tarek M. Harchaoui is assistant director of research in the Microeconomic Analysis Division of Statistics Canada and is associated with the CRIW.

We are indebted to Barry Bosworth, Paul-Emmanuel Piel, Dale Jorgenson, Ann Lawson, Karen Wilson, and Simon Zheng for valuable comments made on an earlier draft. The comments made by the participants of the National Bureau of Economic Research (NBER)–CRIW Conference on the New Architecture for the U.S. National Accounts are also acknowledged with thanks. The usual disclaimers apply.

stimulated by changes in data availability, by new developments in the economics literature, by the needs of data users, and by the increase in the profile of the economy's productivity performance in Canadian public policy circles.

Following the development of the CSNA after the Second World War, Statistics Canada introduced labor productivity measures for the aggregate business sector and its major constituent subsectors.[1] In recent years, the CPA has added multifactor productivity growth measures, which consider the productivity of a bundle of inputs (labor, capital, and purchased goods and services[2]), for the business sector and its constituent subsectors and industries to meet the demands of the user community.

The conceptual framework of the CPA corresponds closely to the standards set out in the Organisation for Economic Co-operation and Development (OECD) productivity manual (OECD 2001). The concepts and definitions used in the CPA generally conform to the standards set out in the 1993 SNA (United Nations et al. 1993) and OECD (2001)—though some minor variations have been adopted to allow for particular Canadian data supply conditions or user requirements.

This chapter discusses the extent to which the CPA is integrated into the CSNA, with emphasis on the benefits and the challenges that are associated with the integration. By way of background, the first section reviews the status of the integration and how the approach adopted by the CPA embodies internationally recommended standard practices for productivity measurement as are laid out in OECD (2001). It highlights how the CPA uses industry production and expenditure accounts from the CSNA to derive a consistent set of outputs and inputs that are suitable for productivity measurement. The chapter then discusses the benefits of integration and possible extensions of the existing program.

10.2   Integration in the Canadian National Accounts

10.2.1   Overview

Measures of productivity are derived by comparing outputs and inputs. The SNAs provide a useful framework for organizing the information re-

---

1. The definition of business sector used for productivity measures excludes all noncommercial activities as well as the rental value of owner-occupied dwellings. Corresponding exclusions are also made to the inputs. Business gross domestic product (GDP) as defined by the productivity program represents 77 percent of total economy GDP in 1992. The business sector is split into the following major subsectors: goods-producing, services, and manufacturing. The goods-producing subsector consists of agriculture, fishing, forestry, mining, manufacturing, construction, and public utilities. Services comprise transportation and storage, communications, wholesale and retail trade, finance, insurance and real estate, and the group of community, business, and personal services.

2. Purchased goods and services are known as intermediate inputs in the CSNA.

quired for comparisons of this type. Integrated systems of economic accounts provide coherent, consistent alternate estimates of the various concepts that can be used to measure productivity.

Statistical systems that provide measures of productivity that are not compatible one with another tend to subtract from, rather enhance, the coherency of public debate. On occasion differences in productivity values are the result of the use of alternate formulas. Alternate methods of measuring productivity are quite legitimate. Economists have long drawn attention to the limitations inherent in a unique measure of productivity performance. In comparing alternative states of an economy, it is difficult to summarize all the relevant information in a single measure.

But the most common cause for inconsistencies across productivity measures is inconsistency in the data that are used. Productivity estimates can be derived using different data sources from the SNA, and these data may not be consistent.

On the one hand, productivity estimates for the aggregate business sector can be constructed from a set of final expenditures accounts—what is sometimes referred to as a top-down approach. Under this approach, "output" is measured as final demand gross domestic product (GDP) and capital input is based on investment series that are also part of the final demand, thereby making it possible to construct a coherent multifactor productivity series for the aggregate business sector.

On the other hand, multifactor productivity measures can be derived from a set of industry accounts—the so-called bottom-up approach. Under this approach, a variety of productivity series at the industry level are constructed using alternate measures of output along with their corresponding inputs. This approach permits the construction of bottom-up multifactor productivity measures for the aggregate business sector as a weighted average of industry productivity growth rates, where the weights are defined in terms of the ratio of industry current-dollar "output" to the current-dollar bottom-up GDP.

The top-down and the bottom-up approach rely on separate sources of data—the first on expenditure accounts and the second on production accounts. Unless the measures of output that are derived from the different sets of accounts are integrated with one another, the two sets of productivity estimates will not be consistent with each other. In Canada, the expenditure and the production accounts are integrated within a unified framework defined by the input-output tables (IOTs). These IOTs are used to derive the estimates of output and inputs by industry and major sectors in current and constant prices as well as the construction of final demand GDP and the cost of primary inputs for the aggregate business sector. In the following section, we describe how these various components are brought together in Canada into a consistent whole that facilitates productivity estimation.

10.2.2   The Production Account of the Canadian System of National Accounts

The Canadian IOTs provide two sets of interrelated accounts: the commodity accounts and the industry accounts. The former details the supply and disposition of individual commodities (goods and nonfactor services). The latter details the commodity composition of the output of industries and the complete costs of production (including earnings of the primary inputs—labor and capital) of industries.

The Canadian IOTs consist of five matrices that outline the disposition or production on the one hand and the use of goods and services and primary inputs on the other hand (see Lal 1986 and Statistics Canada 1990). The format of the "make" matrices that provide a description of the commodities produced by industry is shown in figure 10.1, and the "use" matrices that provide a description of the commodities and primary inputs used by industry are provided in figure 10.2. Under the 1980 Standard Industrial Classification (SIC), the tables contain 243 industries, 671 commodities, 162 categories of final demand, and eight primary inputs. The make and use matrices are used to derive multifactor productivity estimates at the industry level, while the final demand matrix is employed to generate multifactor productivity growth in the aggregate business sector.

Commodity Accounts

Commodities are goods or services and include items normally intended for sale on the market at a price designed to cover production costs, as well as nonmarket services delivered by institutions such as hospitals and schools. Matrix **V** of figure 10.1 contains the commodities produced by business (market) and nonbusiness (nonmarket) industries. While commodities produced by business-sector industries are valued at market prices, the value of nonbusiness commodities is measured by the sum of

Industries	Commodities								Other including fictive	Total
	Business Sector					Non-business Sector				
	Primary Commodities	Manufacturing Commodities	...	...		Non-profit	Government			
Business Primary Manufacturing .... **Non-business** Non-profit Government				**V**						**g**
Fictive										
Total				**q′**						

Fig. 10.1   Make (output) matrix

Notes: Matrix of the values of outputs. **g** = vector of the values of total industry outputs; **q′** = vector of the values of total commodity output.

	Industries	Final demand							Total
		PE	GFCF	VPCI	GCE	X_d	X_r	M	
Commodities									
Primary									
Manufacturing									
...	**U**				**F**				**q**
Government									
Other including fictive									
Total									
Primary inputs					**YF**				
Taxes on products									
Other taxes on production									
Less subsidies									
Labor income	**YI**								**n**
Mixed income									
Other operating surplus									
GDP at basic price									
Total (GDP at market prices)									
Total use	**g′**				**e′**				

Fig. 10.2   Industry and final use matrices

Notes: PE = personal expenditure; GFCF = gross fixed capital formation; VPCI = value of physical change of inventories; GCE = government current expenditures; X_d = domestic exports of goods and services; X_r = re-exports of goods and services; M = imports of goods and services; **U** = matrix of the values of intermediate inputs; **F** = matrix of the values of commodity inputs of final demand categories; **YI** = matrix of the values of the cost of primary inputs of industries; **YF** = matrix of the values of taxes on products or other production of final demand categories; **g** = vector of the values of total industry outputs; **q′** = vector of the values of total commodity output; **e** = vector of the values of total inputs (commodities plus primary) of final demand categories; **n** = vector of the values of total primary inputs (industries plus final demand categories).

Source: Statistics Canada (1990)

their costs of production. Where a nonbusiness industry produces market commodities as secondary output, the value of the nonbusiness commodity is obtained residually as the difference between the industry's total input and its market output.

The disposition of commodities by industry and final demand category is shown in matrices **U** and **F** of figure 10.2. Matrix **U** shows the use of commodities by industries as intermediate inputs for the production of other commodities.[3] Matrix **F** contains the demand for each commodity by final demand categories. They include personal expenditure, gross fixed capital formation, additions to (the value of physical change in) inventories, government expenditure on goods and services, and exports. Another column (matrix **F**) covers imports.

Industry Accounts

Industries are groups of operating units (establishments) engaged in the same or similar kinds of economic activity, whether they produce market, own-account, or nonmarket output.

---

3. Data sources for the intermediate inputs are based on industry surveys and administrative data such as those collected by the Office of the Superintendent of Financial Institutions. In recent years, Statistics Canada has substantially increased the coverage of many services industries (see Smith 2000).

The industry accounts are depicted in matrices **V** and **U** and **YI** (in figures 10.1 and 10.2). Each row of matrix **V** details the commodity composition of each industry's output. The output of business-sector industries is produced for either sale or disposal on the market (e.g., department stores, clothing factories, and restaurants) or for own final use (e.g., owner-occupants of housing and subsistence farming). Production for the market is sold at prices that are economically significant, in the sense that they have a significant influence on the amounts producers are willing to supply or buyers are willing to purchase. Items for own use are valued at the prices of similar products sold on the market. Production of nonbusiness industries is measured by the sum of the costs of production: that is, as the sum of intermediate consumption, compensation of employees, consumption of fixed capital, and taxes less subsidies on production.

For the business sector, the compensation of primary inputs consists of (a) labor income, (b) mixed income of unincorporated business enterprises, (c) other operating surplus, (d) taxes on products, (d) other taxes on production, (e) subsidies on products, and (f) other subsidies on production.

The primary inputs for nonbusiness industries in matrix **YI** also consist of net taxes (taxes less subsidies) on production, labor income, and other operating surplus. Labor income consists of wages and salaries and supplementary labor income paid to persons employed in nonprofit institutions serving households and the government sector. The surplus of nonbusiness industries reflects the depreciation on assets owned in the government sector and by nonprofit institutions serving households. Assets such as buildings, roads, and equipment that are charged to fixed capital formation are depreciated.

Primary inputs are also recorded in matrix **YF** (figure 10.2). These include taxes on products bought by final demand categories, and other taxes on production associated with those categories. The latter includes licences for motor vehicles, cellular telephones, fishing, and hunting, as well as land and deed transfer taxes. Taxes on products make up the difference between the price paid by the purchasers and the price received by the producers.

The production accounts are constructed so as to meet several basic identities. These are as follows:

1. *Industry accounts basic identity:* The gross output of any industry (g in figure 10.1) equals its total intermediate inputs plus its total primary inputs (g' in figure 10.2).

2. *Commodity accounts basic identity:* The total output of any commodity (q' in figure 10.1) equals its total use as an intermediate input and for final demand (q in figure 10.1).

3. *Primary inputs and final demand identities:* In terms of figure 10.1, the output of all commodities ($i\mathbf{q}'$) equals the gross output of all industries ($\mathbf{g}i'$). Intermediate inputs (**U**) being common to both outputs (of industries

and of commodities), primary inputs of all industries together (**YI**) equal commodity inputs of all final demand categories (**F**). Hence, the sum of all elements of **YI** equals those of **F**. And total GDP at market prices (income based)—**YI** plus **YF**—equals total GDP at market prices (expenditure based), **F** plus **YF**.

Measurement and Valuation of Outputs

All of these identities hold for both current price and constant price tables. Input-output flows can be recorded either in market prices, basic prices, or factor costs.

GDP measured at *market prices* is defined as the aggregate expenditure on all goods and services (consumption, investment, government, and net exports) measured at consumer purchasers' prices (including taxes paid). GDP at *basic prices* is GDP calculated at market prices less taxes paid on products plus any subsidies on consumption. GDP at factor cost is GDP at basic prices less indirect taxes on factor inputs less subsidies on these inputs.

At the industry level, the IOT value output at what they refer to as modified basic prices—the price received on products that excludes any product taxes but that also excludes subsidies received.[4] However, for the total economy, Canada produces measures at market prices, basic prices, and factor costs.

The IOTs allow for a variety of measures of output at different levels of aggregation using different measures of valuation—all of which are consistent with one another. At the aggregate level, GDP at market prices, or the sum of all elements of primary inputs in matrices **YI** and **YF**, is equal to final demand expenditures GDP, or the sum of all elements of matrices **F** and **YF** (see figure 10.2). This is true both at current and constant prices.

The industry distribution of GDP for the business sector is shown in matrix **YI** on an industry basis (Standard Industrial Classification [SIC] or North American Industrial Classification System [NAICS]). The compensation of primary inputs of the nonbusiness industries in the matrix **YI** are not shown by industry. However, they may be reallocated to the same classification as that of the business sector so that GDP may be presented for an industry or separately for the business and nonbusiness components of an industry.

Industry value added is calculated as a residual—that is, the difference between the gross output of industries and the total of intermediate inputs and taxes less subsidies on production (net taxes on production). Intermediate inputs are valued at purchaser prices for firms. These components of income include all personal income and corporate income taxes. Summed across all industries, these estimates of value added are equal to the GDP

---

4. Statistics Canada argues that this corresponds to the invoice price and therefore is more easily collected in its production surveys.

calculated from market price final expenditures less taxes on products less subsidies on production.

Industrial product price indexes collected by the Prices Division constitute the main source of deflators for manufactured commodities. Unit value indexes are developed for commodities where there are no measured price indexes but where quantity and value information are available. Unit value indexes are widely used for primary commodities, such as agriculture products, mining commodities, and fish landings.

Less data are available for services than for manufacturing. Here data are available for those services purchased by households and a few price indexes that have recently been developed by the Prices Division.

For the production account at constant prices, real GDP at modified basic prices for business-sector industries is constructed using a double deflation technique. Unlike the IOTs at current prices, which are completely integrated with the income and expenditure accounts (IEAs), there are minor differences across the constant-price tables in the two sets of accounts. Values in the IEAs are at purchaser prices, while they are expressed in the IOTs at modified basic prices. Deflation of commodities in the IOTs by basic prices does not yield the same result as deflation using purchaser prices. However, the deflation of the value of personal expenditure in the final demand matrix of the IOTs with consumer price indexes tends to make the two estimates more consistent (see Statistics Canada 1990). A reconciliation process is implemented to assure consistency between the growth rates of constant-dollar measures of the industry and expenditure accounts in the IOTs.

This set of industry accounts represented by the IOTs is valuable for several reasons. First, it benchmarks the rest of the accounts, including the final demand GDP employed for aggregate productivity measures. Thus, the CPA's estimates at the industry level are consistent with those at the more aggregate level. Second, considerable time and effort are spent in checking the concordance of industry-level measures of outputs and inputs and in valuing outputs and inputs consistently. Since the IOTs are at the core of the statistical system, they provide an audit tool that permits the statistical system to monitor the various sources that are used in different parts of the process that builds data on expenditure, on factor income, and on commodity production and use.

10.2.3   The Canadian Productivity Accounts

Integration of the Data

The integrated CSNA's production and expenditures set of accounts is necessary but not sufficient for multifactor productivity measurement. Multifactor productivity measurement also requires measures of capital and labor services (see Hulten 1995).

The CPA begins with the available production and expenditure accounts available from the CSNA and supplements them with coherent measures of labor services and capital services. This permits the CPA to produce a variety of productivity measures that (a) are consistent with one another and (b) meet different analytical needs.[5]

Output. Data on output and inputs in current and constant prices are obtained from the existing production and expenditure accounts available from the IOTs up to the benchmark or reference year—the last year for which a set of IOTs have been produced. This is two years from the current period. They are updated for recent years from two subannual set of accounts: the quarterly IEA and the monthly real value added by industry accounts.

The aggregate output data that are used for aggregate business-sector productivity estimates are based on the final demand GDP available from the final expenditure accounts. The output concept for the business sector is similar to the one used in the Bureau of Labor Statistics (BLS) for its productivity estimate of the aggregated business sector.[6] Like the BLS, the CPA excludes the government sector and owner-occupied dwellings. The consumption of durable goods is measured in terms of personal expenditures and not as the service flows from consumers' durables and owner-occupied housing.[7]

At the industry level, the production accounts make available a variety of "output" measures in both current and constant prices: value added and gross output. In addition, using information on intrasectoral transactions and on trade available from the IOTs, the CPA constructs a third measure—sectoral output at the industry level.[8] Unlike the other conventional two measures of output, the notion of sectoral output has the particularity of being constructed by the CPA for the purpose of international comparison with the United States.

Labor. The CPA is responsible for constructing labor estimates from various sources that accord with the recommendations of SNA 1993 and that are consistent with the data that are produced by the production accounts.

5. For more information on methodology, see http://www.statcan.ca/english/concepts/15-204/appendix.pdf.

6. With the recent NIPA revisions, the business-sector concepts used by the BEA and the BLS are similar.

7. Recent work that implemented this approach includes Jorgenson and Stiroh (2000) and Jorgenson (2001) for the U.S. economy; Jorgenson (2003) for international comparisons; and Harchaoui and Tarkhani (2005) and Harchaoui, Tarkhani, and Khanam (2004) for a Canada–United States comparison of economic growth and productivity performance. Jorgenson and his associates generally include general government and owner-occupied dwellings and measure the flow of services of consumer durables for productivity estimates.

8. Sectoral output is the value of production, adjusted for inventory change, shipped to purchasers outside of the industry and not just final users.

Other sources are available within Statistics Canada on employment that do not completely satisfy the requirements of the SNA. And none of these other sources are reconciled to events that are occurring at the industry level in terms of output changes or income receipts. The CPA produces a set of labor estimates to accomplish both objectives.

Estimates of jobs and hours worked are produced at a detailed industry level and by class of workers (see Baldwin et al. 2004). These estimates have recently been extended to all provinces and territories. Hours worked is the base measure used for productivity estimates because it represents a better measure of labor input than employment. The hours-worked measure captures changes in overtime worked, standard weekly hours, leave taken, and changes in the proportion of part-time employees.

Data on hours and number of jobs by province and territory and by industry are obtained from a number of different sources—both household and business surveys. The primary benchmark is a household-based survey—the Labor Force Survey (LFS). LFS employment series, which are based on the notion of persons employed, are adjusted to the SNA concept of jobs by adding multiple job holders and excluding those persons absent from work with pay during the reference week. While the LFS is felt to provide the most accurate benchmark for the total economy and for some industry groupings, other sources (employer-based surveys) are felt to provide a better split of employment across detailed industries because firms are more accurately assigned to industries than are households.[9] Therefore, a number of other sources are used to split estimates of labor inputs at the aggregate level into detailed industry estimates.

The CPA then constructs hours worked in a way that is consistent with the SNA 1993.

Statistics on hours worked that are calculated for Statistics Canada's productivity program include

- hours actually worked during normal periods of work;
- time worked in addition to hours worked during normal periods of work, and generally paid at higher rates than the normal rate (overtime);
- time spent at the place of work on work such as the preparation of the workplace, repairs and maintenance, preparation and cleaning of tools, and the preparation of receipts, time sheets, and reports;
- time spent at the place of work waiting or standing by for such reasons as lack of supply of work, breakdown of machinery, or accidents, or time spent at the place of work during which no work is done but for which payment is made under a guaranteed employment contract; and

9. Another disadvantage of firm-based surveys is that they do not easily produce data on the number of persons employed—they only produce estimates of jobs. Household surveys directly measure number of people employed, and when they ask questions about whether an individual holds multiple jobs, they can provide measures of jobs as well.

- time corresponding to short periods of rest at the workplace, including tea and coffee breaks.

Statistics of hours actually worked exclude

- hours paid for but not actually worked, such as paid annual leave, paid public holidays, and paid sick leave; and
- meal breaks and time spent on travel to and from home and work.

Productivity measures need to capture hours worked and not hours paid if they are to accurately represent effort. Both employer and household surveys have potential problems with capturing data on hours worked. Firm-based employer surveys typically collect data on hours paid (or standard hours paid), rather than hours worked. Records of hours paid are the usual measure that employers keep in their management information systems and that therefore can be collected from an employer survey. Hours paid includes hours not worked because of vacation, illness, holiday, and so on, and excludes hours worked but not paid (e.g., unpaid overtime). While a correction can be made to hours paid, as measured in employer surveys, to derive hours worked using a supplementary employer survey (as is done in the United States), this adds an additional possibility of error that has become more important in the last two decades.

In contrast, a well-designed household survey can ask the respondent directly for hours paid. With a well-crafted set of questions, household surveys at least focus directly on the concept that is required for productivity purposes. Employer surveys do not do this. Furthermore, even if this was attempted in an employer survey, the employer would be highly unlikely to be able to report the unpaid overtime of employees that need to be included in the hours-worked estimate for productivity measures. Comparisons of hours-worked estimates from employee surveys with time-use surveys in both Canada and the United Kingdom indicate that hours worked per job are virtually the same in both (Baldwin et al. 2004). For all of these reasons, the CPA uses the household labor survey to develop data on average hours worked by job. Total hours worked are then created by multiplying jobs by hours worked per job.

Changes in the skill level of the labor force are not captured in a simple sum of hours worked across all workers. To obtain a measure of productivity that excludes the effect of changing skill levels, the CPA adjusts hours worked for changes in the "quality" or composition of the labor force.

Our primary data sources for the derivation of hours adjusted for changes in composition are the quinquennial Censuses of Population, the CPA, and the annual LFS surveys. The CPA provides totals for hours worked by class of workers and by industry, while the Census and LFS together allows us to estimate the growth in labor "quality."

Details on the construction of the labor data can be found in Gu et al. (2003). Briefly, the Censuses of Population provide detailed data on employment, hours, and labor compensation across demographic groups in census years. The annual LFS and Survey of Consumer Finance (SCF) data are used to interpolate similar data for intervening years, and the CPA data provide control totals.

The demographic groups include 112 different types of workers, cross-classified by class of workers (employee, self-employed, or unpaid), age (15–17, 18–24, 25–34, 35–44, 45–54, 55–64, 65+), and education (0–8 years grade school, 1–3 years high school, 4 years high school, 1–3 years college, 4 years college, 5+ years college). Adjustments to the data include allocations of multiple job-holders and an estimation procedure to maintain consistent definitions of demographic groups over time. These detailed data cover 1961 to present and allow us to estimate the quality of labor input for the private business sector as well as for individual industries down to the three-digit (L) level of the IOTs.

The CPA's task in creating the labor input numbers is twofold. On the one hand, it is responsible for creating data that meet the conceptual challenges outlined above. But it also is responsible for integrating these data into the supply and use system—by generating hours worked by cell of the industry IOTs that accord with the rest of the data being generated by the SNA. This requires numerous consistency checks that involve comparison of labor trends against known events—shutdowns due to strikes, or blackouts; new plant and firm openings; and so on. It also involves constant comparisons against other variables—perhaps the most important of which is labor remuneration that is being produced within the SNA. For labor income divided by hours worked produces estimates of hourly remuneration that should accord with other exogenous information on wage rates if the system is to be fully coherent within itself and with outside information.

Capital Services. Much like labor input, the CPA also produces internally consistent estimates of capital services. Other sources are available within Statistics Canada for estimates of capital that do not completely satisfy the consistency needs of the CPA—partly because they provide only estimates of capital (not capital services) and partly because they are not fully integrated into the production framework—that is, they are not reconciled to industry-level data. The CPA produces a set of capital service estimates to accomplish both objectives.

In order to estimate productivity at the aggregate business sector, the CPA use an aggregate production function approach and requires an aggregate measure of capital services $K_t = \phi(K_{1t}, K_{2t}, \ldots, K_{Mt})$, where M includes all types of tangible fixed assets. For the industry-level estimates, a similar notion of capital services is developed for each industry i, that is, $K_{it} = \phi(K_{i1t}, K_{i2t}, \ldots, K_{iMt})$. The CPA employ individual quantity indexes to generate aggregate capital services, capital stock, and investment series.

The growth rate of aggregate capital services is defined as a share-weighted average of the growth rate of the components, where the weights are the value share of capital income.

The CPA begin with investment data, estimates capital stocks using the perpetual inventory method, and aggregates capital stocks using rental prices as weights. This approach, originated by Jorgenson and Griliches (1967), is based on the identification of rental prices with marginal products of different types of capital. The estimates of these prices incorporate differences in asset prices, service lives and depreciation rates, and the tax treatment of capital incomes. A broad definition of capital is employed, which includes tangible assets such as equipment and structures, as well as land, and inventories. A service flow is then estimated from the installed capital stock.[10]

The process begins with investment data available from the final demand matrix in the IOTs that is constructed from a comprehensive establishment capital spending survey that covers the entire economy and a variety of asset classes. The final demand matrix of the IOTs contains current price and chain-type quantity indices for 476 types of commodities from 1961 to 2000.

Data on inventories and land complete the capital estimates. The inventory data come primarily from the IEAs in the form of farm and nonfarm inventories, but are bolstered by data from various industry surveys. Inventories are assumed to have a depreciation rate of zero and do not face an investment tax credit or capital consumption allowance, so the rental price formula is a simplified version of the one employed for reproducible assets. Data on land are obtained from the Canadian Balance Sheet Accounts in current prices and in volume terms from the environmental accounts. Like inventories, depreciation, the investment tax credit, and capital consumption, allowances for land are taken to be zero.

As is the case for output, the investment series of the IOTs are only available for the years up to the "reference" year. This is two years from the current period. The CPA makes several adjustments to extend the investment series through to the most current year and to make the investment series by industry consistent with those of national accounts. The investment series is extended through to the present based on the quarterly IEAs. The total value of investment in major categories—structures, equipment and software, residential structures—is set equal to the corresponding total derived from the income and expenditures aggregates.

The CPA approach to capital services generates a complete time series of investment reclassified into twenty-eight private assets (eighteen types of equipment and software, six types of nonresidential structures, and four types of residential structures; see table 10.1). Capital stocks are then estimated using the perpetual inventory method and a geometric depreciation

10. See Harchaoui and Tarkhani (2003a) for methodology.

Table 10.1   Classification of total capital by asset classes

Computers and office equipment
Communication equipment
Software—own account
Software—prepackaged
Software—custom design

Office furniture, furnishing
Household and services machinery and equipment
Electrical industrial machinery and equipment
Nonelectrical industrial machinery and equipment
Industrial containers
Conveyors and industrial trucks
Automobiles and buses
Trucks (excluding industrial trucks) and trailers
Locomotives, ships, and boats and major replacement parts
Aircraft, aircraft engines, and other major replacement parts
Other equipment

Nonresidential building construction
Road, highway, and airport runway construction
Gas and oil facility construction
Electric power, dams, and irrigation construction
Railway and telecommunications construction
Other engineering construction
Cottages
Mobiles
Multiples
Singles

Inventories
Land

rate based on age-price profiles developed by Gellatly, Tanguay, and Yan (2002). Important exceptions are the depreciation rates for assets in the structures category. Owing to a lack of an active transaction markets for structures, depreciation rates were derived here from the existing information on length of lives from a survey done by the Investment and Capital Stock Division that produces expected length of life by asset type.

Capital services for the aggregate business sector are constructed using the information on capital stock and rental prices for these twenty-eight assets. The construction of the aggregate capital services proceeds in two steps: the twenty-eight assets are grouped into three asset classes—information technology, other machinery and equipment, and structures. In the second stage, the three asset classes are aggregated into an index of tangible capital services.

Capital services at the industry level are estimated in three steps. First, a detailed array of capital stocks is developed for various asset types in different industries. The investment flows that are available from the final demand matrix of the IOTs exist only at a relatively high level of industry aggregation. The CPA therefore takes the investment flows from the Investment and Capital Stock Division and uses these to derive more detailed industry flows for the finest level of industry detail—following much the same procedure as is done for the labor data where household data are used for aggregate benchmarks and then spread at finer levels of industry detail using other sources of information. In this case, it is the investment data from Investment and Capital Stock Division that are used to spread the IOT industry aggregate investments to investment by asset type.

Once the investment flows are edited for consistency, asset-type capital stocks are aggregated for each industry to measure capital input for the industry; and industry capital inputs are aggregated to measure sectoral-level capital input. The end result is an estimate of capital services at the industry level that is coherent with that of the aggregate business sector.

The Variety of Productivity Measures

The CPA produces several productivity measures for the aggregate business sector. Annual labor productivity for the Canadian business sector was the first measure of productivity introduced by Statistics Canada in the early sixties. More recently, quarterly labor productivity estimates for the business sector have been introduced to provide more timely estimates of productivity performance.[11] For this measure, output is measured as real GDP—deliveries in constant chained dollars of final goods and services by the business-sector industries to domestic households, investment, government and nonprofit institutions, and net exports—and is compared to labor input, measured as hours worked.

In addition, a multifactor productivity measure has been developed for the business sector, in recognition of the role that capital growth plays in output growth. As is the case for the labor productivity measure calculated for the aggregate business sector, output is measured as final demand GDP, but the input measure is an aggregate of hours worked adjusted for compositional changes in the workforce and capital services flows.

For both these aggregate business-sector measures, aggregate output F_t consists of investment goods I_t, consumption goods C_t, and net exports N_t. These outputs are produced from aggregate input X_t, consisting of capital services K_t and labor services L_t. Productivity is represented as a "Hicks-neutral" augmentation A_t of aggregate input:

$$(1) \qquad F(C_t, I_t, N_t) = A_t \cdot X(K_t, L_t)$$

The outputs of investment, consumption goods, and net exports and the inputs of capital and labor services are themselves aggregates, each with many subcomponents. Under the assumptions of competitive product and

---

11. Quarterly estimates for two-digit-level industries have just been introduced.

factor markets, and constant returns to scale, growth accounting gives the share-weighted growth of outputs as the sum of the share-weighted growth of inputs and growth in multifactor productivity:

(2) $\overline{w}_{C,t}\Delta \ln C_t + \overline{w}_{I,t}\Delta \ln I_t + \overline{w}_{N,t}\Delta \ln N_t$

$$= \overline{v}_{K,t}\Delta \ln K_t + \overline{v}_{L,t}\Delta \ln L_t + \Delta \ln A_t,$$

where $\overline{w}_{C,t}$ is consumption average share of nominal output, $\overline{w}_{I,t}$ is investment's average share of nominal output, $\overline{w}_{N,t}$ is net exports', $\overline{v}_{K,t}$ is capital's average share of nominal income, $\overline{v}_{L,t}$ is labor's average share of nominal income, Δ refers to a first difference, and $\overline{w}_{C,t} + \overline{w}_{I,t} + \overline{w}_{N,t} = \overline{v}_{K,t} + \overline{v}_{L,t} = 1$. Note that the CPA reserves the term multifactor productivity for the augmentation factor in the first equation.[12] The second equation enables us to identify the contributions of outputs as well as inputs to economic growth.

In addition to the aggregate business-sector productivity measures, the CPA produces a comprehensive set of industry productivity measures that are based on the IOTs and that enable users to trace aggregate productivity growth to its source in individual industries.[13] The labor productivity estimates are produced at various levels of detail provided by the IOTs for business or commercial industries—the L (167 industries), M (58 industries), and S (21 industries) level.[14] The multifactor productivity estimates are produced at the P (123 industries), M (58 industries), and S (21 industries) levels.[15] Complete detail is provided up to the benchmark or reference year of the IOTs. While the CPA works at the same level of detail in the postbenchmark years, less industry detail is released for public use since output for the postbenchmark years is based on projections.

Labor productivity measures are produced for real value added per hour worked. Three separate measures of multifactor productivity are produced, using different measures of output (gross output, valued added, and sectoral output). These measures are (a) real value added per unit of capital and labor inputs; (b) gross output per combined unit of capital, labor, and intermediate inputs; and (c) sectoral output[16] per combined unit of capital, labor, and sector intermediate inputs.

Domar's (1961) approach is utilized to link industry-level productivity growth with aggregate multifactor productivity growth. This link is established by expressing the rate of aggregate multifactor productivity growth

---

12. Preferring the term *multifactor* to *total factor productivity.*

13. These are produced with a two-year lag because the detailed IOTs come out only with a lag.

14. These industry numbers apply to the SIC classification system. The NAICS is slightly different.

15. The finest level of industry detail for multifactor productivity estimates is less than that for labor productivity because investment data are not available for the L level.

16. This is the measure used by the BLS.

as a weighted average of industry productivity growth rates, with weights equal to the ratios of industry output to aggregate GDP. Because of the internal consistency between the industry estimates and aggregate GDP, these weights are internally consistent. This internally consistent framework makes it possible to trace aggregate productivity growth to its sources.

Over the entire 1997 to 2003 period, agriculture, trade industries, manufacturing, and professional services have posted the most rapid labor productivity growth of the business sector. Labor productivity gains result from several factors: the increase in capital deepening, the increase in skilled workers (change in labor composition, reflecting a larger share of workers with more education and more experience), and a number of other factors captured by multifactor productivity, the overall efficiency with which resources are employed.

In general, changes in labor composition make a positive, albeit small, contribution to labor productivity growth (see table 10.2). The 1997 to 2003 period is no exception. During this time, labor composition made a 0.2 percentage point contribution to the 2.1 percent annual growth of the business-sector labor productivity. Capital deepening made only a 0.4 percentage point contribution, a reflection of the collapse of investment in

Table 10.2   Labor productivity and its sources of growth, 1997–2003 (percentage points contribution)

	Labor productivity	Capital deepening	Labor quality	Multifactor productivity
Business sector	2.1	0.4	0.2	1.5
Agriculture, forestry, fishing, and hunting	4.8	1.8	0.2	2.9
Mining and oil and gas extraction	1.1	3.3	0.6	–2.8
Utilities	–0.9	0.6	0.1	–1.6
Construction	1.5	0.1	0.2	1.2
Manufacturing	2.9	0.5	0.5	1.8
Wholesale trade	4.2	1.0	0.3	2.9
Retail trade	3.1	0.5	–0.3	2.9
Transportation and warehousing	1.8	1.1	0.6	0.2
Information and cultural industries	3.0	0.9	0.7	1.4
Professional, scientific, and technical services	3.8	4.2	0.0	–0.4
Administrative and support services, waste management and remediation services	–0.8	–0.5	0.4	–0.6
Finance, insurance, real estate, and rental and leasing	1.4	0.4	0.1	0.9
Educational services	1.3	1.8	–0.9	0.4
Health care and social assistance	0.0	0.6	–0.5	–0.1
Arts, entertainment, and recreation	–1.8	–0.6	–1.9	0.7
Accommodation and food services	0.6	–0.4	–0.5	1.6
Other services (except public administration)	3.1	1.3	0.5	1.3

machinery and equipment and the relatively rapid growth in hours at work. Multifactor productivity has added 1.5 percentage points, accounting for the bulk of labor productivity growth. Multifactor productivity was the main source of labor productivity not only during the rapid economic growth period of 1997 to 2000 but also during the economic slowdown period of 2000 to 2003.

In general, the industries that posted the largest labor productivity gains were also those with the most rapid multifactor productivity growth rates, indicating that major improvements in overall efficiency have taken place in recent years.

10.2.4   Comparison with Other Countries

This section compares the Canadian experience in the integration of its productivity accounts and the SNA to the experience of the United States, Australia, the United Kingdom, and France. Table 10.3 lists the various productivity measures produced by these countries and the type of output employed and an indication of the extent to which the productivity program is integrated to the rest of the economic accounts. For example, the lack of gross output measures of multifactor productivity suggests the absence of information on interindustry transactions that can only be available from a comprehensive set of industry production accounts in current and constant prices.

All these countries have a productivity program that relies on an output measure derived from a limited set of industry accounts that are not necessarily reconciled with final demand GDP. With the exception of the United States, the majority of other countries rely on the notion of value added derived from industry accounts. For example, the Office for National Statistics (ONS) in the United Kingdom publishes quarterly labor productivity estimates based on value added for the whole economy, the production sector, total manufacturing, and eleven manufacturing subsectors. A lack of reconciliation is partly the result of imperfections in the production accounts that do not permit the measurement of accurate valued added that would be expected to add up to the total economy GDP.

Recently, the ONS has introduced annual labor productivity estimates at a more detailed industry level based on a new survey vehicle (Annual Business Inquiry [ABI]). This data source has the advantage of bringing together accounting and employment data and improving the consistency between output and labor measures, making the compilation of detailed labor productivity measures feasible. It recognized, however, that the gross value-added measures compiled from the ABI are approximate, as the full range of variables necessary to calculate the true value added is not available, and the estimates differ from input-output final numbers (Daffin and Lau 2002).

The ONS does not have a multifactor productivity program. Recently,

Table 10.3   Across-country comparison in the integration between the productivity program and the System of National Accounts (SNA)

Country	Productivity measures	Nature of output measure	Integration to the SNA	Remarks
Canada	MFP and LP	Business sector: final demand GDP Industry: gross output, value added and sectoral output	Yes. Integrated production account and expenditure account available from the SNA. These are extended to include measures of capital services and labor services that are consistent with the SNA at the aggregate and industry levels by the productivity group. Feedback occurs.	Canada and the United States (Jorgenson and his associates and BLS) are the only countries that have exploited so far the final demand GDP for productivity measurement. As a result, these are the only countries that have employed the top-down approach to productivity measurement. Industry productivity measures are also used to implement the bottom-up approach.
United States	MFP and LP	Business sector: final demand GDP Industry: sectoral output	Output series from NIPAs but labor and capital inputs constructed independently by the BLS. No integration at the industry level between BLS estimate and BEA estimate.	
Australia	MFP and LP	Business sector: aggregate value added Industry: value added	Consistent set of input-output tables in current and constant prices in progress	Bottom-up approach to productivity measurement.
United Kingdom	LP	Total economy: aggregate value added Industry: value added	No.	
France	LP. The French statistical system does not consider MFP a concept that falls under the purview of the official statistical system.	LP	No productivity accounts integrated into the SNA.	

Notes: MFP = multifactor productivity; LP = labor productivity; GDP = gross domestic product; NIPAs = national income and product accounts; sectoral output = gross output net of intra-industrial transactions. Integration is defined as a productivity program that produces alternate measures of productivity based on an established production account (input-output and income and expenditures accounts).

however, the ONS has given priority to the development of experimental multifactor productivity estimates (Lau and Vaze 2002) for two reasons:

- Most countries have experienced a multifactor productivity revival, but independent estimates developed at the Bank of England and at the National Institute of Economic and Social Research have shown that U.K. multifactor productivity performance deteriorated relative to the United States in the post-1995 period compared to the early 1990s. Public pressure has led the ONS to find out whether this is a real phenomenon or a result of a data problem (adequate deflators in particular).
- The ONS recognizes the usefulness of multifactor productivity estimates as a valuable quality assurance tool to check consistency of output and input data.

Australia has also a regular productivity program that produces annual labor productivity and multifactor productivity measures based on real value added derived from industry accounts.

Aggregate multifactor and labor series for the market sector are maintained from the early 1960s to the most recent years. These multifactor productivity series are based on hours at work and capital services. Recently, the Australian Bureau of Statistics has introduced multifactor productivity series for the period 1982 onward with labor input estimates that account for compositional changes. Subsector productivity series are only available for labor productivity measures, and they are maintained from 1992 to the most recent years.

In contrast to the United Kingdom, the United States, and Australia, France does not maintain an ongoing multifactor productivity program. While the majority of statistical offices view productivity measures as an ongoing statistical program, the Institut National de la Statistique et des Études Économiques (INSEE) views them more as an input for analytical papers with little connection to the system of national accounts. INSEE does not produce "official" multifactor productivity series, but its various directorates release occasional studies on multifactor productivity based on real value added series.

There are some striking differences in terms of data sources used for productivity purposes between these countries. First, despite the development of the IEAs in all these countries, only Canada and the United States have employed them for the aggregate productivity measures. The top-down approach is not used by the official statistics in Australia, the United Kingdom, or France. In these countries, value added is the primary vehicle used to measure output. And these countries focus primarily on productivity only for aggregate sectors.

10.3   Benefits of the Integration of the Productivity Accounts

There are several benefits of having a productivity account integrated to the SNA.

10.3.1   Consistency

The IOTs play a central role in the integration of the CSNA, and the CPA contributes to this interactive system. As noted by Wilson (chap. 2 in this volume), the IOTs provide the framework that is used to identify gaps and point to inconsistencies.

The IOTs provide a framework for checking the consistency of data on flows of goods and services obtained from a variety of statistical sources—industrial surveys, household expenditures, investment surveys, foreign trade statistics, and so on. The IOTs serve as a coordinating framework for productivity statistics, both conceptually for ensuring the consistency of the definitions and classifications used and as an accounting framework for ensuring the numerical consistency of data drawn from different sources.

While the productivity accounts benefit from having a coherent unified production framework, they also provide important feedback that helps to identify inconsistencies and to improve the consistency of the framework. The basic production framework worries primarily about balancing commodity supply and disposition, about the relationship between sales and factor incomes. The productivity accounts provide additional checkpoints—asking whether the increase in real outputs is reasonable relative to both labor and capital inputs.

The CPA also provides a set of summary data series that serve to provide a constant check on the time series validity of the SNA. As part of its estimation system, the CPA creates a database containing coherent data on prices and volumes along with data on capital and labor inputs—KLEMS. The KLEMS database allows additional perusal of relationships that emerge from the data produced by the IOTs—especially during research projects.[17]

These projects allow the productivity program to improve both data accuracy and data suitability by contributing to the production of time series that are consistent over time. By their nature, the survey systems that provide data to the national accounts are often not "time series" consistent. Among other events that lead to inconsistencies, industry classification systems have changed from being SIC based to being NAICS based. Surveys (such as the Annual Survey of Manufactures) have changed their coverage. Each of these changes may improve survey estimates at a given point in time—but they serve to render analysis over time less coherent. While

17. Statistics Canada publications on productivity may be found at http://www.statcan.ca/english/studies/eaupdate/prod.htm

rough corrections are often provided by survey programs to account for the impact of changes in coverage or classification, the survey programs rarely provide all of the changes that are required to provide time series coherence. One of the primary focuses of the productivity program, as it prepares the time series used for the program and as it feeds back information to the production divisions, is to improve the time series consistency of the data.

Time series consistency is important since the CPA often is used to quantify the sources of Canadian economic growth using a variety of data for individual industries. Industry-level data enable us to trace the sources of Canadian economic growth to their industry origins, to isolate and analyze specific industries, and to assess the relative importance of productivity growth and factor accumulation at the level of both individual industry and the business sector. Having a set of productivity accounts integrated to the SNA permits the "bottom-up" approach to complement the "top-down" analysis approach cast in the production possibility frontier framework.

One way to ascertain the consistency of the KLEMS data is to inquire whether alternate productivity measures derived at the industry level yield a similar story on the sectoral allocation of aggregate productivity growth. Consider, for example, the direct contribution to aggregate productivity growth from two distinct groups of industries—those that produce information technology and those that use information technology.

A recent Statistics Canada study used both the top-down and the bottom-up approach to study this issue.[18] Regardless of the methodology used, the data show a positive contribution to aggregate productivity in the 1990s from both groups, although the majority comes from information technology–using industries. Using the notion of gross output, information technology–using industries contributed 0.89 percentage points to the 1.10 percent growth of the Canadian business sector's multifactor productivity growth during the late 1990s. This result remains robust to alternate measures of output (value added and sectoral output), albeit with significant differences in the order of magnitude of the results, as one would expect.

10.3.2   Quality Assessment

Because productivity estimates "integrate" data on outputs and inputs in current and constant prices that are collected from a variety of different sources, they constitute a convenient way to ascertain the quality of data obtained from the CSNA. This constitutes more than just improving the coherency of existing data, but also suggesting major data gaps.

For example, the perusal of productivity results at the industry level may

---

18. See Harchaoui and Tarkhani (2005) and Harchaoui, Tarkhani, and Khanam (2004).

suggest sectors where deficiencies need to be addressed. For an analyst who is confirming GDP estimates, finding a positive output growth of an industry that does not show any sign of decline may be sufficient. But when productivity estimates have been integrated into the production system, that same analyst can compare the trend of output to the trend of inputs based on consistent data and ask whether the long-term trends in productivity are reasonable. For example, Gullickson and Harper (1999) suggest that a negative—or even a sluggish—productivity growth over a long period of time for an industry that is not declining is indicative of problems in the quality of the output and/or input estimates.

There are a number of Canadian sectors that display sluggish multifactor productivity performance (an average annual growth rate less than 1 percent) for the period 1981–2000. These include a number of service-sector industries—accommodation and food, business service, personal and household service, amusement and recreational services. As a result, Statistics Canada has mounted an initiative to improve price measurement in these areas.

Elsewhere, in finance, real estate and insurance, growth rates are also relatively low. Here the problem probably has more to do with the development of markets for leased capital. The Canadian system attributes investment to the sector of capital ownership not of capital use. The lower productivity growth rates here conceivably could be the result of very high capital input due to this leasing phenomenon.

10.3.3   Flexibility

The integration between the productivity accounts and the SNA gives flexibility to the CPA in that it allows for the production of a variety of productivity measures that are needed to provide measures for specific purposes that are consistent with those produced by the core program.

Alternate Productivity Measures

Neither the economics profession nor international statistical agencies have settled on a single productivity measure for all purposes. Producing a variety of productivity measures allows Statistics Canada to meet diverse requests for alternate summary statistics for specific purposes—in particular, for cross-country comparisons.

Many national productivity programs like those of Australia and the United Kingdom exclusively produce value-added productivity measures at different levels of aggregation. In contrast, depending on the level of aggregation, the BLS uses different notions of output. The source of the real output measures for the BLS business and nonfarm business productivity measures is the National Income and Product Accounts (national accounts), produced by the Bureau of Economic Analysis of the U.S. Department of Commerce.

The BLS also used the notion of value added (or gross output originating) for its manufacturing productivity measures until 1996 and has subsequently used a "sectoral output" concept to measure manufacturing output.

The notion of gross output has been extensively used by Dale Jorgenson and his associates in a variety of research projects on productivity (see Jorgenson and Stiroh 2000, for example).

The integration of the CPA to the SNA allows Statistics Canada to produce productivity estimates based on value added, sectoral output, and gross output. In doing so, it has established a program allowing comparisons between Canada and the United States. In recent years, several research projects that seek to expand the international scope of the CPA have been initiated.[19]

Producing alternate productivity measures satisfies a range of analytical needs that otherwise cannot be met by a single measure of productivity. Recent requests have been received to consider the role of intermediate inputs and changing levels of intermediation on productivity performance. Increases in imports and the use of business services, such as equipment leasing, computer services, and temporary labor—all of which can have an important impact on production and employment—may have affected productivity. The role of intermediate inputs is invisible when value added is used, which is a "net output" measure. On the other hand, the use of gross output measures that consider the role of materials directly allows for analysts to study what is happening with intermediate materials and services. Flexibility due to the integrated nature of the CSNA permits the development of alternate productivity measures to meet different analytical needs.

Testing Assumptions

Despite the professionalism and energy that is devoted to the CSNA, there are areas where improvements can be made. And occasionally, queries will be made as to whether these improvements would change the nature of the story that productivity numbers are telling.

Having an integrated system allows the CPA to produce productivity estimates with slight changes in the underlying system in order to test the robustness of the productivity estimates. For example, the CPA recently tested the effect of alternate price deflators for information technology products on Canada/United States productivity estimates.

Differences in the measurement of information technology prices have recently attracted professional interest. The construction of a consistent time series of constant price series for information technology requires the

19. See Harchaoui, Jean, and Tarkhani (2005) for a Canada-Australia comparison in terms of standards of living and productivity and Harchaoui, Tarkhani, and Khanam (2004) for a Canada–United States comparison based on the notion of gross output utilized by Dale Jorgenson, and Harchaoui and Tarkhani (2005) for a Canada–United States comparison based on official productivity measures produced by Statistics Canada and the BLS.

availability of "constant-quality price indexes." These prices capture quality improvements across successive generations of information technology products and treat these quality gains as a reduction in the price of information technology.

The use of different techniques to measure quality changes by different countries has been cited as a reason for a lack of comparability in international estimates. For example, Wyckoff (1995) examines computer price methodologies for several countries and finds that both matched-model and hedonic techniques are employed. He argues that the difference in price behavior can be significant, depending upon the technique chosen. Further, based on the results of studies of U.S. data, he notes that typically the matched model index falls at a slower rate than the hedonic index.

The U.S. statistical system has been at the forefront of the development of quality-adjusted price indexes for information technology goods over the last twenty years. Over the same period, Canada has made sustained efforts to monitor these developments and to implement them in its statistical system. Quality changes are reflected to varying degrees in commodities and assets of final demand categories of information technology that appear in Canada's IEAs and in the IOTs.

Although there are some major differences in terms of the structures of the two economies and data sources that might lead to differences in price indices, it is still useful to benchmark the behavior of Canadian information technology prices to those of the United States at both the aggregate and industry levels to ascertain whether Canadian prices differ much from their U.S. counterparts.

There are important similarities between Canada and the U.S. in some categories of final demand. The implicit price index of Canadian imports of information technology tracks the U.S. information technology export price index fairly closely over the 1981–2000 period. On the investment side, important similarities in the price behavior also exist for computers. Similarities also exist between Canadian and U.S. implicit prices of personal expenditures' goods and services. In contrast, Canada's prices for telecommunication equipment on the investment side are different (see Harchaoui and Tarkhani 2005).

Differences in the behavior of information technology prices also exist at the industry level, and their impact on the productivity performance of these industries can be quite significant. Two recent papers have compared the impact of information technology on economic growth in Canada and the United States, while asking how different deflators affect the results. These papers used an "internationally harmonized" deflator for output and intermediate inputs, based on the implicit prices (adjusted for the exchange rate) from the U.S. KLEMS database. The harmonized deflator drops much faster than the prices in the Canadian productivity accounts.

Even with the harmonized price indexes, there is still a multifactor productivity growth gap in favor of U.S. information technology–producing industries. Moreover, overall conclusions about the sources of the productivity revival in Canada in the late 1990s and comparisons of overall differences to the United States are not affected by the replacement of Canadian with U.S. prices. The use of a harmonized price index does not alter the result that Canada's productivity revival is to a large extent attributable to information technology–using industries (see Harchaoui and Tarkhani 2005 and Harchaoui, Tarkhani, and Khanam, 2004).

Extending Coverage

The CPA constructs productivity measures that cover the business sector, which is defined as the total economy less general government (including publicly provided health and education) and owner-occupied dwellings. But for some analytical purposes, there is need for a different sectoral coverage. The availability of a set of productivity accounts allows relatively minor variations in output measures to be readily constructed in aid of special projects.

One such example comes from a recent project done in conjunction with Industry Canada and Dale Jorgenson of Harvard, which required a productivity measure that treated owner-occupied dwellings and consumer durables as investments rather than as consumption, as is done in the traditional estimates.

For this exercise, expenditures on owner-occupied dwellings were treated as investments in assets that provide a flow of services over many periods. The purchase of new housing was considered as an investment, while the flow of services from the installed stock was allocated to consumption and housing capital services were considered as part of capital input.

For the sake of consistency, consumers' durable goods were also treated symmetrically with housing capital since both are essentially long-lived assets that generate a flow of services over the life span of the asset. Capitalizing consumer durables reallocates expenditures that are made on them from personal consumption expenditures to gross private domestic investment and increases GDP by the amount of services they provide.

To implement these changes, the CPA adopted a methodology similar to that used for the calculation of capital services. A rental price was used to impute a flow of services from consumers' durables to be included in consumption and a measure of capital invested in consumer durables was added to capital input. The rate of return on the service flow of housing was imputed from rental values available from the income and expenditures accounts and the capital stock.[20] Capital services were then estimated using the same methodology used for other assets.

---

20. See Harchaoui and Tarkhani (2004a) for a description of the methodology.

10.4   The Challenges Ahead

Statistics Canada has made sustained efforts to improve its productivity measures. These efforts have been devoted to enhancing the reliability of the measures, improving the quality of product, and improving the range of information provided to the public. Despite the progress that has been made by the program, there is room for improvement.

Efforts are underway to expand the CPA coverage to consider unpriced goods and assets such as environment and public capital. These efforts depend once more on the existence of data sources that can be merged and integrated with the economic and productivity accounts.

10.4.1   Unpriced Goods and Assets

While the environment is affected by economic activity, most measurement is done of the two separately; measures of the environment tend to be collected by environmental agencies, while measures of economic activity tend to be collected by national accountants.

As part of the CSNA, the mandate of the environmental statistical accounts (ESAs) is to collect and integrate environmental data into the larger framework of supply and use that provides the foundation for the Canadian Accounts. The ESAs allow the CPA to ask how productivity measures can be expanded to take into account the extent to which the industrial system makes use of the environment.

Ideally, estimates of productivity growth should take account of all inputs and outputs associated with a production process, including changes to the environment. In practice, productivity growth is normally estimated using techniques that only take account of inputs and outputs that are priced. There are two reasons for this. First, data on environmental conditions are rarely collected that can be merged with data on economic activity. Second, since most environmental impacts are not traded in markets, they rarely have observable prices and are not measured by the traditional economic accounting system, and so they tend to be ignored when estimating productivity growth.

The impact of the environment on the productive performance of firms is an important issue facing society. However, detailed evaluation is difficult to obtain since the price paid for the use of the environment is sometimes either zero or below its opportunity cost. Because the consumption of the environment involves true opportunity costs no less than does the consumption of labor, capital, or material inputs, the standard multifactor productivity growth measure may be viewed as an incomplete barometer of efficiency improvements in the economy.

The purpose of extensions of the productivity program under this broad theme is to develop productivity measures that incorporate unpriced environmental impacts and apply them in an experimental way to two of the environmental issues facing Canada—greenhouse gas emissions and water use.

The methodology that has been adopted uses a cost-function-based model of production processes in the Canadian business sector to represent producers' input and output decisions and to estimate productivity in the face of unpriced factor inputs and outputs (see Harchaoui and Lasserre 2002). Earlier work in this area includes the paper by Gollop and Swinand (2001). Emissions are joint outputs of the industrial process and can be included in the output index with weights determined by their marginal costs. And the latter can be estimated with the help of the type of industry cost functions that can be generated using the CPA's KLEMS database.

The experimental framework takes into account a potential source of productivity growth that the conventional methodology misses: a more rapid growth in the value of total output due to a shift toward highly valued marketable products and away from negatively valued waste products. This is as valid an efficiency gain as any other. In some Canadian industries, it has been an important source of improvement in productivity performance.

The experimental estimates show that when the standard productivity framework is modified to take into account undesirable by-products, the conventional measure of productivity growth increases in value—by about 15 percent. This occurs because the economy has been increasing the amount of GDP that is produced faster than the amount of CO_2 emissions that is produced.

10.4.2   Natural Resources and Capital Stock

Most productivity estimates take into account only produced machinery and equipment, or buildings, or engineering construction. While this is adequate for the majority of sectors, it is not for the mining sector, since natural capital (mineral reserves stocks) is important here and it is generally not correctly incorporated by the conventional productivity framework.

The CPA has therefore been engaged in efforts to modify the framework that it uses to estimate multifactor productivity in the extractive sector. Once more, these efforts depend upon the integration of the environmental and the productivity accounts. The environmental group within the CSNA has also produced estimates of the stock of natural resources—various minerals, petroleum, gas, and timber. Both quantities and values of these stocks are maintained. Using these, more direct values of the actual resources that are used in production and the depletion thereof can be directly considered in the productivity analysis.

Those efforts have led the CPA to experiment with new productivity estimates in the natural resource sector—by separating the activities of the mining sector into extraction as opposed to exploration and by specifying the corresponding production framework by introducing natural capital for the extraction sector. The result has been a threefold increase of multifactor productivity for the extraction activity of the mining sector over the 1981–2000 period. In addition, the study recognized that the exploration sector produces "new reserves" as a good and includes this as an output. When this is done, the natural resource sector becomes the second-best-performing sector after the computer manufacturing industry.[21]

10.4.3   Public Capital and Productivity

Public infrastructure assets, defined in terms of dams, roads, highways, railways, ports, bridges, airports, streets, and water and sewer systems, have long been part of the balance sheet accounts and GDP.

They are not part of the official productivity estimates. This is primarily because it is more difficult to estimate their flow of services than it is for private capital. In particular, it is probably not appropriate to use the convention used in the national accounts that treats the net operating surplus of public capital as consisting only of depreciation. At present, the net return to fixed assets used by general government and nonprofit institutions serving households for nonmarket production is assumed to be zero (United Nations et al. 1993, 6.91).

Use of depreciation as a measure of the value of services of government fixed assets is a partial measure. In theory, the service value of an asset in the private sector should equal the reduction in the value of the asset due to its use during the current period (depreciation) plus a return equal to the current value the asset could earn if invested elsewhere (net return).

Unfortunately, the theory that suggests this relationship for the private sector does not provide us with guides as to what the rate of return should be in the public sector. There are alternate ways of estimating the rate of return to general government fixed capital formation, and one of them consists of using econometric models. Many of these regress output on labor, private capital, general government capital, and a constant for the level of technology. The estimated coefficient for government capital can be used to derive an estimate of the marginal product of government capital.

The CPA has been developing new productivity estimates that take into account the role that public capital plays in the private sector and incidentally produces a rate of return for public capital. A recent Statistics Canada study (see Harchaoui and Tarkhani 2003b) has employed a dual cost function and estimated the private cost saving arising from public capital services.

10.5   Concluding Remarks

Statistics Canada measures the quality of its product using five criteria—timeliness, accuracy, coherence, relevance, and interpretability. The integrated set of productivity accounts makes a contribution to each of

---

21. See Harchaoui and Tarkhani (2004b).

these objectives. As indicated previously, the feedback from the productivity group to the production accounts directly contributes to improvements with respect to accuracy. By integrating labor and capital services into the production accounts, the CPA improves the coherence of the overall product. By developing the KLEMS database, it aids in improving time-series consistency and overall coherence. By expanding the type of products that are produced into the area of the environment, it has contributed to improvements in relevance. By developing a set of compatible products that can be used in cross-country comparisons, it contributes to the goal of interpretability—by providing data that allow appropriate use for cross-country comparisons. By building on the integrated system of accounts, it provides both timely quarterly data and more detailed industry data that are fully compatible.

All of this is and could only have been done within the framework of an integrated set of national accounts. The productivity accounts are an integral part of that framework. This has not always been the case. Fifteen years ago, productivity was calculated by a group that was only imperfectly integrated into the main production accounts. Reorganizations have reduced the gap between the two. Closer integration has developed partially as a result of a general improvement in the degree of consistency across the various national accounts programs. Cost pressures have caused the production process to seek ways to improve the general editing process and seek inputs from sources not previously consulted. In addition, the productivity program recognized that it was increasingly important to be using estimates of output and inputs that were replicable by outsiders from published series of outputs. In the end, the productivity group at Statistics Canada has become an integral part of the accounts—similar to the input-output, the income and expenditure, the industry measures and the balance-of-payments groups.

The 1993 SNA stresses the need for a set of integrated national accounts that provide for consistency. As more and more countries move toward the standards of the SNA, productivity accounts are likely to develop that make use of the same type of consistent data that have facilitated the development of the Canadian productivity program. Indeed, the extent to which productivity accounts develop elsewhere can probably be taken as a sign of the progress that the system of accounts in a particular country is making. However, if cross-country comparisons of productivity performance are to be made, international standards need to be adopted for productivity measurement. While progress had recently been made by the OECD in providing a basic manual, international consensus is still required. Because of the close connection between a set of productivity accounts and the national accounts, it is time to consider incorporating standards for productivity measurement into the international guidelines of the SNA.

References

Baldwin, J. R., J.-P. Maynard, M. Tanguay, F. Wong, and B. Yan. 2004. A comparison of Canadian and U.S. productivity levels: An exploration of measurement issues. Economic Analysis Series no. 28. Analytical Studies Branch. Ottawa: Statistics Canada.

Daffin, C., and E. Lau. 2002. Labour productivity measures from the annual business inquiry. *Economic Trends* 589 (December): 54–63.

Domar, E. 1961. On the measurement of technological change. *Economic Journal* 71:709–29.

Gellatly, G., M. Tanguay, and B. Yan. 2003. An alternative methodology for estimating economic depreciation: New results using a survival model. In *Productivity growth in Canada,* ed. J. R. Baldwin and T. M. Harchaoui, 25–56. Ottawa: Statistics Canada.

Gollop, F., and G. Swinand. 2001. Total resource productivity: Accounting for changing environmental quality. In *New directions in productivity analysis,* ed. E. Dean, M. Harper, and C. Hulten, 587–685. Chicago: University of Chicago Press.

Gu, W., M. Kaci, J. P. Maynard, and M. Sillamaa. 2003. The changing composition of the Canadian workforce and its impact on productivity growth. In *Productivity growth in Canada—2002,* ed. J. R. Baldwin and T. Harchaoui, 67–100. Ottawa: Statistics Canada.

Gullickson, W., and M. Harper. 1999. Possible measurement bias in aggregate productivity growth. *Monthly Labor Review* 122 (2): 47–67.

Harchaoui, T., J. Jean, and F. Tarkhani. 2005. Comparisons of economic performance: Canada versus Australia, 1983–2000. *Monthly Labor Review* 128 (4): 36–347.

Harchaoui, T., and P. Lasserre. 2002. Assessing the impact of greenhouse gas emissions on Canada's productivity growth 1981–1996: An experimental approach. Economic Analysis Series no. 9. Ottawa: Statistics Canada.

Harchaoui, T., and F. Tarkhani. 2003a. A comprehensive revision of the capital input methodology for Statistics Canada multifactor productivity. In *Productivity growth in Canada—2002,* ed. J. R. Baldwin and T. Harchaoui, 101–58. Ottawa: Statistics Canada.

———. 2003b. Public capital and its contribution to the productivity performance of the Canadian business sector. Economic Analysis Series no. 17. Analytical Studies Branch. Ottawa: Statistics Canada.

———. 2004a. Accounting for housing and services flow of consumers' durables in the Canadian productivity accounts. Paper presented at the SSHRC Conference on Index Number Theory and the Measurement of Prices and Productivity. 30 June–3 July 20, Vancouver, Canada.

———. 2004b. Integrating natural capital in the Canadian productivity accounts. Paper presented at the SSHRC Conference on Index Number Theory and the Measurement of Prices and Productivity. 30 June–3 July 20, Vancouver, Canada.

———. 2005. Whatever happened to Canada-U.S. Economic growth and productivity performance in the information age? *OECD Economic Studies* no. 40, 2005/1.

Harchaoui, T. M., F. Tarkhani, and B. Khanam. 2004. Information technology and economic growth in the Canadian and U.S. private economies. In *Economic growth in Canada and the United States in the information age,* ed. D. Jorgenson, 7–56. Ottawa: Industry Canada.

Hulten, C. R. 1995. Capital and wealth in the revised SNA. In *The new System of National Accounts,* ed. J. W. Kendrick, 149–81. Boston: Kluwer Academic.

Jorgenson, D. W. 2001. Information technology and the U.S. economy. *American Economic Review* 91:1–32.

Jorgenson, D. W., and Z. Griliches. 1967. The explanation of productivity change. *Review of Economic Studies* 34 (99): 249–83.

Jorgenson, D. W. 2003. Information technology and the G7 Economies. *World Economics* 4:139–69.

Jorgenson, D. W., and K. J. Stiroh. 2000. Raising the speed limit: U.S. economic growth in the information age. *Brookings Papers on Economic Activity,* Issue no. 1:125–211.

Lal, K. 1986. Canadian input-output tables and their integration with other subsystems of the National Accounts. In *Problems of compilation of input-output tables,* ed. A. Franz and N. Rainer, 147–63. Proceedings of an international meeting organized by the Austrian Statistical Society, Vienna, Austria. Vienna: Wirtschaftsverlag Dr. Anton Orac.

Lau, E., and P. Vaze. 2002. Accounting growth: Capital, skills and output. Office for National Statistics, Productivity Workshop.

Organisation for Economic Co-operation and Development (OECD). 2001. *OECD productivity manual: A guide to the measurement of industry-level and aggregate productivity growth.* Paris: OECD.

Smith, P. 2000. Statistics Canada's broad strategy for business statistics. Paper presented at the second International Conference on Establishment Surveys. 17–21 June, Buffalo, New York.

Statistics Canada. 1990. *A guide to the System of National Accounts.* Catalogue 13–589. Ottawa: Statistics Canada.

United Nations, Commission of the European Communities, International Monetary Fund, Organisation for Economic Co-operation and Development and World Bank. 1993. *System of National Accounts 1993.* Series F, no. 2, rev. 4. New York: United Nations.

Wyckoff, A. A. 1995. The impact of computer prices on international comparisons of labor productivity. *Economics of innovation and new technology* 3:277–93.

Integrated Macroeconomic
Accounts for the United States
Draft SNA-USA

Albert M. Teplin, Rochelle Antoniewicz,
Susan Hume McIntosh, Michael G. Palumbo,
Genevieve Solomon, Charles Ian Mead, Karin Moses,
and Brent Moulton

11.1   Introduction

This chapter reports on an ongoing effort at the Federal Reserve Board (FRB) and the Bureau of Economic Analysis (BEA), henceforth the agencies, to integrate the nation's macroeconomic accounts. The BEA publishes the National Income and Product Accounts (NIPAs) and international transaction accounts (ITAs). The NIPAs convey production and income flows in the United States—the current accounts. The NIPAs also include data on the accumulation and value of reproducible, tangible assets. The presentation in the NIPAs is heaviest on national aggregates, with a mixture of sector and transaction detail. The ITAs record the nation's transactions and balances with the rest of the world. They provide detail on the U.S. external position and changes in that position, in many cases by region and country.

The FRB publishes the flow-of-funds accounts (FFAs). The focus of the presentation is on sector activity. For each sector, the FFAs combine a cap-

The analysis and conclusions set forth are those of the authors and do not indicate concurrence by other members of their respective research staffs, the Board of Governors of the Federal Reserve System, the Bureau of Economic Analysis, the Department of Commerce, or the Investment Company Institute. Data in this publication are estimates based on incomplete source material and are not official figures of the U.S. Government or the Federal Reserve System.

Albert M. Teplin is a private consultant. He was chief of the Flow of Funds Section at the Federal Reserve Board from 1989 to 2001. Rochelle Antoniewicz is senior economist at the Investment Company Institute. Susan Hume McIntosh and Michael G. Palumbo are, respectively, senior economist and chief of the Flow of Funds Section at Federal Reserve Board. Genevieve Solomon is economic research assistant at the Federal Reserve Bank of Dallas. Charles Ian Mead and Karin Moses are economists at the Bureau of Economic Analysis. Brent Moulton is the associate director of National Economic Accounts at Bureau of Economic Analysis.

ital account (showing saving and capital expenditures) and a financial account (showing net acquisition of financial assets and net incurrence of liabilities). The FFAs include detail on flows of financial instruments and stocks of financial assets and liabilities. For certain private sectors, the FFAs have balance sheets, which combine information on tangible assets with stocks of financial assets and liabilities. The FFAs offer considerable detail for specific financial instruments, such as mortgages, corporate bonds, and deposits.

The three published accounts—NIPAs, ITAs, and FFAs—are major elements of a full set of integrated national accounts outlined in standards developed by a consortium of international agencies and published as the *System of National Accounts 1993* (United Nations et al. 1993; hereafter SNA93). The U.S. accounts provide a long history of macroeconomic activity, using a consistent methodology, and with a level of detail and quality rarely matched in accounts of other countries. The publications are available quarterly and are produced in a timely fashion.

Over the past decade, many changes to the U.S. accounts have moved them closer to SNA93 standards. For example, in the NIPA comprehensive revision that was released in December 2003, the tables and definition of transactions were changed to make them much more consistent with SNA93 (Moulton and Seskin 2003; Mayerhauser, Smith, and Sullivan 2003). Nonetheless, the agencies and the user public have recognized that the accounts could be more fully integrated.[1] Closer coordination between the agencies would ensure that certain critical elements—such as sector boundaries, alternative data sources, and treatment of transactions—are handled in a way that minimizes distortions to important analytical concepts. Integration likely would align U.S. statistics more closely with those of other nations, and allow policymakers and researchers to analyze more fully and accurately the interrelationships of the nation's financial and nonfinancial activities. Integration of the accounts also would provide a common terminology and a uniform presentation that highlighted connections between the activities described in separate accounts.

The U.S. effort toward a better or more fully integrated set of economic accounts has a history, with a particularly noteworthy undertaking by Richard Ruggles and Nancy Ruggles (1982) about a quarter century ago.[2] While retaining much of the existing account structure, they showed a framework for all economic statistics that embraced both stocks and flows using the then-existing NIPAs, ITAs, and FFAs. The commentary on their effort highlighted significant conceptual issues and considerable disagreement on the form of such accounts. Some of those issues and disagreements

1. For example, references to the integration of the NIPAs and FFAs are contained in both general and specific terms in BEA (2002, 8–32).
2. Discussion by other experts is contained in Adler et al. (1982).

remain, but over the years, international consensus, published in SNA93, has eliminated many.

Given the consensus, our work focuses on the actual production of accounts. With regard to the Ruggleses' 1982 paper, James Tobin noted that "their experiment . . . illustrate[d] the well-known problem. It is difficult to reconcile data from the different sources, and disturbingly large, unexplained discrepancies remain. . . . Conceptual integration needs to be matched by a concerted effort to diagnose and remedy these inconsistencies" (Adler et al. 1982, 74).

Diagnosing and remedying inconsistencies has been our goal. Indeed, preparing this chapter, including the tables, is perhaps the most significant joint effort on the accounts since the Tobin comment was made. The agencies have looked closely at sector boundaries and the nature of discrepancies that arise from using different data sources, judgmental adjustments, and estimating techniques. We have uncovered many issues and have solved a number of them; others remain for future work.

We have also considered ways to present the vast amount of data that lie within integrated accounts. As matters stand, the FFA quarterly release is more than a hundred pages, and the number of tables in the NIPAs and ITAs could easily fill an equal number of pages. Even if done parsimoniously and coherently, a combined set of accounts likely will require considerable navigation by the user.

Other countries and economic areas are in various stages of providing a fully integrated set of macroeconomic accounts. Canada, for example, has published integrated accounts for some time. The integration extends to benchmarking to the input-output accounts. Moreover, within Statistics Canada there is coordination so that common estimation methods are used among the accounts; and, where issues arise, implications are considered for the full range of accounts, rather than a single portion.[3]

Eurostat provides a coordinating role within Europe. They have published standards in the European System of Accounts (ESA95), patterned on SNA93. European Union (EU) member countries are legally required to meet the standards for national income and product accounts and financial accounts over a set time schedule. They are requested to transmit regularly annual financial and nonfinancial accounts to Eurostat. The European Central Bank is coordinating development of quarterly financial accounts for the euro area, and, thus far, countries have provided quarterly national data, which are used, together with other euro-area financial statistics, to compile a subset of quarterly Monetary Union financial accounts for nonfinancial sectors, insurance companies, and pension funds. They are working toward expanding the integrated system to seven sectors—

3. A more thorough description of three countries' integrated accounts is provided in K. Wilson (chap. 2 in this volume).

households, nonfinancial corporations, government, monetary financial institutions, insurance corporations and pension funds, other financial intermediaries, and the rest of the world.

International agencies are also providing impetus to the efforts. The International Monetary Fund (IMF) guides and manuals for national statistics are increasingly ensuring that accounting and other elements are consistent with SNA93 standards.[4] Moreover, international agencies have sponsored ongoing committees and conferences during which issues pertaining to SNA93 standards are addressed. Currently, an effort is underway to update SNA93. The Organisation for Economic Co-ordination and Development (OECD) is coordinating dissemination of integrated accounts among member countries.[5]

The next section of this paper offers an overview of the contents of an integrated set of accounts and reviews how those accounts are related to current publications in the U.S. Section 11.3 discusses draft SNA-USA sector tables produced with the recent data in the NIPAs, ITAs, and FFAs. Section 11.4 highlights several issues that affect the quality of the accounts, mainly those dealing with the statistical discrepancies between the capital and financial accounts. Section 11.5 has a few concluding remarks.

11.2   What Are Integrated Accounts, and Where Do We Stand with Current Publications?

The SNA93 structure envisions separate statements for sectors of the economy. Each statement contains accounts for production, income, saving, investment, and financial flows for that sector. Those sector flow accounts are combined with information on changes in value of assets and liabilities due to factors not related directly to production and saving. All together, the integrated accounts offer a means to track the sources of change in sectors' net worth; the SNA93 structure begins with a balance sheet position and fully explains how that position evolves. Along the way, it provides detail on transactions, the distribution of income by factors of production, saving, capital formation, financial intermediation, and other aspects of national and sector economic activity.

The types of accounts are listed in table 11.1, along with comments on how each account relates to what is currently published. The first, the current account, is composed of production and income subaccounts that provide the familiar measures for gross domestic product (GDP), national income, and their components.

Although there are nearly three hundred NIPA tables that provide ex-

---

4. Examples include Bloem, Dipplesman, and Mæhle (2001) and International Monetary Fund (1995, 2000).
5. The BEA prepares estimates for the OECD on an SNA basis; these estimates and their relationship to the NIPAs are described in Mead, Moses, and Moulton (2004).

Table 11.1   Structure of integrated macroeconomic accounts

Account	Subaccounts	What it shows	What is published now	Significant issues
Current	Production	Gross value added and consumption of fixed capital by sector. For the economy as a whole, sum is gross (net) domestic product	National aggregates in the NIPAs with some sector detail.	Gross output and intermediate consumption not available for nongovernment sectors. No production accounts for subsectors
	Distribution and use of income, including saving	Generation of income within sectors and payment to factors of production supplied by other sectors. Shows taxes and transfers. Use of income provides a derivation of saving as difference between disposable income and consumption.	National aggregates in NIPAs with some sector detail.	Accounts for some financial subsectors not provided.
Accumulation	Capital	Capital outlays for structures, equipment, and software, net lending or net borrowing of funds.	National aggregates in NIPAs with some sector detail. Additional detail provided by the BEA for FFAs. Truncated account shown for all sectors.	Detail for all sectors is notprovided
	Financial	How net lending/net borrowing was satisfied through increase in financial assets and incurrence of liabilities.	Sector and instrument detail in the FFAs and ITAs.	Sector boundaries in the FFAs may not match those in the NIPAs: some differences between rest-of-world sector in FFAs and ITAs.
	Other changes in volume	Changes in net worth that arise from factors unrelated to revaluation and net saving, such as bad debts, accounting changes, data discontinuities.	Some sector and instrument detail in FFAs and ITAs.	Not provided for all sectors. More limited than the revaluation account.
	Revaluation	Nominal changes in net worth arising from holding gains/losses. Splits gains/losses into real and relative price changes.	Some sector and instrument detail in FFAs and ITAs.	Not provided for all sectors. In the FFAs, limited to equity shares and real estate.
Balance sheet	Opening position	Beginning period value of assets, liabilities, and net worth.	Published for some sectors in the FFAs.	Not provided for all sectors.
	Changes in stock positions	Summary of changes in net worth due to (a) capital formation, (b) net lending/ borrowing, (c) revaluation of assets and liabilities, and (d) other changes in volume.	Published for some sectors in the FFAs, but not in the form envisioned in the SNA	A change in format might be helpful, using international terminology.
	Closing position	Ending period value of assets, liabilities, and net worth.	Published for some sectors in the FFAs.	Not provided for all sectors.

tensive detail on the flows underlying the major aggregates, there are still some gaps relative to what would be needed for a complete set of integrated accounts. In addition to what is currently in the NIPAs, the integrated accounts envision providing such information by major sectors and subsectors. In the production account, SNA93 recommends a presentation of gross output, intermediate consumption, and value added by each sector. The BEA provides this type information *by industry* in its input-output and GDP-by-industry accounts, and provides value-added information *by sector* in tables 1.3.5 and 1.14. However, the NIPA tables do not provide information on gross output or intermediate consumption for nongovernment sectors. The more familiar presentation of GDP in NIPA table 1.1.5, though, presents it as the sum of final expenditures (a calculation that SNA93 presents only in the input-output or "supply-use" tables). The SNA93 distribution and use of income accounts are similar to the NIPA private enterprise income, personal income and outlay, government receipts and expenditures, and foreign transactions accounts, but would show more detail on financial and nonfinancial corporations and noncorporate business. Published integrated accounts may retain the information shown on these or similar tables, but they would also clearly derive the saving for each sector and for the total economy.

The most important shortcoming of the NIPAs relative to the integrated accounts envisioned by SNA93 is an inconsistency in sector definitions between the production account and the distribution and use of income account. While SNA93 calls for using consistently defined sectors throughout, the sectors emphasized in the NIPA production account differ from those presented in the distribution and use of income accounts. The NIPA production account, as shown in table 1.3.5, presents three major domestic sectors—business (including private and government noncorporate business), general government, and households and institutions. In contrast, the distribution and use of income accounts feature a personal sector (which includes income derived from private noncorporate business), a government account (which includes government business enterprises—that is, the full public sector), and, implicitly, a corporate business sector, which is defined by corporate legal form of organization.[6] Some production information is presented for corporate business, but these estimates are based on the income approach and, therefore, differ from the expenditure-approach estimates for the other production account sectors. Consequently, the statistical discrepancy between these two types of estimates prevents the derivation of an estimate of value added for the non-

6. The distribution and use of income accounts are presented in table 2.1 for the NIPA personal sector, in table 3.1 for the government (including government enterprises), and in table 1.14 for the corporate business sector.

corporate business sector as the difference between value added for corporate business and for the full business sector. Developing estimates for a consistent set of sectors is a major objective of this chapter.[7]

A second set of accounts is accumulation accounts. Much of the information for the capital account, the first accumulation account, is provided in the current NIPAs. Data for capital outlays and saving are compiled by major sectors. Although not currently labeled as such, FFA sector statements—such as table F.100 for the household sector and tables F.101 through F.104 for the major nonfinancial business sectors—typically begin with a capital account. However, the terminologies in the NIPAs and FFAs are not similar to each other, among the sectors, or with that in SNA93.

Financial accounts, the mainstay of the FFAs, are available in considerable detail. The FFA tables offer information for more than thirty sectors, many of which are financial intermediaries. Data for about fifty instruments are published in the FFAs, with a separate set of tables describing the issuers and purchasers of each instrument. Again, the terminology in the tables differs from international norms, and the organization of the tables varies slightly among sectors.

SNA93 structure has additional accumulation accounts for revaluations of stocks and changes in volume of stocks due to neither holding gains and losses nor net purchases. The information in the United States for revaluation accounts and other changes in volume accounts is less developed than that for other types of flows. The FFA reconciliation tables (labeled R.100 through R.103) enumerate factors that lead to changes in net worth. They estimate holding gains and losses for equity, real estate, and other instruments and other factors that change the level of assets and liabilities. The ITAs also provide figures in some tables on revaluations due to currency and price changes of assets and liabilities.

The SNA format envisions balance sheet positions for each sector. The FFAs publish balance sheet tables for three sectors—the household and nonprofit organizations sector (table B.100 in the FFA), nonfinancial noncorporate business sector (B.103), and nonfinancial corporate business sector (B.102). For other sectors in the FFAs, balance sheet data are limited to financial assets and liabilities. The necessary information for tangible assets of private subsectors has not been fully developed; and, of course, there are many issues concerning valuation of tangible assets of governments other than reproducible assets.

The listing in table 11.1 implies that most of the elements of integrated accounts are in currently published material, although the missing pieces are critical in many instances. Moreover, data for some elements are incomplete or thin. Sophisticated users of the NIPAs, ITAs, and FFAs likely

---

7. See also Lal (2003).

are aware that this is the case, but because the information is diffused over different publications, there is a perception by a new or occasional user that the accounts are unrelated. Use of the combined accounts is cumbersome, at best. For anyone analyzing international transactions, for example, the differences between the FFA rest-of-world sector and the BEA's international transactions tables seem enormous. In fact, they are not, as both agencies rely on the same information, but they present it differently. Less well known are the inconsistencies between accounts that remain in the published data and the dangers of drawing analytical conclusions from a combination of the accounts.

11.3   Draft SNA-USA Tables

This section presents draft SNA-USA tables, an integration of the agencies' accounts. We were able to construct virtually all the series required from existing data in the NIPAs, ITAs, and FFAs. In those instances where information was incomplete, we made estimates. We are reasonably confident that the figures in the tables are near what would be derived from a more sustained effort, but they remain unofficial estimates from the agencies.

Each sector table is lengthy, and the accounts are quite a bit to absorb in a single sitting, even though we have limited them to the major sectors. Little attempt was made at this stage to whittle down the information to ease the presentation, because a goal is to understand and show the structure of the accounts. We maintained the traditional time series format, with tables that have annual figures for 1985 to 2002.[8] The estimates are based on official data available on June 10, 2004.[9]

In draft SNA-USA, the economy is divided into five sectors—households and nonprofit institutions serving households, nonfinancial business, financial business, government, and the rest of the world (table 11.2). Draft SNA-USA tables show subsectors for nonfinancial corporate business, nonfinancial noncorporate business, the federal government, and state and local governments.

There are several differences between draft SNA-USA sectors and those in SNA93 and current publications.

- The household sector includes nonprofit institutions serving households (NPISHs). Over the past decade, both agencies developed and published separate sets of estimates for NPISHs, but their definitions

8. The draft SNA-USA tables 11.3–11.11 show the year 1995 through 2002. A set of these tables that also includes data for 1985–94 is available at http://www.bea.gov in XLS format.

9. June 10, 2004, marked the release of the FFAs for 2004:Q1 and revisions to prior periods. Preliminary estimates of the NIPAs for 2004:Q1 were published on May 27, 2004. International transaction accounts for 2003 were made available on March 12, 2004; revisions to the official estimates made after June 10, 2004, are not reflected in draft SNA-USA.

Table 11.2   **Sectors in draft SNA-USA**

Sector	Subsectors	Comments
1. Households and nonprofit institutions serving households	None	Current efforts seek to coordinate the NIPA and FFA information for consistency in sector boundary and data sources.
2. Nonfinancial business	Nonfinancial corporate business Nonfinancial noncorporate business (partnerships and sole proprietorships)	In SNA93, the unincorporated business sector sector is divided into units that are not separate from households that own them (for example, most sole proprietorships) which is included in the household sector, and units that are distinct and maintain separate accounts (for example, partnerships), which are included in the non-financial corporate business sector. At present, available source data do not permit this treatment for the U.S., nor is it clear that the SNA93 treatment is most useful for analysis, although agencies may consider this treatment, if additional source data are developed.
3. Financial business	None	Financial businesses in the U.S. represent a diverse set of institutions that carry out inter-mediation of funds. Additional subsectors and detail on their types of transactions are provided in the FFAs. Data for revaluations, other changes in volume (such as for loan write-offs), and value of tangible assets need to be developed.
4. General government	Federal government, including federal government enterprises State and local governments, including regional government enterprises	Developing information for the market value of tangible assets remains problematic, particularly land or the combination of land and tructures. Monuments, parks, and other public facilities present difficult valuation issues.
5. Rest of world	None	SNA measures an increase in purchases of national securities by foreigners as an increase in rest of world assets. In the balance of payments, such flows are a positive capital inflow to the nation. Draft SNA-USA provides an integration of foreign activity with other sectors.

of the sector boundary differ enough at this time that combining separately estimated financial and nonfinancial flows was not possible. In addition, assets of bank personal trusts are part of assets of the household sector in draft SNA-USA; in the FFAs, such trusts are a separate financial sector, with the level and change in the total value of the sector assets a separate instrument held by households.

- The division of the nonfinancial business sector in draft SNA-USA into corporate and noncorporate sectors closely matches current publications.[10] The noncorporate sector includes both partnerships and sole proprietors, the latter of which would be within the household sector boundary in SNA93, while the former would be merged with corporations.[11]
- Draft SNA-USA treatment of housing, specifically owner-occupied and tenant-occupied housing, differs in some respects from SNA93 guidance, but is the same as in the NIPAs and FFAs. Owner-occupied housing production and finances are in the household sector, and the transactions associated with such activity are treated as business-type transactions within the sector. Rental housing transactions are also of a business type, but they are part of the nonfinancial noncorporate business sector in draft SNA-USA. As suggested above, SNA93 would include activities of individuals that provide rental homes in the household sector.
- Draft SNA-USA, SNA93, and the NIPAs differ in their placement of government enterprises, such as the Postal Service and Tennessee Valley Authority. In draft SNA-USA and the FFAs, their activity is within the government sector. In the NIPAs, there is a mixed treatment of government business enterprises; their activities are presented as part of the business sector in the production account; but, for calculating net saving, they are consolidated with the government sector in the government receipts and expenditures account.

In addition, as indicated in the comments in table 11.2, portions of the other changes in volume, revaluation, and balance sheet accounts are unavailable or underdeveloped for some sectors. In particular, balance sheet accounts for the government sectors and financial business sector reflect only the reproducible portion of tangible assets. Thus, buildings are included, but the full market value of real estate is not.

The following narrative introduces significant elements of draft SNA-USA. It also highlights differences from currently published series. After some brief comment about the total economy current account, the discus-

10. SNA93, and international statistical terminology generally, defines *corporation* more broadly than in the United States. In the international terminology, a corporation sector refers to institutional business enterprises grouped together because of the type of function they perform, while, in the United States, a corporation sector refers to a legal form of business. Except in instances where the meaning should be clear or where the statistical consequences are judged insignificant, draft SNA-USA has retained the terminology in the NIPAs and FFAs, using *business* to refer to type of sector and *corporation* to refer to a specific legal form of business.

11. SNA93 defines *quasi-corporations* as unincorporated enterprises operated as if they were separate corporations whose de facto relationship to their owner is that of a corporation to its shareholders. It specifically notes one form of quasi-corporation is an unincorporated enterprise, including an unincorporated partnership, owned by households, which is operated as if it were a privately owned corporation. Quasi-corporations are not limited to those owned by households, however; they may include government business enterprises and partnerships.

sion turns to the sectors, with more detailed comments for the household sector to explain the terminology and structure common to all the tables.

11.3.1   Total Economy—Current Account (table 11.3)

Draft SNA-USA table 11.3 shows the current account for the economy as a whole, and illustrates that the account reflects an *income-side* approach. We have used SNA93 terminology—GDP/gross value added in line 1, and net domestic product (line 3), while in the NIPAs we refer to these figures as gross (net) domestic income. That is, in the NIPAs there are two methods of calculating GDP. The featured measure, known as GDP, is based on the sum of final expenditures (personal consumption, private investment, net exports, and government consumption and investment). The other measure, known as gross domestic income, is based on the sum of incomes generated from production. Because these measures, which are conceptually identical, are estimated from separate source data, they differ by a statistical discrepancy. For this paper we avoid dealing with the effects of this discrepancy by focusing on the income-side measure, or gross domestic income; the more familiar expenditure-side measure is shown in line 44.[12]

The specific income factors are shown in lines 4 through 8. One term, *operating surplus* (line 8), is a concept that has only recently appeared in U.S. accounts. In SNA93, it is defined as "the surplus accruing from processes of production before deducting any explicit or implicit interest charges, rents, or other property incomes payable on the financial assets, land, or other tangible nonproduced assets required to carry on the production" (para. 7.82). In other words, it is a broad income concept that includes interest, rent, and profits.

Lines 9 and 10 of table 11.3 account for the difference between domestic product and national income. Specifically, they add to gross product income receipts from the rest of the world and remove income payments made to the rest of the world.

The middle section of the current account describes the factors of net national income (line 11). These include the compensation received by employees and operating surplus. Net saving for the total economy (line 41) is derived by subtracting final consumption expenditures (line 40) from disposable income (line 39).[13] Table 11.4 reports how a number of key

---

12. Total gross value added NIPA table 1.3.5 ("Gross Value Added by Sector") is similar but not identical to the draft SNA-USA gross value added. The NIPA table subsumes the statistical discrepancy and puts value added of government enterprises in the business sector; draft SNA-USA has not allocated the discrepancy, and government enterprises are in the government sector.

13. Draft SNA-USA table 11.4, "Selected Aggregates for Total Economy and Sectors," is an example of the supplementary information that can be provided in a full set of accounts. It summarizes the contribution of sectors for several important aggregates. Table 11.4 was produced mainly as a way to check the consistency of our compilations of sectors with published aggregates. However, it appeared to be of interest on its own and is offered, without narrative, in the overall set of draft SNA-USA tables.

Table 11.3   **Total economy: Current account (billions of dollars)**

Row No.		1995	1996	1997	1998	1999	2000	2001	2002
1	*Gross domestic product (GDP)/Gross value added (income approach)*	7296.4	7723.1	8233.6	8761.7	9304.2	9944.1	10213.0	10558.0
2	*Less consumption of fixed capital*	878.4	918.0	974.4	1030.1	1101.2	1187.8	1266.9	1288.6
3	*Equals net domestic product/Net value added*	6418.1	6805.0	7259.2	7731.6	8202.9	8756.3	8946.2	9269.3
4	Compensation of employees (paid)	4197.3	4394.7	4666.0	5023.9	5362.3	5787.3	5945.4	6024.4
5	Wages and salaries	3439.7	3627.3	3879.1	4187.3	4476.6	4833.8	4947.9	4979.8
6	Employers' social contributions	757.6	767.4	787.1	836.7	885.7	953.5	997.7	1044.6
7	Taxes on production and imports less subsidies	524.2	546.8	579.1	604.5	629.9	664.5	674.6	721.8
8	Operating surplus, net	1696.4	1863.5	2014.1	2103.1	2210.7	2304.5	2326.2	2523.2
9	*Plus income receipts from the rest of the world*	234.0	248.7	286.7	287.1	320.8	382.7	319.0	299.1
10	*Less income payments from the rest of the world*	198.2	213.7	253.7	265.8	287.1	343.7	283.8	277.7
11	*Equals net national income/Balance of primary incomes, net*	6454.0	6840.0	7292.2	7752.9	8236.5	8795.1	8981.1	9290.8
12	Operating surplus, net	1696.4	1863.5	2014.1	2103.1	2210.7	2304.5	2326.2	2523.2
13	Compensation of employees (received)	4193.3	4390.5	4661.7	5019.4	5357.1	5782.7	5940.4	6019.1
14	Wages and salaries	3435.7	3623.2	3874.7	4182.7	4471.4	4829.2	4942.9	4974.6
15	Employers' social contributions	747.7	767.3	787.0	836.7	885.7	953.4	997.6	1044.5
16	Taxes on production and imports, receivable	558.3	581.1	612.0	639.9	674.1	708.9	729.8	760.1
17	Subsidies, payable	-34.0	-34.3	-32.8	-35.4	-44.2	-44.3	-55.3	-38.2
18	Property income (received)	2892.8	3107.0	3379.3	3620.3	3787.3	4302.6	4274.8	4146.6
19	Interest	1935.0	2030.8	2208.0	2390.2	2491.8	2877.1	2833.0	2643.0
20	Distributed income of corporations	882.0	997.4	1086.5	1158.1	1202.8	1297.9	1331.1	1370.5
21	Dividends	335.5	396.8	451.7	472.2	465.8	509.9	498.5	509.1

22	Withdrawals from income of quasi-corporations	546.5	600.6	634.8	685.9	737.0	788.0	832.6	861.4
23	Reinvested earnings on foreign direct investment	68.8	70.3	75.5	63.6	84.1	116.2	97.3	121.0
24	Rents	7.0	8.6	9.3	8.4	8.6	11.4	13.5	12.1
25	Less uses of property income (paid)	2852.9	3067.8	3342.0	3594.4	3748.4	4259.2	4234.7	4119.9
26	Interest	1987.8	2093.5	2281.7	2467.3	2574.3	2979.3	2954.2	2769.6
27	Distributed income of corporations	849.4	957.0	1035.9	1115.7	1161.1	1268.5	1295.9	1331.3
28	Dividends	302.9	356.4	401.1	429.8	424.1	480.4	463.3	469.8
29	Withdrawals from income of quasi-corporations	546.5	600.6	634.8	685.9	737.0	788.1	832.6	861.5
30	Reinvested earnings on foreign direct investment	8.7	8.7	15.2	3.0	4.4	0	−28.9	6.9
31	Rents	7.0	8.6	9.2	8.4	8.6	11.4	13.5	12.1
32	*Net national Income/Balance of primary incomes, net*	6454.0	6840.0	7292.2	7752.9	8236.5	8795.1	8981.1	9290.8
33	Plus current taxes on income, wealth, etc. (received)	959.0	1060.9	1168.5	1271.9	1362.2	1498.0	1442.8	1246.1
34	Less current taxes on income, wealth, etc. (paid)	962.7	1063.8	1172.4	1275.3	1366.1	1500.8	1444.8	1248.1
35	Plus social benefits (received)	1391.2	1457.4	1519.0	1576.8	1649.4	1744.3	1871.2	1999.7
36	Less social contributions (paid)	1393.1	1459.5	1521.1	1579.2	1651.8	1746.9	1873.8	2002.6
37	Plus other current transfers (received)	262.2	280.1	285.9	314.3	347.6	383.5	428.1	452.6
38	Less other current transfers (paid)	292.1	314.1	321.6	357.4	388.4	434.1	470.5	507.2
39	*Equals disposable income, net*	6418.5	6800.9	7250.6	7703.9	8189.2	8739.1	8934.1	9231.5
40	Less final consumption expenditures	6112.4	6427.9	6764.0	7135.5	7616.5	8156.5	8543.2	8980.7
41	*Equals net saving*	306.1	373.0	486.6	568.5	572.7	582.7	390.9	250.8

Memo:

42	GDP (row 1)	7296.4	7723.1	8233.6	8761.7	9304.2	9944.1	10213.0	10558.0
43	Plus statistical discrepancy (NIPA)	101.2	93.7	70.6	−14.7	−35.7	−127.2	−112.3	−77.0
44	Equals GDP (NIPA, expenditure approach)	7397.6	7816.8	8304.3	8747.0	9268.5	9817.0	10100.8	10480.9

Table 11.4   Selected aggregates for total economy and sectors (billions of dollars)

Row No.		1995	1996	1997	1998	1999	2000	2001	2002
1	*Gross domestic product (GDP)/gross value added*	7296.4	7723.1	8233.6	8761.7	9304.2	9944.1	10213.0	10558.0
2	Households and nonprofit institutions serving households	817.7	854.5	898.1	952.1	1014.8	1083.3	1155.8	1229.3
3	Nonfinancial noncorporate business	1052.8	1120.5	1184.8	1284.8	1372.4	1475.7	1569.5	1629.3
4	Nonfinancial corporate business	3879.5	4109.5	4401.8	4655.0	4950.8	5272.2	5299.3	5410.6
5	Financial business	541.0	601.9	679.2	764.3	813.8	899.8	917.7	949.0
6	Federal government	338.7	343.7	349.3	352.9	361.9	378.7	386.9	408.9
7	State and local government	666.7	693.0	720.4	752.6	790.5	834.4	883.8	930.9
8	*Net saving*	306.1	373.0	486.6	568.5	572.7	582.7	390.9	250.8
9	Households and nonprofit institutions serving households	267.2	231.9	215.5	275.9	163.6	168.3	127.1	183.1
10	Nonfinancial corporate business	186.5	226.8	248.7	191.3	210.7	155.2	118.9	197.7
11	Financial business	37.4	30.3	39.1	10.5	44.4	19.7	77.1	113.2
12	Federal government	-197.0	-141.8	-55.8	38.8	103.6	189.5	50.5	-240.0
13	State and local government	12.0	25.8	39.1	52.0	50.4	50.0	17.3	-3.2
	Net capital transfers								
14	Households and nonprofit institutions serving households	-20.7	-23.7	-27.8	-33.1	-37.4	-36.5	-36.7	-34.2
15	Federal government	-12.8	-10.7	-8.5	-3.6	-7.4	-8.1	-12.9	-18.7
16	State and local government	32.4	33.9	35.3	36.0	39.9	43.7	48.5	51.7
17	*Gross fixed capital formation*	1345.6	1454.4	1570.0	1700.7	1845.6	1983.5	1960.3	1921.0
18	Households and nonprofit institutions serving households	292.1	320.3	345.0	388.2	418.5	440.4	467.8	495.0
19	Nonfinancial noncorporate business	135.0	141.5	122.8	151.6	199.5	225.1	205.7	195.4
20	Nonfinancial corporate business	597.5	635.4	684.6	709.7	800.5	882.1	847.0	771.2
21	Financial business	88.2	112.2	165.5	188.9	140.2	131.4	122.9	122.2
22	Federal government	78.7	81.1	73.2	75.8	80.8	79.5	81.2	88.7
23	State and local government	154.0	163.8	178.9	186.5	206.1	225.1	235.8	248.4

24 *Consumption of fixed capital*	878.4	918.0	974.4	1030.1	1101.3	1187.9	1266.9	1288.6
25 Households and nonprofit institutions serving households	113.2	118.2	125.1	132.9	144.5	154.8	167.4	175.2
26 Nonfinancial noncorporate business	111.2	114.8	119.1	126.5	134.6	142.1	148.0	150.9
27 Nonfinancial corporate business	415.0	436.5	467.1	493.3	523.9	567.9	610.5	618.2
28 Financial business	74.0	79.3	89.0	98.4	111.4	126.1	135.1	133.5
29 Federal government	81.9	82.0	82.5	82.8	84.8	87.2	88.2	89.1
30 State and local government	83.1	87.2	91.6	96.2	102.1	109.8	117.7	121.7
31 *Change in inventories*	31.1	30.8	72.0	70.8	66.9	56.5	−36.1	5.4
32 Nonfinancial noncorporate business	−9.0	9.7	6.7	4.8	0.8	1.6	−1.7	−2.9
33 Nonfinancial corporate business	40.1	21.0	65.3	65.9	66.1	54.9	−34.4	8.3
34 *Net lending/borrowing*	−193.0	−194.8	−181.9	−173.5	−243.1	−270.2	−267.5	−388.4
35 Households and nonprofit institutions serving households	67.7	6.2	−32.3	−12.3	−147.7	−153.6	−209.9	−171.0
36 Nonfinancial noncorporate business	−14.8	−36.5	−10.3	−29.9	−65.7	−84.6	−56.0	−41.5
37 Nonfinancial corporate business	−36.7	8.8	−36.0	−89.4	−124.3	−205.5	−75.3	45.2
38 Financial business	23.2	−2.6	−37.4	−80.0	15.6	14.4	89.3	124.5
39 Federal government	−199.3	−147.8	−47.3	47.9	101.3	189.3	45.4	−258.7
40 State and local government	−33.0	−22.9	−18.8	−9.9	−22.3	−30.3	−61.0	−86.9
Memo:								
41 Statistical discrepancy (NIPA)	101.2	93.7	70.6	−14.7	−35.7	−127.2	−112.3	−77.0
42 Rest of the world	92.1	101.0	111.2	188.1	278.8	397.4	379.6	465.4
Total other volume changes								
43 Households and nonprofit institutions serving households	113.4	307.1	186.9	301.9	248.1	52.0	381.6	36.0
44 Nonfinancial noncorporate business	19.7	−21.1	−64.9	−76.6	−72.5	−26.9	−21.5	−36.0
45 Nonfinancial corporate business	177.3	125.5	128.0	438.5	491.4	651.4	26.4	7.3
46 Financial business	49.8	−7.3	21.7	−4.3	−48.7	−156.5	−104.3	−205.3
47 Federal government	29.8	−48.2	−11.6	−28.7	46.0	36.2	−4.5	−29.2
48 State and local government	29.6	15.5	−44.0	45.1	22.6	22.0	33.1	25.2
49 Rest of the world	−60.0	86.9	−56.8	−202.2	−264.0	238.9	50.9	−39.9

(continued)

Table 11.4 (continued)

Row No.	1995	1996	1997	1998	1999	2000	2001	2002
Holding gains/losses								
50 Households and nonprofit institutions serving households	2501.9	2040.3	3405.7	2961.3	4577.7	-458.7	-1245.5	-1839.7
51 Nonfinancial noncorporate business	173.3	196.6	314.2	325.0	280.1	395.7	113.7	226.2
52 Nonfinancial corporate business	-1547.9	-1164.0	-1846.6	-1674.3	-3513.9	2823.8	1614.3	2879.4
53 Financial business	-267.3	-239.9	-584.6	-21.4	395.1	-509.6	322.0	464.1
54 Federal government	46.0	32.7	39.1	28.3	43.2	40.3	32.4	29.4
55 State and local government	101.5	86.5	116.5	100.1	141.6	176.8	79.1	76.9
56 Rest of the world	74.7	-111.5	80.7	105.3	-295.1	-54.9	119.4	47.9
Change in net worth								
57 Households and nonprofit institutions serving households	2861.9	2555.8	3780.2	3506.2	4952.0	-274.7	-773.4	-1654.8
58 Nonfinancial noncorporate business	193.0	175.5	249.4	248.4	207.6	368.7	92.2	190.2
59 Nonfinancial corporate business	-1184.1	-811.7	-1469.9	-1044.5	-2811.7	3630.4	1759.6	3084.4
60 Financial business	-180.2	-216.9	-523.8	-15.2	390.9	-646.4	294.7	372.0
61 Federal government	-133.9	-168.0	-36.6	34.9	185.5	257.8	65.6	-258.6
62 State and local government	175.5	161.7	146.9	233.2	254.6	292.5	178.0	150.5

macroeconomic aggregates (such as GDP, net saving, gross fixed capital formation) are distributed among the sectors in draft SNA-USA.

11.3.2   Households and Nonprofit Organizations Serving Households Sector (table 11.5)

Production in the household sector (table 11.5, line 1) and net domestic product (line 3) are measured largely by compensation paid (line 4) and net operating surplus in draft SNA-USA (line 8). In the context of the household sector, the operating surplus is that part of GDP associated with owner-occupied housing. It also includes net interest on fixed assets used by NPISHs. In both cases, the operating surplus is net of taxes on production and imports less subsidies (line 7).

While output of the sector is relatively small, it receives the bulk of net national income (line 9) in the form of employee compensation (line 11) and property income (line 14), including "withdrawals from income of quasi-corporations" (line 18), which is the sum of proprietors' income and rental income of tenant-occupied housing in the NIPAs.

In draft SNA-USA, household-sector disposable income (line 26) is slightly different from "disposable personal income" in the NIPAs. In draft SNA-USA, interest received (line 15) and interest paid (line 19) are part of the derivation of net national income for the sector. In addition, current transfers paid (line 25) are subtracted from net national income. In the NIPAs, disposable personal income includes interest paid and other current transfers paid.

Net saving (line 28) in draft SNA-USA differs from that in the NIPAs by the amount of wage accruals less disbursements, which are included in compensation received by the household sector in draft SNA-USA. In addition, in draft SNA-USA, net saving is calculated as disposable income (line 26) less sector consumption expenditures (line 27), instead of the more comprehensive personal outlays concept in the NIPAs. When calculating the household sector saving rate, the smaller denominator in draft SNA-USA and difference in the level of net saving results in a slightly higher level for the rate (fig. 11.1, panel A).

The capital account for the household sector is straightforward. Net saving is reduced by capital transfers (net; line 31). For this sector, such transfers are negative, on net, reflecting estate and gift taxes paid to the government and net migrants' transfers received by the rest of the world.

Importantly, net capital formation (line 32) excludes consumer durable goods purchases, which are a component of consumption expenditures (line 27). The accounting treatment of consumer durable goods outlays in the current and capital account is consistent with SNA93 (and NIPA).[14] However, because in draft SNA-USA we chose to show the value of the

---

14. See also Fraumeni and Okubo (2001).

Table 11.5   Households and nonprofit institutions serving households (billions of dollars)

Row No.		1995	1996	1997	1998	1999	2000	2001	2002
	Current account								
1	*Gross domestic product (GDP)/Gross value added*	817.7	854.5	898.1	952.1	1014.8	1083.3	1155.8	1229.3
2	*Less consumption of fixed capital*	113.2	118.2	125.1	132.9	144.5	154.8	167.4	175.2
3	*Equals net domestic product/Net value added*	704.5	736.3	773.0	819.2	870.3	928.5	988.4	1054.1
4	Compensation paid by households and NPISHs	320.3	333.7	349.8	374.3	394.2	421.4	443.4	474.6
5	Wages and salaries	276.3	289.9	306.1	327.2	344.0	367.4	387.0	412.9
6	Employers' social contributions	44.0	43.8	43.8	47.2	50.2	54.0	56.5	61.7
7	Taxes on production and imports less subsidies	83.7	87.8	92.4	95.8	100.6	105.6	112.0	121.2
8	Operating surplus, net	300.5	314.8	330.8	349.0	375.5	401.6	433.0	458.3
9	*Net national income/Balance of primary incomes, net*	5692.6	6003.3	6388.7	6894.7	7267.2	7844.1	8037.2	8173.8
10	Operating surplus, net	300.5	314.8	330.8	349.0	375.5	401.6	433.0	458.3
11	Compensation of employees (received)	4193.3	4390.5	4661.7	5019.4	5357.1	5782.7	5940.4	6019.1
12	Wages and salaries	3435.7	3623.2	3874.7	4182.7	4471.4	4829.2	4942.9	4974.6
13	Employers' social contributions	757.7	767.3	787.0	836.7	885.7	953.4	997.6	1044.5
14	Property income (received)	1563.9	1690.8	1817.6	1970.1	2002.3	2176.2	2208.7	2241.3
15	Interest	764.2	794.0	849.8	934.3	929.7	1012.1	1004.9	983.7
16	Distributed income of corporations	799.7	896.8	967.8	1035.8	1072.6	1164.1	1203.8	1257.6
17	Dividends	253.2	296.2	333.0	349.9	335.6	376.1	371.2	396.2
18	Withdrawals from income of quasi-corporations	546.5	600.6	634.8	685.9	737.0	788.0	832.6	861.4
19	Less uses of property income (interest paid)	365.1	392.8	421.4	443.8	467.7	516.4	544.9	544.9
20	*Net national income/Balance of primary incomes, net*	5692.6	6003.3	6388.7	6894.7	7267.2	7844.1	8037.2	8173.8
21	*Less current taxes on income, wealth, etc. (paid)*	744.1	832.1	926.3	1027.0	1107.5	1235.7	1243.7	1053.1
22	Plus social benefits (received)	858.4	902.1	931.8	952.6	988.0	1041.6	1142.6	1249.5
23	Less social contributions (paid)	532.8	555.2	587.2	624.2	661.4	702.7	728.5	750.3
24	Plus other current transfers (received)	19.0	22.9	19.4	26.0	34.1	42.4	49.9	42.6
25	Less other current transfers (paid)	50.1	52.3	63.5	66.7	74.3	82.0	85.0	94.1

26 *Equals disposable income, net*	5243.0	5488.7	5762.9	6155.4	6446.1	6907.7	7172.5	7568.4
27 Less final consumption expenditures	4975.8	5256.8	5547.4	5879.5	6282.5	6739.4	7045.4	7385.3
28 *Equals net saving*	267.2	231.9	215.5	275.9	163.6	168.3	127.1	183.1
Capital account								
29 *Net saving and capital transfers*	246.6	208.3	187.6	243.0	126.3	132.0	90.5	148.9
30 Net saving	267.2	231.9	215.5	275.9	163.6	168.3	127.1	183.1
31 Capital transfers received (net)	-20.7	-23.7	-27.8	-33.1	-37.4	-36.5	-36.7	-34.2
32 *Capital formation, net*	178.9	202.1	219.9	255.3	274.0	285.6	300.4	319.8
33 Gross fixed capital formation, excluding consumer durables	292.1	320.3	345.0	388.2	418.5	440.4	467.8	495.0
34 Residential	254.8	280.8	293.2	329.9	359.8	377.3	401.6	429.8
35 Nonresidential (nonprofit organizations)	37.3	39.5	51.8	58.3	58.7	63.1	66.2	65.3
36 Less consumption of fixed capital	113.2	118.2	125.1	132.9	144.5	154.8	167.4	175.2
37 *Net lending or borrowing, capital account (rows 29–32)*	67.7	6.2	-32.3	-12.3	-147.7	-153.6	-209.9	-171.0
Financial account								
38 *Net lending or borrowing, capital account (row 37)*	67.7	6.2	-32.3	-12.3	-147.7	-153.6	-209.9	-171.0
39 *Net acquisition of financial assets*	455.9	507.6	383.9	601.2	415.5	305.7	589.4	419.3
40 *Currency and deposits*	90.4	91.2	105.7	144.6	38.9	188.3	342.9	281.1
41 Currency and transferable deposits	-40.8	-72.9	-33.7	-16.2	-75.4	-120.5	93.7	-18.2
42 Other deposits	131.2	164.1	139.4	160.9	114.3	308.7	249.2	299.3
43 Foreign deposits	4.6	12.4	6.5	0.1	5.2	20.0	-5.0	10.7
44 Time and savings deposits	126.6	151.7	132.9	160.7	109.1	288.8	254.2	288.7
45 *Securities other than shares*	30.3	127.4	-43.3	95.6	138.5	-98.7	-138.3	-71.3
46 Open market paper	2.0	4.1	1.3	3.0	4.7	2.4	-33.9	5.6
47 U.S. savings bonds	5.1	2.0	-0.5	0.1	-0.2	-1.7	5.6	4.5
48 Treasury securities	-30.0	-14.2	-150.2	-40.9	29.5	-170.5	-88.9	-71.2
49 Agency- and GSE-backed securities	27.3	100.8	52.7	39.8	114.0	79.1	-57.6	-143.9
50 Municipal securities	-58.9	-35.3	23.5	5.0	34.4	9.2	47.7	108.0
51 Corporate and foreign bonds	84.8	70.0	30.0	88.5	-44.0	-17.4	-11.2	25.7

(continued)

Table 11.5 (continued)

Row No.		1995	1996	1997	1998	1999	2000	2001	2002
52	*Loans*	11.1	27.9	44.4	58.3	54.8	99.8	50.2	-31.1
53	Short-term (security credit)	18.6	35.3	52.6	61.2	47.2	88.6	41.9	-41.6
54	Long-term (mortgages)	-7.5	-7.4	-8.2	-3.0	7.6	11.3	8.3	10.5
55	*Shares and other equity*	103.7	53.9	4.8	17.3	-4.6	-116.1	47.8	-54.8
56	Corporate equities	-101.2	-187.1	-240.1	-321.8	-110.7	-476.7	-264.4	-112.4
57	Mutual fund shares	87.4	195.2	228.5	278.5	65.8	217.5	186.5	154.8
58	Money market mutual fund shares	101.4	58.3	75.9	139.5	119.6	152.7	150.6	-41.6
59	Equity in noncorporate business	16.0	-12.5	-59.4	-78.8	-79.3	-9.6	-24.9	-55.6
60	*Insurance technical reserves*	221.2	203.3	273.6	276.9	190.5	231.2	279.0	298.1
61	Net equity in life insurance and pension funds	204.5	192.8	261.0	264.9	178.0	224.7	260.5	269.4
62	Net equity in life insurance reserves	45.8	44.5	59.3	48.0	50.8	50.2	77.2	60.1
63	Net equity in pension fund reserves	158.7	148.3	201.7	216.9	127.3	174.5	183.4	209.3
64	Prepayments of premiums and reserves against claims	16.7	10.6	12.7	12.1	12.4	6.5	18.5	28.7
65	Net equity in reserves of other insurance companies	8.7	2.7	2.0	1.8	1.1	-0.3	11.9	18.5
66	Net equity in other life insurance company reserves	8.0	7.8	10.7	10.3	11.4	6.9	6.5	10.2
67	*Other accounts receivable (miscellaneous assets)*	-0.9	3.9	-1.4	8.4	-2.5	1.2	7.7	-2.6
68	*Net incurrence of liabilities*	337.4	357.1	350.5	465.2	571.3	574.9	599.1	700.0
69	*Securities other than shares (municipal)*	0.7	6.6	10.0	12.0	10.4	5.8	13.8	12.9
70	*Loans*	328.1	341.7	331.3	445.9	554.7	565.2	581.7	679.2
71	Short-term	180.0	125.8	108.6	125.8	175.0	181.2	83.0	30.2
72	Consumer credit	147.0	103.6	62.1	96.8	112.1	165.2	137.7	81.4
73	Bank loans, nec	17.4	0.5	8.0	7.7	-6.9	6.8	-16.5	-3.1
74	Other loans and advances	12.0	5.8	1.7	-0.3	-5.4	2.0	0.6	0.1
75	Security credit	3.5	15.8	36.8	21.6	75.2	7.2	-38.8	-48.2
76	Long-term (mortgages)	148.1	215.8	222.7	320.1	379.7	383.9	498.7	649.0

77 *Insurance technical reserves (unpaid premiums)*	0.7	0.8	0.3	-1.4	2.1	0.1	-0.4	0.9
78 *Other accounts payable (trade debt)*	7.9	8.0	8.9	8.7	4.1	3.8	4.0	7.0

Memo:

79 Net lending or borrowing, financial account (rows 39–68)	118.5	150.5	33.4	136.0	-155.8	-269.2	-9.7	-280.6

Other changes in volume account

80 Total other volume changes	113.4	307.1	186.9	301.9	248.1	52.0	381.6	36.0
81 Net investment in consumer durable goods	96.0	111.2	129.3	161.0	197.0	205.9	193.5	200.3
82 Other volume changes	-33.4	51.5	-8.1	-7.3	59.1	-38.3	-12.1	-54.6
83 Less statistical discrepancy (rows 37–[39–68])[a]	-50.9	-144.4	-65.6	-148.2	8.1	115.6	-200.2	109.7

Revaluation account

84 *Nonfinancial assets*	329.7	159.2	313.1	586.7	600.5	814.6	734.4	903.0
85 Real estate	325.8	174.4	350.1	627.6	645.6	841.2	799.2	978.6
86 Consumer durable goods	4.3	-14.5	-35.5	-39.2	-44.5	-26.1	-64.1	-74.6
87 Equipment and software	-0.4	-0.8	-1.5	-1.7	-0.6	-0.5	-0.8	-0.9
88 *Financial assets*	2172.2	1881.2	3092.6	2374.6	3977.2	-1273.4	-1979.9	-2742.7
89 Shares and other equity	1695.0	1507.1	2547.8	1876.5	3319.6	-1045.4	-1503.6	-2081.8
90 Corporate equities	1356.4	1080.2	1960.6	1327.9	2438.3	-1148.1	-1255.8	-1843.8
91 Mutual fund shares	136.9	176.5	236.6	217.8	569.2	-295.3	-380.8	-483.9
92 Equity in noncorporate business	201.7	250.5	348.9	330.8	312.0	398.0	132.9	246.0
93 Insurance technical reserves	477.2	374.0	544.8	498.1	657.6	-228.0	-476.3	-660.9
94 Changes in net worth due to nominal holding gains/losses	2501.9	2040.3	3405.7	2961.3	4577.7	-458.7	-1245.5	-1839.7

Changes in balance sheet account

95 *Change in net worth (rows 32 + 37 + 80 + 94)*	2861.9	2555.8	3780.2	3506.2	4952.0	-274.7	-773.4	-1654.8

Balance Sheet Account (end of period)

96 *Total assets*	32618.1	35531.0	39661.9	43633.3	49157.1	49468.3	49293.9	48339.1
97 *Nonfinancial assets*	11048.3	11512.8	12171.1	13173.6	14243.8	15559.3	16789.0	18201.6
98 Real estate	8687.8	9053.5	9613.5	10488.6	11399.9	12529.0	13624.4	14907.8
99 Consumer durable goods	2296.0	2392.8	2486.6	2608.3	2760.9	2940.7	3070.1	3195.7
100 Equipment and software	64.6	66.6	71.0	76.7	83.0	89.5	94.5	98.0

(continued)

Table 11.5 (continued)

Row No.	1995	1996	1997	1998	1999	2000	2001	2002
101 *Financial assets*	21569.8	24018.1	27490.9	30459.7	34913.3	33909.0	32505.0	30137.5
102 *Currency and deposits*	2859.0	2949.9	3050.8	3196.5	3235.3	3423.6	3766.5	4047.6
103 Currency and transferable deposits	544.3	471.4	437.7	421.5	346.0	225.5	319.2	301.0
104 Other deposits	2314.7	2478.5	2613.1	2775.0	2889.3	3198.1	3447.3	3746.6
105 Foreign deposits	23.4	35.5	37.2	38.3	43.5	63.5	58.5	69.2
106 Time and savings deposits	2291.3	2443.1	2575.9	2736.7	2845.8	3134.6	3388.8	3677.4
107 *Securities other than shares*	2051.4	2238.7	2196.5	2384.1	2483.5	2348.2	2196.3	2080.9
108 Open market paper	71.7	75.8	77.1	80.2	84.9	87.3	53.4	59.0
109 U.S. savings bonds	185.0	187.0	186.5	186.6	186.4	184.8	190.3	194.9
110 Treasury securities	626.0	673.7	570.0	528.5	629.6	426.1	327.6	221.2
111 Agency- and GSE-backed securities	116.7	215.3	260.4	292.8	397.5	468.9	407.5	254.6
112 Municipal securities	539.7	504.5	511.1	516.1	550.5	559.8	607.5	715.5
113 Corporate and foreign bonds	512.3	582.3	591.4	679.9	634.6	621.3	610.0	635.7
114 *Loans*	247.2	275.1	319.5	377.8	432.6	532.4	582.6	551.5
115 Short-term (security credit)	127.6	162.9	215.5	276.7	323.9	412.4	454.3	412.7
116 Long-term (mortgages)	119.6	112.3	104.1	101.1	108.7	120.0	128.3	138.8
117 *Shares and other equity*	10120.7	11681.7	14234.3	16128.1	19443.1	18281.7	16825.8	14689.2
118 Corporate equities	4640.3	5533.3	7253.8	8259.8	10587.5	8962.7	7442.6	5486.2
119 Mutual fund shares	1406.6	1778.3	2243.4	2739.7	3374.7	3296.9	3102.7	2773.6
120 Money market mutual fund shares	483.8	542.1	619.6	759.1	878.7	1031.4	1181.9	1140.3
121 Equity in noncorporate business	3590.0	3828.0	4117.5	4369.4	4602.2	4990.6	5098.7	5289.0
122 *Insurance technical reserves*	6279.4	6856.7	7675.2	8450.2	9298.3	9301.5	9104.2	8741.5
123 Net equity in life insurance and pension funds	5963.1	6529.9	7335.7	8098.7	8933.9	8930.6	8714.9	8323.5
124 Net equity in life insurance reserves	566.2	610.6	665.0	718.3	783.9	819.1	880.0	920.9

125 Net equity in pension fund reserves	5396.9	5919.3	6670.7	7380.4	8150.1	8111.5	7834.9	7402.5
126 Prepayments of premiums and reserves against claims	316.3	326.8	339.5	351.5	364.3	370.9	389.4	418.1
127 Net equity in reserves of other insurance companies	194.7	197.5	199.5	201.3	202.3	202.0	214.0	232.4
128 Net equity in other life insurance company reserves	121.5	129.3	140.0	150.3	162.0	168.9	175.4	185.6
129 *Other accounts receivable (miscellaneous assets)*	12.1	16.0	14.6	23.0	20.5	21.7	29.4	26.8
130 *Total liabilities and net worth*	32618.1	35531.0	39661.9	43633.3	49157.1	49468.3	49293.9	48339.1
131 *Liabilities*	5072.8	5429.9	5780.6	6245.8	6817.5	7403.5	8002.6	8702.6
132 *Securities other than shares (municipals)*	98.3	104.9	114.9	126.9	137.3	143.0	156.9	169.8
133 *Loans*	4855.9	5197.6	5529.1	5975.0	6529.9	7106.2	7687.9	8367.1
134 Short-term	1419.7	1545.5	1654.6	1780.4	1955.7	2148.1	2231.1	2261.3
135 Consumer credit	1168.0	1271.7	1333.8	1430.6	1542.7	1719.0	1856.7	1938.1
136 Bank loans, nec	57.4	58.0	66.5	74.2	67.3	74.1	57.6	54.6
137 Other loans and advances	115.7	121.5	123.2	122.9	117.8	199.8	120.4	120.5
138 Security credit	78.6	94.4	131.2	152.8	227.9	235.1	196.4	148.2
139 Long-term (mortgages)	3436.2	3652.0	3874.5	4194.5	4574.2	4958.1	5456.8	6105.8
140 *Insurance technical reserves (unpaid premiums)*	17.5	18.3	18.6	17.2	19.4	19.6	19.1	20.0
141 *Other accounts payable (trade debt)*	101.1	109.1	118.0	126.8	130.9	134.7	138.7	145.7
142 *Net worth*	27545.3	30101.1	33881.3	37387.5	42339.5	42064.8	41291.3	39636.5

[a]The discrepancy is the difference between net lending or borrowing derived in the capital account and the same concept derived in the financial account. The discrepancy reflects differences in source data, timing of recorded flows, and other statistical differences between the capital and financial accounts.

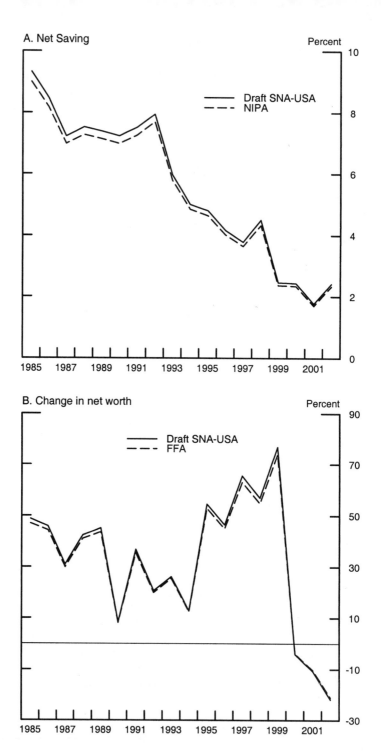

Fig. 11.1 Measures of household-sector saving and net worth as a percentage of disposable income

stock of consumer durable goods as household sector assets (as is done in the FFAs), this treatment has implications for our revaluation and balance sheet accounts (discussed below).

The difference between saving and capital formation is net lending or borrowing (line 37), the amount the sector supplies to financial markets for other sectors or requires from the financial markets to meet its own needs. The figures in table 11.5 indicate the household sector has been a net borrower since 1997.

The details of how the sector meets its borrowing requirement is revealed in the financial account, which is analogous to table F.100 in the FFAs. In the financial account, accounting identities require net lending/net borrowing to equal the net acquisition of financial assets (line 39) less the net incurrence of liabilities (line 68). The "net" in the financial account refers to purchases less sales of assets, and the extensions less repayment of liabilities.

Although conceptually the same, the value of household-sector net lending/net borrowing derived in the financial account (line 79) differs substantially from that in the capital account. Indeed, it is less clear from the figures in line 79 whether the sector has consistently borrowed over the past six years.

The difference between the net lending/net borrowing derived in the capital account and that derived in the financial account is defined in draft SNA-USA as the sector's statistical discrepancy (line 83). The treatment of the statistical discrepancy is problematic and has implications for the estimates of household-sector net worth.

Some nations do not show a discrepancy between the two measures of net lending/net borrowing. Rather, they force equality in some way, such as splitting the difference between the financial account and the current and capital accounts. (There is no recognition of such discrepancies in SNA93.) Our practice is to report the discrepancy as a component of the "other changes in volume" account. An indication, albeit a crude indication, of the success of our efforts to bring the accounts into better alignment in the future will be the reduction of the statistical discrepancies between the financial account and the current and capital accounts for sectors.[15] We examine the alternative values of net lending/net borrowing derived in each sector in the next section.

The remaining accumulation accounts provide additional information on how estimates of net worth of the sector are affected in the period. The account for "other changes in volume" allows for recording factors that are not defined as financial transactions or holding gains and losses in the

---

15. In the household sector, the sum of net lending/net borrowing in the financial account and net capital formation is an alternative, but conceptually equivalent, measure of saving from the FFAs.

period, such as the statistical discrepancy noted above. The revaluation account (analogous to table R.100 in the FFAs) lists changes in value of assets due to holding gains and losses.

We used the other changes in volume account to insert net investment in consumer durable goods (line 81). Our view, not reflected in SNA93, is that the value of such goods is an important household-sector asset that belongs with other tangible assets on the balance sheet account. The BEA estimates the value of the stock consistent with the expenditures in the current account, including depreciation and revaluations. The FRB uses the data to complete estimates of tangible assets in the FFA sector balance sheet statement (table B.100 in the FFAs). Draft SNA-USA retains that balance sheet treatment.

The revaluation account (lines 84 to 94) records nominal holding gains and losses for nonfinancial assets and financial assets. We have carried over the practice of estimating the gains for real estate (combined land and structures), because the agencies have found no acceptable way, on a macro-sector basis, to separate changes in the value of land from changes in the value of structures on the land.[16]

The change in net worth for the household sector is shown in line 95 at the beginning of the balance sheet account. It is the sum of net capital formation, net lending/net borrowing, other changes in volume, and nominal holding gains/losses. The change in net worth is the same as that published in the FFAs, but the components differ. The net lending/net borrowing figure used for calculation of net worth is that from the capital account, rather than the financial account. The statistical discrepancy between the financial and capital account enters into the "other changes in volume" account. The change in net worth as a percent of disposable income differs slightly from that currently published only because the denominator (disposable income) in draft SNA-USA is different (fig. 11.1, panel B).

End-of-period stocks in the household balance sheet are similar to those published in the FFAs, although the terminology for asset and liability items is consistent with international terminology, which should allow for easier comparison across countries. Instruments have been grouped as recommended in SNA93. This was also done in the financial account in draft SNA-USA.

11.3.3 Nonfinancial Noncorporate Business Sector (table 11.6)

As noted above, the nonfinancial noncorporate business sector includes partnerships and sole proprietorships (including tenant-occupied housing). Draft SNA-USA has a full set of accounts for this sector.

---

16. No attempt was made to separate nominal holding gains into neutral gains (those due to changes in the general price level) and real gains (those due to changes in the relative prices of assets), as SNA93 would dictate.

Table 11.6 Nonfinancial noncorporate business (billions of dollars)

Row No.		1995	1996	1997	1998	1999	2000	2001	2002
		Current account							
1	*Gross domestic product (GDP)/Gross value added*	1052.8	1120.5	1184.8	1284.8	1372.4	1475.7	1569.5	1629.3
2	*Less consumption of fixed capital*	111.2	114.8	119.1	126.5	134.6	142.1	148.0	150.9
3	*Equals net domestic product/Net value added*	941.6	1005.7	1065.7	1158.3	1237.8	1333.6	1421.5	1478.4
4	Compensation of employees (paid)	255.3	269.7	286.2	311.4	341.2	367.6	390.7	405.9
5	Wages and salaries	222.3	235.9	351.6	273.7	299.8	322.6	343.8	355.8
6	Employers' social contributions	33.0	33.8	34.6	37.7	41.4	45.0	46.9	50.1
7	Taxes on production and imports less subsidies	52.6	56.7	65.0	72.5	72.5	74.1	80.6	91.5
8	Operating surplus, net	633.6	679.2	714.5	774.4	824.1	891.8	950.2	980.9
9	*Net national income/Balance of primary incomes, net*	6.2	7.8	8.5	7.4	8.8	9.0	7.8	12.4
10	Operating surplus, net	633.6	679.2	714.5	774.4	824.1	891.8	950.2	980.9
11	Property income (interest received)	9.1	10.4	11.8	12.6	13.3	13.3	15.8	17.4
12	*Less* uses of property income (paid)	636.6	681.8	717.8	779.6	828.5	896.1	958.2	986.0
13	Interest	126.1	128.8	136.1	148.7	159.7	182.7	192.7	194.4
14	Withdrawals from income of quasi-corporations	510.4	553.0	581.6	630.9	668.8	713.4	765.6	791.6
15	Reinvested earnings on foreign direct investment	0.1	0	0.1	0	0	0	−0.1	0
16	Rents	0	0	0	0	0	0	0	0
17	*Net national income/Balance of primary incomes, net*	6.2	7.8	8.5	7.4	8.8	9.0	7.8	12.4
18	*Less* other current transfers (paid)	6.2	7.8	8.5	7.4	8.8	9.0	7.8	12.4
19	*Equals disposable income, net*	0	0	0	0	0	0	0	0
20	*Equals net saving*	0	0	0	0	0	0	0	0

(continued)

Table 11.6   (continued)

Row No.	1995	1996	1997	1998	1999	2000	2001	2002
	Capital account							
21 *Net saving*	0	0	0	0	0	0	0	0
22 *Capital formation, net*	14.8	36.5	10.3	29.9	65.7	84.6	56.0	41.5
23 Gross fixed capital formation	135.0	141.5	122.8	151.6	199.5	225.1	205.7	195.4
24 Nonresidential	92.4	95.2	81.0	109.9	139.4	159.0	142.3	127.4
25 Residential	42.6	46.3	41.8	41.7	60.1	66.1	63.4	68.0
26 Less consumption of fixed capital	111.2	114.8	119.1	126.5	134.6	142.1	148.0	150.9
27 Change in inventories	-0.0	9.7	6.7	4.8	0.8	1.6	-1.7	-2.9
28 *Net lending or borrowing, capital account (rows 21–22)*	-14.8	-36.5	-10.3	-29.9	-65.7	-84.6	-56.0	-41.5
	Financial account							
29 *Net lending or borrowing (row 28)*	-14.8	-36.5	-10.3	-29.9	-65.7	-84.6	-56.0	-41.5
30 *Net acquisition of financial assets*	75.6	92.8	127.7	211.4	176.8	237.4	148.2	143.5
31 *Currency and deposits*	18.0	22.8	33.2	47.2	58.4	76.7	8.3	15.4
32 Currency and transferable deposits	13.7	19.3	22.5	34.4	39.3	56.6	1.1	13.2
33 Time and savings deposits	4.3	3.5	10.7	12.7	19.1	20.1	7.1	2.2
34 *Securities other than shares*	5.9	5.3	4.2	5.4	-0.9	2.7	3.7	2.5
35 Treasury securities	5.3	4.9	3.7	5.7	-0.8	3.0	2.7	2.3
36 Municipal securities	0.6	0.4	0.5	-0.4	-0.1	-0.3	1.1	0.2
37 *Loans*	-2.1	-1.4	-1.6	7.9	-2.0	-1.4	3.3	1.2
38 Short-term (consumer credit)	0	0	0	0	0	0	0	0
39 Long-term (mortgages)	-2.1	-1.4	-1.6	7.9	-2.0	-1.4	3.3	1.2
40 *Shares and other equity*	1.9	2.2	3.7	9.7	8.1	8.7	9.6	2.4
41 Money market mutual fund shares	1.9	2.2	3.7	9.7	8.1	8.7	9.6	2.3
42 Equity in government-sponsored enterprises	-0.1	0.0	0	0.1	-0.0	-0.0	0.0	0.1

43 Insurance technical reserves (net equity in reserves of other insurance companies)	3.9	1.2	0.9	0.8	0.5	-0.2	3.9	8.2
44 Other accounts receivable	50.0	64.8	91.0	150.1	120.8	159.6	129.0	116.2
45 Trade receivables	15.3	29.5	35.1	28.2	39.4	69.6	1.8	22.8
46 Other (miscellaneous assets)	34.7	35.2	55.9	121.9	81.4	90.0	127.3	93.4
47 Net incurrence of liabilities	90.4	129.3	138.0	241.4	242.5	321.9	204.2	185.1
48 Loans	48.9	72.2	100.9	190.0	194.8	203.7	166.7	156.9
49 Short-term	19.7	31.3	50.1	39.3	54.0	59.7	38.0	16.0
50 Bank loans, nec	11.8	29.5	47.3	26.0	45.6	47.0	37.8	12.5
51 Other loans and advances	7.9	1.8	2.8	13.3	8.4	12.8	0.3	3.5
52 Long-term (mortgages)	29.2	40.9	50.8	150.7	140.8	144.0	128.7	140.9
53 Shares and other equity	14.0	-6.5	-55.6	-76.4	-70.1	-26.9	-14.2	-22.2
54 Equity in noncorporate business	14.1	-6.8	-56.1	-76.6	-70.3	-27.0	-14.3	-22.4
55 Foreign direct investment in U.S.	-0.1	0.3	0.5	0.2	0.2	0.1	0.1	0.2
56 Other accounts payable	27.6	63.6	92.7	127.8	117.7	145.1	51.7	50.4
57 Trade payables	13.4	31.8	32.4	31.5	35.1	47.5	-7.5	21.9
58 Taxes payable	0.6	2.3	4.3	4.1	8.9	11.7	4.0	8.1
59 Other (miscellaneous liabilities)	13.6	29.4	56.0	92.1	73.7	85.9	55.2	20.3
Memo:								
60 Net lending or borrowing, financial account (rows 30–47)	-14.8	-36.5	-10.3	-29.9	-65.7	-84.6	-56.0	-41.5
Other changes in volume account								
61 Total other volume changes	19.7	-21.1	-64.9	-76.6	-72.5	-26.9	-21.5	-36.0
Revaluation account								
62 Nonfinancial assets	173.3	196.6	314.2	325.0	280.1	395.7	113.7	226.2
63 Real estate	142.0	165.7	285.1	281.6	241.1	344.8	68.9	202.6
64 Residential	119.7	144.6	190.6	178.7	218.6	268.2	119.9	171.0
65 Nonresidential	22.2	21.2	94.5	102.9	22.6	76.6	-51.1	31.6

(continued)

Table 11.6   (continued)

Row No.		1995	1996	1997	1998	1999	2000	2001	2002
66	Equipment and software	30.1	30.9	30.5	45.0	37.8	49.5	46.7	22.3
67	Residential	0.2	0.9	0.2	0.5	0.3	1.1	0.8	0.3
68	Nonresidential	30.0	30.0	30.3	44.4	37.5	48.4	45.8	22.0
69	Inventories	1.2	-0.0	-1.4	-1.6	1.1	1.4	-1.8	1.3
70	*Changes in net worth due to nominal holding gains/losses*	173.3	196.6	314.2	325.0	280.1	395.7	113.7	226.2
	Changes in balance sheet account								
71	*Change in net worth (rows 22 + 28 + 61 + 70)*	193.0	175.5	249.4	248.4	207.6	368.7	92.2	190.2
	Balance sheet account (end of period)								
72	*Total assets*	4207.2	4514.8	4950.1	5504.9	6019.9	6725.9	7028.5	7416.7
73	*Nonfinancial assets*	3659.1	3871.7	4176.2	4512.2	4843.1	5303.1	5450.1	5696.9
74	Real estate	3215.0	3397.9	3674.5	3949.9	4230.5	4639.1	4751.5	4983.8
75	Residential	2361.5	2522.5	2723.5	2912.6	3157.2	3456.3	3604.1	3811.0
76	Nonresidential	853.6	875.5	951.0	1037.3	1073.3	1182.8	1147.4	1172.9
77	Equipment and software	387.8	416.3	442.3	501.0	546.7	593.8	632.0	644.8
78	Residential	37.1	39.0	39.9	41.3	42.8	45.2	47.0	48.1
79	Nonresidential	350.7	377.3	402.3	459.7	503.9	548.7	585.0	596.7
80	Inventories	56.3	57.4	59.5	61.3	65.9	70.2	66.6	68.3
81	*Financial assets*	548.1	643.2	773.8	992.7	1176.8	1422.7	1578.4	1719.8
82	*Currency and deposits*	176.2	199.0	232.0	277.4	335.1	411.6	419.3	434.2
83	Currency and transferable deposits	104.7	124.0	146.2	178.9	217.6	274.1	274.5	287.3
84	Time and savings deposits	71.5	75.0	85.7	98.5	117.5	137.6	144.7	146.9
85	*Securities other than shares*	25.8	31.2	35.4	40.8	39.9	42.6	46.3	48.9
86	Treasury securities	23.6	28.6	32.2	38.0	37.2	40.2	42.8	45.2
87	Municipal securities	2.2	2.6	3.2	2.8	2.7	2.4	3.5	3.7

88	*Loans*	21.7	20.4	18.7	26.7	24.7	23.3	26.6	27.8
89	Short-term (consumer credit)	0	0	0	0	0	0	0	0
90	Long-term (mortgages)	21.7	20.4	18.7	26.7	24.7	23.3	26.6	27.8
91	*Shares and other equity*	18.0	20.9	24.6	34.2	42.3	51.0	60.5	62.9
92	Money market mutual fund shares	17.0	19.2	22.9	32.6	40.7	49.4	59.0	61.3
93	Equity in government-sponsored enterprises	1.0	1.7	1.7	1.6	1.6	1.6	1.5	1.5
94	*Insurance technical reserves (net equity in reserves of other insurance companies)*	44.2	44.8	45.2	45.6	45.9	45.8	48.3	52.5
95	*Other accounts receivable*	262.2	326.9	417.9	568.0	688.8	848.4	977.4	1093.6
96	Trade receivables	140.3	169.8	204.9	233.1	272.6	342.1	343.9	366.7
97	Other (miscellaneous assets)	121.9	157.1	213.0	334.9	416.3	506.2	633.5	726.9
98	*Total liabilities and net worth*	4207.2	4514.8	4950.1	5504.9	6019.9	6725.9	7028.5	7416.7
99	*Liabilities*	1396.4	1528.6	1714.5	2020.9	2328.3	2665.5	2876.0	3073.9
100	*Loans*	1062.0	1130.7	1225.4	1405.3	1595.5	1788.4	1944.7	2093.0
101	Short-term	257.0	287.4	334.5	370.2	425.3	480.7	515.9	531.7
102	Bank loans, nec	164.7	193.6	237.3	262.1	308.6	352.9	390.7	404.1
103	Other loans and advances	92.3	93.9	97.2	108.1	116.7	127.8	125.3	127.6
104	Long-term (mortgages)	805.0	843.2	890.9	1035.1	1170.1	1307.6	1428.8	1561.3
105	*Shares and other equity (direct investment in U.S.)*	2.8	4.0	3.9	3.4	3.3	3.4	3.2	3.4
106	*Other accounts payable*	331.6	393.9	485.2	612.2	729.5	873.8	928.0	977.5
107	Trade payables	86.2	116.8	147.8	178.6	213.3	259.9	255.0	276.0
108	Taxes payable	33.4	35.7	39.9	44.1	53.0	64.6	68.7	76.8
109	Other (miscellaneous liabilities)	212.0	241.5	389.6	463.2	549.2	604.3	624.7	
110	*Net worth*	2810.8	2986.2	3235.6	3484.0	3691.6	4060.3	4152.5	4342.8

Income generated in the sector is paid out to the household sector as withdrawals from income of quasi-corporations (table 11.6, line 14).[17] As a result, the sector has no net saving. Nonetheless, there is capital formation and financial transactions in the noncorporate business sector. The financial account in draft SNA-USA—lines 29 through 60 in table 11.6—is analogous to table F.103 in the FFAs. The additions to net worth (line 71) result mainly from capital gains on real estate shown in the revaluation account (line 63).[18]

11.3.4   Nonfinancial Corporate Business Sector (table 11.7)

We have been able to provide a full set of accounts for the nonfinancial corporate business sector. The sector's value added (table 11.7, line 1) is more than half of total output of the economy. Consumption of fixed capital (line 2) in this sector, as with other sectors, is on an economic basis, reflecting the capital consumption adjustment to book (tax) depreciation. Similarly, in the capital account, inventory investment (line 32) reflects the NIPA valuation adjustment so that inventories are at current prices and on a consistent accounting basis.

The draft SNA-USA current account arguably offers a more comprehensive and intuitive view of flows through the sector, although the terminology is probably unfamiliar to users of NIPA tables. Measures of profits and cash flow, which are fairly prominent in the NIPAs and FFAs, are noticeably missing from SNA93 and, thus, our presentation of draft SNA-USA. Providing them likely would be a useful addition to some analysts of the U.S. economy.

The sector has no final consumption expenditures, and the SNA format shows disposable income (line 23) as net saving (line 24); net saving in this sector and the financial business sector is the same as undistributed corporate profits in the NIPAs. Again, the presentation lacks a measure of total internal funds that is used to derive the financing gap shown in the FFAs (in table F.102 of the FFAs)—a sometimes-cited measure of the impetus for corporate borrowing. Net lending/net borrowing (line 33) is nearly the same concept, but it includes undistributed profits of foreign subsidiaries, which are not in the FFA calculation of U.S. internal funds.

The statistical discrepancy resulting from the difference in net lending/ net borrowing in the capital account and in the financial account was handled the same way as for the household sector. Net saving in the capital account was used to derive changes in net worth (line 93), and the discrepancy is reported in the other changes in volume account (line 80).

The calculation and interpretation of net worth in the nonfinancial

17. Households withdraw income from both financial and nonfinancial quasi-corporations.
18. We considered a number of ways to treat household equity in nonfinancial noncorporate business, and, although the method chosen is consistent within the sequence of accounts in draft SNA-USA, it is not necessarily consistent with SNA93.

Table 11.7   Nonfinancial corporate business (billions of dollars)

Row No.		1995	1996	1997	1998	1999	2000	2001	2002
		Current account							
1	*Gross domestic product (GDP)/Gross value added*	3879.5	4109.5	4401.8	4655.0	4950.8	5272.2	5299.3	5410.6
2	*Less consumption of fixed capital*	415.0	436.5	467.1	493.3	523.8	567.8	610.5	618.2
3	*Equals net domestic product/Net value added*	3464.5	3673.0	3934.7	4161.7	4427.0	4704.3	4688.9	4792.4
4	Compensation of employees (paid)	2509.8	2630.8	2812.9	3045.6	3267.7	3544.4	3597.0	3570.1
5	Wages and salaries	2076.7	2197.0	2367.9	2567.2	2758.0	2989.8	3016.7	2971.8
6	Employers' social contributions	433.1	433.8	445.1	478.4	509.7	554.5	580.4	598.3
7	Taxes on production and imports less subsidies	356.9	369.1	385.5	398.7	416.6	443.4	440.3	464.5
8	Operating surplus, net	597.8	673.1	736.3	717.4	742.7	716.5	651.5	757.7
9	*Net national income/Balance of primary incomes, net*	357.7	417.9	449.6	385.1	426.9	373.8	303.2	388.7
10	Operating surplus, net	597.8	673.1	736.3	717.4	742.7	716.5	651.5	757.7
11	Property income (received)	295.8	331.0	367.8	349.3	384.0	453.6	413.5	398.0
12	Interest	189.9	216.7	239.5	235.9	251.3	291.3	273.0	242.9
13	Distributed income of corporations (dividends)	45.4	52.8	62.4	58.2	59.7	62.0	57.1	54.8
14	Reinvested earnings on foreign direct investment	60.5	61.5	65.9	55.2	73.0	100.3	83.4	100.3
15	Less uses of property income (paid)	535.9	586.2	654.5	681.6	699.8	796.3	761.8	767.0
16	Interest	298.0	319.9	354.2	371.3	402.9	471.5	465.3	437.7
17	Distributed income of corporations (dividends)	223.4	250.2	278.3	299.2	284.4	313.4	305.3	312.0
18	Reinvested earnings on foreign direct investment	7.5	7.5	12.8	2.7	3.9	0	−22.3	5.2
19	Rent	7.0	8.6	9.2	8.4	8.6	11.4	13.5	12.1
20	*Net national income/Balance of primary incomes, net*	357.7	417.9	449.6	385.1	426.9	373.8	303.2	388.7
21	Less current taxes on income, wealth, etc. (paid)	141.0	153.1	161.9	158.6	171.2	170.2	134.3	131.9
22	Less other current transfers (paid)	30.2	38.0	39.0	35.2	45.0	48.4	50.0	59.1
23	*Equals disposable income, net*	186.5	226.8	248.7	191.3	210.7	155.2	118.9	197.7
24	*Equals net saving*	186.5	226.8	248.7	191.3	210.7	155.2	118.9	197.7

(continued)

Table 11.7   (continued)

Row No.		1995	1996	1997	1998	1999	2000	2001	2002
	Capital account								
25	*Net saving and capital transfers*	186.5	226.6	248.7	191.1	210.8	155.2	118.8	197.7
26	Net saving	186.5	226.8	248.7	191.3	210.7	155.2	118.9	197.7
27	Capital transfers received (net)	0	0	0	0	0	0	0	0
28	*Capital formation, net*	223.2	217.8	284.7	280.5	335.1	360.7	194.1	152.5
29	Gross fixed capital formation (acq. of produced nonfinancial assets)	597.5	635.4	684.6	709.7	800.5	882.1	847.0	771.2
30	Less consumption of fixed capital	415.0	436.5	467.1	493.3	523.9	567.9	610.5	618.2
31	Acq. of nonproduced nonfinancial assets	0.6	-2.2	1.8	-1.9	-7.7	-8.5	-8.0	-8.8
32	Inventory change including inventory valuation adjustment	40.1	21.0	65.3	65.9	66.1	54.9	-34.4	8.3
33	*Net lending or borrowing, capital account (rows 25–28)*	-36.7	8.8	-36.0	-89.4	-124.3	-205.5	-75.3	45.2
	Financial account								
34	*Net lending or borrowing, capital account (row 33)*	-36.7	8.8	-36.0	-89.4	-124.3	-205.5	-75.3	45.2
35	*Net acquisition of financial assets*	426.4	454.0	272.4	569.9	969.9	1209.2	177.6	121.3
36	*Currency and deposits*	9.5	50.1	22.2	23.6	81.2	43.5	-64.2	10.4
37	Currency and transferable deposits	4.5	39.3	7.6	23.0	56.0	50.5	-49.5	9.5
38	Time and savings deposits	3.3	-0.0	19.7	-6.8	24.3	0.5	-6.2	-3.6
39	Foreign deposits	1.7	10.8	-5.1	7.4	0.9	-7.4	-8.5	4.4
40	*Securities other than shares*	-8.8	0.7	-39.8	1.1	5.0	18.8	-0.1	21.4
41	Open market paper	1.3	11.4	4.6	3.3	8.2	10.2	2.4	4.5
42	Treasury securities	6.3	-10.0	-20.2	-3.2	-4.2	-1.3	-1.6	14.8
43	Agency- and GSE-backed securities	3.5	5.1	-20.5	2.6	1.8	3.0	1.7	-1.2
44	Municipal securities	-19.9	-5.8	-3.6	-1.6	-0.7	6.9	-2.6	3.3
45	*Loans*	0.3	-0.4	27.7	-16.1	-22.0	4.7	2.5	4.1
46	Short-term (security RPs and consumer credit)	-1.3	-5.9	1.8	-3.1	4.1	2.4	-0.6	2.1
47	Long-term (mortgages)	1.6	-3.6	25.9	-13.0	-26.0	2.3	3.1	2.0

48 *Shares and other equity*	122.5	95.0	94.3	168.1	257.0	184.3	207.9	148.9
49 Mutual fund shares	4.6	8.7	-6.4	6.7	7.4	12.0	2.0	10.5
50 Money market mutual fund shares	22.9	7.7	20.2	38.6	28.4	36.5	110.5	26.9
51 U.S. direct investment abroad	90.3	76.8	84.3	129.2	194.4	128.4	97.0	117.0
52 Equity in government-sponsored enterprises	0	0	0	0	0	0	0	0
53 Investment in finance company subsidiaries	4.6	1.8	-3.7	-6.4	26.8	7.4	-1.7	-5.5
54 *Insurance technical reserves (net equity in reserves of other insurance companies)*	8.2	2.6	1.9	1.7	1.0	-0.3	10.3	17.4
55 *Other accounts receivable*	294.7	315.2	166.0	391.5	647.6	958.2	21.3	-80.8
56 Trade receivables	78.0	88.1	93.5	85.0	203.4	283.0	-129.4	-34.4
57 Other (miscellaneous assets)	216.7	227.1	72.5	306.5	444.1	675.2	150.7	-46.4
58 *Net incurrence of liabilities*	390.8	398.5	283.5	616.0	987.6	1237.4	95.2	107.0
59 *Securities other than shares*	112.3	118.4	168.4	265.3	264.1	212.0	263.7	71.2
60 Open market paper	18.1	-0.9	13.7	24.4	37.4	48.1	-88.3	-64.2
61 Municipal securities	3.1	3.1	4.2	5.8	5.1	1.4	3.5	3.1
62 Corporate bonds	91.1	116.3	150.5	235.2	221.7	162.6	348.5	132.3
63 *Loans*	114.8	64.4	123.4	127.1	108.4	145.2	-36.4	-30.2
64 Short-term	106.8	54.6	90.9	130.5	67.6	114.0	-95.5	-80.5
65 Bank loans, nec	74.5	40.4	51.1	76.2	44.1	48.0	-103.3	-96.5
66 Other loans and advances	32.3	14.2	39.8	54.3	23.4	65.9	7.8	16.0
67 Long-term (mortgages)	8.0	9.8	32.5	-3.3	40.8	31.2	59.0	50.2
68 *Shares and other equity*	-4.8	24.3	22.8	-71.1	136.7	62.9	24.0	-18.9
69 Corporate equities	-58.3	-47.3	-77.4	-215.5	-110.4	-118.2	-47.4	-41.6
70 Direct investment in U.S.	53.6	71.7	100.2	144.4	247.0	181.1	71.4	22.7
71 *Insurance technical reserves (contributions payable)*	4.1	4.1	7.1	21.4	-7.6	1.2	1.3	1.3
72 *Other accounts payable*	164.4	187.3	-38.3	273.3	486.1	816.0	-157.3	83.7
73 Trade payables	81.0	49.5	65.1	57.6	178.5	313.3	-103.7	-15.8
74 Other	83.5	137.8	-103.3	215.7	307.6	502.8	-53.6	99.5

(continued)

Table 11.7 (continued)

Row No.		1995	1996	1997	1998	1999	2000	2001	2002
75	Taxes payable	-0.0	9.6	9.3	4.8	7.0	7.0	3.1	11.9
76	Miscellaneous liabilities	83.5	128.3	-112.7	210.8	300.6	495.8	-56.6	87.6
Memo:									
77	Net lending or borrowing, financial account (rows 35–58)	35.5	55.5	-11.1	-46.1	-17.7	-28.2	82.4	14.4
Other changes in volume account									
78	*Total other volume changes*	177.3	125.5	128.0	438.5	491.4	651.4	26.4	7.3
79	Other volume changes	86.8	81.8	117.2	415.4	385.8	460.0	-122.2	35.9
80	Less statistical discrepancy (rows 33–[35–38])[a]	-72.3	-46.7	-24.9	-43.3	-106.6	-177.3	-157.8	30.0
81	Less inventory valuation adjustment	-18.3	3.1	14.1	20.2	0.9	-14.1	9.1	-2.2
Revaluation account									
82	*Nonfinancial assets*	110.2	74.4	308.6	355.9	106.4	315.9	-227.1	136.6
83	Real estate	82.4	77.9	348.9	393.2	93.3	306.2	-186.7	134.4
84	Equipment and software	23.4	-6.5	-28.0	-27.2	-8.7	-2.8	-14.9	-19.8
85	Inventories	4.4	2.9	-12.3	-10.2	21.8	12.5	-25.5	22.0
86	*Financial assets*	12.7	19.6	0.7	-5.0	13.9	-50.8	-62.7	-15.0
87	Mutual fund shares	10.0	8.6	18.4	16.3	21.6	-15.0	-15.0	-24.5
88	Direct investment abroad	2.8	11.0	-17.6	-21.3	-7.8	-35.7	-47.8	9.5
89	*Liabilities*	1670.9	1258.0	2155.9	2025.2	3634.1	-2558.7	-1904.1	-2757.9
90	Corporate equity	1675.6	1272.4	2203.9	2027.7	3688.2	-2358.6	-1835.2	-2847.7
91	Direct investment in U.S.	-4.7	-14.5	-48.0	-2.4	-54.1	-200.1	-68.9	89.8
92	*Changes in net worth due to nominal holding gains/losses*	-1547.9	-1164.0	-1846.6	-1674.3	-3513.9	2823.8	1614.3	2879.4
Changes in balance sheet account									
93	*Change in net worth (rows 28 + 33 + 78 + 92)*	-1184.1	-811.7	-1469.9	-1044.5	-2811.7	3630.4	1759.6	3084.4

Balance sheet account (end of period)

94 *Total assets*	11580.7	12363.1	13269.9	14866.4	16582.1	18939.8	19014.9	19345.5
95 *Nonfinancial assets*	6622.2	6905.4	7461.2	8050.2	8488.3	9167.3	9116.0	9412.4
96 Real estate	3125.1	3265.2	3665.8	4108.9	4283.8	4671.2	4573.0	4770.5
97 Equipment and software	2376.0	2496.0	2614.1	2722.7	2891.2	3092.8	3200.7	3258.3
98 Inventories	1069.8	1090.7	1129.6	1165.2	1252.1	1333.6	1264.5	1297.0
99 Nonproduced nonfinancial assets	51.3	53.5	51.6	53.5	61.2	69.7	77.7	86.5
100 *Financial assets*	4958.5	5457.7	5808.7	6816.1	8093.8	9772.5	9898.9	9933.1
101 *Currency and deposits*	322.2	372.2	394.4	418.1	499.3	542.8	478.6	488.9
102 Currency and transferable deposits	205.1	244.3	251.9	275.0	331.0	381.4	331.9	341.4
103 Time and savings deposits	99.7	99.7	119.4	112.6	136.9	137.3	131.1	127.5
104 Foreign deposits	17.4	28.2	23.1	30.5	31.5	24.0	15.5	20.0
105 *Securities other than shares*	137.4	138.1	98.3	99.4	104.4	123.2	123.2	144.5
106 Open market paper	20.1	31.5	36.1	39.4	47.6	57.8	60.2	64.7
107 Treasury securities	57.1	47.1	26.8	23.6	19.4	18.1	16.5	31.3
108 Agency- and GSE-based securities	23.4	28.5	8.0	10.6	12.4	15.4	17.2	15.9
109 Municipal securities	36.8	31.0	27.4	25.7	25.0	31.9	29.3	32.6
110 *Loans*	145.4	136.0	163.7	147.7	125.7	130.4	132.9	137.0
111 Short-term	87.5	81.7	83.5	80.4	84.5	86.9	86.3	88.4
112 Security RPs	2.4	3.9	4.6	4.2	5.8	4.2	4.0	6.2
113 Consumer credit	85.1	77.7	78.9	76.2	78.7	82.7	82.3	82.2
114 Long-term (mortgages)	57.9	54.4	80.2	67.3	41.2	43.5	46.6	48.7
115 *Shares and other equity*	909.8	1024.4	1119.5	1282.6	1553.5	1687.0	1832.1	1966.0
116 Mutual fund shares	45.7	63.0	75.0	98.0	127.0	124.0	111.0	97.0
117 Money market mutual fund shares	60.0	67.6	87.8	126.4	154.9	191.4	301.9	328.8
118 U.S. direct investment abroad	778.7	866.5	933.1	1041.0	1227.7	1320.4	1369.6	1496.1
119 Equity in government-sponsored enterprises	0	0	0	0	0	0	0	0
120 Investment in finance company subsidiaries	25.5	27.3	23.5	17.1	43.9	51.3	49.6	44.1

(continued)

Table 11.7 (continued)

Row No.		1995	1996	1997	1998	1999	2000	2001	2002
121	*Insurance technical reserves (net equity in reserves of other insurance companies)*	183.6	186.2	188.1	189.8	190.8	190.4	200.8	218.2
122	*Other accounts receivable*	3260.0	3600.8	3844.6	4678.6	5620.1	7098.6	7131.4	6978.4
123	Trade receivables	1184.9	1273.1	1366.6	1451.6	1655.0	1938.1	1808.7	1774.3
124	Other (miscellaneous assets)	2075.1	2327.7	2478.0	3227.0	3965.1	5160.5	5322.7	5204.1
125	*Total liabilities and net worth*	11580.7	12363.1	13269.9	14866.4	16582.1	18939.8	19014.9	19345.5
126	*Liabilities*	12423.6	14017.7	16394.4	19035.5	23562.9	22290.2	20605.6	17851.8
127	*Securities other than shares*	1636.2	1754.6	1921.5	2186.8	2450.9	2662.9	2926.6	2997.8
128	Open market paper	157.4	156.4	168.6	193.0	230.3	278.4	190.1	126.0
129	Municipal securities	134.8	137.9	142.0	147.8	152.8	154.2	157.7	160.8
130	Corporate bonds	1344.1	1460.4	1610.9	1846.0	2067.7	2230.3	2578.8	2711.0
131	*Loans*	1273.4	1337.7	1460.9	1588.0	1730.7	1875.9	1840.1	1809.8
132	Short-term	1055.4	1110.0	1200.4	1330.8	1398.4	1512.3	1417.5	1337.0
133	Bank loans, nec	601.8	642.1	692.7	768.8	813.0	861.0	758.3	661.9
134	Other loans and advances	453.7	467.9	507.7	562.0	585.4	651.3	659.1	675.1
135	Long-term (mortgages)	217.9	227.7	260.5	257.2	332.3	363.5	422.6	472.8
136	*Shares and other equity*	7055.2	8337.5	10516.3	12470.4	16241.2	13745.4	11865.2	9088.4
137	Corporate equity	6414.1	7639.2	9765.7	11577.8	15155.6	12678.8	10796.2	7906.9
138	Direct investment in U.S.	641.1	698.2	750.6	892.6	1085.5	1066.6	1069.1	1181.5
139	*Insurance technical reserves (contributions payable)*	84.4	86.4	93.5	114.9	107.3	108.5	109.8	111.1
140	*Other accounts payable*	2376.4	2501.4	2402.3	2675.3	3032.8	3897.4	3864.0	3844.7
141	Trade payables	877.5	927.0	992.1	1049.7	1228.2	1541.4	1437.7	1421.9
142	Taxes payable	40.3	49.9	59.2	64.1	71.0	78.0	81.0	93.0
143	Miscellaneous liabilities	1458.6	1524.5	1351.0	1561.6	1733.6	2278.0	2345.2	2329.9
144	*Net worth*	−842.9	−1654.6	−3124.5	−4169.0	−6980.8	−3350.3	−1590.8	1493.6

[a]The discrepancy is the difference between net lending or borrowing derived in the capital account and the same concept derived in the financial account. The discrepancy reflects differences in source data, timing of recorded flows, and other statistical differences between the capital and financial accounts.

corporate business sector (line 144) is substantially different from that currently published. In table B.102 of the FFAs, net worth is the market (or replacement) value of assets less liabilities, *excluding equity capital.* That measure of net worth is sometimes compared with the market value of shares for nonfinancial corporate businesses or to net worth derived with tangible assets at historical cost. Draft SNA-USA follows the format in SNA93, which calculates net worth as the market (or replacement) value of assets less liabilities, *including the market value of shares and other equity* (line 136).

The currently published measure of net worth has been a large positive figure that has risen from just over $4 trillion in 1985 to about $9.5 trillion in 2002 (fig. 11.2, panel A). In contrast, nonfinancial corporate business-sector net worth in draft SNA-USA has both positive and negative values (fig. 11.2, panel B). Indeed, as would be expected from the elevated equity valuations in the late 1990s, the draft SNA-USA measure of net worth moved down sharply over the 1990s to –$7 trillion, before turning up in 2000 and becoming positive in 2002.

The draft SNA-USA measure of net worth may be interpreted as a variant of Tobin's q. As defined by Tobin, q is the ratio of the market value of the firm (equity plus debt) to the replacement cost of its tangible assets. For the nonfinancial corporate business sector, debt and equity are the bulk of liabilities in the SNA format, and they correspond to the numerator of q. Tangible assets (the denominator in q) are about half of total assets on the sector balance sheet.[19] Therefore, a negative net worth in draft SNA-USA corresponds to a q greater than one, while a positive net worth corresponds to a q of less than one.

11.3.5   Financial Business Sector (table 11.8)

The financial business sector includes the monetary authority, depository institutions, insurance and pension funds, and all other financial intermediaries, such as finance companies, mutual funds, and brokers and dealers. Except for a complete accounting for the value of real estate holdings, we have been able to compile nearly a full set of accounts for the combined sector.

The current account and capital account are structured the same as the nonfinancial corporate business sector, with the exception of withdrawals from quasi-corporations, and the financial account is a summation of lending and borrowing flows of all the financial intermediaries in the flow of funds accounts. For this sector, we did not net intrasector assets and liabilities. For example, issuance of a mortgage-backed security by a government-sponsored enterprise and purchased by a bank is reflected as a net incurrence

---

19. The popular press often uses a variant of q equal to the ratio of the market value of equity of the sector to the published net worth of the sector. The popular version differs from true q by including financial assets and nondebt liabilities in the denominator.

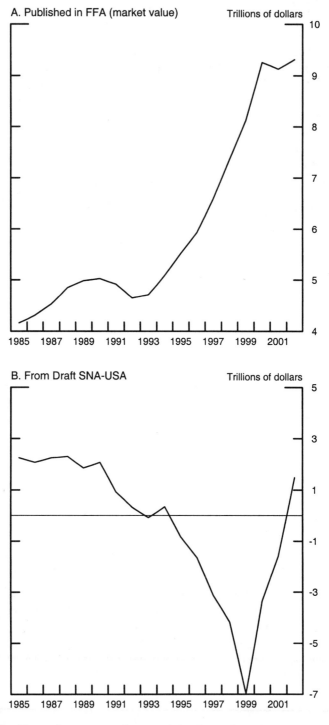

Fig. 11.2   Alternative concepts of net worth for the nonfinancial corporate business sector (trillions of dollars)

Table 11.8   Financial business (includes other financial institutions, depository institutions, insurance companies and pension funds, and monetary authority; billions of dollars)

Row No.		1995	1996	1997	1998	1999	2000	2001	2002
		Current account							
1	*Gross domestic product (GDP)/Gross value added*	541.0	601.9	679.2	764.3	813.8	899.8	917.7	949.0
2	*Less consumption of fixed capital*	74.0	79.3	89.0	98.4	111.4	126.1	135.1	133.5
3	*Equals net domestic product/Net value added*	467.0	522.6	590.2	665.9	702.4	773.7	782.6	815.5
4	Compensation of employees (paid)	282.9	305.7	334.1	376.4	403.9	443.1	450.7	447.6
5	Wages and salaries	238.9	260.1	285.4	322.0	345.5	379.3	384.7	379.4
6	Employers' social contributions	44.0	45.6	48.7	54.4	58.4	63.8	66.0	68.2
7	Taxes on production and imports less subsidies	31.0	33.2	36.2	37.5	40.2	41.4	41.7	44.6
8	Operating surplus, net	153.1	183.7	219.9	252.0	258.3	289.2	290.2	323.5
9	*Net national income/Balance of primary incomes, net*	124.3	116.7	1221.4	120.9	144.1	143.7	181.3	194.5
10	Operating surplus, net	153.1	183.7	219.9	252.0	258.3	289.2	290.2	323.5
11	Property income (received)	931.9	974.6	1078.4	1185.9	1280.9	1542.1	1516.8	1373.8
12	Interest	887.7	919.4	1014.0	1115.1	1201.1	1456.3	1434.7	1297.1
13	Distributed income of corporations (dividends)	35.9	46.4	54.8	62.4	68.7	69.9	68.2	56.0
14	Reinvested earnings on foreign direct investment	8.3	8.8	9.6	8.4	11.1	15.9	13.9	20.7
15	Less uses of property income (paid)	960.7	1041.6	1176.9	1317.0	1395.1	1687.6	1625.7	1502.8
16	Interest	844.0	886.6	998.6	1131.1	1186.7	1445.9	1407.2	1273.4
17	Distributed income of corporations	115.6	153.8	176.0	185.6	207.9	241.7	225.0	227.7
18	Dividends	79.5	106.2	122.8	130.6	139.7	167.0	158.0	157.8
19	Withdrawals from income of quasi-corporations	36.1	47.6	53.2	55.0	68.2	74.7	67.0	69.9
20	Reinvested earnings on foreign direct investment	1.1	1.2	2.3	0.3	0.5	0	-6.5	1.7
21	Rents	0	0	0	0	0	0	0	0

(continued)

Table 11.8 (continued)

Row No.		1995	1996	1997	1998	1999	2000	2001	2002
22	*Net national iacome/Balance of primary incomes, net*	124.3	116.7	121.4	120.9	144.1	143.7	181.3	194.5
23	Less current taxes on income, wealth, etc. (paid)	77.6	78.6	84.2	89.7	87.4	94.9	66.8	63.1
24	Less other current transfers (paid)	9.3	7.8	-1.9	20.7	12.3	29.1	37.4	18.2
25	*Equals disposable income, net*	37.4	30.3	39.1	10.5	44.4	19.7	77.1	113.2
26	*Equals net saving*	37.4	30.3	39.1	10.5	44.4	19.7	77.1	113.2
	Capital account								
27	*Net saving*	37.4	30.3	39.1	10.5	44.4	19.7	77.1	113.2
28	*Capital formation, net*	14.2	32.9	76.5	90.5	28.8	5.3	-12.2	-11.3
29	Gross fixed capital formation (nonresidential)	88.2	112.2	165.5	188.9	140.2	131.4	122.9	122.2
30	Less consumption of fixed capital	74.0	79.3	89.0	98.4	111.4	126.1	135.1	133.5
31	*Net lending or borrowing, capital account (rows 27–28)*	23.2	-2.6	-37.4	-80.0	15.6	14.4	89.3	124.5
	Financial account								
32	*Net lending or borrowing (row 31)*	23.2	-2.6	-37.4	-80.0	15.6	14.4	89.3	124.5
33	*Net acquisition of financial assets*	1511.3	1512.4	1984.0	2568.5	2467.9	2359.4	2771.5	1987.6
34	*Monetary gold and SDRs*	2.1	-0.5	-0.5	-0.0	-3.0	-4.0	-0.0	-0.0
35	*Currency and deposits*	55.8	43.7	57.1	89.4	43.8	25.0	204.7	24.4
36	*Securities other than shares*	543.2	399.7	717.5	876.7	927.3	632.1	1003.4	933.4
37	*Loans*	583.8	554.6	639.6	950.8	1093.6	947.6	768.9	837.6
38	Short-term	375.1	264.5	333.9	453.8	511.0	398.1	99.5	10.7
39	Long-term (mortgages)	208.8	290.1	305.7	497.0	582.5	549.6	669.4	826.8
40	*Shares and otaer equity*	222.1	392.3	362.7	441.4	334.8	535.0	502.5	214.1
41	Corporate equities	74.0	176.3	110.0	157.1	-3.6	289.6	219.1	99.6
42	Mutual fund shares	49.4	27.6	50.4	6.7	113.8	9.0	7.6	15.1

43 Money market mutual fund shares	15.0	77.2	56.1	99.5	93.0	35.4	157.9	-4.4
44 Equity in government-sponsored enterprises	2.0	1.4	1.8	4.0	6.1	2.2	2.8	1.9
45 U.S. direct investment abroad	8.4	15.1	20.5	13.5	30.5	30.8	22.9	20.8
46 Stock in Federal Reserve Banks	0.3	0.6	0.8	0.5	0.5	0.6	0.4	1.0
47 Investment in subsidiaries	72.9	94.1	123.0	160.1	94.6	167.4	91.9	80.0
48 *Insurance technical reserves*	22.5	19.3	6.4	5.1	-15.4	-10.4	3.3	15.2
49 *Other accounts receivable*	81.8	103.2	201.3	205.1	86.8	234.1	288.6	-37.1
50 *Net incurrence of liabilities*	1442.6	1494.0	2002.0	2632.3	2415.7	2496.2	2790.5	1997.7
51 *Currency and deposits*	162.7	174.1	239.2	268.5	334.4	248.7	520.9	384.2
52 *Securities other than shares*	435.4	484.2	527.8	919.6	954.9	754.5	846.4	823.6
53 *Loans*	144.9	126.4	260.9	314.4	297.1	300.4	113.4	89.8
54 *Short-term*	139.5	118.6	246.0	289.6	292.0	294.1	112.1	83.9
55 *Long-term (mortgages)*	5.3	7.9	14.9	24.8	5.1	6.2	1.3	5.9
56 *Shares and other equity*	381.4	484.5	535.1	770.2	618.2	846.1	851.6	326.8
57 Corporate equity issues	-5.6	-20.8	-26.6	0.9	-2.4	16.8	37.3	71.0
58 Mutual fund shares	147.4	237.6	265.1	279.5	191.2	239.4	201.2	182.4
59 Money market mutual fund shares	141.2	145.4	155.9	287.2	249.1	233.3	428.6	-16.8
60 Equity in government-sponsored enterprises	2.0	1.5	1.8	4.1	6.1	2.2	2.8	2.0
61 Foreign direct investment in U.S.	4.3	14.5	4.9	34.4	42.2	140.1	80.0	16.7
62 Equity in noncorporate business	14.4	9.9	13.9	9.9	10.2	39.0	11.2	-4.1
63 Investment by parent	77.5	95.9	119.3	153.7	121.4	174.8	90.2	74.5
64 Stock in Federal Reserve Banks	0.3	0.6	0.8	0.5	0.5	0.6	0.4	1.0
65 *Insurance technical reserves*	250.0	220.9	273.6	263.3	180.6	217.6	294.2	335.2
66 *Other accounts payable*	68.3	3.8	165.3	96.2	30.5	128.9	164.0	38.1

Memo:

67 Net lending or borrowing, financial account (rows 33–50)	68.7	18.3	-18.0	-63.7	52.2	-136.7	-19.1	-10.1

(continued)

Table 11.8 (continued)

Row No.	1995	1996	1997	1998	1999	2000	2001	2002
	Other changes in volume account							
68 *Total other volume changes*	49.8	−7.3	21.7	−4.3	−48.7	−156.5	−104.3	−205.3
69 Other volume changes	4.2	−28.2	2.3	−20.5	−85.2	−5.4	4.1	−70.7
70 Less statistical discrepancy (rows 31–[33–50])[a]	−45.5	−20.9	−19.4	−16.2	−36.5	151.1	108.4	134.6
	Revaluation account							
71 *Nonfinancial assets*	90.0	84.4	81.3	91.0	182.5	187.8	137.8	203.2
72 Structures	79.5	80.3	83.8	94.7	177.2	177.4	131.2	213.2
73 Equipment and software	10.5	4.1	−2.5	−3.7	5.3	10.4	6.6	−10.0
74 *Financial assets*	738.5	657.1	989.7	887.4	1421.7	−615.0	−1043.9	−1423.1
75 Corporate equities	660.0	588.7	873.4	770.7	1277.3	−574.8	−934.8	−1258.5
76 Mutual fund shares	81.1	67.0	126.9	110.1	143.3	−32.2	−105.3	−171.1
77 U.S. direct investment abroad	−2.6	1.4	−8.9	6.6	1.2	−8.1	−3.8	6.5
78 *Liabilities*	1095.9	981.3	1655.5	999.8	1209.2	82.3	−1228.1	−1684.0
79 Corporate equity issues	395.6	371.2	711.6	174.3	−128.6	715.1	−230.8	−354.0
80 Mutual fund shares	228.0	252.0	381.9	344.2	734.1	−342.5	−501.0	−679.6
81 Foreign direct investment in U.S	10.9	−7.4	21.6	0.6	−19.7	−21.1	−15.3	8.4
82 Equity in noncorporate business	−15.9	−8.5	−9.3	−12.1	−19.0	−56.1	−21.0	−17.2
83 Pension fund reserves	477.2	374.0	549.8	492.8	642.4	−213.1	−460.0	−641.7
84 Changes in net worth due to nominal holding gains/losses	−267.3	−239.9	−584.6	−21.4	395.1	−509.6	322.0	464.1
	Changes in balance sheet account							
85 Change in net worth (rows 28 + 31 + 68 + 84)[b]	−180.2	−216.9	−523.8	−15.2	390.9	−646.4	294.7	372.0
	Balance sheet account (end of period)							
86 *Total assets*	23097.8	25366.6	28490.4	32128.5	36225.4	38162.8	40012.1	40706.1

#		C1	C2	C3	C4	C5	C6	C7	C8
87	*Nonfinancial assets*	2836.5	2730.9	2624.0	2450.4	2262.6	2111.0	1983.3	1883.5
88	Structures	2081.0	1985.4	1899.2	1781.1	1663.5	1562.9	1467.7	1402.9
89	Equipment and software	755.6	745.6	724.8	669.4	599.1	548.2	515.5	480.5
90	*Financial assets*	37869.6	37281.1	35538.9	33775.0	29865.9	26379.4	23383.4	21214.3
91	*Monetary gold and SDRs*	13.2	13.2	13.2	17.2	20.2	20.2	20.8	21.2
92	*Currency and deposits*	985.7	960.8	757.6	734.0	692.2	600.8	544.5	498.9
93	*Securities other than shares*	12727.9	11794.4	10792.8	10160.6	9230.9	8354.2	7653.2	7279.8
94	Open market paper	1014.4	1129.5	1225.6	1058.7	835.6	714.4	578.1	525.7
95	Treasury securities	1593.0	1447.9	1424.8	1432.8	1492.7	1557.7	1514.5	1606.8
96	Agency- and GSE-backed securities	4391.4	3800.6	3243.2	3012.1	2610.3	2254.5	2099.7	1967.3
97	Municipal securities	1010.8	961.5	885.1	878.0	855.7	773.1	719.0	684.5
98	Corporate and foreign bonds	3928.0	3689.2	3309.2	3094.9	2793.7	2452.9	2180.6	1989.2
99	Nonmarketable government securities	790.3	765.8	704.9	684.0	642.9	601.7	561.4	506.3
100	*Loans*	13106.9	12269.3	11500.7	10542.0	9446.7	8495.9	7856.3	7301.7
101	Short-term	5187.5	5176.8	5077.6	4668.4	4157.1	3703.3	3369.4	3104.9
102	Long-term (mortgages)	7919.4	7092.5	6423.1	5873.6	5289.6	4792.6	4486.9	4196.8
103	*Shares and other equity*	8161.8	9370.8	9912.2	9992.3	8235.7	6906.9	5554.6	4505.2
104	Corporate equities	5049.1	6207.9	6923.6	7208.8	5935.0	5007.2	4023.8	3258.8
105	Mutual fund shares	734.3	890.3	988.0	1011.2	754.2	637.4	460.0	365.5
106	Money market mutual fund shares	693.5	697.9	540.0	504.6	411.6	312.2	257.7	180.5
107	Equity in government-sponsored enterprises		35.2	33.3	30.5	22.3	18.3	16.5	15.1
108	U.S. direct investment abroad	255.8	228.5	209.4	186.6	155.0	134.9	123.3	106.8
109	Stock in Federal Reserve Banks	8.4	7.4	7.0	6.4	6.0	5.4	4.6	4.0
110	Investments and subsidiaries	1385.6	1305.6	1213.7	1046.3	951.7	791.5	668.5	574.4
111	*Insurance technical reserves*	497.6	501.1	509.4	523.1	516.7	494.1	465.8	432.1
112	*Other accounts receivable*	2376.5	2371.4	2052.9	1805.8	1723.4	1507.2	1288.2	1175.4
113	*Total liabilities and net worth*	40706.1	40012.1	38162.8	36225.4	32128.5	28490.4	25366.6	23097.8

(continued)

Table 11.8 (continued)

Row No.	1995	1996	1997	1998	1999	2000	2001	2002
114 *Liabilities*	21864.6	24350.3	27997.9	31651.1	35357.2	37941.0	39495.5	39817.6
115 *Currency and deposits*	4295.6	4471.5	4709.0	4979.4	5311.7	5564.2	6069.0	6450.3
116 *Securities other than shares*	4122.2	4606.4	5125.1	6044.7	6999.6	7758.1	8601.9	9425.5
117 Agency- and GSE-backed securities	2376.8	2608.2	2821.1	3292.0	3884.0	4317.4	4944.1	5498.1
118 Corporate bonds	1258.5	1419.1	1558.3	1846.0	2032.7	2226.0	2488.4	2821.5
119 Commercial paper	486.9	579.1	745.7	906.7	1082.9	1214.7	1169.4	1105.9
120 *Loans*	1097.7	1224.1	1485.0	1799.4	2096.5	2396.8	2522.9	2612.7
121 Short-term	1073.6	1192.2	1438.2	1727.8	2019.8	2313.9	2438.7	2522.6
122 Long-term (mortgages)	24.1	31.9	46.8	71.6	76.7	82.9	84.2	90.1
123 *Shares and other equity*	4537.7	5629.5	7270.3	8547.6	9732.5	10874.0	10957.6	10242.0
124 Corporate equity issues	1284.0	1634.3	2319.3	2494.5	2363.4	3095.3	2901.8	2618.8
125 Mutual fund shares	1852.8	2342.4	2989.4	3613.1	4538.5	4435.3	4135.5	3638.4
126 Money market mutual fund shares	741.3	886.7	1042.5	1329.7	1578.8	1812.1	2240.7	2223.9
127 Equity in government-sponsored enterprises	18.3	19.7	21.5	25.5	31.6	33.8	36.5	38.5
128 Foreign direct investment in U.S.	36.1	43.2	69.7	104.7	127.2	246.2	310.9	336.1
129 Equity in noncorporate business	1.4	2.8	7.4	5.2	-3.6	-20.7	-30.5	-51.7
130 Investment by parent	599.9	695.8	815.1	968.8	1090.2	1265.0	1355.2	1429.8
131 Stock in Federal Reserve Banks	4.0	4.6	5.4	6.0	6.4	7.0	7.4	8.4
132 *Insurance technical reserves*	6851.7	7461.1	8301.5	9080.4	9940.2	9926.6	9733.0	9388.6
133 *Other accounts payable*	959.7	957.7	1107.0	1199.7	1276.6	1421.2	1611.2	1698.4
134 *Net worth*	1233.2	1016.3	492.5	477.4	868.2	221.8	516.6	888.5

[a]The discrepancy is the difference between net lending or borrowing derived in the capital and the same concept derived in the financial account. The discrepancy reflects differences in source data, timing of recorded flows, and other statistical differences between the capital and financial accounts.
[b]Partial—does not include revaluation of tangible assets.

of a liability (included in line 50 of table 11.8) and as an acquisition of a financial asset (included in line 33).

A consequence of showing gross flows of the sector is that there are sizable revaluations of financial assets (line 74) and liabilities (line 78). As with other sector accounts, shares and other equity instruments were revalued for capital gains and losses. Other types of liabilities, such as bonds and mortgages, were not revalued. Past efforts by staff at the FRB found little impact on net worth of sector balance sheets when liabilities other than equities were revalued. However, that work predated the recent down-shift in interest rates, and it was not applied to the financial business sector as defined in draft SNA-USA.

While draft SNA-USA shows an account for other changes in volume for financial corporations, the data are not well developed. In particular, debt write-offs are not included. Rather, they are reflected in changes in the flows in the financial account. A better articulation of such information would likely make analysis of business and household financing in the economy clearer, and the draft SNA-USA format provides a focused means for eventually recording the figures as they are developed.

The change in net worth for the financial business sector (and for the government sectors that follow) is calculated using the same factors as for the household and nonfinancial business sectors, with an important exception. Data are available only for reproducible assets, which include structures; data are not available for the market value of real estate, which combines the value of structures and land. As a result, the change in net worth (line 85) and the level of net worth (line 134) are limited. The change excludes revaluations of real estate, and the level excludes the market value of real estate but includes the current cost value of structures.

11.3.6   Government Sectors (tables 11.9 and 11.10)

In the government sectors, current surpluses (deficits) are measured by net saving (line 24 of both tables 11.9 and 11.10). Net lending or borrowing (line 32) in the capital account provides a broader measure of the surplus/deficit, by taking into account investment in fixed assets; it is the measure most akin to the budget surplus/deficit reported by U.S. Office of Management and Budget (OMB).

The capital account also shows the net acquisition of *nonproduced* nonfinancial assets (line 31 in both tables). The federal government has been a seller of such assets, which include the sale of electromagnetic spectrum rights and leasing of offshore drilling rights. For state and local governments, acquisition of nonproduced assets reflects net purchases of land and access rights for roads. The counterparty for the government sales, leases, and purchases is the nonfinancial corporate business sector.

The revaluation and balance sheet account for the government sectors is limited by the lack of information for real estate values, the same as is the

Table 11.9   **Federal government (billions of dollars)**

Row No.		1995	1996	1997	1998	1999	2000	2001	2002
	Current account								
1	*Gross domestic product (GDP)/Gross value added*	338.7	343.7	349.3	352.9	361.9	378.7	386.9	408.9
2	*Less consumption of fixed capital*	81.9	82.0	82.5	82.8	84.8	87.2	88.2	89.1
3	*Equals net domestic product/Net value added*	256.9	261.6	266.8	270.1	277.0	291.6	298.7	319.8
4	Compensation of employees (paid)	257.5	262.9	266.5	270.0	277.4	293.9	302.8	323.0
5	Wages and salaries	174.7	175.7	177.3	179.7	184.3	195.8	200.5	213.3
6	Employers' social contributions	82.8	87.2	89.2	90.3	93.1	98.1	102.3	109.7
7	Operating surplus, net	−0.6	−1.2	0.3	0.1	−0.3	−2.3	−4.1	−3.1
8	*Net national income/Balance of primary incomes, net*	−225.1	−232.3	−228.0	−231.1	−221.4	−216.3	−199.0	−161.5
9	Operating surplus, net	−0.6	−1.2	0.3	0.1	−0.3	−2.3	−4.1	−3.1
10	Taxes on production and imports, receivable	75.9	73.2	78.2	81.1	83.9	87.8	86.0	87.6
11	Subsidies (paid)	−33.7	−34.0	−32.4	−35.0	−43.8	−43.8	−47.6	−37.2
12	Property income (received)	23.7	26.9	25.9	21.5	21.5	25.2	24.4	20.6
13	Interest	21.2	23.0	21.4	17.7	18.0	20.1	17.9	15.9
14	Rents	2.5	4.0	4.5	3.8	3.5	5.1	6.5	4.7
15	Less uses of property income (interest paid)	290.4	297.3	300.0	298.8	282.7	283.3	257.5	229.3
16	*Net national income/Balance of primary incomes, net*	−225.1	−232.3	−228.0	−231.1	−221.4	−216.3	−199.0	−161.5
17	Plus current taxes on income, wealth, etc. (received)	769.2	859.2	952.4	1035.8	1111.9	1225.8	1168.9	993.1
18	Plus social benefits (received)	519.2	542.8	576.4	613.8	651.6	691.7	715.4	736.7
19	Less social contributions (paid)	642.7	680.0	706.3	719.2	738.0	772.5	840.2	920.0
20	Plus other current transfers (received)	19.1	23.1	19.9	21.5	22.7	25.7	27.4	25.8
21	Less other current transfers (paid)	196.3	208.2	212.5	227.4	248.0	265.6	290.3	323.4
22	*Equals disposable income, net*	243.5	304.5	401.9	493.4	578.7	688.8	582.2	350.8
23	*Less final consumption expenditures*	440.5	446.3	457.7	454.6	475.1	499.3	531.7	590.8
24	*Equals net saving*	−197.0	−141.8	−55.8	38.8	103.6	189.5	50.5	−240.0

Capital account

25 *Net saving and capital transfers*	−209.8	−152.5	−64.2	35.3	96.3	181.4	37.7	−258.8
26 Net saving	−197.0	−141.8	−55.8	38.8	103.6	189.5	50.5	−240.0
27 Capital transfers received (net)	−12.8	−10.7	−8.5	−3.6	−7.4	−8.1	−12.9	−18.7
28 *Capital formation, net*	−10.5	−4.7	−17.0	−12.6	−5.0	−8.0	−7.8	−0.2
29 Gross fixed capital formation (acq. of produced nonfinancial assets)	78.7	81.1	73.2	75.8	80.8	79.5	81.2	88.7
30 Less consumption of fixed capital	81.9	82.0	82.5	82.8	84.8	87.2	88.2	89.1
31 Acq. of nonproduced nonfinancial assets	−7.4	−3.8	−7.6	−5.7	−1.0	−0.3	−0.7	0.2
32 *Net lending or borrowing, capital account (rows 25–28)*	−199.3	−147.8	−47.3	47.9	101.3	189.3	45.4	−258.7

Financial account

33 *Net lending or borrowing (row 32)*	−199.3	−147.8	−47.3	47.9	101.3	189.3	45.4	−258.7
34 *Net acquisition of financial assets*	−11.5	2.5	−12.6	−8.6	71.4	−70.7	51.2	16.6
35 *Monetary gold and SDRs*	0.8	−0.4	0.4	0.1	−0.0	0.7	0.6	0.8
36 *Currency and deposits*	6.1	9.8	2.5	−9.6	60.4	−65.5	49.2	6.4
37 Official foreign exchange	3.2	−3.8	−1.5	0.8	−1.6	0.9	0.3	1.9
38 Net IMF position	2.5	1.3	3.6	5.1	−5.5	−2.3	3.6	6.1
39 Currency and transferable deposits	−0.0	11.0	−0.5	−16.7	66.2	−65.1	41.1	−18.7
40 Time and savings deposits	0.3	1.4	1.0	1.3	0.7	1.0	4.2	17.1
41 Nonofficial foreign currencies	0.3	−0.1	−0.0	−0.1	0.6	0.0	−0.1	0.1
42 *Loans*	−7.0	−1.3	3.1	11.6	6.4	11.6	6.0	9.8
43 Short-term	6.6	5.9	7.6	12.5	6.4	12.5	7.1	9.2
44 Consumer credit	3.2	7.7	10.8	9.0	13.6	16.1	13.1	12.7
45 Other loans and advances	3.4	−1.8	−3.1	3.4	−7.1	−3.6	−5.9	−3.4
46 Long-term (mortgages)	−13.5	−7.2	−4.5	−0.8	−0.1	−0.9	−1.1	0.5
47 *Shares and other equity*	1.5	1.8	1.6	1.6	1.5	1.5	1.7	1.7
48 Equity in international organizations	1.5	1.8	1.6	1.6	1.5	1.5	1.7	1.7

(continued)

Table 11.9   (continued)

Row No.	1995	1996	1997	1998	1999	2000	2001	2002
49 Equity in government-sponsored enterprises	0	0	0	0	0	0	0	0
50 *Other accounts receivable*	-13.0	-7.4	-20.1	-12.4	3.2	-19.1	-6.3	-2.0
51 Trade receivables	-1.6	0.9	-3.2	1.5	4.6	5.3	7.3	-3.3
52 Taxes receivable	-7.5	0.0	-10.0	-8.9	1.6	-21.5	-13.4	2.8
53 Other (miscellaneous assets)	-3.8	-8.4	-7.0	-5.0	-3.0	-2.9	-0.3	-1.5
54 *Net incurrence of liabilities*	169.0	198.1	56.5	-24.6	-34.0	-268.7	53.5	285.9
55 *Monetary gold and SDRs (SDR certificates)*	2.2	-0.5	-0.5	0	-3.0	-4.0	0	0
56 *Currency and deposits (treasury currency)*	0.7	0.5	0.5	0.6	1.0	2.4	1.3	1.0
57 *Securities other than shares*	144.4	144.9	23.1	-52.6	-71.2	-295.9	-5.6	257.5
58 Treasury securities including savings bonds	142.9	146.6	23.2	-54.6	-71.0	-294.9	-5.0	257.0
59 Federal agency securities	1.5	-1.6	-0.1	2.0	-0.2	-1.0	-0.5	0.5
60 *Insurance technical reserves*	21.8	55.7	42.0	42.5	42.5	22.3	62.2	26.1
61 Insurance reserves	1.0	0.6	1.7	1.3	1.4	1.4	1.4	1.6
62 Nonmarketable securities held by pension plans	20.8	55.1	40.3	41.2	41.1	20.9	60.8	24.5
63 *Other accounts payable*	-0.1	-2.6	-8.6	-15.1	-3.4	6.4	-4.5	1.3
64 Trade payables	-4.6	0.7	-8.8	-8.0	-0.4	4.4	3.4	1.8
65 Other (miscellaneous liabilities)	4.5	-3.3	0.3	-7.1	-2.9	2.0	-7.8	-0.4
Memo:								
66 Net lending or borrowing, financial account (rows 34–54)	-180.4	-195.6	-69.1	16.0	105.4	198.0	-2.3	-269.3
Other changes in volume account								
67 *Total other volume changes*	29.8	-48.2	-11.6	-28.7	46.0	36.2	-4.5	-29.2
68 Other volume changes	11.0	-0.4	10.3	3.2	41.9	27.5	43.2	-18.5
69 Less statistical discrepancy (rows 32–[34–54])[a]	-18.8	47.9	21.8	31.9	-4.1	-8.7	47.7	10.6

Revaluation account

70 *Nonfinancial assets*	45.7	33.6	40.7	27.0	44.1	41.6	33.4	30.8
71 Structures	38.0	33.7	40.9	30.3	38.4	43.0	32.6	30.0
72 Equipment and software	7.6	-0.2	-0.2	-3.3	5.7	-1.4	0.8	0.8
73 *Financial assets*	0.3	-0.8	-1.6	1.3	-0.9	-1.3	-1.0	-1.4
74 Currency and checkable deposits	-5.6	5.2	3.8	-1.7	-1.4	1.4	1.5	-0.6
75 Monetary gold, SDRs, and official foreign exchange	6.0	-6.0	-5.4	3.1	0.5	-2.7	-2.5	-0.8
76 *Changes in net worth due to nominal holding gains/losses*	46.0	32.7	39.1	28.3	43.2	40.3	32.4	29.4

Changes in balance sheet account

77 *Change in net worth (rows 28 + 32 + 67 + 76)*[b]	-133.9	-168.0	-36.6	34.9	185.5	257.8	65.6	-258.6

Balance sheet account (end of period)

78 *Total assets*	1756.3	1790.3	1809.3	1826.8	1981.0	1967.9	2094.6	2122.2
79 *Nonfinancial assets*	1314.4	1343.2	1367.0	1381.4	1420.5	1454.1	1479.8	1510.4
80 Structures	787.7	819.0	848.5	869.4	901.9	936.5	959.2	987.0
81 Equipment and software	526.7	524.3	518.4	511.9	518.6	517.6	520.6	523.4
82 *Financial assets*	441.9	447.1	442.3	445.4	560.5	513.8	614.9	611.8
83 *Monetary gold and SDRs*	11.0	10.3	10.0	10.6	10.3	10.5	10.8	12.2
84 *Currency and deposits*	68.1	77.4	79.0	70.3	130.0	63.7	112.3	116.8
85 Official foreign exchange	28.0	19.0	13.8	16.2	16.0	15.6	14.4	16.9
86 Net IMF position	14.7	15.5	18.2	24.2	18.0	14.9	17.9	22.1
87 Currency and transferable deposits	22.2	38.3	41.6	23.2	87.9	24.3	66.9	47.5
88 Time and savings deposits	0.9	2.4	3.4	4.7	5.4	6.3	10.5	27.6
89 Nonofficial foreign currencies	2.3	2.2	2.1	2.0	2.6	2.6	2.6	2.7
90 *Loans*	207.8	206.5	209.8	221.6	261.1	272.7	278.7	288.5
91 Short-term	150.3	156.3	164.1	176.7	183.3	195.8	203.0	212.2
92 Consumer credit	9.9	17.6	28.3	37.4	50.9	67.0	80.1	92.8
93 Other loans and advances	140.5	138.7	135.7	139.3	132.4	128.8	122.9	119.4
94 Long-term (mortgages)	57.5	50.3	45.7	44.9	77.7	76.9	75.8	76.3

(continued)

Table 11.9   (continued)

Row No.		1995	1996	1997	1998	1999	2000	2001	2002
95	*Shares and other equity*	27.4	29.2	30.8	32.4	33.9	35.4	37.1	38.7
96	Equity in international organizations	27.4	29.2	30.8	32.4	33.9	35.4	37.1	38.7
97	Equity in government-sponsored enterprises	0	0	0	0	0	0	0	0
98	*Other accounts receivable*	127.5	123.6	112.6	110.5	125.3	131.5	176.0	155.7
99	Trade receivables	23.1	24.0	20.8	22.3	22.9	28.1	35.5	32.2
100	Taxes receivable	17.3	20.7	20.0	21.4	38.5	42.4	79.8	64.3
101	Other (miscellaneous assets)	87.2	78.8	71.9	66.9	63.9	61.0	60.7	59.2
102	*Total liabilities and net worth*	1756.3	1790.3	1809.3	1826.8	1981.0	1967.9	2094.6	2122.2
103	*Liabilities*	4289.2	4491.2	4546.8	4529.4	4498.1	4227.2	4288.3	4574.5
104	*Monetary gold and SDRs (SDR certificates)*	10.2	9.7	9.2	9.2	6.2	2.2	2.2	2.2
105	*Currency and deposits (treasury currency)*	18.3	18.9	19.3	19.9	20.9	23.2	24.5	25.5
106	*Securities other than shares*	3636.7	3781.7	3804.8	3752.2	3681.0	3385.1	3379.5	3637.0
107	Treasury securities including savings bonds	3608.5	3755.1	3778.3	3723.7	3652.7	3357.8	3352.7	3609.8
108	Federal agency securities	28.2	26.6	26.5	28.5	28.3	27.3	26.8	27.3
109	*Insurance technical reserves*	536.2	591.9	634.0	676.5	719.0	741.3	803.6	829.7
110	Insurance reserves	29.9	30.5	32.3	33.6	35.0	36.4	37.8	39.4
111	Nonmarketable securities held by pension plans	506.3	561.4	601.7	642.9	684.0	704.9	765.8	790.3
112	*Other accounts payable*	87.7	89.0	79.6	71.7	71.1	75.4	78.6	80.1
113	Trade payables	81.1	81.8	72.9	65.0	64.5	69.0	72.3	74.1
114	Other (miscellaneous liabilities)	6.7	7.3	6.6	6.7	6.6	6.4	6.2	6.0
115	*Net worth*	−2532.9	−2700.9	−2737.6	−2702.6	−2517.2	−2259.3	−2193.7	−2452.3

[a]The discrepancy is the difference between net lending or borrowing derived in the capital account and the same concept derived in the financial account. The discrepancy reflects differences in source data, timing of recorded flows, and other statistical differences between the capital and financial accounts.
[b]Partial—does not include revaluation of tangible assets.

Table 11.10 State and local governments (excludes employee retirement funds; billions of dollars)

Row No.		1995	1996	1997	1998	1999	2000	2001	2002
	Current account								
1	*Gross domestic product (GDP)/Gross value added*	666.7	693.0	720.4	752.6	790.5	834.4	883.8	930.9
2	*Less consumption of fixed capital*	83.1	87.2	91.6	96.2	102.1	109.8	117.7	121.7
3	*Equals net domestic product/Net value added*	583.6	605.8	628.8	656.4	688.4	724.6	766.1	809.1
4	Compensation of employees (paid)	571.5	591.9	616.5	646.2	677.9	716.9	760.8	803.2
5	Wages and salaries	450.8	468.7	490.8	517.5	545.0	578.9	615.2	646.6
6	Employers' social contributions	120.7	123.2	125.7	128.7	132.9	138.1	145.6	156.6
7	Operating surplus, net	12.0	13.9	12.3	10.2	10.4	7.7	5.4	5.9
8	*Net national income/Balance of primary incomes, net*	498.3	526.6	552.0	575.9	610.9	640.8	650.6	682.9
9	Operating surplus, net	12.0	13.9	12.3	10.2	10.4	7.7	5.4	5.9
10	Taxes on production and imports, receivable	482.4	507.9	533.8	558.8	590.2	621.1	643.8	672.5
11	Subsidies (paid)	-0.3	-0.3	-0.4	-0.4	-0.4	-0.5	-7.7	-1.0
12	Property income (received)	68.4	73.3	77.8	80.9	85.3	92.2	95.6	95.5
13	Interest	62.9	67.3	71.5	74.6	78.4	84.0	86.7	86.0
14	Distributed income of corporations (dividends)	1.0	1.4	1.5	1.7	1.8	1.9	2.0	2.1
15	Rents	4.5	4.6	4.8	4.6	5.1	6.3	7.0	7.4
16	Less uses of property income (interest paid)	64.2	68.1	71.4	73.6	74.6	79.5	86.6	89.9
17	*Net national income/Balance of primary incomes, net*	498.3	526.6	552.0	575.9	610.9	640.8	650.6	682.9
18	Plus current taxes on income, wealth, etc. (received)	189.8	201.7	216.1	236.1	250.3	272.2	273.9	253.0
19	Plus social benefits (received)	13.6	12.5	10.8	10.4	9.8	11.0	13.2	13.5
20	Less social contributions (paid)	217.6	224.3	227.6	235.8	252.4	271.7	305.1	332.3
21	Plus other current transfers (received)	224.1	234.1	246.6	266.8	290.8	315.4	350.8	384.2
22	*Equals disposable income, net*	708.1	750.6	798.0	853.3	909.3	967.7	983.4	1001.4
23	Less final consumption expenditures	696.1	724.8	758.9	801.4	858.9	917.8	966.1	1004.6
24	*Equals net saving*	12.0	25.8	39.1	52.0	50.4	50.0	17.3	-3.2

(continued)

Table 11.10 (continued)

Row No.		1995	1996	1997	1998	1999	2000	2001	2002
	Capital account								
25	*Net saving and capital transfers*	44.4	59.7	74.4	88.0	90.3	93.8	65.8	48.4
26	*Net saving*	12.0	25.8	39.1	52.0	50.4	50.0	17.3	-3.2
27	*Capital transfers received (net)*	32.4	33.9	35.3	36.0	39.9	43.7	48.5	51.7
28	*Capital formation, net*	77.4	82.6	93.2	97.9	112.6	124.0	126.8	135.3
29	Gross fixed capital formation (acq. of produced nonfinancial assets)	154.0	163.8	178.9	186.5	206.1	225.1	235.8	248.4
30	Less consumption of fixed capital	83.1	87.2	91.6	96.2	102.1	109.8	117.7	121.7
31	Acq. of nonproduced nonfinancial assets	6.6	6.1	5.9	7.6	8.6	8.8	8.6	8.6
32	*Net lending or borrowing, capital account (rows 25–28)*	-33.0	-22.9	-18.8	-9.9	-22.3	-30.3	-61.0	-86.9
	Financial account								
33	*Net lending or borrowing (row 32)*	-33.0	-22.9	-18.8	-9.9	-22.3	-30.3	-61.0	-86.9
34	*Net acquisition of financial assets*	-31.7	13.8	25.4	146.9	77.5	35.8	91.5	86.6
35	*Currency and deposits*	10.0	5.1	10.2	8.9	14.9	10.4	12.7	25.6
36	Currency and transferable deposits	3.4	-5.5	4.4	-3.9	3.9	1.0	5.1	8.5
37	Time and savings deposits	6.6	10.6	5.8	12.8	11.0	9.4	7.7	17.1
38	*Securities other than shares*	-94.7	-37.5	-3.6	130.3	24.1	-22.3	55.9	20.8
39	Open market paper	17.1	20.3	14.3	28.0	6.9	22.6	-26.5	-3.8
40	Treasury securities	-80.2	-32.8	-17.7	30.0	-2.5	-29.1	50.2	22.1
41	Agency- and GSE-backed securities	-35.1	-35.3	-0.8	63.6	11.0	-18.0	19.9	2.1
42	Municipal securities	-3.5	-0.5	-0.7	-1.4	-1.5	0.6	0.3	-1.4
43	Corporate and foreign bonds	7.1	10.7	1.3	10.2	10.1	1.7	11.9	1.8

44 *Loans*	0.3	35.9	7.2	11.3	9.3	24.2	-8.7	2.8
45 Short-term (security RPs)	-3.0	32.1	3.6	7.2	5.0	19.7	-13.4	-2.1
46 Long-term (mortgages)	3.3	3.8	3.7	4.1	4.3	4.5	4.7	5.0
47 *Shares and other equity*	18.0	20.5	9.4	-2.9	7.8	-0.3	27.9	8.6
48 Corporate equities	12.1	14.5	16.8	9.4	3.5	-1.2	22.8	6.7
49 Mutual fund shares	5.9	6.0	-7.4	-12.3	4.3	0.8	5.1	2.0
50 *Other accounts receivable*	34.6	-10.1	2.1	-0.6	21.5	23.7	3.6	28.7
51 Taxes receivable	-9.1	-4.6	0.3	2.8	10.5	14.8	3.6	10.4
52 Other (miscellaneous assets)	43.7	-5.5	1.9	-3.5	11.0	8.9	-0.0	18.4
53 *Net incurrence of liabilities*	-31.7	15.0	72.9	98.2	67.6	42.8	131.0	168.4
54 Securities other than share (municipals)	-61.4	-16.2	42.8	66.5	38.9	16.5	105.5	143.4
55 Short-term	1.2	6.3	8.3	-6.3	2.6	1.4	23.8	25.2
56 Other	-62.6	-22.5	34.4	72.7	36.3	15.1	81.7	118.2
57 *Loans (short-term)*	0.5	0.4	-1.2	1.2	-0.4	-1.0	0.2	0.5
58 *Other accounts payable (trade payables)*	29.2	30.9	31.4	30.5	29.1	27.4	25.2	24.5
Memo:								
59 Net lending or borrowing, financial account (rows 34–53)	0.0	-1.2	-47.5	48.8	9.9	-7.1	-39.5	-81.7
Other changes in volume account								
60 *Total other volume changes*	29.6	15.5	-44.0	45.1	22.6	22.0	33.1	25.2
61 Other volume changes	-3.5	-6.2	-15.3	-13.7	-9.5	-1.2	11.6	20.1
62 Less statistical discrepancy (rows 32–[34–53])[a]	-33.1	-21.7	28.7	-58.7	-32.1	-23.2	-21.5	-5.2

(continued)

Table 11.10 (continued)

Row No.		1995	1996	1997	1998	1999	2000	2001	2002
	Revaluation account								
63	*Nonfinancial assets*	98.1	80.3	101.2	86.5	132.1	175.6	90.7	97.0
64	Structures	96.2	81.3	104.1	88.6	132.5	175.5	83.8	90.0
65	Equipment and software	1.9	-0.9	-2.9	-2.1	-0.4	0.0	6.9	7.0
66	*Shares and other equity*	3.5	6.2	15.3	13.7	9.5	1.2	-11.6	-20.1
67	*Changes in net worth due to nominal holding gains/losses*	101.5	86.5	116.5	100.1	141.6	176.8	79.1	76.9
	Changes in balance sheet account								
68	*Change in net worth (rows 28 + 32 + 60 +67)*[b]	175.5	161.7	146.9	233.2	254.6	292.5	178.0	150.5
	Balance sheet account (end of period)								
69	*Total assets*	4212.7	4389.5	4609.3	4940.6	5262.8	5598.1	5907.1	6226.0
70	*Nonfinancial assets*	3218.6	3381.5	3575.9	3760.3	4005.0	4304.6	4522.1	4754.4
71	Structures	3059.7	3213.9	3400.8	3574.6	3805.6	4091.2	4288.7	4501.0
72	Equipment and software	158.9	167.7	175.1	185.7	199.4	213.4	233.4	253.4
73	*Financial assets*	994.1	1007.9	1033.3	1180.3	1257.8	1293.5	1385.0	1471.6
74	*Currency and deposits*	95.3	100.3	110.5	119.4	134.3	144.7	157.4	183.0
75	Currency and transferable deposits	33.3	27.8	32.2	28.3	32.2	33.2	38.2	46.7
76	Time and savings deposits	62.0	72.6	78.4	91.1	102.1	111.5	119.2	136.3
77	*Securities other than shares*	524.8	487.2	483.7	614.0	638.1	615.8	671.6	692.4
78	Open market paper	39.4	59.7	74.0	102.0	108.9	131.5	105.0	101.2
79	Treasury securities	289.8	257.0	239.3	269.3	266.8	237.7	287.9	310.0
80	Agency- and GSI-backed securities	151.5	116.2	115.4	179.0	190.0	172.0	191.9	194.0

81 Municipal securities	5.1	4.6	3.9	2.5	1.0	1.6	1.9	0.5
82 Corporate and foreign bonds	39.0	47.7	51.0	61.2	71.3	73.0	84.9	86.7
83 *Loans*	229.5	265.4	272.7	284.0	293.3	317.5	308.8	311.7
84 Short-term (security RPs)	115.7	147.8	151.4	158.5	163.5	183.3	169.9	167.7
85 Long-term (mortgages)	113.8	117.6	121.3	125.4	129.8	134.3	139.0	143.9
86 *Shares and other equity*	61.2	87.9	112.6	123.3	140.6	141.5	157.8	146.4
87 Corporate equities	26.2	46.8	79.0	102.0	115.0	115.1	126.3	112.9
88 Mutual fund shares	35.0	41.0	33.6	21.3	25.6	26.4	31.5	33.5
89 *Other accounts receivable*	83.4	67.1	53.9	39.6	51.6	74.1	89.3	138.2
90 Taxes receivable	27.9	26.1	26.9	28.1	33.5	45.6	50.1	59.5
91 Other (miscellaneous assets)	55.4	41.0	27.0	11.5	18.1	28.5	39.2	78.6
92 *Total liabilities and net worth*	4212.7	4389.5	4609.3	4940.6	5262.8	5598.1	5907.1	6226.0
93 *Liabilities*	1531.7	1546.7	1619.7	1717.8	1785.4	1828.3	1959.2	2127.6
94 *Securities other than shares (municipals)*	1035.3	1019.0	1061.8	1128.2	1167.1	1183.6	1289.2	1432.6
95 Short-term	32.9	39.1	47.5	41.2	43.7	45.1	69.0	94.2
96 Other	1002.4	979.9	1014.3	1087.1	1123.4	1138.5	1220.2	1338.4
97 *Loans (short-term)*	9.8	10.1	8.9	10.1	9.7	8.7	8.9	9.4
98 *Other accounts payable (trade payables)*	486.7	517.6	549.0	579.5	608.6	635.9	661.1	685.6
99 *Net worth*	2681.0	2842.7	2989.6	3222.8	3477.3	3769.8	3947.8	4098.4

[a]The discrepancy is the difference between net lending or borrowing derived in the capital account and the same concept derived in the financial account. The discrepancy reflects differences in source data, timing of recorded flows, and other statistical differences between the capital and financial accounts.

[b]Partial—does not include revaluation of tangible assets.

case for the financial businesses sector. Estimates for real estate—actually for structures and land—are available in supplementary information in the federal government budget documents produced each year by OMB (OMB 2004). However, as noted by OMB, the data are somewhat rough and are provided for illustrative purposes in showing how a national balance sheet could be constructed; they have not been fully vetted by the agencies for use in national accounts. Moreover, there are no estimates for state and local governments. As a result, stocks in the balance sheet in draft SNA-USA are for reproducible tangible assets, financial assets, and liabilities.

In the past, the BEA and FRB have collaborated to compile a consolidated government sector. Both the NIPAs and FFAs have a consolidated sector, and doing so in SNA format should be a relatively straightforward exercise for the agencies in the future.

11.3.7   Rest-of-World Sector (table 11.11)

The rest-of-world sector is a mirror image of the international transactions accounts published by the BEA. In the current account, net saving, or the current external balance (table 11.11, line 8), is derived as the difference in foreign income received from U.S. residents and foreign outlays to U.S. residents. The capital account adds net capital transfers and subtracts acquisitions of nonproduced nonfinancial assets to derive net lending and borrowing to U.S. residents from the rest of the world. That figure must offset the sum of net lending/net borrowing for domestic sectors.[20]

Data for the draft SNA-USA financial, other changes in volume, and revaluation accounts are taken from the BEA's international transaction accounts and underlying source data. The nature of the presentation is the same as the domestic sectors. It differs from the ITAs, however, because many financial transactions are netted in draft SNA-USA (and the FFAs), while they are shown gross in the ITAs.

The statistical discrepancy in the rest-of-world sector—the difference between net lending calculated in the current and capital account and net lending in the financial account reflects the statistical discrepancy in the recorded balance of payments as well as a combination of other differences in residency definitions in the NIPAs, the ITAs, and the FFAs. The agencies have a project underway to reconcile differences between the accounts.

11.4   Issues Concerning the Integration of the Accounts

As noted above, the agencies are working to minimize sector discrepancies that result from using alternative data sources and methods. Those

---

20. Net lending from the rest of the world does in fact equal the net borrowing from the domestic sectors after accounting for the NIPA statistical discrepancy, wage accruals less disbursements, and rounding differences. The statistical discrepancy is a factor because we used data for capital formation from the NIPA product side and net saving from the NIPA income side. The figures for all the sectors are shown in draft SNA-USA table 11.4.

Table 11.11   **Rest of the world (billions of dollars)**

Row No.		1995	1996	1997	1998	1999	2000	2001	2002
	Current account								
1	*Foreign income from U.S.*	1137.2	1217.7	1352.2	1430.4	1586.0	1875.6	1732.5	1770.1
2	U.S. imports of goods and services	903.6	964.8	1056.9	1115.9	1251.8	1475.8	1401.7	1433.1
3	U.S. income payments to rest of world	198.2	213.7	253.7	265.8	287.1	343.7	283.8	277.7
4	Current taxes and trans. payments to rest of world	35.4	39.1	41.6	48.8	47.2	56.1	47.1	59.3
5	*Foreign outlays to U.S.*	1046.2	1117.3	1242.1	1243.1	1312.1	1479.0	1354.1	1306.0
6	U.S. exports of goods and services	812.2	868.6	955.4	955.9	991.3	1096.3	1035.1	1006.8
7	U.S. income receipts from rest of world	234.0	248.7	286.7	287.1	320.8	382.7	319.0	299.1
8	*Equals net saving (current external balance)*	91.0	100.4	110.2	187.4	273.9	396.6	378.5	464.1
	Capital account								
9	*Net saving*	91.0	100.4	110.2	187.4	273.9	396.6	378.5	464.1
10	*Net capital transfers*	1.1	0.6	1.0	0.7	4.9	0.3	1.1	1.3
12	*Net lending or borrowing, capital account (rows 9 + 10 − 11)*	92.1	101.0	111.2	188.1	278.8	397.4	379.6	465.4
	Financial account								
13	*Net lending or borrowing (row 12)*	92.1	101.0	111.2	188.1	278.8	397.4	379.6	465.4
14	*Net acquisition of U.S. financial assets*	419.2	521.8	597.3	393.4	708.5	942.2	640.3	680.0
15	*Monetary gold and SDRs*	−0.8	0.4	−0.4	−0.1	0.0	−0.7	−0.6	−0.8
16	*Currency and deposits*	17.9	−21.1	38.6	0.7	49.2	18.5	−41.6	39.4
17	*Currency*	12.3	17.4	24.8	16.6	26.6	5.3	23.8	21.5
18	*Transferable deposits*	1.1	2.6	5.1	−1.8	13.3	−9.5	0.4	1.7
19	*Time deposits*	−6.6	10.9	13.1	13.0	15.0	1.9	−20.1	12.0
20	*Net interbank items due from U.S. banks*	11.1	−52.0	−4.3	−27.1	−5.7	20.8	−45.6	4.2

(continued)

Table 11.11   (continued)

Row No.		1995	1996	1997	1998	1999	2000	2001	2002
21	*Securities other than shares*	246.8	375.7	242.3	173.4	162.5	228.1	321.4	428.9
22	Open market paper	18.6	14.4	19.9	37.6	-13.0	9.5	6.2	17.3
23	Treasury securities	160.5	262.7	123.7	18.7	-32.3	-87.2	3.3	139.4
24	Agency- and GSE-backed securities	17.6	26.8	30.3	11.1	63.4	137.3	106.1	106.7
25	Corporate bonds	50.1	71.8	68.4	106.2	144.4	168.4	205.8	165.6
26	*Loans (short-term)*	21.0	7.1	37.2	-19.8	-14.8	9.2	57.8	49.5
27	Security RPs	21.0	3.2	20.0	-18.8	8.0	11.4	59.4	39.4
28	Loans to U.S. corporate business	0.0	3.9	17.3	-1.0	-22.7	-2.2	-1.6	10.1
29	*Shares and other equity*	74.3	97.6	172.6	221.0	401.7	514.9	273.0	92.8
30	Corporate equities	16.5	11.1	67.0	42.0	112.3	193.6	121.4	53.2
31	Foreign direct investment in U.S.	57.8	86.5	105.6	179.0	289.4	321.3	151.6	39.6
32	*Other accounts receivable*	60.0	62.2	106.9	18.2	109.9	172.3	30.3	70.2
33	Trade receivables	0.7	5.5	0.9	-6.5	-5.1	-0.4	-3.1	3.1
34	Other (miscellaneous assets)	59.2	56.7	106.0	24.7	115.0	172.6	33.4	67.1
35	*Net incurrence of liabilities*	332.6	383.9	377.8	318.4	476.8	486.7	225.8	153.3
36	*Currency and deposits*	44.4	79.5	108.3	12.9	53.0	133.8	34.9	33.9
37	Official foreign exchange	6.3	-7.6	-2.9	1.5	-3.3	1.9	0.7	3.8
38	Net IMF position	2.5	1.3	3.6	5.1	-5.5	-2.3	3.6	6.1
39	U.S. private deposits	35.3	85.9	107.7	6.5	61.1	134.2	30.7	23.9
40	U.S. government deposits	0.3	-0.1	-0.0	-0.1	0.6	0.0	-0.1	0.1
41	*Securities other than shares*	70.6	78.3	65.1	30.6	18.2	46.9	-38.7	2.6
42	Commercial paper	13.5	11.3	3.7	7.8	16.3	31.7	-14.2	36.1
43	Bonds	57.1	67.0	61.4	22.8	1.9	15.2	-24.5	-33.5
44	*Loans (short-term)*	7.9	10.1	6.7	0.6	-5.3	10.1	-11.0	3.2
45	Acceptance liabilities to banks	0.3	1.8	-0.2	-5.0	-0.9	-0.7	-2.6	-0.4
46	U.S. government loans	-0.8	-0.7	-1.6	-1.0	-4.8	-0.6	-1.1	-1.8
47	Bank loans, nec	8.5	9.1	8.5	6.6	0.5	11.4	-7.3	5.3

48 *Shares and other equity*	165.7	176.6	164.0	245.6	340.7	267.4	230.8	157.2
49 Corporate equities	65.4	82.8	57.6	101.4	114.3	106.7	109.1	17.7
50 U.S. government equity in BRD, etc.	1.5	1.8	1.6	1.6	1.5	1.5	1.7	1.7
51 U.S. direct investment abroad	98.8	91.9	104.8	142.6	224.9	159.2	120.0	137.8
52 *Other accounts payable*	44.1	39.4	33.7	28.7	70.1	28.5	9.8	-43.6
53 Trade payables	5.8	-1.7	5.2	-3.9	4.2	0.8	-2.2	-10.1
54 Other (miscellaneous liabilities)	38.3	41.1	28.5	32.6	65.9	27.6	12.0	-33.5
Memo:								
55 Net lending, financial account (rows 14–35)	86.6	137.9	219.6	75.0	231.7	455.5	414.5	526.7

Other changes in volume account

56 *Total other volume changes*	-60.0	86.9	-56.8	-202.2	-264.0	238.9	50.9	-39.9
57 Other volume changes	-54.5	50.0	-165.2	-89.1	-217.0	180.8	15.9	-101.3
58 Less statistical discrepancy (rows 12–[14–35])[a]	5.6	-36.9	-108.4	113.1	47.1	-58.1	-35.0	-61.3

Revaluation account

59 *Financial assets*	170.2	57.4	185.0	261.0	111.5	-360.0	-285.0	-222.2
60 *Securities other than shares*	30.6	-33.5	-1.4	8.0	-63.3	40.6	12.7	44.1
61 Treasury securities	27.1	-35.6	-5.3	0.6	-72.2	32.9	10.3	35.2
62 Agency- and GSE-backed securities	3.5	2.1	3.9	7.4	8.9	7.7	2.5	8.9
63 *Shares and other equity*	139.6	90.9	186.4	253.0	174.8	-400.6	-297.7	-266.3
64 Corporate equities	135.3	111.8	213.5	255.5	248.9	-179.5	-213.1	-364.4
65 Foreign direct investment in U.S.	4.3	-20.9	-27.1	-2.5	-74.1	-221.1	-84.6	98.2
66 *Liabilities*	95.4	168.9	104.3	155.7	406.6	-305.1	-404.4	-270.1
67 *Currency and deposits*	11.3	13.2	-16.4	4.6	-1.2	-3.6	-3.5	-0.9
68 Official foreign exchange	1.5	-3.2	-4.6	3.7	-0.6	-2.8	-2.9	1.0
69 Net IMF position	0.2	-0.5	-0.9	0.9	-0.7	-0.8	-0.6	-1.9

(continued)

Table 11.11 (continued)

Row No.		1995	1996	1997	1998	1999	2000	2001	2002
70	*Shares and other equity*	84.1	155.7	120.7	151.2	407.8	-301.4	-400.9	-269.2
71	Corporate equities	83.9	143.3	147.3	165.8	414.4	-257.6	-349.3	-285.2
72	U.S. direct investment abroad	0.2	12.4	-26.6	-14.7	-6.6	-43.8	-51.6	15.9
73	*Changes in net worth due to nominal holding gains/losses*	74.7	-111.5	80.7	105.3	-295.1	-54.9	119.4	47.9
	Changes in balance sheet account								
74	*Change in net worth (rows 12 + 56 + 73)*	106.8	76.4	135.1	91.2	-280.4	581.4	549.9	473.3
	Financial balance sheet account (end of period)								
75	*Total financial assets*	3434.5	4042.1	4627.3	5199.3	5819.9	6590.6	6979.2	7375.3
76	*Currency and deposits*	472.7	451.6	490.2	490.9	540.1	558.7	517.1	556.5
77	Currency	169.2	186.6	211.4	228.0	254.6	259.9	283.7	305.2
78	Transferable deposits	24.5	27.1	32.2	30.4	43.7	34.2	34.6	36.3
79	Time deposits	49.6	60.6	73.6	86.6	101.6	103.5	83.3	95.3
80	Net interbank items due from U.S. banks	229.3	177.3	173.0	145.9	140.3	161.1	115.5	119.7
81	*Securities other than shares*	1371.3	1713.5	1954.4	2135.9	2235.1	2503.8	2837.9	3310.9
82	Open market paper	43.4	57.9	77.8	115.3	102.3	111.9	118.1	135.4
83	Treasury securities	820.2	1047.3	1165.7	1185.0	1080.4	1026.1	1039.7	1214.2
84	Agency- and GSE-backed securities	146.2	175.1	209.4	227.8	300.2	445.2	553.8	669.4
85	Corporate bonds	361.5	433.2	501.6	607.8	752.1	920.6	1126.3	1291.9
86	*Loans (short-term)*	189.7	196.9	234.1	214.3	199.5	208.7	266.4	316.0
87	Security RPs	67.6	70.9	90.8	72.0	79.9	91.3	150.7	190.1
88	Loans to U.S. corporate business	122.1	126.0	143.3	142.3	119.5	117.3	115.7	125.8
89	*Shares and other equity*	1229.6	1418.0	1777.0	2251.0	2827.5	2941.8	2917.1	2743.7
90	Corporate equities	549.5	672.4	952.9	1250.3	1611.5	1625.6	1533.9	1222.7
91	Foreign direct investment in U.S.	680.1	745.6	824.1	1000.7	1216.0	1316.2	1383.2	1521.0

92 *Other accounts receivable*	171.2	262.2	171.6	107.7	17.6	377.6	440.5	448.2
93 Trade receivables	52.6	58.1	59.0	52.5	47.4	47.0	43.9	47.0
94 Other (miscellaneous assets)	118.6	204.1	112.6	55.2	−29.7	330.6	396.7	401.2
95 *Total liabilities and net worth*	3434.5	4042.1	4627.3	5199.8	5819.9	6590.6	6979.2	7375.3
96 *Total liabilities*	2788.5	3319.7	3769.8	4251.1	5151.6	5340.9	5179.5	5102.3
97 *Currency and deposits*	484.8	577.6	669.5	687.0	738.8	869.0	900.4	933.4
98 Official foreign exchange	49.1	38.3	30.8	36.0	32.2	31.2	29.0	33.8
99 Net IMF position	14.6	15.4	18.1	24.1	18.0	14.8	17.9	22.0
100 U.S. private deposits	418.8	521.7	618.5	624.9	686.1	820.1	851.0	874.9
101 U.S. government deposits	2.3	2.2	2.1	2.0	2.6	2.6	2.6	2.7
102 *Securities other than shares*	355.5	433.8	492.8	523.5	541.7	588.6	549.9	552.6
103 Commercial paper	56.2	67.5	65.1	72.9	89.2	120.9	106.7	142.8
104 Bonds	299.4	366.3	427.7	450.6	452.5	467.7	443.2	409.8
105 *Loans (short-term)*	98.1	108.3	115.1	115.8	110.8	120.9	109.8	113.0
106 Acceptance liabilities to banks	8.2	9.9	9.7	4.7	3.9	3.1	0.5	0.2
107 U.S. government loans	55.4	54.7	53.2	52.4	47.8	47.2	46.0	44.3
108 Bank loans, nec	34.6	43.7	52.1	58.7	59.2	70.5	63.2	68.6
109 *Shares and other equity*	1689.7	2022.0	2306.7	2703.4	3451.9	3417.9	3247.8	3135.8
110 U.S. government equity in BRD, etc.	27.4	29.2	30.8	32.4	33.9	35.4	37.1	38.7
111 U.S. direct investment abroad	885.5	989.8	1068.1	1196.0	1414.4	1529.7	1598.1	1751.9
112 Corporate equities	776.8	1002.9	1207.8	1475.0	2003.7	1852.9	1612.7	1345.2
113 *Other accounts payable*	160.3	178.0	185.7	221.4	308.4	344.5	371.6	367.6
114 Trade payables	45.3	43.6	48.8	44.9	49.1	49.9	47.8	37.6
115 Other (miscellaneous liabilities)	115.0	134.4	136.9	176.5	259.3	294.6	323.8	330.0
116 *Net worth (external account)*	646.0	722.4	857.5	948.7	668.3	1249.7	1799.6	2273.0

[a]The discrepancy is the difference between net lending or borrowing derived in the capital account and the same concept derived in the financial account. The discrepancy reflects differences in source data, timing of recorded flows, and other statistical differences between the capital and financial accounts.

discrepancies are summarized by the net lending/net borrowing measures compared in the panels of figure 11.3. The figure indicates that the pattern of net lending/net borrowing is similar in each sector whether measured by the capital account or the financial account. Even so, there are significant differences for some sectors and in some years.

For the household sector (fig. 11.3, panel A), the differences in net lending/net borrowing between draft SNA-USA capital account and financial account are significant, but relatively stable in sign for the earlier period shown. Until about 1998, net lending derived in the financial account averaged about 2 percentage points (of disposable income) more than in the current account. In recent years, the differences have narrowed on average. Put another way, the financial account implies that households accumulated more assets than suggested by flows from the capital account, and household-sector net worth is about 6 percent higher than would be the case without the discrepancy that is included in the "other changes in volume" account. (The 6 percent represents the value of the discrepancy accumulated over time.)

The household-sector discrepancy in the FFAs has been the subject of several studies over the years.[21] The residual calculation of some categories in the current account and the residual calculation of most asset categories and some liability categories in the financial and balance sheet accounts leave considerable room for speculation on the sources of the difference. A benefit of integrating the national accounts as we have done for this chapter is that the nature of the problem is more clearly defined in terms of stocks and flows of the sector.

An additional concern to the agencies has been the difference in net lending/net borrowing for the nonfinancial corporate business sector (panel B of fig. 11.3). Creating draft SNA-USA pointed to several likely sources for the discrepancy. A particularly vexing one lies in the agencies' separation of nonfinancial and financial businesses, a boundary that is important for analysis of disintermediation and evaluation of flows, such as interest paid and interest received. The boundary also has implications for measuring stocks and net worth in the sectors.

The business boundary problem reflects in part differences in source data for the NIPAs and the FFAs. The NIPAs rely heavily on tax return data, and the FFAs supplement tax data with surveys and regulatory information to compile accounts for financial corporations. In the NIPAs, corporations that file consolidated returns, which combine data for nonfinancial and financial subsidiaries, are in either the financial or nonfinancial business sectors, depending on the predominant business. In the financial accounts, adjustments are made with the supplementary information to split consolidated corporations into financial and nonfinancial enterprises. The

21. See, for example, Wilson et al. (1989).

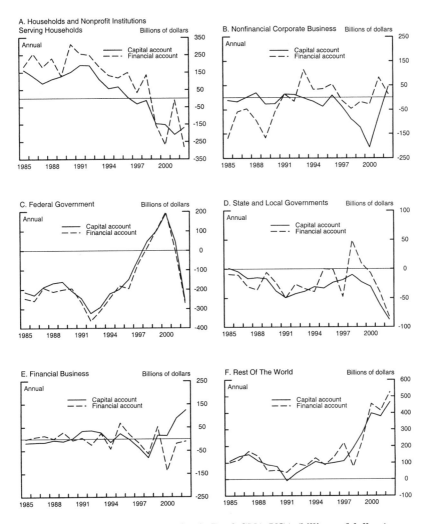

Fig. 11.3   Net lending/net borrowing in Draft SNA-USA (billions of dollars)

issue is particularly acute in cases for firms with captive finance companies, such as General Motor's GMAC and General Electric's GE Capital.

Some encouragement that solving the boundary problem will reduce the discrepancy is evident in figure 11.4. The net lending/net borrowing estimates of the two sectors combined align somewhat better than for the sectors separately.

In addition to the boundary problem, part of the difference between net lending/net borrowing measures in the nonfinancial corporate business sector likely reflects the booking of miscellaneous financial assets. In the fi-

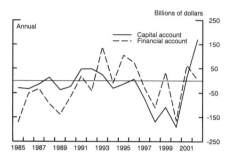

Fig. 11.4   Net lending/net borrowing for combined financial and nonfinancial corporate business (billions of dollars)

nancial accounts, changes to goodwill and other intangible assets are included in flows of miscellaneous financial assets. Such flows are large and positive during periods of heavy merger activity; they are large and negative during periods of economic weakness. The impact of changes in such assets is not reflected in the current and capital accounts. SNA93 standards would relegate a portion of the changes in the value of such assets to the "other changes in volume" account. An effort to reclassify them into revaluations and/or other changes in volume is likely to have a sizable impact on the statistical discrepancy. No changes were made for draft SNA-USA for the business sectors' boundary or other accounting issues.

Finally, net lending/net borrowing estimates for the federal government sector (panel C of figure 11.3) are close, reflecting a generally high quality of information available and recent efforts by the agencies to ensure consistent use of that data. In contrast, net lending/net borrowing estimates for the state and local government sector (panel D)—where the data tend to be of lower quality—diverge by significant amounts. It would appear that coordination of estimation methods for missing data would more tightly integrate the accounts of the state and local government sector.

11.5   Where Do We Go from Here?

Aside from reformulating the structure of the accounts to international standards, it has been our intention to use the integration of the accounts to improve the quality and usefulness of the estimates published. Specific items that require joint work by the agencies have been identified, including further work on ensuring that sector boundaries are consistent across accounts, developing additional source material for sectors where information is not available, and sharing data sources and methods for estimating missing data.

We have shown that SNA-USA tables can be produced for the period

1985–2002. Considerable work is still required if the agencies chose to rework the published figures into the draft SNA-USA structure for the period before 1985. The exercise indicated, moreover, that considerable investment is needed to produce the integrated accounts on a continuing basis, and even greater investment to carry out the improvements identified.

The BEA's strategic plan outlines a number of research and development activities related to the development of integrated accounts. Work is already underway to examine sector definitions, with particular consideration given to the development of improved source data on government business enterprises. Other research is being conducted on improving the consistency of source data between the NIPAs and FFAs—for example, to improve consistency of NIPA interest flow estimates with FFA estimates of interest-bearing assets and liabilities. Efforts are also underway to improve the estimates of fixed assets and to provide more reliable information on valuation and legal form of ownership of these assets, along with the efforts to improve integration with other BEA accounts, such as the input-output accounts, and with the Bureau of Labor Statistics productivity statistics, which are described in many of the other chapters in this volume.

Among other prospective projects that should improve integration of the U.S. macroeconomic accounts, FRB staff are initiating new research into the accounting of miscellaneous assets and liabilities by nonfinancial businesses. These categories include a wide range of financial activities and, indeed, are the largest items on the balance sheets of nonfinancial corporations in the United States. Once more detailed information about these financial activities has been analyzed, FRB staff intend to reconsider how changes in miscellaneous assets and liabilities should be apportioned into flows, revaluations, and other changes in volume. Although the work involved is expected to be considerable, it offers the potential to improve the integration of the FFAs of the U.S. with the NIPAs and to bring them into closer alignment with the SNA93 guidelines.

In addition, efforts at the Federal Reserve are directed toward improving integration in the capital accounts, particularly adapting the draft SNA-USA framework to show estimates for as many detailed financial sectors as are included in the FFAs of the United States. In conjunction with that work will be a consideration of developing detailed information for the "other changes in volume" accounts, particularly estimates of debt writedowns.

The BEA and FRB are jointly advancing other efforts to improve the integration of the accounts. These efforts include estimating the general degree to which captive finance companies are included in consolidated tax return data for nonfinancial corporations, so that more is known about the importance that disparities between the sector boundaries might play in examining the financing of the corporate sector. BEA and FRB staff are also working together to further examine the possible use of alternative data sources to improve the NIPA estimates for state and local governments that are made before complete data from the Census of Governments become available.

An important and useful result of integrated macroeconomic accounts would be an ability to produce on a regular basis a national balance sheet. Several deficiencies, some already noted, would need to be resolved before such a balance sheet is completed. Three of the most important are

- Further development of the "other changes in volume" and revaluation accounts. Although the "other changes in volume" accounts in draft SNA-USA are more advanced than found in other countries' publications, they are still limited. The effort to expand the accounts would require a closer review of the accounting techniques used in data sources and whether those techniques align with what is needed for macroeconomic accounts so that differences in flows, revaluations, and other changes in volume can be separated.
- Improved data for real estate values in some sectors, especially for the government sector, and techniques for separating the market value of land and structures.
- Removal or reconciliation of remaining differences between the current and accumulation accounts and the international transactions accounts.

References

Adler, Hans J., Preston S. Sunga, Carol S. Carson, George Jaszi, Edward F. Denison, John A. Gorman, Martin L. Marimont, et al. 1982. Comments on "Integrated economics accounts for the United States, 1947–80. *Survey of Current Business* 62 (May): 54–75.
Bloem, Adriann M., Robert J. Dipplesman, and Nils Ø. Mæhle. 2001. *Quarterly national accounts manual: Concepts, data sources, and compilation.* Washington, DC: International Monetary Fund.
Bureau of Economic Analysis (BEA). 2002. BEA's strategic plan for FY 2001–2005. *Survey of Current Business* 82 (May): 8–32.
Fraumeni, Barbara M., and Sumiye Okubo. 2001. Alternative treatments of consumer durables in the national accounts. Paper prepared for the Bureau of Economic Analysis Advisory Committee Meeting. 11 May, Washington, DC.
International Monetary Fund. 1995. *Balance of payments compilation guide.* Washington, DC: International Monetary Fund.
———. 2000. *Monetary and financial statistics manual.* Washington, DC: International Monetary Fund.
Lal, Kishori. 2003. Measurement of Output, Value Added, GDP in Canada and the United States: Similarities and Differences. Research Paper 13F0031MIE no. 010. Ottawa: Statistics Canada, June.

Mayerhauser, Nicole, Shelly Smith, and David F. Sullivan. 2003. Preview of the 2003 comprehensive revision of the National Income and Product Accounts: New and redesigned tables. *Survey of Current Business* 83 (August): 7–31.

Mead, Charles Ian, Karin Moses, and Brent R. Moulton. 2004. The NIPAs and the System of National Accounts. *Survey of Current Business* 84 (December): 17–32.

Moulton, Brent R., and Eugene P. Seskin. 2003. Preview of the 2003 comprehensive revision of the National Income and Product Accounts: Changes in definitions and classifications. *Survey of Current Business* 83 (June): 17–34.

Ruggles, Richard, and Nancy D. Ruggles. 1982. Integrated economic accounts for the United States, 1947–80. *Survey of Current Business* 62 (May): 1–53.

Wilson, John F., James L. Freund, Frederick O. Yohn, Jr., and Walter Lederer. 1989. Measuring household saving: Recent experience from the flow-of-funds perspective. In *The measurement of saving, investment, and wealth,* ed. Robert E. Lipsey and Helen Stone Tice, 101–52. Chicago: University of Chicago Press.

United Nations, Commission of the European Communities, International Monetary Fund, Organisation for Economic Co-operation and Development, and World Bank. 1993. *System of national accounts 1993.* Series F, no. 2, rev. 4. New York: United Nations.

U.S. Office of Management and Budget (OMB). 2004. *Analytical perspective: Budget of the United States government, fiscal year 2005.* Part II: *The federal government's assets and liabilities.* Washington, DC: OMB.

Micro and Macro Data Integration
The Case of Capital

Randy A. Becker, John Haltiwanger, Ron S. Jarmin,
Shawn D. Klimek, and Daniel J. Wilson

12.1   Introduction

It seems natural that statistical agencies would strive for internal consistency between macro- and microeconomic measures of key economic variables quantifying the activities of businesses. That is, ideally a given measure should be collected at the micro level (i.e., the firm or, even better, the establishment level) either from the universe of firms or from representative surveys, and macro aggregates of the measure should reflect appropriately weighted aggregation (e.g., sums or means) of the underlying microdata. Unfortunately, this ideal is achieved for very few of the key economic variables; the measures that come closest to this ideal are employment and

Randy Becker is a senior economist at the Center for Economic Studies of the U.S. Census Bureau. John Haltiwanger is a professor of economics at the University of Maryland, and a research associate of the Center for Economic Studies of the U.S. Census Bureau and of the National Bureau of Economic Research (NBER). Ron Jarmin is assistant division chief for research at the Center for Economic Studies of the U.S. Census Bureau. Shawn Klimek is an economist at the Center for Economic Studies (CES) of the U.S. Census Bureau. Daniel Wilson is an economist in applied microeconomic research at the Federal Reserve Bank of San Francisco.

This chapter was written, in part, by Census Bureau staff. It has undergone a more limited review than official Census Bureau publications. Any views, findings, or opinions expressed in this chapter are those of the authors and do not necessarily reflect those of the Census Bureau or the Federal Reserve system. All results were reviewed to ensure confidentiality. We thank Douglas Meade and Michael Glenn, Adriano Rampini, Andrea Eisfeldt, John Seabold, Robert Parker, and other participants at this NBER Conference on Research in Income and Wealth (CRIW) conference, and members of the Census Advisory Committee of Professional Associations, as well as seminar participants at the Center for Economic Studies for many helpful discussions concerning the various data sources used in this paper. We thank the participants of the NBER/CRIW preconference in August 2003 for their many helpful comments on the direction of this research.

payroll. Measures of outputs and inputs are typically far from this ideal, even for nominal measures.

In this chapter, we focus on the measurement of capital stocks and flows, which are arguably the measures that are the furthest from this ideal. Specifically, we compare and contrast the measurement methodology for investment and capital at the aggregate (i.e., industry and asset) and micro (i.e., firm and establishment) levels. In so doing, we examine the extent of the micro/macro measurement inconsistencies and the associated limitations of both measurement and interpretation of capital dynamics at the micro and macro levels.

A key theme of this chapter is that the micro/macro inconsistency for capital measurement stems from dramatically different approaches to capital measurement at the micro and the macro levels. In the United States, aggregate capital measurement is based upon a top-down, supply-side approach. Production data for the capital goods producing industries, along with export and import data by product (asset) class yield measures of the domestic supply of each type of capital good. Measures of capital purchases/usage by government and consumers are then deducted from domestic supply to obtain gross investment totals by asset class. That is, gross investment totals are constructed using a commodity flow methodology that allocates the commodity totals among private and government consumption and fixed business investment. To construct a measure of the capital stock for each asset class, perpetual inventory methods are used that require the historical gross investment series, depreciation rates and investment price deflators by asset class.

Measuring economic (as opposed to accounting) depreciation and investment price deflators are difficult issues in their own right, but much of our focus is on other dimensions of capital measurement. Our analysis of aggregate capital measurement focuses on two closely related issues: (a) how the gross investment totals by asset class are allocated to industries and (b) how the gross investment measures by asset and industry classes from the top-down approach differ from the gross investment measures by asset and industry classes that can be constructed from a bottom-up approach. That is, there are data on capital expenditures in business surveys that can be aggregated to industry-asset totals as well.

Currently, the top-down approach for generating industry aggregates is based on the construction of capital flow tables that permit the allocation of the top-down asset totals to industries. The periodic capital flow tables (produced by the Bureau of Economic Analysis, hereafter BEA) are developed every five years as part of the input-output tables for the United States. Historically there have been limited data available to generate such capital flows tables and the BEA has, in lieu of direct information, used indirect methods and very strong assumptions to generate the capital flows tables. The limited information problem has been improved lately with the development of the Annual Capital Expenditures Survey (ACES), and the BEA has begun to incorporate the information from these data into their capital flows tables. However, for the most recent capital flow table released (i.e., the 1997 capital flow table, released in 2003), the BEA uses ACES data only to help construct the structures portion of the capital flows table and still uses indirect methods to construct the equipment portion of the capital flows table. At least part of the reason for this is that, as will become clear, it is difficult to reconcile the industry-asset statistics generated from the top-down and bottom-up approaches.

Another closely related focus of this paper is the nature and difficulties of measuring capital at the micro level. Increasingly, analysts interested in even macro issues seek to use firm-level data to understand the dynamics of key variables like productivity, job growth, and investment. Thus, getting capital measurement right at the micro level needs to be viewed as a critical part of the data infrastructure used to measure capital in the United States. In this paper, we review some sources of business-level data on capital and discuss the measurement methods that are available.

Even if the data are not fully reconcilable at the micro and macro levels, it is in principle desirable to have the measurement methodology be consistent. However, data limitations render this impossible. The aggregate approach uses perpetual inventory methods to construct capital stocks by asset (or industry-asset class). At the micro level, a number of limitations make this difficult. First, even though there has been progress via the development of ACES, data on investment by detailed asset are available at the firm level only periodically (currently every five years). The key annual business-level surveys (ACES and the Annual Survey of Manufactures) collect annual data on capital expenditures only by broad asset classes: equipment and structures. Second, business-level surveys have enormous sample rotation, especially for smaller businesses, and (as we will highlight below) underrepresent young businesses. These limitations make using perpetual inventory methods difficult at the broad asset class level and impossible at the level of detailed asset classes. Instead, a modified perpetual inventory approach is used to the extent possible, by initializing the capital stock based upon book value data when available and then using perpetual inventory methods for businesses that have sequential years of investment data. We examine the properties of the microdata in light of these limitations.

Another key theme of this chapter is that the internal inconsistency makes it very difficult to investigate the nature and sources of the variation in key economic variables. That is, given the internal inconsistency, it is not easy to drill down from the published aggregates to the microdata to investigate the (measurement or economic) factors generating the observed aggregate fluctuations.

For measurement reasons alone, it would be useful to be able drill down from the aggregates to the micro level. However, recent theory and empirical evidence from the micro behavior of businesses make clear that micro/ macro data integration may be essential for understanding the economic factors driving aggregate fluctuations. For example, recent evidence has emphasized that to understand macro aggregates it is important to measure and understand the contribution of the dynamics of the entry and exit of businesses (and in a related fashion the dynamics of young and small businesses). The basic reason is that the U.S. economy (like most advanced market economies) is constantly restructuring and this restructuring is associated with a large and continuing change in the composition of businesses. Entering businesses are quite different on a number of dimensions than the businesses that are exiting. Likewise, young and small businesses are quite different from large and mature businesses.

All of this restructuring is quite important for measuring and understanding economic change and, unfortunately, the economic aggregates published by the statistical agencies both neglect some important aspects of the contribution of this restructuring and typically do not permit quantifying the contribution of this restructuring. Part of the problem stems from the natural focus on large and mature businesses in the collection and processing of data by the statistical agencies. While large and mature businesses account for a very large share of the *level* of economic activity, the dynamics of entry and exit and the associated dynamics of young and small businesses account for a disproportionate share of the *change* in activity. This perspective suggests that measuring and understanding aggregate changes require a measurement approach that permits the decomposition of the contribution of different types of businesses (and not simply just along industry boundaries, but by entry and exit, young and mature, large and small). However, such decompositions require micro/macro consistency—that is, in the current context, to decompose the contribution of entering and exiting businesses to capital investment we would need to be able to quantify the capital investment of continuing, entering, and exiting businesses in an internally consistent manner. However, since the capital investment data are not internally consistent at the micro and macro levels, this approach is generally not possible.[1]

The chapter proceeds as follows. Section 12.2 provides a more detailed overview of capital measurement from the top-down (macro) and bottom-

1. A related argument is that recent evidence suggests that micro investment is a highly nonlinear function of fundamentals. Prima facie evidence for this is that investment at the micro level is highly skewed to the right and has a mass around zero and a fat right tail. It is unlikely that the distribution of shocks affecting businesses has this same shape (indeed, measures of the distribution of shocks at the micro level suggest that the distribution is approximately normal). The nonlinear nature of micro investment behavior implies that the response of aggregate investment dynamics to aggregate shocks will be complex and depend upon the cross-sectional distribution of the circumstances faced across firms (see, e.g., Caballero, Engel, and Haltiwanger 1995). Viewed from this perspective, micro/macro consistency is fundamentally important for understanding the aggregate response of the economy to aggregate shocks.

up (micro) approaches. The source data and measurement methods are discussed for both the micro and the macro approaches. Section 12.3 presents an analysis of some of the limitations of the top-down approach. The focus here is on the measurement of capital at the industry level and an analysis of the relationship between industry-level data from the top-down and bottom-up approaches. Analysis of the discrepancies at the industry level makes sense because the top-down and bottom-up approaches can both yield industry-level measures. Moreover, accurate industry level measurement is obviously critical for understanding the dynamics of the U.S. economy. For example, the adoption of advanced technologies like computers has been far from uniform across industries, and thus understanding the impact of changing technology depends critically on high-quality industry measures. Section 12.4 presents an analysis of the microdata with a focus on both the measurement limitations and the key properties of the distribution of capital and investment at the micro level. Alternative measurement methods and alternative data sources for micro measurement are presented and discussed. The last section provides concluding remarks.

12.2 An Overview of the Measurement of Capital in the United States

12.2.1 Aggregate Capital Stocks and Flows: A Top-Down Approach

The supply-side, top-down approach toward capital measurement utilizes production data from the capital goods–producing industries, data on capital exports and imports, and personal consumption and government use of capital goods. The primary source for the production data is the Census Bureau's Annual Survey of Manufactures (ASM), which collects data on a nationally representative sample of manufacturing establishments. The ASM collects information on the total value of shipments and inventories in nominal terms, and establishments are classified at the detailed industry (Standard Industrial Classification [SIC] and now North American Industrial Classification System [NAICS]) level. The Census Bureau also collects data on U.S. exports and imports via the U.S. Merchandise Trade Statistics, which uses a variety of sources (e.g., U.S. Customs, shipper's export declarations, etc.) to collect data on a detailed transaction basis of the products shipped and the countries of origin and destination. For capital goods industries, combining the shipments, exports, and imports data yields a nominal domestic use total by product (asset) class. Private and government consumption are subtracted from these commodity totals to obtain nominal use by the business sector.

Price deflators for these products are derived primarily from the Bureau of Labor Statistics' Producer Price Index (PPI; other sources include import/export price deflators). The BEA measures real gross investment by asset type as nominal investment divided by the appropriate price deflator.

The capital stock for asset type a is measured using a perpetual inventory specification given by

$$(1) \qquad K_{at} = \sum_{j=0}^{\infty} \theta_{ajt} I_{at-j}$$

where θ_{ajt} provides the period t weight for the vintage j real gross investment of asset a and I_{at-j} is the real gross investment of vintage j. The weights given to vintages depend upon whether the measure of the capital is to measure wealth or productive use. The BEA uses age-price (depreciation) profiles for its weights to construct its estimates of wealth by the perpetual inventory method. For the BEA, these weights emerge from assumptions that the depreciation patterns of most assets decline geometrically over time. In contrast, the Bureau of Labor Statistics (hereafter BLS) and the Federal Reserve Board (hereafter FRB) use age-efficiency schedules intended to capture the remaining productive value of assets of vintage j.

While the measurement of capital stocks and flows is already difficult enough, in large part because price deflators for capital goods are inherently difficult to measure, our focus (for the most part) is on the limitations associated with measuring capital stocks and flows at the industry level.[2] To compute industry-by-asset gross investment totals, the BEA constructs data on the shares of each asset type in each industry's total investment.

Historically, there have been limited data available to produce these shares, and in lieu of direct measurement the BEA has used alternative indirect source data together with strong assumptions. In particular, the historical capital flows tables prior to 1997 are based upon information from the occupational distribution of employment (largely drawn from decennial census data) and strong assumptions about the relationship between the occupational and asset distributions (essentially fixed coefficient technology assumptions). Starting with the 1997 capital flows table (CFT; released in late 2003), the BEA has begun to incorporate industry-by-asset information from a direct survey of asset purchases by businesses (namely, the ACES). However, for the 1997 CFT (which will be the source of the in-

---

2. There is a very large literature on the measurement of depreciation and obsolescence. It is obviously of fundamental importance and also inherently difficult to measure. For the most part, this is not our focus, given our focus on micro/macro inconsistencies. However, one area of overlap is the role of entry and exit of businesses and the measurement of depreciation. Depreciation and obsolescence schedules are based upon service life distributions of assets. The latter reflect the physical service life of an asset, and to some extent the schedules reflect obsolescence via estimates from the secondary markets for capital (see, e.g., Hulten and Wykoff 1981). However, when businesses exit, the extent of irreversibility is unclear and the nature of secondary markets for businesses that are liquidated is in a related fashion unclear. To be fair, the BEA does provide an adjustment to its depreciation rates to deal with "selection bias," which significantly increases depreciation rates. However, the adjustment factors for selection are based upon limited information and provide little guidance to the role of exit across asset types, across industries, and over time. In our view, this is a neglected area of the measurement of depreciation and obsolescence, and our findings in section 12.4 below suggest that this could be important.

dustry capital data for the last five years and the succeeding five years) the BEA only uses the structures detail data from the ACES. For the 1997 CFT equipment industry-by-asset shares, the standard method of using the occupational distribution of employment is used.

The BEA combines the industry-by-asset shares and the gross investment totals by asset to generate annual gross investment by industry and asset class. To provide more discipline on this allocation, the BEA uses industry expenditure control totals at a broad asset class (i.e., equipment or structures) from other sources (e.g., ASM and ACES) to produce its final statistics for capital stocks and expenditures by industry and asset classes reported in the CFT and the Fixed Reproducible Tangible Wealth (FRTW).[3]

To produce capital stocks (in the FRTW), the BEA uses the perpetual inventory approach using the industry-asset gross investment totals and the price deflators and depreciation profiles as described above. Since the FRTW is intended to reflect wealth and ownership of wealth, the depreciation profiles used reflect this conceptual objective. Adjustments are also made for the leasing versus ownership of capital (more on this in section 12.3 below).

The obvious micro/macro inconsistency in this top-down approach is that, for the most part, the CFT does not reflect actual data on the expenditures on assets by industries. Thus, by construction, there is a potential inconsistency between the business-level survey data on capital expenditures and the top-down-based measures. In section 12.3 below, we analyze the nature and extent of the discrepancies between the top-down and bottom-up approach.

Before proceeding to our discussion of the micro approaches to capital measurement, it is useful to emphasize that the U.S. statistical agencies have been at the lead of innovations to capital measurement. The adoption of hedonic methods for computers and the user cost approach for measuring capital in the 1980s are two examples. It is our hope that the U.S. statistical agencies will in turn take a lead in improving measures of the usage of capital and, in turn, the consistency between the micro and the macro measurement of capital.

12.2.2 Business-Level Measurement of Capital: A Bottom-Up Approach

The U.S. Census Bureau conducts a number of surveys that provide data that can be used for capital measurement at the microeconomic level. The nature of these surveys has changed substantially over the last two decades, so it is useful to review the changes in the survey instruments.

---

3. The use of such control totals is complicated by the fact that the expenditure totals at even a broad asset level summed across all industries do not match up that well with the gross investment totals at a broad asset level from the top-down approach. As will become clear in section 12.3, this is one of several sources of difficulties in reconciling the top-down and bottom-up approaches.

Statistical agencies historically have had the most complete and detailed measurement of capital at the business (micro) level in the manufacturing sector. The ASM, through 1987, collected data on book value at the beginning and end of year, new expenditures, used expenditures and retirements (including sales). In addition, all these items were collected separately for equipment and structures. Since 1987, the book value questions have been asked in the ASM only during economic census years (years ending in 2 or 7), and since 1997, the book value questions ask only about the *total* capital (rather than equipment and structures separately). Moreover, the retirement and sales questions have been dropped from the ASM.[4] The ASM is an establishment-based survey, so measures of capital can obviously be constructed at the establishment level and then, through information in the Census Bureau's Business Register, can be aggregated to the firm level if desired.

For the nonmanufacturing sectors, data on book values and expenditures have historically been very sparse. In economic census years, a sample of nonmanufacturing businesses had been asked questions about their total book value of capital and total capital expenditures in the Asset and Expenditure Survey (AES). The sampling unit employed in the AES is not the establishment (as in the ASM), or the firm (as in the ACES). The AES sampling unit can be thought of as a taxpaying entity (i.e., a particular Employer Identification Number) or a line of business (e.g., a two-digit SIC) within a firm. Due to the difficulty in matching data across these different survey units, we choose not to use AES investment data in this study.[5]

Since 1993, the Census Bureau has been collecting capital stock and expenditures data on an economywide basis using ACES as the survey instrument.[6] The ACES is a firm-level survey, although firms are asked to break out at least some of their responses on an industry basis (e.g., on a two- to three-digit SIC basis). The ACES collects data annually on capital expenditures (new and used) by broad asset class (i.e., equipment and structures) and periodically (e.g., 1998 and 2003) by detailed asset class. The ACES also collects total book value of capital and retirement/sales of assets.

One obvious use of these surveys is to generate expenditure totals (by either broad asset category or detailed asset classes) at the industry level. These expenditure totals by industry and broad asset category are used as control totals in the top-down approach discussed in section 12.2.1. Additionally, the industry-level data have been used in their own right to construct capital stocks by detailed industry for the manufacturing sector. For

---

4. The deterioration of the ASM in terms of capital measurement is unfortunate, as the expenditures and retirements/sales data have been used at the micro level successfully to analyze the capital adjustment processes across businesses (see, e.g., Caballero, Engel, and Haltiwanger 1995 and Cooper and Haltiwanger 2000). The type of analysis in these studies is no longer feasible.

5. See Doms, Jarmin, and Klimek (2004) for more detailed descriptions of the investment data and sampling units in the AES.

6. A pilot version of ACES was in the field prior to 1993.

example, the NBER/CES/FRB productivity database relies on these data to produce capital stock estimates for four-digit SIC manufacturing industries for the 1958–96 period.

These business-level data have also been used extensively by the research community to study investment dynamics at the micro level (the ASM data have been used much more extensively than ACES to date). Several measurement challenges immediately arise in the use of these data for this purpose.

First, the historical availability of the microdata as well as the sample rotation of the surveys makes literally applying the perpetual inventory measurement specification in equation (1) impossible for all but a small subset of the largest survey units. Consider the ASM for which data are available for a much longer period of time than for ACES. The ASM data at the CES are available from 1972 to the present. For businesses that existed in 1972, the data are left-censored and there are a large number of manufacturing establishments in the ASM that are left-censored. In addition, the ASM sample rotation is every five years with only large establishments sampled with certainty across panels. As such, data for small establishments are typically left-censored in the first year of a five-year ASM panel and right-censored in the last. To overcome these limitations, researchers have typically applied the following variant of the perpetual inventory measurement methodology:

$$(2) \qquad\qquad K_{et} = (1 - \delta_{it})K_{et-1} + I_{et},$$

where K_{et} is the capital stock for a broad asset type for establishment e at time t, I_{et} is real gross expenditures (ideally new plus used less retirement/sales, but often just new plus used given lack of retirement/sales data), and δ_{it} is the depreciation rate.[7] The latter is indexed by i and t to denote that plant-level depreciation schedules are not available so the typical practice is to use the depreciation rate schedule for industry i at time t. The depreciation rate at the industry level varies over time as the asset mix of an industry changes over time.

Several measurement difficulties are immediately apparent in imple-

---

7. The depreciation rates and the age-price or age-efficiency schedules from equation (1) are obviously closely related. A standard method for generating industry depreciation rates is to use equation (2) along with the real measures of capital and investment at the industry level to back out the implied rate of depreciation at time t in industry i. Those researchers who use the implied depreciation schedules from the NBER-CES Productivity Database are using depreciation schedules that reflect the productive capital stock, since the NBER-CES Productivity Database relies upon age-efficiency schedules from the FRB. Note further that Caballero, Engel, and Haltiwanger (1995) and Cooper and Haltiwanger (2000) use the retirement/sales data in their measures of gross capital expenditures. Use of the latter permits these studies to study the propensity for negative gross investment that is indeed observed in the data. However, these studies find that the distribution of gross investment rates is highly skewed to the right, with relatively little negative gross investment suggesting the presence of substantial irreversibilities.

menting equation (2). Left-censoring implies that the capital stock needs to be initialized in the initial year of observation (rather than initial year of operation). The standard practice is to use the book value to initialize the capital stock. Typically, since book values don't reflect price and efficiency factors, there is a crude adjustment to this initial capital stock. The statistical agencies (e.g., BLS and BEA) produce capital stocks on a historical-cost and real basis (the real capital stock is measured using the methods described above) at an industry level. Microdata researchers often use this information to make the following adjustment of the initial capital stock:

$$(3) \qquad\qquad K_{e0} = \frac{BV_{e0}}{\dfrac{BV_{i0}}{K_{i0}}},$$

where BV_{e0} is the book value for the establishment in the initial year 0, BV_{i0} is the historical-cost value at the industry level (from BEA or BLS) for the industry i that establishment e is located in for year 0, and K_{i0} is the real capital stock at the industry level (from BEA or BLS) for year 0. This adjustment of the book value corrects for price and efficiency differences in the asset mix at the industry level but obviously generates mismeasurement for establishments within the same industry with different vintages and asset mixes.

In addition to the problem of initializing the capital stock, investment price deflators are typically not available at the establishment level either. Instead, researchers use the industry-level investment price deflator so that asset mix differences across establishments in the same industry also are a source of measurement error.

While implementation of this methodology for ASM establishments already raises various measurement issues, the problems are even more severe in attempting to measure real capital stocks and flows at the firm level with ACES.[8] For one, given that ACES only started in 1993, the left-censoring problem is large for even the businesses that are regularly sampled in ACES. For another, the sample rotation in ACES is annual so that for small businesses the adjusted book value (as in equation [3]) is the only measure of the capital stock available. In addition, ACES is a firm-level survey and only asks firms to break out industry data at a two- to three-digit level. As will become clear below, there are questions about the qual-

---

8. Another data source for firm-level capital stocks that has been widely used in the literature is the COMPUSTAT data. The methods for measuring capital stocks and flows from COMPUSTAT are typically very similar to the methods described in this section (with similar limitations). Future work needs to be done comparing and contrasting the ACES data with COMPUSTAT data as a further check on the quality of the ACES data. We do not focus on the COMPUSTAT data in this chapter since they reflect only publicly traded companies, so that the sample selection makes micro/macro comparisons not very informative.

ity of the industry-level data in ACES, as firms apparently truncate the set of industries for which they should be reporting capital expenditures. Finally, and this is another theme we return to in section 12.4, ACES adds new businesses with a considerable lag. The paucity of data on new businesses raises a variety of questions. Among other things, new businesses are arguably quite different in the rate and mix of investment across asset classes. This heterogeneity is masked in the ACES since young businesses are undersampled.

This brief overview makes transparent that the micro and macro capital stock measures are not internally consistent. Even for nominal capital expenditures the micro and the macro data are not internally consistent, much less the real capital expenditures and real capital stocks. In what follows, we quantify and explore the nature of the micro and macro approaches on a variety of dimensions.

12.3   Top-Down versus Bottom-Up: The Industry Allocation of Asset-Specific Investment

One of the primary objectives of this chapter is to quantify the extent to which the top-down and bottom-up approaches to capital measurement differ. In this section, we focus on how the two approaches yield different allocations of asset-specific investment across industries. The primary set of data on investment flows by asset and industry is the CFT, constructed at five-year intervals by the BEA. We describe the methodology for constructing the CFT as "top-down" since the BEA first obtains economy-wide investment totals at the detailed asset level and industry investment totals at the broad asset level (equipment or structures), and then allocates detailed asset-level investment to using industries based not on micro expenditures data, but based rather on occupational employment data. As it is derived from the CFT, the BEA's annual investment by asset type and by industry data, the FRTW, can also be characterized as top-down. An alternative, bottom-up approach would be to aggregate up to the industry level from micro-level data on expenditures by detailed asset type. Until recently, this could not be done as such microdata did not exist. However, detailed asset-type investment data were collected in the 1998 ACES, allowing us to create a bottom-up investment-by-type-and-by-industry matrix.

Section 12.3.2 below describes a number of exercises we performed to quantify the differences and similarities between the BEA's top-down investment allocations and the bottom-up allocations we obtained from the 1998 ACES. The ACES itself is discussed in more detail in section 12.3.3, including some of its important limitations as well as potential remedies. First, though, we provide some necessary background regarding the construction of two BEA investment matrices and their conceptual differences.

12.3.1   Background

Conceptual Differences

There are two substantial conceptual differences between the CFT and the FRTW. First, the CFT is on a use basis, whereas the FRTW is on an ownership basis. The distinction primarily has to do with how the two data sets treat operating leases. The CFT allocates leased capital to the lessee (user) industry while the FRTW allocates it to the lessor (owner) industry. The choice of treatment has an enormous impact on the distribution of certain types of capital goods such as autos, trucks, and aircraft.

The second conceptual difference is that the CFT measures only flows of *new* capital, whereas the FRTW seeks to track flows of used capital as well. For instance, for autos, the CFT provides estimates of each industry's use of autos produced in the current year. Purchases or leases of used autos would not be counted. In contrast, the FRTW attempts to first obtain each industry's expenditures on new and used autos and then net out the industries' sales of used autos to consumers or other industries (though, in practice, they can only net out sales to consumers since there is no data on interindustry transfers).

Construction of the Capital Flows Table

The methodology used by BEA to construct the CFTs in general, and the 1997 CFT in particular, is fully documented in Meade, Rzeznik, and Robinson-Smith (2003). Here we provide a brief synopsis. First, the BEA obtains asset-type (row) control totals (i.e., economywide investment by asset type), which are taken straight from the data on private fixed investment by asset type in the BEA's benchmark input-output (IO) tables.[9] These totals are also published in the private fixed investment tables of the National Income and Product Accounts (NIPAs). For structures, data on private (nonresidential) fixed investment by type of structure comes from the Census Bureau's "Value of Construction Put in Place," which is based on a survey of builders of construction projects. For equipment, private fixed investment by asset in the IO tables is obtained from source data on domestic supply (shipments minus net exports), from which measures of private and government consumption are then subtracted.[10] Thus, we refer to the CFT's approach to obtaining asset-type control totals as the "supply-side" approach.

Second, the BEA obtains industry (column) control totals from aggre-

9. For more information on the BEA's supply-side approach to obtaining asset investment totals, see Lawson et al. (2002).

10. For certain asset types, special adjustments are made to private fixed investment numbers. For example, for autos, a portion of consumers' purchases of autos is added to the business fixed investment total according to Census data on the average fraction of mileage consumers use their autos for business purposes.

gated firm- or establishment-level data on capital expenditures (over all asset types). The primary sources of these data are the Economic Census (EC) and the ACES (after 1992) or the Plant and Equipment (P&E) survey (before 1992). Note, however, that the ACES source data referred to here are those on total investment (available every year since 1992), not the data on investment by asset type (available only in certain years). The industry control totals, as derived from the source data, are adjusted for some industries so that expenditures on operating leases are allocated to the lessee (using) industry rather than the lessor (owner) industry.

Third, the asset-type control totals are allocated to using industries via two methods: "direct" and "distributive." With direct allocation, capital goods thought to be used by a small set of industries are directly allocated (in total) to those industries in proportion to their output. For example, *mining and oil field equipment* is distributed to the following industries: oil and natural gas extraction, coal mining, metal ores mining, nonmetallic mineral mining and quarrying, support activities for mining, and natural gas distribution. For capital goods thought to be used by multiple industries, their investment totals are *distributed* to using industries based on BLS data on occupational employment by industry. As Meade, Rzeznick, and Robinson-Smith (2003) describe it, "[c]ertain occupations or sets of occupations are assumed to be good indicators of which industries use a specific type of capital good; for example, machine tools are allocated to industries by the employment of machine tool operators." In the 1997 CFT, 85 percent of total new equipment investment was allocated to industries using this latter method. For the recently released 1997 CFT, investment for a subset of structures types (constituting 37 percent of total structures investment) was allocated using the published data on investment by industry and by asset type from the 1998 ACES. Prior to the 1997 CFT, these structures types were allocated to industries using the occupational employment data.

Construction of the Fixed Reproducible Tangible Wealth investment matrix

Now, consider the BEA's methodology for constructing the annual FRTW investment matrices.[11] First, as with the CFT, they obtain "supply-side" asset-type control totals from the private fixed investment tables of the NIPAs. In contrast to the CFT, for some asset types, this total is then adjusted for net transfers of used capital into the business sector (from consumers, government, or foreign countries), which are estimated using various sources of data. In the case of autos, for example, sales of used autos to consumers by businesses (e.g., rental car companies) are estimated using auto registration data and subtracted from total business fixed investment in autos.

---

11. For a full description of the FRTW methodology, see BEA (1999).

Second, the BEA obtains industry control totals from aggregated firm- or establishment-level survey data on capital expenditures. Starting with 1993 (the first year of the ACES), the survey data primarily consist of the ASM for manufacturing industries and the ACES (and sometimes the P&E survey as well) for nonmanufacturing industries. For years before 1993, the BEA primarily uses the Economic Census for years in which it's available, and uses the ASM and P&E survey for other years. Notice that for Economic Census years, the FRTW and CFT use essentially the same source data for industry control totals. However, a major difference in the CFT's and FRTW's industry control totals comes from the fact that the FRTW adjusts industry totals for transfers of used assets. For example, an industry's exports of used assets are subtracted from the industry's capital expenditures to arrive at the industry's investment total.

Third, asset-type investment totals are allocated to purchasing industries. The *initial* allocation is based on the adjacent CFT(s), which, as described above, are based on BLS occupational employment data. Since the FRTW is on an ownership basis and the CFT is on a use basis, this initial allocation is adjusted to an ownership basis "using data from unpublished I-O studies, industry trade associations, and secondary sources" (BEA 1999). For years between two CFTs, they interpolate the capital flows distribution. For years after the most recent CFT (1992 at the time of this writing), they extrapolate.[12]

Uses of the BEA's Investment Matrices

The importance of the BEA's data on investment distributions by industry and by capital type is far greater than is generally recognized. These distributions are frequently used in academic studies relating to the economic effects of industry information technology (IT) usage (see, e.g., Autor, Levy, and Murname 2003; Wolff 2002; Stiroh 2004; Wilson 2003). In fact, some studies even use these data to analyze the relationship between occupational mix and capital mix, which, given that the distributions are based on occupational mix in the first place, is rather disconcerting. These distributions are also used by other governmental and non-governmental data programs. For instance, these distributions provide the weights used (e.g., by the FRB, the BLS, and Jorgenson, Ho, and Stiroh 2005) to generate aggregate investment deflators from asset-specific price indices. These aggregate deflators, in turn, are used throughout empirical macroeconomics. Likewise, the distributions are also used by the BLS and others to generate measures of aggregate capital services by industry. The BLS uses these measures in their estimates of multifactor productivity (MFP). Lastly, the BEA's investment

---

12. Unfortunately, the version of the FRTW that makes use of the 1997 CFT was not released in time for use in our study.

distribution data are used by businesses, academia, and the government to do forecasting, marketing studies, and impact analysis.[13]

12.3.2   Comparing the Top-Down and Bottom-Up Investment Matrices

Given the important and wide-ranging uses of the investment distribution data, evaluating their accuracy is crucial. Until recently, however, such an evaluation was difficult (if not impossible) as there was no alternative data to compare to, at least for the United States. That changed with the 1998 ACES, which collected firm-level ("bottom-up") data on investment by detailed industry and asset type. These data can be aggregated up and used to assess the accuracy of the BEA's investment matrices, built using their "top-down" methodology. In this section, we conduct such an assessment.

First, though, we must decide which BEA investment matrix to compare to the 1998 ACES-derived investment matrix. Since the ACES data are conceptually most comparable to the FRTW, given that both are ownership based and they pertain to the same year, this seems a natural place to start.

In order to assess the similarity of the ACES and FRTW investment matrices, we look at three statistical measures of similarity: correlation, distance, and cosine. We report only the correlation statistics here; the distance and cosine measures yielded virtually identical results (available from authors upon request).

The two investment matrices can be compared along either the industry dimension or the asset-type dimension. That is, let V_{ij} denote investment by industry i in asset type j. Let v_{ij} denote an industry's investment share of some asset type:

$$(4) \qquad v_{ij}^{Source} = \frac{V_{ij}}{\sum_i V_{ij}}; \text{ where Source} = \text{FRTW or ACES.}$$

One can compute a correlation (or other similarity index) for each asset type between the vectors $\{v_{ij}^{FRTW}\}_j$ and $\{v_{ij}^{ACES}\}_j$. Alternatively, one can define an asset type's investment share as

$$(5) \qquad s_{ij}^{Source} = \frac{V_{ij}}{\sum_j V_{ij}},$$

and one can compute a correlation for each industry between the vectors $\{s_{ij}^{FRTW}\}_i$ and $\{s_{ij}^{ACES}\}_i$.

The mean and median (over industries) of the within-industry, cross-type correlations (see equation [5]) between the FRTW and the ACES are

---

13. See Meade, Rzeznick, and Robinson-Smith (2003) for a more thorough description of the uses of the CFT.

Table 12.1   Summary of within-industry, cross-type correlations

Correlations between investment shares from:	Mean	Median
1998 FRTW and 1998 ACES (raw)		
Equipment		
Unweighted correlations	0.653	0.774
Weighted correlations	0.833	0.967
Structures		
Unweighted correlations	0.816	0.960
Weighted correlations	0.882	0.999
1998 FRTW and 1998 ACES-FRTW hybrid		
Equipment		
Unweighted correlations	0.703	0.821
Weighted correlations	0.864	0.971
Structures		
Unweighted correlations	0.809	0.960
Weighted correlations	0.885	0.999
1997 CFT and 1998 ACES-FRTW hybrid		
Equipment		
Weighted correlations	0.835	0.947
Structures		
Weighted correlations	0.928	1.000

Note: Mean and median are calculated over 59 industries.

given in table 12.1 (along with the mean and median for the other comparisons discussed below). The statistics for equipment and structures are reported separately. We find that the mean correlation over industries for equipment is 0.65 and the median is 0.77. For structures, the mean is 0.82 and the median is 0.96. If, in computing an industry's correlation, we weight asset types by their investment share (i.e., the average between the FRTW and ACES shares), the mean for equipment rises to 0.83 and the median rises to 0.97. For structures, the mean rises to 0.88 and the median rises to (virtually) 1. Clearly, weighting helps since the FRTW and ACES tend to align more closely for asset types that are a larger share of investment. Furthermore, as the high median suggests, there are a fair number of industries with weighted correlations close to one.

However, there are also a fair number of industries with very low correlations. This can be seen in figure 12.1, which shows two histograms of weighted correlations over industries—one for within-industry correlations across equipment investment shares (panel A) and one for within-industry correlations across structures shares (panel B). For the cross-equipment-types correlations, forty of the fifty-nine industries had a correlation between 0.9 and 1.0. Nonetheless, a few industries had very low correlations: Metal Mining (correlation = 0.03), Petroleum Refining (0.28), Miscellaneous Manufacturing (0.55), Pipelines (0.06), Gas Transmission, Distribution, and Storage (0.05), Nondepository Credit Institutions (0.27),

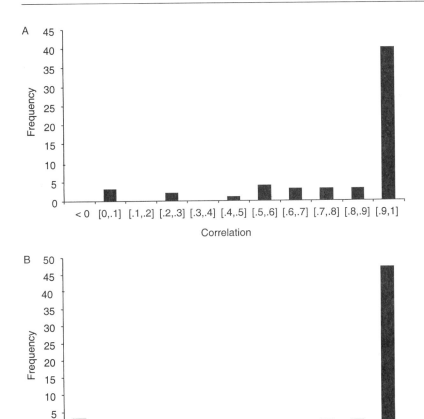

Fig. 12.1   FRTW versus ACES, within-industry, across-type correlations: *A,* **Equipment;** *B,* **Structures**

Security and Commodity Brokers (0.58), Insurance Agents, Brokers, and Service (0.43), Personal Services (0.53), and Repair Services (0.56). As for structures, there were fewer industries with very low correlations. Those that did have low correlations were Public Transportation (–0.07), Water Transportation (–0.11), Transportation Services (0.55), Real Estate Offices (0.47), and Health Services (0.33). Thus, it seems that there are still some substantial discrepancies between the FRTW and ACES.

Looking at the within-type, cross-industry correlations (see equation [4]), we find a mean of 0.68 and a median of 0.76. If, in computing a type's correlation, we weight industries by their investment share, the mean rises to 0.79 and the median rises to 0.95. Thus, the FRTW and ACES seem to have lower discrepancies for industries with larger investment (in each asset type). However, as with the within-industry correlations, there are still quite a few within-type correlations that are low. The especially low correlations were for the following types: Mobile Structures (correlation = 0.01), Educational Buildings (0.08), Religious Buildings (–0.02), Other Mining Exploration (0.03), Other Nonfarm Structures (0.15), Electrical Equipment, not elsewhere classified (0.10), Other Nonresidential Equipment (0.64), and General Purpose Machinery (0.65). The weak correlations for more general forms of equipment are not surprising since presumably it is difficult to identify which occupations intensively use such equipment. Apparently, there are some types of structures that are difficult to allocate across industries, but the outliers here don't appear to fit any general pattern. Also, given the wide use of the data on computer investment, it is worth noting that the unweighted correlation across industries for the computer investment share from FRTW and ACES is 0.76—the weighted correlation for computers is 0.81. While this is a reasonably high correlation, it is far from one suggesting that those studies that use the computer investment by industry data from the FRTW are subject to potentially nontrivial measurement error that is, by construction, correlated with the distribution of occupations across industries.

Which Is Right?

From the results discussed above, we conclude that the BEA's "top-down" FRTW investment matrix and the "bottom-up" matrix derived from the ACES largely agree on the capital distributions for the most important asset types, but there are serious differences for particular industries and particular asset types. In the face of these discrepancies, the obvious question is: which is right?

Both have their advantages and shortcomings. Clearly, the primary advantage of the ACES investment matrix is that it is survey based—that is, bottom-up. In contrast, the allocation of asset-type investment to purchasing industries (i.e., the investment shares) in the FRTW is derived from the most recent CFT. In turn, the investment shares in the CFT are based on arguably suspect assumptions. Specifically, as described above, the CFT investment shares are based on assumed relationships between capital use of particular asset types and employment in particular occupations. We are aware of little or no empirical support for these relationships.[14]

The fact that ACES is survey based, however, doesn't mean that its data are necessarily entirely accurate. There are in fact a number of potential sources of reporting error in the ACES. First, due to incomplete records or lack of effort on the part of the respondent, firms may not break out their investment into every industry in which they operate (as they are instructed to do). Indeed, we know from matching ACES respondents to their corre-

---

14. In principle, one could match ACES microdata to the Occupation Employment Survey to test the strength of the fixed coefficients implicit in this allocation method.

sponding Business Register (BR) records that there is such "industry truncation"—an issue we explore in more depth in section 12.3.3. An implication of this is that the BEA's industry control totals derived from ACES may be incorrect.

Similarly, ACES respondents may fail to fully break out their investment into all of the appropriate asset types. Unfortunately, we have no alternative data source with which to evaluate the extent of this "type truncation," nor do we have any way to treat it (as we do in the case of industry truncation). Third, firms may *expense* some of their expenditures, where the BEA would (properly) consider it capital investment. This may be particularly problematic for particular asset types, such as computers and software.[15] Fourth, ACES does not allocate the investment done by nonemployers either by industry or by asset type. In 1998, capital expenditure by nonemployers accounted for some 10 percent of nationwide investment. Note that these last three issues should mainly affect the asset-type control totals in the ACES-based investment matrix rather than the industry allocations, though it is possible that some industries are more susceptible to these types of reporting errors than others.

The FRTW, on the other hand, may be more accurate when it comes to the asset-type control totals. The FRTW captures economywide investment by asset type using the supply-side approach, described above, which is based on micro source data on domestic supply (shipments minus net exports) combined with measures of government and personal consumption of each asset type. In principle, this approach captures expenditures on an asset type irrespective of how purchasing firms account for these expenditures.

Note that the supply-side approach is not above reproach: investment is computed as a residual (i.e., $I = Y - NX - C - G$). While Y (shipments) may be relatively well measured, measurement error in any of the remaining components will also manifest itself in I. This certainly may impact some asset classes more than others—for example, assets in which personal consumption (C) or government expenditure (G) may be particularly difficult to measure, such as computers. Also, net exports (NX) are subject to a host of potential measurement problems. Nonetheless, in this paper, we assume that the BEA's supply-side asset investment totals are more accurate than the ACES totals, given the shortcomings of ACES described above. However, further research on the accuracy of the supply-side approach would be useful.

It is clear that the asset-type control totals in FRTW and ACES differ greatly. Table 12.2 shows the ratio of economywide investment by asset type from the FRTW to that of ACES. In most cases, ACES has lower asset-type investment than does FRTW.

15. In 2003, the Census Bureau addressed this issue in its supplemental Information and Communications Technologies (ICT) survey, which elicited information from firms regarding their expensing of ICT equipment. Unfortunately, these data were not yet available at the time of this writing.

Table 12.2   **Ratio of economywide investment by asset type**

Asset type	Ratio of FRTW to ACES investment by type	Share of economy-wide investment in FRTW	Share of economy-wide investment in ACES
Structures			
Other nonfarm buildings	0.168	0.007	0.041
Mobile structures	9.034	0.003	0.000
Hotels, motels, and inns	1.847	0.068	0.036
Industrial buildings	0.891	0.130	0.143
Office buildings	1.156	0.180	0.152
Other commercial buildings, NEC	0.821	0.137	0.163
Commercial warehouses	1.304	0.048	0.036
Hospital and institutional buildings	0.656	0.057	0.085
Amusement and recreational buildings	1.727	0.029	0.016
Air, land, and water transportation facilities	0.673	0.021	0.031
Telecommunications facilities	0.435	0.030	0.068
Electric, nuclear, and other power facilities	1.454	0.102	0.069
Educational buildings	1.063	0.040	0.037
Religious buildings	0.696	0.024	0.033
Other mining exploration	0.314	0.005	0.015
Petroleum and natural gas wells	1.500	0.106	0.069
Other nonfarm structures	2.107	0.012	0.005
Equipment			
Instruments	1.799	0.053	0.035
Computer and peripheral equipment	1.043	0.125	0.142
Office equipment except computers and peripherals	2.096	0.031	0.017
Communications, audio, and video equipment	1.366	0.121	0.105
Capitalized software purchased separately	4.256	0.072	0.020
Fabricated metal products	1.355	0.014	0.012
Metalworking machinery	0.930	0.051	0.065
Special industrial machinery	0.479	0.054	0.134
Ventilation, heating, air-conditioning, refrigeration, and other general purpose machinery	1.425	0.049	0.041
Autos	0.130	0.019	0.174
Trucks, buses, and truck trailers	6.271	0.140	0.026
Aircraft	0.926	0.030	0.039
Other transportation equipment	0.458	0.014	0.036
Mining and oil field-machinery	0.350	0.006	0.021
Engine, turbine, and power transmission equipment	0.980	0.007	0.008
Electrical transmission and distribution equipment	3.622	0.034	0.011
Electrical equipment, NEC	3.805	0.021	0.006
Furniture and related products	1.269	0.053	0.050
Agricultural equipment	3.815	0.009	0.003
Construction machinery	1.767	0.034	0.023
Service industry equipment	2.070	0.022	0.013
Other nonresidential equipment	2.727	0.037	0.016

Note: NEC = not elsewhere classified.

As for the FRTW's (or the CFT's) industry control totals, for most non-manufacturing industries, the totals are actually based on the ACES microdata, so the industry totals for the FRTW matrix do not differ much from our ACES-based matrix.

Creating a Hybrid Matrix Combining the Advantages of FRTW and ACES

So clearly the ACES and FRTW investment matrices each have some advantages over the other. Can the advantages of each be combined to create a hybrid investment matrix that is conceptually superior to either individually? We believe they can. First, we can rescale the ACES investment matrix to have the same asset-type control totals as those in FRTW. This should address the last three shortcomings of the ACES investment matrix that we mentioned above—namely, type truncation, expensing, and nonemployer investment. And as for industry truncation, we've developed a methodology to help treat this problem. This is described below in section 12.3.3. These two corrections yield a 1998 ACES/FRTW hybrid that is potentially superior to both.

As earlier, we computed the within-industry, cross-type correlations between the investment shares from the hybrid matrix and those from the FRTW. The correlations are computed separately for equipment types and structures types. The mean and median across industries are reported in table 12.1, and the histograms (for equipment and structures, separately) are shown in figure 12.2. Not surprisingly, the correlations generally are higher than those between the FRTW and the original ACES matrix. Similarly, the mean and median of the within-type, cross-industry correlations are also higher when comparing FRTW to the hybrid than when comparing FRTW to the original ACES.

The individual correlations for each type and each industry are also generally higher between the FRTW and the hybrid than between it and the original ACES. However, there remain a number of asset types and a number of industries for which there are substantial discrepancies. The industries with the lowest correlations for equipment are Petroleum Refining (correlation = 0.36); Stone, Clay, Glass, and Concrete (0.58); Pipelines (0.47); Gas Transmission, Distribution, and Storage (−0.01); Nondepository Credit Institutions (0.36); Insurance Agents, Brokers, and Service (0.39). Those with the lowest correlations for structures are Mining and Quarrying Nonmetallic Minerals (0.35); Tobacco (0.43); Public Transportation (−0.07); Water Transportation (−0.10); Air Transportation (−0.08); and Health Services (0.56). The types with the lowest cross-industry correlations are for these types: Mobile Structures (0.04); Educational Buildings (0.08); Religious Buildings (−0.02); Other Mining Exploration (0.03); Other Nonfarm Structures (0.17); and Electrical Equipment, not elsewhere classified (0.11).

In order to help assess which data source is more accurate, it is useful to

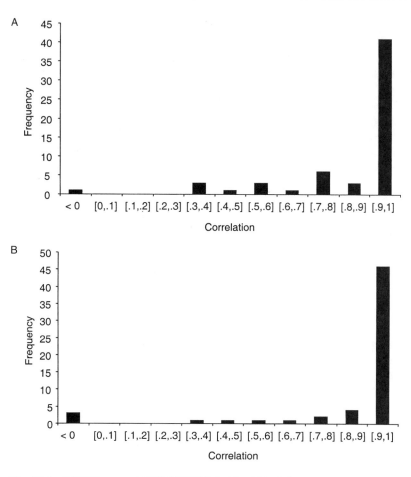

Fig. 12.2   FRTW versus ACES-FRTW hybrid; within-industry, across-type corre-lations: *A*, Equipment; *B*, Structures

look at an independent third source. One possible alternative source is the survey-based investment matrix constructed by Statistics Canada (Stat-Can). Table 12.3 shows the investment shares for selected asset-industry pairs from three sources: the FRTW, the FRTW-ACES hybrid, and Stat-Can. These selected pairs are every possible pair for which a common asset-type and industry aggregate could be obtained (since each of the three sources has its own industry and type classification systems). Of the eighty-two comparable pairs that we obtained, StatCan was closer to the FRTW-ACES hybrid in terms of industry investment shares in fifty pairs (60 percent). In terms of asset type investment shares, StatCan was closer to the hybrid in forty-seven pairs (57 percent). The sum across all pairs of the absolute difference between StatCan's industry investment shares and those

Table 12.3   Comparing selected investment shares across three data sources: BEA (FRTW), FRTW-ACES hybrid and StatCan

Industry	Asset type	Share of industry investment (within equipment or structures)			Share of economywide investment in that asset type		
		StatCan	FRTW share minus StatCan share	Hybrid share minus StatCan share	StatCan	FRTW share minus StatCan share	Hybrid share minus StatCan share
Business services	Computers, excluding production process	80.6	-38.0	-26.9	17.2	-6.5	-5.6
Communications and other utilities		16.9	-7.1	-8.7	15.3	-9.1	-9.8
Construction		5.0	2.8	-0.4	1.1	-0.1	-0.3
Educational services		32.6	7.3	18.3	3.2	-3.1	-1.1
Finance and insurance		11.5	28.3	16.6	23.2	5.7	0.3
Health and social services		20.8	-1.3	4.8	2.3	-0.6	3.0
Hotels and restaurants		9.2	1.8	6.5	0.6	-0.3	-0.1
Manufacturing		4.8	11.5	6.8	8.9	6.5	9.3
Mining and oil well		0.6	6.5	4.3	0.2	0.5	0.5
Retail		22.4	3.2	2.0	4.9	1.0	3.2
Wholesale		28.7	18.2	5.2	8.2	8.6	1.7
Business services	Communication equipment	1.7	6.7	4.2	0.6	3.4	1.6
Communications and other utilities		53.5	-5.2	16.4	80.1	-22.8	1.2
Educational services		0.8	24.2	4.7	0.1	0.1	0.3
Finance and insurance		0.5	6.9	1.5	1.8	8.3	1.1
Health and social services		0.7	-0.2	0.5	0.1	0.0	0.4
Hotels and restaurants		0.1	3.0	1.1	0.0	0.1	0.1
Manufacturing		0.3	3.2	2.4	0.8	5.4	6.4
Retail		1.5	2.0	0.1	0.6	0.9	0.3
Wholesale		1.7	7.1	-0.3	0.8	5.1	-0.1
Business services	Instruments	6.9	-3.7	-4.8	8.6	-5.1	-6.2
Communications and other utilities		0.1	2.0	0.3	0.6	5.3	0.8

(continued)

Table 12.3   (continued)

Industry	Asset type	Share of industry investment (within equipment or structures)			Share of economywide investment in that asset type		
		StatCan	FRTW share minus StatCan share	Hybrid share minus StatCan share	StatCan	FRTW share minus StatCan share	Hybrid share minus StatCan share
Educational services		34.7	-32.7	-23.9	19.8	-19.8	-17.5
Finance and insurance		0.5	1.8	-0.5	5.9	1.3	-5.7
Health and social services		51.4	0.1	11.2	33.4	-14.1	34.7
Mining and oil well		1.1	10.7	-0.9	2.2	3.1	-2.0
Wholesale		0.8	-0.1	0.2	1.4	-0.3	0.1
Communications and other utilities	Fabricated metal products and metalworking machinery	0.7	1.5	-0.5	2.0	2.8	-1.6
Construction		0.0	4.1	1.6	0.0	1.9	0.6
Manufacturing		12.0	11.1	13.5	72.1	4.2	21.7
Mining and oil well		0.3	2.5	-0.1	0.3	0.7	-0.2
Wholesale		2.7	0.6	0.2	2.5	1.6	-0.5
Finance and insurance	Industrial, energy, electrical and related equipment	0.2	2.9	0.2	3.1	4.1	-1.9
Health and social services		4.1	17.1	-2.8	3.4	2.5	-2.4
Manufacturing		1.9	10.8	3.9	26.7	12.3	8.3
Mining and oil well		2.6	19.1	-0.6	6.8	0.4	-5.7
Retail		3.5	1.3	10.8	5.7	-2.1	12.5
Wholesale		2.6	2.9	15.9	5.4	1.0	15.3
Communications and other utilities	Autos	0.6	0.0	1.4	0.3	4.1	1.1
Finance and insurance		66.6	-61.3	-5.3	79.0	-33.3	-25.1
Manufacturing		0.1	0.0	2.3	0.1	1.5	3.9

		1	2	3	4	5	6
Mining and oil well		1.5	-1.6	0.0	0.3	-0.4	-0.1
Retail		8.6	-6.9	-4.0	1.1	3.6	0.5
Wholesale		3.1	-5.1	5.1	0.5	-8.9	2.0
Construction	Trucks, buses, and truck trailers	25.0	15.1	-18.1	10.9	-2.3	-3.0
Educational services		5.0	-4.2	-4.7	1.0	-1.0	-0.9
Manufacturing		0.4	1.9	0.4	1.6	1.9	7.0
Mining and oil well		6.6	-2.3	-4.7	4.6	-3.9	-2.8
Communications and other utilities	Aircraft	0.2	-0.2		1.4	-1.2	
Manufacturing		0.2	0.0	1.4	3.9	-2.8	7.6
Communications and others utilities	Motors, generators, transformers, turbines and pumps	1.5	8.0	11.2	9.5	23.7	78.5
Manufacturing		1.3	5.6	-0.9	17.4	18.7	-10.6
Mining and oil well		0.9	6.5	-0.3	2.1	2.1	-1.2
Retail		4.3	-3.7	-4.2	6.6	-5.8	-6.3
Wholesale		1.4	1.0	-1.2	2.7	2.0	-2.1
Business services	Furniture and related products	6.5	-1.4	-1.0	2.3	3.2	2.1
Communications and other utilities		2.0	1.2	-0.3	2.9	5.7	1.2
Construction		10.0	-5.8	-8.9	3.6	-1.2	-2.9
Educational services		23.6	-15.3	-12.9	3.8	-3.7	-2.2
Finance and insurance		5.4	1.2	-1.2	17.8	2.7	-4.9
Health and social services		21.3	-17.6	-15.7	3.9	-2.5	0.4
Hotels and restaurants		83.8	-52.0	-22.1	8.7	-5.3	-1.3
Manufacturing		1.5	2.2	-0.4	4.6	10.3	1.6
Retail		54.8	-37.7	-22.8	19.4	-2.4	19.3
Wholesale		28.7	-24.4	-20.9	13.4	-6.8	-5.1
Construction	Agricultural and construction equipment	60.0	-32.2	-15.4	23.4	-3.8	30.1
Finance and insurance		1.3	0.9		4.7	3.7	4.8
Manufacturing		0.5	0.0	0.1	1.5	1.1	
Mining and oil well		17.3	-3.1	-8.4	10.8	-3.0	-1.8

(continued)

Table 12.3 (continued)

Industry	Asset type	Share of industry investment (within equipment or structures)			Share of economywide investment in that asset type		
		StatCan	FRTW share minus StatCan share	Hybrid share minus StatCan share	StatCan	FRTW share minus StatCan share	Hybrid share minus StatCan share
Business services	Industrial buildings	34.9	-33.4	-30.1	2.5	-2.3	-2.1
Communications and other utilities		0.0	3.1	0.0	0.0	4.1	0.0
Construction		0.0	11.6	21.9	0.0	0.5	0.6
Health and social services		1.0	-0.9	-0.8	0.3	-0.3	-0.2
Manufacturing		86.8	-7.5	2.7	93.7	-27.8	-7.7
Mining and oil well		0.1	4.0	4.8	0.5	3.2	2.6
Retail		0.0	2.3	1.1	0.0	1.4	0.8
Business services	Office buildings	26.8	29.0	37.2	2.1	4.6	3.5
Communications and other utilities		3.5	13.1	-0.5	7.3	8.8	-4.8
Construction		35.0	-4.6	5.1	3.5	-2.6	-2.5
Finance and insurance		94.0	-45.8	-32.8	28.5	-1.6	17.0
Manufacturing		3.1	4.1	2.4	3.6	0.7	1.3
Mining and oil well		0.4	0.2	0.1	2.2	-1.8	-1.9
Retail	Other commercial buildings, NEC	87.3	-3.8	8.8	33.0	4.7	16.6
Mining and oil well	Electric, nuclear, and other power facilities	3.9	-2.5	-3.3	14.3	-12.6	-13.5
Total of absolute differences			794.1	570.6		420.0	489.9

of FRTW turns out to be considerably larger than that between StatCan and the hybrid matrix. However, in terms of asset-type investment shares, the hybrid-StatCan differences are somewhat larger in total than the FRTW-StatCan differences.

Thus, in general, we find StatCan's investment distributions are more similar to the hybrid matrix than the FRTW. This begs the question: should the BEA use this hybrid instead of the current methodology for constructing FRTW?

The hybrid still is not immune to the ACES shortcoming of type truncation (which could explain agreement between the hybrid and StatCan, since StatCan may also be prone to similar type truncation). But this is arguably a smaller problem than the problems introduced by using occupational employment to allocate investment to industries. In fact, the BEA seems to be moving towards this hybrid, as indicated by the changes in methodology introduced in the 1997 CFT. With the 1997 CFT, investment in certain types of structures (covering 35 percent of structures investment) was allocated to industries according to 1998 ACES distribution. Ideally, we would like to compare this 1998 ACES-FRTW hybrid to a 1998 FRTW matrix that incorporates the 1997 CFT (not just because it uses the ACES distribution for some structures types, but also because it is based on more up-to-date information). Unfortunately, these revised FRTW data were not available at the time of this writing.

So as an alternative, we can compare the 1998 hybrid matrix directly to the 1997 CFT. The shortcoming of this approach is that 1997 CFT is use based (where ACES is ownership based) and covers a different year. Nonetheless, in table 12.1 we show the mean and median of the correlations, and figure 12.3 presents the histograms. Not surprisingly, the correlations for structures are extremely high. In fact, the median correlation for structures is almost exactly 1 (and the mean is 0.93). For equipment, the median correlation is 0.95 and the mean is 0.84. Thus, with the BEA's recent changes in methodology, the industry allocations of detailed asset investment have, in effect, partly switched from a top-down to a bottom-up approach, bringing increased consistency between micro and macro data on capital flows. However, for a fair number of important equipment types, large discrepancies remain between the ACES microdata and the CFT (and FRTW) macrodata. Further consideration by the BEA of using the ACES as a source for equipment investment allocations seems warranted.

In the section that follows, we introduce some of the key features of the ACES and further explore and discuss the issue of industry truncation, which (as we've noted) is an important limitation in using the ACES as a source of information about asset-industry shares and for building aggregate data. We discuss the methodology we've designed to treat the issue of industry truncation, and we demonstrate its effect on reallocating capital expenditure across industries and sectors.

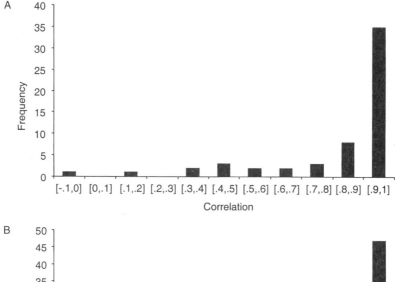

Fig. 12.3   CFT versus ACES-FRTW hybrid; within-industry, across-type correlations: *A,* **Equipment;** *B,* **Structures**

12.3.3   Working with the Annual Capital Expenditures Survey

In existence for over a decade, the ACES is a nationally representative firm-level survey designed to produce industry-level estimates of capital investment in new and used structures and equipment.[16] Among our earliest discoveries in using the ACES microdata (and we are among the very first researchers to have used these data) is that firms may be providing insufficient industry detail on the ACES—that is, they "truncate" the list of industries that they record investment for. In particular, we noticed that many firms acknowledged far fewer industries on their ACES form than we observe employment and payroll data for in the Census Bureau's BR.[17] If

16. See, for example, U.S. Census Bureau (2000).
17. This observation relies on at least one critical assumption: If a firm had zero investment in an industry, it recorded the industry, reported zero, *and* the Census Bureau actually "keyed

true, an implication is that ACES may incorrectly distribute total capital expenditures across industries, particularly if some industries are systematically excluded more often than others and the impacts are not perfectly off-setting.

Correcting for Industry Truncation

A description of the industry truncation (and details about the ACES survey in general) is located in the appendix, but in this section of the paper we attempt to correct the problem. To do so, we first assume that the information in the BR reflects a firm's true industrial composition. We then split the sample into two: "Complete reporters" are those firms whose list of industries on the ACES is absolutely identical to their list of industries in the BR. We employ these particular firms' ACES and BR data to compute investment-to-payroll ratios for each asset type and industry pair, simply calculated as total weighted capital expenditure in that industry-asset pair divided by total weighted payroll in that industry. All other firms are designated "incomplete reporters" and their capital expenditures will be reallocated across industries using (a) their industry-level payroll from the BR and (b) the investment-to-payroll ratios computed from the complete reporters.[18]

Specifically, for incomplete reporters with nonzero expenditure in a particular asset type, we sum up their investment in that asset to the firm level. We then completely replace the industries they recorded on the ACES with the list of industries they have payroll in according to the BR. We then multiply the payroll in these industries by the investment-to-payroll ratios specific to the asset-industry pair. This yields a firm-level capital expenditure that should not be used directly—it is the *implied distribution* of investment across industries that we are interested in, however. We use this distribution to allocate the *actual* firm-level capital expenditure in said asset type to the full list of BR industries for the firm. Should this particular methodology fail—as will be the case when the investment-to-payroll ratio is zero

in" at least the industry (if not also the zero). We know from other Census Bureau surveys, however, that zeros are often not keyed into the database (because they do not impact aggregation). By extension, in order to conserve time and resources, the Census Bureau may not key in a line of data from an ACES form if it contributes nothing to the aggregate capital expenditure. That industry entries do sometimes appear in the ACES database with zero investment suggests that the Census Bureau does *sometimes* key in such data. But the prevalence of missing data in the database also suggests that—just like in other surveys—zeros are very often disregarded in the ACES. For our purposes, we assume that if the database shows any trace of an industry associated with a firm then the firm in fact "acknowledged" that industry and we backfill zeros into the missing values as appropriate.

18. Actually, we allow firms to cross the boundaries of these groups on an asset-by-asset basis. Suppose, for example, that a firm reports zero investment in metalworking machinery in five industries. And say that the firm in fact truncated its industry detail—it actually operated in those five industries plus three others. Because we assume that firm-level totals are correct, capital expenditure in metalworking machinery in the three omitted industries must also be zero. This firm, and its eight industries, will enter the complete reporter group for at least this one asset type.

for all of a firm's industries—we instead use the distribution of payroll to allocate capital expenditure across industries. The end result is a new distribution of capital expenditures across industries by detailed asset type, which served as the basis for the hybrid ACES-FRTW matrix we discussed and used in Section 12.3.2.

One can certainly imagine more refined reallocation mechanisms than the one used here. One of the less desirable features of the current algorithm, for example, is that a report of zero investment in a particular asset for a particular industry may be overwritten with a positive value, or a positive value may be replaced with an even larger value. Yet neither of these changes has anything to do with the problem of industry truncation per se. In principle, constraints can be placed on this type of reallocation, but these are rather difficult to implement empirically, for a variety of reasons. We have also experimented with the possibility of imputing zero investment for a particular firm's investment in a particular asset in a particular industry, recognizing that investment is often "lumpy" at the micro level.[19] This too is quite difficult to implement empirically and if done improperly may lead to unintended biases. So while we acknowledge that more sophisticated methodologies certainly exist, much more understanding of their side effects is necessary. Therefore, for now, we have chosen a simple and (arguably) more benign treatment.

We are also intentionally conservative—along a number of dimensions—in our approach to reallocating capital expenditure. Because we are mainly interested in matching ACES to the BEA's FRTW and CFT, we first collapse the ACES data down to the lowest common denominator of industrial classification, reducing the number of industries from some ninety-eight down to sixty-three. One effect of this is that there are *fewer* mismatches between the ACES and the BR.[20] Similarly, we aggregate asset types to the lowest common denominator, which reduces the fifty-five ACES types to forty.[21] The net effect of both of these actions is larger

19. In essence, this variation of the algorithm would use the group of complete reporters to compute a *probability* of nonzero investment and an investment-to-payroll ratio *conditional on investment being positive.* This probability and conditional ratio would then be applied to the incomplete reporters. In a further refinement, the probability of investment could be set to one (zero) in cases where the firm already reports positive (zero) capital expenditure. And to remove the element of chance from the resulting estimates, this exercise can be replicated a number of times and an average of the outcomes taken.

20. For instance, suppose a firm reports its activity in chemicals (SIC 289) on the ACES but not drugs (SIC 283). Because the BEA recognizes no distinction within SIC 28, these data are collapsed. Therefore, the firm is seen as reporting data in SIC 28, which matches what is found in the (collapsed) BR, and is classified as a complete reporter, where normally it would not have been.

21. For example, office, bank, and professional buildings are combined with medical offices. Note that there are also instances in which the BEA recognizes more asset detail than the ACES—for example, the eight different types of computer and peripheral equipment. And there are two asset types that the ACES do not recognize at all: custom software and own-account software. This changed with the 2003 ACES.

samples in the asset-industry cells, resulting in more robust estimates of investment-to-payroll ratios.[22]

For various reasons, we also decided *not* to reallocate capital expenditures in Cars and Light Trucks. Like the CFT, ACES measures just the flow of new capital, ignoring the sale of used capital. This is a very important distinction for asset types with extensive resale markets, as is the case with automobiles. To demonstrate the importance of this distinction: ACES tallies over $98 billion of business investment in automobiles in 1998 (a total that does not include expenditure by nonemployers) while BEA's FRTW, which does adjust for resales, recognizes just $12.8 billion. Surely some industries play more of a role here than others. For example, rental car agencies (SIC 751) invest heavily in automobiles but also sell off a tremendous number, generally after a few years of use. (Automobiles leased by the automakers face a similar fate.) FRTW reports $4.8 billion of investment in automobiles by all of SIC 75 (Auto Repair, Services, and Parking), while firms in the ACES reported $27.9 billion of (weighted) automobile investment in this industry—a difference of over $23 billion.[23] We found that reallocating automobiles needlessly contaminated our analyses (particularly in certain industries) and we therefore left them in their original industries.

The Reallocation of ACES Capital Expenditure

Despite our rather conservative approach to treating the industry truncation issue, we see some significant reallocation of capital expenditure across industries and sectors. Table 12.4 shows the reallocation of capital expenditure across broad sectors (in millions of 1998 dollars). Interestingly, the sector that gained the most from reallocation was Wholesale Trade, while Manufacture of Durable Goods lost the most. In light of our discussion in the appendix of industry truncation at manufacturing firms, these findings are not at all surprising. Besides Wholesale Trade, other sectors gaining large amounts of capital expenditure are Transportation, Finance, and Manufacture of Nondurable Goods. Other sectors losing large amounts of investment are Services; Insurance and Real Estate; and the ACES category "serving multiple industries." A virtue of our algorithm is that capital expenditure in the latter is actually allocated to industries.

---

22. Though not our interest here, if assets were further collapsed into two types—equipment and structures—one could introduce investment-to-payroll ratios that varied by industry and size class. In early work with the 1995 ACES (not reported here), we did exactly that.

23. Interestingly, firms that are classified as *primarily* in SIC 75 in the ACES reported over $20 billion in "retirements and dispositions" of capital assets, which presumably includes the sale of used autos. Since this is based on firm-level totals, however, this value may also include any retirement of nonautomobile assets as well as the retirement of assets these firms may have had outside of SIC 75. And the retirement of automobiles in this industry by firms *not* primarily engaged in this activity is excluded from this figure. Nonetheless, we see that this magnitude is similar to the $23 billion gap between FRTW's and ACES's estimates of automobile investment in this industry.

Table 12.4   Reallocation of capital expenditure by sector

Sector	Millions of 1998 dollars
Agricultural services, forestry, and fishing	+61
Mining	–1,008
Construction	+98
Manufacturing (nondurables)	+1,615
Manufacturing (durables)	–5,074
Transportation	+7,395
Communications	–1,127
Utilities	–609
Wholesale trade	+8,641
Retail trade	–252
Finance	+2,000
Insurance and real estate	–4,074
Services	–5,013
Health services	+111
Serving multiple industries	–2,766

Underlying table 12.4 is a much larger table by detailed industry and detailed asset type (not presented here). This table reveals that the reallocation of the $8.6 billion of capital expenditure toward Wholesale Trade is unusually broad, in the sense that nearly every asset type experienced a net gain in expenditure. This sort of robust reallocation does not appear to be the norm in other industries experiencing large net changes.

For example, in terms of the increase in investment in the transportation sector, roughly half of the $7.4 billion is accounted for by the industry Motor Freight Transportation and Warehousing (SIC 42), which had most of its increase from nonautomobile transportation equipment. In the finance sector, Holding, Charitable Trusts, and Other Investment Offices (SIC 67), in particular, experienced a large increase in capital expenditure, most of which was in commercial buildings. Meanwhile, in the Manufacture of Nondurable Goods sector, the industry experiencing the largest gain was Chemicals and Allied Products (SIC 28), mainly in industrial buildings. It is important to note that not all industries in a sector necessarily move in the same direction. Food and Kindred Products (SIC 20), for example, experienced a decrease similar in magnitude to the increase in Chemicals, chiefly through a loss of miscellaneous equipment.

In terms of the sectors experiencing large losses of capital expenditure as a result of reallocation, Manufacture of Durable Goods leads the list. Here we find that Communications Equipment and Electronic Components and Equipment (SIC 36) are the largest of the losers, mostly in various types of industrial equipment. Again, however, there is heterogeneity within the sector; for instance, Primary Metals (SIC 33) experiences substantial gains. The decline in investment in the Service sector comes mainly in Business

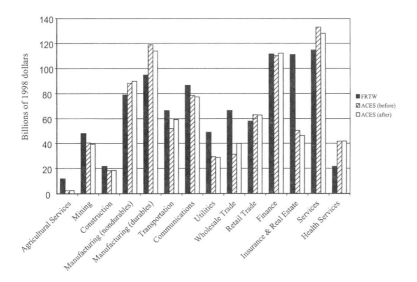

Fig. 12.4   Total capital expenditures

Services (SIC 73) and Automotive Repair, Services, and Parking (SIC 75), and the vast majority of that are accounted for by a decline in nonautomobile transportation equipment. And in the Insurance and Real Estate sector, Real Estate Offices (SIC 65) are found to lose a large amount of capital expenditure in commercial buildings.

Finally, in figure 12.4 we show how these reallocations affect sectoral totals vis-à-vis BEA's FRTW. This is done for the assets and industries that ACES and FRTW have in common.[24] We see that our reallocation efforts moved ACES noticeably closer to FRTW totals in Manufacturing (Durables), Transportation, Wholesale Trade, and Services, but large differences still exist, particularly in Insurance and Real Estate, Wholesale Trade, Health Services, Utilities, and Manufacturing (Durables). Part of these discrepancies might be due to remaining conceptual differences. First, recall that capital investment by nonemployers (totaling $95 billion in 1998) are not included in ACES totals, which may certainly explain at least part of the gap seen in an industry like Insurance and Real Estate. Second, ACES

24. In particular, ACES does not recognize investment in two types of software, nor does it tally capital expenditure for Agricultural Production (SIC 01-02). FRTW, on the other hand, does not contain capital expenditure for Combination Electric and Gas, and Other Utility Services (SIC 493), Water Supply (SIC 494), Steam and Air-Conditioning Supply (SIC 496), Irrigation Systems (SIC 497), and Social Services (SIC 83). Neither recognizes the U.S. Postal Service (SIC 43), Private Households (SIC 88), and Public Administration (SIC 9). With these restrictions, the FRTW contains $939.9 billion in capital expenditure in 1998 while ACES contains $860.1 billion. These totals cannot be easily compared because conceptual differences still remain.

does not attempt to adjust for the sale of used capital, which we know from our example above amounts to $23 billion in just one particular service industry. Third, there may be issues with the expensing of capital expenditure by firms in the ACES. And then there are the issues surrounding leasing. Therefore, while our correction for industry truncation in the ACES may matter, it is not the whole story.

12.4   Business-Level Capital and Investment: A Bottom-Up Approach

High-quality business surveys on capital stocks and flows are critical for building aggregates from the bottom up, but the microdata are also critical for understanding the behavior of investment at the micro and the macro levels. The longitudinal business datasets developed in the United States have increasingly been used by analysts to study the behavior of productivity, investment, employment, and price and wage dynamics. Part of the motivation for analysts to use such microdata is obvious, as the decision-making unit is the firm or the establishment. Therefore, testing alternative economic models of business behavior is best achieved with microdata. Aggregate data (at the industry- or economywide level) can only be used if firms within a given industry are relatively homogeneous in their behavior. However, the recent literature using microdata shows that micro- and macrodata provide very different pictures of investment dynamics. Macro investment dynamics are volatile in the sense that investment is highly procyclical but the aggregate data changes over a relatively narrow range of investment rates and in a smooth fashion. In contrast, investment at the micro level is very lumpy—there is a mass of businesses with zero or little investment and a fat right tail of businesses that exhibit what has been denoted an investment spike (see, e.g., Caballero, Engel, and Haltiwanger 1995; Doms and Dunne 1998; and Cooper, Haltiwanger, and Power 1999). Recent literature emphasizes that lumpy micro behavior implies complex aggregation. That is, movements in the aggregates will reflect both intensive and extensive margins, with the latter reflecting businesses discretely switching from inaction to action ranges for investment.

In this section, we explore the properties of the micro distribution of investment using the two key business-level surveys the Census Bureau uses to collect data on capital stocks and flows—the ASM and ACES. Our primary goal is to illustrate key properties of the micro distribution that highlight the idiosyncratic features of the micro distribution with a particular focus on those features that raise questions about aggregation and aggregate fluctuations. As noted in section 12.2.2, data limitations in these surveys unfortunately make it difficult to apply exactly the same measurement methodology (e.g., perpetual inventory) used in constructing investment rates using aggregate data. Instead, either an adjusted book values or a modified perpetual inventory method is used to construct capital stocks (and in turn act as the denominator in calculating an investment rate). As such, we also explore the sensitivity of the distributions at the micro level to these measurement issues.

12.4.1   The Annual Survey of Manufactures

In this subsection, we explore the measurement and properties of business-level capital and investment using the ASM. Our objectives are broadly threefold. First, we explore the limitations of alternative measurement methods outlined in section 12.2. In particular, we examine the properties of investment and capital measures using the modified perpetual inventory specification given in equation (2) versus the adjusted book value specification given in equation (3). We compare and contrast the properties of the micro and macro capital and investment using these alternative measurement specifications. In addition, we explore the sensitivity of analyses using such alternative capital stock measures—here our metric is the impact that alternative measures have on the measurement of total factor productivity. Second, we summarize and explore key features of the micro distribution of investment. In so doing, we highlight the features of the micro distribution that suggest an internally consistent and fully integrated micro/macro measurement of capital would be important for understanding aggregate fluctuations. Third, we explore basic aggregation issues by comparing and contrasting the properties of the distribution of investment at the establishment and at the firm level. The ASM has the advantage that analysis can be conducted at the establishment level, and it is of interest to understand how the properties of business-level investment change as we aggregate data from the establishment to the firm level.

Perpetual Inventory versus Adjusted Book Values

The ASM is the only data set that measures capital stocks and flows at the establishment level. There have, however, been some major changes in the collection of capital data on the ASM. As mentioned earlier, the ASM collected beginning- and end-of-year book values broken out by equipment and structures each year until the 1987 Census of Manufactures (CM). After 1987, the book value question is only asked during economic census years. In the 1997 CM, only total book value was collected. For these reasons, we can only construct adjusted book values of capital stocks for the period 1972–87, 1992, and 1997. Fortunately, investment data, broken out by both equipment and structures, has been collected in the ASM continuously for the entire 1972–2000 period. Using the detailed investment data along with the book value data to initialize the series, the modified perpetual inventory method described in section 12.2.2 (equation [2]) can be used to construct capital stocks at the establishment level for the vast majority of plants in the ASM.

In what follows, we often compare our measures for all plants and then for a subset of plants that have at least five years of prior continuous plant history. The reason for focusing on the latter subset in this context is that the difference between the capital stocks computed on an adjusted book value basis (equation [3]) and on the modified perpetual inventory basis (equation [2]) will be zero, by construction, in the year the plant first appears in the ASM and can only grow over time based upon the plant having a different vintage structure of capital relative to the average plant in its two-digit industry (see section 12.2.2 for a more complete discussion). We denote this subset of plants the "five-year continuers" in the analysis that follows.

Figure 12.5 provides a comparison of the distribution of adjusted book value capital stock and the modified perpetual inventory capital stock, using the five-year continuers. We observe that the distribution of perpetual inventory capital is slightly to the left of the adjusted book value distribution, with more mass in the center of the distribution. Thus, one difference is that the adjusted book value yields a higher mean and cross-section variance of the capital stock relative to the preferred perpetual inventory measures. However, the distributions are remarkably similar and the correlation at the micro level is above 0.9 (overall and in each year separately).

We now turn to properties of the investment rate, defined as real investment divided by the beginning of year capital stock. As figure 12.6 shows, investment rates computed using the two alternative measures of the capital stock are also highly correlated. We find that the correlation is generally higher when we include all establishments and is always greater than 0.6. This is sensible considering that the full sample includes the years when the

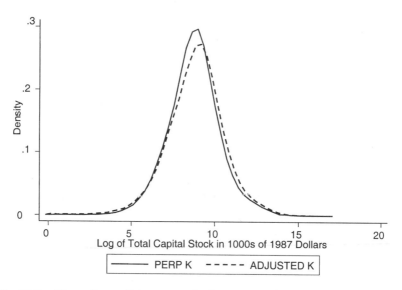

Fig. 12.5   Alternative capital measures for five-year continuers

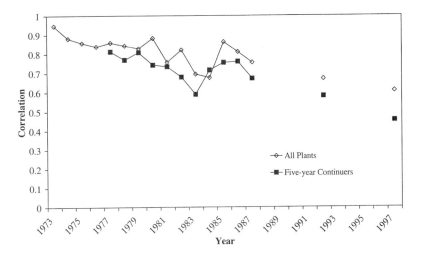

Fig. 12.6   Correlation of Adjusted and Perpetual Inventory Investment Rates

capital stocks are initialized in the perpetual inventory method (i.e., when the two measures of capital stocks are equal). When we only look at the five-year continuers, we find that the correlation of the two measures is not as strong, but is still relatively high (in the 0.6 to 0.8 range) in the period prior to 1987 when the ASM still collected data on capital stocks. In 1992 and 1997 the correlation falls off, but this also would include a set of long-lived establishments that would have significantly different measures of capital stocks across the two measures.

While these correlations are quite high they are far from one, and they are also time varying. These findings thus serve as a caution to the micro-data analyst who is studying investment rate behavior with microdata and only can construct capital stocks using an adjusted book value. Put differ-ently, while the capital stock distributions are very similar, the investment rate distributions are apparently less so. In what follows, we further explore some of the key features of these distributions. For the remainder of the analysis, we focus our attention on the five-year continuers, since they are the more interesting comparison for this purpose.

In figure 12.7, we show the annual time series fluctuations for the median investment rate using the alternative two capital measures. First, we note that the perpetual inventory method yields higher medians. On the low side, the median investment rate ranges from 5.5 percent of capital in the previous period to just over 9 percent. The two measures yield the same time series variation, with both series showing increases in median invest-ment rates during the boom periods of the business cycle, and declines dur-ing recessionary periods. The median investment rate also exhibits little if any secular trend.

In addition to examining the fluctuations in the median of the micro dis-

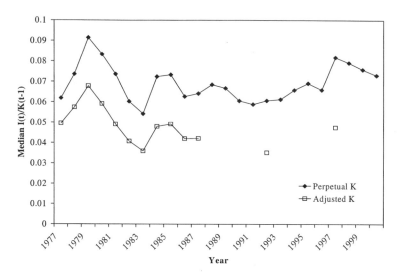

Fig. 12.7   Median $I(t)/K(t-1)$ for five-year continuers

tributions, we also examine how the shape of the distribution is changing over time. In figure 12.8, we show the interquartile range for the investment rate distributions. Interestingly, we find that the interquartile range widens during boom periods and declines during contractionary ones. If we focus on the boom in the late 1970s, we find that the 75th percentile invests roughly 16 percent more of its capital stock than the 25th percentile did. This difference is large given that the median investment rate is roughly 9 percent at this time.

We also look at how the upper tail of the distribution fluctuates over time. In figure 12.9, we look at the difference between the median establishment investment rate and the investment rate of the 90th percentile. The right tail is more spread out using the perpetual inventory–based measure compared to the adjusted book value. We also find that the upper tail of the distribution spreads out in cyclical upturns, and this pattern holds for both capital measures. For example, in 1978 (a boom year), the 90th percentile of the establishment distribution invests nearly 28 percent more than does the median establishment, while during the recession of the early 1980s, there is a large decline in the 90-50 differential to about 18 percent. Looking at figure 12.7, the change in the median investment rate from peak to trough over this period is roughly 3.5 percent, while the change in the 90-50 differential is about three times that large. Since the changes in the median are relatively modest, it must be the case that this wide swing over the business cycle is caused by firms in the upper tail of the investment rate distribution.

Another dimension over which to check the respective merits of the alternative capital stock measures is to consider the aggregate behavior of

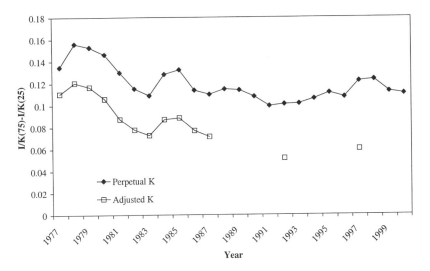

Fig. 12.8   Interquartile range of $I(t)/K(t-1)$

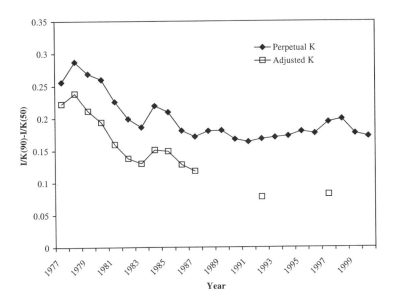

Fig. 12.9   90-50 differential for $I(t)/K(t-1)$

the measures at the industry and total manufacturing level. For this purpose, we consider the sample of five-year continuers and generate capital stock and flow (investment) aggregates using ASM sample weights. Figure 12.10 shows the implied aggregate investment rates using this aggregation compared to the aggregate investment rate from the NBER/CES/FRB productivity database. While the latter is based on the ASM data, the capital

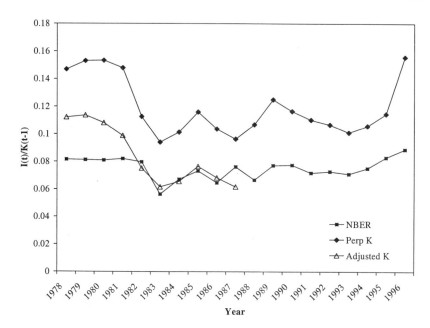

Fig. 12.10   Manufacturing $I(t)/K(t-1)$

stock series is generated using a long time series of real gross investment rates and perpetual inventory methods.[25] The perpetual inventory micro-data yield a higher average aggregate investment rate than either the NBER or the micro adjusted rate. Both of the total manufacturing aggregates from the microdata are highly correlated with the NBER series (0.76 for the perpetual inventory and 0.75 for the adjusted book value). Figure 12.11 presents the annual average of the pairwise correlations across the four-digit industry investment rates using the four-digit aggregate from the microdata and the NBER rate. For the perpetual inventory–based method the correlation averages 0.53, while for the adjusted book value method the correlation averages 0.42.

As an additional check of the sensitivity of micro patterns to these alternative capital stock measures, we consider how the alternative capital stock measures compare in terms of estimating production functions and measuring total factor productivity. Table 12.5 presents ordinary least squares (OLS) estimates of production functions using the alternative measures.[26] It is apparent that both capital stock measures yield very sim-

25. While perpetual inventory with a long time series is used in the NBER/CES/FRB data set, the investment series is from the ASM and thus is not based upon a top-down, supply-side approach.
26. The micro sample used for these regressions is the same sample used to produce the five-year continuer statistics on investment rates described in this section. In particular, the sample is five-year continuers over the period 1977 to 1987 and 1992 and 1997.

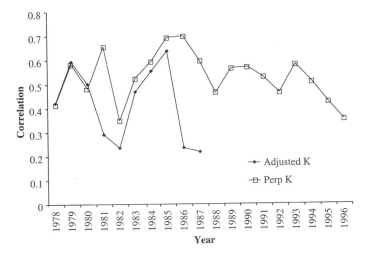

Fig. 12.11   Correlation across aggregate industry *I/K*

**Table 12.5   Sensitivity of production function estimation to alternative
                      capital measurement**

Production function estimation	Perpetual inventory	Adjusted book values
Equipment	0.037 (0.0070)	0.023 (0.0006)
Structures	0.062 (0.0009)	0.076 (0.0008)
Labor	0.287 (0.0008)	0.284 (0.0008)
Material	0.593 (0.0007)	0.597 (0.0007)
Energy	0.016 (0.0007)	0.012 (0.0008)
Correlation of TFP	0.994	
Correlation of TFP (cost shares)	0.995	

Notes: Sample consists of five-year continuers in the ASM/CM for the period 1977–87 and including the years 1992 and 1997 as well. Note that book value data on K are only collected in Census years after 1987. TFP = total factor productivity.

ilar results in terms of factor elasticities. While OLS estimates have limitations (e.g., endogeneity bias) so that the factor elasticities should be treated with appropriate caution, it is instructive that the alternative measures yield very similar estimates. Moreover, the correlation of the implied total factor productivity (TFP; the residual) is very high. As a related cross-check, we calculated TFP using cost shares but again with the alternative capital stock series. Again, the correlation of TFP is very high using these alternative capital stock measures.

To sum up, the adjusted book value and perpetual inventory capital stocks are highly correlated at the micro level. They perform about the same if the use of the capital stocks is to estimate production functions and TFP. Moreover, their aggregate properties are similar and match fairly well and yield aggregate fluctuations at the industry and total manufacturing level similar to those from published aggregates for the manufacturing sector. There are enough differences between them that there are some notable differences in the mean and dispersion of the capital stocks, which translate into differences in the mean and dispersion of investment rates. Fortunately, these latter differences, while notable, are fairly stable over time. These patterns are reassuring for analysts who are restricted to use microdata sets where the only measure of capital available is the book value.

Key Properties of Micro Distribution

The previous section focused on the sensitivity of the distribution of capital and investment rates at the micro level to alternative measures of the capital stock. In this section, we focus on key properties of the micro distribution that are not present in the aggregate data and in turn are likely to be important for both micro studies of investment but also for our understanding of the aggregate dynamics of capital stocks and flows. In particular, in this section, we focus on the lumpy nature of investment as well as the related tremendous dispersion of investment rates at the plant level. From the previous section one could believe that all establishments invest each year, and that in some years their investment is high relative to their capital stock and other years it is low relative to their capital stock. As we will show in this section, this is hardly the case.

In figure 12.12 we show the fraction of establishments that report zero investment in each year, broken out by total investment, equipment, and structures. We look at all establishments and the five-year continuers. The two series track each other quite well, but in nearly every case five-year continuers have a smaller share of plants with zero investment. Establishments are much more likely to have zero investment in structures. The share of establishments with zero investment in structures is as high as 62 percent in 1974, and as low as 38 percent in 1997. The fraction of establishments with zero total investment varies quite a bit, from nearly 28 percent of all establishments in 1973 to a low of 9 percent in 2000. It is also interesting to note the time series pattern in the data. The share of establishments with zero investment shows a secular decline over time, but also is countercyclical (e.g., the correlation between the median investment rate and the fraction of plants with zeroes among the five-year continuers is –0.25). The secular trend is somewhat weaker for the five-year continuers. We don't have a ready explanation for the declining fraction of zeroes, but taken at face value the results suggest less inertia in capital adjustment over time. It may be that capital adjustment costs have been reduced (part of this might reflect improved functioning of capital markets) or perhaps there have been secular shifts in the asset mix toward shorter-lived equipment such as computers.

At the other end of the distribution, we are interested in investments

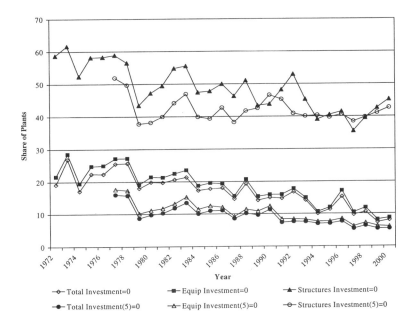

Fig. 12.12   Fraction of plants with zero investment

spikes, defined here as investment that equals more than 20 percent of the capital stock. Figure 12.13 show that spikes are highly procyclical (e.g., the correlation between the median investment rate and share of plants with an equipment spike is 0.48 for the five-year continuers). Spikes occur much more commonly in equipment investment than they do with structures. Spikes in structures decline in frequency during this time period, but spikes in equipment occur as often in the early 1970s as they do in 2000. As we saw before, five-year continuers are less likely to have zero investment. They are also more likely to have investment spikes. During recessionary periods we still observe roughly 15 percent of all establishments investing over 20 percent of the value of their entire capital stock.

As evidenced by the large fraction of zeros and the large fraction of investment spikes, it is clear that investment at the establishment level is quite lumpy. In order to quantify this in more detail, we construct the share of cumulative investment that is due to the largest year for two samples of establishments: five-year continuers and a panel of long-lived establishments that have been in the ASM from 1972 to 2000 continuously. The results of this exercise are reported in table 12.6. For the group of five-year continuers in each year, we find that (on average across all years from 1977 to 2000) the largest year of investment over any given five-year period accounts for over 40 percent of investment in terms of both total investment and invest-

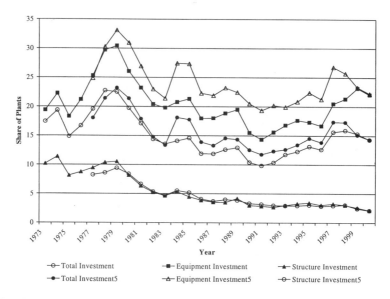

Fig. 12.13   Investment spikes: $I(t)/K(t-1) > .2$

ment in equipment.[27] In general, these two numbers have been monotonically decreasing over time, from the 47 percent range in the mid-1970s to roughly 39 percent in 2000. A similar pattern shows up in the data for structures, but on average the largest year of structures investments accounts for a much larger fraction of cumulative investment for the five-year continuers, over 60 percent in the average year, and the decline in the average is much less pronounced than in the total and equipment investment.

Looking at our panel of long-lived establishments we see that roughly 17 percent of their total investment in the past thirty years comes in just one year, and the three-year total is roughly twice that or 32 percent. At least 5 percent of investment comes from the largest year of investment, and in some cases all investment comes in one year. While the results are quite similar for equipment, the results for structures are even more striking. On average, 32 percent of structures investment comes from the largest year of investment, and the largest three-year average is nearly 60 percent of the cumulative investment in structures. At least 16 percent of cumulative investment in structures at these establishments comes from the largest single year of investment.

The findings on lumpy investment indicate that understanding investment dynamics at the micro level requires understanding both the intensive

---

27. This exercise is closely related to the much more detailed and more sophisticated analyses of investment spikes in Doms and Dunne (1998) and Cooper, Haltiwanger, and Power (1999).

Table 12.6   **Share of cumulative investment**

Time period	Variable	Mean	Min.	Max.
Last five years	The largest total investment/cumulative total investment[a]	.414	.389	.475
Last five years	The largest equipment investment/cumulative equipment investment[a]	.414	.391	.467
Last five years	The largest structures investment/cumulative structures investment[a]	.627	.608	.675
Twenty-nine years	The largest total investment/cumulative total investment[b]	.169	.056	1
Twenty-nine years	The largest equipment investment/cumulative equipment investment[b]	.167	.053	1
Twenty-nine years	The largest structures investment/cumulative structures investment[b]	.325	.064	1
Twenty-nine years	The largest three years of total investment/ cumulative total investment[b]	.362	.162	1
Twenty-nine years	The largest three years of equipment investment/ cumulative equipment investment[b]	.362	.157	1
Twenty-nine years	The largest three years of structures investment/ cumulative structures investment[b]	.594	.171	1

[a]Distribution across all years 1977–2000 for five-year continuers.
[b]Distribution across all establishments in the 29-year balance panel with approximately 6,600 observations.

(how much investment) and the extensive (invest or not invest) margins. The finding that the extensive margin and relatedly the fraction of spikes are so procyclical, suggests that understanding the procyclicality of investment at the micro level requires understanding the forces that cause plants to change from inaction to action. As has been highlighted in the recent theoretical and empirical literature, the models that can account for these dynamics are models where there is some type of nonconvexity in capital and other adjustment costs. The latter models inherently have a range of inaction and also have the interesting feature that aggregate dynamics depend critically on the entire distribution of micro behavior because it is critical to know how many plants are close to their extensive margin thresholds to understand how aggregate behavior responds to aggregate shocks.

We now turn to another key property of the micro distribution of investment. As is evident from the characterization of the distribution of investment in the prior section, there is substantial dispersion in investment rates across businesses. There are a large fraction of zeros and a large fraction of spikes. Those with zero investment are, given depreciation, experiencing a decline in their capital stock. Those with spikes are, even taking into account depreciation, experiencing large increases in their capital stock. Thus, one inference that immediately emerges from the distribution of investment rates is that there are considerable changes in the allocation of capital across establishments all the time. In addition, what is not evident in the results presented thus far is that another potentially important source of capital reallocation is the entry and exit of establishments. Entry and exit rates in U.S. manufacturing are not as large as they are in other sectors, but still it is of interest to consider the role of entry and exit in the reallocation of capital across establishments. A related issue that we explore in more depth in the next section is that the exit of establishments (or firms) may not be properly accounted for in the measurement of depreciation used to build aggregate capital stocks. That is, the standard measurement of depreciation is based upon the service life of an asset. The latter does not explicitly consider whether the exit of a firm or establishment changes the useful service life of an asset. Instead, efficiency or depreciation schedules implicitly assume that the capital from an exiting business is still in use—put differently, it is implicitly assumed that the capital from an exiting business is transferred to another business (presumably through the secondary market for capital).

To explore these issues, we use the (perpetual inventory–based) capital stock measures for the ASM from 1972 to 1998, along with longitudinal identifier links created by Davis, Haltiwanger, and Schuh (1996), extended by Haltiwanger and Krizan (1999) and Foster, Haltiwanger, and Kim (2005), as well as longitudinal identifiers from the Longitudinal Business Database (LBD) created from the BR (Jarmin and Miranda 2002). These identifiers permit us to take any pair of consecutive years and classify plants as being entrants, exits, or continuers.

Using this classification, we compute the growth rate of the capital stock at each plant as

$$(6) \qquad gk_{et} = \frac{K_{et} - K_{et-1}}{X_{et}} \text{ where } X_{et} = .5 \cdot (K_{et} + K_{et-1}),$$

where K_{et} is the real capital stock for establishment e at time t. For this purpose, we used the real capital stocks computed using the modified perpetual inventory method, and since we are interested in entry and exit we use all plants.[28] This growth rate measure mimics the growth rate measure used in the job creation and destruction literature (see Davis, Haltiwanger, and Schuh 1996). It has the desirable feature that it is symmetric like a log first difference (indeed, it can be shown that this is a second-order approximation to a log first difference), but unlike the log first difference it incorporates establishment entry and exit. Using this growth rate measure, aggregate gross capital creation and destruction measures are defined respectively as

---

28. Note that our neglect of retirement/sales implies that we are potentially missing an important part of the gross capital destruction for continuing establishments. Caballero, Engel, and Haltiwanger (1995) find that the average gross investment rate (not net investment rate) for businesses with negative gross real investment is around 3 percent. We are missing that three percent in this analysis in part although it may be partly captured in the depreciation rates we are using. See Caballero, Engel, and Haltiwanger (1995) for further discussion.

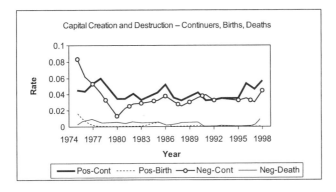

Fig. 12.14   Capital creation and destruction: Continuers, births, deaths

(7)
$$POSK_{et} = \sum_{gk_{et} \geq 0} \frac{X_{et}}{X_t} gk_{et}$$

(8)
$$NEGK_{et} = \sum_{gk_{et} < 0} \frac{X_{et}}{X_t} |gk_{et}|$$

Using these measures, note that by definition the aggregate net capital stock growth rate is equal to $POSK_{et} - NEGK_{et}$.

Figure 12.14 depicts the capital creation and destruction rates from the mid-1970s to the late 1990s for equipment investment.[29] The net growth rate in capital is on average much smaller than the gross capital creation and destruction rates calculated in this manner. Not surprisingly, gross capital creation is procyclical and gross capital destruction is countercyclical. However, the cyclical patterns vary considerably across cycles. In the late 1970s, those businesses that were exiting and/or had very low gross investment (so the net capital stock was falling) decreased their capital destruction, and this led to a rise in the net capital stock. In contrast, the booms of the 1980s and 1990s were driven more by entrants and/or businesses whose gross investment was considerably larger than depreciation so that their net capital stocks grew substantially. One way of viewing these findings is that they illustrate that the changes in the aggregate capital stock in the manufacturing level at cyclical frequencies varies in terms of what part of the micro distribution is changing. It is also interesting to note that, like net job creation in manufacturing, net capital growth in manufacturing is driven more by fluctuations in capital destruction than by cap-

29. We exclude the first year of each ASM panel (1974, 1979, 1984, 1989, and 1994) since the ASM does not have a representative sample of entrants and exits in those years. This is somewhat unfortunate since many of these years (1974 excluded) are boom years, so we miss some of the story on what happens during booms. This also yields the average net growth to be considerably lower than it would be if these years were included. Note that we use all plants in the ASM that are identified to be either an entrant, an exit, or a continuer and we also use sample weights.

ital creation. The standard deviation of capital destruction is 1.5 times the standard deviation of capital creation (although this appears to be driven primarily by the cyclical variation in the 1970s and early 1980s).

An interesting question here is the role of entry and exit. Figure 12.14 shows the components of gross capital creation accounted for by continuers (businesses that are present in year $t-1$ and t) and entrants (businesses not present in period $t-1$ but present in period t) as well as the components of gross capital destruction accounted for by continuers and exits (businesses present in year $t-1$ but not present in year t). Figure 12.14 shows that the contribution of entry and exit is quite modest in this setting although the share of capital creation accounted for by entry and the share of capital destruction accounted for by exit both exceed 20 percent in specific years. Part of the reason that the contribution of entry and exit is modest in this case is that as a share of the capital stock in any given year, entering and exiting plants account for a very small share (less than 1 percent each). This is because entering and exiting plants tend to be younger and smaller plants. However, the latter suggests that these annual calculations may be somewhat misleading regarding the contribution of entry and exit. As we will explore in the next section, the investment rates of young businesses (e.g., less than ten years old) are very high so the cumulative contribution of entry taking into account the immediate post-entry growth is substantially higher. Still, it is striking that figure 12.14 shows that most of the fluctuations in gross capital creation and destruction rates in manufacturing are from continuers. For example, the large decline in capital destruction during the boom in the late 1970s is entirely driven by a decline in capital destruction by continuers. The role of entry and exit in nonmanufacturing may be much larger, as we will see in the next section, since the entry and exit rates are much larger in nonmanufacturing. To sum up our plant-level evidence on the properties of the micro distributions, we emphasize two key points. First, the micro distribution of investment is very lumpy, and second, the micro distribution is very heterogeneous, with some businesses rapidly expanding their capital stocks through large gross investments and others contracting their capital stocks either by depreciation or exit.

Firm versus Establishment Micro Properties

As the only data set that collects measures of investment and capital at the establishment level, the ASM is a unique data set that permits exploration of the differences between establishment data and data aggregated to the firm level. In this section, we summarize the findings from an investigation of the comparison between establishment and firm effects but for the sake of brevity do not include the underlying tables and figures (available on request). For this analysis, we restrict our attention to those plants that are classified as five-year continuers. The median of the firm distribution exhibits that same overall time series pattern as the establishment-level data, but with the median firm investment rate being slightly higher than the establishment investment rate. The correlation of our two measures of capital, perpetual inventory and adjusted book value, show that the two measures are also highly correlated at the firm level, ranging from 0.6 to 0.8 and exhibiting a slight trend upward during this period. The correlation at the firm level is slightly lower than at the establishment level, and the series shows less variation over time. The interquartile range and 90-50 difference show exactly the same time series patterns and are roughly identical in terms of levels. In terms of the micro properties of the firm series, the fraction of firms with zero investment is somewhat lower for equipment and total investment, but the fraction of firms with zero investment in structures is significantly lower than the fraction of establishments with zero investment. Investment spikes in structures exhibit the same patterns and levels at the firm and establishment level, but the incidence of spikes in equipment and total investment are much lower for firms than for establishments. These last two points suggest that firm investment is somewhat less lumpy than plant investment, smoothing structures investment across the firm but concentrating investment at particular plants within the firm. Equipment and total investment also exhibit smoother investment patterns, with slightly fewer zero-investment firms and fewer investment spikes. While the results for the ASM establishment versus firm level are roughly equivalent, some differences do exist. In the following section, we describe the micro properties of another firm-level data set, the ACES.[30]

12.4.2   Investment Dynamics at the Micro Level for the Entire Economy

In this section, we look at patterns of investment across firms in all sectors of the economy (not just manufacturing as in the preceding section). For this purpose we use the ACES data on gross investment at the firm level along with the book value information.[31] The ACES is now the primary source of data on business investment in the U.S. statistical system. To date, however, it has been used sparingly by researchers looking at invest-

---

30. For the analysis reported here we are using the distributions across plants versus the distributions across firms without weighting by some measure of activity (in this case the most appropriate weight would probably be capital). It turns out that most firms are single units (i.e., have one plant) so the micro distributions of firms and plants are quite similar. However, multi-unit plant firms account for a large fraction of activity. Thus, it would be interesting to explore the activity-weighted distributions. Put differently, it would be interesting to focus some attention on the large, complex multi-units who have many establishments. The behavior of the latter at the firm level is likely to look quite different from the plant-level data.

31. We have not constructed real investment flows and capital stocks with the ACES data. Many large firms in the ACES span many industries, which somewhat complicates the choice of appropriate deflators for constructing real values for investment flows and capital stocks. Most of the calculations using ACES in this paper are within year. In addition, we don't construct perpetual inventory capital stocks using ACES. Therefore, deflating ACES investment and capital stocks was not a high priority for this paper.

ment dynamics. This is partly due to its relatively recent introduction and to researchers' unfamiliarity with the survey. We hope to shed light on the usefulness of the ACES for understanding investment dynamics and to suggest ways the survey can be changed to improve its utility in this area. Before moving on to this analysis, it is useful to briefly compare the ACES to the ASM on some key measures.

Comparing the ACES and ASM

Differences in the sampling units and survey design make comparisons between the ACES and ASM difficult. Both surveys sample larger units (firms and manufacturing establishments, respectively) with certainty. The surveys differ markedly in how they handle the noncertainty cases, however. In particular, the ASM selects a sample of smaller establishments that it follows over a five-year panel. This allows the use of the perpetual inventory methods discussed above. The ACES, on the other hand, selects a new probability sample each year. Thus, perpetual inventory methods can only be used to construct firm-level capital stocks for the largest ACES firms.

Despite the differences between the two surveys it is possible to compare various statistics computed from each. Here we focus on the investment rates and the share of firms experiencing spikes in investment. Figure 12.15 compares the median investment rate (I/K, computed as total capital expenditures divided by total fixed assets) and the share of businesses with investment rates exceeding 0.2 (i.e., those experiencing spikes) across ACES firms and ASM establishments. The differences in units and industry focus notwithstanding, we see that the results are broadly consistent. Firms in the ACES have slightly higher investment rates than the manufacturing establishments in the ASM, and a larger proportion of ACES firms experience investment spikes. While measurement differences could play a role (for instance, we believe the capital stock measures available for the ASM are more reliable than the book value information collected but not published on the ACES), the differences between the ACES and ASM seen in figure 12.15 may stem largely from higher investment rates in the nonmanufacturing sector over the 1990s. All of the series trend up over the 1990s following the business cycle.

Now we turn our attention to the contribution of entry and exit and also to a closely related idea raised in the prior subsection—that is, the contribution of young businesses to investment. We focus on these issues in this context because, in the nonmanufacturing sectors, entry and exit are much more important in accounting for the reallocation of outputs and inputs and for growth (see, e.g., Foster, Haltiwanger, and Krizan 2001, 2002). As mentioned in the introduction, one of the limitations of aggregate data on capital stocks and flows is that it is difficult to capture the contribution of young versus mature businesses or the contribution of entry and exit. It is

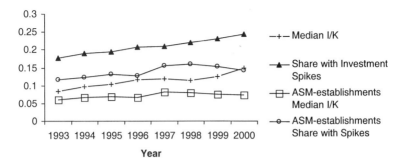

Fig. 12.15   Median investment rates and proportion of firms with spikes: ACES versus ASM

also the case that typical business surveys (including ACES) have some limitations when it comes to capturing the roles of entry and young businesses, as often the focus of these surveys is on large, mature businesses. Accordingly, the analysis in this section serves the purpose both of illustrating the importance of considering the age distribution of businesses (and entry and exit) and also of highlighting some of the limitations in trying to assess the contribution of these factors given the traditional emphasis in data collection on larger, more mature businesses. Another reason to be particularly interested in the investment behavior of young firms is that we believe they are among the first to adopt new technologies and business practices. This may have been particularly true over the period covered by the ACES: the 1990s.

Incorporating Age Information into the ACES

The ACES is not designed to provide statistics on investment by firm age. However, the ACES can be easily linked to the LBD, which contains longitudinally linked establishment-level data with firm ownership information from 1975 to the present. The LBD contains two sources of information on firm age. First, one can use the first year a firm's numeric identifier (FIRMID) is observed in the LBD. However, numeric firm identifiers in the LBD are not intended for longitudinal analysis. For example, events such as mergers and acquisitions can result in changes to numeric firm identifiers for continuing businesses. An alternative measure of firm age is the age of the oldest establishment owned by the firm. While this measure is not ideal either, it yields a much more plausible age distribution of firms than that which results from using only numeric firm identifiers.[32]

32. Work is currently underway at the CES to create firm-level longitudinal linkage in the LBD. Once completed, this work will allow researchers to construct more sophisticated measures of firm age.

Basic Facts about Investment and Firm Dynamics by Firm Age

Table 12.7 provides information on the distribution of employment across the firm age distribution for 1998. The LBD contains the universe of firms with paid employees and thus provides the benchmark to compare with those employer firms covered in the ACES. The first column in the table shows the 1998 distribution of employment in the LBD. Note the mass point at age twenty-three. This results from the fact that the LBD extends back only to 1975. Thus, all firms owning establishments born on or before 1975 have the same age. These older firms tend to be large and, therefore, account for large portion of overall economic activity.

The second and third columns of table 12.7 show the unweighted and weighted percentages of total LBD employment by age for ACES firms. The table clearly shows that young firms are undersampled in the ACES. For example, good responses for the 1998 ACES were received from firms accounting for only 1.5 percent of all employment at age 1 firms. Using ACES sample weights, these firms represent only 15 percent of age 1 employment. Recall, however, that ACES is not stratified by firm age. Coverage is much better for the more mature firms that account for a lot of economic activity. Thus, ACES is representative of total investment spending.

Figure 12.16 looks at investment rates over the age distribution. Because there are limited observations on young firms within each year, we use pooled data to construct the figure. That is, each age category (below twenty-five) is made up of observations from multiple years.[33] The figure clearly shows that investment rates, measured as the ratio of total capital expenditures to fixed assets, decline with firm age. Younger firms invest much more intensively than do older firms. In addition, younger firms pursue more varied investment strategies relative to older firms, as shown in the decline of 90-10 differential in investment intensity as firms age.

An alternative way to examine investment behavior across the age distribution of firms is to follow a cohort of firms over time. This is difficult with the ACES as there is no explicit panel nature to the survey. The ACES does a good job of longitudinally tracking only larger certainty case businesses. These, of course, are mostly all old. Young firms are mostly small and are, therefore, only observed in the ACES once over the 1993–2000 period (111,446 out of 141,605 ACES-1 firms observed over the 1993–2000 period are observed only once). Thus, the only way to follow a cohort over time is to construct a synthetic cohort of firms that were all born in the same year but where the composition of the observed cohort changes over different survey years.

Table 12.8 looks at a synthetic cohort of 1993 births over the period cov-

33. Note that the oldest firms in the LBD (i.e., those born or owning establishments born before 1975) dominate the age categories from eighteen on up.

Table 12.7   **Distribution of paid employment by firm age—1998**

Firm age	Employment LBD	ACES coverage Unweighted (%)	Weighted (%)	Age share of total LBD (%)	ACES (unweighted; %)	ACES (weighted; %)
0	1,452,603	D	D	1.31	D	D
1	3,146,743	1.50	15.02	2.85	0.10	0.55
2	3,193,107	2.99	47.21	2.89	0.20	1.76
3	2,711,276	2.80	45.47	2.45	0.16	1.44
4	2,551,283	3.76	45.14	2.31	0.20	1.34
5	2,377,135	5.13	51.89	2.15	0.25	1.44
6	2,553,304	7.44	54.91	2.31	0.39	1.63
7	2,315,490	5.71	53.51	2.09	0.27	1.44
8	2,006,223	5.11	54.66	1.81	0.21	1.28
9	2,174,030	9.95	63.45	1.97	0.44	1.61
10	2,263,811	12.95	65.44	2.05	0.60	1.73
11	2,584,330	14.43	59.58	2.34	0.76	1.80
12	2,671,816	8.31	48.36	2.42	0.45	1.51
13	2,296,896	13.55	66.72	2.08	0.64	1.79
14	2,078,559	12.69	63.81	1.88	0.54	1.55
15	1,648,923	14.60	60.48	1.49	0.49	1.16
16	2,376,955	21.71	78.26	2.15	1.06	2.17
17	1,558,257	18.20	66.93	1.41	0.58	1.22
18	1,386,752	16.09	70.97	1.25	0.46	1.15
19	1,410,778	22.09	77.46	1.28	0.64	1.27
20	1,376,125	18.92	69.44	1.24	0.53	1.11
21	2,453,113	39.00	84.61	2.22	1.96	2.42
22	2,019,449	65.59	154.43	1.83	2.71	3.64
23	59,953,493	70.43	92.98	54.23	86.38	65.00
Total	110,560,451	44.21	77.57			

Notes: LBD = Longitudinal Business Database. D indicates that the statistic is suppressed in order to avoid disclosing data for individual companies.

ered by the ACES. The first four columns of the table highlight the small share of total activity accounted for by any given birth cohort (the payroll and employment shares in the first two columns are based on universe information from the LBD). It is interesting to note that young firms account for a smaller share of investment and assets than they do payroll and employment. This is true even though they invest more intensively than do more mature firms.

The behavior of investment intensities for this synthetic cohort is not as clean as that depicted in figure 12.16. Within a year, we generally find that the mean and median investment intensities are higher for younger firms. Figure 12.16 essentially pools statistics across time and shows the downward trend in investment intensity as firms age. However, since the ACES does not track individual young firms over an extended period of time, it's

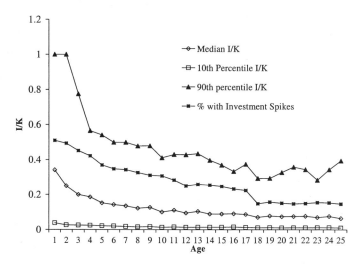

Fig. 12.16   Firm age distribution of *I/K* (ACES-1 firms)

Table 12.8   Share of activity for the 1993 birth cohort (%)

Year	Share of payroll	Share of employment	Share of investment	Share of capital	Relative share of investment	Relative share of capital	Median of investment/ capital
1993	1.38	1.12	D	D	D	D	D
1994	2.04	3.02	0.48	0.30	15.89	9.93	19.63
1995	1.93	2.79	1.13	0.86	40.50	30.82	18.54
1996	1.82	2.58	1.10	0.80	42.64	31.01	20.57
1997	1.64	2.36	1.18	0.62	50.00	26.10	25.00
1998	1.72	2.15	1.35	0.53	62.79	24.65	16.36
1999	1.74	2.06	0.71	0.59	34.47	28.64	14.89
2000	1.12	1.97	0.73	0.57	37.06	28.93	19.08

Note: D indicates that the statistic is suppressed in order to avoid disclosing data for individual companies.

difficult to make inferences about the behavior of a given cohort since the composition of the sample changes from year to year. Obviously, the sample in out years would only contain successful entrants, which most likely invested more intensively than did the unsuccessful ones that were in the sample in previous periods. This may explain why we don't see the same patterns for a synthetic cohort as we do across the age distribution within a given year.

Another reason to be interested in understanding the investment behavior of young firms is that they may chose a different mix of capital than more mature firms. New firms are often more likely to experiment with new

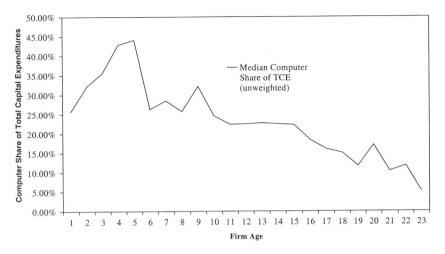

Fig. 12.17   Median computer share of TCE (unweighted): 1998

technologies. Figure 12.17 looks at this issue by comparing the share of total capital expenditure accounted for by IT equipment in 1998 across the firm age distribution. Here we see that older firms devote a smaller share of their investment budgets to IT equipment. This is admittedly a very limited analysis. The small number of observations in the ACES for younger firms limits our ability to control for other factors such as industry and size and we only have one year with detailed asset information.[34] Nevertheless, figure 12.17 demonstrates that asset mix is a function of firm age.

We compare the share of different measures of economic activity at young firms across the 1990s in table 12.9. The table shows that the share of employment accounted by firms less than four years old is roughly constant, over the 1990s, at just under 10 percent. The contribution of young firms to net employment growth is much larger as most age cohorts usually experience reductions in employment.

The striking feature of table 12.9 is the low share of total investment accounted for by young firms. These firms account for nearly 10 percent of total employment (at firms with paid employees) yet only account for, on average, 3 percent of total investment. New firms seem to enter the ACES with some lag. For instance, the ACES has very limited coverage of age 0 and 1 firms. It is possible that if we imputed missing ACES investment for age 0 and 1 firms in 1997 and 1998, we would see more investment by younger firms in these years as well.

34. That is, at the time of this research, data on investment by detailed asset type were only available for 1998. Such data have since been released for 2003, but too late for inclusion herein. See Wilson (2004) for more details regarding the asset mix of firms using the 1998 ACES microdata.

Table 12.9   **Share of activity at young firms over the 1990s (%)**

Firm age	1993	1994	1995	1996	1997	1998	1999	2000
			Share of total ACES-1 investment					
0	D	D	D	D	D	D	D	D
1	0.39	0.48	0.21	0.37	0.65	0.84	2.54	1.80
2	0.81	1.00	1.11	2.50	1.01	1.04	2.46	1.96
3	0.68	0.77	0.96	1.10	0.65	0.96	1.53	1.10
Total	1.88	2.25	2.29	3.97	2.31	2.85	6.52	4.85
			Share of LBD employment					
0	1.12	1.11	1.24	1.59	1.31	1.31	1.24	1.39
1	3.02	3.02	3.01	2.93	3.20	2.85	2.69	2.87
2	3.01	2.84	2.79	2.76	2.71	2.89	2.65	2.89
3	2.53	2.75	2.64	2.58	2.55	2.45	2.71	2.55
Total	9.67	9.72	9.68	9.86	9.77	9.50	9.29	9.70
			Contribution to net employment growth					
0		61.50	35.23	61.29	28.28	33.78	123.97	58.94
1		103.93	54.31	66.49	48.70	40.81	139.17	70.65
2		−6.42	−3.47	−6.66	−3.58	−4.85	−17.12	−1.59
3		−11.16	−3.00	−5.49	−3.45	−3.94	−14.84	−1.64
Total		147.86	83.06	115.63	79.95	65.80	231.18	126.37

Note: D indicates that the statistic is suppressed in order to avoid disclosing data for individual companies.

The Contribution of Exit

As discussed above, we are also interested in the contribution of entry and exit to capital and investment dynamics. The results and discussion in the prior subsection make clear, however, that ACES is not well suited to a study of the contribution of entry since new firms seem to enter ACES with a lag. Since we cannot adequately measure entry in this context we do not adopt the capital creation and destruction measures used in our plant-level analysis. ACES can be used to study the contribution of exit to capital destruction. Thus, we undertake a more limited analysis and simply try to quantify the value of assets that are impacted by firm exit.

For this exercise, we are looking at firm rather than plant exit. In this context, we consider two alternative types of firm exit. Using the LBD we can differentiate between firms that disappear from the data but whose establishments (or subset of those establishments) continue to operate under a different firm, and firms whose establishments cease to be active. We call the latter cases "pure deaths" and the former "FIRMID deaths." We note that ACES does not provide sufficient information to investigate what happens to the capital assets for establishment deaths for multi-unit firms. The latter is a related topic worthy of further investigation.

Table 12.10 shows the current dollar value of fixed assets for both pure and FIRMID deaths from 1993 to 1999. These numbers give us the fixed

Table 12.10   **Disposition of assets from firm closures and used capital expenditures (billions of current $)**

	1993	1994	1995	1996	1997	1998	1999
Fixed assets: Pure deaths	10.1	26.7	8.3	19.1	25.6	30.5	22.3
Fixed assets: FIRMID deaths	124.9	145.0	166.1	284.9	295.1	270.4	348.5
Year $t + 1$ used capital expenditures	30.7	35.0	34.6	31.2	63.5	42.0	62.7
Year $t + 1$ other additions and acquisitions	38.3	67.8	101.6	123.0	152.6	186.6	173.3

Note: This table is based on our calculations using only ACES-1 firms that reported positive capital expenditures. Thus, our totals are slightly below published estimates. We chose to use only this subsample due to data quality considerations. The Census Bureau does not publish either fixed assets or other additions and acquisitions. Therefore, these fields were only edited for ACES-1 firms with positive capital expenditures.

assets from ACES for the last year the firm operated. FIRMID deaths can include mergers and other activities that result in the disappearance of an active FIRMID in the LBD with little or no real consequences for the operating establishments the firm controlled.

To put these numbers into perspective and also to raise a related measurement issue, we consider possible outcomes for the assets of dying firms. These assets can be purchased by domestic firms in used capital markets, acquired by domestic firms through merger and acquisition (M&A) activity, exported, or scrapped. On the ACES form, the Census Bureau asks firms to give two pieces of information that shed light on how the assets of dying firms are disposed. First it asks for expenditures on used capital. This would capture any assets of dying firms that are purchased in used capital markets. But these markets also deal in capital sold by continuing firms. So not all used capital expenditures captured on the ACES would be from dying firms.

Table 12.10 shows that the value of assets at FIRMID deaths far exceeds that of pure deaths. Most of these assets are absorbed by the firms that acquire the establishments of the dying FIRMID businesses. The Census Bureau asks firms to include as used capital expenditures assets acquired through M&A activity in cases that the firm considers these capital expenditures (i.e., when the firm maintains depreciation or amortization accounts for the acquired assets). If assets acquired through M&A activity are not considered capital expenditures, the Census Bureau asks ACES respondents to enter the value of these assets under "Other Additions and Acquisitions."

Thus, it should be the case that those assets impacted by firm deaths (pure and FIRMID deaths) that remain in use by other domestic firms should be reflected in the used expenditures and other additions and acquisitions numbers in ACES. The last two rows of table 12.10 show the total used capital expenditures and other additions and acquisitions, respectively, in the ACES for the year following the death of the firms whose fixed assets are reported in the first two rows of the table. The idea here is that we should see deaths in year t be reflected in increased assets in year $t + 1$ for the firms acquiring the assets of the dying firms. Thus, in this context, the sum of the first two rows can be taken to represent the stock of used assets available from firm deaths. The last two rows represent the domestic absorption of these assets plus assets sold on used capital markets by continuing firms. Hence, the last two rows serve as an upper bound on the absorption of used assets from dying firms.

We see from the table that, depending on the year, between 51 percent and 78 percent (64 percent on average) of the assets of pure and FIRMID deaths are absorbed either through M&A activity, in the case of FIRMID deaths, or outright purchases of used capital. The ACES data suggest that the total absorption is substantially below the amount of fixed assets made available through FIRMID deaths (i.e., the transfer of assets through M&A activity). Moreover, much of this absorption is measured via the "other additions and acquisitions" category. This category is not included in published capital expenditures statistics, and thus users of the published statistics would miss much of these expenditures.

In short, this preliminary investigation reveals two different but related problems in the treatment of firm exits. First, the total value of assets associated with firm exits (either pure deaths or FIRMID deaths) is not captured through measures of used capital expenditures or through measures of other acquisitions. An open question is whether this measurement gap reflects capital that is scrapped but not captured in the measurement of capital and depreciation. A related question here which we could not investigate is the possible scrapping of capital from establishments that shut down that are part of multi-unit firms. In addition to the measurement gap we have detected, the composition of capital acquisition raises further questions. Much of the transfer of assets appears to be captured in ACES via an unpublished category denoted as other acquisitions. The fact that these capital transfers are apparently not captured in used expenditures and, in turn, are not part of published statistics raises further questions about the treatment of firm exits in the measurement of capital.

The work reported here is just a small step toward a better understanding of how the assets of dying firms are disposed. Its clear there is much more to be learned about how firm entry and exit affect the stock and flows of capital. Understanding the role for firm dynamics on capital is important from both the micro and macro perspectives. Further progress will require addressing several difficult measurement issues such as the valuation of the fixed assets stock versus the cost of acquiring them, the role of exports of used assets, and price deflators to both new and used capital.

We also believe that the measurement problems induced by exits do not simply imply measurement error in the average level of the capital stock but likely cause problems in the measurement of cyclical variations in the capital stock as well as capital utilization. As we have emphasized, studies of firm dynamics highlight the volatile nature of firm-level adjustment whether in terms of entry and exit or in terms of lumpy adjustment of capital. Important for this point is the fact that establishment exits are highly countercyclical. Accordingly, the scrappage rate of capital as well as the reallocation rate of capital is not just a constant but likely varies across industries, time periods, and types of businesses. A related open question is the utilization rates of capital that are engaged in capital reallocation. Presumably it takes time and resources to reallocate capital (even if it is primarily a change of ownership rather than the physical location of the capital), and utilization rates during such periods might be very low. All of these factors suggest that the problems induced by exits are not likely to be fixed with simple adjustment factors to depreciation rates but will require direct data collection and analysis.

Summing Up Firm-Level Evidence

This brief exploration of the micro properties of the distribution of firm-level investment yields a number of insights. First, it is difficult to apply perpetual inventory measurement and, in a related fashion, difficult to use ACES as a panel data set given the annual panel rotation. Second, ACES appears to get entrants with a lag. Third, there are dramatic differences in the patterns of investment by firm age. Young businesses have much greater investment rates than do mature businesses. This latter pattern mimics the patterns of employment growth. However, unlike for employment, young businesses account for a relatively small fraction of gross investment. This finding is partly because young businesses have much smaller capital stocks than do more mature businesses, so even high gross investment rates contribute relatively little to aggregate gross investment. Moreover, for employment growth we tend to find mature businesses exhibiting little growth, while for capital we still find that mature businesses exhibit robust positive gross investment. Finally, we find that there are substantial assets associated with firm exit (via either exit of all plants or acquisition).

12.5   Concluding Remarks

Micro and macro data integration should be an objective of economic measurement, as it is clearly advantageous to have internally consistent measurement at all levels of aggregation—firm, industry, and aggregate. Such internal consistency permits transparent accounting of the sources of changes in aggregates, whether due to economic factors or problems of measurement, and it permits micro-level analysis in a context where the aggregate implications can be clearly investigated. There are a rich range of firm characteristics over which recent research suggests it is useful to decompose aggregate changes such as age and size of business as well as decomposing the contribution of continuing, entering, and exiting businesses. In spite of these apparently compelling arguments, there are few measures of business activity that achieve anything close to micro/macro data integration. The measures of business activity that are arguably the worst on this dimension are capital stocks and flows. In this chapter, we have documented and quantified the widely different approaches to the measurement of capital from the aggregate (top-down) and micro (bottom-up) approaches.

Capital stock and flow aggregates are based on a top-down, supply-side approach. Measures of the domestic production, exports, and imports of capital goods yield reasonably accurate measures of domestic supplies of these commodities. These supply totals are the strength of the top-down approach. Somewhat more challenging is to allocate the domestic supply across personal consumption, government consumption, and fixed business investment by detailed asset class since there are limited expenditure data available by these categories by detailed asset class. Still, the top-down approach arguably yields reasonably accurate measures of aggregate capital stocks and flows by detailed asset classes (to be cautious, there are inherently difficult problems with measuring investment deflators for capital goods and depreciation given both data limitations and difficult conceptual problems).

The weakest link in the top-down approach is not the capital stocks and flows by asset class but the capital stock and flows by detailed asset type and by industry. Currently, this latter allocation is based upon indirect methods and very strong assumptions about the relationship between asset use by industry and the occupational distribution of an industry. These problems are most severe for allocating equipment investment—for example, in the most recently released 1997 capital flows table, about 85 percent of the total value of equipment investment is allocated across industries based upon the occupational distribution of employment.

The core problem has been the lack of direct measures of detailed asset use by industry. Recently, there have been some improvements in the collection of capital expenditures at the firm level for all sectors with the development of the ACES. However, data from the ACES are only beginning to be used in the national accounts. We have taken advantage of these new data in our analysis in this paper to explore the limitations of the top-down approach for measuring capital stocks and flows by industry.

In exploring the new ACES data, we have also learned about the many limitations of building up capital expenditures data from the bottom up. For one, firms that are asked to break out their assets by industry too often truncate the set of industries for which they report (where we know from other sources that the firms are engaged in activity in those industries). For another, expensing and leasing issues plague measurement of capital expenditures by firms, particularly for some types of assets.

In this chapter, we develop a hybrid approach to allocating assets by industry that attempts to take advantage of the strengths of both the top-down and bottom-up approach and also minimizes (or at least adjusts for) the limitations of each of the approaches. We believe our hybrid approach has promise for improved measurement of capital stocks and flows by asset and industry. Moreover, our hybrid methodology has the promise of making the micro and macro data more internally consistent so that there is a greater ability to conduct internally consistent analyses of capital stocks and flows at the micro and the macro levels. Our actual implementation of this hybrid methodology has numerous limitations of its own that could be improved upon by further study as well as by improved source data and improved integration of the business data at the Census Bureau.

A closely related objective of this chapter is to characterize the state of economic measurement for micro-level capital stocks and flows. Measurement from the bottom up is important for improving the aggregates, as discussed above, but is also important in its own right. Analysts have increasingly been using longitudinal business-level data sets to study business dynamics even when the objective is to understand aggregate fluctuations in business activity.

Creating a data infrastructure that permits high-quality analysis at the micro level poses many challenges. Panel rotation of surveys makes measurement of capital stocks by perpetual inventory methods difficult. Moreover, the data collected are quite sparse at the micro level on an annual basis—at best, data are collected by broad asset class annually. Among other things, this makes generating investment price deflators and depreciation rates that are firm specific difficult if not impossible. There has also unfortunately been some deterioration in the collection of capital stocks and flows at the establishment level for the manufacturing sector in the ASM. The deterioration of the ASM capital data is unfortunate since the ASM has successfully been linked longitudinally, permitting a rich range of analysis of business dynamics. As we have emphasized, while ACES has yielded an improvement on some dimensions, ACES has many limitations as a longitudinal microdata set given the sampling procedures used for ACES (e.g., the annual sample rotation and the underrepresentation of entrants and young businesses).

In spite of these measurement challenges at the micro level, the facts that emerge from the micro analysis are quite striking. Investment activity at the business level is very lumpy and in turn very heterogeneous. A large fraction of businesses in any given year have literally zero investment while a small fraction of businesses have large investment spikes. These investment spikes account for a large fraction of aggregate investment and also account for a large fraction of the cumulative investment of the individual business over a long period of time. All of this lumpiness implies that some businesses are shrinking their capital stocks (via depreciation primarily) while others are expanding their capital stocks substantially. The implied heterogeneity of capital growth rates across businesses implies that the allocation of capital across producers is constantly in a state of flux. Moreover, the entry and exit of businesses yields important contributions to this reallocation of capital inputs across production sites. A related dynamic is that young businesses have high failure rates but conditional on survival have very high average investment (and output and employment) growth rates. Putting all of these factors together suggests that the aggregate dynamics are driven by a complex set of factors and that understanding the aggregates requires decomposing the aggregate changes into the contribution of businesses with zero investment versus those with investment spikes, the contribution of entry and exit, and the contribution of young versus more mature businesses. Moreover, our findings suggest that the contribution of these factors is time varying both across cycles and across secular episodes. For example, the investment boom in the late 1970s is more associated with a fall in what we denote as gross capital destruction (capital contraction by continuing and exiting businesses) than gross capital creation, while the investment booms in the 1980s and 1990s are more associated with increases in gross capital creation.

In addition to raising interesting questions about the driving forces for micro and macro investment dynamics, our preliminary findings raise an interesting question about the treatment of plant and firm exits in the measurement of capital. The standard treatment of the service life of an asset ignores plant and firm exit issues. That is, the service life is given by the technological use of the asset and neglects the role of plant and firm exits. The current methods used to estimate capital stocks do take into account the impact of secondary markets on the efficiency schedules in a crude fashion with some adjustments for selection bias. Still, at the end of the day we don't know very much about the implications of firm exits and capital reallocation for capital measurement. We make some progress on determining the extent of this problem by undertaking some exercises that compare the assets from exiting businesses with used capital expenditures and estimates of other acquisitions that in principle should capture the capital reallocation from firm exits. We find that the value of assets released into the economy from firm exits substantially exceeds our upper-bound estimates of domestic absorption of used assets through purchases and acquisitions. While there are a number of measurement limitations from our analysis, we believe this issue deserves further attention and also highlights the importance of micro/macro data integration. One reason that this is important is that firm and plant exits are highly cyclical and vary considerably across industry so that any measurement error induced has consequences for our understanding of variation over time and industries.

We believe these micro properties provide prima facie evidence that understanding aggregates requires the micro/macro internal consistency. However, we clearly recognize that our analysis of the properties of the micro distributions have limitations, given the limitations in the microdata (and the associated measures at the micro level), so these inferences should be treated with appropriate caution.

An open question is what can be done to improve micro/macro data consistency—in general and in particular for the case of capital. From our vantage point, considerable progress could be made if (a) there were a concerted effort to develop the type of hybrid methodology proposed here to integrate the micro and the macro approaches to capital measurement, and (b) the survey design for the collection of the data on capital stocks and flows (primarily by the ASM and ACES) clearly recognized that one of the uses of the data is for microdata analysis and closely related micro/macro data integration. As such, statistical agencies should consider changes to surveys of business investment, such as the ACES, that put increased attention on entrants and young business and rethink sample rotation strategies to enhance longitudinal analysis.

Appendix

First collected in 1993, the Annual Capital Expenditure Survey (ACES) is designed to tabulate industry level totals for capital investment, split out into equipment and structures, new and used. Its coverage includes nearly the entire nonfarm private-sector economy. In particular, prior to 1999, capital expenditure data were collected and published on nearly 100 industries at the two- to three-digit SIC level of detail, and since 1999 data have been collected on a NAICS basis, with about 134 three- to four-digit nonfarm industries. An additional "industry" is provided for reporting a firm's structures and equipment expenditures that serve multiple industries (e.g., headquarters, regional offices, and central research laboratories). From 1993 to 1995, the ACES sample consisted of 27,000–30,000 companies with five or more employees, and in 1993 and 1995, an abbreviated survey form (ACES-2) was sent to 15,000 companies with under five employees or no employees at all (i.e., nonemployers). Since 1996, the sample has consisted of roughly 32,000–44,000 companies with employees and 12,000–15,000 nonemployers. The former group receives the long-form version of the survey (ACES-1), while the others receive the abbreviated ACES-2.

Recipients of both these forms are asked their firm-level expenditures on new and used structures and equipment. The ACES-2 form essentially stops there. Firms receiving the ACES-1, however, are also asked to report firm-level totals on the book value of assets, depreciation, and retirements, new structures and equipment acquired under capital lease agreements entered into during the survey year, and capitalized interest incurred to produce or construct new fixed assets during the survey year. Most important, these firms are asked to provide capital expenditures data *for each industry* in which they had activity and to classify these expenditures as new or used and as structures, equipment, or other.

In certain years, recipients of the ACES-1 are asked to further break down their investment expenditures by type of structure and by type of equipment, in addition to breaking them down by industry. For example, in 1994, firms were asked to provide detail on their structure expenditure, and in 1998 they were asked for detail on both structure and equipment expenditure. In 1998, ACES collected data on expenditures on twenty-nine distinct categories of structures, twenty-six distinct categories of equipment. The 2003 ACES, which was in the field at the time of this research and was published in mid-2005, also collected the full structure and equipment detail by industry.

As above, we focus on just the 1998 ACES. Overall, 45,997 firms were sampled in 1998, with 33,815 employers receiving the ACES-1 and the 12,182 nonemployers receiving the ACES-2. Because we are interested in investment by industry and by asset type, we focus on just the recipients of ACES-1. Unfortunately, as we noted above, the capital expenditure accounted for by nonemployers—totaling $95 billion, or about 9.7 percent of the national total—is allocated to neither industry nor asset type in the ACES, which is an important limitation and an important difference from the BEA estimates.[35] It is also important to note that this missing investment is likely to affect some industries (and probably some asset types) more than others. In any event, of the 33,815 firms that were sent ACES-1 forms, 27,710 (82 percent) responded with quality data that entered into the published aggregates. The employer universe accounted for $879 billion of (weighted) capital expenditures. With the $95 billion of investment by nonemployers, the ACES measured $973.6 billion in total capital expenditure in 1998.[36]

While we note several issues with the data collected in ACES in section 12.2, one important phenomenon is that survey respondents truncate the number of industries that they report relative to the number of industries in the BR. To document this phenomenon, we examine a subsample of 26,470 ACES-1 reporters.[37] Employing ACES definitions of industries, we

---

35. In 1995, when firms with one to four employees also received the ACES-2, almost 18 percent of national investment was unallocated to industry by ACES.

36. In contrast, the FRTW recognized $1,067.1 billion in investment and the CFT $1,160.7 billion, though it is important to note that the industrial scope and the assets captured are somewhat different between these three sources, in addition to some of the other conceptual differences discussed above.

37. For various reasons, 1,024 firms are excluded from the original sample: Most are dropped for not having industries with positive payroll in the BR. Others are dropped for having activity in various out-of-scope industries, such as agricultural production. Including these firms would complicate the analyses. Still other firms are dropped for having establish-

find that these firms acknowledged 1.35 industries in the ACES on average, while the same firms had nonzero payroll in 1.85 industries according to the Business Register, or 37 percent more. The omitted industries however appear to be among these firms' lesser industries, at least on average. In particular, the unacknowledged industries accounted for just 11.0 percent of the weighted payroll.[38] Even so, if capital expenditures are distributed identically to payroll (hypothetically), this implies that total investment in the *reported* industries would be 12 percent too high on average (i.e., 1/[1 − 0.110] = 1.124).[39] In terms of the 8,122 firms that actually operated in more than one industry (according to the BR), they acknowledged an average of 2.08 industries in the ACES, while the BR had nonzero payroll in 3.78 industries, or 82 percent more. Here, the unacknowledged industries accounted for 16.8 percent of these firms' weighted payroll—suggesting an upward bias in the capital expenditures of the remaining industries of almost 20 percent on average. Industry truncation, therefore, appears to be a potentially serious concern.

Next, we explore whether certain industries go unreported in ACES more often than others. Table 12A.1 lists the top ten industries in terms of how frequently these 26,470 firms failed to acknowledge them and in terms of the weighted payroll at stake (in billions of 1998 dollars). By either measure, Wholesale Trade of Durable Goods (Except Motor Vehicles) is the top omitted industry, and the related Wholesale Trade of Nondurable Goods (Except Groceries and Petroleum Products) is not very far behind. This is not an entirely new finding. In their attempt to reconcile why firms responding to both the 1996 ACES and the 1996 ASM reported more capital expenditure in manufacturing on their ACES form, Becker and Dunne (1999) found that firms primarily engaged in manufacturing regularly failed to acknowledge their wholesaling activities in the ACES, presumably misallocating that expenditure to their manufacturing industries instead. It seems that any industry that is secondary to a firm's primary activity runs a greater risk of being shortchanged in ACES. And to the extent that some industries are "inherently secondary," they may be systematically shortchanged by ACES. Indeed, some of the other industries in table 12A.1 might certainly be deemed "support" industries, such as Engineering, Accounting, Research, and Management Services as well as Computer Programming, Data Processing, and Other Computer Services.

---

ments in the BR that have insufficient SIC codes and could not be reasonably assigned proper codes. These excluded firms account for 6.4 percent of the weighted investment in the original sample.

38. While relatively rare, firms sometimes acknowledge industries that are not in the BR. Here, 3.2 percent of weighted capital expenditure appeared in such industries.

39. This of course presumes that firms correctly report *firm-level* capital expenditure and distribute it over too few industries. Another possibility is that firms underreport the firm-level total, by omitting the investment in the unacknowledged industries. Given the structure of the ACES survey, however, this scenario doesn't seem likely.

Table 12A.1   Industries most often omitted by firms in the ACES

Rank/Industry	Frequency
1 Wholesale trade of durable goods (except motor vehicles)	1,301
2 Holding, charitable trusts, and other investment offices	1,251
3 Engineering, accounting, research, and management services	1,137
4 Other retail dealers[a]	851
5 Wholesale trade of nondurable goods (except groceries and petroleum products)	748
6 Business services, NEC[b]	646
7 Real estate offices	509
8 Other health care and allied services[c]	399
9 Computer programming, data processing, and other computer services	380
10 Social services (including child day care and residential care)	370

	Weighted payroll (billions of 1998 dollars)
1 Wholesale trade of durable goods (except motor vehicles)	31.5
2 Engineering, accounting, research, and management services	24.0
3 Wholesale trade of nondurable goods (except groceries and petroleum products)	18.6
4 Business services, NEC[b]	15.6
5 Other retail dealers[a]	15.2
6 Securities and commodity brokers and services	13.3
7 Computer programming, data processing, and other computer services	12.2
8 Measuring, analyzing, and controlling instruments; etc.[d]	9.9
9 Fabricated metal products (except machinery and transportation equipment)	9.2
10 Other health care and allied services[c]	8.7

Note: NEC = not elsewhere classified.

[a]Excludes retail stores dealing in general merchandise (including department stores), food, apparel & accessories, and shoes

[b]Includes all of SIC 73 except equipment rental and leasing (SIC 735) and computer programming, data processing, and other computer services (SIC 737).

[c]Includes medical and dental laboratories, kidney dialysis centers, specialty outpatient facilities NEC, and other NEC activities.

[d]SIC 38. Also includes photographic, medical, and optical goods, as well as watches and clocks.

A corollary to the above is that some industries may be "inherently primary" and therefore systematically have too much capital expenditure attributed to them. In table 12A.2, we list the top ten types of firms (according to their primary industry) that are most likely to provide insufficient industry detail on the ACES, as measured by the percent of their collective payroll in industries unacknowledged on their forms. Two things are im-

Table 12A.2   **Types of firms most likely to provide insufficient industry detail on the ACES**

		Payroll unacknowledged in ACES	
Rank/Firm's primary industry		Percent	Billions of 1998 dollars
1	Water supply and sanitary service (SIC 494-497)	46.2	3.2
2	Suppressed	39.0	D
3	Holding, charitable trusts, and other investment offices (SIC 67)	37.9	4.1
4	Measuring, analyzing, and controlling instruments, etc. (SIC 38)	34.0	12.5
5	Miscellaneous services (SIC 89)	33.5	1.5
6	Other health care and allied services (SIC 807 and 809)	30.0	5.1
7	Computer and office equipment (SIC 357)	29.0	5.3
8	Communications equipment and electronic components and equipment (SIC 36)	24.7	19.7
9	Other depository institutions (SIC 608 and 609)	21.4	1.0
10	Wholesale trade of nondurable goods (except groceries and petroleum products)	21.1	10.0

Note: D indicates that the statistic is suppressed in order to avoid disclosing data for individual companies.

mediately apparent. First, some of the industries here are also among those in table 12A.1. This finding suggests that these industries experience offsetting effects—of having unreported capital expenditure by some firms and overreported expenditure by others. It could also indicate that there are some discrepancies in how these firms classify their primary industry and how the Census Bureau classifies it. Second, more manufacturing industries appear here than in the prior table, and they are relatively high-tech industries at that. And not only do these particular manufacturing firms miss a large portion of their activities in percentage terms, but these activities account for quite a bit of weighted payroll.

Isolating the firms in just these manufacturing industries, we examined the industries that they were least likely to acknowledge in ACES despite having payroll in them (according to the BR). Perhaps not surprisingly, the single industry that these firms failed to report more than all others is Wholesale Trade of Durable Goods, which was also the top industry in table 12A.1.[40] The point is that manufacturing firms tend not to think of themselves as being engaged in wholesale activity. Other unreported industries high on the list of these high-tech firms are Holding, Charitable Trusts, and Other Investment Offices (SIC 67); Engineering, Accounting, Research, and Management Services (SIC 87); and Computer Programming, Data Processing, and Other Computer Services (SIC 737).

40. In fact, these three manufacturing industries account for over 40 percent of the $31.5 billion of the uncovered payroll in Wholesale Trade of Durable Goods seen in table 12.4.

References

Autor, David H., Frank Levy, and Richard J. Murnane. 2003. The skill content of recent technological change: An empirical explanation. *Quarterly Journal of Economics* 118 (4): 1279–1333.

Becker, Randy, and Timothy Dunne. 1999. Annual Capital Expenditure Survey (ACES) and Annual Survey of Manufactures (ASM) comparison. Washington, DC: Center for Economic Studies. Memorandum, March.

Caballero, Ricardo, Eduardo Engel, and John C. Haltiwanger. 1995. Plant-level adjustment and aggregate investment dynamics. *Brookings Papers on Economic Activity,* Issue no. 2:1–39.

Cooper, Russell, and John C. Haltiwanger. 2000. On the nature of capital adjustment costs. NBER Working Paper no. 7925. Cambridge, MA: National Bureau of Economic Research.

Cooper, Russell, John C. Haltiwanger, and Laura Power. 1999. Machine replacement and the business cycle: Lumps and bumps. *American Economic Review* 89:921–46.

Davis, Steven, John C. Haltiwanger, and Scott Schuh. 1996. *Job creation and destruction.* Cambridge, MA: MIT Press.

Doms, Mark, and Timothy Dunne. 1998. Capital adjustment patterns in manufacturing plants. *Review of Economic Dynamics* 1:409–29.

Doms, Mark, Ron S. Jarmin, and Shawn D. Klimek. 2004. IT investment and firm performance in U.S. retail trade. *Economics of Innovation and New Technology* 13 (7): 595–613.

Foster, Lucia, John C. Haltiwanger, and Namsuk Kim. 2005. Gross job flows from the Annual Survey of Manufactures: 1993–98. Washington, DC: Center for Economic Studies. Mimeograph.

Foster, Lucia, John C. Haltiwanger, and C. J. Krizan. 2001. Aggregate productivity growth: Lessons from microeconomic evidence. In *New developments in productivity analysis,* ed. Edward Dean, Michael Harper, and Charles Hulten, 303–63. University of Chicago Press.

———. 2002. The link between aggregate and micro productivity growth: Evidence from retail trade. NBER Working Paper no. 9120. Cambridge, MA: National Bureau of Economic Research. August.

Haltiwanger, John C., and C. J. Krizan. 1999. Small business and job creation in the United States: The role of new and young businesses. In *Are small firms important? Their role and impact,* ed. Zoltan Acs, 79–97. Boston: Kluwer Academic.

Hulten, Charles, and Frank Wykoff. 1981. The estimation of economic depreciation using vintage asset prices: An application of the Box-Cox power transformation. *Journal of Econometrics* 15:367–96.

Jarmin, Ron, and Javier Miranda. 2002. The longitudinal business database. Washington, DC: Center for Economic Studies Working Paper no. WP-02-17.

Jorgenson, Dale, Mun Ho, and Kevin Stiroh. 2005. Growth of U.S. industries and investments in information technology and higher education. In *Measurement of capital in the new economy,* ed. Carol Corrado, John Haltiwanger, and Daniel Sichel. Chicago: University of Chicago Press, forthcoming.

Lawson, Ann, Kurt Bersani, Mahnaz Fahim-Nader, and Jiemin Guo. 2002. Benchmark input-output accounts of the United States, 1997. *Survey of Current Business* 82 (12): 19–109.

Meade, Douglas, Stanislaw Rzeznik, and Darlene Robinson-Smith. 2003. Business investment by industry in the U.S. economy for 1997. *Survey of Current Business* 83 (11): 18–70.

Stiroh, Kevin J. 2004. Reassessing the impact of IT in the production function: A meta-analysis and sensitivity tests. New York: Federal Reserve Bank of New York. Mimeograph.

U.S. Bureau of Economic Analysis. 1999. *Fixed reproducible tangible wealth in the United States, 1925–1994.* Washington, DC: U.S. Government Printing Office.

U.S. Census Bureau. 2000. *Annual capital expenditures 1998.* Washington, DC: U.S. Department of Commerce.

Wilson, Daniel J. 2003. Embodying embodiment in a structural, macroeconomic input-output model. *Economic Systems Research* 15 (3): 371–98.

———. 2004. Investment behavior of U.S. firms over heterogeneous capital: A snapshot. FRBSF Working Paper no. 2004-21. October. San Francisco: Federal Reserve Bank of San Francisco.

Wolff, Edward. 2002. Computerization and structural change. *Review of Income and Wealth* 48 (2): 59–75.

Panel Remarks

Thomas L. Mesenbourg

It's a pleasure to have the opportunity to describe the Census Bureau initiatives to improve the National Accounts. We at the Census Bureau regard the BEA as our most important customer, and much of what we do to improve our programs is guided by the needs of the BEA. We like to say that about three-quarters of the source data the BEA uses to develop its quarterly GDP estimates depends directly or indirectly upon the data generated by the Census Bureau. That number points out that improvements in the National Accounts call for the BEA and the Census Bureau to move forward in lockstep.

Let me touch on our plans to improve our data in three broad areas—better and more timely services data, more detailed data to help BEA to develop its input-output table, and additional data on capital inputs. In the case of services, I'll describe some improvements that you probably heard about earlier in the conference. The point is that we are now doing what we promised we would do a year ago. We are now implementing the new initiatives we received funds for as part of the fiscal 2003 economic statistics initiatives.

We are now collecting data on selected service industries on a quarterly basis. Our first quarterly survey actually went into the field on March 31, 2004, with the initial focus on information, communications, and technology intensive industries. We're covering three sectors in the first year and selected industries within those sectors. We're starting by requesting data for the first quarter of 2004 and the fourth quarter of 2003. We will mail the

Thomas L. Mesenbourg is the assistant director for economic programs at the U.S. Census Bureau.

second-quarter survey at the end of June. We are going to collect three quarters of data, making sure we have established consistent reporting arrangements with surveyed companies. This is a voluntary survey, and we will publish data in about mid-September 2004. The first release will cover the fourth quarter 2003 through the second quarter of 2004. After that, we will be releasing quarterly data no later than seventy-five days after the end of the referenced quarter.

With the funding we have on hand as part of the 2003 appropriation, we will expand the new quarterly survey next year to include hospitals, nursing and residential care facilities. The president's 2006 budget, which is pending, includes a request for additional funding to expand the quarterly survey to add coverage of eight additional service sectors.

I should add that the president's 2006 budget also includes an initiative to fund the expanded annual collection of industry data from about 117 additional service industries, adding coverage of some critical sectors that are now covered only in the economic census, once every five years. Namely, finance, insurance, real estate, utilities, and those transportation industries that we don't cover annually now. We had hoped to get funding in that this initiative in the 2004 or 2005 budgets. It didn't happen, but everybody, including the Office of Management and Budget (OMB) agreed that remedying this glaring shortcoming in our services data justified resubmitting the request to Congress in fiscal year (FY) 2006.

Turning back to improvement activities that we actually have underway, we have begun a phased-in expansion of the Services Annual Survey (SAS). Right now SAS covers 269 service industries. The content expansion includes first time product data from these service industries. The 2003 SAS showed product data for the information sector. Starting in survey year 2004, we began collecting annual information on the cost of purchased services and materials. This new collection includes data on what companies in the various service industries are spending on such things as purchased materials, contract labor, software, data processing, telecommunication services and management and consulting.

Greater detail on outputs and more detail on intermediate inputs will help BEA strengthen its estimates of value added service activity. Here again the president's 2006 budget includes funds to keep this momentum going and we hope to collect more product detail for retailers and wholesalers, about forty to fifty industries in those two sectors. As regards information on capital expenditures, the Census Bureau is mailing in mid-April 2004 an expanded version of our Annual Capital Expenditures Survey, which you just heard about in the last session.

For the first time, we are going to be able to provide annual, detailed information on business expenditures, both capitalized and expensed, on hardware, software and communication services. On an annual basis, starting with data year 2003, we will be collecting data on business purchases of computers, communications equipment, and high-tech medical equipment. We will publish information by the industry categories we publish in ACES. We also will be providing data on software, capitalized and expensed by industry, we hope, and total software by the categories of prepackaged, custom, and developed in-house, though that data will not be available by industry. The first release of this new information is scheduled for May 2005.

I'm aware of the view that federal statistics give a fair picture of who makes capital investments but not such a good picture of where those capital goods are actually purchased. We think the expansion of the ACES survey will remedy that shortcoming.

I've been describing steps we are taking in our current economic statistics programs to help the BEA improve the National Accounts. I should also mention that we built improvements into the 2002 Economic Census aimed at helping BEA. On March 29, 2004, we released the first of the 1,700 data reports that will flow out of the 2002 Economic Census. That was the advanced summary statistics for the United States. The data release schedule for the 2002 Economic Census has been accelerated to support BEA's efforts to improve the timeliness of the I-O tables.

For the first time the Economic Census will publish an industry series for both the goods-producing and the non-goods-producing sectors of the economy. Between now and the end of December 2004, we will produce 651 individual industry series reports. This accelerated schedule will provide BEA with the manufacturing and mining data four months earlier than five years ago; the manufacturing product class information, eleven months earlier; and the retail and wholesale trade commodity line information, about twenty months earlier than five years ago.

Let me conclude by mentioning one other improvement activity. We have expanded our 2003 Annual Survey of Wholesale Trade to cover sales branches and sales offices of domestic manufacturers. We refer to them as nonmerchant wholesalers. Measures of economic performance for those firms have been covered only once every five years in the economic census. Now we'll start providing these data annually. In March 2004, we started collecting data on these nonmerchant wholesalers and plan to release data in April 2005. The big payoff from this collection will be in terms of better inventory data.

For a long time the BEA has wanted to have better data on what amounts to about $50 billion in wholesale inventories held by manufacturers' sales offices and branches. And given how inventory swings can affect GDP estimates, improvements in this area should certainly be welcome.

To sum up, we recognize the vital importance of the macro measures of our economy and we craft our improvement efforts in close collaboration with BEA and BLS and the Federal Reserve Board, I might add. At the Census Bureau, our job is to gather data—and that, as a task, is not getting any easier. Indeed, it's becoming more and more of a challenge. But as we wrestle with these challenges, I can guarantee you that we will be keeping your needs in mind.

Kathleen Utgoff

The first thing that I want to do is affirm the eagerness of those of us at the BLS to work with BEA to improve our contributions to the National Accounts and to reconcile and coordinate the measures that are produced by both the BEA and BLS. As you know, the National Accounts are among the most important and most closely watched measures in the U.S. statistical system. BLS provides much of the information used by BEA in constructing its accounts and we use BEA information for productivity measures. As a result, close cooperation between our agencies is absolutely essential.

Let me just briefly talk about some of the things that we are doing that are related to the National Accounts. You heard about one of these efforts this morning at a session that discussed the integration of BEA and BLS production accounts. That paper compared a theoretical set of consistent measures with those that are produced now. And the last part of the paper begins the enormous task of comparing the many detailed industry output measures prepared by the two agencies.

Steve Landefeld really deserves an enormous amount of credit for this effort. And I know that both the BEA and BLS are committed to further progress. We're also working with BEA to compare the CPI-U and the PCE chain weight index. I think that, undoubtedly, this work will lead to better, more transparent measures. We're now engaged in other efforts that should improve the National Accounts. Our payroll survey, which is called the CES, or the 790, will be modified to produce better measures of personal income. The earnings measure as well as the hours measure will be broadened to include all employees, rather than just production and non-supervisory workers. The BEA needs were very important in the consideration to make this change. But I have to say another impetus was that in an economy where there is declining manufacturing and increasing service sector activity, it's becoming increasingly more difficult to distinguish between non-production workers and non-supervisory workers and other workers. Respondents tell us that this is a significant problem. So we want to move in another direction.

Another change to the payroll survey is the addition of a total wage series. That will include non-wage cash payments, such as bonuses. We expect the publication for both of these changes to begin early in 2006. We're also working on improvements to both the consumer price index and the

Kathleen P. Utgoff is the commissioner of the Bureau of Labor Statistics.

producer price index. In the consumer price index we're increasing the frequency of outlet rotation and then we're resampling within outlets to keep our sample more current. And we're continuing with many of the additional initiatives that we had including refining our hedonic models to measure quality change.

Improvements in the PPI include coverage expansions. The PPI was expanded to include half the industries in retail trade, completing PPI coverage for that sector. The PPI measures the change in margin for this sector, which is consistent with the treatment in the input-output accounts. This coverage expansion will continue. Indexes will be added for additional industries in the service sector and for non-residential construction.

One of the noteworthy additions is the anticipated publication next year of indexes for the banking industry. This project has been conducted with the close cooperation of BEA. The intent was to make the price changes measure consistent with the output measure. The methodology that is currently being tested is the user cost approach.

The last upcoming event that I want to talk about is the publication of the first estimates from the American Time Use Survey in summer 2005. The survey produces a wealth of information from a sample of 1,800 households a month that are exiting from the Current Population Survey. This survey will provide important data for nonmarket national accounting, and it will also be invaluable in understanding and assessing available hours data for measuring productivity. Micro data will be available from the ATUS as well. I should point out that I think the Time Use Survey is a major advance, and Katharine Abraham deserves all the credit for getting that done. It was a wonderful project to get started and a great job.

Larry Slifman

Tom Mesenbourg and Kathleen Utgoff have just stated what their institutions are doing, and plan to do, to help further the integration of the national accounts. Although I am the Federal Reserve's representative on this panel, I do not want to repeat what Al Teplin and his co-authors have already said about the Federal Reserve's efforts (chap. 11 in this volume). Consequently, I will offer more general comments on some of the issues raised at this conference regarding the integration of the accounts.

Three types of integration. It seems to me that at this conference the word "integration" has been used in three ways. The first way, as exemplified by the SNA, is integration as providing a unified accounting framework. The second way is what I would call process consistency, which involves such things as making sure that the various statistical agencies use consistent

Larry Slifman is associate director of the Division of Research and Statistics at the Federal Reserve Board.

definitions of sectors, sector boundaries, and transactions. The papers by Teplin et al. (chap. 11 in this volume) and by Fraumeni and her co-authors (chap. 9 in this volume) are examples of this type of integration. The third way, and one that received a good deal of discussion in this conference, is the elimination of statistical discrepancies.

The benefits of integration. As with most things, each type of integration of the national accounts has both benefits and costs. Let me start with some of the benefits. With regard to the unified accounting framework, one benefit is obvious: Integrated accounts are more consistent with economic and accounting theory. In addition, full integration makes the accounts seamless, which makes it easier for researchers to trace out a greater variety of relationships.

Process consistency is clearly critical for the implementation of a unified accounting framework. Unless the statistical agencies agree about exactly where to draw sector boundaries or exactly how to define specific transactions, fully integrating the accounts will be impossible. Such work is very time consuming and detailed, but it is also very important. One behind-the-scenes benefit of this conference has been the progress made by the BEA and the Federal Reserve in identifying inconsistencies of treatment between the NIPAs and the Flow of Funds Accounts and in resolving many of those inconsistencies. I know that we at the Federal Reserve look forward to continuing our collaboration with the BEA and to making further progress in achieving process consistency.

Finally, what are the benefits of eliminating statistical discrepancies? As best I can tell, the primary benefit is that doing so removes confusion (or, at least, reduces it) for less sophisticated users. That, in my opinion, is not an inconsequential benefit.

The costs of integration. But integration also comes with costs. For example, achieving complete process consistency may involve appreciable resource costs for the statistical agencies, and we must keep these costs in mind when we are thinking about new architectures and integration. But I don't think that there are any significant analytical costs to moving forward with achieving complete process consistency.

The same cannot be said for eliminating statistical discrepancies. I like the way Jack Triplett put it: Discrepancies tell us that there is something mushy in the data. Knowing that something is mushy in the data is valuable information, and throwing it away, I believe, comes at a significant cost. Let me give you one example of the potential cost. During the mid-1990s, the contemporaneous data for the income side of the national accounts began to capture the acceleration in productivity considerably sooner than the product side.[1] Had the BEA been using methods at that time that elimi-

---

1. See, for example, L. Slifman and C. Corrado, "Decomposition of Productivity and Unit Costs," November 18, 1996, available at http://www.federalreserve.gov/pubs/oss/oss1/oss1 .doc.html.

nated the statistical discrepancy, the information would have been un-available to analysts and government officials, and important policy errors might have occurred.

Recommendations. What are my recommendations? First, process consistency is something that is good for its own sake. The more the statistical agencies can harmonize the accounts and make them seamless, the better off all of us are. To the extent that resources allow, the agencies should be moving forward vigorously with their efforts at process consistency.

Next, as I suggested previously, with regard to statistical discrepancies, the first rule should be: don't throw away any information. In practical terms, this rule means that the BEA should make available to researchers all the unpublished "atoms" used to construct the accounts before any algorithms are applied to eliminate statistical discrepancies. Doing so will enable sophisticated users to see for themselves whether there is something mushy in the data and draw their own conclusions.

Finally, I am not saying, however, that the BEA should necessarily abandon its plan to eliminate statistical discrepancies. But, before it makes a final decision on the method, the BEA needs to examine more options for the best way to eliminate discrepancies. These options should be systematic and reproducible, and they should be guided by economic theory, as Joe Beaulieu and Eric Bartelsman were in their chapter (chap. 8 in this volume), and by the principles of information theory for optimally combining alternative measures.[2]

Katharine G. Abraham

A major challenge in the integration of the national economic accounts or of economic statistics more generally is how to deal with discrepancies in the behavior of different but obviously related measures. Sometimes the fact that data collected from different perspectives tell a different story may be illuminating, though even in these cases, it often would be helpful to have more information about the reasons for the disagreement than typically is available. On the other hand, data inconsistencies that arise simply because different agencies have made different operational decisions—classifying businesses in different industries, using different deflators or deflation methods to produce real output estimates, and so on—seem, as a general rule, very unlikely to be useful to anyone. Although I recognize that it may be difficult to reach agreement on common approaches in such cases, I nonetheless would argue that we are doing data users a serious disservice if we fail to work toward that goal.

A good example of a case in which differences in related series seem

2. See Beaulieu and Bartelsman (this volume).

Katharine G. Abraham is a professor of survey methodology and adjunct professor of economics at the University of Maryland, and a research associate of the National Bureau of Economic Research.

likely to contain useful information can be found in the two measures of employment derived from the monthly establishment survey and the Current Population Survey. These two measures are designed to measure different things. The establishment survey measures the number of jobs, while the household survey measures the number of employed people; the establishment survey excludes jobs in agriculture and private households, while people employed in these sectors are included in the household survey; the establishment survey excludes the self-employed, who are included in the household survey; and so on. Having information about employment on both conceptual bases should enrich our understanding of labor market conditions. These conceptual differences are not, however, the only reason for the observed differences between the establishment and the household survey employment measures. Even after adjusting the household survey employment figures so that they align conceptually with the payroll survey employment figures, employment as measured by the household survey grew more slowly during most of the 1990s, and has grown more rapidly over the past several years. The fact that large discrepancies in measured employment growth remain even after adjusting for the difference in underlying concepts suggests that, despite the considerable efforts made to ensure both series' accuracy, at least one of them must be wrong! There is a clear need for research designed to shed light on this rather troubling discrepancy.[3]

To take another example, the Consumer Price Index (CPI) and the Personal Consumption Expenditure (PCE) deflator are related but not equivalent data series. Both relate to trends in the prices that consumers pay, but there are important scope and concept differences between the two series. These include the significantly broader coverage of the PCE deflator and the use of a chain-weighted Fisher formula rather than a fixed-weight Laspeyres formula in its calculation (see Fixler and Jaditz 2002 for further discussion). But scope and concept differences are not the whole story; the selective use of different component price indexes even where the CPI and the PCE deflator overlap also has caused the two series to behave differently. It may be that there are compelling conceptual or other reasons for these choices, but absent some compelling reason to do otherwise, it would make life simpler for the data user if CPI component price indexes were used where available in producing the PCE deflator.

Differences in the behavior of the Bureau of Economic Analysis (BEA) and Bureau of Labor Statistics (BLS) industry output measures, discussed in detail by Fraumeni, Harper, Powers, and Yuskavage (chap. 9 in this volume), provide another example of potentially confusing data discrepancies. The BEA and the BLS have made considerable progress in harmoniz-

---

3. See Nardone, Bowler, and Kropf (2003) for a discussion and exploration of possible explanations for the divergence between the two series during the 1990s.

ing their manufacturing industry output measures, largely by agreeing that they would use a common set of price deflators, but significant differences across alternative measures of nonmanufacturing industry output remain. As explained by Fraumeni et al., there are differences in the output concepts underlying the alternative series, but as an empirical matter these conceptual differences appear relatively unimportant. Considerably more important are differences in the source data used to produce the different nonmanufacturing measures and differences in the deflators and deflation methods adopted for their construction. The BEA and the BLS are committed to developing a better understanding of the sources of observed differences in their industry output measures and to working toward greater consistency "where appropriate." I applaud this commitment and hope that the two agencies will be aggressive in their pursuit of greater consistency, rather than being content to develop explanations for why their output measures differ and leave it at that.

To take another example, although they rely on essentially the same underlying source data, BEA and BLS capital stock measures embody different assumptions about how the services provided by different types of capital assets decline with the age of the asset. The BEA assumes that the efficiency of capital assets declines geometrically with age; the BLS, on the other hand, assumes a hyperbolic age-efficiency function (see Fraumeni 1997 and Dean and Harper 1998). The BLS also has not adopted the longer assumed service lives for residential structures implied by the depreciation rates that the BEA adopted in 1997 (U.S. Bureau of Labor Statistics 2003). As has been pointed out to me by both BEA and BLS staff members, the different assumptions made by the two agencies in this case generally lead to similar results in practice, which arguably means that the differences in methodology aren't worth worrying much about. Still, these methodological differences can be confusing to those who would like to understand how the two agencies' capital stock series relate to one another. Surely this is a case where at least in principle there is a right answer and we should be able to come to a mutual agreement about the assumption that most closely approximates that right answer.

The differences in the industry classification of business establishments on the BLS and Census Bureau business registers, something that came up in passing during discussion of the Lawson, Moyer, Okubo, and Planting paper (chap. 6 in this volume), highlight a case in which having one solution clearly would be preferable to having competing solutions. Given the applicable classification structure, there is in principle one and only one correct industry code for each business establishment. It may be that both the source data used by the BLS and the source data used by the Census Bureau can be helpful for determining the proper industry assignment, but maintaining two separate registers is difficult to defend on anything other than historical grounds. Differences in industry classification on the two business registers cause real problems for data users who seek to combine industry information based on the two lists. The same comment applies to differences in geographic coding across the two lists. Joint work is underway at the BLS and Census Bureau to *understand* these differences, and I would commend the staff involved for the progress that has been made to date on this important project. Still, it seems clear that, from the data user perspective, *eliminating* the differences between the two lists rather than simply *understanding* them ought to be the ultimate goal.

Working toward the harmonization of different but related statistical series, especially those produced by different agencies, is of course easier said than done. Those responsible for producing any individual data series are, understandably enough, concerned primarily with getting that data series out the door. Moreover, the conscientious and well-qualified staff members who produce each of the separate data products understandably may be reluctant to give up the freedom to apply their own best professional judgment about exactly how their product should be constructed. Their reluctance may be heightened by the time and energy that negotiating common approaches unavoidably requires and skepticism that common solutions will in any way improve their own data products. Still, to the extent that coordination among the producers of related data products is neglected, the cumulative effect will be to make life unnecessarily difficult for users of the data.

What can be done about this situation? Given the opportunity to redesign the statistical system from scratch, I might make the Director of the Bureau of Economic Analysis the final arbiter regarding problematic differences in methodology across economic data programs, especially those that feed the national accounts. It is, after all, the work of the BEA for which these differences cause the most severe problems, as inconsistent data from different sources must somehow be reconciled. In one particularly important case—the differences in industry classification between the BLS and Census Bureau business registers—harmonization almost certainly will require changes in the law governing access to Internal Revenue Service records for statistical purposes. But even without making Steve Landefeld the economic data czar and even without the remaining changes in the law that governs statistical data sharing that we all have been awaiting, there is much that can be done. Given all of the day-to-day demands that are placed upon them, the senior management and the staffs of the BEA, the BLS, and the Census Bureau deserve our praise for the considerable progress made to date toward harmonizing their data products. I would inveigh all of them to continue to make this both a goal and a priority for our economic data programs.

J. Steven Landefeld

There are many ways that a statistical system can achieve integration and consistency among its various statistics. One option is to establish a central statistical agency and mandate that it use a single and consistent set of concepts, methods, and source data for each of its interrelated statistics. However, within the long-established decentralized U.S. statistical system, marginal change through increased coordination and data sharing is likely to be a more practical solution than attempting to change the myriad of laws and organizational structures necessary to merge the various U.S. statistical agencies. It also likely to be a solution that produces more accurate and relevant data than that produced by a monolithic central statistical agency since it preserves the innovation that can be sparked within a decentralized system.

Despite the many working groups formed over the years to explore the creation of a central statistical agency, there has been little progress in moving toward such a system. Part of the problem is the many structures and laws that would have to be changed and the absence of a compelling argument for consolidation. What has developed in recent years is a series of changes in the various statistical agencies producing economic statistics that attempt to capture the benefits of both centralized and decentralized systems. These changes include

- increased coordination in filling gaps in source data, in updating classification systems, and in confronting and reconciling differences in the data produced by the separate agencies;
- changes in laws and regulations that permit limited sharing of microdata across the separate agencies with the ultimate goals of improving data consistency and accuracy and of reducing the burden on respondents from the separate agencies' economic surveys; and
- development of more easily accessible and consistent information on central databases available through common (www.fedstats.gov) and linked web sites (www.bea.gov, www.bls.gov, and www.census.gov).

The papers in this conference provide numerous examples of the efficacy of this approach to achieving the benefits of a centralized statistical system within a decentralized system. For example, the development of BEA GDP-by-industry and input-output accounts that are consistent with each other and ultimately with the BLS productivity estimates illustrate how improved coordination in filling data gaps along with coordination in developing consistent source data and methods can produce more consistent *and* more accurate data.

In developing more consistent GDP by industry and I-O value-added

J. Steven Landefeld is the director of the Bureau of Economic Analysis.

estimates, the BEA—on the advice of its advisory committee—decided against using a single methodology based on benchmarking to the I-O tables. Instead, it embarked on a two-pronged approach that involved (a) working with the Census Bureau and BLS to improve the accuracy and timeliness of the source data on services and intermediate inputs[4] while at the same time (b) developing a set of new and consistent estimates that essentially used a weighted average of two estimates for each industry, with each estimate depending on separate source data and methods. The weights are based on the assessment of the relative accuracy of the source data and methods for each of the components. With this approach no information is lost, and the resulting estimate—which uses all available data—is not only more consistent but more accurate.[5]

The BEA and BLS have also adopted a strategy of confronting and reconciling the differences in their gross output and value-added series with the goal of picking the best possible combination of source data and methods rather than simply adopting one of the agencies' estimates. In some cases, however, such as the definition of business product, the BEA has simply adopted the BLS definition in the interest of consistency, sacrificing the small marginal advantage of the BEA's definition for users of its accounts.

Data sharing offers the largest potential gains to integration. One of the most significant inconsistencies confronted in U.S. industry data is illustrated by the differences in the industry data from the Census Bureau and BLS used in the BEA's I-O accounts. The BEA uses Census industry and product data in measuring commodity and industry output, intermediate products, and final demand in the I-O accounts, but use BLS wage and salary and other data in measuring value added. The differences can be quite large and indirectly account for a large share of the inconsistencies in the industry account estimates.

For example, while the aggregate sum of compensation across industries is roughly the same whether BLS or Census data are used, the differences in individual industries can be quite large, with differences in levels as large as 15 percent and differences in growth rates that are nearly twice as large. As was found in an earlier microdata linkage of BEA-BLS-Census data authorized by the International Investment and Trade and Services Act, a large share of the differences in the industry data appear to be due to differences in the classification of individual firms to specific industries or differences in the treatment of auxiliary units.

4. See the panel remarks by Kathleen Utgoff and Thomas Mesenbourg for a complete catalogue of the improvements that BLS and Census have embarked upon in filing gaps in the data provided by the BEA, BLS, and Census.
5. For a further discussion of consistency versus accuracy and the need for a statistical technique—rather than forcing estimates to a single method and control total—see the accompanying panel remarks by Lawrence Slifman and Katherine Abraham.

While the papers presented at this conference point the way toward collaboration within a decentralized system, much work remains. Additional changes in rules and legislation are required for data sharing that extends beyond those limited kinds of sharing now permitted. Only with those changes can we achieve the larger benefits of data sharing envisioned by the initial data-sharing legislation. The statistical agencies, the Office of Management and Budget, and the Congress will need to build on their success in developing and funding cross-cutting initiatives that fill gaps, integrate, and update the nation's economic statistics. Despite major success in recent years, for example, large gaps remain in measures of services output and prices, international trade in services, and incomes. Progress over the next five years comparable to the last five should yield a set of U.S. economic statistics from this decentralized system that are even more consistent, more accurate, and more relevant than what is available today.

References

Dean, Edwin R., and Michael J. Harper. 1998. The BLS productivity measurement program. Paper presented at the Conference on Research in Income and Wealth conference on New Directions in Productivity Analysis. 20–21 March, Washington, DC.

Fixler, Dennis, and Ted Jaditz. 2002. An examination of the difference between the CPI and the PCE deflator. Bureau of Labor Statistics Working Paper no. 361. June. Washington, DC: Bureau of Labor Statistics.

Fraumeni, Barbara. 1997. The measurement of depreciation in the U.S. National Income and Product Accounts. *Survey of Current Business* 77 (July): 7–23.

Nardone, Thomas, Mary Bowler, and Jurgen Kropf. 2003. Examining the discrepancy in employment growth between the CPS and the CES. Paper prepared for presentation to the Federal Economic Statistics Advisory Committee. 17 October, Washington, DC.

U.S. Bureau of Labor Statistics. 2003. Revisions to capital inputs for the BLS multifactor productivity measures. Available at http://www.bls.gov/web/mprcaptl.htm. Last updated April 8, 2003; accessed October 19, 2004.

Contributors

Katharine G. Abraham
Joint Program in Survey Methodology
1218 LeFrak Hall
University of Maryland
College Park, MD 20742

Rochelle Antoniewicz
Investment Company Institute
1401 H Street, NW
Washington, DC 20005

John R. Baldwin
Microeconomic Analysis Division
R. H. Coats, 18-F
Statistics Canada
Ottawa, Ontario K1A 0T6, Canada

Eric J. Bartelsman
Department of Economics, 4A-14
Free University
De Boelelaan 1105
1081 HV Amsterdam, The Netherlands

J. Joseph Beaulieu
1776 Eye Street, NW
Suite 250
Washington, DC 20006

Randy Becker
U.S. Census Bureau
4700 Silver Hill Road
Washington, DC 20233-6300

Carol Corrado
Division of Research and Statistics
Federal Reserve Board
20th Street and Constitution Avenue,
    NW
Washington, DC 20551

W. Erwin Diewert
Department of Economics
University of British Columbia
#997-1873 East Mall
Vancouver, BC V6T 1Z1, Canada

Barbara M. Fraumeni
Muskie School of Public Service
University of Southern Maine
96 Falmouth Street
Portland, Maine 04104-9300

John Haltiwanger
Department of Economics
University of Maryland
College Park, MD 20742

Tarek M. Harchaoui
Microeconomic Analysis Division
R. H. Coats, 18-F
Statistics Canada
Ottawa, Ontario K1A 0T6, Canada

Michael J. Harper
Bureau of Labor Statistics
2 Massachusetts Avenue, NE
Washington, DC 20212-0001

Charles R. Hulten
Department of Economics
University of Maryland
Room 3105, Tydings Hall
College Park, MD 20742

Ron Jarmin
U.S. Census Bureau
4700 Silver Hill Road
Washington, DC 20233-6300

Dale W. Jorgenson
Department of Economics
Littauer 122
Harvard University
1805 Cambridge Street
Cambridge, MA 02138

Shawn D. Klimek
U.S. Census Bureau
4700 Silver Hill Road
Washington, DC 20233-6300

J. Steven Landefeld
Bureau of Economic Analysis
1441 L Street, NW
Washington, DC 20230

Ann M. Lawson
Bureau of Economic Analysis
1441 L Street, NW
BE-51
Washington, DC 20230

Christopher Mackie
Committee on National Statistics
National Academy of Sciences
500 Fifth Street, NW
11th Floor
Washington, DC 20001

Charles Ian Mead
Bureau of Economic Analysis
1441 L Street, NW
Washington, DC 20230

Thomas L. Mesenbourg
U.S. Census Bureau
4700 Silver Hill Road
Washington, DC 20233-0001

Susan Hume McIntosh
Flow of Funds Section
Federal Reserve Board
20th Street and Constitution Avenue,
NW
Washington, DC 20551

Karin Moses
Bureau of Economic Analysis
1441 L Street, NW
Washington, DC 20230

Brent Moulton
Bureau of Economic Analysis
1441 L Street, NW
Washington, DC 20230

Brian C. Moyer
Bureau of Economic Analysis
1441 L Street, NW
Washington, DC 20230

William D. Nordhaus
Department of Economics
Yale University
28 Hillhouse Avenue, Box 208264
New Haven, CT 06520-8264

Sumiye Okubo
Bureau of Economic Analysis
1441 L Street, NW
Washington, DC 20230

Michael G. Palumbo
Flow of Funds Section
Federal Reserve Board
20th Street and Constitution Avenue,
NW
Washington, DC 20551

Mark A. Planting
Bureau of Economic Analysis
1441 L Street, NW
Washington, DC 20230

Susan G. Powers
Bureau of Labor Statistics
2 Massachusetts Avenue, NE
Washington, DC 20212

Marshall B. Reinsdorf
Bureau of Economic Analysis
1441 L Street, NW
Washington, DC 20230

Larry Slifman
Federal Reserve Board
20th Street and Constitution Avenue,
   NW
Washington, DC 20551

Genevieve Solomon
Federal Reserve Bank of Dallas
2200 N. Pearl Street
Dallas, TX 75201

Albert M. Teplin
6617 Paxton Road
Rockville, MD 20852

Kathleen P. Utgoff
Bureau of Labor Statistics
2 Massachusetts Avenue, NE
Washington, DC 20212-0001

Dan Wilson
Federal Reserve Bank of San Francisco
101 Market Street
San Francisco, CA 94105

Karen Wilson
System of National Accounts
Statistics Canada
R. H. Coats Building
120 Parkdale Avenue
Ottawa, Ontario, K1A 0T6, Canada

Robert E. Yuskavage
Bureau of Economic Analysis
1441 L Street, NW
Washington, DC 20230

Author Index

Abraham, Katharine, 4–5, 170n5, 617–20
Adelman, M. A., 154
Adler, Hans J., 472n2, 473
Antoniewicz, Rochelle, 8

Bacharach, Michael, 324
Baily, Martin N., 29
Baker, Dean, 311
Baldwin, John R., 8, 448, 449
Bartlesman, Eric J., 6–7, 311, 315, 322, 324n5, 343, 344, 345, 346
Bates, J. M., 324n5
Beaulieu, J. Joseph, 6–7, 311, 315, 322, 343, 344, 345, 346
Becker, Randy, 9
Berndt, Ernest R., 206
Bishop, Y. M., 324
Bloem, Adriann M., 474n4
Bolt, Katharine, 153
Bosworth, Barry P., 29, 311, 356n1
Bureau of Labor Statistics, 28n6
Byushgens, S. S., 64

Caballero, Ricardo, 544n1, 548n4, 549n7, 574, 586n28
Champernowne, G., 322
Chen, Baoline, 341
Christensen, Lauritis R., 14n1, 22n2, 34, 44, 75n21, 194, 205, 211
Clemens, Michael, 153
Constanza, Robert, 151n4

Cooper, Russell, 548n4, 549n7, 574, 584n27
Corrado, Carol, 34, 74, 207, 207n7, 616n1

David, Martin H., 175
Davis, Steven, 586
Dean, Edwin R., 312, 619
Debreu, Gerard, 304
De Mesnard, Louis, 345
Denison, Edward F., 22n2, 27, 44
Diewert, W. Erwin, 28n5, 64, 204n5, 275n6, 288n5, 294n16, 303n22, 305nn25–26
Dikhanov, Y., 288n5
Dipplesman, Robert J., 474n4
Domar, Evsey, 368–69, 454
Doms, Mark, 74, 548n5, 574, 584n27
Dulberger, Ellen R., 73
Dunne, Timothy, 574, 574n27

Ehemann, C. A., 288n5
Eisner, Robert, 30, 34
Engel, Eduardo, 544n1, 548n4, 549n7, 574, 586n28

Fahim-Nader, Mahnaz, 282
Faruqui, Umar, 265
Fienberg, S. E., 324
Fisher, Irving, 64
Fixler, Dennis J., 167, 340, 341, 618
Flamm, Kenneth, 73–74
Fogel, Robert W., 170
Forini, Mario, 345

Foss, Murray F., 1
Foster, Lucia, 586
Fraumeni, Barbara M., 7, 14n1, 34, 45,
    48n13, 70, 70n19, 145n2, 173n6, 207n7,
    357, 365n11, 487n14, 619
Fuss, Melvyn A., 206

Gale, William G., 30, 99
Gellatly, G., 452
Godbey, Geoffrey, 156n10
Gollop, Frank M., 7, 14n1, 48n13, 70n19,
    357, 365n11, 466
Gordon, Robert J., 29, 73, 74
Greenspan, Alan, 312
Griliches, Zvi, 27, 211, 301n20
Grimm, Bruce T., 74
Gu, W., 449
Gullickson, William, 364n10, 367n13,
    369n17, 461
Günlük-Senesen, G., 324n5
Guo, Jiemin, 359n4

Hall, Bronwyn H., 34
Hall, Robert E., 34, 209, 210, 211
Haltiwanger, John, 34, 544n1, 548n4,
    549n7, 574, 584n27, 586, 586n28
Harchaoui, Tarek M., 8, 447n7, 451n10,
    460n18, 462n19, 463, 464, 464n20,
    466, 467n21
Harper, Michael J., 7, 312, 364n10, 367n13,
    369n17, 461, 619
Harrington, C., 161
Herman, Shelby W., 70
Hicks, J., 288n2
Hill, Peter, 44
Ho, Mun S., 29n7, 48n13, 51n15, 68n17,
    70n18, 70n19, 77n23
Holland, P. W., 324
Holloway, Sue, 175
Horvath, Michael, 345n8
Hulten, Charles R., 5, 73, 88n25, 204, 207,
    207nn7–9, 208nn9–10, 209, 344, 357n3,
    446, 546n2

Jaditz, Ted, 618
Jarmin, Ron, 9, 548n5
Jaszi, George, 34
Jean, J., 462n19
Jorgenson, Dale W., 3, 7, 14n1, 22n2, 27,
    29n7, 34, 44, 47n11, 48n13, 49n14,
    51n15, 68n17, 70nn18–19, 75n21,
    76n22, 77n23, 79n24, 93, 95, 194,

204n5, 205, 208n9, 211, 301n20,
    305n26, 356n1, 357, 365n11, 447n7,
    462, 462n19, 464
Juster, F. Thomas, 156n9

Kahneman, Daniel, 157–58
Kang, T., 161
Katz, Arnold, 178n9, 288n5
Kazemier, Brugt, 183
Kendrick, John, 30, 34, 166, 166n3
Kern, Paul V., 282
Keuning, Steven, 183
Khanam, B., 447n7, 460n18, 464
Kim, Namsuk, 586
Klein, L. R., 311
Klimek, Shawn D., 9, 548n5
Kokkelenberg, Edward, 4, 145, 149, 151,
    177n8
Konus, Alexander A., 64
Koopman, Tjalling, 194
Krizan, C. J., 586
Krueger, Alan B., 157–58
Kuznets, Simon S., 161

Lal, Kishori, 477n7
Landefeld, J. Steven, 2n1, 3, 27n3, 64, 164,
    614, 621–22
LaPlante, M. P., 161
Lasserre, P., 466
Lau, E., 458
Lawrence, D. A., 305n26
Lawrence, Robert Z., 29
Lawson, Ann M., 5, 216n2, 218n5, 359n4,
    552n9
Lebow, David E., 345
Leontief, Wassily, 345
Lum, Sherlene K., 216n2, 221n9

Mackie, Christopher, 4, 170n5
Mæhle, Nils Ø., 474n4
Makino, J., 311
Marshall, Alfred, 166
Matete, Mampite, 153
Mayerhauser, Nicole, 472
McCahill, Robert J., 266n2
McCulla, Stephanie, 164
McIntosh, Susan Hume, 8
Mead, Charles Ian, 8, 139, 474n5
Meade, J. E., 322
Meadows, Donnella H., 35n9
Mesenbourg, Thomas L., 6, 611–14
Moses, Karin, 8, 139, 474n5

Moulton, Brent, 8, 44, 45, 64, 74n20, 76n22, 139, 288n5, 311, 373n24, 472, 474n5
Moyer, Brian C., 5, 6, 216n2, 221n9, 266n2, 282

Nordhaus, William D., 1, 4, 29, 34, 34n9, 47n12, 145, 149, 151, 173, 177n8, 311, 356n1

Okubo, Sumiye, 5, 45, 173n6, 216n2, 487n14
Oliner, Stephen D., 70n19, 74
Otto, Phyllis F., 312

Palumbo, Michael G., 8
Parker, Robert P., 64, 74
Patinkin, Don, 194n1
Pigou, A. C., 166–67
Planting, Mark A., 5, 216n2, 282, 359n4
Popkin, Joel, 166
Power, Laura, 574, 584n27
Powers, Susan G., 7

Reichlin, Lucrezia, 345
Reid, Margaret, 171–72
Reinsdorf, Marshall B., 6, 99, 167, 288nn4–5, 340
Robinson, John, 156n9
Ruggles, Nancy D., 9, 30, 472
Ruggles, Richard, 9, 30, 472

Sabelhaus, John, 30, 99
Samuelson, Paul A., 1, 47n12
Schkade, David A., 157–58
Schneider, M. H., 324n5
Schreyer, Paul, 205
Schuh, Scott, 586
Schwartz, Norbert, 157–58
Seskin, E. P., 288n5, 373n24, 472
Short, Sandra, 175
Sichel, Daniel E., 34, 70n19, 74, 207, 207n7
Slater, Courtenay M., 175
Slifman, Larry, 9, 615–17, 616n1

Smith, George M., 167, 340
Smith, P., 443n3
Smith, Shelly, 472
Solomon, Genevieve, 8
Stiroh, Kevin J., 13, 29, 29n7, 47n11, 51n15, 68n17, 70nn18–19, 77n23, 447n7, 462
Stone, Arthur A., 157–58
Stone, Richard D., 322
Strassner, Erich H., 311n1
Sullivan, David F., 472
Swinand, G., 466

Tamplin, Sarah, 175
Tanguay, M., 452
Tarkhani, F., 447n7, 451n10, 460n18, 462n19, 463, 464, 464n20, 467n21
Teplin, Albert M., 8
Tobin, James, 4, 34, 34n9, 47n12, 473
Triplett, Jack E., 29, 73, 207, 311, 356n1, 616

Utgoff, Kathleen, 6, 614–15

Van de Ven, Peter, 183
Vartia, Y. O., 275n6
Vaze, P., 458

Watkins, G. C., 154
Weale, Martin, 312, 348
Weitzman, Martin L., 47n12, 88, 98, 209
Whelan, Karl, 346
Wilson, Dan, 9
Wilson, Karen, 3
Wright, Gavin, 34
Wyckoff, A. A., 463
Wykoff, Frank C., 73, 207n8, 208n10, 546n2

Yan, B., 452
Yun, Kun-Young, 76n22
Yuskavage, Robert E., 6, 7, 216nn2–3, 221n9, 275, 288n4, 311n1

Zenios, S. A., 324n5

Subject Index

Accounting framework, 144–55; adjustments necessary to conform to economic welfare and, 145–46; nonmarket activities and, 146–48
Accounting system, U.S., blueprint for, 45–49
Accounts. *See specific type of account*
Accumulation accounts, 52–54
ACES. *See* Annual Capital Expenditures Survey (ACES)
American Time Use Survey (ATUS), 4, 178, 185–90
Annual Capital Expenditures Survey (ACES), 9–10, 543, 548, 550–51, 600–601, 603–7; compared to ASM, 590–91; compared to FRTW investment matrix, 555–68; expansion of, 613; incorporating firm age information into, 591–96; incorporating firm exit into, 596–99; industries sampled in, 603–5; industries unreported in, 605–7; working with, 568–74
Annual Survey of Manufacturers (ASM), 319, 543, 545, 548–49, 574; compared to ACES, 590–91; measuring business-level capital with, 575–89
Annual Survey of Wholesale Trade, 613
ASM. *See* Annual Survey of Manufacturers (ASM)
ASNA. *See* Australian System of National Accounts (ASNA)

Asset and Expenditures Survey (AES), 548
Assets, natural, measuring, for nonmarket accounts, 152
ATUS. *See* American Time Use Survey (ATUS)
Augmented national accounts: accounting framework for, 144–55; defined, 143; principles for designing, 143. *See also* Satellite accounts
Australia: cross-country comparison of SNA of, 456–58; implementation of SNA93 in, 126–30; system of national accounts in, 3
Australian System of National Accounts (ASNA), 126–30

Balance sheet accounts, 13
BEA. *See* Bureau of Economic Analysis (BEA)
Beyond the Market (Abraham), 4–5
BLS. *See* Bureau of Labor Statistics (BLS)
Blue Book (UK), 133–34
Bridge tables, 317, 319–21
Britain. *See* United Kingdom
Bureau of Economic Analysis (BEA), 2, 13, 355–58, 611–13; capital and financial accounts of, 22; comparison of output measures for sectors and industries of BLS and, 378–403; vs. FRB measurements, 29; function of international wealth accounts of, 15; function of

Bureau of Economic Analysis (*cont.*)
wealth accounts of, 15; goal of integrating GDP-by-industry accounts with input-output accounts of, 6; integration of accounts and, 621–22; international and regional accounts of, 22; national accounts of, 167; preference for GDP as measure of domestic output, 312; responsibilities of, 14. *See also* National Income and Product Accounts (NIPAs)

Bureau of Labor Statistics (BLS), 2, 3, 6, 13, 355–58; comparison of output measures for sectors and industries of BEA and, 378–403; national accounts and, 614–15; productivity estimates of, 22. *See also* Productivity statistics

Cambridge Growth Project, 323
Canada: cross-country comparison of SNA of, 456–58; implementation of SNA93 in, 134–38; integration of production and productivity accounts of, 8
Canadian Productivity Accounts (CPAs), 439–40, 446–56
Canadian System of National Accounts (CSNA), 3, 134–38, 439–40; future challenges for, 465–67; overview of, 440–41; production accounts of, 442–46; productivity accounts and, 446–56
Capital: as deferred consumption, 198–200; defined, 5; depreciation and, 207–11; as inventory of goods, 200–202; measuring, 541–45; measuring business-level, with ASM, 575–89; obsolescence and, 207–11; overview of U.S. measurement of, 545–51; as produced means of production, 202–4; producer-operated fixed, 204–6
Capital accounting, overview of, 193–95
Capital accounts: circular flow model for, 5; conceptual issues in designing, 5
Capital flows tables (CFTs), 546–47, 551–52; construction of, 552–53; vs. FRTW, 552
Capital income, 70–83
Census Bureau, 2, 6, 545; attempts to improve national accounts at, 611–14
CFM. *See* Circular flow model (CFM)
CFTs. *See* Capital flows tables (CFTs)

Circular flow model (CFM), 5, 194–95; overview of, 195–98
CNStat. *See* Committee on National Statistics (CNStat)
Committee on National Statistics (CNStat), 4
Commodity taxes: input-output tables with, 298–303; input-output tables with no, 289–98
Communications investment, 74
COMPUSTAT data, 550n8
Consumer durables, measuring, 45
Consumer Price Index (CPI), 618
Consumer surplus issue, for nonmarket accounts, 151–52
Consumption, capital as deferred, 198–220
Contributions formula, 278; empirical results for, 283–84
Council of Economic Advisors, 311
Counting issues, for nonmarket accounting, 183–84
CPA. *See* Canadian Productivity Accounts (CPAs)
CPI. *See* Consumer Price Index (CPI)
CSNA. *See* Canadian System of National Accounts (CSNA)

Data sources, for nonmarket accounts, 4
DDI. *See* Gross domestic income (GDI)
Depreciation, capital and, 207–11
Discrepancy. *See* Statistical discrepancy
Domestic Capital Account, 47, 59–61, 88; change in wealth, 91–92t; investment, 90t
Domestic Income and Product Account, 49, 53–54t, 69t; capital income, 80–81; in constant prices, 68–83; labor income, 71–72t; productivity, 82t
Double-entry bookkeeping, NIPAs and, 173–75

Economic accounts, overview of existing sets of, 14–16
Economic Census, 613
Economic growth, sources and uses of, 93–105
Environmental accounting, 35–36, 176–77
Environmental statistical accounts, 465
European System of Accounts (ESA95), 130–31, 473
Eurostat, 473

Expenditure accounts, 52, 55–56t, 83–88, 84–85t; net, 83–88, 89t
Externalities, 176–77

Federal Reserve Board (FRB), 2, 3, 13, 471–72; balance sheet accounts of, 23; vs. BEA measurements, 29; flow-of-funds accounts of, 23
Female labor force participation, 163–64
FFAs. *See* Flow-of-funds accounts (FFAs)
Financial accounts, integration of income accounts and, 8–9
Firm age information, incorporating, into ACES, 591–96
Firm exit information, incorporating, into ACES, 596–99
Fisher ideal index, 62–66
Fixed Reproducible Tangible Wealth (FRTW) investment matrix, 547, 551; vs. CFTs, 552; compared to ACES, 555–68; construction of, 553–54; uses of, 554–55
Flow-of-funds, 2
Flow-of-funds accounts (FFAs), 13, 471–72
Foreign Transaction Capital Account, 48, 62t
Foreign Transactions Current Account, 48, 57t, 58–59
France, cross-country comparison of SNA of, 456–58
FRB. *See* Federal Reserve Board (FRB)
FRTW. *See* Fixed Reproducible Tangible Wealth (FRTW) investment matrix

GDP. *See* Gross domestic product (GDP)
GNP. *See* Gross national product (GNP)
Goods and services accounts, of SNA93, 124

Great Britain. *See* United Kingdom
Greenspan, Alan, 26
Gross domestic income (GDI), 3, 16, 50, 309; constructing measure of, in constant prices, 44; desirable properties of, 312; methodology and data for determining, 313–25; statistical discrepancy and results controlled to, 325–41. *See also* Statistical discrepancy
Gross domestic product (GDP), 2, 3, 16, 49, 309; BEA's preference as measure of domestic output, 312; methodology and data for determining, 313–25;

statistical discrepancy and results controlled to, 325–41. *See also* Statistical discrepancy
Gross domestic product (GDP)-by-industry accounts, 263; combining I-O methodology with methodologies of, 221–25; contributions formula for, 278; empirical results for factors contributing to discrepancies for, 278–86; factors contributing to discrepancies for, 267–78; integration of, with annual input-output accounts, 5–7; integration with annual input-output accounts, 216; methodologies, 221; statistical discrepancy of, 265–67, 277–78
Gross national product (GNP), 25
Gross output, defined, 5
Gross state product (GSP), 16
GSP. *See* Gross state product (GSP)

Household production, 169–70
Human capital, investments in, 13

IEESAs. *See* Integrated economic and environmental satellite accounts (IEESAs)
IMF. *See* International Monetary Fund (IMF)
Imputations, in NIPAs, 167–68
Income, accounts for measuring, 49–57
Income accounts, 50, 52, 55–56t, 83–88, 86–87t; integration of financial and, 8–9; net, 88, 89t
Income and Expenditures Account, 47
Indexes, price and quantity, 57–68
Index of Industrial Production (FRB), 74
Industries: sampled, in ACES, 603–5; unreported, in ACES, 605–7
Industry accounts, integration of, 615–17; BEA and, 621–22; full, 225–28; future research issues for full, 240–50; methodology of partial, 228–49; overview of, 215–18; partial, 218–25
Input-output accounts: combining GDP-by-industry methodologies with methodology of, 221–25; constructing consistent, 5; development of, 25; integration of, with GDP-by-industry accounts, 5–7, 216; methodology, 218–21
Input-output tables (IOTs): Canadian, 442; with commodity taxes, 298–303; with no commodity taxes, 289–98

Integrated accounts, 5
Integrated economic and environmental satellite accounts (IEESAs), 36–43; asset account, 40–41t; production account, 37–39t
Integration, of industry accounts, 615–17; BEA and, 621–22; full, 225–28; future research issues for full, 249–50; methodology of partial, 228–49; overview of, 215–18; partial, 218–25
International accounts, of BEA, 22
International Monetary Fund (IMF), 474
International transaction accounts (ITAs), 471, 472
Inventory of goods, capital as, 200–202
Investments: defined, 5; in human capital, 5
IOTs. See Input-output tables (IOTs)
ITAs. See International transaction accounts (ITAs)

KLEMS database, 459–60, 468
Knight, Frank, 194n1
Kuznets, Simon, 3, 13, 25, 34, 161

Labor income, 68–70
Laspeyres index, 62–63
Leontief, Wassily, 25, 323

Marginal valuation, for nonmarket accounting, 184–85
Market accounts, nonmarket accounts and, 4, 149. See also Nonmarket accounting; Nonmarket accounts
Measurement issues, 2–3
MFP. See Multifactor productivity (MFP) estimates
Mitchell, Wesley C., 25
Multifactor productivity (MFP) estimates, 357, 446

NAICS. See North American Industry Classification System (NAICS)
National accounts, U.S., 4; applications of prototype system of, 93–105; augmented, 143, 144–45; of BEA, 167; BLS and, 614–15; blueprint for accounting system for, 45–49; building integrated and consistent system of, 43–45; comprehensiveness of, 15–16; constructing measure for rental prices for, 44; constructing measure of GDI for, 44; emerging issues in, 2–3; history of, 166–67; income, 5, 25–27; integrat-

ing estimates of tangible wealth for, 44; measuring consumer durables and, 45; need for integration of, 14; overview of existing sets of, 14–16; references for, 107–9; remaining challenges for, 27–30. See also National Income and Product Accounts (NIPAs); Nonmarket accounting; Nonmarket accounts
National economic accounts (NEA) design, models of, 144–45
National income accounts: constructing consistent, 5; history of, 25–27
National Income and Product Accounts (NIPAs), 1, 2, 16–21, 144, 355–58, 471, 472; domestic and income product account of, 16–20; domestic capital account of, 21; double-entry bookkeeping approach and, 173–75; expansion of existing accounts of, 30–34; foreign capital account of, 21; foreign sector account of, 21; function of, 15; government sector of, 21; imputations in, 167; personal-sector account of, 20–21; private enterprise income account of, 20; scope of coverage in, 166–68; shortcomings of, 161–62. See also Bureau of Economic Analysis (BEA); National accounts, U.S.; Nonmarket accounting; Nonmarket accounts; Satellite accounts
NEA. See National economic accounts (NEA) design
Net expenditure accounts, 83–88, 89t
New economy, measures for studying, 29
NIPAS. See National Income and Product Accounts (NIPAs)
Nonmarket accounting: assigning prices for, 179–83; benefits of extending, 152; classifying nonmarket inputs and outputs for, 175–76; counting and valuation issues for, 183–84; current state of, 162; data for, 185–90; double-entry bookkeeping for, 173–75; externalities and, 176–77; marginal valuation for, 184–85; measuring quantities for, 177–79; objective for improving, 162–63; total valuation for, 184–85. See also National accounts, U.S.; National Income and Product Accounts (NIPAs)
Nonmarket accounts: consumer surplus issue for, 151–52; data sources for, 4; European vs. American views on measuring, 152–55; imputing price issues

for, 150–51; lack of data issue for, 149–50; market accounts and, 4, 149; measuring natural assets for, 152; "satellite" systems of accounts and, 4–5; time-use data for, 155–59; "zero problem" issue for, 151–52. *See also* National Income and Product Accounts (NIPAs)

Nonmarket activities: measuring economic, 34–43; national accounts including, 13

Nonzero-rent economy, 211

North American Industry Classification System (NAICS), 8

Obsolescence, capital and, 207–11

Operating surplus, defined, 481

Output income, 68–70

Paasche index, 62–63

Personal Consumption Expenditure (PCE) deflator, 618

Pollution, accounting for, 176–77

Price deflators, 545–46; measuring, 542

Price indexes, 57–68

Producer-operated fixed capital, 204–6

Producer price index (PPI), 615

Product accounts, 50

Production accounts: constructing measure of GDI in constant prices and, 44; of CSNA, 442–46; framework for, 7–8; illustration of relationship between GDP and major-sector estimates using, 371–77; integration of productivity and, in Canada, 8; theoretical foundation for, 358–71

Productivity accounts: benefits of integrating, to SNA, 459–64; Canadian, 446–56; of CSNA, 446–56; integration of production and, in Canada, 8

Productivity statistics, 2, 13. *See also* Bureau of Labor Statistics (BLS)

Quantities, measuring, for nonmarket accounting, 177–79

Quantity indexes, 57–68

RAS technique, 323, 324–25

Regional accounts, of BEA, 22

Rental prices, 44, 75

SAS. *See* Services Annual Survey (SAS)

Satellite accounting, 35–36

Satellite accounts, 164–66; nonmarket accounts and, 4–5; scope of, 168–72. *See*

also Augmented national accounts; National Income and Product Accounts (NIPAs)

Satellite systems of accounts, 4–5

Saving, issues in measuring, 29

SEEA. *See* System of environmental and economic accounting (SEEA)

Sequence economic accounts, of SNA93, 119–24; in Australia, 127–28; in Canada, 135–37

Services Annual Survey (SAS), 612

SNA93, 357, 468; central framework of, 116; changes to U.S. accounts and, 472; implementation of, in Australia, 126–30; implementation of, in Canada, 134–38; implementation of, in United Kingdom, 130–34; infrastructure of, 117–19; integrated data system of, 119–26; structure of, 474–78; supply and use tables of, 124–26, 125t, 128–30, 131–32, 133, 137. *See also* System of National Accounts (SNA)

SNA-USA tables, draft, 478–81; current account, 481–87; financial business sector, 509–17; future and, 537–38; government sectors, 517–28; households and nonprofit organizations serving households sector, 487–96; integration issues for, 528–39; nonfinancial corporate business sector, 502–9; nonfinancial noncorporate business sector, 496–502; rest-of-world sector, 528, 529–33

Software investment, 74–75

SOI division. *See* Statistics of Income (SOI) division, of Internal Revenue Service

Statistical discrepancy, 617–20; defined, 277; of GDP-by-industry accounts, 265–67, 277–78; optimal combinations of GDI and GDP data for, 341–48; overview of, 309–13; results controlled to GDI data for, 325–41; results controlled to GDP data for, 325–41. *See also* Gross domestic income (GDI); Gross domestic product (GDP)

Statistics Canada, 8, 439–40. *See also* Canada

Statistics of Income (SOI) division, of Internal Revenue Service, 2

Stone, Richard, 114, 323

Supply and use tables, of SNA93, 124–26, 125t; in Australia, 128–30; in Canada, 137; in United Kingdom, 131–32, 133

Surplus: consumer, nonmarket accounts and, 151–52; operating, defined, 481

System of environmental and economic accounting (SEEA), 35–36

System of National Accounts (SNA), 3, 144–45, 144n1; analytic underpinnings of, 115t; in Australia, 3, 126–30; benefits of integrating productivity accounts to, 459–64; in Canada, 439–40, 446–56; cross-country comparisons of, 456–58; development of, 113–16; international comparison of, 3; overview of, 23–25, 24t; in United Kingdom, 130–34. *See also* SNA93

Taxes, 66–68, 75–76

TFP. *See* Total factor productivity (TFP)

Third-party criterion, for nonmarket output, 171–72

Time-use data, for nonmarket accounts, 155–59

Total factor productivity (TFP), 345

Total valuation, for nonmarket accounting, 184–85

United Kingdom: *Blue Book* for, 133–34; cross-country comparison of SNA of, 456–58; implementation of SNA93 in, 130–34; system of national accounts in, 3

United States: blueprint for accounting system for, 45–49; efforts to integrate economic accounts of, 472–73; national accounts of, 4. *See also* National accounts, U.S.; National Income and Product Accounts (NIPAs); SNA-USA tables, draft

U.S. International Investment Position, 54–57, 67t

U.S. International Position, 48

U.S. national accounts. *See* National accounts, U.S.; National Income and Product Accounts (NIPAs)

Valuation, total, for nonmarket accounting, 184–85

Valuation issues, for nonmarket accounting, 183–84

Wealth, accounts for measuring, 49–57

Wealth Account, 47–48, 93, 94t

Wealth accounts, 54–57; function of, BEA and, 15

"Zero problem" issue, for nonmarket accounts, 151–52

Zero-rent economy, 211